Study Guide

to Accompany

McConnell

Economics

achieved only if there are full employment and full production in the economy; the best combination of products depends upon the (values, resources, technology) _____ of that society and is a (scientific, nonscientific) _____ matter.

10. The quantity of other goods and services an economy must go without in order to produce more low-cost housing is the _____ _____ of producing the additional low-cost housing.

11. The cost of producing a commodity tends to increase as more of the commodity is produced because _____ _____

12. The more an economy consumes of its current production, the (more, less) _____ it will be capable of producing in future years if other things are equal.

13. List the Five Fundamental Questions which every economy must answer.

a. _____
b. _____
c. _____
d. _____
e. _____

14. The changes which occur almost continuously in modern industrial economies and which these economies must accommodate if they are to be efficient are changes in:

a. _____
b. _____
c. _____

15. In:

a. pure capitalism property resources are (publicly, privately) _____ owned and the means employed to direct and coordinate economic activity is the _____ system.

b. a command economy the property resources are _____ owned and the coordinating device is central _____

■ PROBLEMS AND PROJECTS

1. Below is a list of resources. Indicate in the space to the right of each whether the resource is land, capital (C), labor, entrepreneurial ability (EA), or some combinations of these.

a. Fishing grounds in the North Atlantic _____
b. A cash register in a retail store _____
c. Uranium deposits in Canada _____
d. An irrigation ditch in Nebraska _____
e. The work performed by the late Henry Ford _____
f. The oxygen breathed by human beings _____
g. The U.S. Steel plant in Gary, Indiana _____
h. The goods on the shelf of a retail store _____
i. The work done by a laborer on an assembly line _____
j. The tasks accomplished in perfecting color television for commercial sales _____

2. A production possibilities table for two commodities, wheat and automobiles, is found below. The table is constructed employing the usual assumptions. Wheat is measured in units of 100,000 bushels and automobiles in units of 100,000.

Combination	Wheat	Automobiles
A	0	7
B	7	6
C	13	5
D	18	4
E	22	3
F	25	2
G	27	1
H	28	0

a. Follow the general rules for making graphs (see Chapter 1); plot the data from the table on the graph below to obtain a production possibilities curve. Place wheat on the vertical axis and automobiles on the horizontal axis.

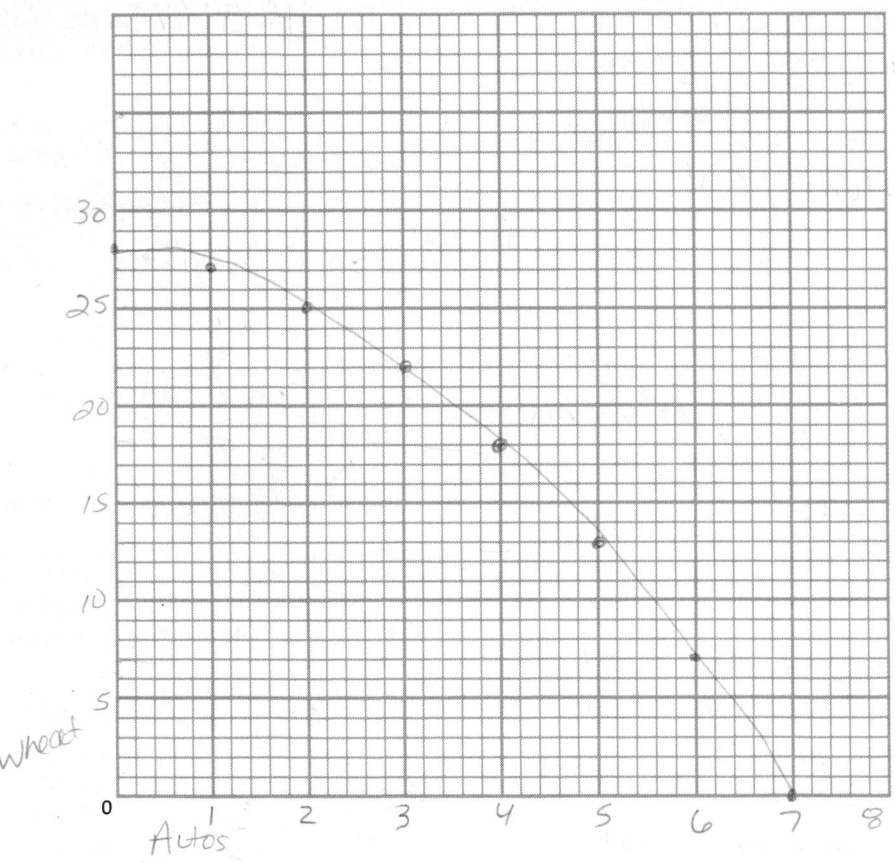

b. Fill in the table below showing the opportunity cost per unit of producing the 1st through the 7th automobile.

Automobiles	Cost of production
1st	1
2d	2
3d	3
4th	4
5th	5
6th	6
7th	7

3. Below is a production possibilities curve.

Draw on this graph:

a. A production possibilities curve which indicates greater efficiency in the production of good *A*.

b. A production possibilities curve which indicates greater efficiency in the production of good *B*.

c. A production possibilities curve which indicates an increase in the resources available to the economy.

4. Below is a list of economic goods. Indicate in the space to the right of each whether the good is a consumer good (CON), a capital good (CAP), or that it depends (DEP) upon who is using it and for what purpose.

a. An automobile ______

b. A tractor ______

c. A taxicab ______

d. A house ______

e. A factory building ______

f. An office building ______

g. An ironing board ______

h. A refrigerator ______

i. A telephone ______

j. A quart of Scotch whisky ______

k. A cash register ______

l. A screwdriver ______

■ SELF-TEST

Circle the T if the statement is true, the F if it is false.

1. The wants with which economics is concerned include only those wants which can be satisfied by goods and services. T F

2. Money is a resource and is classified as "capital." T F

3. Profit is the reward paid to those who provide the economy with capital. T F

4. Resources are scarce because society's material wants are unlimited. T F

5. The opportunity cost of producing antipollution devices is the other goods and services the economy is unable to produce because it has decided to produce these devices. T F

6. The opportunity cost of producing a good tends to increase as more of it is produced because resources less suitable to its production must be employed. T F

7. Drawing a production possibilities curve concave to the origin is the geometric way of stating the law of increasing costs. T F

8. It is not possible for an economy capable of producing just two goods to increase its production of both. T F

9. Economic growth means an increase in the ability of an economy to produce goods and services; and it is shown by a movement of the production possibilities to the right. T F

10. The more capital goods an economy produces today, the greater will be the total output of all goods it can produce in the future, other things being equal. T F

11. It is economically desirable for a nation to have unemployed resources at the outset of a war because it can increase its production of military goods without having to decrease its production of civilian goods. T F

12. In the economic system called authoritarian capitalism most property is publicly owned but the market system is used to coordinate economic activity. T F

Circle the letter that corresponds to the best answer.

1. An "innovator" is defined as an entrepreneur who: (*a*) makes basic policy decisions in a business firm; (*b*) combines factors of production to produce a good or service; (*c*) invents a new product or process for producing a product; (*d*) introduces new products on the market or employs a new method to produce a product.

2. An economy is efficient when it has achieved: (*a*) full employment; (*b*) full production; (*c*) either full employment or full production; (*d*) both full employment and full production.

3. When a production possibilities schedule is written (or a production possibilities curve is drawn) four assumptions are made. Which of the following is *not* one of those assumptions? (*a*) Only two products are produced; (*b*) the nation is not at war; (*c*) the economy has both full employment and full production; (*d*) the quantities of all resources available to the economy are fixed.

4. At point *A* on the production possibilities curve in the following illustration: (*a*) more wheat than tractors is being produced; (*b*) more tractors than wheat are being produced; (c) the economy is employing all its resources; (d) the economy is not employing all its resources.

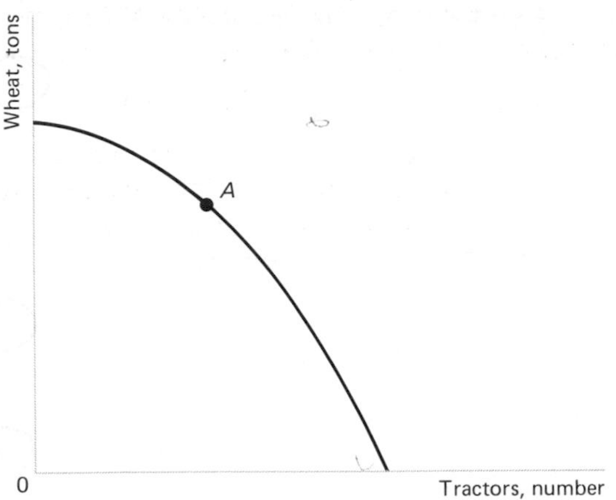

5. The combinations of products in a society's production possibilities table which is its optimum product-mix depends upon that society's: (a) resources; (b) technology; (c) level of employment; (d) values.

6. The production possibilities curve is: (a) concave; (b) convex; (c) linear; (d) positive.

7. A farmer who produces his crops by inefficient methods is: (a) an unemployed worker; (b) an underemployed worker; (c) a fully employed worker; (d) an apparently unemployed worker.

8. If there is an increase in the resources available within the economy: (a) more goods and services will be produced in the economy; (b) the economy will be capable of producing more goods and services; (c) the standard of living in the economy will rise; (d) the technological efficiency of the economy will improve.

9. If the production possibilities curve on the graph below moves from position A to position B, then: (a) the economy has increased the efficiency with which it produces wheat; (b) the economy has increased the efficiency with which it produces tractors; (c) the economy has put previously idle resources to work; (d) the economy has gone from full employment to less-than-full employment.

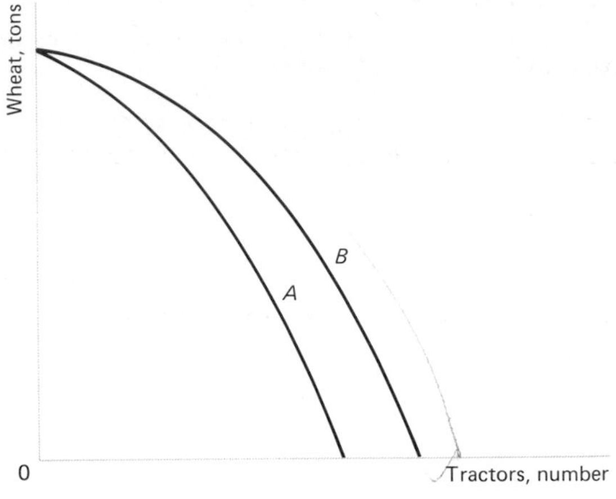

10. Which one of the following is *not* one of the Five Fundamental Questions which every economy must answer? (a) What level of resource use to have; (b) what goods and services to reproduce; (c) how to distribute the output of the economy; (d) how to enforce the law of increasing costs.

11. The private ownership of property resources and use of the market system to direct and coordinate economic activity is characteristic of: (a) pure capitalism; (b) the command economy; (c) market socialism; (d) the traditional economy.

12. The public ownership of property resources and the use of a market system to direct and coordinate economic activity is characteristic of: (a) pure capitalism; (b) the command economy; (c) market socialism; (d) authoritarian capitalism.

■ DISCUSSION QUESTIONS

1. Explain what is meant by the "economizing problem." Why are resources scarce?

2. In what sense are wants satiable and in what sense are they insatiable?

3. What are the four economic resources? How is each of these resources defined? What is the income earned by each of them called?

4. When is a society economically efficient? What is meant by "full production" and how does it differ from "full employment"?

5. What four assumptions are made in drawing a production possibilities curve or schedule? How do technological advance and an increased supply of resources in the economy affect the curve or schedule?

6. Why cannot an economist determine which of the combinations in the production possibilities table is "best"? What determines the optimum product-mix?

7. What is opportunity cost? What is the law of increasing cost? Why do costs increase?

8. What is the important relationship between the *composition* of the economy's current output and the *location* of future production possibilities curves?

9. What are the Five Fundamental Questions?

10. Pure capitalism and the command economy differ in two important ways. Compare these two economic systems with each other and with authoritarian capitalism and market socialism.

3
Pure capitalism and the circular flow

Chapter 3 has three principal aims: to outline six ideological and institutional characteristics of pure capitalism, to explain three practices found in all modern economies, and to sketch in extremely simple terms the fundamental operation of a capitalistic economy. A more detailed explanation of the institutions, practices, and behavior of the American economy—which is not *purely* capitalistic—is found in the chapters that follow. If the aims of this chapter are accomplished, you can begin to understand the system and methods employed by our economy to find answers to the Five Fundamental Questions discussed in Chapter 2.

The resources of the American economy are owned by its citizens, who are free to use them as they wish in their own self-interest; prices and markets serve to express the self-interests of resource owners, consumers, and business firms; and competition serves to regulate self-interest—to prevent the self-interest of any person or any group from working to the disadvantage of the economy as a whole and to make self-interest work for the benefit of the entire economy.

The three practices of all modern economies are the employment of large amounts of capital, extensive specialization, and the use of money. Economies use capital and engage in specialization because it is a more efficient use of their resources; it results in larger total output and the greater satisfaction of wants. But when workers, business firms, and regions within an economy specialize they become dependent on each other for the goods and services they do not produce for themselves. To obtain these goods and services they must engage in trade. Trade is made more convenient by using money as a medium of exchange.

The circular-flow-of-income model (or diagram) is a device which illustrates for a capitalistic economy the relation between households and businesses, the flow of money and economic goods and services between households and businesses, their dual role as buyers and sellers, and the two basic types of markets essential to the capitalistic process.

Understand these essentials of the economic skeleton first; then a little flesh—a little more reality, a little more detail—can be added to the bones. Understanding the skeleton makes it much easier to understand the whole body and its functioning.

■ CHECKLIST

When you have studied this chapter you should be able to:

☐ Identify and explain the six important institutional characteristics of capitalism.

☐ Name and explain the three characteristics of all modern economies.

☐ Draw the circular flow diagram; and correctly label the real and money flows and the two major types of markets.

■ CHAPTER OUTLINE

1. The American economy is not pure capitalism, but it is a close approximation of pure capitalism. Pure capitalism has the following six peculiarities that distinguish it from other economic systems.

a. Private individuals and organizations own and control its property resources by means of the institution of private property.

b. These individuals and organizations possess both the freedom of enterprise and the freedom of choice.

c. Each of them is motivated largely by self-interest.

d. Competition prevents them as buyers and sellers from exploiting others.

e. Markets and prices (the price system) are used to communicate and coordinate the decisions of buyers and sellers.

f. And the role of government is limited in a competitive and capitalistic economy.

2. In common with other advanced economies of the world, the American economy has three major characteristics.

a. It employs complicated and advanced methods of production and large amounts of capital equipment to produce goods and services efficiently.

b. It is a highly specialized economy; and this specialization increases the productive efficiency of the economy.

c. It also uses money extensively to facilitate trade and specialization.

3. The circular flow model is a device used to clarify the relationships between households and business firms in a purely capitalistic economy.

a. In resource markets households supply and firms demand resources and in product markets the firms supply and households demand products. Households use the incomes they obtain from supplying resources to purchase the goods and services produced by the firms; and in the economy there is a real flow of resources and products and a money flow of incomes and expenditures.

b. The circular flow model has at least four limitations.

■ IMPORTANT TERMS

Private property	**Money**
Self-interest	**Medium of exchange**
Competition	**Barter**
Freedom of choice	**Coincidence of wants**
Freedom of enterprise	**Circular flow model**
Roundabout production	**Household**
Specialization	**Resource market**
Division of labor	**Product market**

■ FILL-IN QUESTIONS

1. The ownership of property resources by private individuals and organizations is the institution of ________

2. Two basic freedoms encountered in a capitalistic economy are the freedoms of ________
____
and ________

3. Self-interest means that each economic unit attempts to ________; this self-interest might work to the disadvantage of the economy as a whole if it were not regulated and constrained by ________

4. According to the economist, competition is present if two conditions prevail; these two conditions are:

a. ________

b. ________

5. If the number of buyers and sellers in a market is large, no single buyer or seller is able to ________ the price of the commodity bought and sold in that market.

6. In a capitalistic economy individual buyers communicate their demands and individual sellers communicate their supplies in the ________ of the economy; and their decisions are coordinated by the ________ determined there by demand and supply.

7. In the ideology of pure capitalism government is assigned (no, a limited, an extensive) ________ role.

8. The three practices or institutions common to all modern economies are ________
________,
________,
and ________

9. Modern economies make extensive use of capital goods and engage in roundabout production because it is more ________ than direct production.

10. If an economy engages in extensive specialization the individuals living in the economy are extremely ________; and if these individuals are to enjoy the benefits of specialization there must be ________ among them.

11. Modern economies practice specialization and the division of labor because the self-sufficient producer or worker tends to be an inefficient one.

12. In modern economies money functions chiefly as a medium of exchange

13. Barter between two individuals will take place only if there is a coincidence of wants

14. For an item to be "money," it must be accepted by sellers in exchange

15. In the circular flow model:

a. Households are demanders and businesses are suppliers in the product, ~~resource~~ markets; and businesses are demanders and households are suppliers of the resource markets of the economy.

b. The two flows are called the real flow and the money flow.

c. The expenditures made by businesses are a cost to them and become the income of households.

■ PROBLEMS AND PROJECTS

1. In the circular flow diagram below, the upper pair of flows (*a* and *b*) represent the product market and the lower pair (*c* and *d*) the resource market.

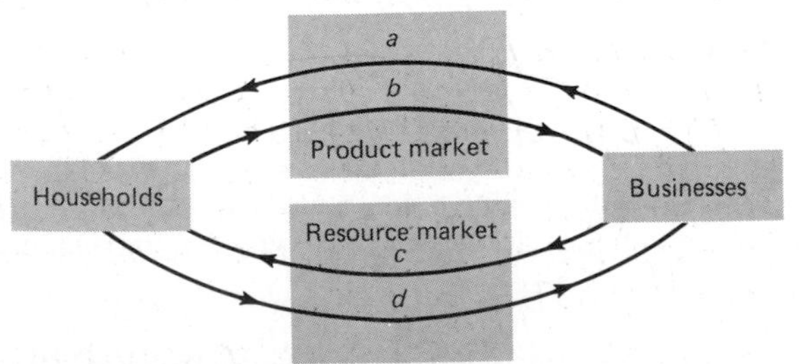

Supply labels or explanations for each of the four flows:

a. goods & services

b. Consumption expenditures

c. Money income (wages, profits, etc.

d. Services of resources — land, L, K, entr. abil.

■ SELF-TEST

Circle the T if the statement is true, the F if it is false.

1. The American economy can correctly be called "pure capitalism." T F

2. There are in the United States legal limits to the right of private property. T F

3. The freedom of business firms to produce a particular consumer good is always limited by the desires of consumers for that good. T F

4. When a market is competitive the individual sellers of the commodity are unable to reduce the supply of the commodity enough to drive its price upward. T F

5. In a purely capitalistic economy it is consumers who ultimately decide what goods and services the economy will produce. T F

6. The price system is not employed in communistic and socialistic economies. T F

7. The employment of capital to produce goods and services requires that there be "roundabout production" but it is more efficient than "direct" production. T F

8. Increasing the amount of specialization in an economy generally leads to the more efficient use of its resources. T F

9. Money is a device for facilitating the exchange of goods and services. T F

10. "Coincidence of wants" means that two persons desire to acquire the same good or service. T F

11. Cigarettes may serve as money if sellers are generally willing to accept them as money. T F

12. In the circular flow model, the household functions on the demand side of the resource and product market. T F

Circle the letter that corresponds to the best answer.

1. Which of the following is *not* one of the six characteristics of capitalism? (*a*) Competition; (*b*) central economic planning; (*c*) private property; (*d*) freedom of enterprise and choice.

2. Maximization of profits appears to be in the self-interest of (*a*) business firms; (*b*) landowners; (*c*) workers; (*d*) consumers.

3. To decide how to use its scarce resources to satisfy human wants pure capitalism relies on (*a*) central planning; (*b*) roundabout production; (*c*) a price system; (*d*) the coincidence of wants.

4. In pure capitalism the role of government is best described as (*a*) nonexistent; (*b*) limited; (*c*) significant; (*d*) extensive.

5. Which of the following is *not* a necessary consequence of specialization? (*a*) People will use money; (*b*) people will engage in trade; (*c*) people will be dependent upon each other; (*d*) people will produce more of some things than they would produce in the absence of specialization.

6. In an economy in which there are full employment and full production, constant amounts of resources, and unchanging technology (*a*) to increase the production of capital goods requires an increase in the production of consumer goods; (*b*) to decrease the production of capital goods necessitates a decrease in the production of consumer goods; (*c*) to increase the production of capital goods is impossible; (*d*) to increase the production of capital goods a decrease in the production of consumer goods is needed.

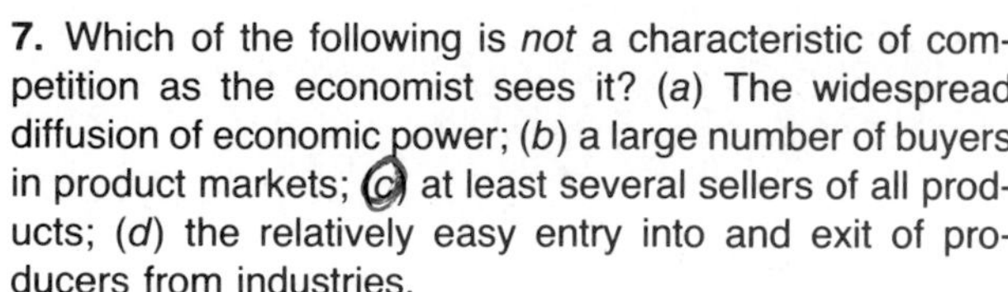

7. Which of the following is *not* a characteristic of competition as the economist sees it? (*a*) The widespread diffusion of economic power; (*b*) a large number of buyers in product markets; (*c*) at least several sellers of all products; (*d*) the relatively easy entry into and exit of producers from industries.

8. The two kinds of market found in the circular flow model are (*a*) the real and the money markets; (*b*) the real and the product markets; (*c*) the money and the resource markets; (*d*) the product and the resource markets.

9. In the circular flow model businesses (*a*) demand both products and resources; (*b*) supply both products and resources; (*c*) demand products and supply resources; (*d*) supply products and demand resources.

10. One of the limitations of the circular flow model found in this chapter is that (*a*) no mention is made of the role of government; (*b*) it is assumed households save some of their income; (*c*) too much attention is paid to how resource and product prices are determined; (*d*) it "ensnares the viewer in a maze of detail."

■ DISCUSSION QUESTIONS

1. Explain the several elements—institutions and assumptions—embodied in pure capitalism.

2. What do each of the following seek if they pursue their own self-interest? Consumers, resource owners, and business firms.

3. Explain what economists mean by competition. Why is it important to have competition in an economy whose members are motivated by self-interest?

4. What are the advantages of "indirect" or "roundabout" production?

5. How does an economy benefit from specialization and the division of labor?

6. What disadvantages are there to specialization and the division of labor?

7. What are the principal disadvantages of barter?

8. What is money? What important function does it perform? Explain how money performs this function and how it overcomes the disadvantages associated with barter. Why are people willing to accept paper money in exchange for the goods and services which they sell?

9. In the circular-flow-of-income model: (*a*) What two markets are involved? (*b*) What roles do households play in each of these markets? (*c*) What roles do businesses play in each of these markets? (*d*) What two income flows are pictured in money terms? In real terms? (*e*) What two expenditure flows are pictured in money terms? In real terms?

10. What are the four shortcomings of the circular-flow-of-income model?

4
The mechanics of individual prices: demand and supply

Chapter 4 is an introduction to the most fundamental tools of economic analysis: demand and supply. If you are to progress successfully into the later chapters it is essential that you understand what is meant by demand and supply and how to use these powerful tools.

Demand and supply are simply "boxes" or categories into which all the forces and factors that affect the price and the quantity of a good bought and sold in a competitive market can conveniently be placed. Demand and supply determine price and quantity exchanged and it is necessary to see *why* and *how* they do this.

Many students never do understand demand and supply because they never learn to *define* demand and supply *exactly* and because they never learn (1) what is meant by an increase or decrease in demand or supply, (2) the important distinctions between "demand" and "quantity demanded" and between "supply" and "quantity supplied," (3) the equally important distinctions between an increase (or decrease) in demand and an increase (or decrease) in quantity demanded and between an increase (or decrease) in supply and an increase (or decrease) in quantity supplied.

Having learned these, however, it is no great trick to comprehend the so-called "law of supply and demand." The equilibrium price—that is, the price which will tend to prevail in the market as long as demand and supply do not change—is simply the price at which *quantity demanded* and *quantity supplied* are equal. The quantity bought and sold in the market (the equilibrium quantity) is the quantity demanded and supplied at the equilibrium price. If you can determine the equilibrium price and quantity under one set of demand and supply conditions, you can determine them under any other set and so will be able to analyze for yourself the effects of changes in demand and supply upon equilibrium price and quantity.

The chapter includes a brief examination of the factors that determine demand and supply and of the ways in which changes in these determinants will affect and cause changes in demand and supply. A graphic method is employed in this analysis in order to facilitate an understanding of demand and supply, equilibrium price and quantity, changes in demand and supply, and the resulting changes in equilibrium price and quantity. In addition to understanding the *specific* definitions of demand and supply, it is necessary to understand the two counterparts of demand and supply: the demand *curve* and the supply *curve*. These are simply graphic (or geometric) representations of the same data contained in the schedules of demand and supply.

If you wonder why an entire chapter has been devoted to demand and supply you will find the answer in the last major section of the chapter. Demand and supply have so many applications that they are the most important single tool in economics. You will employ this tool over and over again. It will turn out to be as important to you as jet propulsion is to the pilot of a DC-10. You can't get off the ground without it.

■ CHECKLIST

When you have studied this chapter you should be able to:

☐ Define a market.

☐ Define demand, quantity demanded, supply, and quantity supplied.

☐ Graph demand and supply when you are given demand and supply schedules.

☐ State the law of demand and the law of supply.

☐ List the major determinants of demand and of supply.

☐ Determine when you are given the demand for and the supply of a good what the equilibrium price and the equilibrium quantity will be.

☐ Explain why the price of a good and the amount of the good bought and sold in a competitive market will be the equilibrium price and the equilibrium quantity, respectively.

☐ Predict the effects of changes in demand and supply on equilibrium price and equilibrium quantity; and on the prices of substitute and complementary goods.

☐ Explain the meaning of the rationing function of prices; and the economic effects of legally established prices.

■ CHAPTER OUTLINE

1. A market is any institution or mechanism that brings together the buyers and the sellers of a particular good or service; and in this chapter it is assumed that markets are perfectly competitive.

2. Demand is a schedule of prices and the quantities which buyers would purchase at each of these prices during some period of time.

a. As price rises, other things being equal, buyers will purchase smaller quantities, and as price falls they will purchase larger quantities; this is the law of demand.

b. The demand curve is a graphic representation of demand and the law of demand.

c. Market (or total) demand for a good is a summation of the demands of all individuals in the market for that good.

d. The demand for a good depends upon the tastes, income, and expectations of buyers; the number of buyers in the market; and the prices of related goods.

e. A change (either an increase or a decrease) in demand is caused by a change in any of the factors (in *d*) which determine demand, and means that the demand schedule and demand curve have changed.

f. A change in demand and a change in the quantity demanded are *not* the same thing.

3. Supply is a schedule of prices and the quantities which sellers will offer to sell at each of these prices during some period of time.

a. The law of supply means, other things being equal, that as the price of the good rises larger quantities will be offered for sale, and that as the price of the good falls smaller quantities will be offered for sale.

b. The supply curve is a graphic representation of supply and the law of supply; the market supply of a good is the sum of the supplies of all sellers of the good.

c. The supply of a good depends upon the techniques used to produce it, the prices of the resources employed in its production, the extent to which it is taxed or subsidized, the prices of other goods which might be produced, the price expectations of sellers, and the number of sellers of the product.

d. Supply will change when any of these determinants of supply changes; a change in supply is a change in the entire supply schedule or curve.

e. A change in supply must be distinguished from a change in quantity supplied.

4. The market or equilibrium price of a commodity is that price at which quantity demanded and quantity supplied are equal; and the quantity exchanged in the market (the equilibrium quantity) is equal to the quantity demanded and supplied at the equilibrium price.

a. The rationing function of price is the elimination of shortages and surpluses of the commodity.

b. A change in demand, supply, or both changes both the equilibrium price and the equilibrium quantity in specific ways.

c. In resource markets suppliers are households and demanders are business firms, and in product markets suppliers are business firms and demanders are householders; and supply and demand are useful in the analysis of prices and quantities exchanged in both types of markets.

d. When demand and supply schedules (or curves) are drawn up it is assumed that all the nonprice determinants of demand and supply remain unchanged.

5. Understanding how demand and supply determine price and quantity in a competitive market is a powerful tool which:

a. has a large number of applications;

b. can be used to predict the effects of legally established price supports and price ceilings; and

c. may be employed to solve such problems as pollution and congestion.

■ IMPORTANT TERMS

Market	**Law of demand**
Demand schedule	**Diminishing marginal utility**
Quantity demanded	

Income effect
Substitution effect
Demand curve
Individual demand
Total or market demand
Nonprice determinant of demand
Increase (or decrease) in demand
Normal (superior) good
Inferior good
Substitute (competing) goods
Complementary goods
Independent goods
Supply schedule
Quantity supplied
Law of supply
Supply curve
Nonprice determinant of supply
Increase (or decrease) in supply
Equilibrium price
Equilibrium quantity
Rationing function of prices
Price-increasing (-decreasing) effect
Quantity-increasing (-decreasing) effect
Price support
Price ceiling

■ FILL-IN QUESTIONS

1. A market is the institution or mechanism that brings together the buyers and the sellers of a particular good or service.

a. In resource markets prices are determined by the demand decisions of (business firms, households) bus. firms and the supply decisions of households

b. In product markets they are determined by demand of households and supply of businesses

2. The relationship between price and quantity in the demand schedule is a(n) (direct, indirect) indirect relationship; in the supply schedule the relationship is a(n) direct one.

3. The added satisfaction or pleasure obtained by a consumer from additional units of a product decreases as her or his consumption of the product increases. This phenomenon is called diminishing marginal utility

4. A consumer tends to buy more of a product as its price falls because:

Product market
households demand; businesses supply
resource market
households supply businesses demand

a. the purchasing power of the consumer is increased and the consumer tends to buy more of this product (and of other products); this is called the (income, substitution) income effect;

b. the product becomes less expensive relative to similar products and the consumer tends to buy more of this and less of the similar products; and this is called the substitution effect.

5. When demand or supply is graphed, price is placed on the (horizontal, vertical) vertical axis and quantity on the horizontal axis.

6. When a consumer demand schedule or curve is drawn up, it is assumed that five factors that determine demand are fixed and constant. These five determinants of consumer demand are:

a. change in buyer tastes
b. Change in # of buyers
c. change in income
d. Change in price of related goods
e. Change in expectations (weather etc)

7. A decrease in demand means that consumers will buy (larger, smaller) Smaller quantities at every price or will pay (more, less) less for the same quantities.

8. A change in income or in the price of another product will result in a change in the (demand for, quantity demanded of) demand for the given product, while a change in the price of the given product will result in quantity demanded change

9. The fundamental factors which determine the supply of any commodity in the product market are:

a. Change in technology
b. Change in resource prices

c. changes in taxes & subsidies

d. changes in prices of other goods

e. change in expectation

f. change in # of suppliers

10. The equilibrium price of a commodity is the price at which quantity demanded & quantity supplied are equal

11. If quantity demanded exceeds quantity supplied, price is (above, below) below the equilibrium price; and the (shortage, surplus) shortage will cause the price to (rise, fall) rise

12. In the spaces below each of the following, indicate the effect [*increase* (+), *decrease* (−), or *indeterminate* (?)] upon equilibrium price *and* equilibrium quantity of each of these changes in demand and/or supply.

a. Increase in demand, supply constant + +

b. Increase in supply, demand constant − +

c. Decrease in demand, supply constant − −

d. Decrease in supply, demand constant + −

e. Increase in demand, increase in supply ? +

f. Increase in demand, decrease in supply + ?

g. Decrease in demand, decrease in supply ? −

h. Decrease in demand, increase in supply − ?

13. If supply and demand establish a price for a good such that there is no shortage or surplus of the good, then price is successfully performing its rationing.

14. To assume that all the nonprice determinants of demand and supply do not change is to employ the others things equal assumption.

15. The effect of a price support for a good is a (shortage, surplus) Surplus of that good; and the effect of a price ceiling is a shortage

■ **PROBLEMS AND PROJECTS**

1. Using the demand schedule below, plot the demand curve on the graph on the next page. Label the axes and indicate for each axis the units being used to measure price and quantity.

Price	Quantity demanded, 1,000 bushels of soybeans
$7.20	10
7.00	15
6.80	20
6.60	25
6.40	30
6.20	35

a. Plot the supply schedule which follows on the same graph.

Price	Quantity supplied, 1,000 bushels of soybeans
$7.20	40
7.00	35
6.80	30
6.60	25
6.40	20
6.20	15

b. The equilibrium price of soybeans will be $6.60

c. 25 thousand bushels of soybeans will be exchanged at this price.

d. Indicate clearly on the graph the equilibrium price and quantity by drawing lines from the intersection of the supply and demand curves to the price and quantity axes.

e. If the Federal government supported a price of $7.00 per bushel there would be a (shortage, surplus) ~~shortage~~ surplus of ~~10~~ 20 bushels of soybeans.

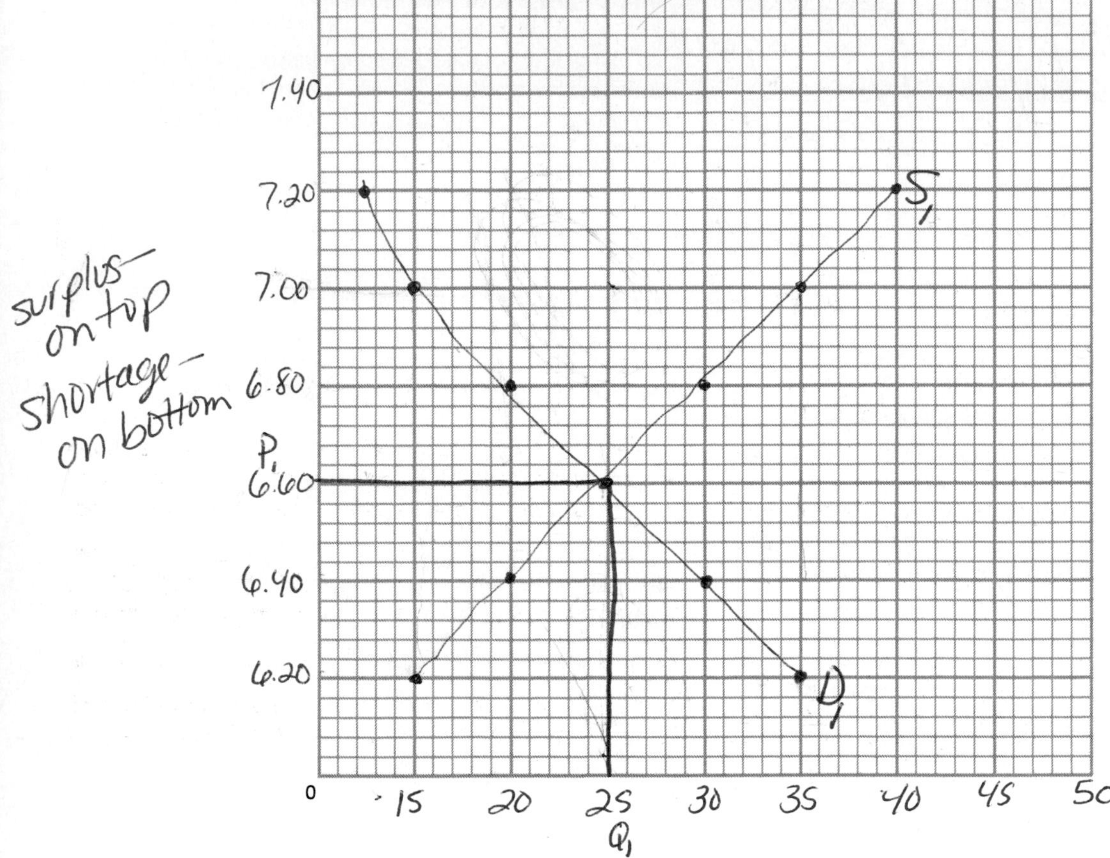

2. The demand schedules of three individuals (Roberts, Charles, and Lynn) for loaves of bread are shown below. Assuming there are only three buyers of bread, draw up the total or market demand schedule for bread.

Price	Quantity demanded, loaves of bread			Total
	Roberts	Charles	Lynn	
$.40	1	4	0	5
.36	3	5	1	9
.32	6	6	5	17
.28	10	7	10	27
.24	15	8	16	39

3. Below is a demand schedule for bushels of apples. In columns 3 and 4 insert *any* new figures for quantity which represent in column 3 an increase in demand and in column 4 a decrease in demand.

(1) Price	(2) Quantity demanded	(3) Demand increases	(4) Demand decreases
$6.00	400		
5.90	500		
5.80	600		
5.70	700		
5.60	800		
5.50	900		

Demand for A (per week)			Demand for B (per week)		
(1) Price	(2) Quantity demanded	(3) Quantity demanded	(4) Price	(5) Quantity demanded	(6) Quantity demanded
$.90	10	0	$5.00	4	7
.85	20	10	4.50	5	8
.80	30	20	4.00	6	9
.75	40	30	3.50	7	10
.70	50	40	3.00	8	11
.65	60	50	2.50	9	12
.60	70	60	2.00	10	13

4. Assume that O'Rourke has, when his income is $100 a week, the demand schedule for good A shown in columns 1 and 2 of the table above and the demand schedule for good B shown in columns 4 and 5. Assume that the prices of A and B are $.80 and $5, respectively.

a. How much A will O'Rourke buy? 30

How much B? 4

b. Suppose that, as a consequence of a $10 increase in O'Rourke's weekly income, the quantities demanded of A become those shown in column 3 and the quantities demanded of B become those shown in column 6.

(1) How much A will he now buy? 20

How much B? 7

(2) Good A is (normal, inferior) inferior (demand varies inversely)

(3) Good B is normal

5. The market demand for good X is shown in columns 1 and 2 of the next table. Assume the price of X to be $2 and constant.

(1) Price	(2) Quantity demanded	(3) Quantity demanded	(4) Quantity demanded
$2.40	1,600	1,500	1,700
2.30	1,650	1,550	1,750
2.20	1,750	1,650	1,850
2.10	1,900	1,800	2,000
2.00	2,100	2,000	2,200
1.90	2,350	2,250	2,450
1.80	2,650	2,550	2,750

price of good & demand vary inversely

a. If as the price of good Y rises from $1.25 to $1.35 the quantities demanded of good X become those shown in column 3, it can be concluded that X and Y are (substitute, complementary) complementary goods.

b. If as the price of good Y rises from $1.25 to $1.35 the quantities of good X become those shown in column 4, it can be concluded that X and Y are substitute goods.

6. In a local market for hamburger on a given date, each of 300 sellers of hamburger has the following supply schedule.

(1) Price	(2) Quantity supplied—one seller, lb.	(3) Quantity supplied—all sellers, lb.
$2.05	150 × 300	4500
2.00	110 × 300	3300
1.95	75 × 300	2250
1.90	45 × 300	1300
1.85	20	6000
1.80	0	0

a. In column 3 construct the market supply schedule for hamburger.

b. On the next page is the market demand schedule for hamburger on the same date and in the same local market as that given above.

Price	Quantity demanded, lb.
$2.05	28,000
2.00	31,000
1.95	36,000
1.90	42,000
1.85	49,000
1.80	57,000

c. If the Federal government set a ceiling price on hamburger at $1.90 a pound the result would be a (shortage, surplus) ______ of ______ pounds of hamburger in this market.

7. Each of the following events would tend to increase or decrease either the demand for or the supply of video games and, as a result, increase or decrease the price of these games. In the first blank indicate the effect upon demand or supply; and in the second indicate whether price would rise or fall.

a. It becomes known that a local department store is going to have a sale on these games three months from now. ______; ______

b. The workers who produce the games go on strike for over two months. ______; ______

c. The workers in the industry receive a 90-cent-an-hour wage increase. ______; ______

d. The average price of movie tickets increases. ______; ______

e. The firms producing the games undertake to produce a large volume of missile components for the Defense Department. ______; ______

f. It is announced by a private research institute that children who have taken to playing video games also improve their grades in school. ______; ______

g. Because of the use of mass-production techniques, the amount of labor necessary to produce a game decreases. ______; ______

h. The price of high-fidelity phonograph sets decreases. ______; ______

i. The average consumer believes that a shortage of games is developing in the economy. ______; ______

j. The Federal government imposes a $5 per game tax upon the manufacturers of video games. ______; ______

■ SELF-TEST

Circle the T if the statement is true, the F if it is false.

1. A market is any arrangement that brings the buyers and sellers of a particular good or service together. **T F**

2. Demand is the amount of a commodity or service which a buyer will purchase at a particular price. **T F**

3. The law of demand states that as price increases, other things being equal, the quantity of the product demanded increases. **T F**

4. In graphing supply and demand schedules, supply is put on the horizontal axis and demand on the vertical axis. **T F**

5. If price falls, there will be an increase in demand. **T F**

6. If the demand curve moves from D_1 to D_2 in the graph shown below, demand has increased. **T F**

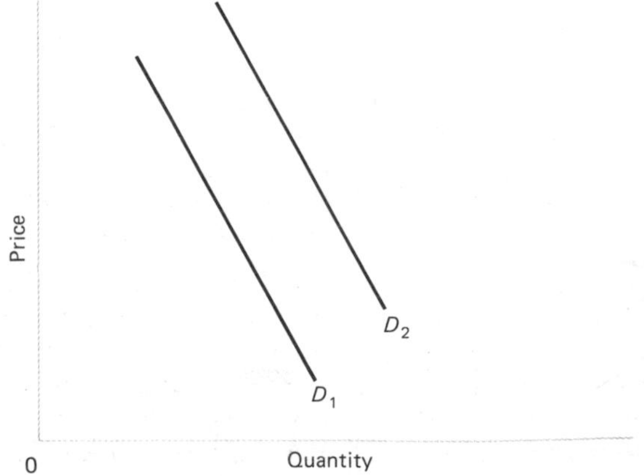

7. A fall in the price of a good will cause the demand for goods which are substitutes for it to increase. **T F**

8. If two goods are complementary, an increase in the price of one will cause the demand for the other to increase. **T F**

9. If the market price of a commodity is for a time below its equilibrium price, the market price will tend to rise because demand will decrease and supply will increase. **T F**

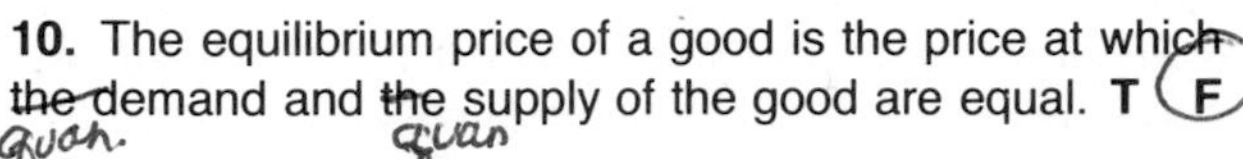

10. The equilibrium price of a good is the price at which the demand and the supply of the good are equal. **T F**

11. The rationing function of prices is the elimination of shortages and surpluses. **T F**

Circle the letter that corresponds to the best answer.

1. The markets examined in this chapter are: (*a*) perfectly competitive markets; (*b*) markets for goods and services; (*c*) markets for products and resources; (*d*) all of the above.

2. Which of the following could cause a decrease in consumer demand for product X? (*a*) A decrease in consumer income; (*b*) an increase in the prices of goods which are good substitutes for product X; (*c*) an increase in the price which consumers expect will prevail for product X in the future; (*d*) a decrease in the supply of product X.

3. If two goods are substitutes for each other, an increase in the price of one will necessarily: (*a*) decrease the demand for the other; (*b*) increase the demand for the other; (*c*) decrease the quantity demanded of the other; (*d*) increase the quantity demanded of the other.

4. The income of a consumer decreases and his/her demand for a particular good increases. It can be concluded that the good is: (*a*) normal; (*b*) inferior; (*c*) a substitute; (*d*) a complement.

5. If the supply curve moves from S_1 to S_2 on the graph, in the next column, there has been: (*a*) an increase in supply; (*b*) a decrease in supply; (*c*) an increase in quantity supplied, (*d*) a decrease in quantity supplied.

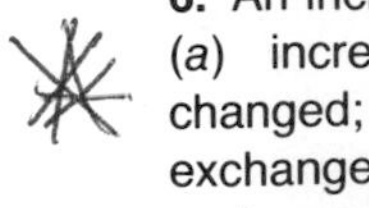

6. An increase in demand and a decrease in supply will: (*a*) increase price and increase the quantity exchanged; (*b*) decrease price and decrease the quantity exchanged; (*c*) increase price and the effect upon quantity exchanged will be indeterminate; (*d*) decrease price and the effect upon quantity exchanged will be indeterminate.

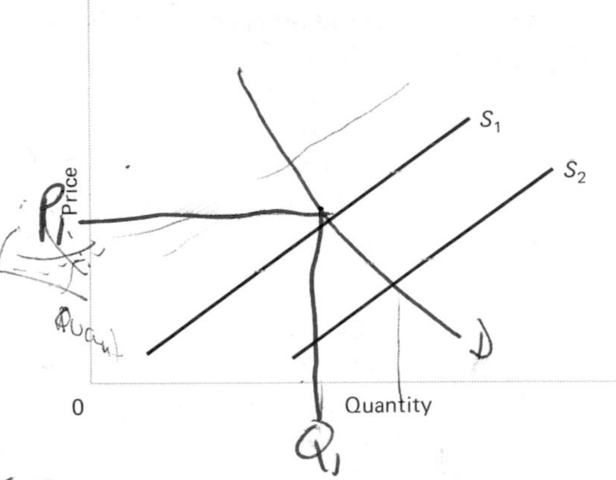

7. An increase in supply and an increase in demand will: (*a*) increase price and increase the quantity exchanged; (*b*) decrease price and increase the quantity exchanged; (*c*) affect price in an indeterminate way and decrease the quantity exchanged; (*d*) affect price in an indeterminate way and increase the quantity exchanged.

8. Which of the following could *not* cause an increase in the supply of cotton? (*a*) An increase in the price of cotton; (*b*) improvements in the art of producing cotton; (*c*) a decrease in the price of the machinery and tools employed in cotton production; (*d*) a decrease in the price of corn.

9. The law of supply states that other things being constant as price increases: (*a*) supply increases; (*b*) supply decreases; (*c*) quantity supplied increases; (*d*) quantity supplied decreases.

10. Demand and supply may be employed to explain how price is determined in: (*a*) product markets; (*b*) resource markets; (*c*) markets for foreign currency; (*d*) all of the above markets.

11. When government places a ceiling on the price of a good and that ceiling is below the equilibrium price the result will be: (*a*) a surplus of the good; (*b*) a shortage of the good; (*c*) an increase in the demand for the good; (*d*) a decrease in the supply of the good.

■ DISCUSSION QUESTIONS

1. How is a market defined?

2. Carefully define demand and state the law of demand. Now define supply and state the law of supply.

3. Several years ago the price of coffee in the United States rose as a result of bad weather in coffee-producing regions. Employ the income-effect and the substitution-effect concepts to explain why the quantity of coffee demanded in the U.S. declined dramatically. A few years later when the weather became normal the price of coffee fell. Use the diminishing-marginal-utility notion to explain why the quantity of coffee demanded rose.

4. Explain the difference between an increase in demand and an increase in quantity demanded, and between a decrease in supply and a decrease in quantity supplied.

5. Neither demand nor supply remains constant for long because the factors which determine demand and supply do not long remain constant. What are these factors? How do changes in them affect demand and supply?

6. How are normal, inferior, substitute, complementary, and independent goods defined, and how can these concepts be used to predict the way in which a change in income or in the price of another good will affect the demand for a given good?

7. Early in 1981 the ceiling price imposed by the Federal government (in 1971) on crude oil produced in the United States was eliminated in order to reduce the energy shortage in the United States. Explain why this increase in the price petroleum producers were allowed to receive helped to ease the oil shortage.

8. Given the demand for and the supply of a commodity, what price will be the equilibrium price of this commodity? Explain why this price will tend to prevail in the market and why higher (lower) prices, if they do exist temporarily, will tend to fall (rise).

9. Analyze the following quotation and explain the fallacies contained in it. "An increase in demand will cause price to rise; with a rise in price, supply will increase and the increase in supply will push price down. Therefore, an increase in demand results in little change in price because supply will increase also."

10. What is meant by the "rationing function of prices"? How do legally established price supports and price ceilings interfere with the rationing function and what are the effects of these legally established prices?

11. What is the difference between individual and market demand; and what is the relationship between these two types of demand? Does this distinction and relationship also apply to individual and market supply?

12. The interest rates received by those who lend money have in recent years been higher in the United States than in most foreign countries. This has led many foreigners to increase their purchases of American dollars (for which they pay with foreign money) and to lend these dollars in the United States. The price which foreigners have to pay to obtain an American dollar is the exchange rate for the dollar. What do you think has been the effect of higher interest rates in the United States on the exchange rate for the dollar—has it risen or fallen?

13. The interest rate is a price. It is the price paid by borrowers for the use of money and the price received by the lenders of the money. Unless government interferes, the demand for borrowed money and the supply of loanable money determine the interest rate. What would be the effect of (*a*) a government imposed interest-rate ceiling on this money market; (*b*) the deduction of interest expenses from the taxable incomes of borrowers on the demand for borrowed money and the rate of interest; and (*c*) the exclusion of interest incomes from the taxable incomes of lenders on the supply of loanable money and the rate of interest?

5
The price system and the Five Fundamental Questions

In Chapters 2, 3, and 4 you examined the institutions and characteristics of pure capitalism and saw how supply and demand determine equilibrium prices and equilibrium quantities in resource and product markets. Chapter 5 draws these elements together into an explanation of the ways in which the market system finds answers for the first four of the Five Fundamental Questions. This explanation is only an approximation—a simplified version or a model—of the methods actually employed by the American economy. Yet this simple model, like all good models, contains enough realism to be truthful and is general enough to be understandable.

The model is intentionally and specifically unrealistic because the economic role of government is ignored and because actual competition in the American economy is probably much less effective than is assumed in Chapter 5. These shortcomings, however, do not weaken the major points made in the chapter about the functioning of the price-market system; and the shortcomings are corrected in later chapters to make the model less unrealistic.

The first of the two major sections is entitled "Operation of the Price System" and is both the most important part of this chapter and the part you will find most difficult. If you will try to understand how the American system of prices and markets finds answers for each of the four basic questions by examining them *individually* and in the order in which they are presented, you will more easily understand how the price system as a whole operates. Actually the price system finds answers for all these questions simultaneously, but it is much simpler to consider them as if they were separate questions.

In addition to explaining how the price system operates, Chapter 5 also takes up the question of *how well* it operates. Here you will find the going much easier. It should be particularly noted, however, that the price-market system is a widely accepted method of allocating scarce resources because it is economically quite efficient in the allocation of resources. But even so, it, like every other economic system devised by humans, is not so efficient as it might be. The specific criticisms leveled against the price-market system are well worth noting because, as will be seen in Chapter 6, many of government's functions in the economy are directed toward the correction of the system's faults which have been pointed out by its critics; in fact, one of the reasons for ignoring the role of government in Chapter 5 is to emphasize the shortcomings of pure capitalism in the absence of government.

A few final words of advice to you. Be sure to understand the *importance* and *role* of each of the following in the operation of the price-market system: (1) the rationing and directing functions of prices, (2) the profit motive of business firms, (3) the entry into and exodus of firms from industries, (4) competition, and (5) consumer sovereignty.

■ CHECKLIST

When you have studied this chapter you should be able to:

☐ Explain how a competitive price system determines what will be produced.

☐ Distinguish between normal profit and economic profit.

☐ Predict what will happen to the price charged by and the output of a prosperous and an unprosperous industry; and explain why these events will occur.

☐ Explain how production is organized in a competitive price system.

☐ Find the least-cost combination of resources when you are given the technological data and the prices of the resources.

☐ Explain how a competitive price system determines the distribution of total output.
☐ List the three kinds of change to which an economy must be able to adapt itself if it is to remain efficient; and explain how a competitive price system both adjusts to and initiates desirable changes.
☐ Present the case for and the case against the price system.
☐ Identify the two basic differences between an ideal price system and the price system found in the United States.

■ CHAPTER OUTLINE

1. The system of prices and markets and the choices of households and business firms furnish the economy with answers to the first four Fundamental Questions.

a. The demands of consumers for products and the desires of business firms to maximize their profits determine what and how much of each product is produced (and its price).

b. The desires of business firms to maximize profits by keeping their costs of production as low as possible guide them to employ the most efficient techniques of production and determine their demands for and prices of the various resources; competition forces them to use the most efficient techniques and ensures that only the most efficient will be able to stay in business.

c. With resource prices determined, the money income of each household is determined; and with product prices determined, the quantity of goods and services which these money incomes will buy is determined.

d. The price-market system is able to accommodate itself to changes in consumer tastes, technology, and resource supplies.

(1) The desires of business firms for maximum profits and competition lead the economy to make the appropriate adjustments in the way it uses its resources.

(2) Competition and the desire to increase profits promote both better techniques of production and capital accumulation.

e. Competition in the economy compels firms seeking to promote their own interests to promote (as though led by an "invisible hand") the best interest of society as a whole: an allocation of resources appropriate to consumer wants, production by the most efficient means, and the lowest possible prices.

2. The price system has been praised and damned because it has both merits and faults.

a. The major merits of the system are that it efficiently allocates scarce resources and allows individuals large amounts of personal freedom.

b. The chief faults are the decline in the competitiveness of markets and wasteful and inefficient production.

c. The analysis of the price system found in this chapter is only a rough approximation of how the American economy actually operates because the bigness of some buyers and sellers has weakened competition in some markets because the economic role of government has been ignored.

■ IMPORTANT TERMS

Normal profit	**Derived demand**
Economic cost	**Guiding function of prices**
Economic profit	**Self-limiting adjustment**
Expanding (prosperous) industry	**Invisible hand**
Declining (unprosperous) industry	**Market failure**
Dollar votes	**External (spillover) benefit**
Consumer sovereignty	**External (spillover) cost**

■ FILL-IN QUESTIONS

1. The competitive price system is a mechanism for both Communicating the decisions of producers and households and Synchronizing these decisions.

2. A *normal* profit (is, is not) is an economic cost because it is a payment that (must, need not) must be paid to (workers, landowners, suppliers of capital goods, entrepreneurs) entrepreneurs; but a *pure* (or *economic*) profit (is, is not) isn't an economic cost because it (must, need not) need not be paid to them to obtain and retain the services they provide to the firm.

3. Pure or economic profits are equal to the total revenue of a firm less its total costs

4. Business firms tend to produce those products from which they can obtain:

a. at least a (pure, normal) normal profit; and

b. the maximum pure profit.

5. If firms in an industry are obtaining economic profits, firms will (enter, leave) enter the industry, the price of the industry's product will (rise, fall) fall, the industry will employ (more, fewer) more resources, produce a (larger, smaller) ~~smaller~~ larger output, and the industry's economic profits will (increase, decrease) decrease until they are equal to 0

6. Consumers:

a. vote with their dollars for the production of a good or service when they buy that good or service;

b. are said, because firms are motivated by their desire for profits to produce the goods and services consumers vote for in this way, to be (dependent, sovereign) sovereign

c. (restrict, expand) restrict the freedom of firms and resource suppliers.

7. Because firms are interested in obtaining the largest economic profits possible the technique they select to produce a product is the one that enables them to produce that product in the least cost ly way.

8. In determining how the total output of the economy will be divided among its households the price system is involved in two ways:

a. it determines the money income each of the households receives; and

b. it determines the price they have to pay for each of the goods and services produced.

9. In industrial economies:

a. the changes which occur almost continuously are changes in consumer tastes, in technology, and in the supplies of resources;

b. to make the adjustments in the way it uses its resources that are appropriate to these changes a market economy allows price to perform its guiding function.

10. The competitive price system tends to foster technological change.

a. The incentive for a firm to be the first to employ a new and improved technique of production or to produce a new and better product is a greater economic profit;

b. and the incentive for other firms to follow its lead is the avoidance of losses

11. The entrepreneur uses money which is obtained either from profits or from borrowed funds to acquire capital goods.

12. If the price system is competitive, there is an identity of public interests and the social interest: firms seem to be guided by an invisible hand to allocate the economy's resources efficiently.

13. The chief economic advantage of the price system, it is said, is that efficiently allocates resources; its chief noneconomic advantage is that it emphasizes personal freedom

14. Critics of the price system argue that:

a. with the passage of time there is a weakening of competition

b. the system is inefficient because

(1) the distribution of income is unequal

(2) even competitive markets fail to recognize external ______ and ______ and to take into account the demand for ______ goods;

(3) it does not ensure the ______ of resources and stable ______

15. This chapter has been (intentionally) unrealistic because it has ignored the existence of ______ business corporations and labor unions and the economic role of ______

■ PROBLEMS AND PROJECTS

1. Assume that a firm can produce *either* product A, product B, or product C with the resources it currently employs. These resources *cost* the firm a total of $50 per week. Assume, for the purposes of the problem, that the firm's employment of resources cannot be changed. The market prices of and the quantities of A, B, and C these resources will produce per week are given below. Compute the firm's profit when it produces A, B, or C; and enter these profits in the table below.

Product	Market price	Output	Economic profit
A	$7.00	8	$______
B	4.50	10	______
C	.25	240	______

a. Which product will the firm produce? ______

b. If the price of A rose to $8, the firm would ______

(Hint: You will have to recompute the firm's profit from the production of A.)

c. If the firm were producing A and selling it at a price of $8, what would tend to happen to the number of firms producing A?

______

2. Suppose that a firm can produce 100 units of product X by combining labor, land, capital, and entrepreneurial ability in three different ways. If it can hire labor at $2 per unit, land at $3 per unit, capital at $5 per unit, and entrepreneurship at $10 per unit; and if the amounts of the resources required by the three methods of producing 100 units of product X are indicated in the table, answer the questions below it.

	Method		
Resource	1	2	3
Labor	8	13	10
Land	4	3	3
Capital	4	2	4
Entrepreneurship	1	1	1

a. Which method is the least expensive way of producing 100 units of X? ______

b. If X sells for 70 cents per unit, what is the economic profit of the firm? $______

c. If the price of labor should rise from $2 to $3 per unit and if the price of X is 70 cents,

(1) the firm's use of:

Labor would change from ______ to ______

Land would change from ______ to ______

Capital would change from ______ to ______

Entrepreneurship would not change.

(2) The firm's economic profit would change from $______ to $______

■ SELF-TEST

Circle the T if the statement is true, the F if it is false.

1. Business firms try to maximize their normal profits. **T F**

2. Industries in which economic profits are earned by the firms in the industry will attract the entry of new firms into the industry. **T F**

3. If firms have sufficient time to enter and leave industries, the economic profits of an industry will tend to disappear. **T F**

4. Business firms are really only free to produce whatever they want in any way they wish if they do not want to maximize profits or to minimize losses. **T F**

5. To say that the demand for a resource is a derived demand means that it depends upon the demands for the products the resource is used to produce. T F

6. Resources will tend to be used in those industries capable of earning normal or economic profits. T F

7. Economic efficiency requires that a given output of a good or service be produced in the least costly way. T F

8. If the market price of resource A increases, firms will tend to employ smaller quantities of resource A. T F

9. Changes in the tastes of consumers are reflected in changes in consumer demand for products. T F

10. The incentive which the price system provides to induce technological improvement is the opportunity for economic profits. T F

11. In a capitalistic economy it is from the entrepreneur that the demand for capital goods arises. T F

12. The tendency for individuals pursuing their own self-interests to bring about results which are in the best interest of society as a whole is often called the "invisible hand." T F

Circle the letter that corresponds to the best answer.

1. The competitive price system is a method of: (*a*) communicating the decisions of consumers, producers, and resource suppliers; (*b*) synchronizing these decisions; (*c*) communicating and synchronizing these decisions; (*d*) neither communicating nor synchronizing the decisions.

2. Which of the following best defines economic costs? (*a*) Total payments made to workers, landowners, suppliers of capital, and entrepreneurs; (*b*) only total payments made to workers, landowners, suppliers of capital, and entrepreneurs which must be paid to obtain the services of their resources; (*c*) total payments made to workers, landowners, suppliers of capital and entrepreneurs less normal profits; (*d*) total payments made to workers, landowners, suppliers of capital, and entrepreneurs plus normal profits.

3. If less than normal profits are being earned by the firms in an industry, the consequences will be that: (*a*) lower-priced resources will be drawn into the industry; (*b*) firms will leave the industry, causing the price of the industry's product to fall; (*c*) the price of the industry's product will rise and fewer resources will be employed by the industry; (*d*) the price of the industry's product will fall and thereby cause the demand for the product to increase.

4. Which of the following would not necessarily result, sooner or later, from a decrease in consumer demand for a product? (*a*) A decrease in the profits of the industry producing the product; (*b*) a decrease in the output of the industry; (*c*) a decrease in the supply of the product; (*d*) an increase in the prices of resources employed by the firms in the industry.

5. If firm A does not employ the most "efficient" or least costly method of production, which of the following will *not* be a consequence? (*a*) Firm A will fail to earn the greatest profit possible; (*b*) other firms in the industry will be able to sell the product at lower prices; (*c*) new firms will enter the industry and sell the product at a lower price than that at which firm A now sells it; (*d*) firm A will be spending less on resources and hiring fewer resources than it otherwise would.

6. Which of the following is *not* a factor in determining the share of the total output of the economy received by any household? (*a*) The price at which the household sells its resources; (*b*) the quantities of resources which the household sells; (*c*) the tastes of the household; (*d*) the prices which the household must pay to buy products.

7. If an increase in the demand for a product and the resulting rise in the price of the product cause the supply of the product, the size of the industry producing the product, and the amounts of resources devoted to its production to expand, price is successfully performing its: (*a*) guiding function; (*b*) rationing function; (*c*) medium-of-exchange function; (*d*) standard-of-value function.

8. In a capitalistic economy characterized by competition, if one firm introduces a new and better method of production, other firms will be forced to adopt the improved technique: (*a*) to avoid less-than-normal profits; (*b*) to obtain economic profits; (*c*) to prevent the price of the product from falling; (*d*) to prevent the price of the product from rising.

9. Which of the following would be an indication that competition does not exist in an industry? (*a*) Less-than-normal profits in the industry; (*b*) inability of the firms in the industry to expand; (*c*) inability of firms to enter the industry; (*d*) wages lower than the average wage in the economy paid to workers in the industry.

10. Economic criticism of the price system is widespread and has pointed out many of the failures of the system. However, the chief economic virtue of the system remains that of: (*a*) allowing extensive personal freedom; (*b*) efficiently allocating resources; (*c*) providing an equitable distribution of income; (*d*) eliminating the need for decision making.

11. Which one of the following is *not* a part of the case *against* the price system? (*a*) With the passage of time competition becomes excessive; (*b*) it distributes income unequally; (*c*) spillover costs and benefits are not registered in the marketplace; (*d*) it does not guarantee either full employment or price stability.

12. This chapter is unrealistic because it ignores: (*a*) the role of government in the economy; (*b*) the impact of large business corporations; (*c*) the existence of big labor unions; (*d*) all of the above.

■ DISCUSSION QUESTIONS

1. In what way do the desires of entrepreneurs to obtain economic profits and to avoid losses make consumer sovereignty effective?

2. Why is the ability of firms to enter industries which are prosperous important to the effective functioning of competition?

3. Explain *in detail* how an increase in the consumer demand for a product will result in more of the product being produced and in more resources being allocated to its production.

4. To what extent are firms "free" to produce what they wish by methods which they choose? Do resource owners have freedom to use their resources as they wish?

5. What is meant when it is said that competition is the mechanism which "controls" the price-market system? How does competition do this? What do critics of the price system argue tends to happen to this controlling mechanism as time passes, and why do they so argue?

6. What are the two important functions of prices? Explain the difference between these two functions.

7. "An invisible hand operates to identify private and public interests." What are private interests and what is the public interest? What is it that leads the economy to operate as if it were directed by an invisible hand?

8. If the basic economic decisions are not made in a capitalistic economy by a central authority, how are they made?

9. Households use the dollars obtained by selling resource services to "vote" for the production of consumer goods and services. Who "votes" for the production of capital goods, why do they "vote" for capital-goods production, and where do they obtain the dollars needed to cast these "votes"?

10. What five arguments do critics of the price system advance to refute the contention that the price system allocates resources efficiently?

11. What are the two principal kinds of market failures? Include in your answer definitions of an external cost and an external benefit.

12. To what extent is this chapter unrealistic?

6
Mixed capitalism and the economic functions of government

Chapter 6 introduces you to the five basic functions performed by the Federal, state, and local governments in America's mixed capitalistic economy. This is an examination of the actual role of government (the public sector) in an economy which is neither a purely planned nor a purely market-type economy. The discussion points out the degree and the ways in which government causes the American economy to differ from pure capitalism. The chapter does not attempt to list all the *specific* ways in which government affects the behavior of the economy. Instead it provides a *general* classification of the tasks performed by government.

Following an explanation of each of the five functions of government in the American economy, the chapter attempts to evaluate the economic role of government in the United States. Here it is pointed out that people generally agree that government should perform these functions. But they disagree on how far government should go in performing them and over whether specific government actions and programs are needed for government to perform these functions.

Governments today frequently employ benefit-cost analysis to determine whether they should or should not undertake some specific action—a particular act, project, or program. This kind of analysis forces government to estimate both the added costs and the additional benefits of the project or program; to expand its activities only where the additional benefits exceed the added costs; and to reduce or eliminate programs and projects when the additional costs exceed the added benefits.

The latter part of Chapter 6 examines two important questions which are related to the economic role of government in the American economy. The first question is whether government fails to solve social problems because the process it uses to make decisions is an inherently inefficient mechanism for allocating resources. The question is whether there has been a public sector failure; and the author presents some of the reasons why the public sector's decision-making process may result in a misallocation of resources in the economy. The second question is whether an increase in the size of government's role in the economy reduces or expands the freedoms of the individual members of the American society. The author presents the case of those who argue that expanded governmental activity reduces personal freedom and the case of those who contend it may actually lead to greater individual freedom.

■ CHECKLIST

When you have studied this chapter you should be able to:

- ☐ Explain in one or two sentences why the American economy is *mixed* rather than *pure* capitalism.
- ☐ Enumerate the five economic functions of government in the United States; and explain the difference between the purpose of the first two and the purpose of the last three functions.
- ☐ Define monopoly and explain why government wishes to prevent monopoly and to preserve competition in the economy.
- ☐ Explain why government feels it should redistribute income and list the three principal policies it employs for this purpose.
- ☐ Define a spillover cost and a spillover benefit; explain why a competitive market fails to allocate resources efficiently when there are spillovers; and list the things government may do to reduce spillovers and improve the allocation of resources.

☐ Define a public good and a private good and explain how government goes about reallocating resources from the production of private to the production of public goods.

☐ Draw a circular flow diagram that includes businesses, households, and government; label all the flows in the diagram; and use the diagram to explain how government alters the distribution of income, the allocation of resources, and the level of activity in the economy.

☐ Use benefit-cost analysis to determine the extent to which government should apply resources to a project or activity when you are given the cost and benefit data.

☐ Explain what is meant by "public sector failure" and list several possible causes of this alleged failure.

☐ Present briefly the case for and the case against the proposition that an expanded public sector reduces personal freedom.

■ CHAPTER OUTLINE

1. The American economy is neither a pure market economy nor a purely planned economy. It is an example of mixed capitalism in which government affects the operation of the economy in important ways.

2. Government in the American economy performs five economic functions. The first two of these functions are designed to enable the price system to operate more effectively; and the other three functions are designed to eliminate the major shortcomings of a purely market-type economy.

3. The first of these functions is to provide the legal and social framework that makes the effective operation of the price system possible.

4. The second function is the maintenance of competition and the regulation of monopoly.

5. Government performs its third function when it redistributes income to reduce income inequality.

6. When government reallocates resources it performs its fourth function.

a. It reallocates resources to take account of spillover costs and benefits.

b. It also reallocates resources to provide society with public (social) goods and services.

c. It levies taxes and uses the tax revenues to purchase or produce the public goods.

7. Its fifth function is stabilization of the price level and the maintenance of full employment.

8. A circular flow diagram that includes the public sector as well as business firms and households in the private sector of the economy reveals that government purchases public goods from private businesses, collects taxes from and makes transfer payments to these firms, purchases labor services from households, and collects taxes from and makes transfer payments to these households; and government can alter the distribution of income, reallocate resources, and change the level of economic activity by affecting the six flows in the diagram.

9. In evaluating government's role in the economy it should be noted that:

a. It is generally agreed that it is desirable for government to perform these five functions; but there is a good deal of controversy about how far it should go in performing them.

b. Benefit-cost analysis may be employed by government to determine whether it should employ resources for a project and to decide upon the total quantity of resources it should devote to a project. Additional resources should be devoted to a project only so long as the marginal benefit to society from using the additional resources for the project exceeds the marginal cost to society of the additional resources.

c. In using benefit-cost analysis, however, government encounters the problem of measuring benefits and costs accurately.

10. Critics of the governmental or public sector of the economy argue that this sector has failed to find solutions for social problems; and public choice theory suggests that the public sector has failed because the process it uses to make decisions is inherently weak and results in an economically inefficient allocation of resources.

a. The weakness of the decision-making process in the public sector and the resulting inefficient allocation of resources is often the result of pressures exerted on Congress and the bureaucracy by special interests.

b. Those seeking election to public office frequently favor (oppose) programs whose benefits (costs) are clear and immediate and whose costs (benefits) are uncertain and deferred even when the benefits are less (greater) than the costs.

c. When the citizen must vote for candidates who represent different but complete programs the voter is unable to select those parts of a program which he or she favors and to reject the other parts of the program.

d. It is argued that the public sector (unlike the private sector) is inefficient because those employed there are offered no incentive to be efficient; and because there is no way to measure efficiency in the public sector.

e. Just as the private or market sector of the economy does not allocate resources perfectly, the public sector does not perform its functions perfectly; and the imperfections of both sectors make it difficult to determine which sector will provide a particular good or service more efficiently.

11. The nature and amount of government activity and the extent of individual freedom may be related to each other.

■ IMPORTANT TERMS

Market economy	**Exclusion principle**
Planned economy	**Quasi-public good**
Mixed capitalism	**Free-rider problem**
Monopoly	**Benefit-cost analysis**
Spillover (externality)	**Public sector**
Spillover cost	**Public sector failure**
Spillover benefit	**Public choice theory**
Subsidy	**Special-interest effect**
Public (social) good	**Fallacy of limited decisions**
Private good	

■ FILL-IN QUESTIONS

1. All actual economies are "mixed" because they combine elements of a ______ economy and a ______ economy.

2. List the five economic functions of government:

a. ______

b. ______

c. ______

d. ______

e. ______

3. To control monopoly in the United States government has:

a. created commissions to ______ the prices and the services of the ______ monopolies; and taken over at the local level the ______ of electric and water companies;

b. enacted ______ laws to maintain competition.

4. The price system, because it is an impersonal mechanism, results in an (equal, unequal) ______ distribution of income. To redistribute income from the upper- to the lower-income groups the Federal government has:

a. enacted ______ programs;

b. engaged in ______ intervention;

c. used the ______ tax to raise much of its revenues.

5. Government frequently reallocates resources when it finds instances of ______ failure; and the two major cases of such failure occur when the competitive price system either:

a. ______

b. or ______

6. Competitive markets bring about an optimum allocation of resources only if there are no ______ costs or benefits in the consumption and production of the good or service.

7. There is a spillover whenever some of the costs of producing a product or some of the benefits from consuming it accrue to ______.

8. Whenever in a competitive market there are:

a. spillover costs the result is an (over-, under-) ______ allocation of resources to the production of the good or service;

b. spillover benefits the result is an ______ allocation of resources to the production of the good or service.

9. What two things can government do to:

a. Make the market reflect spillover costs?

(1) ______

(2) ______________________________

b. Make the market reflect spillover benefits?

(1) ______________________________

(2) ______________________________

10. Public (social) goods tend to be goods which are not subject to the ______________ principle and which are (divisible, indivisible) ______________. Quasi-public goods are goods which could be subjected to the exclusion principle but which are provided by government because they have large spillover ______________

11. To reallocate resources from the production of private to the production of public goods government reduces the demand for private goods by ______________ consumers and firms and then ______________ public goods.

12. To stabilize the economy, government:

a. when there is less than full employment (increases, decreases) ______________ aggregate demand by (increasing, decreasing) ______________ its expenditures for public goods and services and by (increasing, decreasing) ______________ taxes.

b. when there are inflationary pressures ______________ ______________ aggregate demand by ______________ its expenditures for public goods and services and by ______________ taxes.

13. Throughout most of its history government in the United States has performed in some degree each of the five functions except that of ______________ ______________

14. In applying benefit-cost analysis, government should employ more resources in the public sector if the marginal (costs, benefits) ______________ from the additional public goods exceed the marginal (costs, benefits) ______________ that result from having fewer private goods.

15. When government employs benefit-cost analysis it often finds that it is difficult to ______________ the benefits and the costs of a program.

16. When governments use resources to attempt to solve social problems and the employment of these resources does not result in solutions to these problems there has been ______________ sector ______________

17. Four possible reasons for public sector failure are:

a. that government instead of promoting the general interests (or welfare) of its citizens may promote the ______________ interests of small groups in the economy;

b. that the benefits from a program or project are often (clear, hidden) ______________ and its costs are frequently ______________

c. that individual voters are unable to ______________ the particular quantities of each public good and service they wish the public sector to provide;

d. that there are weak ______________ to be efficient in the public sector and no way to ______________ the efficiency of the public sector.

18. Those who allege that there are inherent deficiencies in the processes used to make decisions in the public sector and that these deficiencies produce economic inefficiency are interested in public ______________ theory.

19. Despite the recognition of inefficiency in the public sector:

a. it should be recognized that there is also inefficiency in the ______________ of the economy;

b. the institutions employed in both sectors to allocate resources are ______________

c. it is, therefore, difficult to determine to which sector the production of a particular good or service should be ______________

20. To reason that increased governmental activity necessarily reduces private economic activity is an example of the fallacy of ______________

■ PROBLEMS AND PROJECTS

1. Below is a list of various government activities. Indicate in the space to the right of each into which of the five classes of government functions the activity falls. If it falls under more than one of the functions, indicate this.

a. Maintaining an army reallocate

b. Providing for a system of unemployment compensation redistribute

c. Establishment of the Federal Reserve Banks legal

d. Insuring employees of business firms against industrial accidents reallocate

e. Establishment of an Antitrust Division in the Department of Justice competition

f. Making it a crime to sell stocks and bonds under false pretenses legal

g. Providing low-cost lunches to school children redistribute

h. Taxation of whisky and other spirits reallocate

i. Regulation of organized stock, bond, and commodity markets ______

j. Setting tax *rates* higher for larger incomes than for smaller ones ______

2. The circular flow diagram below includes business firms, households, and government (the public sector).

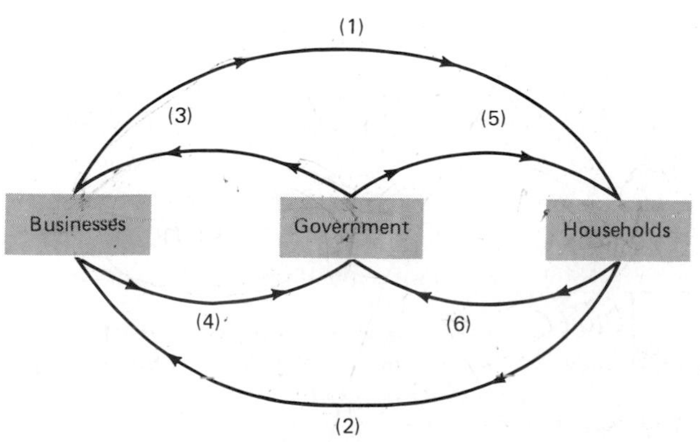

a. The flow labeled

(1) is the expenditures of (households, businesses, government) business for (products, resources) resources obtained from households;

(2) is the expenditures of households for products obtained from businesses;

(3) is the expenditures of government for products obtained from businesses

(4) is the taxes minus the transfer payments collected by government from businesses;

(5) is the expenditures of gov't for resources obtained from households; and

(6) is the taxes minus the transfer payments collected by government from households.

b. If government wished to

(1) expand output and employment in the economy it would increase flows 3 or 5, decrease flows 4 or 6, or do both;

(2) increase the production of public (social) goods and decrease the production of private goods in the economy it would increase flows 4 and 6 or 3;

(3) redistribute income from high-income to low-income households it would (increase, decrease) increase the taxes minus transfers paid by the former and decrease the taxes minus transfers paid by the latter in flow 6

3. On the following graph are the demand and supply curves for a product bought and sold in a competitive market. Assume that there are no spillover benefits or costs.

a. Were this market to produce an output of Q_1 there would be an (optimum, under, over) under allocation of resources to the production of this product.

b. Were this market to produce Q_3 there would be an over allocation of resources to this product.

Supply has to do w/ cost
Benefit has to do w/ demand

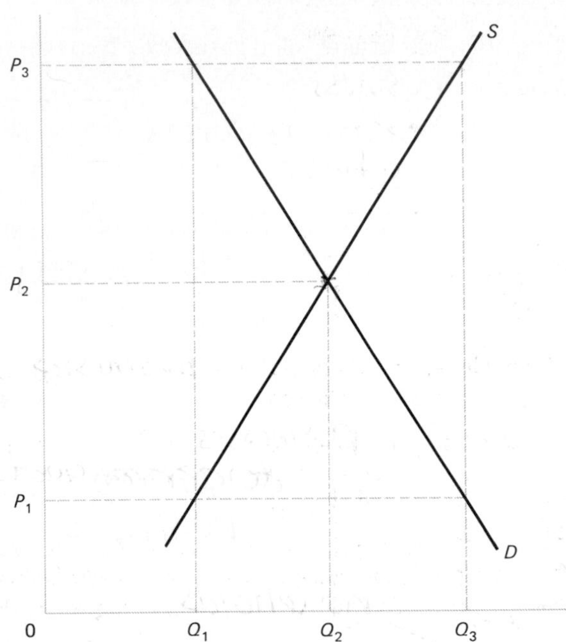

c. The equilibrium output is Q2 and at this output there is an optimum allocation of resources.

4. On two graphs that follow are product demand and supply curves that do *not* reflect either the spillover costs

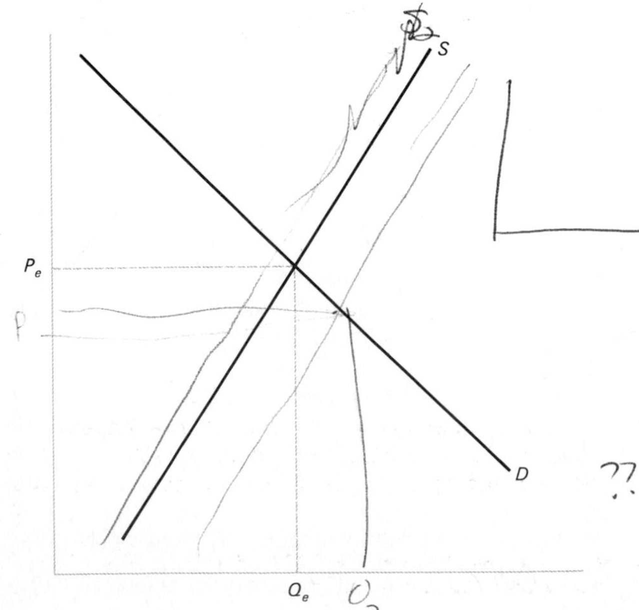

of producing the product or the spillover benefits obtained from its consumption.

a. On the first graph draw in another curve that reflects the inclusion of spillover costs.

(1) Government might force the (demand for, supply of) Supply of the product to reflect the spillover costs of producing it by (taxing, subsidizing) tax the producers.

(2) The inclusion of spillover costs in the total cost of producing the product (increases, decreases) decreases the output of the product and increases its price.

b. On the next graph draw in another curve that reflects the inclusion of spillover *benefits*.

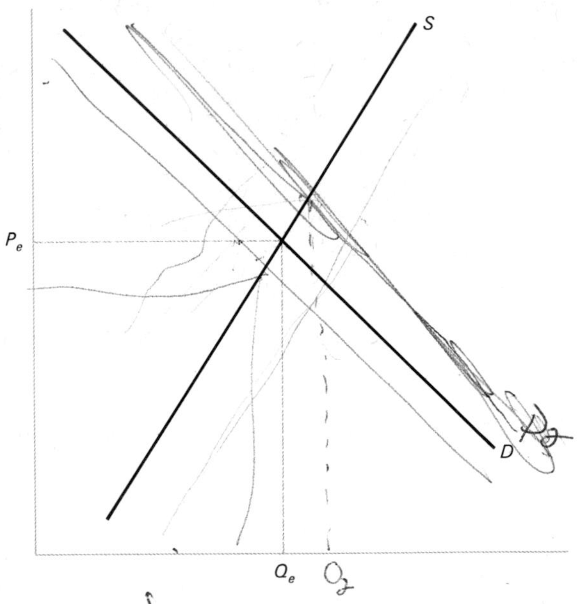

(1) Indicate on the graph the output that is optimum when spillover benefits are included.

(2) To bring about the production of this optimum output government might (tax, subsidize) subsidize the producers of this product and this would (raise, lower) lower the supply curve for the product.

(3) Draw on the graph this new supply curve. It should cross the original demand curve at the optimum output determined in (1) above.

Project	Total cost	Marginal cost	Total benefit	Marginal benefit
No highway	$ 0		$ 0	
2 lane highway	500	$______	650	$______
4 lane highway	680	______	750	______
6 lane highway	760	______	800	______
8 lane highway	860	______	825	______

(4) This optimum output is (greater than, less than, equal to) ______ Q_e; and the price of the product is (above, below, equal to) ______ P_e.

5. Imagine that a state government is considering the construction of a new highway to link its two largest cities. Its estimate of the total costs and the total benefits of building 2, 4, 6, and 8 lane highways between the two cities are shown in the table above. (All figures are in millions of dollars.)

a. Compute the marginal cost and the marginal benefit of the 2, 4, 6, and 8 lane highways.

b. Will it benefit the state to allocate resources to construct a highway? ______

c. If the state builds a highway:

(1) It should be a ______ lane highway.

(2) The total cost will be $______

(3) The total benefit will be $______

(4) The *net* benefit to the state will be $______

■ SELF-TEST

Circle the T if the statement is true, the F if it is false.

1. The American economy cannot be called "capitalistic" because its operation involves some "planning." **T F**

2. When the Federal government provides for a monetary system, it is functioning to provide the economy with public goods and services. **T F**

3. An economy in which strong and effective competition is maintained will find no need for programs designed to redistribute income. **T F**

4. Competitive product markets ensure an optimal allocation of an economy's resources. **T F**

5. In a competitive product market and in the absence of spillover costs, the supply curve or schedule reflects the costs of producing the product. **T F**

6. If demand and supply reflected all the benefits and costs of a product, the equilibrium output of a competitive market would be identical with its optimum output. **T F**

The following graph should be used to answer true-false question 7 and multiple-choice question 3.

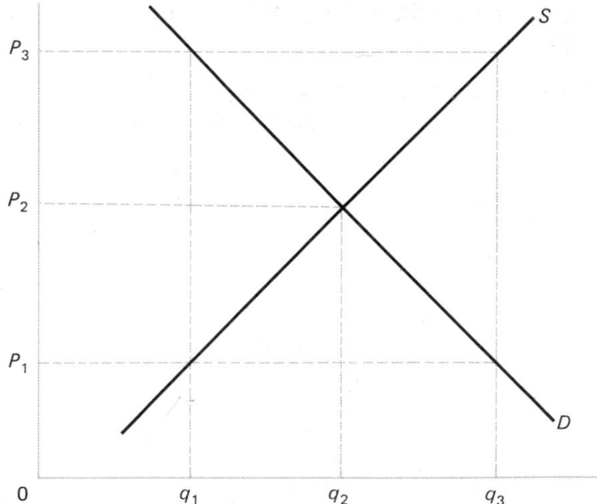

7. Assuming there are no spillover costs or benefits, the production of q_1 units of this product would result in an overallocation of resources to the production of the product. **T F**

8. The inclusion of the spillover benefits would increase the demand for a product. **T F**

9. When there are spillover costs involved in the production of a product, more resources are allocated to the production of that product and more of the product is produced than is optimal or most efficient. T F

10. Subsidizing the firms producing goods which provide spillover benefits will usually result in a better allocation of resources. T F

11. Governments have undertaken to provide lighthouse services because these services have social benefits and private producers of such services encounter the free-rider problem. T F

12. In performing its stabilization function when there is widespread unemployment and no inflation in the economy, government should decrease its spending for public goods and services and increase taxes. T F

13. If the economic role of government in the United States is evaluated objectively, it becomes clear that the scope of the government's activities is too large. T F

14. Reduced government spending is the same as economy in government. T F

15. In practice it is usually quite simple to estimate the costs and the benefits of a project financed by government. T F

16. There is a failure in the public sector whenever a governmental program or activity has been expanded to the level at which the marginal social cost exceeds the marginal social benefit. T F

17. The special-interests effect, it is argued by those concerned with public choice theory, tends to reduce public sector failures because the pressures exerted on government by one special-interest group are offset by the pressures brought to bear by other special-interest groups. T F

18. When the costs of programs are hidden and the benefits are clear vote-seeking politicians tend to reject economically justifiable programs. T F

19. The nonselectivity of citizens refers to the inability of individual voters to select the precise bundle of social goods and services that best satisfies the citizen's wants when he or she must vote for a candidate and the candidate's entire program. T F

20. Both liberals and conservatives agree that the expansion of government's role in the economy has reduced personal freedom in the United States. T F

Circle the letter that corresponds to the best answer.

1. Which of the following is *not* one of the methods utilized by government to control monopoly? (*a*) The imposition of special taxes on monopolists; (*b*) government ownership of monopolies; (*c*) government regulation of monopolies; (*d*) antitrust laws.

2. One of the following is *not* employed by government to redistribute income. Which one? (*a*) The negative income tax; (*b*) direct market intervention; (*c*) income taxes which take a larger part of the incomes of the rich than the poor; (*d*) public assistance programs.

Use the graph on page 41 to answer the following question.

3. If there are neither spillover costs nor spillover benefits, the output which results in the optimum allocation of resources to the production of this product is (*a*) q_1; (*b*) q_2; (*c*) q_3; (*d*) none of these outputs.

4. When the production and consumption of a product entail *both* spillover costs and benefits, a competitive product market results in (*a*) an underallocation of resources to the product; (*b*) an overallocation of resources to the product; (*c*) an optimum allocation of resources to the product; (*d*) an allocation of resources that may or may not be optimum.

5. Which of the following is the best example of a good or service providing the economy with spillover benefits? (*a*) An automobile; (*b*) a drill press; (*c*) a high school education; (*d*) an operation for appendicitis.

6. In the American economy the reallocation of resources needed to provide for the production of public goods is accomplished mainly by means of (*a*) government subsidies to the producers of social goods; (*b*) government purchases of social goods from producers; (*c*) direct control of producers of both private and social goods; (*d*) direct control of producers of social goods only.

7. Which of the following is characteristic of public goods? (*a*) They are indivisible; (*b*) they are sold in competitive markets; (*c*) they are subject to the exclusion principle; (*d*) they can be produced only if large spillover costs are incurred.

8. Quasi-public goods are goods and services (*a*) to which the exclusion principle could not be applied; (*b*) which have large spillover benefits; (*c*) which would not be produced by private producers through the market system; (*d*) which are indivisible.

9. To redistribute income from high-income to low-income households government might (*a*) increase transfer payments to high-income and decrease transfer payments to low-income households; (*b*) increase the taxes paid by high-income and increase the transfer payments to low-income households; (*c*) increase the taxes paid by low-income and decrease the taxes paid by high-income households; (*d*) decrease the taxes paid by high-income and decrease the transfer payments to low-income households.

10. To reallocate resources from the private to the public sector of the economy government should (*a*) increase its expenditures for the goods it purchases from business firms; (*b*) increase the transfer payments it makes to households; (*c*) increase its expenditures for the labor services it purchases from households; (*d*) do either or both *a* and *c*.

11. To prevent or slow inflation in the economy government should (*a*) increase its expenditures for the goods and services it purchases from business firms and households; (*b*) increase the transfer payments it makes to business firms and the public; (*c*) increase the taxes it collects from business firms and the public; (*d*) do either or both *a* and *c*.

12. In asserting the desirability of government performing the five basic economic functions in the United States, there seems to be rather general agreement that (*a*) the functions ought to be increased in number and government's role in the economy expanded; (*b*) the functions ought to be decreased in number and government's role in the economy reduced to a minimum; (*c*) the functions are those which the government ought to perform, but there is no general agreement as to the extent to which government should go in performing them; (*d*) with the exception of stabilizing the economy, these are legitimate tasks for government to perform as long as government, in performing them, does not interfere with the operation of the economy.

13. Assume that a government is considering a new antipollution program and it may choose to include in this program any number of four different projects. The marginal cost and the marginal benefits of each of the four projects are given below. What total amount should this government spend on the antipollution program? (*a*) $2 million; (*b*) $7 million; (*c*) $17 million; (*d*) $37 million.

Project	Marginal cost	Marginal benefit
# 1	$2 million	$5 million
# 2	$5 million	$7 million
# 3	$10 million	$9 million
# 4	$20 million	$15 million

14. Which of the following is *not* one of the reasons for the alleged greater efficiency of the private sector? (*a*) The least efficient workers in the economy gravitate to the public sector; (*b*) strong incentives to be efficient are largely absent in the public sector; (*c*) there is no simple way to measure or test efficiency in the public sector; (*d*) there is a tendency in the public sector to increase the budgets of agencies that have failed to perform efficiently.

15. It is difficult to determine whether provision for a particular good or service should be assigned to the private or public sector of the economy because (*a*) the institutions in both sectors function efficiently; (*b*) the markets function efficiently and the agencies of government perform imperfectly; (*c*) the markets are faulty and government agencies function with much greater efficiency; (*d*) the institutions in both sectors are imperfect.

■ DISCUSSION QUESTIONS

1. Why is it proper to refer to the United States economy as "mixed capitalism"?

2. What are the five economic functions of government in America's mixed capitalistic economy? Explain what the performance of each of these functions requires government to do.

3. Would you like to live in an economy in which government undertook only the first two functions listed in the text? What would be the advantages and disadvantages of living in such an economy?

4. Why does the market system provide some people with lower income than it provides others?

5. What is "market failure" and what are the two major kinds of such failures?

6. What is meant by a spillover in general and by spillover cost and spillover benefit in particular? How does the existence of such costs and benefits affect the allocation of resources and the prices of products? If a market could be required to take these costs and benefits into account, how would the allocation of resources and the price of the product bought and sold in that market be changed?

7. What methods do governments employ to (*a*) redistribute income; (*b*) reallocate resources to take account of spillover costs; (*c*) reallocate resources to take account of spillover benefits?

8. Distinguish between a private and a public good. Include in your answer an explanation of the "exclusion principle" and the distinction between divisible and indivisible goods.

9. What basic method does government employ in the United States to reallocate resources away from the production of private goods and toward the production of social goods?

10. In a circular flow diagram that includes not only business firms and households but also government (or the public sector), what are the four flows of money into or out of the government sector of the economy? Using this diagram, explain how government redistributes income, reallocates resources from the private to the public sector, and stabilizes the economy.

11. Is there agreement on whether government should perform its five economic functions? Why is there criticism of government activity?

12. Explain what benefit-cost analysis is and how it is used. What is the major problem encountered when benefit-cost analysis is utilized by government?

13. Explain what is meant by "public sector failure."

14. Public choice theory suggests that there are a number of possible causes of public sector failures. What are these causes? Explain how each would tend to result in the inefficient allocation of the economy's resources.

15. It is generally agreed that "national defense must lie in the public sector while wheat production can best be accomplished in the private sector." Why isn't there agreement on where many other goods or services should be produced?

16. Do you think government limits or expands personal freedom by performing its economic functions?

7
The facts of American capitalism: the private sector

The American economy has two major parts or sectors. This chapter is concerned with the private sector: the eighty-five million households and the roughly fifteen million business firms in the economy. The next chapter deals with the public sector of the economy: the approximately eighty thousand governments found in the United States. These two chapters aim to acquaint you with a few of the facts relevant to an understanding of our economy.

The first part of Chapter 7 examines the households of the economy, the distribution of income in the United States, and the uses to which the households put their incomes. Two different distributions of income are examined. American households earn five kinds of income and receive transfer payments. The way in which the total personal income received by all American households is divided among the five types of earned income and transfer payments is called the *functional distribution.* The way in which the total personal income received by all households is distributed among the various income classes is called the *personal* distribution of income. Attention should be concentrated on the *general* facts of income distribution (not the exact figures), the conclusions which are drawn from these general facts, and the definitions of the new terms employed. In the examination of the different uses households make of their incomes, several new terms and concepts are introduced; and figures are employed in the discussion. Again, attention should be paid to the generalizations and to the new terms.

The latter part of the chapter is concerned with the business firms of the United States. It is apparent that what most characterizes American business is the differences among firms insofar as their size and legal form are concerned, as well as in the products they produce. You should note the distinction between a proprietorship, a partnership, and a corporation and the advantages and disadvantages of each.

In the last section of the chapter you will find that the American economy can be divided into ten sectors or industry classes. The privately owned business firms are found in eight of these industry classes. These eight sectors are not equal in terms of the number of firms in the class, the contribution to the national income made by the industry class, and the number of full-time workers employed by the sector. These facts serve as an introduction to two major observations. In the economy as a whole and in the manufacturing sector a relatively few firms produce a relatively large part of the output of that sector. And in this sector are to be found many specific industries in which the four largest firms produce a high percentage of the output of that industry. These two observations indicate that big business is an important characteristic of the American economy. The corollary of these observations is that the American economy also has a large number of small business firms. But the problems created by big business and the ways in which government deals with these problems are topics examined later in the text.

■ CHECKLIST

When you have studied this chapter you should be able to:

☐ Define and distinguish between a functional and a personal distribution of income.

☐ State the relative size of the six sources of personal income in the functional distribution.

☐ Explain the relationship between the personal distribution and the composition and the size of the national output.

☐ Explain the determinants of a household's income in a capitalistic economy.

☐ List the three uses to which households put their personal incomes and state the relative size of each.

☐ Distinguish among durable goods, nondurable goods, and services.

☐ Explain the difference between a plant, a firm, and an industry; and between limited and unlimited liability.

☐ State the advantages and disadvantages of the three legal forms of business enterprise.

☐ Report the relative importance of each of the legal forms of business enterprise in the American economy.

☐ State which two industry classes contain the largest and the smallest number of privately owned business firms, produce the largest and the smallest percentages of the national income, and employ the greatest and the smallest number of full-time workers.

☐ Cite evidence to indicate that large corporations dominate the economy and some major American industries; and indicate in which industry classes big business is and is not a dominant force.

■ CHAPTER OUTLINE

1. Households play a dual role in the economy: They supply the economy with resources, and they purchase the greatest share of the goods and services produced by the economy. They obtain their personal incomes in exchange for the resources they furnish the economy and from the transfer payments they receive from government.

a. The functional distribution of income indicates the way in which total personal income is divided among the five sources of earned income (wages and salaries, proprietors' income, corporate profits, interest, and rents) and transfer payments.

b. The personal distribution of income indicates the way in which total personal income is divided among households in different income classes and is of particular importance because it affects the types of goods and services demanded by households and the total output of the economy. The personal income of a household depends roughly on its contribution to the total output of the economy.

2. Households use their incomes to purchase consumer goods, to pay taxes, and to accumulate savings.

a. Personal taxes constitute a deduction from a household's personal income; what remains after taxes can be either saved or spent.

b. Saving is what a household does not spend of its after-tax income.

c. Households spend for durable goods, nondurable goods, and services.

3. The business population of the American economy consists of many imperfectly defined and overlapping industries; business firms which operate one or more plants and produce one or more products are the components of these industries.

4. The three principal legal forms of organization of firms are the proprietorship, the partnership, and the corporation; each form has special characteristics, advantages, and disadvantages. The form of organization which any business firm should adopt depends primarily upon the amount of money capital it will require to carry on its business. Although the proprietorship is numerically dominant in the United States, the corporation accounts for the major portion of the economy's output.

5. An examination of the ten industry classes found in the American economy reveals at least four important facts and leads to the conclusion that large firms are a characteristic of the American economy and that many of its industries are dominated by big businesses.

■ IMPORTANT TERMS

Private sector
Functional distribution of income
Personal distribution of income
Personal consumption expenditures
Durable good
Nondurable good
Service
Personal taxes
Personal saving
Plant
Firm
Industry
Horizontal combination
Vertical combination
Conglomerate combination
Sole proprietorship
Partnership
Corporation
Unlimited liability
Limited liability
Double taxation
Separation of ownership and control

■ FILL-IN QUESTIONS

1. The approximately 63 million households in the United States play a dual role in the

p. 108 economy because they supply economic res's and major spending group in economy

2. The largest single source of income in the United States is wages & salaries and is equal to about 74% of total income.

3. In the United States the poorest 20% of all American families receive about 5 % of total personal income and the richest 20% of these families receive about 43 % of total personal income.

4. The personal distribution of income is of particular importance because it affects the composition of output and the levels of national income, output, and employment.

5. In a price-market system the money income of a family or person depends roughly upon its contribution of res's to the total production of the economy.

6. The total income of households is disposed of in three ways: personal taxes, personal savings, and personal consumption expenditures

7. Households use about 16 % of their total income to pay personal taxes; and the greatest part of their personal taxes are the personal income taxes which they pay to the (Federal, state, local) Federal government.

8. Households save primarily in order to obtain security and for purposes of speculation

9. Based on their durability, consumer spending is classified as spending for durable, nondurable goods, ______, and services

10. There are today about 16 1/2 business firms in the United States. The legal form of the great majority of these firms is the sole proprietorship; but the legal form that produces over one-half the output of the American economy is the corporation

11. The liabilities of a sole proprietor and of partners are unlimited but the liabilities of stockholders in a corporation are limited

12. Indicate in the spaces to the right of each of the following whether these business characteristics are associated with the proprietorship (PRO), partnership (PART), corporation (CORP), two of these, or all three of these legal forms.

a. Much red tape and legal expense in beginning the firm CORP

b. Unlimited liability PRO & PART

c. No specialized management PRO

d. Has a life independent of its owner(s) CORP

e. Modest tax advantage if its profits are large CORP

f. Greatest ability to acquire funds for the expansion of the firm CORP

g. Permits some but not a great degree of specialized management PART

h. Possibility of an unresolved disagreement among owners over courses of action PART

i. Makes it possible for a businessman to avoid responsibility for illegal actions CORP

13. Of the eight industry classes in which privately owned business firms are found:

a. The two which contain the greatest number of firms are ag, forestry, fisheries and services

b. The two which make the largest contribution to the national income and employ the most full-time workers are manufacturing and wholesale & retail trades trade.

14. The public sector produces roughly one-eighth -th of all the goods and services produced in the American economy.

15. The United States is often called a big business economy because a relatively ______ firms produce a relatively ______ part of the output of the economy and of some industries.

■ PROBLEMS AND PROJECTS

1. The table below shows the functional distribution of total income in the United States in 1984.

	Billions of dollars
Wages and salaries	$2000
Proprietors' income	154
Corporate profits	78
Interest	434
Rents	64
Total earnings	2729

Of the total earnings about ______% were wages and salaries, and about ______% were corporate profits.

2. Below are six numbers and each of them is a percentage. Match these six numbers with the six phrases that follow

81	17
60	12
51	9

A. Percentage of the manufacturing assets owned by the 200 largest manufacturing firms. ______

B. Percentage of the national income which is contributed by the government sector of the economy. ______

C. Percentage of the privately owned business firms in the United States which are in the agriculture, forestry, and fishing sector of the economy. ______

D. Percentage of business firms in the United States which are partnerships. ______

E. Percentage of personal consumption expenditures which are for services. ______

F. Percentage of the income of consumers which is used for personal consumption expenditures. ______

3. Indicate to the best of your ability what you would call the industries in which the following firms operate:

a. Sears, Roebuck and Company
b. The General Electric Company
c. A used-car dealer in your town
d. Gimbels department stores
e. Your local electric company
f. A new-car dealer
g. The Mars Candy Company
h. The Aluminum Company of America
i. The Revere Copper and Brass Company
j. The William Wrigley Chewing Gum Company

4. Look at the list of firms in question 3 above.

a. In which industry *class* would you put each of these firms?

b. Are any of these firms in industries which Table 30-1 of the text lists as highly concentrated manufacturing industries?

■ SELF-TEST

Circle the T if the statement is true, the F if it is false.

1. The personal distribution of income describes the manner in which society's total personal income is divided among wages and salaries, corporate profits, proprietors' income, interest, and rents. **T F**

2. Limited liability refers to the fact that all members of a partnership are liable for the debts incurred by one another **T F**

3. A distribution of income which is based on the productivity of resources usually results in considerable *inequality* in the size of incomes. **T F**

4. In both relative and absolute terms, personal taxes have exceeded personal saving in recent years. **T F**

5. Most of the personal saving in the American economy is done by those households in the top 10% of its income receivers. **T F**

6. *Dissaving* means that personal consumption expenditures exceed after-tax income. **T F**

7. A "durable good" is defined as a good which has an expected life of one year or more. **T F**

8. A plant is defined as a group of firms under a single management. **T F**

9. An industry is a group of firms that produce the same or nearly the same products. **T F**

10. The corporate form of organization is the least used by firms in the United States. **T F**

11. The corporation in the United States today always has a tax advantage over other legal forms of business organization. **T F**

12. Whether a business firm should incorporate or not depends chiefly upon the amount of money capital it must have to finance the enterprise. **T F**

13. The wholesale and retail trade and the service industries contain a relatively large number of firms but are not important sources of income and employment in the American economy. **T F**

14. Corporations produce over one-half the total output produced by privately owned business firms in the United States. **T F**

15. Historical data show quite clearly that economic concentration has tended to increase in the U.S. with the passage of time. **T F**

Circle the letter that corresponds to the best answer.

1. There are in the United States approximately how many households (families)? (*a*) 63 million; (*b*) 75 million; (*c*) 80 million; (*d*) 85 million.

2. The functional distribution for the United States shows that the largest part of personal income is: (*a*) wages and salaries; (*b*) proprietors' income; (*c*) corporate profits; (*d*) interest and rents.

3. Which of the following is *not* a factor affecting the amount of money income received by the individual household? (*a*) The quantity of resources the household has available to supply to business firms; (*b*) the amount of saving done by the household; (*c*) the prices paid for the various resources in the market; (*d*) the actual level of employment of the household's resources.

4. The personal distribution of income affects: (*a*) the total output of the economy; (*b*) the number of people who find employment in the economy; (*c*) the composition of the total output of the economy; (*d*) all of the above.

5. Expenditures for *nondurable* goods in recent years have amounted to approximately what percentage of personal consumption expenditures? (*a*) 30%; (*b*) 40%; (*c*) 50%; (*d*) 60%.

6. Which of the following is a true statement? (*a*) The durable goods and service parts of personal consumption expenditures vary more over time than do the expenditures for nondurables; (*b*) expenditures for nondurables vary more than do the expenditures for durable goods and services; (*c*) expenditures for nondurables vary more than the expenditures for services and less than the expenditures for durables; (*d*) expenditures for nondurables vary more than the expenditures for durables and less than the expenditures for services.

7. In recent years personal taxes have been approximately what percentage of total income? (*a*) 16%; (*b*) 22%; (*c*) 24%; (*d*) 80%.

8. If we include self-employed farmers and professional people, there are approximately how many million business firms in the United States? (*a*) 5; (*b*) 8; (*c*) 16; (*d*) 20.

9. A group of three plants which is owned and operated by a single firm and which consists of a farm growing wheat, a flour milling plant, and a plant which bakes and sells bakery products is an example of: (*a*) a horizontal combination; (*b*) a vertical combination; (*c*) a conglomerate combination; (*d*) a corporation.

10. Limited liability is associated with: (*a*) only proprietorships; (*b*) only partnerships; (*c*) both proprietorships and partnerships; (*d*) only corporations.

11. Which of the following forms of business organization can most effectively raise money capital? (*a*) Corporation; (*b*) partnership; (*c*) proprietorship; (*d*) vertical combination.

12. Which of the following industry classes has the largest number of firms? (*a*) Agriculture, forestry, and fishing; (*b*) manufacturing; (*c*) wholesale and retail trade; (*d*) mining.

13. Which of the following industry classes produces the largest percentage of the national income? (*a*) Agriculture, forestry, and fishing; (*b*) manufacturing; (*c*) wholesale and retail trade; (*d*) government.

14. About what percentage of the national income of the United States is produced by government? (*a*) 3%; (*b*) 5%; (*c*) 10%; (*d*) 12%.

15. The 100 largest manufacturing firms in the United States today own approximately what percentage of the assets of all manufacturing firms? (*a*) 40%; (*b*) 45%; (*c*) 50%; (*d*) more than 50%.

■ DISCUSSION QUESTIONS

1. Explain the difference between a functional and a personal distribution of income. Rank the five types of earned income in the order of their size.

2. The present personal distribution of income affects both the level of resource use and the allocation of resources in the economy. What is the connection between the distribution of income and the employment and allocation of resources?

3. What determines how large a money income an individual household will have? In what way is a household's income related to its productivity? Why does a personal distribution of income based on productivity lead to personal income inequality?

4. Which would result in greater total saving and less consumption spending out of a national income of a given size: a more or less nearly equal distribution of income?

5. The purchase of what type of consumer goods is largely postponable? Why is this? How is it possible for a family's personal consumption expenditures to exceed its after-tax income?

6. What is the difference between a plant and a firm? Between a firm and an industry? Which of these three concepts is the most difficult to apply in practice? Why? Distinguish between a horizontal, a vertical, and a conglomerate combination.

7. What are the principal advantages and disadvantages of each type of the three legal forms of business organization? Which of the disadvantages of the proprietorship and partnership accounts for the employment of the corporate form among the big businesses of the American economy?

8. Explain what "separation of ownership and control" of the modern corporation means. What problems does this separation create for stockholders and the economy?

9. What figures can you cite to show that the typical firm engaged in agriculture is relatively small and that the average firm engaged in manufacturing is relatively large? Are firms engaged in wholesaling and retailing; mining; finance, insurance, and real estate; and services relatively large or relatively small?

10. Is the American economy and manufacturing in the United States dominated by big business? What evidence do you use to reach this conclusion?

8
The facts of American capitalism: the public sector

The facts of public-sector or government finance in the United States presented in Chapter 8 center on two questions: Where do governments get their incomes? On what do they spend these incomes?

The organization of the chapter is relatively simple. First, the trends which taxes collected and expenditures made by all levels of government—Federal, state, and local—have taken since 1929 and the causes of the increases in expenditures and taxes are examined briefly. Second, a closer look is taken at the major items upon which the Federal government spends its income, the principal taxes it levies to obtain its income, and the relative importance of these taxes. Third, the chapter looks at the major expenditures of and the major taxes of the state and the local governments, and at revenue sharing. Fourth, the chapter examines the principles applied in levying taxes, the way tax rates vary as personal incomes change, who really pays the taxes levied against various groups in the economy, and how much of their incomes Americans pay to government in the form of taxes. Finally, Chapter 8 takes a look at three controversial issues related to the reform of the American tax system.

What should you get out of this chapter? There are at least five important sets of facts: (1) the trends which taxes and government expenditures have taken in recent years and why; (2) the relative importance of the principal taxes and the relative importance of the various expenditure items in the budgets of the three levels of government; (3) the meaning of the benefits-received and the ability-to-pay principles; (4) the meaning of progressive, regressive, and proportional taxation, the shifting and incidence of taxes, and the incidence of the major types of taxes; and (5) estimates of the degree of progressiveness of the American tax system.

Avoid memorizing statistics. You should look instead for the trends and generalizations which these statistics illuminate. Spend your time, also, on the terms used, the classifications employed, and the conclusions which are drawn and which embody these terms and classifications.

■ CHECKLIST

When you have studied this chapter you should be able to:

☐ List the six causes of the historical expansion and the present size of government tax revenues and expenditures.

☐ Explain the differences between government purchases and transfer payments; and the effect of each of these two kinds of expenditures on the composition of the national output.

☐ Describe the three largest categories of expenditures and the two greatest sources of revenue of the Federal government.

☐ Define and explain the difference between the marginal and the average tax rate.

☐ State three charges critics make against the Federal personal income tax; and describe several of the loopholes in it.

☐ List the two largest sources of tax revenue and the three largest types of expenditures of state governments; and the largest single source of tax revenue and the largest category of expenditures of local governments.

☐ Distinguish between the ability-to-pay principle and the benefits-received principle.

☐ Define and explain the differences among a regressive, proportional, and progressive tax; and identify the taxes levied in the American economy that fall into each of these categories.

☐ State the probable incidence of personal income, corporate income, sales and excise, and property taxes.

☐ Describe the estimates made by Joseph Pechman of how the tax burden in the American economy is distributed among different income classes, the progressivity of the American tax system, and the effect of this tax system on the distribution of income in the United States.

☐ Explain the three tax-related issues that have been paramount in recent years.

■ CHAPTER OUTLINE

1. Government's functions in the economy are felt most directly when it collects revenue by taxation and expends this revenue for goods and services; but there is an important difference between the voluntary transactions in the private and the compulsory transactions in the public sector of the economy.

2. In both absolute and relative terms, government tax collections and spending have increased during the past sixty or so years.

a. The increased tax collections and spending are the result of hot and cold wars, population increases, urbanization and the greater demand for social goods, pollution of the environment, egalitarianism, and inflation.

b. Government spending consists of purchases of goods and services and of transfer payments; but these two types of spending have different effects on the composition of the national output.

3. At the Federal level of government:

a. 41% of the total expenditure is for income security, about 27% is for national defense, and some 13% is for interest on the national debt;

b. the major sources of revenue are personal income, payroll, and corporate income taxes;

c. tax-exempt securities and capital gains are tax loopholes for some persons and firms;

d. illegal tax evasion reduces the revenues of the Treasury by an estimated $100 billion a year.

4. At the other two levels of government:

a. state governments depend largely on sales and excise taxes and personal income taxes, and use a large part of their revenues for education and public welfare;

b. local governments rely heavily upon property taxes and spend the greatest part of their revenues for education;

c. tax revenues are less than expenditures and the Federal government shares some of its revenues with these governments by making grants to them.

5. Although the overall level of taxes is important to the economy, the question of who pays the tax bill is equally important.

a. The benefits-received principle and the ability-to-pay principle are widely employed to determine how the tax bill should be apportioned among the economy's citizens.

b. Taxes can be classified as progressive, regressive, or proportional according to the way in which the average *tax rate* changes as income increases.

c. A tax levied upon one person or group of persons may be shifted partially or completely to another person or group; and to the extent that a tax can be shifted or passed on through lower prices paid or higher prices received, its incidence is passed on. The incidence of the four major types of taxes is only probable and is not known for certain.

d. Because some taxes levied in the American economy are progressive and some are regressive it appears that the American tax system is only slightly progressive, has very little effect on the distribution of income in the United States, and has become less progressive over the past 20 years; but estimates of the progressivity of the tax system depend on the assumed incidence of the various taxes; and the transfer payments made by governments do reduce income inequality in the United States.

6. Over the past 15 or so years three tax-related issues have been debated in the United States.

a. The first of these has been how to limit the size of government expenditures and taxes; and the Economic Recovery Tax Act of 1981 resulted in substantial reductions in Federal personal and corporate income taxes.

b. How to "reindustrialize" the American economy by significantly increasing spending for modern machinery and equipment is the second of these issues; and it has been suggested that the corporate income tax be reduced and a value-added tax on consumer goods be levied.

c. The third issue surrounds the suggestion that the Federal personal income tax be modified to eliminate all exemptions, deductions, and loopholes and to apply the same tax rate to all incomes.

■ IMPORTANT TERMS

Government purchase

Government transfer payment

Personal income tax

Marginal tax rate

Average tax rate

Payroll tax

Corporate income tax

Economic Recovery Tax Act of 1981

Double taxation
Sales tax
Excise tax
Capital gain
Property tax
Revenue sharing
Fiscal federalism
Restricted ("categorical") grant
Unrestricted ("block") grant
Benefits-received principle
Ability-to-pay principle
Progressive tax
Regressive tax
Proportional tax
Tax incidence
Tax shifting
Proposition 13
Value-added tax (VAT)
Flat-rate income tax

■ FILL-IN QUESTIONS

1. It is through the __expenditures__ it makes and the __taxation__ it collects that the functions of government are most directly felt by the economy.

2. Transactions in the private sector of the economy are (voluntary, compulsory) __voluntary__ while those in the public sector, by and large, are __compulsory__

3. An examination of the public sector of the American economy reveals that:

a. between 1929 and 1985 government *purchases* of goods and services as a percentage of national output have tended to (increase, decrease, remain constant) __increase__ and since the early 1950s have been about (10, 20, 33) __20__ percent of the GNP;

b. but government *transfer payments* as a percentage of national output during the past 20 or so years have (increased, decreased, remained constant) __increase__

c. and the tax revenues required to finance both government expenditures and transfer payments are today about (10, 20, 33) __33__ percent of the GNP.

4. Government transfer payments are defined as __do not absorb resources or account from production__ and are a(n) (exhaustive, nonexhaustive) __nonexhaustive__

5. When government raises $20 billion by taxation and uses it to purchase goods it shifts resources from the production of (private, social) __private__ goods to the production of __social__ goods; but when it uses the $20 billion to make transfer payments it changes the __composition__ of the output of private goods.

6. The most important source of revenue for the Federal government is the __personal income__ tax; next in importance are the __payroll__ taxes. The three largest categories of Federal expenditures are for __income security__, for __nat'l defense__, and for interest on the __public debt__

7. The Federal government uses the personal income tax to obtain most of the __revenue__ it requires to finance its expenditures; the personal income tax also has the potential to __redistribute__ income, and can be employed to __stabilize__ the economy.

8. Three criticisms of the Federal personal income tax are that the tax code is too __complex__, that special deductions and exemptions have decreased __equity__, and that the tax reduces __incentive__ to work, invest, and assume risks.

9. Two principal loopholes in the Federal tax system are the __tax-exempt__ securities of state and local governments and the way in which __capital gains__ are taxed.

10. Illegal tax evasion is the result of activities in the "__underground__ economy" and the failure of individuals to report all of their incomes; and costs the Federal government an estimated $__100__ billion a year.

11. The state governments rely primarily upon __sales__ and __property__ taxes for their incomes which they spend mostly on __education__ and __public welfare & highway maintenance & construction.__

12. At local levels of government the single most important source of revenue is the ____________ tax and the single most important expenditure is for ____________.

13. The amount by which the expenditures of state and local governments exceed their tax revenues is largely filled by grants from the ____________ government; and these grants are called revenue ____________.

14. The two philosophies of apportioning the tax burden which are most evident in the American economy are the ____________ principle and the ____________ principle.

15. As income increases: if a tax is proportional the average tax rate ____________; if it is progressive the average rate ____________; and if it is regressive the average rate ____________.

16. Indicate in the space to the right of each of the following taxes whether that tax (as applied in the United States) is regressive (R) or progressive (P) or whether it is uncertain (U) which it is.

a. Personal income tax ____________
b. Sales tax ____________
c. Payroll tax ____________
d. Property tax ____________
e. Corporation income tax ____________

17. What is the probable incidence of each of the following taxes?

a. Personal income tax: ____________
b. Sales and excise tax: ____________
c. Corporate income tax: ____________
d. Property tax: ____________

18. The American tax structure is mildly (regressive, progressive) ____________

a. As a result it has a (small, great) ____________ effect on the distribution of income in the United States.
b. But these conclusions depend on the assumed ____________ of the various taxes used in the American economy.
c. Over the last 20 years the American tax structure has become (more, less) ____________ progressive.
d. Income inequality in the United States is, however, reduced by the system of ____________ payments made by governments.

19. The major issues related to taxes during the 1970s and 1980s have been of:

a. limiting the expenditures of and lowering the taxes collected by the public sector and resulted in

(1) the approval in California of ____________

(2) and the passage by the United States of the ____________ Act in 1981;

b. reindustrializing the U.S. economy and increasing the ____________ of American workers.

(1) This would require that consumption be (increased, decreased) ____________ and investment be ____________

(2) This might be accomplished by lowering the (personal, corporate) ____________ income tax and establishing a ____________ tax on consumption;

c. eliminating the progressive ____________ income tax and replacing it with a ____________ rate tax on personal income which would

(1) do away with all the ____________, ____________, and ____________ in the present tax system

(2) and tax all income at the ____________ rate.

20. The Reagan proposal for tax reform would (increase, decrease) ____________ the marginal tax rates on the incomes of individuals and corporations in exchange for the elimination of many existing deductions and exclusions; and would reduce the number of marginal tax brackets on personal incomes from eleven to ____________

■ PROBLEMS AND PROJECTS

1. In the table below are several levels of taxable income and hypothetical marginal tax rates for each $1000 increase in income.

Taxable income	Marginal tax rate, %	Tax	Average tax rate, %
$1500		$300	20
2500	22	520	20.8
3500	25	____	____
4500	29	____	____
5500	34	____	____
6500	40	____	____

a. Compute at the four income levels the tax and the average tax rate.

b. As the marginal tax rate:

(1) increases the average tax rate (increases, decreases, remains constant) ________

(2) decreases the average tax rate ________

2. In the table below are five levels of taxable income and the amount that would be paid at each of the five levels under three tax laws: A, B, and C. Compute for each of the three tax laws the *average* rate of taxation at each of the four remaining income levels and indicate whether the tax is regressive, proportional, progressive, or some combination thereof.

	Tax A		Tax B		Tax C	
Income	Tax paid	Av. tax rate %	Tax paid	Av. tax rate %	Tax paid	Av. tax rate %
$ 1,500	45.00	3 %	30.00	2 %	135.00	9 %
3,000	90.00	____	90.00	____	240.00	____
5,000	150.00	____	150.00	____	350.00	____
7,500	225.00	____	187.50	____	450.00	____
10,000	300.00	____	200.00	____	500.00	____
Type of tax:	____		____		____	

3. Assume a state government levies a 4% sales tax on all consumption expenditures. Consumption expenditures at six income levels are shown in the table below.

Income	Consumption expenditures	Sales tax paid	Average tax rate, %
$ 5,000	$5,000	$200	4.0
6,000	5,800	232	3.9
7,000	6,600	____	____
8,000	7,400	____	____
9,000	8,200	____	____
10,000	9,000	____	____

a. Compute the sales tax paid at the next four incomes.

b. Compute the average tax rate at these incomes.

c. Using income as the tax base, the sales tax is a ________ tax.

■ SELF-TEST

Circle the T if the statement is true, the F if it is false.

1. Transactions in the public sector of the economy are largely compulsory and those in the private sector are voluntary. **T F**

2. Government purchases of goods and services are called *nonexhaustive* and government transfer payments are called *exhaustive* expenditures. T F

3. When a government levies taxes and uses the tax revenue to make transfer payments it shifts resources from the production of private goods to the production of social goods. T F

4. The level of Federal expenditures in 1984 was about $850 billion. T F

5. The chief source of revenue for the Federal government is the corporation income tax. T F

6. Because the Federal personal income tax is a progressive tax, if a taxpayer had a taxable income of $20,000 and his or her marginal tax rate was 35%, the taxpayer would be required to pay a total tax of less than $7,000. T F

7. Personal income tax rates have been "indexed" since 1985 to prevent inflation from pushing taxpayers into higher marginal tax brackets. T F

8. Because the marginal tax rate on all taxable corporate profits in excess of $100,000 is 46%, beyond $100,000 the Federal corporate income tax is proportional. T F

9. The Federal government levies sales taxes on tobacco and gasoline. T F

10. Evading taxes is legal, but avoiding taxes is illegal. T F

11. There is a major loophole in the Federal tax system because personal income tax rates are progressive. T F

12. In sharing revenue with state and local governments the Federal government has in recent years tended to switch from making restricted (or "categorical") grants to making unrestricted (or "block") grants. T F

13. Total taxes collected by the Federal government are approximately equal to the amount of taxes collected by all state and local governments. T F

14. The chief difficulty in applying the benefits-received principle of taxation is determining who receives the benefits of many of the goods and services which government supplies. T F

15. A sales tax generally turns out to be a proportional tax. T F

16. The state and Federal taxes on gasoline are good examples of taxes levied on the benefits-received principle. T F

17. Estimates of the overall structure of the American tax system depend on the assumed incidence of taxes. T F

18. A value-added tax is a tax on the difference between the value of goods sold by a firm and the value of the goods it purchased from other firms. T F

19. Advocates of "reindustrializing" the American economy have proposed increasing the tax rate imposed by the Federal government on corporate incomes to force corporations to be more efficient. T F

20. A value-added tax, its proponents argue, would tend to reduce consumption and increase saving in the economy and release resources for the production of more investment goods. T F

Circle the letter that corresponds to the best answer.

1. Today all government expenditures equal approximately what percentage of the American economy's total output? (*a*) 10%; (*b*) 18%; (*c*) 23%; (*d*) 33%.

2. Which of the following is *not* one of the causes of the present size of government expenditures in the United States? (*a*) Inflation; (*b*) double taxation; (*c*) population growth; (*d*) egalitarianism.

3. Which of the following would *not* be a government transfer expenditure? (*a*) Contributions of employers to support the social security program; (*b*) social security payments to the aged; (*c*) unemployment compensation benefits; (*d*) payments to the widows of war veterans.

4. Which of the following accounts for the largest percentage of all Federal expenditures? (*a*) Income security; (*b*) national defense; (*c*) interest on the public debt; (*d*) veterans' services.

5. Which of the following is the largest source of the tax revenues of the Federal government? (*a*) Sales and excise taxes; (*b*) property taxes; (*c*) payroll taxes; (*d*) personal income taxes.

6. The Federal personal income tax (*a*) is used to obtain the revenue to pay for the purchases of social goods and services; (*b*) can be used to redistribute income from those with greater to those with smaller incomes; (*c*) helps to stabilize the economy; (*d*) does or can do all of the above.

7. Critics of the Federal personal income tax contend that (*a*) it reduces the incentives to work, invest, and assume risks; (*b*) special exemptions and deductions make it inequitable; (*c*) the tax law is so complex that filing a tax return is difficult, time-consuming, and expensive; (*d*) all of the above are true.

8. Which of the following is a loophole in the application of the Federal tax on personal income? (*a*) The taxing of capital gains at a marginal rate which is lower than the rate on other kinds of income; (*b*) the exempting of the interest received by owners of the bonds of state and local governments from the tax; (*c*) allowing taxpayers to deduct mortgage-interest payments and property taxes when computing their taxable incomes; (*d*) all of the above.

9. Tax evasion is estimated by the U.S. Treasury to cost the Federal government each year (*a*) $50 billion; (*b*) $100 billion; (*c*) $150 billion; (*d*) $200 billion.

10. Which of the following pairs represents the chief source of income and the most important type of expenditure of *state* governments? (*a*) Personal income tax and expenditures for education; (*b*) personal income tax and expenditures for highways; (*c*) sales and excise taxes and expenditures for public welfare; (*d*) sales and excise taxes and expenditures for education.

11. Which of the following pairs represents the chief source of income and the most important type of expenditure of *local* governments? (*a*) Property tax and expenditures for highways; (*b*) property tax and expenditures for education; (*c*) sales and excise taxes and expenditures for public welfare; (*d*) sales and excise taxes and expenditures for police, fire, and general government.

12. Which of the following is *not* true of the ability-to-pay principle as applied in the United States? (*a*) It is more widely applied than the benefits-received principle; (*b*) income is generally taken as the measure of the ability to pay; (*c*) it is more widely applied by state and local than by the Federal government; (*d*) as the tax base increases, taxes paid increase both absolutely and relatively.

13. When the income of a taxpayer increases and a tax is regressive, the amount of the tax paid by the taxpayer (*a*) increases; (*b*) decreases; (*c*) remains unchanged; (*d*) may do any of the above.

14. Which of the following tends to be a progressive tax in the United States? The (*a*) income tax; (*b*) property tax; (*c*) sales tax; (*d*) payroll tax.

15. Which of the following taxes can be least easily shifted? A (*a*) personal income tax; (*b*) corporation income tax; (*c*) sales tax; (*d*) business property tax.

16. The Pechman study of the American tax structure shows it to be (*a*) very progressive; (*b*) slightly progressive; (*c*) slightly regressive; (*d*) very regressive.

17. The Economic Recovery Tax Act of 1981 (*a*) established a value-added tax on certain consumer goods; (*b*) reduced tax rates on personal and corporate incomes; (*c*) introduced a flat-rate tax on personal and corporate incomes; (*d*) decreased the number of tax brackets on personal income from fifteen to three.

18. The advocates of "reindustrializing" the American economy argue that (*a*) the production of consumer goods must be increased; (*b*) the productivity of American workers must be improved; (*c*) corporate income taxes should be increased; (*d*) the production of investment goods needs to be reduced by a substantial amount.

19. Proponents of replacing the progressive Federal personal income tax with a flat-rate tax contend it would (*a*) redistribute the Federal tax burden from the poor to the rich; (*b*) improve the incentives to work, invest, and take risks; (*c*) increase the built-in stability of the economy; (*d*) expand the progressivity of the American tax system.

20. President Reagan has proposed to reform the present tax system by doing all but one of the following. Which one? (*a*) Establish a value-added tax on certain consumer goods; (*b*) decrease the number of tax brackets on consumer income from fifteen to three; (*c*) reduce the maximum marginal tax rate on personal income from 50 to 35 percent; (*d*) lower the maximum marginal tax rate on corporate profits from 46 to 33%.

■ DISCUSSION QUESTIONS

1. How do transactions in the public sector differ from those in the private sector of the economy?

2. What are the causes of the historical growth and the present size of government spending and taxes in the American economy?

3. Government expenditures fall into two broad classes: expenditures for goods and services, and transfer payments. Explain the difference between these and give examples of expenditures which fall into each of the two classes.

4. Explain the difference between exhaustive and nonexhaustive government spending.

5. When government collects taxes and spends the tax revenues it affects the composition of the total output of the economy. What is the effect on the composition of total output if government uses the tax revenues to purchase goods and services? What is the effect if it uses them to make transfer payments?

6. Explain precisely the difference between the marginal tax rate and the average tax rate.

7. Explain how the Federal personal income tax enables the Federal government to perform three (of the five) economic functions discussed in Chapter 6 of the text.

8. What are the three major criticisms of the Federal personal income tax?

9. What is a tax "loophole"? What are the two principal loopholes in the Federal tax system? How do these loopholes affect the distribution of income?

10. What is the difference between avoiding taxes and evading them? How are taxes evaded in the United States and why is the Treasury so concerned by the evasion of taxes?

11. Explain in detail the differences that exist among Federal, state, and local governments in the taxes upon which they primarily rely for their revenues and the major purposes for which they use these revenues.

12. Why does the Federal government share its tax revenues with state and local governments? What is the difference between a categorical and a block grant, and why does the Reagan administration endorse the shift from block to categorical grants?

13. What are the two basic philosophies for apportioning the tax burden in the United States? Explain each. What are the difficulties encountered in putting these philosophies into practice?

14. Explain the differences among progressive, regressive, and proportional taxes. Which taxes fall into each of these three categories? What can be said about the progressivity or regressivity of the overall structure of the American tax system?

15. Which of the following taxes tends to be shifted? (*a*) Personal income tax; (*b*) corporate income tax; (*c*) sales and excise taxes; (*d*) property tax. From whom is the tax shifted and upon whom is the tax incidence?

16. Explain what is meant by the "taxpayers' revolt" and its basic causes. How did the approval of Proposition 13 and the enactment of the Economic Recovery Tax Act of 1981 attempt to redress the grievances felt by taxpayers?

17. What does the term "reindustrialize" mean when applied to the American economy? Why do the proponents of reindustrialization feel the economy is in need of it and what steps would they take to accomplish it?

18. How would the proposed flat-rate tax differ from the current Federal tax on personal income? What advantages do its proponents see in such a tax and what have its critics had to say about this proposal? What proposals has President Reagan made to change the present Federal tax system?

9
National income accounting

The subject matter of Chapter 9 is national income (or social) accounting. This type of accounting measures or estimates the size of (1) the gross national product, (2) the net national product, (3) the national income, (4) the personal income, and (5) the disposable income of the economy.

This is national income (or social) accounting because it involves estimating output or income for the nation society as a whole, rather than for an individual business firm or family. Note that the terms "output" and "income" are interchangeable because the nation's output and its income are identical. The value of the nation's output equals the total expenditures for this output, and these expenditures become the income of those in the nation who have produced this output. Consequently, there are two equally acceptable methods, both discussed in the chapter, for obtaining each of the five income-output measures listed above. These two methods are the expenditures method and the income method.

Accounting is essentially an adding-up process. This chapter explains in detail and lists the items which must be added to obtain by both methods each of the five income-output measures. It is up to you to learn precisely *what* to add, i.e., how to compute GNP, NNP, NI, PI, and DI by both methods. This is a fairly difficult chapter, and the only way to learn the material is simply to sit down and learn it—memorize it if necessary! A careful reading of the chapter, however, will enable you to avoid the necessity of memorizing. You should first try to understand what each of the five income-output measures measures and the two alternative approaches to these measurements. Remembering the items to be added will then be much simpler.

In addition to explaining the two methods of computing the five income-output measures and each of the items used in the computation process, the chapter discusses the purpose of social accounting; the means by which income-output measures for different years may be adjusted to take account of changes in the price level so that comparisons between years are possible; and the shortcomings and dangers inherent in using these income-output measures. It is especially dangerous to assume that the GNP is a good overall measure of the welfare of society as a whole. Chapter 9 is, however, the essential background for Parts Two and Three, which explain the history of and the factors that determine the level of total output and income in the economy. The chapter is important in itself because it presents one of the several means of measuring the well-being of the economy and the individuals comprising the economy in a given year and over the years.

■ CHECKLIST

When you have studied this chapter you should be able to:

☐ State the purposes of national income accounting.

☐ Define GNP; and compute it using either the expenditures or the income approach when you are given the necessary data.

☐ Explain: the difference between gross and net investment; why changes in inventories are investment; and the relation between net investment and economic growth.

☐ Define each of the following; and, when you are given the needed data, compute each by two different methods: NNP, NI, PI, and DI.

☐ Adjust the money GNP (or nominal GNP), when you are given the relevant price index, to find the real GNP.

☐ Present several reasons why GNP is not an index of social welfare.

■ CHAPTER OUTLINE

1. National income (or social) accounting consists of concepts which enable those who use them to measure the economy's output, to compare it with past outputs, to explain its size and the reasons for changes in its size, and to formulate policies designed to increase it.

2. The gross national product (GNP) is the market value of all final goods and services produced in the economy during a year.

a. GNP is measured in dollar terms rather than in terms of physical units of output.

b. To avoid double counting, GNP includes only *final* goods and services (goods and services that will not be processed further during the *current* year).

c. Nonproductive transactions are not included in GNP; purely financial transactions and second-hand sales are, therefore, excluded.

d. Measurement of GNP can be accomplished by either the expenditures or the income method but the same result is obtained by the two methods.

3. Computation of the GNP by the expenditures method requires the addition of the total amounts of the four types of spending for final goods and services.

a. Personal consumption expenditures (C) are the expenditures of households for durable and nondurable goods and for services.

b. Gross private domestic investment (I_g) is the sum of the spending by business firms for machinery, equipment, and tools; spending by firms and households for new buildings; and the changes in the inventories of business firms.

(1) A change in inventories is included in investment because it is the part of output of the economy which was not sold during the year.

(2) Investment does not include expenditures for stocks or bonds or for second-hand capital goods.

(3) Gross investment exceeds net investment by the value of the capital goods worn out during the year.

(4) An economy in which net investment is positive (zero, negative) is an expanding (a static, a declining) economy.

c. Government purchases of goods and services (G) are the expenditures made by all governments in the economy for products produced by business firms and for resource services from households.

d. Net exports (X_n) in an economy equal the expenditures made by foreigners for goods and services produced in the economy less the expenditures made by the consumers, governments, and investors of the economy for goods and services produced in foreign nations.

e. In symbols, $C + I_g + G + X_n = \text{GNP}$

4. Computation of GNP by the income method requires the addition of the nine uses to which the income derived from the production and sales of final goods and services are put. These nine items are:

a. Depreciation (capital consumption allowance).

b. Indirect business taxes.

c. Compensation of employees (the sum of wages and salaries *and* wage and salary supplements).

d. Rents.

e. Interest (only the interest payments made by business firms are included and the interest payments made by government are excluded).

f. Proprietors' income (the profits or net income of unincorporated firms).

g. Corporate profits which are subdivided into:

(1) Corporate income taxes

(2) Dividends

(3) Undistributed corporate profits

5. In addition to GNP, four other national income measures are important in evaluating the performance of the economy. Each has a distinct definition and can be computed by making additions to or deductions from another measure.

a. NNP is the annual output of final goods and services over and above the capital goods worn out during the year; and is equal to the GNP minus depreciation (capital consumption allowance).

b. NI is the total income *earned* by owners of land and capital and by the suppliers of labor and entrepreneurial ability during the year; and equals NNP less indirect business taxes.

c. PI is the total income *received*—whether it is earned or unearned—by the households of the economy before the payment of personal taxes; and is found by *adding* transfer payments to and *subtracting* social security contributions, corporate income taxes, and undistributed corporate profits from the NI.

d. DI is the total income available to households after the payment of personal taxes; and is equal to PI less personal taxes and also equal to personal consumption expenditures plus personal saving.

e. The relations among the five income-output measures are summarized for you in Table 9-5.

f. Figure 9-2 is a more realistic and complex circular flow diagram that shows the flows of expenditures and incomes among the households, business firms, and governments in the economy.

6. Because price levels change from year to year it is necessary to adjust the money GNP (or nominal GNP) computed for any year to obtain the real GNP before year-to-year comparisons between the outputs of final goods and services can be made.

a. To adjust the money GNP figures, divide the nominal GNP in any year by the price index for that year; the result is the adjusted or real GNP.

b. When the price index in a year is below (above) the 100 it was in the base year the nominal GNP figure for that year is inflated (deflated) by this adjustment.

7. The GNP is not, for the following reasons, a measure of social welfare in the economy.

a. It excludes the value of final goods and services not bought and sold in the markets of the economy.

b. It excludes the amount of leisure the citizens of the economy are able to have.

c. It does not record the improvements in the quality of products which occur over the years.

d. It does not measure changes in the composition and the distribution of the national output.

e. It is not a measure of per capita output because it does not take into account changes in the size of the economy's population.

f. It does not record the pollution costs to the environment of producing final goods and services.

g. It does not measure the market value of the final goods and services produced in the underground sector of the economy.

■ IMPORTANT TERMS

National income (social) accounting
Gross national product
Final goods
Intermediate goods
Double counting
Value added
Nonproductive transaction
Nonmarket transaction
Expenditures approach
Income approach
Personal consumption expenditures
Government purchases of goods and services
Gross private domestic investment
Noninvestment transaction
Net private domestic investment
Expanding economy
Static economy
Declining economy
Net exports
Nonincome charges
Capital consumption allowances (depreciation)
Indirect business taxes
Compensation of employees
Wage and salary supplements
Net national product
National income
Personal income
Disposable income
Personal saving
Real gross national product
Price index
Base year
Given year
Inflating
Deflating
GNP deflator

■ FILL-IN QUESTIONS

1. Social accounting is valuable because it provides a means of keeping track of the level of __________ in the economy and the course it has followed over the long run; and the information required to devise and put into effect the public __________ that will improve the performance of the economy.

2. Gross national product is a monetary measure of all final goods and services produced during a year; to measure the value of these goods and services, the goods and services are valued at their __________

3. In measuring GNP only final goods and services are included; if intermediate goods and services were included, the accountant would be __________

4. A firm buys materials for \$200 from other firms in the economy and produces from them a product which sells for \$315. The \$115 is the __________ by the firm.

5. The total value added to a product at all stages of production equals the __________ value of the __________ product; and the total value added to all products produced in the economy during a year is the __________ product.

6. Personal consumption expenditures are the expenditures of households for __________ and __________ goods and for __________

7. Gross private domestic investment basically includes ____________, ____________, and ____________. Net private domestic investment is less than gross private domestic investment by an amount equal to ____________

8. If gross private domestic investment is less than depreciation, net private domestic investment is (positive, zero, negative) ____________ and the economy is (static, declining, expanding) ____________

9. An economy's *net* exports equal its ____________ less its ____________

10. In symbols, the GNP by the expenditures approach = ____ + ____ + ____ + ____

11. The capital consumption allowance and indirect business taxes, by the income approach, are referred to as ____________ charges or allocations.

12. The compensation of employees in the system of social accounting consists of actual wages and salaries *and* wage and salary ____________

The latter are the payments employers make to social ____________ programs and to ____________ pension, health, and welfare funds.

13. Corporate profits are disposed of in three ways: ____________, ____________, and ____________

14. Gross national product overstates the economy's net production because it fails to make allowance for that part of the output which replaces the ____________ worn out or used up in producing the output. To compute the net national product it is, therefore, necessary to subtract the ____________

15. National income equals net national product minus ____________

16. Personal income:

a. equals national income plus ____________ and minus the sum of ____________, ____________, and ____________;

b. also equals ____________ plus ____________ plus ____________

17. Disposable income:

a. equals personal income minus ____________;

b. also equals ____________

18. In order to compare the real gross national product in two different years, it is necessary to adjust the nominal GNP because ____________

19. For several reasons the real GNP is not a measure of social welfare in an economy.

a. It does not include the ____________ transactions that result in the production of goods and services or the amount of ____________ enjoyed by the citizens of the economy.

b. It fails to record improvements in the ____________ of the products produced, changes in the composition and distribution of the economy's total ____________, the undesirable effects of producing the GNP upon the ____________ of the economy, and the goods and services produced in the ____________ economy.

c. And because it is a measure of the *total* output of the economy it does not measure the ______ output of the economy.

20. When the population of an economy grows at a more rapid rate than its real GNP grows, the standard of living in that economy (rises, falls, remains constant) ______

■ PROBLEMS AND PROJECTS

1. Below are social accounting figures for the United States.

	Billions of dollars
Exports	$ 367
Dividends	60
Capital consumption allowance	307
Wages and salaries	1442
Government purchases of goods and services	577
Rents	33
Indirect business taxes	255
Wage and salary supplements	280
Gross private domestic investment	437
Corporate income taxes	88
Transfer payments	320
Interest	201
Proprietors' income	132
Personal consumption expenditures	1810
Imports	338
Social security contributions	148
Undistributed corporate profits	55
Personal taxes	372

a. Compute each of the following.

(1) Compensation of employees: $______

(2) Net exports: $______

(3) Net private domestic investment: $______

b. Use any of these figures and any of your computations in (*a*) above to prepare in the table below an Income Statement for the Economy similar to the one found in Table 9-4 (on page 152 of the text).

Receipts: Expenditures approach		Allocations: Income approach	
	$______		$______
	$______		$______
	$______		$______
	$______		$______
			$______
			$______
			$______
			$______
			$______
Gross national product	$______	Gross national product	$______

c. In this economy:

(1) Net national product is $______

(2) National income is $______

(3) Personal income is $______

(4) Disposable income is $______

2. A farmer who owns a plot of ground sells the right to pump crude oil from his land to a crude-oil producer. The crude-oil producer agrees to pay the farmer $20 a barrel for every barrel pumped from the farmer's land.

a. During one year 10,000 barrels are pumped.

(1) The farmer receives a payment of $______ from the crude-oil producer.

(2) The value added by the farmer is $______

b. The crude-oil producer sells the 10,000 barrels pumped to a petroleum refiner at a price of $25 a barrel.

(1) The crude-oil producer receives a payment of $______ from the refiner.

(2) The value added by the crude-oil producer is $______

c. The refiner employs a pipeline company to transport the crude oil from the farmer's land to the refinery and pays the pipeline company a fee of $1 a barrel for the oil transported.

(1) The pipeline company receives a payment of $10,000 from the refiner.

(2) The value added by the pipeline company is $10,000

d. From the 10,000 barrels of crude oil the refiner produces 315,000 gallons of gasoline and various by-products which are sold to distributors and gasoline service stations at an average price of $1 per gallon.

(1) The total payment received by the refiner from its customers is $315,000

(2) The value added by the refiner is $55,000

e. The distributors and service stations sell the 315,000 gallons of gasoline and by-products to consumers at an average price of $1.30 a gallon.

(1) The total payment received by distributors and service stations is $________

(2) The value added by them is $________

f. The total value added by the farmer, crude-oil producer, pipeline company, refiner, and distributors and service stations is $________ and the market value of the gasoline and by-products (the final good) is $________

3. Below is a list of items which may or may not be included in the five income-output measures. Indicate in the space to the right of each which of the income-output measures includes this item; it is possible for the item to be included in none, one, two, three, four, or all of the measures. If the item is included in none of the measures, indicate why it is not included.

a. Interest on the national debt ________

b. The sale of a used computer ________

c. The production of shoes which are not sold by the manufacturer ________

d. The income of a bootlegger in a "dry" state ________

e. The purchase of a share of common stock on the New York Stock Exchange ________

f. The interest paid on the bonds of the General Motors Corporation ________

g. The labor performed by a homemaker ________

h. The labor performed by a paid baby-sitter ________

i. The monthly check received by an idler from his rich aunt ________

j. The purchase of a new tractor by a farmer ________

k. The labor performed by an assembly-line worker in repapering his own kitchen ________

l. The services of a lawyer ________

m. The purchase of shoes from their manufacturer by a shoe retailer ________

n. The monthly check received from the Social Security Administration by a college student whose father has died ________

o. The rent a homeowner would receive if he did not live in his own home ________

4. In the table below are money (or unadjusted) GNP figures for three years and the price indices for each of the three years. (The GNP figures are in billions.)

Money GNP / price index = adjusted GNP

Year	Money GNP	Price index	Adjusted GNP
1929	$104	121	$86
1933	56	91	62
1939	91	100	91

a. Which of the three years appears to be the base year? 1939

b. Between:

(1) 1929 and 1933 the economy experienced (inflation, deflation) deflation

(2) 1933 and 1939 experienced inflation

c. Use the price indices to compute the adjusted GNP in each year. (You may round your answers to the nearest billion dollars.)

d. The nominal GNP figure:

(1) for 1929 was (deflated, inflated, neither) ________

(2) for 1933 was ________

(3) for 1939 was ________

■ SELF-TEST

Circle the T if the statement is true, the F if it is false.

1. Gross national product measures at their market values the total output of all goods and services produced in the economy during a year. T F

2. Both the nominal GNP and the real GNP of the American economy are measured in dollars. T F

3. The total market value of the wine produced in the United States during a year is equal to the number of bottles of wine produced in that year multiplied by the (average) price at which a bottle sold during that year. T F

4. The total value added to a product and the value of the final product are equal. T F

5. The two approaches to the measurement of the gross national product yield identical results because one approach measures the total amount spent on the products produced by business firms during a year while the second approach measures the total income of business firms during the year. T F

6. In computing gross national product, net national product, and national income by the expenditures approach, transfer payments are excluded because they do not represent payments for currently produced goods and services. T F

7. The expenditure made by a household to have a new home built for it is a personal consumption expenditure. T F

8. In national income accounting any increase in the inventories of business firms is included in gross private domestic investment. T F

9. If gross private domestic investment is greater than capital consumption during a given year, the economy has declined during that year. T F

10. The net exports of an economy equal its exports of goods and services less its imports of goods and services. T F

The data in the following table should be used to answer true-false questions 11 through 14 and multiple-choice questions 8 through 14.

	Billions of dollars
Net private domestic investment	$ 32
Personal taxes	39
Transfer payments	19
Indirect business taxes	8
Corporate income taxes	11
Personal consumption expenditures	217
Capital consumption allowance	7
United States exports	15
Dividends	15
Government purchases of goods and services	51
Undistributed corporate profits	10
Social security contributions	4
United States imports	17

11. The stock of capital goods in the economy has expanded. T F

12. Gross private domestic investment is equal to $25 billion. T F

13. National income equals the net national product minus $8 billion. T F

14. Disposable income is equal to $245 billion. T F

15. Comparison of a gross national product with the gross national product of an earlier year when the price level has risen between the two years necessitates the "inflation" of the GNP figure in the later year. T F

16. To adjust money gross national product for a given year so that a comparison between GNP in that year and in the base year can be made, it is necessary to divide nominal GNP in the given year by the price index—expressed as a decimal—for that year. T F

17. The price index used to adjust nominal GNP to measure the real GNP is the consumer price index (CPI). T F

18. The GNP is a measure of the social welfare of society. T F

Circle the letter that corresponds to the best answer.

1. Which of the following is *not* an important use to which social accounting is put? (*a*) Provides a basis for formulation and application of policies designed to improve the economy's performance; (*b*) permits measurement of the economic efficiency of the economy; (*c*) makes possible an estimate of the output of final goods and services in the economy; (d) enables the economist to chart the growth or decline of the economy over a period of time.

2. To include the value of the parts used in producing the automobiles turned out during a year in gross national product for that year would be an example of: (a) including a nonmarket transaction; (b) including a nonproductive transaction; (c) including a noninvestment transaction; (d) double counting.

3. Which of the following is *not* a purely financial transaction? (a) The sale of a used (second-hand) ironing board at a garage sale; (b) the sale of shares of stock in the United States Steel Corporation; (c) the payment of social-security benefits to a retired worker; (d) the birthday gift of a check for $5 sent by a grandmother to her grandchild.

4. The sale in 1979 of an automobile produced in 1978 would not be included in the gross national product for 1979; doing so would involve: (a) including a nonmarket transaction; (b) including a nonproductive transaction; (c) including a noninvestment transaction; (d) double counting.

5. The service a baby-sitter performs when she stays at home with her baby brother while her parents are out and for which she receives no payment is not included in the gross national product because: (a) this is a nonmarket transaction; (b) this is a nonproductive transaction; (c) this is a noninvestment transaction; (d) double counting would be involved.

6. Which of the following does *not* represent investment? (a) An increase in the quantity of shoes on the shelves of a shoe store; (b) the construction of a house which will be occupied by its owner; (c) the purchase of newly issued shares of stock in the General Motors Corporation; (d) the construction of a factory building using money borrowed from a bank.

7. A refrigerator is produced by its manufacturer in 1978, sold during 1978 to a retailer, and sold by the retailer to a final consumer in 1979. The refrigerator is: (a) counted as consumption in 1978; (b) counted as investment in 1979; (c) counted as investment in 1978 and consumption and disinvestment in 1979; (d) not included in the gross national product of 1978.

Questions 8 through 14 use the national income accounting data given in the table in the true-false section.

8. The nonincome charges are equal to: (a) $11 billion; (b) $15 billion; (c) $17 billion; (d) $19 billion.

9. Corporate profits are equal to: (a) $15 billion; (b) $25 billion; (c) $26 billion; (d) $36 billion.

10. Net exports are equal to: (a) −$2 billion; (b) $2 billion; (c) −$32 billion; (d) $32 billion.

11. The gross national product is equal to: (a) $298 billion; (b) $302 billion; (c) $317 billion; (d) $306 billion.

12. The net national product is equal to: (a) $298 billion; (b) $302 billion; (c) $317 billion; (d) $321 billion.

13. National income exceeds personal income by: (a) $6 billion; (b) $15 billion; (c) $21 billion; (d) $44 billion.

14. Personal saving is equal to: (a) −$28 billion; (b) −$8 billion; (c) $8 billion; (d) $28 billion.

15. If both money gross national product and the level of prices are rising, it is evident that: (a) real GNP is constant; (b) real GNP is rising but not so rapidly as prices; (c) real GNP is declining; (d) no conclusion can be drawn concerning the real GNP of the economy on the basis of this information.

16. Suppose GNP rose from $500 billion to $600 billion while the GNP deflator increased from 125 to 150. The real GNP: (a) remained constant; (b) increased; (c) decreased; (d) cannot be calculated from these figures.

17. The GNP includes: (a) the goods and services produced in the underground economy; (b) expenditures for equipment to reduce the pollution of the environment; (c) the value of the leisure enjoyed by citizens; (d) the goods and services produced but not bought and sold in the markets of the economy.

18. Changes in the real GNP from one year to the next do *not* reflect: (a) changes in the quality of the goods and services produced; (b) changes in the size of the population of the economy; (c) changes in the average length of the workweek; (d) any of the above changes.

■ DISCUSSION QUESTIONS

1. Of what use is national income accounting to the economist and to the policy makers in the economy?

2. Why are GNP, NNP, etc., monetary measures, and why is it necessary that they be monetary measures?

3. Why does GNP exclude nonproductive transactions? What are the two principal types of nonproductive transactions? List some examples of each.

4. Why are there two ways, both of which yield the same answers, of computing GNP, NNP, etc.?

5. Why are transfer payments excluded from GNP, NNP, and NI?

6. Is residential construction counted as investment or consumption? Why? Why is a change in inventories an investment?

7. How do you define a static, an expanding, and a declining economy? What is the relationship between gross private domestic investment and the capital consumption allowance in these three economies?

8. What is meant by a nonincome charge or allocation? What are the two principal non-income charges included in GNP? Why are they excluded from NI?

9. Why do economists find it necessary to inflate and deflate GNP when comparing GNP in different years? How do they do this?

10. Why is GNP not a measure of the social welfare of society?

9. Corporate Profits { Corp Y tax 11
undistrib. Corp π - retained 10
dividends 15

14. Saving Y = C + S + Tx
Disposable Inc - personal taxes } don't need

15 Money GNP (↑)
100 → 200
↑ Price lev
100 120

Formula
Real GNP = money GNP ↑ / P index ↑

10
Macroeconomic instability: unemployment and inflation

In the last chapter you learned how to define and how to compute the gross and net national product and national, personal, and disposable income in any year. This chapter begins the explanation of what determines how large each of these five income-output measures will tend to be. In the chapters that follow you will learn what causes the income and output of the economy to be what they are, what causes them to change, and how they might be controlled for the welfare of society.

Chapter 10 is concerned with the instability of the American economy or with what is commonly called the business cycle: the ups and downs in the employment of labor and the real output of the economy that occur over the years. That there have been expansions and contractions in economic (or business) activity since the end of the American Civil War is evident from even a casual look at American economic history. What is not immediately evident, however, is that these alternating and relatively short periods of prosperity and "hard times" have taken place over a longer period in which the trends in output, employment, and the standard of living have been upward. During this long history booms and busts have occurred quite irregularly; and their duration and intensity have been so varied that it is better to think of economic instability than of business cycles.

There are two principal problems that result from the instability of the economy—from the business cycle. After a brief look in the first major section of the chapter at the business cycle, its phases, and its impact on the production of different kinds of goods, Professor McConnell turns to the first of these two problems in the second major section. Here you will find an examination of the unemployment that accompanies a downturn in the level of economic activity in the economy. You will discover that there are three different kinds of unemployment, that full employment means about 6% of the labor force is unemployed, and that there are at least three problems encountered in measuring the percentage of the labor force actually unemployed at any time. That unemployment has an economic cost and that this cost is unequally distributed among different sectors of our society you will also learn; and you probably won't be too surprised to discover that widespread unemployment can be the cause of other social problems.

The second of the two problems that result from economic instability is inflation and it is examined in the remainder of the chapter. Inflation is an increase in the general (or average) level of prices in an economy. It does not have a unique cause: it may result from increases in demand; increases in costs; or from both. But regardless of its cause, it works a real hardship on certain sectors within the economy. If it occurs at too rapid a rate it may bring about a severe breakdown in the economy.

One last word. The thing to keep your eye on when you consider economic fluctuations and unemployment and inflation in the American economy is the changes in aggregate expenditures which can occur because consumers, business firms, or the public sector decides to spend more or less for goods and services.

■ CHECKLIST

When you have finished this chapter you should be able to:

☐ Explain what is meant by the business cycle; describe the four phases of an idealized cycle; and identify the two types of noncyclical fluctuations.

☐ Identify the "immediate determinant" or cause of the levels of output and employment.

☐ Distinguish between the impact of cyclical fluctuations on industries producing capital and consumer durable goods and on those producing consumer nondurable goods; and on high- and low-concentration industries.

☐ Distinguish between frictional, structural, and cyclical unemployment; and explain the causes of these three kinds of unemployment.

☐ Define full employment and the full-employment unemployment rate (the natural rate of unemployment).

☐ Describe the process employed (by the Bureau of Labor Statistics) to measure the rate of unemployment; and list the three criticisms of the BLS data.

☐ Identify the economic cost of unemployment and three groups that bear the unequal burdens of unemployment.

☐ Define the GNP gap, and state Okun's law.

☐ Define inflation and the rate of inflation; and describe the two kinds of inflation.

☐ Explain the effects of an increase in total spending on real output and employment *and* on the rate of increase in the price level in ranges 1, 2, and 3.

☐ List three groups that are hurt and two groups that benefit from inflation.

☐ Present three scenarios that describe the possible effects of inflation on real output and employment.

■ CHAPTER OUTLINE

1. The history of the American economy is a record of exceptional economic growth.

a. But this growth has been accompanied by periods of inflation, of depression, and of both.

b. The business cycle means alternating periods of prosperity and depression. These recurrent periods of ups and downs in employment, output, and prices are irregular in their duration and intensity; but the typical pattern is peak, recession, trough, and recovery to another peak.

c. Changes in the levels of output and employment are largely the result of changes in the level of aggregate spending or demand in the economy.

d. Not all changes in employment and output which occur in the economy are cyclical; some are due to seasonal and secular influences.

e. The business cycle affects almost the entire economy, but it does not affect all parts in the same way and to the same degree: the production of capital and durable consumer goods fluctuates more than the production of consumer nondurable goods during the cycle because

(1) the purchase of capital and durable consumer goods can be postponed, and

(2) the industries producing these goods are largely dominated by a few large firms that hold prices constant and let output decline when demand falls.

2. Full employment does not mean that all workers in the labor force are employed and that there is no unemployment; some unemployment is normal.

a. There are at least three kinds of unemployment.

(1) There is always some frictional unemployment; and this kind of unemployment is generally desirable.

(2) And in addition there is the structural unemployment that is the result of changes in technology and in the types of goods and services consumers wish to buy.

(3) Cyclical unemployment is the result of insufficient aggregate demand in the economy.

b. Because some frictional and structural unemployment is unavoidable, the full-employment unemployment rate (the natural rate of unemployment) is the sum of frictional and structural unemployment; is achieved when cyclical unemployment is zero (the real output of the economy is equal to its potential output); and is about 6% of the labor force.

c. Surveying 60,000 households each month, the Bureau of Labor Statistics finds the unemployment rate by dividing the number of persons in the labor force who are unemployed by the number of persons in the labor force; but the figures collected in the survey have been criticized for at least three reasons.

d. Unemployment has an economic cost.

(1) The economic cost is the unproduced output (or the GNP gap), and Okun's law is that for every 1% the actual unemployment rate exceeds the natural rate of unemployment there is 2.5% GNP gap.

(2) This cost is unequally distributed among different groups of workers in the labor force.

e. Unemployment also leads to serious social problems.

3. Over its history the American economy has experienced not only periods of unemployment but periods of inflation.

a. Inflation is an increase in the general level of prices in the economy; and a decline in the level of prices is deflation.

b. The rate of inflation in any year is equal to the percentage change in the price index between that year and the preceding year; and the rule of 70 can be used to calculate the number of years it will take for the price level to double at any given rate of inflation.

c. There are at least two causes of inflation; and these two causes may operate separately or simultaneously to raise the price level.

(1) Demand-pull inflation is the result of excess aggregate demand in the economy; and while increases in aggregate demand do not increase the price level when the unemployment rate is high (in a depression) they do bring about inflation as the economy nears and reaches full employment.

(2) Cost-push inflation is the result of the ability of strong labor unions and large business firms with market power to raise wage rates and prices; and it may occur when aggregate demand is not excessive and output and employment are declining.

4. Even if the total output of the economy did not change, inflation would arbitrarily redistribute real income and wealth; and would benefit some groups and hurt other groups in the economy.

a. Inflation injures those whose nominal incomes rise less rapidly and benefits those whose nominal incomes rise more rapidly than the price level.

b. It also injures savers because it decreases the real value of any savings the money value of which is fixed.

c. And it benefits debtors and hurts creditors because it lowers the real value of debts.

d. But when the inflation is anticipated and people can adjust their nominal incomes to reflect the expected rise in the price level the redistribution of income and wealth is lessened.

e. Since World War II inflation in the United States has redistributed wealth from the household to the public sector of the economy.

f. In short, inflation acts to tax some groups and to subsidize other groups.

5. Inflation may also affect the total output of the economy but economists disagree over whether it is likely to expand or contract total output.

a. Mild demand-pull inflation seems likely to expand output and employment in the economy.

b. Cost-push inflation is apt to contract output and employment.

c. And hyperinflation may well lead to the breakdown of the economy.

■ IMPORTANT TERMS

Business cycle
Seasonal variation
Secular trend
Frictional unemployment
Structural unemployment
Cyclical unemployment
Full employment
Full-employment unemployment rate
Natural rate of unemployment
Potential output
Unemployment rate
Labor force
Discouraged workers
GNP gap
Okun's law
Inflation
Deflation
Rule of 70
Demand-pull inflation
Cost-push inflation
Nominal income
Real income
Cost-of-living adjustment (COLA)
Anticipated inflation
Unanticipated inflation
Hyperinflation
Wage-price inflationary spiral

■ FILL-IN QUESTIONS

1. The history of the American economy is one of (steady, unsteady) unsteady economic growth; and at times its growth has been accompanied by inflation and at other times its expansion has been interrupted by low levels of employment and output

2. The business cycle is a term which means the recurrent ups and downs in the level of business activity in the economy; and the four phases of a typical business cycle are peak, recession, trough, and recovery

3. The basic determinant of the levels of employment and output in an economy is the level of total spending or aggregate ~~expenditures~~ (demand) in the economy.

4. In addition to the changes brought about by the operation of the business cycle, changes in output and employment may be due to seasonal variations and to a secular trend.

5. Production and employment in the (durable, nondurable) durable and (capital, consumer) capital goods industries are affected to a greater extent by the expansion and contraction of the economy than they are in the ~~hard~~ nondurable goods industries; and prices vary to a greater extent in the (low-, high-) low concentration industries.

6. The three types of unemployment are:

a. frictional - between-jobs

b. structural - have to retrain

c. cylical - unemp. caused by recessional phase of cycle

7. The full-employment unemployment rate is:

a. sometimes called the natural rate of unemployment;

b. equal to the total of the frictional and the structural unemployment in the economy;

c. realized when the cylical unemployment in the economy is equal to zero and when the actual output of the economy is equal to its potentiial output; and

d. assumed in this chapter to be about 6 %.

8. When the economy achieves its natural rate of unemployment the number of job seekers is (greater than, less than, equal to) equal the number of job vacancies; and the price level is (rising, falling, constant) constant

9. The unemployment *rate* is found by dividing unemployment by the labor force X 100

10. The GNP gap is equal to actual GNP *minus* potential GNP; and for every percentage point the unemployment rate rises above the natural rate of unemployment the GNP gap will, according to Okun's law, (increase, decrease) increase by $2\frac{1}{2}$ %

11. The burdens of unemployment are borne more heavily by (black, white) black, (adult, teenage) teenage, and (white-collar, blue-collar) blue collar workers; and the percentage of the labor force unemployed for 15 or more weeks is (greater, less) less than the unemployment rate.

12. Inflation means a rising in the general level of prices in the economy; and the rate of inflation in year 1987 is equal to the price index for year 1987 less the price index for year 86 all divided by the price index for year 86

13. The basic cause of:

a. demand-pull inflation is (an increase, a decrease) increase in aggregate demand;

b. cost-push inflation is the result of the market power of strong businesses (corp) and large unions

14. Inflation:

a. hurts those whose nominal incomes are relatively (fixed, flexible) fixed

b. penalizes savers when the inflation is (expected, unexpected) unexpected

c. hurts (creditors, debtors) creditors and benefits debtors

d. has since World War II shifted wealth from (the public sector, households) households to public sector

15. Despite considerable disagreement and uncertainty among economists it seems that:

a. demand-pull inflation, unless there is full employment in the economy, will (increase, decrease) increase total output and employment;

b. cost-push inflation will decrease output and employment in the economy;

c. hyperinflation may bring about an economic breakdown (collapse)

PROBLEMS AND PROJECTS

1. In the table below are statistics showing the labor force and total employment in the United States during 1970 and 1975. Make the computations necessary to complete the table. (Numbers of persons are in thousands.)

	1970	1975
Labor force	84,889	95,453
Employed	80,796	87,524
Unemployed		
Unemployment rate		

a. How is it possible that *both* employment and unemployment increased? ______

b. In relative terms, if unemployment increases employment will decrease. Why? ______

c. Would you say that 1975 was a year of full employment? ______

d. Why is the task of maintaining full employment over the years more than just a problem of finding jobs for those who happen to be employed at any given time? ______

2. In the space below, indicate for each of the following situations the effects of an increase in total spending on *real GNP, nominal GNP,* the *unemployment rate,* and the *price level,* respectively, using the following symbols: A, little or no effect; B, increase; C, decrease; and D, sharp increase.

a. Depression and widespread unemployment

b. Prosperity, but moderate unemployment

c. Prosperity and full employment

3. Indicate in the space to the right of each of the following the effect—beneficial (B), detrimental (D), or indeterminate (I)—of inflation on these persons:

a. A retired self-employed businessman who now lives by spending each month a part of the amount he saved and deposited in a savings and loan association. ______

b. A retired private-school teacher who lives on the dividends she receives from the shares of stock she owns. ______

c. A farmer who (by mortgaging his farm) borrowed at the local bank $500,000 that must be repaid during the next ten years. ______

d. A retired couple whose sole source of income is the pension they receive from her former employer. ______

e. A widow whose income consists entirely of interest received from the corporate bonds she owns. ______

f. A public school teacher. ______

g. A member of union who works for a firm that produces computers. ______

4. Suppose that in 1987 the economy is at full employment, has a potential and actual real GNP of $3000 billion, and an unemployment rate of 6%.

a. Compute the GNP gap in 1987 and enter it in the table below.

Year	Potential GNP	Actual GNP	GNP gap
1987	$3000	$3000	$
1988	3800	3705	
1989	4125	3712.5	

b. The potential and actual real GNPs in 1988 and 1989 are also shown in the table. Compute and enter into the table the GNP gaps in these two years.

c. In 1988 the actual real GNP is ____% of the potential real GNP. (*Hint:* divide the actual real GNP by the potential real GNP.)

(1) The actual real GNP is ____% *less* than the potential real GNP.

(2) Using Okun's law, the unemployment rate will rise from 6% in 1987 and be 7 % in 1988.

d. In 1989 the actual real GNP is 90 % of the potential real GNP.

(1) The actual real GNP is 10 % *less* than the potential real GNP.

(2) The unemployment rate, according to Okun's law, will be 10 %.

5. The table below shows the price index in the economy at the end of four different years.

Year	Price index	Rate of inflation
1	100.00	
2	112.00	12 %
3	123.20	10
4	129.36	5

a. Compute and enter in the table the rates of inflation in years 2, 3, and 4.

b. Employing the "rule of 70," how many years would it take for the price level to double at each of these three inflation rates? ____________

6. On the two graphs in the next column the price *level* is measured along the vertical axis and real *national* output is measured along the horizontal axis. The demand for and the supply of national output are shown by the curves labeled *D* and *S*.

a. Applying the principles of demand and supply which you learned in Chapter 4, the equilibrium price level is the price level at which the national output demanded and the national output supplied are equal and the equilibrium national output is the nat'l outpt demanded & supplied at the equil. price level

b. Draw on the first graph a new demand curve which represents an *increase* in the demand for national output.

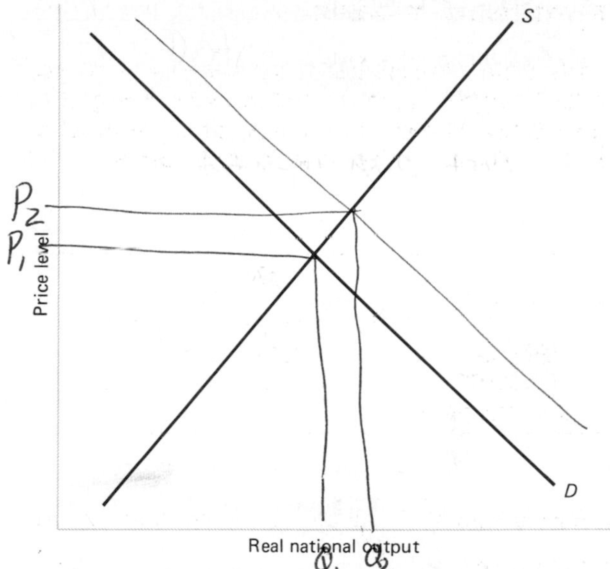

(1) The effect of this increase in demand is a rise in the equilibrium price level and a(n) increase in the equilibrium national output.

(2) This rise in the price level is an example of demand-pull inflation.

c. On the graph below draw a new supply curve which represents a *decrease* in the supply of national output.

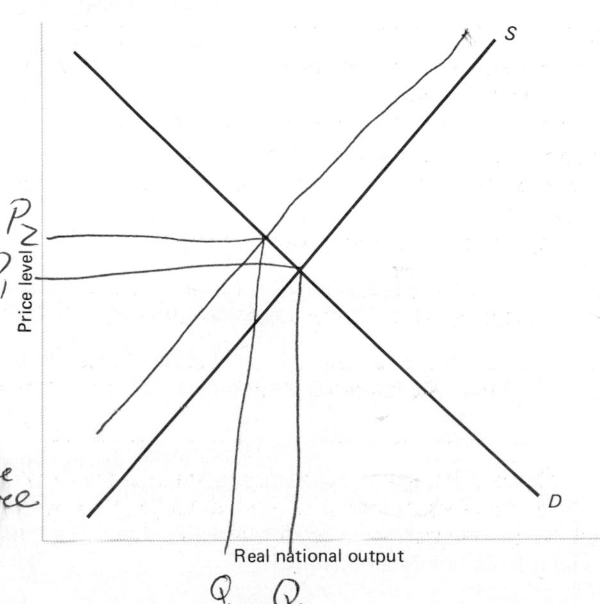

(1) The effect of this decrease in supply is a ________ in the equilibrium price level and a ________ in the equilibrium national output.

(2) These effects are an example of ________
____

■ **SELF-TEST**

Circle the T if the statement is true, the F if it is false.

1. The American economy has experienced a long period of substantial economic growth and shorter periods of inflation and of high unemployment. **T F**

2. The business cycle is best defined as alternating periods of increases and decreases in the rate of inflation in the economy. **T F**

3. Individual business cycles tend to be of roughly equal duration and intensity. **T F**

4. Not all changes which occur in output and employment in the economy are due to the business cycle. **T F**

5. Industries which are highly concentrated show small relative decreases in output and large relative decreases in prices during a downswing of the business cycle. **T F**

6. Frictional unemployment is not only inevitable but largely desirable. **T F**

7. The essential difference between frictionally and structurally unemployed workers is that the former do *not* have and the latter do have salable skills. **T F**

8. When the number of people seeking employment is less than the number of job vacancies in the economy the actual rate of unemployment is less than the natural rate of unemployment and the price level will tend to rise. **T F**

9. If unemployment in the economy is at its natural rate the actual and potential outputs of the economy are equal. **T F**

10. The natural rate of unemployment in the American economy is a constant 6% of the labor force. **T F**

11. An economy cannot produce an actual real GNP that exceeds its potential real GNP. **T F**

12. The unemployment rate is equal to the number of persons in the labor force divided by the number of people who are unemployed. **T F**

13. The percentage of the labor force unemployed for fifteen or more weeks is always less than the unemployment rate and tends to rise during a recession. **T F**

14. The economy's GNP gap is measured by deducting its actual GNP from its potential GNP. **T F**

15. The economic cost of cyclical unemployment is the goods and services that are not produced. **T F**

16. Inflation is defined as an increase in the total output of an economy. **T F**

17. Between 1968 and 1969 the consumer price index rose from 104.2 to 109.8. The rate of inflation was, therefore, 5.6%. **T F**

18. If the price level increases by 10% each year the price level will double every ten years. **T F**

19. With a moderate amount of unemployment in the economy, an increase in aggregate spending will generally increase both the price level and the output of the economy. **T F**

20. If the economy is operating at full employment a decrease in total spending can be expected to reduce both the price level and employment in the economy. **T F**

21. A person's real income is the amount of goods and services which the person's money (or nominal) income will enable him or her to purchase. **T F**

22. Whether inflation is anticipated or unanticipated, the effects of inflation on the distribution of income are much the same. **T F**

23. Suppose a household has $10,000 on deposit in a savings and loan association upon which it earns 7% interest during a year and the rate of inflation is 9% in that year. By the end of the year the purchasing power of the $10,000 and the interest it has earned will have decreased to about $9,817. **T F**

24. Deflation would benefit creditors and hurt debtors. **T F**

25. Inflation in the United States has transferred wealth from the public sector to the households of the economy. **T F**

Circle the letter that corresponds to the best answer.

1. Which one of the following is *not* one of the four phases of an idealized business cycle? (*a*) inflation; (*b*) recession; (*c*) recovery; (*d*) trough.

2. Most economists believe that the immediate determinant of the levels of national output and employment is (*a*) the price level; (*b*) the size of the civilian labor force; (*c*) the nation's stock of capital goods; (*d*) the level of aggregate spending.

3. Total employment in December of this year was greater than total employment in December of 1928. This is no doubt due to the effect of: (*a*) seasonal variations; (*b*) secular trend; (*c*) the business cycle; (*d*) business fluctuations.

4. If employment in the agricultural sector of the American economy during last August and September was 112% of what it normally is in those months, this is probably a consequence of: (*a*) seasonal variations; (*b*)secular trend; (*c*) the business cycle; (*d*) both seasonal variations and the business cycle.

5. Production and employment in which of the following industries would be least affected by a depression? (*a*) Nondurable consumer goods; (*b*) durable consumer goods; (*c*) capital goods; (*d*) iron and steel.

6. A worker who loses his job at a petroleum refinery because consumers and business firms switch from the use of oil to the burning of coal is an example of (*a*) frictional unemployment; (*b*) structural unemployment; (*c*) cyclical unemployment; (*d*) disguised unemployment.

7. A worker who has quit one job and is taking two weeks off before reporting to a new job is an example of (*a*) frictional unemployment; (*b*) structural unemployment; (*c*) cyclical unemployment; (*d*) disguised unemployment.

8. Insufficient aggregate demand results in (*a*) frictional unemployment; (*b*) structural unemployment; (*c*) cyclical unemployment; (*d*) disguised unemployment.

9. The full-employment unemployment rate in the economy has been achieved when (*a*) frictional unemployment is zero; (*b*) structural unemployment is zero; (*c*) cyclical unemployment is zero; (*d*) the natural rate of unemployment is zero.

10. Which of the following has increased the natural rate of unemployment in the United States? (*a*) The increased participation of women and teenagers in the American labor force; (*b*) the expansion of the unemployment compensation system in the United States; (*c*) the increases in the legal minimum wage; (*d*) all of the above.

11. The labor force includes those who are (*a*) under sixteen years of age; (*b*) in mental institutions; (*c*) not seeking work; (*d*) employed.

12. The data collected by the Bureau of Labor Statistics have been criticized because (*a*) part-time workers are not counted in the number of workers employed; (*b*) discouraged workers are treated as a part of the labor force; (*c*) some workers who are not looking for work are included in the labor force; (*d*) all of the above.

13. Okun's law predicts that when the actual unemployment rate exceeds the natural rate of unemployment by two percentage points the GNP gap will equal (*a*) 2% of the potential GNP; (*b*) 3% of the potential GNP; (*c*) 4% of the potential GNP; (*d*) 5% of the potential GNP.

14. If the GNP gap were equal to 7.5% of the potential GNP the actual unemployment rate would exceed the natural rate of unemployment by (*a*) two percentage points; (*b*) three percentage points; (*c*) four percentage points; (*d*) five percentage points.

15. The burden of unemployment is *least* felt by (*a*) white-collar workers; (*b*) teenagers; (*c*) blacks; (*d*) males.

16. If the resources of the economy are fully employed, an increase in aggregate spending will cause: (*a*) output and employment to increase; (*b*) output and prices to increase; (*c*) nominal incomes and prices to increase; (*d*) employment and nominal incomes to increase.

17. If the economy is experiencing a depression with substantial unemployment, an increase in total spending will cause: (*a*) a decrease in the *real* income of the economy; (*b*) little or no increase in the level of prices; (*c*) an increase in the *real* income and a decrease in the *nominal* income of the economy; (*d*) proportionate increases in the price level, output, and income in the economy.

18. If a person's nominal income increases by 8% while the price level increases by 10% the person's real income will have (*a*) increased by 2%; (*b*) increased by 18%; (*c*) decreased by 18%; (*d*) decreased by 2%.

19. If no inflation were anticipated a bank would be willing to lend a business firm $10 million at an annual interest rate of 8%. If the rate of inflation were expected to be 6% the bank would charge the firm an annual interest rate of (*a*) 2%; (*b*) 6%; (*c*) 8%; (*d*) 14%.

20. Which of the following would *not* be hurt by inflation? (*a*) Those living on fixed nominal incomes; (*b*) those who find prices rising more rapidly than their nominal incomes; (*c*) those who have money savings; (*d*) those who became debtors when prices were lower.

21. Mild demand-pull inflation, many economists argue, results in (*a*) rising output; (*b*) rising real income; (*c*) falling unemployment; (*d*) all of the above.

22. Which of the following is *not* related to the cost-push theory of inflation? (*a*) An increase in employment and output; (*b*) the market power of aggressive labor unions; (*c*) the ability of large corporations to administer prices; (*d*) a decrease in supply.

23. Which of the following is *not* associated with hyperinflation? (*a*) War or its aftermath; (*b*) rising output in the economy; (*c*) the hoarding of goods and speculation; (*d*) a halt to the use of money as both a medium of exchange and a standard of value.

24. Inflation in the American economy has been caused by (*a*) increases in aggregate demand; (*b*) decreases in aggregate supply; (*c*) either *a* or *b*; (*d*) both *a* and *b*.

25. Since 1983 (*a*) both the rate of inflation and the unemployment rate have increased; (*b*) the rate of inflation has increased and the unemployment rate has decreased; (*c*) the rate of inflation has increased and the unemployment rate has decreased; (*d*) both the rate of inflation and the unemployment rate have decreased.

■ DISCUSSION QUESTIONS

1. What is the historical record of American economy with respect to economic growth, full employment, and price-level stability?

2. Define the business cycle. Why do some economists prefer the term "business fluctuations" to "business cycle"? Describe the four phases of an idealized cycle.

3. What, in the opinion of most economists, is the immediate determinant or cause of the levels of output and employment in the economy?

4. The business cycle is only one of three general causes of changes in output and employment in the economy. What are the other influences which affect these variables?

5. Compare the manner in which the business cycle affects output and employment in the industries producing capital and durable goods with industries producing nondurable goods and services. What causes these differences?

6. Distinguish between frictional, structural, and cyclical unemployment.

7. When is there full employment in the American economy? (Answer in terms of the unemployment rate, the actual and potential output of the economy, and the markets for labor.)

8. How is the unemployment rate measured in the United States? What criticisms have been made of the method used by the Bureau of Labor Statistics to determine the unemployment rate?

9. What is the economic cost of unemployment and how is this cost measured? What is the quantitative relationship (called Okun's law) between the unemployment rate and the cost of unemployment?

10. What groups in the economy tend to bear the burdens of unemployment? How are women affected by unemployment and how is the percentage of the labor force unemployed fifteen or more weeks related to the unemployment rate in the economy?

11. What is inflation and how is the rate of inflation measured?

12. Compare and contrast demand-pull and cost-push inflation.

13. What groups benefit from and what groups are hurt by inflation and how has the public sector of the economy been affected by it?

14. What is the difference between the effects of unanticipated and the effects of anticipated inflation on the redistribution of real incomes in the economy?

15. Explain what will tend to happen to employment, output, money income, and the price level if total spending increases and the resources of the economy are: (*a*) widely unemployed, (*b*) moderately unemployed, (*c*) fully employed. If total spending *decreased* would the effects on employment, output, income, and the price level be just the opposite?

16. Write three scenarios that describe the effects of inflation on the national output.

11 Macroeconomics: an overview

You learned in Chapter 9 how the GNP and the NNP are measured and how to adjust them when the price level changes to find the real GNP and the real NNP. Then in Chapter 10 you found that over the years the American economy has at times suffered from unemployment, has at other times experienced inflation, and has at still other times had both unemployment and inflation.

In Chapter 11 you will begin learning what determines how large the real national output (the real GNP or NNP) and the price level at any time will be; what causes them to change; and what policies the Federal government can use to prevent unemployment and inflation.

The tools employed to explain what determines the economy's real output and price level are demand and supply. You first encountered these tools in Chapter 4 where they were used to explain what determines the output and the price of a particular product. These same tools are now employed in a slightly different way. To use these tools of aggregate demand and aggregate supply you will have to think not of the price of a particular good or service but of the price level in the economy. And instead of thinking about the quantity of a particular good or service demanded or supplied it is necessary to think about the total (the aggregate) quantity of all final goods and services demanded (purchased) and supplied (produced) in the economy. You will have no difficulty with the way demand and supply are used in this chapter once you adjust the way you think about them from a particular good or service and its price to all final goods and services and their average price.

Having made this adjustment in your way of thinking about demand and supply, the rest is not too difficult. The aggregate demand curve is downsloping because of the interest-rate, real-balances, and foreign-purchases effects of changes in the price level. The aggregate supply curve is, however, somewhat peculiar. It is horizontal at low levels, vertical at high levels, and upsloping at intermediate levels of real national output.

Like the ordinary demand and supply curves of Chapter 4, the intersection of the aggregate demand and the aggregate supply curves determine equilibrium quantity and price: the equilibrium quantity is the equilibrium real national output and the equilibrium price is the equilibrium price level. With the knowledge of how aggregate demand and supply determine the real national output and the price level you have acquired the ability to explain the basic causes of inflation (an increase in demand or a decrease in supply), of a decrease in national output and employment (a decrease in demand or in supply), and of stagflation (a decrease in supply). You have also acquired the economic principles that will enable you to know what the Federal government might do to increase output and employment, prevent inflation, and eliminate stagflation in the economy.

Aggregate demand and aggregate supply are the skeleton upon which macroeconomic theory and policies are based. The next nine chapters "flesh-out" this skeleton. As you study these chapters you may forget the aggregate-demand-aggregate-supply framework. Don't!

■ CHECKLIST

When you have studied this chapter you should be able to:

☐ Define aggregate demand and aggregate supply.

☐ Explain why the aggregate-demand curve slopes downward.

☐ Describe and name the three ranges on the aggregate-supply curve.

☐ Explain what the equilibrium real national output and the equilibrium price level will be; and why the economy will tend to produce this output (rather than a larger or smaller one).

☐ State the effects on the real national output and on the price level of an increase in aggregate demand when the economy is in the Keynesian, classical, and intermediate ranges.

☐ Explain why a decrease in aggregate demand will not reduce the price level so much as an equal increase in aggregate demand would have raised it.

☐ State what demand-management (fiscal and monetary) policies government might employ to increase the real national output or to prevent a rise in the price level; and cite four real-world examples of the use of such policies.

☐ Explain the basic cause of changes in aggregate supply; and the effects of increases and decreases in aggregate supply upon the real national output and the price level.

☐ Describe the dilemma government faces if it uses demand-management policies to deal with stagflation; and how the use of supply-side policies would enable it to avoid this dilemma.

■ CHAPTER OUTLINE

1. Aggregate demand and aggregate supply determine the real national output and the price level of the economy; and are used in this chapter to explain both why output and the price level fluctuate and what the Federal government may do to control them.

2. Aggregate demand is a curve which shows the total quantity of goods and services that will be purchased (demanded) at different price levels; and the curve slopes downward for three reasons.

a. With the supply of money fixed, an increase in the price level increases the demand for money, increases interest rates, and as a result reduces those expenditures (by consumers and business firms) which are sensitive to increased interest rates; and a decrease in the price level has the opposite effects.

b. An increase in the price level also decreases the real value (purchasing power) of financial assets with a fixed money value, and because those who own such assets are now poorer they spend less for goods and services; and a decrease in the price level has the opposite effects.

c. In addition, an increase in the price level (relative to foreign price levels) will reduce American exports, expand American imports, and decrease the quantity of goods and services demanded in the American economy; and a decrease in the price level (relative to foreign price levels) will have opposite effects.

3. Aggregate supply is a curve that shows the total quantity of goods and services that will be produced (supplied) at different price levels; and the curve has three ranges.

a. In the Keynesian range (when the economy is in a severe recession or depression) the aggregate supply curve is horizontal; the price level need not rise to induce producers to supply larger quantities of goods and services.

b. In the classical range (when the economy is at full employment) the aggregate supply curve is vertical: a rise in the price level cannot result in an increase in the quantity of goods and services supplied.

c. Between these two ranges is the intermediate range in which the supply curve slopes upward: the price level must rise to induce producers to supply larger quantities of goods and services.

4. The equilibrium real national output and the equilibrium price level are at the intersection of the aggregate-demand and the aggregate-supply curves. Were the actual output greater (less) than the equilibrium output producers would find that their inventories were increasing (decreasing) and they would contract (expand) their output to the equilibrium output.

a. An increase in aggregate demand in:

(1) the Keynesian range would result in an increase in real output but the price level would remain unchanged;

(2) the classical range would result in an increase in the price level but the real national output would remain unchanged;

(3) the intermediate range would result in an increase in both real national output and the price level.

b. But a decrease in aggregate demand would not have the opposite effect on the price level because prices (for several reasons) tend to be inflexible (sticky) downward.

c. The Federal government can manage aggregate demand to bring about changes in real output and the price level: to increase (decrease) aggregate demand it employs an expansionary (a contractionary) fiscal policy or an easy (a tight) money policy; and real-world examples of the effects of these policies include:

(1) the large increases in government expenditures during World War II that produced a decline in unemployment and inflation;

(2) the 1964 tax cut and easy money policy which accompanied it that reduced unemployment and increased the price level;

(3) the income tax surcharge levied during the Vietnam war to fight inflation that failed to stem inflation because consumers saw it as temporary and believed the inflation would continue; and

(4) the 1979–1982 period of monetary restraint that slowed the rate of inflation, reduced output, and increased the unemployment rate.

d. An increase (a decrease) in the costs of producing goods and services will decrease (increase) aggregate supply—move the aggregate supply curve to the left (right)—and reduce (expand) the real national output and push the price level upward (downward).

e. To offset the effects of a decrease in aggregate supply the Federal government might increase aggregate demand, but this would bring about a further rise in the price level; or decrease aggregate demand, but this would result in a further decline in real output. This dilemma may be avoided by supply-side policies to increase aggregate supply.

f. To recap, both aggregate demand and aggregate supply affect real national output and the price level; both demand-management and supply-side policies may be used to combat recession and inflation; but using either has problems and limits.

5. Macroeconomic policies to deal with recession and inflation and the theories upon which these policies are based are currently in a state of flux; the older classical theory, reinforced by monetarism and supply-side economics, has attacked the widely accepted conclusions and policies of the Keynesian theory. The remaining eight chapters of Parts Two and Three of the text examine these theories and policies in greater detail.

■ IMPORTANT TERMS

Stagflation	**Demand management**
Aggregate-demand curve	**Expansionary fiscal policy**
Interest-rate effect	**Easy money policy**
Real-balances effect	**Contractionary fiscal policy**
Foreign-purchases effect	**Tight money policy**
Aggregate-supply curve	**Cost-push inflation**
Keynesian range	**Supply-side economics**
Classical range	**Keynesian theory**
Intermediate range	**Classical theory**
Demand-pull inflation	**Monetarism**
Ratchet effect	

■ FILL-IN QUESTIONS

1. Aggregate demand and aggregate supply together determine the equilibrium real national ________ and the equilibrium price ________

2. The aggregate-demand curve shows the quantity of goods and services that will be ________ at various price ________

a. It slopes (upward, downward) ________

b. because of the ________, the ________, and the ________ effects.

3. The aggregate-supply curve shows the quantity of goods and services that will be ________ at various price ________; and in the:

a. Keynesian range is (vertical, horizontal, upsloping) ________

b. the intermediate range is ________

c. the classical range is ________

4. The equilibrium real national output and price level are found at the ________ of the aggregate-demand and the aggregate-supply curves.

a. At this price level the aggregate quantity of goods and services ________ is equal to the aggregate quantity of goods and services ________

b. And at this real national output the prices producers are willing to (pay, accept) ________ are equal to the prices buyers are willing to ________

5. Were the actual real national output:

a. greater than the equilibrium national output producers would find that their inventories are (increasing, decreasing) ________ and they would (expand, reduce) ________ their production;

b. less than the equilibrium national output producers

would find that their inventories are decreasing and they would expand their production.

6. When the economy is producing in:

a. the Keynesian range an increase in aggregate demand will (increase, decrease, have no effect on) increase real national output and will no effect the price level;

b. the intermediate range an increase in aggregate demand will increase real national output and will increase the price level;

c. the classical range an increase in aggregate demand will have no effect on real national output and will increase the price level.

7. Were the economy operating in the intermediate or classical ranges and aggregate demand were to decrease, the price level would decline by (a larger, a smaller, the same) a smaller amount as an equal increase in aggregate demand would have raised the price level; this is called the (interest-rate, real-balances, ratchet) rathet effect.

8. Should the Federal government use demand-management policies:

a. to increase the real national output it might employ either:

(1) a(n) (expansionary, contractionary) expansionary fiscal policy by (increasing, decreasing) increasing its expenditures or by decreasing taxes

(2) or a(n) (tight, easy) ~~tight~~ easy money policy by (increasing, decreasing) ~~decreasing~~ increasing the money supply;

b. to prevent a rise in the price level it might employ either:

(1) a(n) ~~contractionary~~ contractionary fiscal policy by decreasing its expenditures or by increasing taxes

(2) or a(n) tight money policy by reducing the money supply.

9. The basic cause of a decrease in aggregate supply is a(n) (increase, decrease) increase in the costs of producing goods and services; and the basic cause of an increase in aggregate supply is decrease in costs of prod. G & serv.

a. An increase in aggregate supply will not only (raise, lower) raise real national output and (lead to, prevent) prevent inflation but will also (increase, decrease) increase the full-employment level of national output.

b. A decrease in aggregate supply will lower real output and raise the price level.

10. If the Federal government uses demand-management policies to deal with stagflation:

a. an increase in aggregate demand will increase real output but will increase the price level.

b. a decrease in aggregate demand will prevent further inflation but will lower (decrease) real national output.

11. Supply-side policies to deal with stagflation try to (increase, decrease) increase aggregate supply. This will both increase the (price level, real output) real output and reduce (inflation, real output) inflation

12. Demand-pull inflation is the result of a(n) (increase, decrease) increase in aggregate demand and is accompanied by a (rise, fall) rise in real output; but cost-push inflation is the result of a(n) decrease in aggregate supply and is accompanied by a fall in real nat'l outpt.

■ PROBLEMS AND PROJECTS

1. In the table below is an aggregate-supply schedule.

Price level	Real national output produced
$7.00	2000
6.00	2000
5.00	1900
4.00	1700
3.00	1400
2.00	1000
2.00	500
2.00	0

a. The economy is in the:

(1) Keynesian range when the real national output is between ___0___ and ___1000___

(2) classical range when the real national output is ___2000___ and the price level is $__6.00__ or more

(3) intermediate range when the real national output is between ___1000___ and ___2000___

b. Plot this aggregate-supply schedule on the graph below.

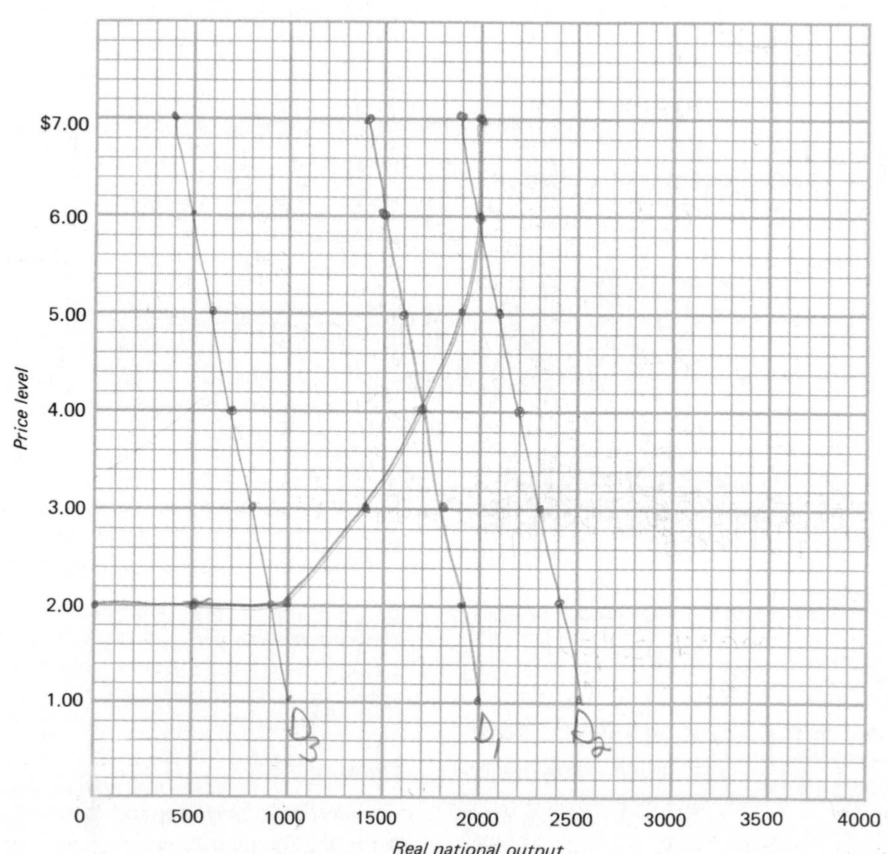

c. In the table below are three aggregate-demand schedules.

Price level	Real national output purchased		
(1)	(2)	(3)	(4)
$7.00	1400	1900	400
6.00	1500	2000	500
5.00	1600	2100	600
4.00	1700	2200	700
3.00	1800	2300	800
2.00	1900	2400	900
1.00	2000	2500	1000

(1) Plot the aggregate-demand curve shown in columns (1) and (2) on the graph on the previous page; and label this curve D_1. At this level of aggregate demand the equilibrium real national output is 1700

and the equilibrium price level is $4.00

(2) On the same graph plot the aggregate-demand curve shown in columns (1) and (3); and label this curve D_2. The equilibrium real national output is 2000

and the equilibrium price level is $6.00

(3) Now plot the aggregate-demand curve in columns (1) and (4) and label it D_3. The equilibrium real national output is 900

and the equilibrium price level is $2.00

2. In the diagram in the next column are an aggregate-supply curve and six aggregate demand curves.

a. The movements of the aggregate-demand curves from D_1 to D_2, from D_3 to D_4, and from D_5 to D_6 all portray (increases, decreases) increases in aggregate demand.

(1) The movement from D_1 to D_2 increases the (real national output, price level) nat'l output but does not change the price level

(2) The movement from D_3 to D_4 will (raise, lower) increase the price level and will (expand, contract) expand the real national output.

(3) The movement from D_5 to D_6 will increase price level but no change in real nat'l output

b. The movements of the aggregate-demand curves to the left all portray (increases, decreases) decreases in aggregate demand.

(1) If prices are flexible in a downward direction, what effects will these changes in aggregate demand have upon the real national output and the price level? ______

(2) If prices are *not* flexible in a downward direction, what effects will these changes in aggregate demand have? reduces real nat'l output but doesn't change price

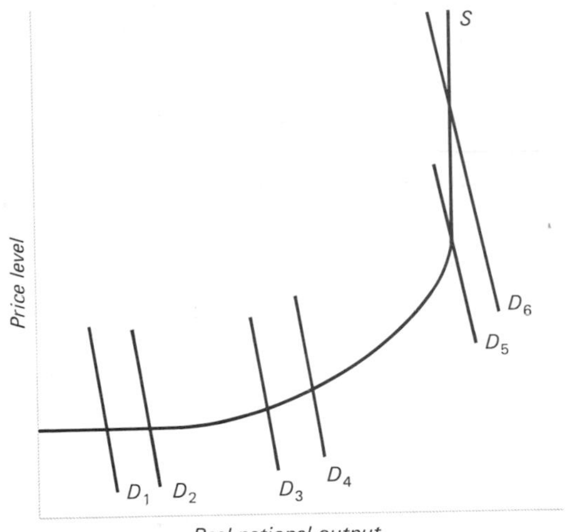

Real national output

3. In the diagram on the next page there are two aggregate-supply curves and three aggregate-demand curves.

a. The movement of the aggregate-supply curve from S_1 to S_2 represents a(n) (increase, decrease) increase in aggregate supply.

(1) If the price level is flexible downward and upward, this change in aggregate supply in each of the three ranges along the aggregate supply curve will (raise, lower) lower the price level and (expand, contract) expand the real national output.

(2) But if prices are inflexible in a downward direction, this change in aggregate supply will (increase, decrease) increase real national output but (will, will not) will not affect the price level.

b. The movement of aggregate supply from S_2 to S_1 portrays a(n) decrease in aggregate supply and in each of the three ranges will raise the price level and decrease the real national output.

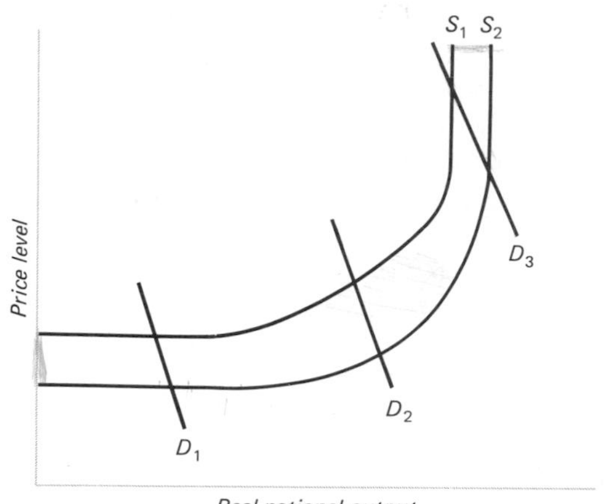

■ SELF-TEST

Circle the T if the statement is true, the F if it is false.

1. The aggregate-demand curve slopes downward. T F

2. A fall in the price level increases the real value of financial assets with fixed money values and, as a result, increases spending by the holders of these assets. T F

3. A fall in the price level reduces the demand for money in the economy and drives interest rates upward. T F

4. A rise in the price level of an economy (relative to foreign price levels) tends to increase that economy's exports and to reduce its imports of goods and services. T F

5. The aggregate-supply curve is horizontal in the classical range. T F

6. At the equilibrium price level the real national output purchased is equal to the real national output produced. T F

7. In the intermediate range on the aggregate-supply curve an increase in aggregate demand will increase both the price level and the real national output. T F

8. A decrease in aggregate demand will lower the price level by the same amount as an equal increase in aggregate demand would have raised it. T F

9. An increase in aggregate supply increases both the equilibrium real national output and the full-employment output of the economy. T F

10. The basic cause of a decrease in aggregate supply is an increase in the costs of producing goods and services. T F

11. When government uses demand-management policies in the intermediate range along the aggregate-supply curve it is able to increase the real national output or reduce the rise in the price level, but it is unable to do both. T F

12. Stagflation is a rise in the price level accompanied by declining or stable levels of real national output and employment in the economy. T F

13. A decrease in aggregate supply is "doubly good" because it increases the real national output and prevents inflation. T F

14. Demand-management policies are an effective method of eliminating stagflation. T F

15. The use of supply-side policies requires the economy to trade higher levels of real output and employment for a more rapid rise in the price level. T F

16. Supply-siders advocate the use of economic policies that stimulate the incentives to work, save, invest, and undertake risks. T F

Circle the letter that corresponds to the best answer.

1. The slope of the aggregate-demand curve is the result of (*a*) the real-balances effect; (*b*) the interest-rate effect; (*c*) the foreign-purchases effect; (*d*) all of the above effects.

2. The aggregate-demand curve is the relationship between the (*a*) price level and the real national output purchased; (*b*) price level and the real national output produced; (*c*) price level which producers are willing to pay; (*d*) real national output purchased and the real national output produced.

3. The aggregate-supply curve is the relationship between the (*a*) price level and the real national output purchased; (*b*) price level and real national output produced; (*c*) price level which producers are willing to accept and the price level purchasers are willing to pay; (*d*) real national output purchased and the real national output produced.

4. In the Keynesian range the aggregate-supply curve is (*a*) upsloping; (*b*) downsloping; (*c*) vertical; (*d*) horizontal.

5. In the intermediate range the aggregate-supply curve is (*a*) upsloping; (*b*) downsloping; (*c*) vertical; (*d*) horizontal.

6. When the price level rises (*a*) holders of financial assets with fixed money values increase their spending; (*b*) the demand for money and interest rates rise; (*c*) spending which is sensitive to interest-rate changes increases; (*d*) holders of financial assets with fixed money values have more purchasing power.

7. If the real national output is less than the equilibrium real national output producers find (*a*) their inventories decreasing and expand their production; (*b*) their inventories increasing and expand their production; (*c*) their inventories decreasing and contract their production; (*d*) their inventories increasing and contract their production.

8. When the economy is in the Keynesian range an increase in aggregate demand will (*a*) increase the price level and have no effect on real national output; (*b*) increase the real national output and have no effect on the price level; (*c*) increase both real output and the price level; (*d*) increase the price level and decrease the real national output.

9. The rachet effect is the result of (*a*) a price level that is inflexible upward; (*b*) a price level that is inflexible downward; (*c*) a national output that cannot be increased; (*d*) a national output that cannot be decreased.

10. A demand-management policy for increasing the real national output is (*a*) an increase in government expenditures; (*b*) an increase in taxes; (*c*) a decrease in the money supply; (*d*) a decrease in government expenditures and an increase in taxes.

11. A contractionary fiscal policy requires (*a*) an increase in government expenditures; (*b*) an increase in taxes; (*c*) a decrease in the money supply; (*d*) an increase in the money supply.

12. An increase in aggregate supply will (*a*) reduce the price level and real national output; (*b*) reduce increases in the price level and increase the real national output; (*c*) increase the price level and real national output; (*d*) reduce increases in the price level and decrease the real national output.

13. When government increases aggregate demand to deal with stagflation (*a*) both real national output and the price level increase; (*b*) the real national output increases and the price level falls; (*c*) the real national output decreases and the price level rises; (*d*) the real national output decreases and the price level falls.

14. If there were stagflation in the economy and aggregate supply were to increase (*a*) both the real national output and the price level would decrease; (*b*) the real national output would increase and rises in the price level would become smaller; (*c*) the real national output would decrease and the price level would rise; (*d*) both the real national output and rises in the price level would become greater.

15. Which of the following seems to be the most effective way of eliminating stagflation? (*a*) An increase in aggregate demand; (*b*) a decrease in aggregate demand; (*c*) an increase in aggregate supply; (*d*) a decrease in aggregate supply.

16. A decrease in aggregate supply generally results in (*a*) inflation and prosperity; (*b*) stagflation; (*c*) deflation and unemployment; (*d*) deflation and prosperity.

■ DISCUSSION QUESTIONS

1. What is an aggregate-demand and an aggregate supply curve?

2. Explain (*a*) the interest-rate effect, (*b*) the real-balances effect, and (*c*) the foreign-purchases effect of change in the price level on the quantity of goods and services demanded in an economy.

3. The aggregate-supply curve is divided into three distinct ranges. Describe the slope of this curve in each of the three ranges. What conditions prevail in the economy in each of the ranges? Why is one range called the Keynesian and another called the classical range?

4. Why does the aggregate-supply curve slope upward in the intermediate range?

5. What real national output is the equilibrium real national output? Why will business firms that produce the national output reduce or expand their production when they find themselves producing more or less than the equilibrium output?

6. What are the effects on the real national output and the price level when aggregate demand increases in each of the three ranges along the aggregate-supply curve?

7. If prices were as flexible downward as they are upward, what would be the effects on real national output and the price level of a decrease in aggregate demand in each of the three ranges along the aggregate-supply curve?

8. Prices in the economy tend to be "sticky" or inflexible in a downward direction. Why? How does this downward inflexibility alter your answers to question 7 (above)?

9. What are the appropriate demand-management policies for dealing with recession and unemployment? (Be sure to include both fiscal and monetary policies.) What are the appropriate demand-management policies for slowing inflation in the economy? Cite two real-world examples of each type of policy.

10. What have been some of the causes of decreases in aggregate supply in the American economy during recent years? What might cause aggregate supply to increase?

11. What are the effects on the real national output and the price level of a decrease in aggregate supply? What are the effects of an increase in aggregate supply on the real national output, the price level, and the maximum real output the economy is able to produce?

12. Why is a decrease in aggregate supply "doubly bad" and an increase in aggregate supply "doubly good"?

13. What is the "tradeoff" faced by the Federal government when it uses demand-management policies in the intermediate range along the aggregate-supply curve?

14. Using the aggregate-demand and aggregate-supply concepts, explain the difference between demand-pull and cost-push inflation.

15. Explain the dilemma faced by the Federal government if it were to employ demand-management policies to deal with stagflation. How can it avoid this dilemma?

16. What policies do the advocates of supply-side economics advocate to reduce unemployment and inflation in the economy?

12
Classical and Keynesian theories of employment

Chapters 12 and 13 are really one chapter which has been divided into two parts. They continue the explanation begun in the last chapter of how aggregate demand and aggregate supply determine the real national output and price level of the economy. In these two chapters you will learn what determines the total quantity of goods and services that will be purchased (or demanded) at various price levels: the focus in these chapters is on aggregate demand.

Most of the material contained in these two chapters deals with the Keynesian theory or explanation of what determines the demand for the real national output (the real NNP) and how the equilibrium level of output (and of employment) is determined. The Keynesian explanation is not the only possible explanation, however. It is with the alternative classical theory that the first part of Chapter 12 deals. The classical theory is described there for several reasons: to impress upon you the fact that an alternative theory does exist; to examine its assumptions and its "cures" for depression; and to prepare you for both Keynesian and "monetarist" macroeconomic theory.

The outstanding thing about the classical theory is its conclusion that the economy will *automatically* function to produce the maximum output it is capable of producing and to provide employment for all those who are willing and able to work. Compare this with the conclusion drawn by the exponents of the Keynesian theory that the economy functions in no such way, that both depression and inflation can prevail with no automatic tendency to be corrected, and that full employment and maximum output, when achieved, are accidental. Compare also the political philosophies of the proponents of the two theories. Those accepting the classical theory have advocated as little government interference with the economy as possible in the belief that such interference prevents the achievement of full employment and maximum output. Adherents of the Keynesian theory argue that government action is necessary to eliminate the periods of depression that occur. The basic proposition contained in the Keynesian theory is that the level of total or aggregate expenditures in the economy determines the location of the economy's aggregate-demand curve and, as a result, determines real output and employment and, as you learned in the last chapter, therefore determines the price level. The latter part of the chapter analyzes the economic factors which determine two principal components of aggregate expenditures—consumption expenditures and investment expenditures. You should pay particular attention to the relationships called the consumption schedule, the saving schedule, and their characteristics; to the four propensity concepts; and to the "non-income" determinants of consumption and saving.

Investment expenditures—that is, the purchase of capital goods—depend upon the rate of net profits which business firms *expect* to earn from an investment and upon the real rate of interest they have to pay for the use of money. Because firms are anxious to make profitable investments and to avoid unprofitable ones, they undertake all investments which have an expected rate of net profit greater than (or equal to) the real rate of interest and do not undertake an investment when the expected rate of net profit is less than the real interest rate. You should see that because business firms behave this way the lower the real rate of interest the larger will be the dollar amount invested; and that this relationship between the real interest rate and the level of investment spending, called the investment-demand schedule, is an inverse one. But you should not confuse the investment-demand schedule (or curve) with the investment schedule (or curve) which relates investment spending to the NNP and which may show investment is either unrelated to or directly related to the NNP. Five noninterest determinants of investment spending influence the profit expectations of business firms; and these are analyzed. You should learn how changes in these determinants affect investment; and why investment spending is unstable.

In the next chapter the tools and ideas developed and explained in Chapter 12 are put together to form a complete and coherent picture of how aggregate expenditures determine the level of NNP in the Keynesian theory.

■ CHECKLIST

When you have studied this chapter you should be able to:

☐ Contrast the views of classical and Keynesian economists on unemployment in a market (or capitalistic) economy and the type of policy government should pursue.

☐ List the three simplifying assumptions made in this and the next chapter and the two implications of these assumptions.

☐ State Say's Law and explain how classical economists were able to reason that all saving would be borrowed and spent for capital goods.

☐ Explain how classical economists were able to reason that price-wage flexibility would eliminate a recession and unemployment.

☐ Present three reasons why the rate of interest may not guarantee the quantity of saving and investment, and two reasons why price-wage flexibility may not guarantee full employment; and state the classical response to the latter Keynesian contention.

☐ Compare the classical and Keynesian aggregate-supply curves and the effects of a decrease in aggregate demand in the two theories; and explain why classical (and monetarist) economists argue that the price level and the real national output are inversely related if the money supply is constant.

☐ State what determines the amount of goods and services produced and the level of employment in the Keynesian theory.

☐ Explain how consumption and saving are related to disposable income.

☐ Compute, when you are given the necessary data, the four propensities.

☐ Explain what happens to the size of the two average propensities as income increases.

☐ List five nonincome determinants of consumption and saving; and explain how a change in each of these determinants will affect the consumption and saving schedules.

☐ Explain the difference between a change in the amount consumed (or saved) and a change in the consumption (or saving) schedule.

☐ List the two basic determinants of investment; and explain when a firm will and will not invest.

☐ Compute, when given the appropriate data, the investment-demand schedule; and explain why the relationship between investment spending and the real rate of interest is inverse.

☐ List the five noninterest determinants of investment; and explain how a change in each of these determinants will affect the investment-demand curve.

☐ Explain the two variables found in an investment schedule; and the two kinds of relationships that might be found to exist between these two variables.

☐ List the four factors which explain why investment spending tends to be unstable.

■ CHAPTER OUTLINE

1. Classical economists contend that full employment is the norm in a market (or capitalistic) economy and laissez-faire is the best policy for government to pursue; but Keynesian economists argue that unemployment is typical of such economies and activist policies are required to eliminate it.

2. To simplify the explanation of Keynesian employment theory in this and the next chapter three assumptions are made: the economy is "closed," government neither spends nor collects taxes, and all saving is personal saving; and these assumptions have two important implications.

3. The classical theory of employment reached the conclusion that the economy would automatically tend to employ its resources fully and produce a full-employment level of output; this conclusion is based on Say's Law and the assumption that prices and wages are flexible.

a. Say's Law stated that the production of goods produced an equal demand for these goods because changes in the rate of interest would ensure that all income not spent (that is, income saved) by consumers would be lent to investors who would spend these borrowed funds for capital goods.

b. If there were an excess supply of goods or an excess supply of labor (unemployment), prices and wages would fall until the excesses were eliminated and full employment and maximum output again prevailed in the economy.

c. Believing that capitalism would automatically ensure a full-employment level of output, the classical economists saw no need for government interference with the operation of the economy.

3. J. M. Keynes, in *The General Theory of Employment, Interest, and Money,* denied that flexible interest rates, prices, and wages would automatically promote full employment; he set forth the theory that there was nothing automatic about full employment and that both depression and inflation might prevail without any tendency existing for them to be self-correcting.

a. According to Keynes, flexible interest rates do not guarantee that all income saved by consumers will be spent by investors for capital goods because savers and investors are different groups and are differently motivated and because saving is neither the only source of the funds to finance investment nor the only use to which consumers can put these funds.

b. Keynes also argued that prices and wages

(1) are not, in fact, flexible downward; and

(2) that even if they were a reduction in prices and wages would not reduce unemployment in the economy; but

(3) the defenders of classical theory responded that they would be flexible downward if it were not for government policies that prevented them from falling.

4. Classical and Keynesian economics can be compared by examining their aggregate demand–aggregate supply models of the economy.

a. In the classical model the aggregate-supply curve is vertical at the economy's full-employment output; and a decrease in aggregate demand will lower the equilibrium price level and have no effect on the real output of (or employment in) the economy.

b. In the Keynesian model the aggregate-supply curve is horizontal at the current price level; and a decrease in aggregate demand will lower the real output of (and employment in) the economy and have no effect on the equilibrium price level.

c. In both the classical and Keynesian models the aggregate-demand curve slopes downward; but in the classical model it slopes downward because (with a fixed money supply in the economy) a fall in the price level increases the purchasing power of money and enables consumers and business firms to purchase a larger real output.

5. Aggregate output and employment in the Keynesian theory are directly related to the level of total or aggregate expenditures in the economy; and to understand what determines the level of total expenditures at any time it is necessary to explain the factors that determine the levels of consumption and investment expenditures.

6. Consumption is the largest component of aggregate expenditures; and saving is disposable income not spent for consumer goods.

a. Disposable income is the most important determinant of both consumption and saving; the relationships between income and consumption and between income and saving are both direct (positive) ones.

b. The consumption schedule shows the amounts that households plan to spend for consumer goods at various levels of income.

c. The saving schedule indicates the amounts households plan to save at different income levels.

d. The average propensities to consume and to save and the marginal propensities to consume and to save can be computed from the consumption and saving schedules.

(1) The APC and the APS are, respectively, the percentages of income spent for consumption and saved; and their sum is equal to 1.

(2) The MPC and the MPS are, respectively, the percentages of *additional* income spent for consumption and saved; and their sum is equal to 1.

e. In addition to income, there are several other important determinants of consumption and saving; and changes in these nonincome determinants will cause the consumption and saving *schedules* to change.

f. A change in the amount consumed (or saved) is not the same thing as a change in the consumption (or saving) schedule. If these schedules change they change in opposite directions; but the schedules are very stable.

7. The two important determinants of the level of net investment spending in the economy are the expected rate of net profits from the purchase of additional capital goods and the real rate of interest.

a. The expected rate of net profits is directly related to the net profits (revenues less operating costs) that are expected to result from an investment and inversely related to the cost of making the investment (purchasing capital goods).

b. The rate of interest is the price paid for the use of money. When the expected real rate of net profits is greater (less) than the real rate of interest a business will

(will not) invest because the investment will be profitable (unprofitable).

c. For this reason, the lower (higher) the real rate of interest, the greater (smaller) will be the level of investment spending in the economy; and the investment-demand curve (schedule) indicates this inverse relationship between the real rate of interest and the level of spending for capital goods.

d. There are at least five noninterest determinants of investment demand; and a change in any of these determinants will shift the investment-demand curve (schedule).

e. Investment spending in the economy may also be either independent or directly related to the real NNP; and the investment schedule may show that investment either remains constant or increases as real NNP increases.

f. Because the five noninterest determinants of investment are subject to sudden changes, investment spending tends to be unstable.

■ IMPORTANT TERMS

Classical theory of employment
Say's Law
Rate of interest
Money market
Savings
Investment
Price-wage flexibility
Keynesian economics
Aggregate total expenditures
Dissaving
Consumption schedule
Saving schedule
Break-even income
Average propensity to consume
Average propensity to save
Marginal propensity to consume
Marginal propensity to save
Nonincome determinants of consumption and saving
Change in amount consumed (saved)
Change in the consumption (saving) schedule
Expected rate of net profits
Real rate of interest
Investment-demand schedule (curve)
Noninterest determinants of investment
Investment schedule (curve)

■ FILL-IN QUESTIONS

1. Classical economists believe a market (or capitalistic) economy will tend to produce an output at which its labor force is (fully, less than fully) __fully__ employed but Keynesian economists argue it will tend to produce an output at which its labor force is __less than fully__ employed; and for this reason the classical economists favor a(n) (activist, laissez faire) __laissez faire__ government policy and the Keynesian economists favor a(n) __activist__ policy.

2. Three "simplifying assumptions" used throughout most of the chapter are that the economy is a(n) (open, closed) __closed__ economy, that all saving is (personal, business) __personal__ saving, and that government does not collect __taxes__, make __transfer__ payments, or __spend__ for goods and services.

The implications of these assumptions are:

a. NNP = __NI__ = __PI__ = __DI__

b. total spending = __consumption__ + __investment__

3. Full employment, in the classical theory, was ensured by the operation of __Say's__ Law and price-wage __flexibility__

4. According to Say's Law, the production of goods and services creates an equal __demand (purchase) for the goods & services__

5. Changes in __interest rate__, according to the classical economists, ensure that what is not spent on consumer goods is spent on capital goods.

6. In the classical theory, if saving is greater than investment the rate of interest will (rise, fall) __fall__; and if investment is greater than saving it will __rise__; and the rate of interest will move to the level at which __saving__ and __investment__ are equal.

7. According to the classical way of thinking, if the interest rate did not equate saving and investment, and if total output exceeded the level of spending, prices in the output markets would tend to (rise, fall) __fall__ because of competition among business firms; this would make some production unprofitable and temporarily cause ______ in labor markets; but competition among workers would tend to drive wage rates (upward, downward) ______ and (increase, decrease) ______ their employment. This process would continue until ______

8. According to the Keynesian theory of employment:

a. saving and investment are done by different ______ and for different ______

b. the funds to finance investment come not only from current saving but from the ______ of households and from ______

c. current saving may not be lent to investors in the money market but added to the money ______ of consumers or used to retire outstanding bank ______

9. Keynes, in attacking the classical theory of employment, contended that in the modern economy prices and wages (do, do not) ______ fall when there is unemployment; and that wage reductions would lead to (smaller, larger) ______ money incomes, a (fall, rise) ______ in total spending, a(n) (increase, decrease) ______ in prices, and little or no change in total ______ in the economy.

10. Reasoning that if a price and wage-rate reduction would increase the output and employment of an individual firm, then a general reduction in prices and wages will increase output and employment in the economy as a whole is an example of the (*post hoc, ergo propter hoc* fallacy, fallacy of composition, fallacy of limited decisions) ______

11. The aggregate-supply curve of the classical economists is (horizontal, vertical) ______ and the aggregate-supply curve of the Keynesian economists is ______. For this reason, a decrease in aggregate demand will have no effect on the price level and will decrease output and employment in the (classical, Keynesian) ______ and will decrease the price level and have no effect on output and employment in the ______ model.

12. In the classical and present-day monetarist way of thinking, if the price level falls and the money supply is constant the purchasing power of money will (fall, rise) ______ and consumers and business firms will (expand, contract) ______ their expenditures for goods and services.

13. Keynes argued that:

a. the national output and employment depend (directly, inversely) ______ upon the level of aggregate ______ in the economy;

b. the most important determinant of consumption and of saving in the economy is the economy's ______

c. and that both consumption and saving are (directly, inversely) ______ related to this determinant.

14. As disposable income falls, the average propensity to consume will (rise, fall) ______ and the average propensity to save will ______

15. The most important determinants of consumption spending, other than the level of income, are:

a. the wealth or the sum of the ______ and the ______ assets households have accumulated

b. ______

c. ______

d. ______

e. ______

16. A change in the consumption (or saving) schedule means that the entire curve moves— there is a shift

but a change in the amount consumed (or saved) means that movement from one pt. to another on same curve

17. Investment is defined as spending for additional capital goods; and the total amount of investment spending in the economy depends upon:

a. the expected rate of net profit

b. the real rate of interest

18. A business firm will invest in more capital if the expected rate of net profits on this investment is (greater, less) greater than the real rate of interest it must pay for the use of money.

19. The relation between the rate of interest and the total amount of investment in the economy is (direct, inverse) inverse

This means that if the real rate of interest:

a. rises, investment will fall ↓

b. falls, investment will rise ↑

20. Five noninterest determinants of investment demand are:

a. acquisition, maintenance & operating costs

b. Business taxes

c. technological change

d. Stock of capital goods on hand

e. expectations

21. The consumption schedule and the saving schedule tend to be (stable or unstable) stable while investment demand tends to be unstable

22. The demand for new capital goods tends to be unstable because of the durability of capital goods, the irregularity of innovation, and the variability of actual and expected profits.

■ PROBLEMS AND PROJECTS

1. Below is a consumption schedule. Assume taxes and transfer payments are zero and that all saving is personal saving.

NNP	C	S	APC, %	APS, %
$1500	$1540	$-40	1.027	−.027
1600	1620	-20	1.025	−.025
1700	1700	0	0	0
1800	1780	+20	.989	.011
1900	1860	+40	.979	.021
2000	1940	+60	.970	.030
2100	2020	+80	.962	.038
2200	2100	+100	.955	.045

APC = C/I APS = S/I

a. Compute saving at each of the eight levels of NNP and the missing average propensities to consume and to save.

b. The break-even level of income (NNP) is $1700

c. As NNP rises the marginal propensity to consume remains constant. Between each two NNPs the MPC can be found by dividing $80 by $100; and is equal to 80 % MPC = ΔC/ΔI

d. The marginal propensity to save also remains constant when the NNP rises. Between each two NNPs the MPS is equal to $20 divided by $100; or to 20 % MPS = ΔS/ΔI

e. Plot the consumption schedule, the saving schedule, and the 45° line on the graph on the next page.

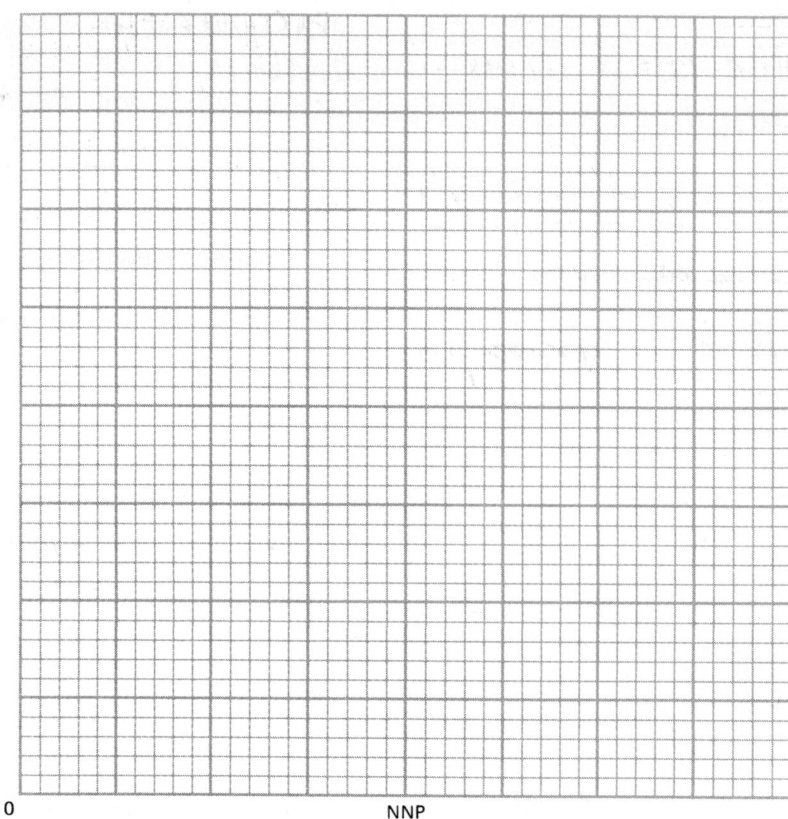

2. Indicate in the space to the right of each of the following events whether the event will tend to increase (+) or decrease (−) the *saving* schedule.

a. Development of consumer expectations that prices will be higher in the future —

b. Gradual shrinkage in the quantity of real assets owned by consumers —

c. Increase in the volume of consumer indebtedness +

d. Growing belief that disposable income will be lower in the future +

e. Rumors that a current shortage of consumer goods will soon disappear +

f. Rise in the actual level of disposable income NONE

g. A build-up in the dollar size of the financial assets owned by consumers —

h. Development of a belief by consumers that the Federal government can and will prevent depressions in the future —

3. The schedule below has eight different rates of net profit and the dollar amounts of the investment projects expected to have each of these net profit rates.

Expected rate of net profit	Investment projects (billions)
18%	$ 0
16	10
14	20
12	30
10	40
8	50
6	60
4	70

a. If the real rate of interest in the economy were 18%, business firms would plan to spend $ 0 billion for investment; but if the real interest rate were 16% they would plan to spend $ 10 for investment.

b. Should the real interest rate be 14% they would still wish to make the investments they were willing to make at real interest rates of 18% and 16%; they would also plan to spend an additional $ 20 billion for investment; and their total investment would be $ 30 billion.

c. Were the real rate of interest 12% they would make all the investments they had planned to make at higher real interest rates plus an additional $ 30 billion; and their total investment spending would be $ 60 billion.

d. Complete the table below by computing the amount of planned investment at the four remaining real interest rates.

Real rate of interest	Amount of investment (billions)
18%	$ 0
16	10
14	30
12	60
10	100
8	150
6	210
4	280

raise by 10's in succession

e. Graph the schedule you completed on the graph in the next column. Plot the real rate of interest on the vertical axis and the amount of investment planned at each real rate of interest on the horizontal axis.

f. Both the graph and the table show that the relation between the real rate of interest and the amount of investment spending in the economy is inversely related This means that when the real rate of interest:

(1) increases, investment will (increase, decrease) decrease

(2) decreases, investment will increase

g. It also means that should we wish to;

(1) increase investment, we would need to ↓ the real rate of interest

(2) decrease investment, we would have to ↑ the real rate of interest

h. This graph (or table) is the investment demand curve (or schedule).

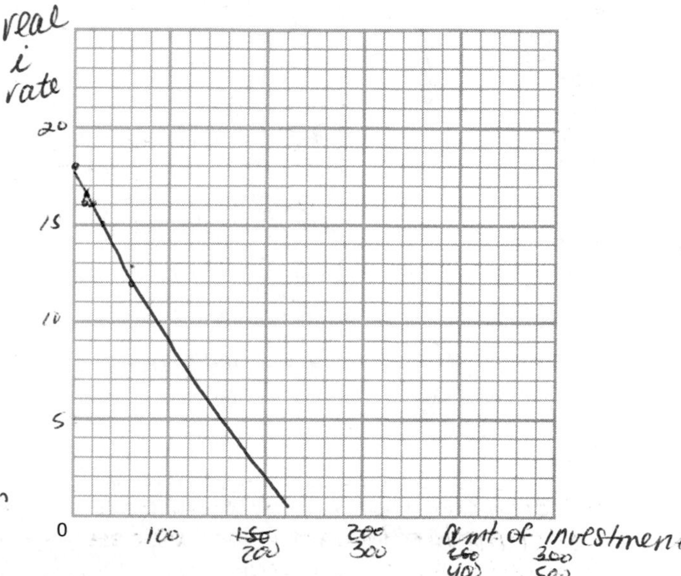

4. Indicate in the space to the right of the following events whether the event would tend to increase (+) or decrease (−) investment expenditures.

a. Rising stock market prices +

b. Development of expectations by businessmen that business taxes will be higher in the future −

c. Step-up in the rates at which new products and new production processes are being introduced +

d. Business belief that wage rates may be lower in the future +

e. A mild recession −

f. A belief that business is "too good" and the economy is due for a period of "slow" consumer demand −

g. Rising costs in the construction industry ______

h. A rapid increase in the size of the economy's population ______

i. A period of a high level of investment spending which has resulted in productive capacity in excess of the current demand for goods and services ______

5. Below are two schedules showing several NNPs and the level of investment spending (*I*) at each NNP. (All figures are in billions of dollars.)

Schedule number 1		Schedule number 2	
NNP	*I*	NNP	*I*
$1850	$90	$1850	$ 75
1900	90	1900	80
1950	90	1950	85
2000	90	2000	90
2050	90	2050	95
2100	90	2100	100
2150	95	2150	105

a. Each of these schedules is an ______ schedule.

b. When such a schedule is drawn up it is assumed that the real rate of interest is ______

c. In schedule:

(1) number 1, NNP and *I* are (unrelated, directly related) ______

(2) number 2, NNP and *I* are ______

d. Should the real rate of interest rise, investment spending at each NNP would (increase, decrease) ______ and the curve relating NNP and investment spending would shift (upward, downward) ______

■ SELF-TEST

Circle the T if the statement is true, the F if it is false.

1. According to the classical economists, full employment is normal in market economies. T F

2. The classical economists believed that government assistance was *not* required to bring about full employment and full production in the economy. T F

3. Say's Law states that demand for goods and services creates an equal supply of goods and services. T F

4. In both the classical and Keynesian theories of employment saving is income not expended for consumer goods and services. T F

5. In the classical theory, if saving exceeds investment the rate of interest will rise until saving and investment are equal. T F

6. Keynesians contend that most saving is done by business firms and most investment is done by households in the economy. T F

7. Classical economists contend that prices and wages would be sufficiently flexible to assure full employment in the economy if it were not for the government policies that reduce their downward flexibility. T F

8. The classical economists' view of aggregate demand is that if the money supply is constant a decrease in the price level will decrease the purchasing power of money and increase the quantities of goods and services demanded by consumers and business firms. T F

9. The level of saving in the economy, according to the Keynesians, depends primarily upon the level of its disposable income. T F

10. The consumption schedule which is employed as an analytical tool is also a historical record of the relationship of consumption to disposable income. T F

11. Statistics show the economists tend to agree that the marginal propensity to consume rises and the marginal propensity to save falls as disposable income rises. T F

12. An increase in the price level will increase the consumption schedule (shift the consumption curve upward). T F

13. An increase in the taxes paid by consumers will decrease both the amount they spend for consumption and the amount they save. T F

14. Both the consumption schedule and the saving schedule tend to be relatively stable over time. T F

15. The *real* interest rate is the nominal interest rate minus the rate of inflation. T F

16. A business firm will purchase additional capital goods if the real rate of interest it must pay exceeds the expected rate of net profits from the investment. T F

17. An increase in an economy's income may induce an increase in investment spending. T F

18. The relationship between the rate of interest and the level of investment spending is called the investment schedule. T F

19. The investment-demand schedule (or curve) tends to be relatively stable over time. T F

20. The irregularity of innovations and the variability of business profits contribute to the instability of investment expenditures. T F

Circle the letter that corresponds to the best answer.

1. Keynesian economists believe that (*a*) unemployment is characteristic of capitalistic economies and in activist government policies; (*b*) unemployment is characteristic of capitalistic economies and in a government policy of laissez-faire; (*c*) full employment is characteristic of capitalistic economies and in activist government policies; (*d*) full employment is characteristic of capitalistic economies and in a government policy of laissez-faire.

2. If government neither taxes nor spends, and all saving done in the economy is personal saving: (*a*) gross national product equals net national product; (*b*) gross national product equals national income; (*c*) net national product equals disposable income; (*d*) disposable income equals personal consumption expenditures.

3. In the classical theory of employment, a decline in the rate of interest will (*a*) decrease saving and investment; (*b*) decrease saving and increase investment; (*c*) increase saving and decrease investment; (*d*) increase saving and investment.

4. The classical theory predicts that an increase in the supply of savings will (*a*) lower interest rates and reduce investment; (*b*) raise interest rates and reduce investment; (*c*) lower interest rates and expand investment; (*d*) raise interest rates and expand investment.

5. If the rate of interest did not equate saving and investment and total output was greater than total spending, the classical economists argued, competition would tend to force: (*a*) product and resource prices down; (*b*) product prices up and resource prices down; (*c*) product prices up and resource prices up; (*d*) product prices down and resource prices up.

6. Which of the following is *not* involved in Keynes's criticism of the classical theory of employment? (*a*) A reduction in wage rates will lead only to a reduction in total spending, not to an increase in employment; (*b*) investment spending is not influenced by the rate of interest; (*c*) prices and wages are simply not flexible downward in modern capitalistic economies; (*d*) saving in modern economies depends largely upon the level of disposable income and is little influenced by the rate of interest.

7. Keynesian economists argue the source of the funds which finance investment are (*a*) current saving; (*b*) the accumulated money balances of households; (*c*) commercial banks; (*d*) all of the above.

8. The Keynesian economists also argue that saving is (*a*) used to finance investment expenditures; (*b*) added to the money balances of savers; (*c*) used to retire the loans made previously by banks; (*d*) utilized for all of the above.

9. The Keynesian aggregate-supply curve (*a*) is horizontal; (*b*) slopes upward; (*c*) is vertical; (*d*) slopes downward.

10. The aggregate-supply curve of classical economists (*a*) is horizontal; (*b*) slopes upward; (*c*) is vertical; (*d*) slopes downward.

11. In the classical theory of employment a decrease in aggregate demand results in (*a*) a decrease in both the price level and national output; (*b*) a decrease in the price level and no change in national output; (*c*) no change in the price level and a decrease in national output; (*d*) no change in either the price level or national output.

12. A decrease in aggregate demand, in the Keynesian theory of employment, results in (*a*) a decrease in both the price level and national output; (*b*) a decrease in the price level and no change in national output; (*c*) no change in the price level and a decrease in national output; (*d*) no change in either the price level or national output.

13. In the Keynesian theory, output and employment in the economy depend (*a*) directly on the level of total expenditures; (*b*) inversely on the quantity of resources available to it; (*c*) directly on the level of disposable income; (*d*) directly on the rate of interest.

14. As disposable income decreases, *ceteris paribus,* (*a*) both consumption and saving increase; (*b*) consumption increases and saving decreases; (*c*) consumption decreases and saving increases; (*d*) both consumption and saving decrease.

15. If consumption spending increases from $358 to $367 billion when disposable income increases from $412 to

$427 billion, it can be concluded that the marginal propensity to consume is: (*a*) 0.4; (*b*) 0.6; (*c*) 0.8; (*d*) 0.9.

16. If when disposable income is $375 billion the average propensity to consume is 0.8, it can be concluded that: (*a*) the marginal propensity to consume is also 0.8; (*b*) consumption is $325 billion; (*c*) saving is $75 billion; (*d*) the marginal propensity to save is 0.2.

17. As the disposable income of the economy increases (*a*) both the APC and the APS rise; (*b*) the APC rises and the APS falls; (*c*) the APC falls and the APS rises; (*d*) both the APC and the APS fall.

18. Which of the following would *not* cause the consumption schedule to increase (that is, cause the consumption curve to rise)? (*a*) A decrease in the expected price level; (*b*) an increase in consumers' ownership of financial assets; (*c*) a decrease in the amount of consumers' indebtedness; (*d*) an increase in the income received by consumers.

19. A decrease in the price level tends to (*a*) increase the amount consumed; (*b*) decrease the amount consumed; (*c*) shift the consumption schedule upward; (*d*) shift the consumption schedule downward.

20. A decrease in the level of investment spending would be a consequence of: (*a*) a decline in the rate of interest; (*b*) a decline in the level of wages paid; (*c*) a decline in business taxes; (*d*) a decline in stock market prices.

21. Which of the following relationships is an inverse one? (*a*) The relationship between consumption spending and disposable income; (*b*) the relationship between investment spending and the rate of interest; (*c*) the relationship between saving and the rate of interest; (*d*) the relationship between investment spending and net national product.

■ DISCUSSION QUESTIONS

1. How do the classical and Keynesian economists differ on (*a*) the normal amount of unemployment that will prevail in a capitalistic (or market) economy; and (*b*) the role they would assign to government in such an economy?

2. What are the three simplifying assumptions used in this chapter and what are the two implications of these assumptions?

3. According to the classical economists, what level of employment would tend to prevail in the economy? On what two basic assumptions did their analysis of the level of employment rest?

4. What is Say's Law? How were the classical economists able to reason that whatever is saved is spent?

5. In the classical analysis Say's Law made it certain that whatever was produced would be sold. How did flexible prices, flexible wages, and competition drive the economy to full employment and maximum output?

6. On what grounds did J. M. Keynes argue that flexible interest rates would not assure the operation of Say's Law? What were his reasons for asserting that flexible prices and wages would not assure full employment; and what was the classical response to his assertion?

7. What is (*a*) the difference between the classical and the Keynesian aggregate-supply curve; and (*b*) the difference between the effects a decrease in aggregate demand would have on the price level and on the real national output in the two models? Why does the classical aggregate-demand curve have a negative (downward) slope?

8. "Savers and investors are largely different groups and are motivated by different factors." Explain in detail who these groups are and what motivates them. Does the rate of interest play any role in determining saving and investment?

9. Describe the relation between consumption and disposable income called the consumption schedule and the one between saving and disposable income known as the saving schedule; and then define the two average propensities and the two marginal propensities.

10. Explain briefly how the average propensity to consume and the average propensity to save vary as disposable income varies. Why do APC and APS behave this way? What happens to consumption and saving as disposable income varies?

11. Why do the sum of the APC and the APS and the sum of the MPC and the MPS always equal exactly one?

12. Explain briefly and explicitly *how* changes in the five nonincome determinants will affect the consumption schedule and the saving schedule and *why* such changes will affect consumption and saving in the way you have indicated.

13. Explain (*a*) when a business firm will or will not purchase additional capital goods; (*b*) how changes in the five noninterest determinants of investment spending will affect the investment-demand curve; (*c*) why investment spending tends to rise when the rate of interest falls; and (*d*) how changes in NNP might affect investment spending.

14. Why does the level of investment spending tend to be highly unstable?

15. Explain why the amount consumers spend and the amount investors spend matter all that much to the performance of the economy.

13
Equilibrium national output in the Keynesian model

Chapter 13, building on the tools developed in the last chapter, continues the Keynesian explanation of what determines the equilibrium level of real NNP—the real NNP an economy will tend to produce. You *must* understand this chapter if you are to acquire an understanding of what causes the real NNP to rise and fall; of what causes unemployment, depression, inflation, and prosperity; and of what can be done to foster price stability, full employment, and economic growth.

In the Keynesian model of the economy the equilibrium level of real NNP is determined *only* by the level of *aggregate expenditures* because it is assumed in this model that the economy is operating in the Keynesian (or depression) range of the aggregate-supply curve (and that the price level does not rise or fall). The two components of aggregate expenditures in an economy which is closed (neither exports nor imports goods and services) and in which governments do not spend or tax are consumption expenditures and net investment expenditures; and they were analyzed in the last chapter. In this chapter the equilibrium level of real NNP is explained with both tables and graphs, first by using the expenditures-output approach and then by employing the leakages-injections approach. These two approaches are complementary and are two different ways of analyzing the same process and of reaching the same conclusions. For each approach it is important for you to know, given the consumption (or saving) schedule and the level of net investment expenditures, *what* real NNP will tend to be produced and *why* this will be the real NNP which will be produced.

It is also important that you understand the significant distinction between *planned* investment and *actual* investment. Saving and actual net investment are always equal because they are defined in exactly the same way: the output of the economy minus its consumption. But saving and planned net investment are not, however, equal by definition. They are equal only when real NNP is at its equilibrium level. When real NNP is *not* at its equilibrium level, saving and planned net investment are *not* equal even though saving and actual investment are, as always, equal because the actual investment includes *un*planned investment or disinvestment. Remember: Equilibrium real NNP is achieved when saving and *planned* net investment—*not* saving and *actual* net investment—are equal.

The consumption (and the saving) schedule and the investment schedule—especially the latter—are subject to change, and when they change equilibrium real NNP will also change. The relationship between an initial change in the investment or consumption schedules and a change in equilibrium real NNP is called the multiplier. Three things to note here are: *how* the multiplier is defined, *why* there is a multiplier effect, and upon *what* the size of the multiplier depends. Because of the multiplier, the paradoxical consequence of an attempt by the economy to save more is either no increase or a decrease in the level of saving in the economy. The explanation of this paradox will be evident to you when you understand the equilibrium real NNP and the multiplier effect.

It is important to be aware that the equilibrium real NNP is not necessarily the real NNP at which full employment with inflationary pressures is achieved. Aggregate expenditures may be greater or less than the full-employment noninflationary real NNP; if they are greater there is an inflationary gap, and if they are less there exists a recessionary gap. Be sure that you know how to measure the size of each of these gaps: the amount by which the aggregate-expenditures schedule (or curve) must change to bring the economy to its full-employment real NNP without there being inflation in the economy.

The price level in the Keynesian model, as noted above, is assumed to be constant; but in the aggregate demand–aggregate supply model (examined in Chapter 11) the price level can rise or fall. These two models do not, however, contradict each other; and the last section of the chapter reconciles them. The important thing to understand is that prices can be constant at different levels. The price index in the economy, for example, might be constant at 100, at 75, or at 120. The AD curve is derived from the Keynesian model by letting prices be *constant at different levels.* Once you realize this it is no great problem to see that the lower (the higher) the level at which prices are constant in the Keynesian model the larger (the smaller) will be the equilibrium real NNP in that model of the economy; and that the AD curve slopes downward.

The AD curve derived in this way from the Keynesian model and the AS curve together determine the price level and the equilibrium real NNP in the aggregate demand–aggregate supply model. But aggregate demand can increase (or decrease); and when it does both the price level and the equilibrium real NNP may be changed. How the price level and real NNP are affected depends upon the range on the aggregate-supply curve in which the economy is initially operating. Here the important thing to see is that because the change in AD may also affect the price level in the economy, the change in AD may not have its *full* multiplier effect on the real NNP of the economy.

The next chapter deals with the fiscal policies that can be employed by government to eliminate recessionary and inflationary gaps in the economy. Chapter 13 has purposely ignored government and assumed an economy in which government neither taxes nor spends. But Chapter 14 does not ignore the role of government in the economy and discusses fiscal policies and their effects upon the equilibrium real NNP and the price level.

■ CHECKLIST

When you have studied this chapter you should be able to:

☐ State the range along the aggregate supply in which the economy is assumed to operate and the assumption made about the price level in the Keynesian model.

☐ Find the equilibrium real NNP, when you are given the necessary tabular or graphical data, by employing either the aggregate expenditures-national output or the leakages-injections approach.

☐ Explain why the economy will tend to produce its equilibrium real NNP rather than some smaller or larger real NNP.

☐ State the difference between planned investment and actual investment; and explain how it is possible for saving and actual investment to be equal when saving and planned investment are not equal.

☐ Determine the economy's new equilibrium real NNP when there is a change in the consumption (or saving) schedule or in the investment schedule.

☐ Find the value of the multiplier when you are given the needed information; and cite the two facts upon which the multiplier effect (a multiplier greater than one) is based.

☐ Draw a graph to explain the paradox of thrift.

☐ Distinguish between the equilibrium real NNP and the full-employment noninflationary level of real NNP.

☐ Find the recessionary and the inflationary gaps when you are provided the relevant data.

☐ Contrast the Keynesian expenditures-output and the aggregate demand-aggregate supply models by comparing the variability of the price level and real NNP in the two models in the three ranges along the aggregate-supply curve.

☐ Derive the aggregate-demand curve (or schedule) from the Keynesian model; and explain the effect of a change in aggregate expenditures (in the Keynesian model) on the aggregate-demand curve (or schedule).

☐ Predict the effects of a change in aggregate demand on the price level and the equilibrium real NNP in the three ranges along the aggregate-supply curve; and explain what determines how large the multiplier effect on the equilibrium real NNP will be in the aggregate demand–aggregate supply model.

■ CHAPTER OUTLINE

1. In this chapter it is assumed (unless otherwise explicitly specified) that the economy is operating within the Keynesian range of the aggregate-supply curve and the price level is, therefore, constant; two approaches are used to explain what *real* national output (or NNP) the economy will tend to produce; but both approaches yield the same conclusion.

2. Employing the aggregate expenditures–national output approach, the equilibrium real NNP is the real NNP at which:

a. aggregate expenditures (consumption plus planned net investment) equal the real NNP; or

b. in graphical terms, the aggregate-expenditures curve crosses the 45-degree line.

3. Using the leakages-injections approach, the equilibrium real NNP is the real NNP at which:

a. saving and planned net investment are equal; or

b. in graphical terms, the saving curve crosses the planned net investment curve

4. The net investment schedule indicates what investors *plan* to do; and when saving is greater (less) than planned net investment,

*a. un*planned net investment (disinvestment) in inventories will occur; and

b. producers will reduce (expand) their production and the real NNP will fall (rise) until there is no unplanned net investment (disinvestment); but the *actual* net investment and saving are always equal because the former includes unplanned investment or disinvestment.

5. Changes in planned net investment (or in the consumption and saving schedules) will cause the equilibrium real NNP to change in the same direction by an amount greater than the initial change in investment (or consumption).

a. This is called the multiplier effect; and the multiplier is equal to the ratio of the change in the real NNP to the initial change in spending.

(1) The multiplier effect occurs because a change in the dollars spent by one person alters the income of another person in the same direction and because any change in the income of one person will change the person's consumption and saving in the same direction by a fraction of the change in income.

(2) The value of the simple multiplier is equal to the reciprocal of the marginal propensity to save.

(3) The significance of the multiplier is that relatively small changes in the spending plans of business firms or households bring about large changes in the equilibrium real NNP.

(4) The simple multiplier has this value only in an economy in which the only leakage is saving; and the complex multiplier takes into account such other leakages as taxes and imports.

b. The paradox of thrift is that an increase in the saving schedule results in no increase, and may result in a decrease, in saving: the increase in the saving schedule causes a multiple contraction in real NNP and at the lower real NNP the same amount or even less saving takes place; but saving is not socially undesirable if it limits demand-pull inflation or if it leads to more investment and growth in the economy.

6. The equilibrium level of real NNP may turn out to be an equilibrium at less than full employment, at full employment, or at full employment with inflation.

a. If the equilibrium real NNP is *less* than the real NNP consistent with full employment, there exists a recessionary gap; the size of the recessionary gap equals the amount by which the aggregate-expenditures schedule must increase (shift upward) to increase the real NNP to its full-employment noninflationary level.

b. If equilibrium real NNP is *greater* than the real NNP consistent with stable prices there is an inflationary gap. The size of the inflationary gap equals the amount by which the aggregate-expenditures schedule must decrease (shift downward) if the economy is to achieve full employment without inflation.

c. It is, however, likely that a full-employment noninflationary real NNP is unattainable in the real world; and this likelihood complicates the elimination of an inflationary gap.

7. The Keynesian expenditures-output model and the aggregate demand–aggregate supply model are reconciled by recalling that the price level is assumed to be constant in the former and is a variable (can rise or fall) in the latter model.

a. The AD curve is derived from the intersections of the aggregate-expenditures curves and the 45-degree curve: as the price level falls (rises) the consumption and the aggregate-expenditures curves shift upward (downward) because of the real balances effect and the equilibrium real NNP increases (decreases); and this inverse relationship between the price level and the equilibrium real NNP is the AD schedule (or curve).

b. If the price level is constant, any change in the nonprice level determinants of consumption and planned investment that shifts the aggregate-expenditures curve upward (downward) will increase (decrease) the equilibrium real NNP and shift the AD curve to the right (left) by an amount equal to the increase (decrease) in aggregate expenditures times the multiplier.

c. If the economy is operating along the

(1) Keynesian range of the AS curve an increase in AD will have no effect on the price level and the increase in the equilibrium real NNP will equal the full multiplier effect of the increase in aggregate expenditures;

(2) intermediate range the increase in AD will increase the price level and the increase in the equilibrium real NNP will be less than the full multiplier effect of the increase in aggregate expenditures;

(3) classical range the increase in AD will increase the price level and have no effect on the equilibrium real NNP.

d. The Keynesian expenditures-output model is expanded in the appendix to this chapter (by adding the effects of an economy's exports and imports on its real NNP); and in the next chapter (by including the effects of government expenditures and tax collections on real NNP).

IMPORTANT TERMS

Real national output (NNP)
Nominal national output (NNP)
Aggregate expenditures–national output approach
Leakages-injections approach
Aggregate expenditures
Aggregate-expenditures schedule (curve)
Planned investment
Equilibrium (real) NNP
45-degree line
Leakage
Injection
Actual investment
Unplanned investment
Multiplier effect
Multiplier
Simple multiplier
Complex multiplier
Paradox of thrift
Recessionary gap
Inflationary gap

FILL-IN QUESTIONS

1. In this chapter (unless explicitly indicated to the contrary),

a. it is assumed that the economy is operating within the (Keynesian, classical) Keynesian range of the aggregate supply and the price level is (variable, constant) constant;

b. the explanation is in terms of the (real, nominal) real national output or (GNP, NNP) NNP

2. Two complementary approaches which are employed to explain the equilibrium level of real national output are the leakage-injections approach and the expenditure-output approach.

3. Assuming a private and closed economy, the equilibrium level of real NNP is the real NNP at which:

$C + I_n = NNP$

a. aggregate expenditures equal real national output

b. real NNP equals consumption plus planned net investment

c. the aggregate-expenditures schedule or curve intersects the 45° line.

4. When the leakages-injections approach is used:

a. In this chapter the only leakage considered is savings and the only injection considered is net investment

b. Later the two additional:

(1) leakages considered are taxes and imports

(2) injections considered are gov't purchases and exports

5. If:

a. Aggregate expenditures are greater than the real national output, saving is (greater, less) less than planned net investment, there is unplanned (investment, disinvestment) disinventment in inventories, and the real NNP will (rise, fall) rise

b. Aggregate expenditures are less than the real national output, saving is greater than planned net investment, there is unplanned investment in inventories, and the real NNP will fall

c. Aggregate expenditures are equal to the real national output, saving is equal to planned net investment, unplanned investment in inventories is zero, and the real NNP will neither ↑ nor ↓

6. At every level of real NNP saving is equal to (planned, actual) actual net investment.

a. But if planned net investment is greater than saving by $10:

(1) there is $10 of unplanned (investment, disinvestment) disinvestment

disinvestment — econ. uses up more capital in a year than it manages to produce.
decline in investment of investment in investories

(2) the real NNP will (rise, fall) ____________

b. And if planned net investment is less than saving by $5:

(1) there is $5 of unplanned ____________

(2) the real NNP will ____________

7. The multiplier:

a. is the ratio of the change in ____________ to an initial change in spending in the economy;

b. has a value equal to one divided by the ____________ which is the same thing as one divided by the quantity of one minus ____________

8. The multiplier effect is based on two facts:

a. an initial increase in spending by business firms or consumers will increase the ____________ of the households in the economy; and

b. the latter increase will expand the (consumption, investment) ____________ spending of the households by an amount equal to the increase in income times the ____________

9. When planned net investment spending increases the equilibrium real NNP (increases, decreases) ____________ and when planned net investment spending decreases the equilibrium real NNP ____________

a. The changes in the equilibrium real NNP are (greater, less) ____________ than the changes in planned net investment spending.

b. The size of the multiplier varies (directly, inversely) ____________ with the size of the marginal propensity to consume.

10. If the economy decides to save more (consume less) at every level of NNP, the equilibrium real NNP will (increase, decrease) ____________ and the equilibrium level of saving in the economy will either remain the same or (increase, decrease) ____________ This consequence of an increased desire to save is called the ____________

11. A recessionary gap exists when equilibrium real NNP is (greater, less) ____________ than the full-employment real NNP; to bring real NNP to the full-employment level, the aggregate-expenditures schedule must (increase, decrease) ____________ by an amount equal to the difference between the equilibrium and the full-employment noninflationary real NNP divided by the ____________

12. When equilibrium *money* NNP is greater than the full-employment real NNP at which prices are stable, there is a(n) ____________ gap; to eliminate this gap ____________ must decrease by ____________ divided by the multiplier.

13. In the aggregate demand–aggregate supply model the price level is a (constant, variable) ____________ in the Keynesian expenditures-output model it is a ____________

a. But if the price level were lower in the Keynesian model the ____________ effect would (raise, lower) ____________ the consumption and aggregate-expenditures curves; and the equilibrium real NNP would (rise, fall) ____________

b. And if the price level were higher in the Keynesian model this effect would ____________ the consumption and aggregate-expenditures curves; and the equilibrium real NNP would ____________

c. This (direct, inverse) ____________ relationship between the price level and the equilibrium real NNP in the Keynesian model is the aggregate (demand, supply) ____________ curve (or schedule).

14. If the price level were a constant, a(n)

a. increase in the aggregate-expenditures curve would shift the aggregate-demand curve to the (right, left) ____________ by an amount equal to the upward shift in aggregate expenditures times the ____________

b. decrease in the aggregate-expenditures curve would

shift the aggregate-demand curve to the ________ by an amount equal to the ________

15. Were aggregate demand to increase,

a. the flatter the aggregate-supply curve, the (greater, smaller) ________ is the multiplier effect on the real equilibrium NNP and the ________ is the effect on the equilibrium price level; and

b. the steeper the aggregate-supply curve, the ________ is the multiplier effect on the equilibrium real NNP and the ________ is the effect on the equilibrium price level.

■ PROBLEMS AND PROJECTS

1. The table below shows consumption and saving at various levels of real NNP. Assume the price level is constant, the economy is closed, and government neither taxes nor spends.

Real NNP	C	S	I	C + I	UI
$1300	$1290	$10	$22	$1312	$−12
1310	1298	12	22	1320	−10
1320	1306	14			
1330	1314	16			
1340	1322	18			
1350	1330	20			
1360	1338	22			
1370	1346	24			
1380	1354	26			
1390	1362	28	22	1384	+6
1400	1370	30	22	1392	+8

a. The next table is an investment-demand schedule which shows the net amounts investors plan to invest at different rates of interest (*i*). Assume the rate of interest is 6% and complete the net investment, the consumption-plus-investment, and the unplanned investment (*UI*) columns—showing unplanned investment with a + and unplanned disinvestment with a −.

i	*I*
10%	$ 0
9	7
8	13
7	18
6	22
5	25
4	27
3	28

b. The equilibrium real NNP will be $________

c. The value of the marginal propensity to consume in this problem is ________ and the value of the marginal propensity to save is ________

d. The value of the simple multiplier is ________

e. If the rate of interest should fall from 6% to 5%, planned net investment would (increase, decrease) ________ by $________; and the equilibrium real NNP would, as a result, (increase, decrease) ________ by $________

f. Suppose the rate of interest were to rise from 6% to 7%. Planned investment would ________ by $________; and the equilibrium real NNP would ________ by $________

g. Assume the rate of interest is 6%.

(1) On the following graph, plot *C*, *C* + *I*, and the 45-degree line, and indicate the equilibrium real NNP.

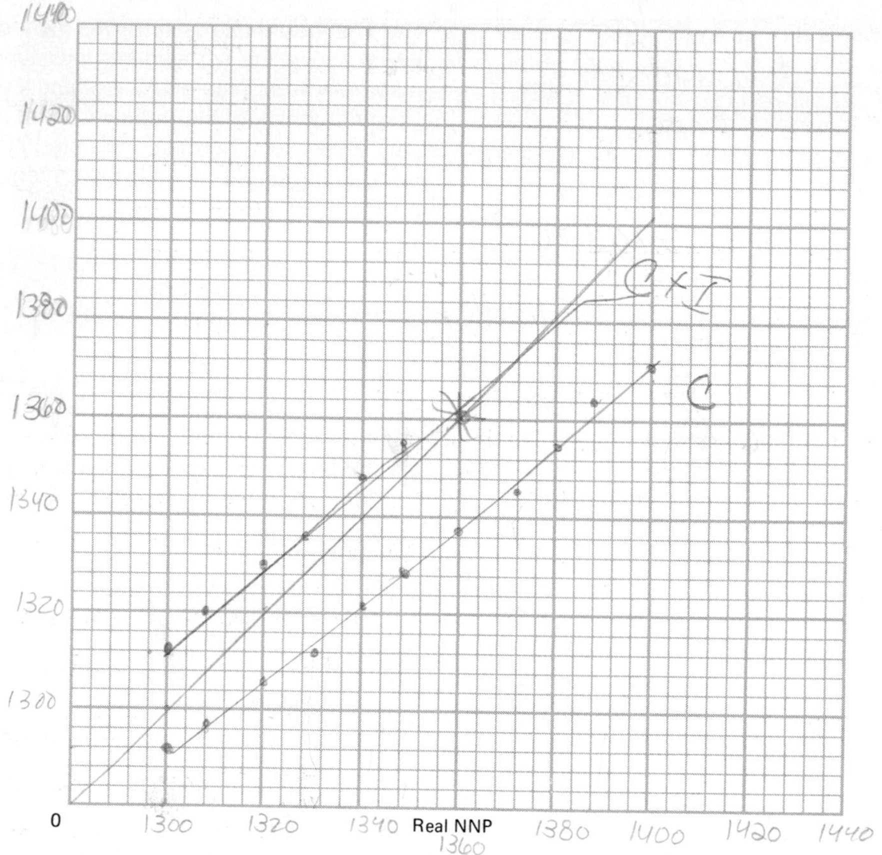

(2) On the graph opposite plot *S* and *I* and indicate the equilibrium real NNP.

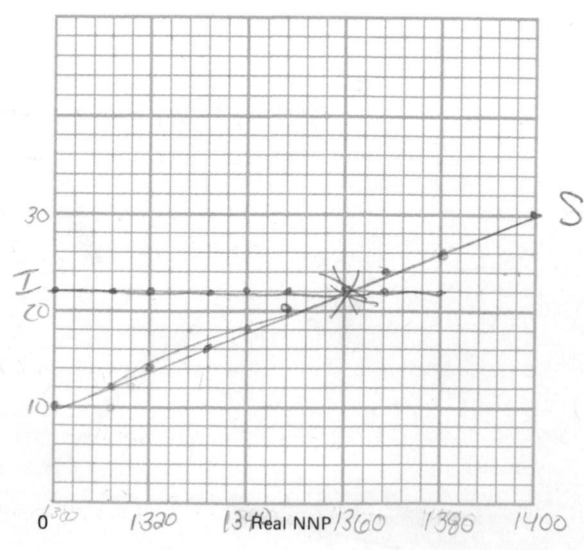

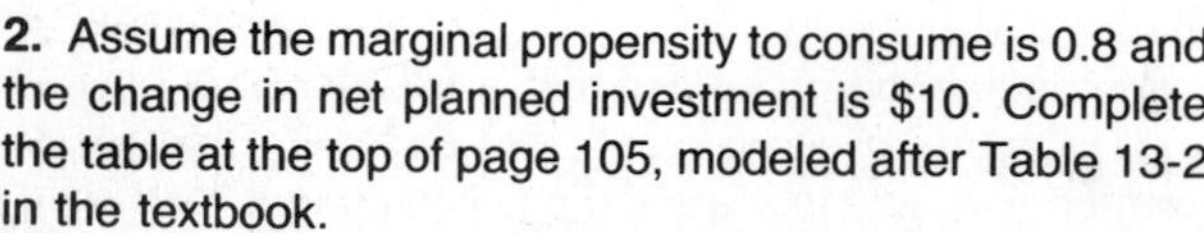
2. Assume the marginal propensity to consume is 0.8 and the change in net planned investment is $10. Complete the table at the top of page 105, modeled after Table 13-2 in the textbook.

	Change in income	Change in consumption	Change in saving
Increase in net investment of $10	$ + 10	$ ____	$ ____
Second round	____	____	____
Third round	____	____	____
Fourth round	____	____	____
Fifth round	____	____	____
All other rounds	16.38	13.10	3.28
Totals	____	____	____

3. Below are a saving schedule and two investment schedules—one (I_a) indicating that planned investment is constant and the other (I_i) indicating that the investment schedule is upsloping.

Real NNP	S	I_a	I_i
$300	$ 5	$15	$10
310	7	15	11
320	9	15	12
330	11	15	13
340	13	15	14
350	15	15	15
360	17	15	16
370	19	15	17
380	21	15	18
390	23	15	19
400	25	15	20

a. Using either investment schedule, the equilibrium real NNP is $____ and saving and planned investment are both $____

b. The marginal propensity to save is ____ and the simple multiplier is ____

c. A $2 rise in the I_a *schedule* will cause real NNP to rise by $____; while a $2 rise in the level of I_i *schedule* will cause real NNP to rise by $____

d. The value of the supermultiplier in the second case is, therefore, ____

e. Use the two investment schedules given in the table and assume a $2 increase in the saving schedule in the table—that is, saving at every real NNP increases by $2.

(1) If the investment schedule is I_a, equilibrium real NNP will ____ to $____ and at this real NNP saving will be $____

(2) If the investment schedule is I_i, equilibrium real NNP will ____ to $____ and at this real NNP saving will be $____

(3) The effect of the increase in the saving schedule is to ____ equilibrium real NNP and either to ____ or to ____ saving; this is called the ____

(4) The amount by which real NNP changes depends upon the size of the change in the saving schedule and the size of ____

4. In the next table are consumption and saving schedules. Assume that the level of real NNP at which full employment without inflation is achieved is $590.

Real NNP	C	S
$550	$520	$30
560	526	34
570	532	38
580	538	42
590	544	46
600	550	50
610	556	54
620	562	58
630	568	62

a. The value of the multiplier is 2.5

b. If planned net investment is $58, the equilibrium money NNP is $620 and exceeds the full-employment noninflationary real NNP by $30.
There is a(n) inflationary gap of $12

c. If planned investment is $38, the equilibrium real NNP is $570 and is less than full-employment real NNP by $20
There is a(n) recessionary gap of $8

5. The real NNP an economy might produce is shown in column (1) below.

(1) Real NNP	(2) $AE_{1.20}$	(3) $AE_{1.00}$	(4) $AE_{0.80}$
$2100	$2110	$2130	$2150
2200	2200	2220	2240
2300	2290	2310	2330
2400	2380	2400	2420
2500	2470	2490	2510
2600	2560	2580	2600

a. If the price level in this economy were $1.20 the aggregate expenditures (AE) at each real NNP would be those shown in column (2) and the equilibrium real NNP would be $2200

b. But if the price level were $1.00 the aggregate expenditures at each real NNP would be those shown in column (3) and the equilibrium real NNP would be $2400

c. And if the price level were $0.80 the aggregate expenditures at each real NNP would be those shown in column (4) and the equilibrium real NNP would be $2600

d. Show in the schedule below the equilibrium real NNP at each of the three price levels.

Price level	Equilibrium real NNP
$1.20	$ 2200
1.00	2400
.80	2600

(1) This schedule is the aggregate-demand schedule; and

(2) in it the equilibrium real NNP is inversely related to the price level.

6. Columns (1) and (2) in the table below are the aggregate-supply schedule of an economy.

(1) Price level	(2) Real NNP	(3) AQD_1	(4) AQD_2	(5) AQD_3	(6) AQD_4	(7) AQD_5	(8) AQD_6
$2.60	$2390	$ 840	$ 940	$1900	$2000	$2190	$2290
2.40	2390	940	1040	2000	2100	2290	2390
2.20	2390	1040	1140	2100	2200	2390	2490
2.00	2390	1140	1240	2200	2300	2490	2590
1.90	2350	1190	1290	2250	2350	2540	2640
1.80	2300	1240	1340	2300	2400	2590	2690
1.60	2200	1340	1440	2400	2500	2690	2790
1.40	2090	1440	1540	2500	2600	2790	2890
1.20	1970	1540	1640	2600	2700	2890	2990
1.00	1840	1640	1740	2700	2800	2990	3090
1.00	1740	1640	1740	2700	2800	2990	3090
1.00	1640	1640	1740	2700	2800	2990	3090

a. The economy is in the

(1) classical range when its real NNP is $______ and the price level is $______ or higher;

(2) Keynesian range when its real NNP is $______ or less and its price level is $______

b. If the aggregate demand in the economy were columns (1) and (3) the equilibrium real NNP would be $______ and the equilibrium price level would be $______; and if aggregate demand should increase by $100 to that shown in columns (1) and (4) the equilibrium real NNP would increase by $______ and the price level would ______

c. Should aggregate demand be that shown in columns (1) and (5) the equilibrium real NNP would be $______ and the equilibrium price would be $______; and if aggregate demand should increase by $100 to that shown in columns (1) and (6) the equilibrium real NNP would increase by $______ and the price level would rise to $______

d. And if aggregate demand were that shown in columns (1) and (7) the equilibrium real NNP would be $______ and the equilibrium price level would be $______; but if aggregate demand increased by $100 to that shown in columns (1) and (8) the price level would rise to $______ and the equilibrium real NNP would ______

■ SELF-TEST

Circle the T if the statement is true, the F if it is false.

1. In the Keynesian model of the economy the price level is constant. T F

Questions 2 and 3 are based on the data supplied in the following table.

Real NNP	*C*
$200	$200
240	228
280	256
320	284
360	312
400	340
440	368
480	396

2. If saving at each level of real NNP decreased by $5 and if planned net investment remained constant at $24, equilibrium real NNP would decrease by $16⅔ and saving in the economy would decrease by $5. T F

3. If consumption spending at each level of real NNP increased by $10, the equilibrium level of real NNP would tend to rise by $30. T F

4. The investment schedule is a schedule of planned investment rather than a schedule of actual investment. T F

5. Saving and actual net investment are always equal. T F

6. Saving at any level of real NNP equals planned net investment plus unplanned investment (or minus unplanned disinvestment). T F

7. If real NNP were to decline by $40, consumers would reduce their consumption expenditures by an amount less than $40. T F

8. A decrease in the rate of interest will, other things remaining the same, result in a decrease in the equilibrium real NNP. T F

9. The larger the marginal propensity to consume, the larger the size of the multiplier. T F

10. If planned net investment increases when the real NNP rises, the size of the multiplier is less than 1/MPS. T F

11. The equilibrium real NNP is the real NNP at which there is full employment in the economy. T F

12. The existence of a recessionary gap in the economy is characterized by the full employment of labor. T F

13. The evidence suggests that the American economy is capable of achieving both full employment and stable prices. T F

14. The higher the level at which the price level is constant in the Keynesian model of the economy the smaller are the real balances of consumers and the lower is the consumption schedule (curve). T F

15. An increase in the price level will shift the aggregate-demand curve to the right. T F

16. In the Keynesian range on the aggregate-supply curve an increase in aggregate demand will have no effect on the real equilibrium NNP of the economy and will raise its price level. T F

17. The greater the increase in the price level that results from an increase in aggregate demand the greater will be the increase in the equilibrium real NNP. T F

18. The Keynesian model of the economy does not adequately predict the effects of changes in aggregate expenditures on the equilibrium real NNP if the price level is not constant. T F

Circle the letter that corresponds to the best answer.

1. The range of the aggregate-supply curve to which the Keynesian model is relevant is (*a*) the horizontal range; (*b*) the intermediate range; (*c*) the vertical range; (*d*) both the intermediate and the vertical range.

2. In the Keynesian model in this chapter the equilibrium real NNP is (*a*) the real NNP at which saving and planned net investment are equal; (*b*) the real NNP at which national output and aggregate expenditures are equal; (*c*) the real NNP which is equal to consumption plus planned net investment; (*d*) all of the above.

Questions 3 and 4 below are based on the consumption schedule preceding true-false questions 2 and 3.

3. If planned net investment is $60, the equilibrium level of real NNP will be: (*a*) $320; (*b*) $360; (*c*) $400; (*d*) $440.

4. If planned investment were to increase by $5, the equilibrium real NNP would increase by: (*a*) $5; (*b*) $7 1/7; (*c*) $15; (*d*) $16 2/3.

5. When the economy's real NNP exceeds its equilibrium real NNP: (*a*) there is unplanned real investment in the economy; (*b*) planned net investment exceeds saving; (*c*) the aggregate expenditures exceed the real national output; (*d*) there is an inflationary gap.

6. If real NNP is $275 billion, consumption $250 billion, and planned investment $30 billion, real NNP: (*a*) will tend to remain constant; (*b*) will tend to increase; (*c*) will tend to decrease; (*d*) equals aggregate expenditures.

7. Which of the following is an injection? (*a*) Investment; (*b*) saving; (*c*) taxes; (*d*) imports.

8. If saving is greater than planned net investment: (*a*) businesses will be motivated to increase their investments; (*b*) aggregate expenditures will be greater than the real national output; (*c*) real NNP will be greater than planned net investment plus consumption; (*d*) saving will tend to increase.

9. On a graph the equilibrium real NNP is found at the intersection of the 45-degree line and (*a*) the consumption curve; (*b*) the investment-demand curve; (*c*) the saving curve; (*d*) the aggregate-expenditures curve.

10. If the value of the marginal propensity to consume is 0.6 and real NNP falls by $25, this was caused by a decrease in the aggregate-expenditures schedule of: (*a*) $10; (*b*) $15; (*c*) $16 2/3; (*d*) $20.

11. If the marginal propensity to consume is 0.6 2/3 and if both planned net investment and the saving schedule increase by $25, real NNP will: (*a*) increase by $75; (*b*) not change; (*c*) decrease by $75; (*d*) increase by $25.

12. The paradox of thrift means that: (*a*) an increase in saving lowers the level of real NNP; (*b*) an increase in the average propensity to save lowers or leaves unchanged the level of savings; (*c*) an increase in the marginal propensity to save lowers the value of the multiplier; (*d*) an increase in real NNP increases investment demand.

13. If the economy's full-employment noninflationary real NNP is $1200 and its equilibrium real NNP is $1100 there is a recessionary gap of: (*a*) $100; (*b*) $100 divided by the multiplier; (*c*) $100 multiplied by the multiplier; (*d*) $100 times the reciprocal of the marginal propensity to consume.

14. To eliminate an inflationary gap of $50 in an economy in which the marginal propensity to save is 0.1, it will be necessary to: (*a*) decrease the aggregate-expenditures schedule by $50; (*b*) decrease the aggregate-expenditures schedule by $5; (*c*) increase the aggregate-expenditures schedule by $50; (*d*) increase the aggregate-expenditures schedule by $5.

15. If the price level in the Keynesian model were lower the consumption and aggregate-expenditures curves would be: (*a*) lower and the equilibrium real NNP would be smaller; (*b*) lower and the equilibrium real NNP would be larger; (*c*) higher and the equilibrium real NNP would be larger; (*d*) higher and the equilibrium real NNP would be smaller.

16. An increase in aggregate expenditures in the Keynesian model shifts the aggregate-demand curve to the: (*a*) right by the amount of the increase in aggregate expenditures; (*b*) right by the amount of the increase in aggregate expenditures times the multiplier; (*c*) left by the amount of the increase in aggregate expenditures; (*d*) left by the amount of the increase in aggregate expenditures times the multiplier.

17. An increase in aggregate demand will increase the equilibrium real NNP if the economy is operating in the: (*a*) Keynesian range; (*b*) intermediate range; (*c*) Keynesian or intermediate ranges; (*d*) classical range.

18. An increase in aggregate demand will increase both the equilibrium real NNP and the price level if the economy is operating in the: (*a*) Keynesian range; (*b*) intermediate range; (*c*) intermediate or classical ranges; (*d*) classical range.

■ DISCUSSION QUESTIONS

1. Why is the price level in the Keynesian model assumed to be constant? How does this Keynesian-model assumption differ from the assumption used in the aggregate demand–aggregate supply model?

2. Why is the equilibrium level of real NNP that level of real NNP at which national output equals aggregate expenditures and at which saving equals planned net investment? What will cause real NNP to rise if it is below this level and what will cause it to fall if it is above this level?

3. Explain what is meant by a leakage and by an injection. What are the three major leakages and the three major injections in the flow of income in the American economy? Which leakage and which injection are considered in this chapter? Why is the equilibrium real NNP the real NNP at which the leakages equal the injections?

4. What is meant by "the distinction between saving and investment plans and the actual amounts which households manage to save and businesses to invest"? Is the net investment schedule planned or actual investment? What adjustment causes planned and actual net investment to become equal?

5. What is the multiplier effect? *Why* does there tend to be a multiplier effect (that is, on what basic economic facts does the multiplier effect depend)? What determines how large the simple multiplier effect will be?

6. What is meant by the paradox of thrift? When would an increase in the saving schedule cause saving (at equilibrium) to decrease?

7. What relationship is there between the equilibrium level of real NNP and the level of real NNP at which full employment without inflation is achieved?

8. Explain what is meant by a recessionary gap and an inflationary gap. What economic conditions are present in the economy when each of these gaps exists? How is the size of each of these gaps measured?

9. How is the aggregate-demand curve used in the aggregate demand–aggregate supply model of the economy derived from the Keynesian model?

10. What is the effect of an increase in aggregate expenditures in the Keynesian model (*a*) on the aggregate demand curve; (*b*) on the equilibrium real NNP and price level in the Keynesian, intermediate, and classical ranges of the aggregate-supply curve; and (*c*) on the size of the multiplier effect on real NNP in each of these three ranges? What is the relationship between the effect of an increase in aggregate expenditures on real NNP and the rise in the price level that accompanies it?

APPENDIX TO CHAPTER 13
INTERNATIONAL TRADE AND EQUILIBRIUM OUTPUT

This appendix expands the Keynesian model of the economy (examined in Chapter 13) by adding the *net* exports of an economy to its aggregate-expenditures schedule. Net exports are nothing more than the economy's exports less its imports of goods and services. Like investment, the exports of a nation are an injection into its circular flow of income; and they increase the flow. But imports are, like saving, a leakage from the circular flow, and decrease the flow.

The generalization used to find the equilibrium real NNP in an open economy (one that exports and imports) is the same one used in Chapter 13: the economy will tend to produce a real NNP (in the Keynesian model) which is equal to aggregate expenditures. The only difference in this appendix is that the aggregate expenditures include not only consumption and planned net investment expenditures but the expenditures for net exports. So the equilibrium real NNP will equal $C + I_n + X_n$ (when X_n is the symbol used for net exports).

An increase in X_n, like an increase in I_n, will increase the equilibrium real NNP; and a decrease in X_n will decrease the equilibrium real NNP. And like a change in I_n, a change in X_n has a multiplier effect on real NNP. But there is a difference between the size of the multiplier effect of a change in I_n in a closed economy (one that doesn't export or import) and the size of the multiplier effect of a change in X_n in an open economy. The multiplier in an open economy is a bit more complex; and it is equal to one divided by the sum of the MPS and the MPI. The MPI is the marginal propensity of the economy to import; and it is equal to the fraction (or percentage) of any increase in its real NNP that is spent by its citizens to purchase additional goods and services in foreign countries.

You won't have much trouble with this appendix if you have mastered the material in Chapter 13. The principles are the same; but aggregate-expenditures schedule has a third component and the multiplier has a different size.

■ CHECKLIST

When you have studied this appendix you should be able to:

☐ Identify the major determinant of a nation's exports and the major determinant of its imports.

☐ Use the concept of net exports to define aggregate expenditures in an open economy.

☐ Explain what the equilibrium real NNP in an open economy will be; and find the equilibrium real NNP in an open economy when you are given the appropriate data.

☐ Identify the two policy options a nation might consider if it wished to expand its net exports, NNP, and employment; and explain the objections of economists to both of these options.

☐ Determine the value of the multiplier in an open economy; and explain how a change in an economy's exports and in its imports would affect the equilibrium real NNP and the level of employment in that economy.

☐ Outline the linkage between the real NNP and the level of employment in one nation with the real NNP and employment in other nations.

■ APPENDIX OUTLINE

1. In an open economy the exports (X) of a nation increase and its imports (M) decrease aggregate expenditures in that economy; and aggregate expenditures are equal to the sum of consumption spending, planned net investment spending, and net exports (X_n) when X_n is defined as X minus M.

a. A nation's X depend primarily upon the levels of income in foreign nations.

b. Its M depend directly upon its own income (real NNP).

2. The equilibrium real NNP in an open economy is the real NNP equal to consumption plus planned net investment plus net exports; and any increase (decrease) in its X_n will increase (decrease) its equilibrium real NNP with a multiplier effect.

3. The policy implications of this conclusion are that the government of a nation might try to expand its X or reduce its M to increase the real NNP of and employment in its economy.

(1) Tariffs and import quotas reduce an economy's M; but there are two serious problems in imposing tariffs and quotas that lead almost all economists to oppose their imposition.

(2) Increasing the price that must be paid for foreign money (the exchange rate) will increase an economy's X and decrease its M; but economists do not favor such a policy for the same reasons they oppose trade barriers.

4. The value of the multiplier in an open economy is equal to one divided by the sum of the nation's marginal propensities to save and to import.

5. The economies of nations that engage in international trade are linked by the effect a change in one nation's real NNP has on the real NNPs of other nations: an increase (a decrease) in real NNP in one nation will expand (contract) its *M*, expand (contract) the *X* of other nations, and increase (decrease) their real NNPs and employment.

■ IMPORTANT TERMS

Open economy	**Import quota**
Closed economy	**Exchange rate**
Net exports	**Marginal propensity to import**
Tariff	**Open-economy multiplier**

■ FILL-IN QUESTIONS

1. When a nation is able to export and import goods and services:

a. Its net exports equal its ________________ minus its ________________

b. The volume of its total exports depends (directly, indirectly) ________________ upon the level of ________________ in foreign countries.

c. The volume of its total imports depends (directly, indirectly) ________________ upon the level of ________________

2. In an open economy:

a. Aggregate expenditures are equal to consumption plus planned net investment plus ________________

b. The equilibrium real NNP is the real NNP which is equal to ________________

c. The value of the multiplier is equal to one divided by the sum of the marginal propensities to ________ and to ________

3. What would be the effect—increase (+) or decrease (−)—of each of the following upon an open economy's equilibrium real NNP?

a. An increase in its imports ________

b. An increase in its exports ________

c. A decrease in its imports ________

d. A decrease in its exports ________

4. To reduce its imports or expand its exports a nation might impose such barriers to imports as ________ and ________ or (increase, decrease) ________ the exchange rate for foreign monies; but such policies are opposed by most economists because they

a. ________________

b. ________________

5. An open economy's marginal propensity to import is equal to the fraction (or percentage) of an increase in its ________________ which is spent on ________________

6. Suppose an economy experienced a recession in which its real NNP and employment fell.

a. Its imports from other nations would (rise, fall) ________ and the exports of the other nations would ________________

b. Real NNP and employment in the other nations would (rise, fall) ________________

■ PROBLEM

1. Next is a schedule showing what aggregate expenditures (consumption plus planned net investment) would be at various levels of real net national product in a closed economy.

Possible levels of real NNP (billions)	Aggregate expenditures, closed economy (billions)	Exports (billions)	Imports (billions)	Net exports (billions)	Aggregate expenditures, open economy (billions)
$ 750	$ 776	$90	$74	$_____	$_____
800	816	90	78	_____	_____
850	856	90	82	_____	_____
900	896	90	86	_____	_____
950	936	90	90	_____	_____
1,000	976	90	94	_____	_____
1,050	1,016	90	98	_____	_____

a. Were this economy to become an open economy the volume of exports would be a constant $90 billion; and the volume of imports at the various levels of real NNP would be the amount shown in the table. Compute the net exports at each of the seven real NNPs and enter them in the table.

b. Compute aggregate expenditures in this open economy at the seven real NNP levels and enter them in the table.

c. The equilibrium real NNP in this open economy would be $________ billion.

d. In this open economy the marginal propensity to save is 0.20 and the marginal propensity to import is ________

e. The value of the multiplier in this open economy is equal to approximately ________________

f. A $10 billion increase in:

(1) exports would (increase, decrease) __________ the equilibrium real NNP by about $________ billion.

(2) imports would (increase, decrease) __________ the equilibrium real NNP by about $________ billion.

■ SELF-TEST

Circle the T if the statement is true, the F if it is false.

1. The total volume of exports from a nation depends directly on the levels of national income in foreign nations. **T F**

2. The net exports of an economy equal the sum of its exports and its imports of goods and services. **T F**

3. An increase in the volume of a nation's exports, other things being equal, will expand the nation's real NNP. **T F**

4. The value of the multiplier in an open economy is equal to the reciprocal of the economy's marginal propensity to import. **T F**

5. The aggregate-expenditures curve in an open economy tends to be steeper than the aggregate-expenditures curve in a closed economy. **T F**

6. An increase in the imports of a nation will increase the exports of other nations. **T F**

Circle the letter that corresponds to the best answer.

Use the data in the table below to answer questions 1, 2, and 3.

Real NNP	$C + I$	Net exports
$ 900	$ 913	$7
920	929	6
940	945	5
960	961	4
980	977	3
1,000	993	2
1,020	1,009	1

1. If exports in this economy are constant, its marginal propensity to import must be (*a*) .04; (*b*) .05; (*c*) .06; (*d*) .07.

2. The equilibrium real NNP is (*a*) $960; (*b*) $980; (*c*) $1,000; (*d*) $1,020.

3. If the marginal propensity to save in this economy is 0.2, a $10 increase in its net exports would increase its equilibrium real NNP by (*a*) $40; (*b*) $50; (*c*) $100; (*d*) $200.

4. Other things remaining constant, which of the following would *not* increase an economy's real NNP and employment? (*a*) The imposition of tariffs on goods imported from abroad; (*b*) the placing of quotas on the quantities of goods that may be imported from abroad; (*c*) a decrease in the exchange rates for foreign monies; (*d*) none of the above.

5. The imposition of trade barriers (*a*) decreases the volume of trade among nations; (*b*) limits international specialization in the production of goods and services; (*c*) reduces the efficiency with which resources are allocated; (*d*) does all of the above.

6. An increase in the real NNP of an economy will, other things remaining constant, (*a*) increase its imports and the real NNPs in other economies; (*b*) increase its imports and decrease the real NNPs in other economies; (*c*) decrease its imports and increase the real NNPs in other economies; (*d*) decrease its imports and the real NNPs in other economies.

■ DISCUSSION QUESTIONS

1. What are the primary determinants of the volume of a nation's exports and imports? How do exports and how do imports affect aggregate expenditures within a nation?

2. To what is the equilibrium real NNP equal in an open economy (in the Keynesian model)? How does a change in the volume of exports and in the volume of imports affect real NNP and employment in a nation?

3. While they might expand the real NNP and employment in a nation, why are economists generally opposed to the use of trade barriers and the manipulation of exchange rates to achieve these ends?

4. What determines the size or value of the multiplier in an open economy? Why is the multiplier larger in a closed than in an open economy?

5. How are real output and employment in one nation linked to real output and employment in other nations?

14
Fiscal policy

Chapter 14 is really a continuation of the two preceding chapters and is concerned with the chief practical application of the principles discussed in those chapters.

It is worth recalling that principles of economics are generalizations about the way the economy works; and that these principles are studied in order that policies may be devised to solve real problems. Over the past one hundred or so years the most serious problems encountered by the American economy have been those problems that resulted from the business cycle. Learning what determines the real output and price levels of an economy and what causes them to fluctuate will make it possible to discover ways to bring about full employment, maximum output, and stable prices. Economic principles, in short, suggest the policies that will lessen both recession and inflation.

Government spending and taxing have a strong influence on the economy's output and employment and its price level. Federal expenditure and taxation policies designed to expand total production and employment or reduce the rate of inflation are called fiscal policies. (The Federal Reserve Banks are also able to affect these variables by applying monetary policy; but the study of monetary policy must wait until the effect of banks on the operation of the economy is examined in Chapters 17, 18, and 19.)

The brief first section of the chapter makes it clear that Congress in the Employment Act of 1946 committed the Federal government to using fiscal (and monetary) policy to achieve a trio of economic goals—economic growth, stable prices, and full employment. This act also established the Council of Economic Advisers to advise the President and the Joint Economic Committee to advise Congress on matters pertaining to national economic policy.

The section entitled "Discretionary Fiscal Policy" is, however, the crucial part of Chapter 14. It introduces government taxing and spending into the analysis of equilibrium real NNP. It is important to note that government purchases of goods and services add to aggregate demand; and that taxation reduces the disposable income of consumers, and thereby reduces both the amount of consumption and the amount of saving that will take place at any level of real NNP. Both "approaches" are again employed, and you are warned that you must know *what* real NNP will tend to be produced and *why.* Special attention should be directed to the exact effect taxes have upon the consumption and saving schedules and to the multiplier effects of changes in government purchases and taxes.

Once you learn how government purchases and taxing affect the equilibrium real NNP it is fairly easy to understand what fiscal policies will be expansionary and reduce unemployment and what fiscal policies will be contractionary and lessen inflation. In addition to this, you should be aware (1) that if the government has a budget deficit or surplus there are several ways of financing the deficit or disposing of the surplus, and the way the deficit or surplus is handled can affect the economy's operation as much as the size of the deficit or surplus; and (2) that the Federal government has the option of changing its expenditures or altering the taxes it collects when it applies fiscal policy to reduce unemployment or lessen inflation in the economy.

Discretionary fiscal policy requires that Congress take action to change tax rates, transfer payment programs, or purchases of goods and services. *Non*discretionary fiscal policy does not require Congress to take any action; and is a built-in stabilizer of the economy. You should be sure that you understand *why* net taxes increase when the NNP rises and decrease when the NNP falls and *how* this tends to stabilize the economy.

Unfortunately, nondiscretionary fiscal policy by itself is not able to eliminate any recessionary or inflationary gap that might develop; and discretionary fiscal policy will be necessary if the economy is to produce its full-employment NNP and avoid inflation. And the built-in stabilizers make it more difficult to use discretionary fiscal policy to achieve this goal because they produce fiscal drag, and create the illusion that the Federal government's policy is expansionary or contractionary when in fact its policy is just the opposite. Because of the illusions created by the built-in stabilizers, economists developed the full-employment budget to enable them to discover whether Federal fiscal policy was actually expansionary or contractionary and to determine what policy should have been followed to move the economy toward full employment or slow the rate of inflation.

In addition to the problems of timing and the political problems encountered in using fiscal problems in the real world, you will discover in the last major section of the chapter that many economists and other people are concerned by two other important complications. They fear, first of all, that all expansionary fiscal policy which requires the Federal government to borrow in the money market will raise the level of interest rates in the economy and reduce (or crowd out) investment spending; this is called the crowding-out effect and if it is large it will reduce the effect of the expansionary fiscal policy on real NNP and unemployment. The second fear is that an expansionary fiscal policy, if the economy is operating in the intermediate range along the aggregate-supply curve, will drive up the price level and have only a small effect on real output and employment. But all is not gloom. The supply-side economists argue that a reduction in tax rates will not only increase aggregate demand but will also (for a number of reasons explained in the text) expand aggregate supply. In this way, they contend, the real equilibrium NNP of the economy can be increased with little or no rise in the price level.

This is, however, the problem of stagflation which will be dealt with in more detail in Chapter 16.

■ CHECKLIST

When you have studied this chapter you should be able to:

☐ State the responsibility imposed on the Federal government by the Employment Act of 1946 and the roles of the CEA and JEC in fulfilling this responsibility.

☐ Find the equilibrium real NNP in an economy in which government purchases goods and services and levies net taxes when you are given the necessary data.

☐ Determine the effect on the equilibrium real NNP of a change in government purchases of goods and services and in net taxes.

☐ Explain why the balanced-budget multiplier is equal to one.

☐ Explain when government should pursue an expansionary and a contractionary fiscal policy; what each of these policies might entail; and the effect of each upon the Federal budget.

☐ Describe the best way to finance a government deficit and to dispose of a surplus.

☐ Distinguish between discretionary and nondiscretionary fiscal policy.

☐ Indicate how the built-in stabilizers help to eliminate recession and inflationary pressures.

☐ Outline the timing and political problems encountered in applying fiscal policy in the real world.

☐ Describe the crowding-out effect of an expansionary fiscal policy and how it may lessen the impact of an expansionary fiscal policy on real output and employment.

☐ Distinguish between the effects of an expansionary fiscal policy in the Keynesian and intermediate ranges of the aggregate-supply curve; and explain how the impact of such a policy is reduced when the economy is in the latter range.

☐ State the effects supply-side economists argue a reduction in tax rates would have on aggregate supply, real NNP, and the price level; and explain why they believe it would have these effects.

■ CHAPTER OUTLINE

1. Fiscal policy is the manipulation by the Federal government of its expenditures and tax receipts in order to expand or contract aggregate expenditures in the economy; and by doing so either increase its real output (and employment) or decrease its rate of inflation.

2. The Employment Act of 1946 set the goals of American fiscal policy and provided for a Council of Economic Advisers to the President and the Joint Economic Committee; and in 1978 the Humphrey-Hawkins Act required the Federal government to develop a plan to reach specific economic goals.

3. Discretionary fiscal policy involves deliberate changes in tax rates and government spending to offset cyclical fluctuations and to increase economic growth.

a. Six assumptions are made in order to simplify the explanation of the effects of government spending and taxes on the equilibrium real NNP.

b. Government purchases of goods and services add to the aggregate-expenditures schedule and increase equilibrium real NNP; and an increase in these purchases has a multiplier effect upon equilibrium real NNP.

c. Taxes decrease consumption and the aggregate-expenditures schedule by the amount of the tax times the MPC (and decrease saving by the amount of the tax times the MPS); and an increase in taxes has a negative multiplier effect on the equilibrium real NNP. When government both taxes and purchases goods and services, the equilibrium NNP is the NNP at which

(1) aggregate expenditures (consumption + planned net investment + government purchases of goods and services) = the real national output (consumption + saving + taxes); or

(2) using the leakages-injections approach, at which planned net investment + government purchases of goods and services = saving + taxes.

d. Equal increases (decreases) in taxes and in government purchases increase (decrease) equilibrium real NNP by the amount of the change in taxes (or in expenditures).

e. The elimination of the inflation (recession) is accomplished by contractionary (expansionary) fiscal policy and by increasing (decreasing) taxes, decreasing (increasing) purchases, and incurring budget surpluses (deficits).

f. In addition to the size of the deficit or surplus, the manner in which the government finances its deficit or disposes of its surplus affects the level of total spending in the economy.

g. Whether government purchases or taxes should be altered to reduce recession and inflation depends to a large extent upon whether an expansion or a contraction of the public sector is desired.

4. In the American economy net tax revenues (tax receipts minus government transfer payments) are not a fixed amount or lump sum; they increase as the NNP rises and decrease as the NNP falls.

a. This net tax system serves as a built-in stabilizer of the economy because it reduces purchasing power during periods of inflation and expands purchasing power during periods of recession.

b. But built-in stability:

(1) can only reduce and cannot eliminate economic fluctuations;

(2) creates fiscal drag and makes it difficult to reduce unemployment during a recession and to maintain full employment in a growing economy;

(3) and requires that the full-employment budget be used to determine whether the Federal budget is actually expansionary or contractionary.

5. Certain problems and complications arise in enacting and applying fiscal policy.

a. There will be problems of timing because it requires time to recognize the need for fiscal policy; to take the appropriate steps in the Congress; and for the action taken there to affect output and employment, and the rate of inflation in the economy.

b. There will also be political problems because:

(1) the economy has goals other than full employment and stable prices;

(2) there is an expansionary bias (for budget deficits and against surpluses);

(3) there may be a political business cycle (if politicians lower taxes and increase expenditures before and then do the opposite after elections).

c. An expansionary fiscal policy may, by raising the level of interest rates in the economy, reduce (or crowd out) investment spending and weaken the effect of the policy on real NNP; but this crowding-out effect may be small and can be offset by an expansion in the nation's money supply.

d. The effect of an expansionary fiscal policy on the real NNP will also be weakened to the extent that it results in a rise in the price level (inflation).

e. Aggregate demand and aggregate supply curves can be used to show how crowding out and inflation weaken the effects of an expansionary fiscal policy on real NNP.

f. But an expansionary fiscal policy that includes a reduction in taxes (tax rates) may, by increasing aggregate supply in the economy, expand real NNP (and employment), and reduce inflation.

■ IMPORTANT TERMS

Fiscal policy
Employment Act of 1946
Council of Economic Advisers
Joint Economic Committee
Humphrey-Hawkins Act of 1978
Discretionary fiscal policy
Lump-sum tax
Balanced-budget multiplier
Expansionary fiscal policy
Contractionary fiscal policy

Nondiscretionary fiscal policy
Net taxes
Built-in stability
Fiscal drag
Actual budget
Full-employment budget
Political business cycle
Crowding-out effect

■ FILL-IN QUESTIONS

1. The use of monetary and fiscal policy to reduce inflation and recession became national economic policy in the Employment Act of 1946.

a. This act also established the Council of Economic Advisors to the President and the Joint Committee in Congress.

b. And in 1978 the Humphrey-Hawkins Act required the Federal government to establish five-year goals for the economy and a plan to achieve them.

2. Taxes tend to reduce consumption at each level of real NNP by an amount equal to the taxes multiplied by the MPC; saving will decrease by an amount equal to the taxes multiplied by the MPS ______

3. In an economy in which government both taxes and purchases goods and services, the equilibrium level of real NNP is the real NNP at which:

a. aggregate expenditures equal the national output;

b. NNP is equal to consumption plus planned net investment plus government purchases of G & S

c. Planned net invest. plus gov't purchases equals savings plus net taxes

$S_a + T = I_n + G / C_a + I_n + G = NNP$

4. Equal reductions in taxes and government purchases will (increase, decrease) decrease real NNP by an amount equal to decrease in taxes & gov't purchases

5. In order to increase real NNP during a recession, taxes should be (increased, decreased) decreased and government purchases should be increased; to decrease the rise in the price level during a period of inflation taxes should be increased and government purchases should be decreased

dir. of deficit

dir. of surplus

6. If fiscal policy is to have a countercyclical effect, it will probably be necessary for the Federal government to incur a budget (surplus, deficit) deficit during a recession and a budget surplus during inflation.

7. The two principal means available to the Federal government for financing budget deficits are borrowing money from public and creating money; and the (former, latter) latter is more expansionary.

8. Those who wish to expand the public sector of the economy would during a period of *inflation* advocate a(n) (increase, decrease) increase in (government purchases, taxes) ~~purchases~~ taxes, and those who wish to contract the public sector during a *recession* would advocate a(n) decrease in taxes

9. Net taxes:

a. equal taxes minus transfers & subsidies

b. in the United States will (increase, decrease) increase as the NNP rises and will decrease as the NNP falls.

10. When net tax receipts are directly related to the NNP the economy has some built-in stability because:

a. when the NNP rises, leakages (increase, decrease) increase and the budget surplus will (increase, decrease) ~~decrease~~ increase (or the budget deficit will decrease);

b. when the NNP falls, leakages decrease

and the budget deficit will increase (or the budget surplus will decrease)

11. Fiscal drag means that when net tax receipts vary directly with the NNP and are not a lump sum it is more difficult for discretionary fiscal policy to raise the level of ~~surpluses~~ employment in the short run and to maintain Full employment in the long run.

12. The full-employment budget:

a. indicates what the Federal budgetary surplus or deficit would have been if the economy had operated at FE during the year;

b. tells us whether the Federal budget was in fact expansionary or contractionary

13. There is a problem of timing in the use of discretionary fiscal policy because of the recognition, administrative, and operationae lags.

14. Political problems arise in the application of discretionary fiscal policy to stabilize the economy because government has Other goals; because voters have a bias in favor of budget (surpluses, deficits) deficits; and because politicians use fiscal policies in a way that creates a politicae business cycle.

15. When the Federal government employs an expansionary fiscal policy to increase real NNP and employment in the economy it usually has a budget (surplus, deficit) deficit and (lends, borrows) borrows in the money market.

a. This will (raise, lower) raise interest rates in the economy and (contract, expand) Contract investment spending.

b. This change in investment spending is the crowding out effect of the expansionary fiscal policy and it tends to (weaken, strengthen) weaken the impact of the expansionary fiscal policy on real NNP and employment.

16. An expansionary fiscal policy when the economy is operating in the intermediate range of the aggregate-supply curve will increase the real NNP and employment in the economy and (raise, lower) raise the price level.

a. This change in the price level will (weaken, strengthen) weaken the impact of the expansionary fiscal policy on output and employment in the economy.

b. But if the expansionary fiscal policy is the result of reduction in taxes, the supply-side effects of the policy may be to (increase, decrease) increase aggregate supply, to increase productivity capacity of the economy, to increase real NNP and employment, to decrease the rate of inflation, and to (weaken, strengthen) Strengthen the impact of the fiscal policy on output and employment.

■ PROBLEMS AND PROJECTS

1. Consumption and saving schedules are shown in the following table.

Real NNP	C	S	C_a	S_a	$S_a + T$	$I + G$	$C_a + I + G$
$1500	$1250	$250	$1160	$240	$340	$350	$1510
1600	1340	260	1260	250	350	350	1600
1700	1430	270	1340	260	360	350	1690
1800	1520	280	1430	270	370	350	1780
1900	1610	290	1520	280	380	350	1870
2000	1700	300	1610	290	390	350	1960
2100	1790	310	1700	300	400	350	2050

a. Assume government levies a lump-sum tax of $100.

(1) Because the marginal propensity to consume in this problem is .9, the imposition of this tax will reduce consumption at all levels of real NNP by $90. Complete the C_a column to show consumption at each real NNP after the levying of this tax.

(2) Because the marginal propensity to save in this problem is .1, this tax will reduce saving at all levels of real NNP by 10. Complete the S_a column to show saving at each real NNP after this tax has been levied.

b. Compute the (after-tax) saving-plus-taxes at each real NNP and put them in the $S_a + T$ column.

c. Suppose that planned net investment is $150 and government purchases of goods and services equal $200. Complete the investment-plus-government-purchases column ($I + G$) and the (after-tax) consumption-plus-investment-plus-government-purchases column ($C_a + I + G$).

d. The equilibrium real NNP is $1600

e. On the graphs on pages 120 and 121 plot:

(1) C_a, $I + G$, $C_a + I + G$, and the 45-degree line. Show the equilibrium real NNP.

(2) $S_a + T$ and $I + G$. Show the real equilibrium NNP.

(To answer the questions below it is *not* necessary to recompute C, S, $S + T$, $I + G$, or $C + I + G$. They can be answered by using the multipliers.)

f. If taxes remained at $100 and government purchases rose by $10, the equilibrium real NNP would (rise, fall) rise by $100

g. If government purchases remained at $200 and the lump-sum tax increased by $10, the equilibrium real NNP would fall by $90

h. The combined effect of a $10 increase in government purchases *and* a $10 increase in taxes is to raise real NNP by $10

2. In the table below are seven real NNPs and the net tax receipts of government at each real NNP.

Real NNP	Net tax receipts	Government purchases	Government surplus
$ 850	$170	$200	$-30
900	180	200	-20
950	190	200	-10
1000	200	200	0
1050	210	200	10
1100	220	200	20
1150	230	200	30

a. Looking at the two columns on the left of the table, it can be seen that:

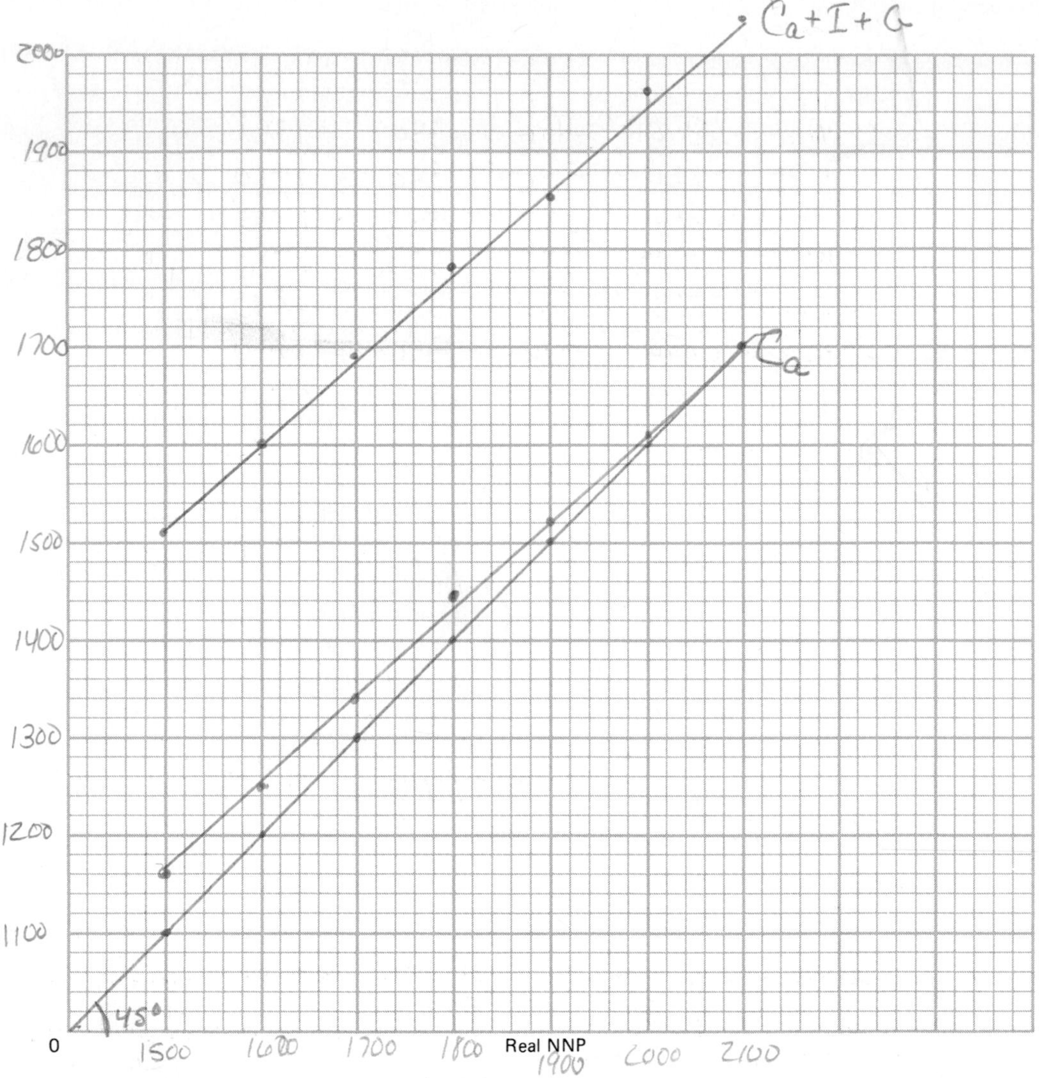

(1) when real NNP increases by $50, net tax receipts (increase, decrease) increase by $ 10

(2) when real NNP decreases by $100, net tax receipts decrease by $ 20

(3) the relation between real NNP and net tax receipts is (direct, inverse) direct

b. Assume the investment multiplier has a value of 10 and that investment spending in the economy decreases by $10.

(1) *If* net tax receipts remained constant, the equilibrium real NNP would decrease by $ 100

(2) But when real NNP decreases, net tax receipts also decrease; and this decrease in net tax receipts will tend to (increase, decrease) increase the equilibrium real NNP.

(3) And, therefore, the decrease in real NNP brought about by the $10 decrease in investment spending will be (more, less) less than $100.

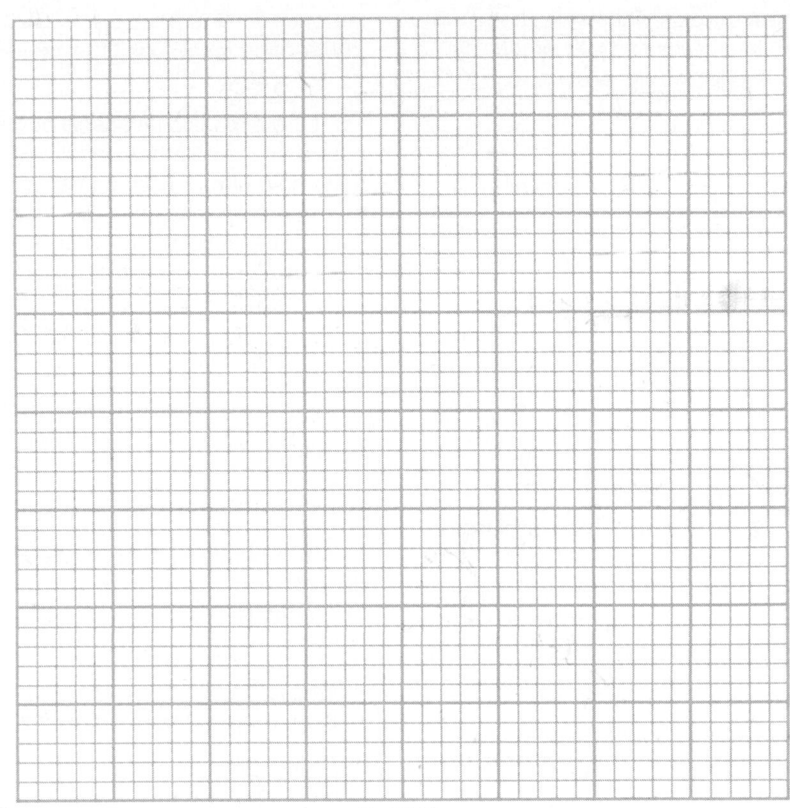

(4) The direct relationship between net tax receipts and real NNP has (lessened, expanded) lessened the impact of the $10 decrease in investment spending on real NNP.

c. Suppose the government purchases multiplier is also 10 and government wishes to increase the equilibrium real NNP by $50.

(1) *If* net tax receipts remained constant, government would have to increase its purchases of goods and services by $ 5

(2) But when real NNP rises, net tax receipts also rise; and this rise in net tax receipts will tend to (increase, decrease) decrease the equilibrium real NNP.

(3) The effect, therefore, of the $5 increase in government purchases will also be to increase the equilibrium real NNP by (more, less) lessened than $50.

(4) The direct relation between net tax receipts and real NNP has (lessened, expanded) lessened the effect of the $5 increase in government purchases; and to raise the equilibrium real NNP by $50 government will have to increase its purchases by (more, less) more than $5.

d. Imagine that the full-employment real NNP of the economy is $1150 and that government purchases of goods and services are $200.

(1) Complete the table on page 119 by entering the government purchases and by computing the budget surplus at each of the real NNPs. (Show a government deficit by placing a minus sign in front of the amount by which expenditures exceed net tax receipts.)

(2) The full-employment surplus equals $ ______

(3) Were the economy in a recession and producing a real NNP of $900, the budget would show a (surplus, deficit) ______ of $ ______

(4) This budget deficit or surplus makes it appear that government is pursuing a(n) (expansionary, contractionary) ______ fiscal policy; but this deficit or surplus is not the result of countercyclical fiscal policy but the result of the ______

(5) If government did not change its net tax *rates* it could increase the equilibrium real NNP from $900 to the full-employment real NNP of $1150 by increasing its purchases by (approximately) $70. At the full-employment real NNP the budget would show a (surplus, deficit) ______ of $ ______

(6) If government did not change its purchases it would increase the equilibrium real NNP from $900 to the full-employment real NNP of $1150 by decreasing net tax receipts at all real NNPs by a lump sum of (approximately) $80. The full-employment budget would have a (surplus, deficit) ______ of $ ______

3. Columns (1) and (2) in the table below are the aggregate-supply schedule and columns (1) and (3) are the aggregate-demand schedule.

(1) Price level	(2) Real NNP_1	(3) AQD_1	(4) AQD_2	(5) Real NNP_2
$2.20	$2390	$2100	$2200	$2490
2.00	2390	2200	2340	2490
1.90	2350	2250	2350	2450
1.80	2300	2300	2400	2400
1.60	2200	2400	2500	2300

a. The equilibrium real NNP is $ ______ and the price level is $ ______

b. Suppose that an expansionary fiscal policy increases aggregate demand from that shown in columns (1) and (3) to that shown in columns (1) and (4).

(1) If the price level remained constant the equilibrium real NNP would increase to $ ______

(2) But the increase in aggregate demand does raise the price level to $ ______; and this rise in the price level results in real NNP increasing to only $ ______

c. If the expansionary fiscal policy that increased aggregate demand also has supply-side effects and increased aggregate supply from that shown in columns (1) and (2) to that shown in columns (1) and (5):

(1) The equilibrium real NNP would increase to $ ______; and

(2) the price level would ______

■ SELF-TEST

Circle the T if the statement is true, the F if it is false.

1. The Employment Act of 1946 committed the Federal government to using monetary and fiscal policy to achieve economic stability. **T F**

2. The purposes of discretionary fiscal policy are reduced inflation, the elimination of unemployment, and the stimulation of economic growth. **T F**

3. If the MPS were 0.3 and taxes were levied by the government so that consumers paid $20 in taxes at each level of real NNP, consumption expenditures at each level of real NNP would be $14 less. **T F**

4. If taxes only are reduced by $10 at all levels of real NNP and the marginal propensity to save is 0.4, equilibrium real NNP will rise by $25. **T F**

5. Even a balanced budget can be a weapon in fighting depression and inflation. **T F**

6. A governmental deficit is contractionary. **T F**

7. A reduction in taxes during a recession would tend to contract the public sector of the economy. **T F**

8. Built-in stabilizers are not sufficiently strong to prevent recession or inflation, but they can reduce the severity of a recession or inflation. **T F**

9. The automatic (or built-in) stabilizers also increase the sizes of the government expenditures and investment multipliers. **T F**

10. The full-employment budget indicates how much government must spend and tax if there is to be full employment in the economy. T F

11. Recognition, administrative, and operational lags in the timing of Federal fiscal policy make fiscal policies more effective in reducing the rate of inflation and decreasing unemployment in the economy. T F

12. The fiscal policies of state and local governments have tended to assist and reinforce the efforts of the Federal government to mitigate depression and inflation. T F

13. The spending and taxing policies of the Federal government are designed solely to reduce unemployment and limit inflation in the economy. T F

14. It is generally easier to induce U.S. Senators and Representatives to vote for decreases in tax rates and for increases in government purchases than for increased taxes and decreased purchases. T F

15. Economists who see evidence of a political business cycle argue that members of Congress tend to increase taxes and reduce expenditures before and to reduce taxes and increase expenditures after elections. T F

16. Supply-side economists maintain that reductions in tax rates decrease aggregate supply and are, therefore, inflationary. T F

Circle the letter that corresponds to the best answer.

1. Which of the following established unemployment-rate and inflation-rate goals for the American economy? (*a*) The Employment Act of 1946; (*b*) the Humphrey-Hawkins Act of 1978; (*c*) the Economic Recovery Act of 1981; (*d*) the Balanced Budget Amendment of 1983.

The next four questions are based on the consumption schedule below. Investment figures are for planned investment.

Real NNP	*C*
$300	$290
310	298
320	306
330	314
340	322
350	330
360	338

2. If taxes were zero, government purchases of goods and services $10, and investment $6, equilibrium real NNP would be: (*a*) $310; (*b*) $320; (*c*) $330; (*d*) $340.

3. If taxes were $5, government purchases of goods and services $10, and investment $6, equilibrium real NNP would be: (*a*) $300; (*b*) $310; (*c*) $320; (*d*) $330.

4. Assume investment is $42, taxes $40, and government purchases of goods and services zero. If the full-employment level of real NNP is $340, the gap can be eliminated by reducing taxes by: (*a*) $8; (*b*) $10; (*c*) $13; (*d*) $40.

5. Assume that investment is zero, that taxes are zero, and the government purchases of goods and services are $20. If the full-employment-without-inflation level of real NNP is $330, the gap can be eliminated by decreasing government expenditures by: (*a*) $4; (*b*) $5; (*c*) $10; (*d*) $20.

6. If the marginal propensity to consume is $0.6\frac{2}{3}$ and both taxes and government purchases of goods and services increase by $25, real NNP will: (*a*) fall by $25; (*b*) rise by $25; (*c*) fall by $75; (*d*) rise by $75.

7. Which of the following policies would do the *most* to reduce inflation? (*a*) Increase taxes by $5 billion; (*b*) reduce government purchases of goods and services by $5 billion; (*c*) increase taxes and government expenditures by $5 billion; (*d*) reduce both taxes and government purchases by $5 billion.

8. If the government wishes to increase the level of real NNP, it might: (*a*) reduce taxes; (*b*) reduce its purchases of goods and services; (*c*) reduce transfer payments; (*d*) reduce the size of the budget deficit.

9. Which of the following by itself is the most expansionary (least contractionary)? (*a*) Redemption of government bonds held by the public; (*b*) borrowing from the public to finance a budget deficit; (*c*) a build-up in the size of the government's checking account in the central banks; (*d*) issuing new money to finance a budget deficit.

10. Which of the following by itself is the most contractionary (least expansionary)? (*a*) Redemption of government bonds held by the public; (*b*) borrowing from the public to finance a budget deficit; (*c*) a build-up in the size of the government's checking account in the central banks; (*d*) issuing new money to finance a budget deficit.

11. If the economy is to have built-in stability, when real NNP falls: (*a*) tax receipts and government transfer payments should fall; (*b*) tax receipts and government transfer payments should rise; (*c*) tax receipts should fall and government transfer payments should rise; (*d*) tax receipts should rise and government transfer payments should fall.

12. A direct relation between net tax receipts and real NNP (*a*) automatically produces budget surpluses during a recession; (*b*) makes it easier for discretionary fiscal policy to move the economy out of a recession and toward full employment; (*c*) makes it easier to maintain full employment in a growing economy; (*d*) reduces the effect of a change in planned investment spending upon the national output and employment.

13. The length of time it takes for the fiscal action taken by Congress to affect output, employment, or the price level is referred to as the (*a*) administrative lag; (*b*) operational lag; (*c*) recognition lag; (*d*) fiscal lag.

14. The crowding-out effect of an expansionary (deficit) fiscal policy is the result of government borrowing in the money market which (*a*) increases interest rates and net investment spending in the economy; (*b*) increases interest rates and decreases net investment spending; (*c*) decreases interest rates and increases net investment spending; (*d*) decreases interest rates and net investment spending.

15. The effect of an expansionary (deficit) fiscal policy on the real NNP of an economy operating in the Keynesian range on the aggregate-supply curve is lessened by (*a*) increases in aggregate supply; (*b*) the crowding-out effect; (*c*) increases in the price level; (*d*) both *b* and *c*.

16. The effect of an expansionary (deficit) fiscal policy on the real NNP of an economy operating in the intermediate range on the aggregate-supply curve is lessened by (*a*) increases in aggregate supply; (*b*) the crowding-out effect; (*c*) increases in the price level; (*d*) both *b* and *c*.

■ DISCUSSION QUESTIONS

1. What is meant by fiscal policy?

2. In the Employment Act of 1946, (*a*) what responsibility was given to the Federal government; (*b*) what tasks were assigned to the Council of Economic Advisers and the Joint Economic Committee; and (*c*) what specific kinds of policy were to be used to achieve the goals established by the act? What did the Humphrey-Hawkins Act require the Federal government to do?

3. What is the exact effect which taxes will have on the consumption schedule? On the saving schedule?

4. Explain why, with government taxing and spending, the equilibrium real NNP is the real NNP at which real NNP equals consumption plus planned investment plus government purchases of goods and services; and saving plus taxes equals planned investment plus government purchases. What will cause NNP to move to its equilibrium level?

5. If both taxes and government purchases increase by equal amounts, real NNP will increase by that amount. Why?

6. What three things might the Federal government do if its fiscal policy were to be (*a*) expansionary and if it were to be (*b*) contractionary? When would it invoke each of these two kinds of policy and what would be their effects on the Federal budget?

7. What are the alternative means of financing deficits and disposing of surpluses available to the Federal government? What is the difference between these methods insofar as their expansionary and contractionary effect is concerned?

8. Explain the fiscal policy that would be advocated during a recession and during a period of inflation (*a*) by those who wish to expand the public sector and (*b*) by those who wish to contract the public sector.

9. What is the difference between discretionary and nondiscretionary fiscal policy? How do the built-in stabilizers work to reduce rises and falls in the level of money NNP?

10. Explain why a tax system in which net tax receipts vary directly with the level of money NNP makes it difficult to achieve and to sustain full employment.

11. What is the full-employment budget? What was the problem which the use of the full-employment budget was designed to solve?

12. Explain the three kinds of time lags that make it difficult to use fiscal policy to stabilize the economy.

13. What are three political problems that complicate the use of fiscal policy to stabilize the economy?

14. How do (*a*) crowding out and (*b*) inflation reduce the effect of an expansionary (deficit) fiscal policy on real NNP and employment?

15. What might be the supply-side effects of a reduction in tax rates on the capacity output of the economy, the equilibrium levels of real NNP and employment, and the price level?

15
Budget deficits and the public debt

When the Federal government applies fiscal policies to lessen inflation in the economy it is apt to have a budget surplus; and when it uses fiscal policies to reduce unemployment it is likely to have a budget deficit. Over the past quarter of a century the Federal government has had very few budget surpluses: it has had budget deficits in all but one year.

Any budget surplus or deficit affects the size of the public (sometimes called the national) debt; surpluses decrease it and deficits increase it. As a consequence of its persistent deficits during and since World War II the public debt has increased; and since 1980 the deficits have grown larger and the public debt has increased by increasing amounts from one year to the next. The Federal government finances the public debt by selling securities (bonds). To those who have purchased these securities the government pays interest each year; and as the size of the debt has increased (and interest rates in the economy have risen) the annual interest payments on the debt have also increased.

These facts are the background for this chapter. After defining a budget deficit and the public debt, the chapter examines three budget philosophies. You should be aware that the philosophies adopted by the Federal government have a significant impact on the output of and employment in the economy *and* on the public debt. A brief explanation of the reasons for the increases in the public debt (wars and recessions) and of the absolute and relative sizes of the debt and the interest payments on the debt is next. Then comes an examination of the economic implications or consequences of the debt. Here you will learn that the debt creates problems for the economy (but these problems do not include bankrupting the Federal government or shifting the cost of a war—or of other government programs—to future generations).

The problems created by the public debt and the payment of interest of the debt are four in number. They appear to make the distribution of income in the economy more unequal, to reduce the incentives which induce people and business firms to produce and expand their outputs, to decrease the American standard of living if a part of the debt is owed to foreigners, and to have a crowding-out effect on investment in plant and equipment in the United States.

Crowding-out is probably the most serious of these four problems; and you should be sure that you understand how crowding-out works and how it imposes a burden on future generations by reducing the growth of the nation's capital stock. To understand why it reduces the growth of the capital stock, borrowing to finance an increase in government expenditures is compared with increasing taxes to finance these expenditures.

Finally the chapter shows that government borrowing not only crowds out investment in the economy but results in a chain of events that lead to the contraction of output and employment in the United States. Be sure you follow each of the steps in this cause-and-effect chain. There is not any new theory in this chapter: only problems and potential solutions.

The next chapter begins the presentation of the information about money and banks in the American economy.

■ CHECKLIST

When you have studied this chapter you should be able to:

☐ Define a budget deficit (and surplus) and the public debt; and explain how the latter is related to the former.

☐ Explain each of the three budget philosophies.

☐ State the absolute and relative size of the public debt and of the annual interest charges on this debt; the principal causes of the debt; and why the public debt is for the most part also a public credit.

☐ Compare the effects of an internal debt with the effects of an external debt on the economy.

☐ Explain how adjusting the size of the nominal public debt for inflation affects the real size of the debt and the real size of a budget deficit; and why the accounting procedures employed by the Federal government do not accurately reflect its financial condition.

☐ Settle the two false issues related to the public debt.

☐ Enumerate the four real issues related to the public debt.

☐ Describe the crowding-out effect of borrowing to finance an increase in government expenditures and the burden this method of financing expenditures places on future generations; compare the burden imposed on future generations by this method of finance with the burden placed on them if the increased expenditures are financed by increased taxation; and qualify in two ways this comparison.

☐ Trace the effects of borrowing to finance an increase in government expenditures on interest rates, the attractiveness of American securities to foreigners, the international debts of the United States, the international value of the dollar, American exports and imports, and output and employment in the United States.

☐ List four possible solutions to the rising budget deficits of the Federal government and to the increasing public debt of the United States; and describe the principal provisions of the Gramm-Rudman Act of 1985.

☐ Explain why increasing debt is necessary in a growing economy if the economy is to remain at full employment and when it is necessary for the public debt to expand.

■ CHAPTER OUTLINE

1. The budget deficit of the Federal government is the amount by which its expenditures exceed its revenues in any year; and the public debt at any time is the sum of the Federal government's previous annual deficits (less any annual surpluses).

2. If the Federal government utilizes fiscal policy to combat recession and inflation its budget is not likely to be balanced in any particular year. Three budgetary philosophies may be adopted by the government; and the adoption of any of these philosophies will affect employment, real output, and the price level of the economy.

a. Proponents of an annually balanced budget would have government expenditures and tax revenues equal in every year; such a budget is pro- rather than countercyclical; but conservative economists favor it to prevent the expansion of the public sector (and the contraction of the private sector) of the economy without the increased payment of taxes by the public.

b. Those who advocate a cyclically balanced budget propose matching surpluses (in years of prosperity) with deficits (in depression years) to stabilize the economy; but there is no assurance that the surpluses will equal the deficits over the years.

c. Advocates of functional finance contend that deficits, surpluses, and the size of the debt are of minor importance; that the goal of full employment without inflation should be achieved regardless of the effects of the necessary fiscal policies upon the budget and the size of the public debt.

3. Any government deficit increases the size of the public debt; and the public debt has grown substantially since 1929.

a. The growth of the debt is the result of Federal borrowing during wartime and during recessions (when the built-in stability of economy generates budget deficits automatically); and in the early 1980s the debt grew as a result of reductions in tax rates without matching reductions in government expenditures.

b. The public debt currently exceeds $2 trillion dollars.

(1) The size of the debt as a percentage of the economy's GNP did not grow so rapidly as the absolute size of the debt between 1940 and 1985; but relative to the GNP it has increased significantly since the early 1970s.

(2) Since the early 1970s the interest payments on the debt (because of increases in the size of the debt and higher interest rates in the economy) have also increased significantly; and interest payments as a percentage of the economy's GNP have grown dramatically.

(3) About one-fourth of the public debt is owed to government agencies and the Federal Reserve Banks and three-fourths to others; but, more importantly, about 11% of it is owed to foreign citizens, firms, and governments.

(4) Because the accounting system used by the Federal government records its debts but not its assets the public debt is not a true picture of its financial position; and when adjusted for inflation, the decrease in the real value of its debt can exceed its nominal deficit and result in a real budget surplus.

4. The contentions that a large debt will eventually bankrupt the government and that borrowing to finance expenditures passes the cost onto future generations are false.

a. The debt cannot bankrupt the government

(1) because the government need not retire (reduce) the debt and can refund (or refinance) it; and

(2) because the government can always print (or create) money to pay both the principal and the interest on it.

b. The debt cannot shift the burdens of the debt to future generations because the debt is largely internally held, and repayment of any portion of the principal and the payment of interest on it does not reduce the wealth or purchasing power of Americans.

5. But the debt does create real and potential problems in the economy.

a. The payment of interest on the debt probably increases the extent of income inequality.

b. The payment of taxes to finance these interest payments may also reduce the incentives to bear risks, to innovate, to invest, and to save, and so slow economic growth in the economy.

c. The portion of the debt that is externally held requires the repayment of principal and the payment of interest to foreign citizens and institutions and transfers a part of the real output of the American economy to them.

d. An increase in government spending may or may not impose a burden on future generations.

(1) If the increase in government spending is financed by increased personal taxes, the burden of the increased spending is on the present generation whose consumption is reduced; but if it is financed by an increased public debt, the increased borrowing of the Federal government will raise interest rates, crowd-out investment spending, and future generations will inherit a smaller stock of capital goods.

(2) The burden imposed on future generations is lessened if the increase in government expenditures is for real or human capital or if the economy were initially operating at less than full employment (and it stimulates an increase in investment demand).

6. In the 1980s the Federal government has incurred deficits and the public debt has risen.

a. This has caused concern because the deficits and the increases in the public debt have grown larger, because interest costs of the debt have risen, and because the deficits have taken place in a peacetime economy operating close to full employment.

b. These large deficits have produced a cause-and-effect chain of events: they have increased interest rates; higher interest rates have crowded-out real private investment and made financial investment by foreigners in the United States more attractive; the latter increased the external debt of the United States and raised the international value of the dollar; and the latter reduced U.S. exports, expanded U.S. imports, and had a contractionary effect on employment and output in the American economy.

c. A number of remedies have been suggested to lessen the deficits and the increases in the public debt.

(1) One suggested remedy is an amendment to the U.S. Constitution that would require Congress to balance the Federal budget each year.

(2) Congress in December of 1985 passed the Gramm-Rudman Act which required it to reduce the deficits annually and to balance the budget by 1981 and which mandated automatic reductions in spending when Congress and the President cannot agree on how to achieve the targeted deficit reductions.

(3) Others would have Congress impose a value-added tax or a tax on imported oil or repeal earlier reductions in the tax rates on personal and corporate incomes.

(4) And the Reagan Administration has proposed privitization of some government assets and programs by selling them to private business firms.

d. Despite the problems associated with deficits and the public debt, private and public debt has an important role to play: it absorbs the saving done in a growing economy at full employment and sustains the aggregate expenditures of consumers, businesses, and governments at the full-employment level; and if consumers and firms do not borrow sufficient amounts, the public debt must be increased to maintain full employment and economic growth in the economy.

■ IMPORTANT TERMS

Budget deficit	**External debt**
Public debt	**Crowding-out effect**
Annually balanced budget	**Gramm-Rudman Act**
Cyclically balanced budget	**Privitization**
Functional finance	

■ FILL-IN QUESTIONS

1. The budget deficit of the Federal government in any year is equal to its (expenditures, revenues) Expenditures less its revenues in that year; and the public debt is equal to the sum of the Federal government's past budget deficits less its budget surpluses.

2. An annually balanced budget is (pro-, counter-) pro cyclical because governments tend to (raise, lower) increase taxes and to decrease their purchases of goods and services during a recession (and to do just the opposite during an inflation).

3. A cyclically balanced budget suggests that to ensure full employment without inflation, the government incur deficits during periods of recession and surpluses during periods of inflation with the deficits and surpluses equaling each other over the business cycle.

4. Functional finance has as its main goal the achievement of full employmt w/out inflation; and would regard budget ~~balances~~ deficits and increases in the public debt as of secondary importance.

5. The principal causes of the public debt are past ~~deficits~~ wars and recessions and recent discretionary reductions in tax rates.

6. The public debt of the United States is:

a. equal to about $ 2112 billion and about 46 % of the GNP, and the annual interest charges on this debt are about $ 140 billion and equal about 3.2 % of the GNP;

b. for the most part an (internal, external) internal debt.

7. About:

a. one-fourth of the public debt is owed to government agencies and to American (commercial, central) Central banks; and

b. about 11 % of this debt is owed to foreigners.

8. The accounting procedures used by the Federal government reflect its (assets, debts) debts but do not reflect its assets

a. Eisner and Pieper demonstrated that in 1980 the value of the government's assets was (greater, less) greater than the public debt.

b. They also showed that because inflation (increases, decreases) decreases the real value of the public debt, when the $61 billion (surplus, deficit) deficit of the Federal government in 1980 was adjusted for the change in the real value of the debt it ended up with a $7 billion Surplus

9. The possibility that the Federal government will go bankrupt is a false issue. It need not (reduce, refinance) reduce its debt; and it can retire maturing securities by refinancing them or by creating money

10. As long as the government expenditures which lead to the increase in the public debt are not financed by borrowing from foreigners, the public debt of the United States is also an asset of the American people who own government securities; and the cost of a government program financed by borrowing from the American public is equal to their decreased consumption of goods and services and is a burden on (the present, a future) present generation.

11. The public debt is a burden on an economy if it is (internally, externally) externally held. It and the payment of interest on it may, however, (increase, decrease) ~~decrease~~ increase income inequality in the economy, dampen the incentive to work, take risks, save, and invest in the economy, and have a ____ effect on investment.

12. A public debt which is internally held imposes a burden on future generations if the borrowing done to finance an increase in government expenditures (increases, decreases) ____ interest rates, ____ investment spending, and leaves future generations with a smaller stock of ____ goods.

a. But if the increased government expenditures are financed by an increase in the taxes on personal income, the present generation will have fewer ____ goods and the burden of the increased government expenditures will be on ____ generation.

b. These generalizations are subject to two qualifications: The size of the burden of increased government expenditures financed by borrowing on future generations is weakened if the government expenditures finance increases in physical or human ____ or if the economy had been operating at (full, less than full) ____ employment.

13. The increased concern of the public with Federal deficits and the expanding public debt in the 1980s is the result of the large ____ of these deficits, the increased interest ____ of the debt, and the fact that the economy was at (peace, war) ____ and operating close to ____.

14. The deficits of the Federal government tend to (increase, decrease) ____ interest rates in the money markets.

a. This change in interest rates (expands, contracts) ____ private investment spending and makes financial investments by foreigners in the U.S. (more, less) ____ attractive.

b. This change in the financial investments of foreigners in the U.S. (increases, decreases) ____ the external debts of the U.S. and (raises, lowers) ____ the international value of the dollar.

c. This change in the international value of the dollar (expands, contracts) ____ American exports, ____ American imports, and ____ net exports.

d. This change in American net exports has a(n) (expansionary, contractionary) ____ effect on real output and employment in the United States.

15. Four possible remedies for the large budget deficits of the Federal government are a ____ amendment requiring the Federal government to balance its budget annually, the ____ Act of 1985, an increase in ____, and the ____ of some of the assets and programs of the Federal government.

16. Public and private debts play a positive role if they absorb a sufficient amount of ____ to enable an economy that is (stationary, growing) ____ to remain at ____.

■ PROBLEMS AND PROJECTS

1. Columns (1) and (2) in the table below are the investment-demand schedule and show planned net investment (*I*) at different rates of interest (*i*). Assume the marginal propensity to consume in the economy is 0.8.

(1) *i*	(2) *I*	(3) *I'*
.08	$115	$125
.07	140	150
.06	165	175
.05	190	200
.04	215	225

a. If the Federal government were to spend an additional $20 for goods and services the equilibrium real NNP would (increase, decrease) ____ by $____

b. If the Federal government had obtained the additional $20 by

(1) increasing taxes by $20 the equilibrium real NNP would have (increased, decreased) ________ a total of $________;

(2) borrowing $20 in the money market and this borrowing had increased the interest rate from 5% to 6%,

(a) planned net investment spending would have (increased, decreased) ____________ by $____________,

(b) the equilibrium real NNP would have ____________ by $________, and

(c) the net effect of the increased government spending of the $20 borrowed in the money market would have been to ______________ the equilibrium real NNP by $________.

c. But if the government deficit-spending had improved business profit expectations and shifted the investment-demand schedule to the one shown in columns (1) and (3) in the table above the total effect of the increased government spending of the $20 borrowed in the money market would have been to ____________ the equilibrium real NNP by $________

■ SELF-TEST

Circle the T if the statement is true, the F if it is false.

1. The budget deficit of the Federal government in any year is equal to its revenues less its expenditures. T F

2. There is no assurance that a nation can both use fiscal policy to promote full employment and balance its budget cyclically. T F

3. Proponents of functional finance argue that a balanced budget, whether it is balanced annually or over the business cycle, is of minor importance when compared with the objective of full employment without inflation. T F

4. The primary reasons for the increase in the public debt since 1929 have been wars, recessions, and reductions in tax rates. T F

5. The public debt was about $1800 billion at the end of 1986. T F

6. Between 1940 and the present both the public debt and the interest charges on this debt as percentages of the GNP have decreased. T F

7. About one-tenth of the public debt is currently held by foreigners and about three-fourths of it is held by agencies of the Federal government and the American central banks. T F

8. Inflation increases the *real* value of the *nominal* public debt. T F

9. When adjusted for inflation, Eisner and Pieper found that the Federal government had a budget surplus rather than a budget deficit in 1980. T F

10. Selling government securities to foreigners to finance increased expenditures by the Federal government imposes a burden on future generations. T F

11. The crowding-out effect of borrowing in the money market to finance an increase in government expenditures is the result of the rise in interest rates in these markets. T F

12. Financing increased government expenditures by increasing personal taxes imposes a burden on future generations. T F

13. Crowding-out shifts the investment-demand curve to the left. T F

14. Higher interest rates in the United States not only crowd-out real investment but make financial investment by foreigners in the United States less attractive. T F

15. Increases in the international value of the dollar tend to have an expansionary effect on output and employment in the United States. T F

16. Privitization would allow the Federal government to acquire the assets of profitable privately owned business firms in order to increase the revenues and reduce the budget deficits of the Federal government. T F

17. The amount of saving done at full employment increases in a growing economy. T F

18. To maintain full employment in a growing economy it is necessary for the total of public and private debt to increase. T F

Circle the letter that corresponds to the correct answer.

1. The public debt is the sum of all previous (*a*) expenditures of the Federal government; (*b*) budget deficits of the Federal government; (*c*) budget deficits less the budget surpluses of the Federal government; (*d*) budget surpluses less the budget deficits of the Federal government.

2. Which of the following would involve reducing government expenditures and increasing tax rates during a depression? (*a*) An annually balanced budget policy; (*b*) functional finance; (*c*) a cyclically balanced budget policy; (*d*) a policy employing built-in stability.

3. As a percentage of the gross national product, the public debt and interest on the debt are, respectively, about (*a*) 50% and 1%; (*b*) 50% and 2%; (*c*) 45% and 2%; (*d*) 45% and 3%.

4. The annual interest payments on the public debt today are about (*a*) $140 billion; (*b*) $120 billion; (*c*) $100 billion; (*d*) $80 billion.

5. Since 1980 (*a*) both the public debt and the interest charges on the debt relative to the GNP have increased; (*b*) the public debt relative to the GNP has decreased and the interest charges on the debt relative to the GNP have increased; (*c*) the public debt relative to the GNP has increased and the interest charges on the debt relative to the GNP have decreased; (*d*) both the public debt and the interest charges on the debt relative to the GNP have decreased.

6. The accounting procedures used by the Federal government record (*a*) only its assets; (*b*) only its debts; (*c*) both its assets and debts; (*d*) its net worth.

7. Inflation is a tax on (*a*) the holders of the public debt and reduces the size of a budget deficit; (*b*) the holders of the public debt and expands the size of a budget deficit; (*c*) the Federal government and reduces the size of a budget deficit; (*d*) the Federal government and expands the size of a budget deficit.

8. The public debt cannot bankrupt the Federal government because the Federal government (*a*) need not reduce the size of the debt; (*b*) is able to refinance the debt; (*c*) can create money to repay the debt and pay the interest on it; (*d*) all of the above.

9. Incurring an internal debt to finance a war does not pass the cost of the war on to future generations because: (*a*) the opportunity cost of the war is borne by the generation that fights it; (*b*) the government need not pay interest on internally held debts; (*c*) there is never a need for government to refinance the debt; (*d*) wartime inflation reduces the relative size of the debt.

10. Which of the following would be a consequence of the retirement of the internally held portion of the public debt? (*a*) A reduction in the nation's productive capacity; (*b*) a reduction in the nation's standard of living; (*c*) a redistribution of the nation's wealth among its citizens; (*d*) an increase in aggregate expenditures in the economy.

11. Which of the following is an important consequence of the public debt of the United States? (*a*) It increases incentives to work and invest; (*b*) it transfers a portion of the American output of goods and services to foreign nations; (*c*) it reduces income inequality in the United States; (*d*) it leads to greater saving at every level of disposable income.

12. The crowding-out effect of borrowing in the money market to finance an increase in government expenditures (*a*) reduces current private investment expenditures; (*b*) decreases the rate at which the privately owned stock of real capital increases; (*c*) imposes a burden on future generations; (*d*) does all of the above.

13. The crowding-out effect of government borrowing to finance its increased expenditures is reduced (*a*) when the economy is operating at less than full employment; (*b*) when the expenditures expand human capital in the economy; (*c*) when the government's deficit financing improves the profit expectations of business firms; (*d*) when any one or more of the above are true.

14. Which one of the following is *not* one of the sources of the recent concern with the deficits of the Federal government and the growth of the public debt? (*a*) The large increases in the size of the deficits and in the public debt; (*b*) the operation of the economy substantially below full employment; (*c*) the mounting interest costs of the debt; (*d*) the fact that the nation was not at war.

15. The increased foreign demand for American securities that results from higher interest rates in the United States (*a*) increases the external debts of the United States and the international value of the dollar; (*b*) increases the external debts of the United States and decreases the international value of the dollar; (*c*) decreases the external debts of the United States and increases the international value of the dollar; (*d*) decreases the external debts of the United States and the international value of the dollar.

16. When the international value of the dollar rises (*a*) American exports tend to increase; (*b*) American imports tend to decrease; (*c*) American net exports tend to decrease; (*d*) all of the above tend to occur.

17. The Gramm-Rudman Act of 1985 requires that (*a*) the sizes of the Federal budget deficits be reduced annually; (*b*) the Federal budget be balanced by 1991; (*c*) the expenditures of the Federal government be automatically reduced if Congress and the President cannot agree on how to reach the targeted reductions in the budget deficits; (*d*) all of the above.

18. Suppose the multiplier is 3. Were the amount of saving done at full employment to increase by $20 and were private borrowing to increase by $5, to maintain full employment the public debt would have to increase by: (*a*) $5; (*b*) $15; (*c*) $45; (*d*) $60.

■ DISCUSSION QUESTIONS

1. What is the difference between the (Federal) budget deficit and the public debt.

2. Explain why an annually balanced budget is not "neutral" and how it can intensify, rather than reduce, the tendencies for NNP to rise and fall.

3. How does a cyclically balanced budget philosophy differ from the philosophy of functional finance? Why do advocates of functional finance argue that budget deficits and a mounting national debt are of secondary importance?

4. How big is the public debt of the United States absolutely and relative to the GNP? How large are the interest payments on this debt absolutely and relative to the GNP? What has happened to the size of the debt and the interest payments on it absolutely and relatively since 1930 and since 1980? Why have these changes occurred?

5. In what way do the accounting procedures of the Federal government misstate its actual financial position (its net worth)? How does inflation affect the *real* size of the public debt and the real size of the Federal government's budget deficits?

6. Why can't the public debt result in the bankruptcy of the Federal government?

7. Explain the difference between an internally held and an externally held public debt. If the debt is internally held government borrowing to finance a war does not pass the cost of the war on to future generations. Why?

8. How does the public debt and the payment of interest on this debt affect (*a*) the distribution of income and (*b*) incentives? Why does the portion of the public debt externally held impose a burden on the economy?

9. How can deficit financing impose a burden on future generations? Why don't increases in government expenditures financed by increased personal taxes impose the same burden on future generations? What will lessen the burden on future generations of deficit financing?

10. What heightened the concern of the public in the early 1980s over budget deficits and the increase in the public debt? How do budget deficits (and the increase in the public debt) affect (*a*) interest rates; (*b*) planned domestic investment in real capital and the financial investment of foreigners in American securities; (*c*) the external debts of the United States and the international value of the dollar; (*d*) American exports and imports of goods and services; and (*e*) employment and real output in the American economy?

11. Explain the remedies that have been suggested for the Federal budget deficits and the increasing public debt. What were the chief provisions of the Gramm-Rudman Act of 1985?

12. What tends to happen to the amount of saving done at full employment as the full-employment real NNP grows? Why, in a growing economy, must debt increase in order to maintain full employment and economic growth?

16
Inflation, unemployment, and aggregate supply

Not too many years ago most economists believed that it was possible for the American economy to have both full employment and stable prices. This belief was based on the assumption that the price level would not rise until the labor force was fully employed. All that was necessary if there was to be full employment without inflation was just the right level of aggregate expenditures. Fiscal and monetary policy, thought economists, could be used to assure that aggregate demand was adequate but not excessive.

But the assumption which was the basis of the economists' belief that monetary and fiscal policy could guarantee a stable price level and the full employment of the labor force was not at all realistic. The price level rises before full employment is achieved; and the closer the economy moves to full employment the more rapid appears to be the rate at which prices rise. This premature inflation (that is, inflation *before* full employment is reached) seems to be the result of the ability of big unions to raise wage rates, of the power of big business firms to raise prices, and of the fact that some types of labor become fully employed while other kinds of workers have not yet all found jobs. But no matter what the causes of this premature inflation, the economy found itself on the spot. It could have full employment with inflation or it could have stable prices with unemployment; *but* it could not have both full employment and stable prices.

Was there any way for the economy to avoid this problem? It might have been possible for the economy to avoid both horns of this dilemma. But whether the market policies and the wage-price policies (discussed in this chapter) would have enabled us to escape from both inflation and unemployment is doubtful.

While this problem and the policy dilemma it created were bad enough, an even worse problem emerged in the United States during the 1970s. This was the problem of stagflation. Rising prices were accompanied not by falling but by rising unemployment rates. This inflation was not the result of excessively high levels of aggregate expenditures and the failure to utilize fiscal and monetary policies to control these expenditures. It was the consequence of decreases in aggregate supply rather than increases in aggregate demand.

When the aggregate-supply curve moves upward (that is, when aggregate supply decreases), the equilibrium price level in the economy will increase and the equilibrium real output will decrease. As a direct result the employment of workers declines: the unemployment rate rises. Rising prices and rising unemployment rates were the experience of the American economy in the 1970s and early 1980s and this *is* stagflation.

The group of economists who explained stagflation by emphasizing the decreases in aggregate supply are labeled supply-side economists; and their brand of economics has been called supply-side economics. This breed of economist pointed to the role of the Federal government in decreasing aggregate supply; and their remedies for stagflation, often referred to as Reaganomics, are less government regulation and massive reductions in personal and corporate taxes.

In sympathy with the contention of the supply-side economists that the Federal government was the chief cause of stagflation are the economists who are called accelerationists (because they accept the accelerationist hypothesis) and rational-expectation theorists. Both contend that the downsloping Phillips Curve is a figment of Keynesian imagination; that it is actually a vertical line; and that government attempts to reduce the unemployment rate below the rate at which the vertical Phillips Curve meets the horizontal axis produce a higher rate of inflation. The only difference between the accelerationists and the rational-expectations theorists is that the former believe that expansionary monetary or fiscal policies can bring about a temporary decline in the unemployment rate and the latter argue that such policies do not even reduce the unemployment rate temporarily.

Whether the supply-side economists and the policies of the Reagan Administration or their Keynesian critics are right is more than a theoretical detail. It is a matter of great practical importance. The selection of the correct policies for controlling inflation and reducing unemployment depends upon it. But regardless of which view and set of policies is correct, the macroeconomic events of the past twenty years in the United States have taught Americans a lot about the problems of unemployment and inflation and of controlling them.

■ CHECKLIST

When you have studied this chapter you should be able to:

☐ Explain how Keynesian analysis was able to conclude that the economy could achieve both full employment and stable prices; and what was needed to reach these two goals simultaneously.

☐ Use the aggregate demand-aggregate supply model to explain and distinguish demand-pull and cost-push inflation.

☐ Draw a traditional Phillips Curve (after properly labeling the two axes); and explain how to derive this curve by using the aggregate demand-aggregate supply model.

☐ Explain what is meant by premature inflation; and state the two basic causes of the premature inflation shown on the Phillips Curve.

☐ Explain and use the Phillips Curve to illustrate the stabilization policy dilemma.

☐ Define stagflation; and contrast stagflation with the relationship shown by a Phillips Curve.

☐ Enumerate the supply-side shocks experienced by the American economy in the 1970s and early 1980s; and use the aggregate demand-aggregate supply model to explain why these shocks led to stagflation.

☐ Explain why demand-management policies cannot reduce or eliminate stagflation.

☐ State the accelerationist hypothesis and the rational-expectations theory; and explain how the economists who employ this hypothesis and this theory come to the conclusion that the Phillips Curve is vertical.

☐ State the two kinds of market policies that might be used to combat stagflation.

☐ Distinguish between wage-price guideposts and wage-price controls; and explain why they are called income policies.

☐ Explain what the advocates of supply-side economics see as the three basic causes of stagflation in the American economy; and the four policies advocated by the Reagan Administration to deal with this stagflation.

☐ Criticize the program of the Reagan Administration (Reaganomics) and evaluate the effectiveness of that program.

☐ List the three macroeconomic lessons of the 1970s and early 1980s.

■ CHAPTER OUTLINE

1. In the Keynesian expenditures-output model it is possible for the economy to experience either a recession or inflation and to achieve both full employment and a stable price level simultaneously; but to understand stagflation it is necessary to use the aggregate demand-aggregate supply model.

2. Aggregate demand and aggregate supply determine the real national output (and employment) and the price level of the economy.

a. In the intermediate range along the aggregate-supply curve, an increase in aggregate demand results in a higher level of output (and employment) and demand-pull inflation; but a decrease in aggregate supply results in a lower level of output (and employment) and cost-push inflation.

b. In the real world it is difficult to distinguish between the two kinds of inflation and difficult to control inflation; and while cost-push inflation tends to be self-limiting, demand-pull inflation continues as long as aggregate demand continues to increase.

3. If aggregate supply is constant and the economy is operating in the intermediate range on the aggregate-supply curve, the greater the rate of increase in aggregate demand the greater is the rate of increase in the price level and in real output, and the lower is the rate of unemployment (and *vice versa*); and there is, therefore, an inverse relationship (or tradeoff) called the Phillips Curve between the inflation rate and the unemployment rate.

a. There are at least two reasons why inflation occurs before the economy reaches full employment.

(1) Scarcities of some kinds of labor develop before the economy's entire labor force is fully employed; and these scarcities increase wage rates, production costs, and prices.

(2) Labor unions and business firms have market power and they raise wage rates and prices as the economy approaches full employment.

b. While fiscal and monetary policy can be employed to manage aggregate demand and to affect unemployment and the rate of inflation, the nation faces a serious policy dilemma: full employment without inflation and price stability without unemployment are impossible and the nation must choose one of the combinations of inflation and unemployment that lies on the Phillips Curve.

c. Events in the 1960s seemed to confirm the inverse relationship between the unemployment and inflation rates; but the relationship is complicated by the downward inflexibility of prices (the reversibility problem) and by shifts in aggregate supply.

4. In the 1970s and early 1980s, however, the American economy experienced both higher rates of inflation and greater unemployment rates; and this stagflation suggests either that there is no dependable relationship between the inflation and unemployment rates or that the Phillips Curve had shifted to the right.

a. During these years six cost- or supply-side shocks decreased aggregate supply (moved the aggregate-supply curve upward) to increase both prices and unemployment in the United States; and the experiences of the American economy suggest that the Phillips Curve is not a stable relationship and cannot be used as the basis for economic policy.

b. Demand-management policies are not an effective means of treating stagflation: restricting aggregate demand will increase unemployment without lowering the price level (because of the reversibility problem) and stimulating aggregate demand will increase the price level without reducing unemployment (because it induces offsetting effects on the supply side).

5. The accelerationist hypothesis is that an increase in aggregate demand sponsored by government which reduces unemployment and increases the price level also reduces the real wages of workers who demand and obtain higher nominal wages; this expands unemployment to its original level; the process is repeated when government again tries to reduce unemployment; and the rise in the price level accelerates. The downsloping Phillips Curve does not, in short, exist; and the real Phillips Curve is a vertical line.

6. In the rational-expectations theory workers anticipate that government policies to reduce unemployment will also be inflationary, and they increase their nominal wage demands to offset the anticipated inflation; and not even temporary increases in employment will occur.

7. Because of the ineffectiveness of demand-management policies in coping with stagflation, the American economy has sought other kinds of policies to prevent decreases in or to increase aggregate supply (to shift the Phillips Curve to the left).

a. Market policies try to eliminate the causes of premature inflation and include:

(1) manpower policies to reduce the scarcities of particular kinds of labor that occur before the labor force is fully employed;

(2) pro-competition policies to reduce the power of labor unions and business firms to raise wage rates and prices.

b. Wage-price (or incomes) policies restrict increases in wages and prices by utilizing either guideposts or controls.

(1) Wage-price guideposts are voluntary restraints. The Kennedy-Johnson guideposts restricted money-wage increases in all industries to the rate at which the productivity of labor in the economy had increased; and allowed an industry to increase the price of its product by an amount equal to the increase in its unit labor cost.

(2) Wage-price controls are mandatory (or legal) restraints; and were employed in 1971 to deal with stagflation in the American economy.

(3) Whether to employ wage-price policies has been a vigorously debated issue; and the proponents and opponents have based their arguments on the questions of workability and compliance, allocative efficiency, and economic freedom of choice.

(4) To improve the effectiveness of income policies it has been suggested that special tax rebates be given to (tax penalties imposed on) those who comply with (ignore) the guideposts.

c. Supply-side economists argue that the Keynesians have overemphasized the aggregate-demand side and neglected the aggregate-supply side in their explanation of the price level and unemployment.

(1) Taxes, they argue, are business costs and increased taxes result in an upward shift in aggregate supply.

(2) They also argue that taxes and transfer payments reduce the incentives to work, to save, and to invest and lead to a misallocation of resources which reduces aggregate supply.

(3) And the increased regulation of industry has adversely affected costs and productivity.

d. Reaganomics was based on supply-side economics and was the policies of the Reagan Administration to reduce almost all government spending (except defense expenditures), reduce government regulation of private business firms, prevent the growth in the money supply from being inflationary, and reduce personal and corporate income tax rates.

(1) Sizable reductions in personal and business tax rates were contained in the Economic Recovery Tax Act of 1981 and were aimed at increasing aggregate supply to bring about a reduction in the rates of inflation and unemployment (and an expansion in real output); and Professor Laffer contended that this would increase tax revenues and prevent inflationary government deficits.

(2) But critics replied that these tax-rate reductions would have little effect on incentives (and would be slow to expand national output), would so increase aggregate demand (relative to supply) that large budget deficits and more rapid inflation would result, would actually decrease tax revenues, and would increase income inequality.

e. While the programs of the Reagan Administration reduced the inflation rate sharply, they appear to have brought on a sharp recession between 1980 and 1982, increased the budget deficits of the Federal government, failed to increase tax revenues, may have crowded-out private investment, and have not increased saving and investment or incentives to work; and the recovery of the economy since 1982 can be attributed to the expansionary effects of the budget deficit.

8. From the American economic experiences of the last one and one-half decades or two have emerged three lessons.

a. Macroeconomic instability in the American economy is more and more related to events outside the United States.

b. Expectations of inflation lead to inflation and make inflation difficult to control.

c. Both aggregate demand and aggregate supply affect output, employment, and the price level of an economy; and both demand-side and supply-side policies have limitations and effects on the other side of a market economy.

■ IMPORTANT TERMS

Demand-pull inflation
Cost-push inflation
Premature inflation
Phillips Curve
Stagflation
Stabilization policy dilemma
Reversibility problem
Supply-side shock
Accelerationist hypothesis
Rational-expectations theory
Wage-price controls
Inflationary expectations
Market policies
Wage-price (incomes) policy
Wage-price guideposts
Wage guidepost
Price guidepost
Tax-based income policy (TIP)
Supply-side economics
Tax "wedge"
Reaganomics
Economic Recovery Tax Act (ERTA)
Tax-transfer disincentives
Laffer Curve

■ FILL-IN QUESTIONS

1. In the Keynesian view, the price level of the economy would not increase until the economy reached ____________ and inflation was the result of (excess, insufficient) ____________ aggregate demand; and the economy can have (either, both) ____________ unemployment or/and inflation.

2. In the aggregate demand-aggregate supply model, when the economy is producing in the intermediate range along the aggregate-supply curve:

a. An increase in aggregate demand will (increase, decrease) ____________ real output and employment and result in ____________ inflation.

b. A decrease in aggregate supply will ____________ real output and employment and result in ____________ inflation.

3. If aggregate supply remains constant, along the intermediate range of aggregate supply:

a. the greater the increase in aggregate demand, the (greater, smaller) ____________ will be the increase in the price level, the greater will be the increase in real output, and the less will be the unemployment rate;

b. there will be a(n) (direct, inverse) inverse relationship between the rate of inflation and the unemployment rate.

4. Premature inflation:

a. means that prices rise before FE is reached

b. is the result of the market power of business firms and labor unions and of imbalances or bottlenecks in labor markets.

5. The Phillips Curve:

a. is the relation between the annual rate of increase in the price level and the unemployment rate;

b. has a (positive, negative) negative slope.

6. The policy dilemma faced by the American economy is that:

a. to have full employment it must also have inflation and to have stable prices it must tolerate UE

b. to reduce the unemployment rate the rate of inflation must (increase, decrease) increase and to reduce the rate of inflation the unemployment rate must increase

7. Demand-management policies can be used to (shift the Phillips Curve, select a point on the Phillips Curve) select a pt. on the Phillips Curve

8. List the six factors (supply-side shocks) that shifted the Phillips Curve to the right after 1972.

a. rise in oil prices of OPEC

b. ↑ in ag prices

c. devaluation of $$

d. abandonment of wage-price controls

e. fall in rate of growth of labor pro.

f. inflationary expectations

9. In the equation that relates unit labor costs to money-wage rates and the productivity of labor:

a. If the rate at which money wages increase is greater than the rate at which productivity increases, unit labor costs will (increase, decrease) increases

b. If the productivity of labor decreases and money-wage rates are constant, unit labor costs will increases

10. The expectation of inflation by workers and employers leads to (higher, lower) higher wage rates and in turn to a (rise, fall) rise in production costs, to a(n) (increase, decrease) decrease in aggregate supply, to a (higher, lower) higher price level, and to a higher rate of unemployment in the economy.

11. The rising unemployment rates and the sharp inflation following the supply-side shocks can be understood by using the aggregate demand-aggregate supply model.

a. The shocks (increased, decreased) decreased aggregate supply.

b. Which in turn increased both the price level and the unemployment rate.

c. And these two events when they occur simultaneously are called stagflation

12. The stagflation of the 1970s led:

a. some economists to believe that the Phillips Curve had shifted to the (right, left) right;

b. and other economists to conclude that the conventional downsloping Phillips Curve did not exist

13. It is the contention of those who accept

a. the accelerationist hypothesis that:

(1) the Phillips Curve is actually a (vertical, horizontal) vertical line at an unemployment rate that is (greater, less) less than the

unemployment rate government would like to achieve; and

(2) attempts by government to reduce the unemployment rate bring about a rate of inflation that (increases, decreases) increases ________

b. the rational expectations theory that:

(1) attempts by government to reduce the unemployment rate lead workers to anticipate perfectly the amount of inflation ________ this will cause and to keep their (real, nominal) real ________ wages constant they obtain a(n) (increase, decrease) increase ________ in their nominal ________ wages; and

(2) this brings about (a rise, a fall, no change) a rise ________ in the price level and no Δ ________ in the unemployment rate.

14. Three kinds of economic policies might be used to deal with stagflation.

a. These three policies are ________ policies, ________-________ policies, and the policies identified with ________ economics.

b. If effective, these policies would move the Phillips Curve to the (right, left) ________

15. Market policies to reduce unemployment include:

a. those designed to reduce bottlenecks in labor markets and are called ________ policies; and

b. those aimed at reducing the market power of business firms and labor unions and are called pro-________ policies.

16. Wage-price policies:

a. are sometimes called ________ policies;

b. involve either:

(1) wage-price (controls, guideposts) ________ which rely upon the voluntary cooperation of labor unions and business firms

(2) or wage-price ________ which have the force of law to make them effective.

17. The wage-price guideposts for curbing inflation during the Kennedy-Johnson administrations limited *wage* increases in an industry to the overall rate of increase in the ________ of labor and limited *price* increases to an amount equal to the increase in ________ costs in that industry.

18. It is the view of supply-side economists that:

a. business costs and product prices have increased because

(1) government has raised taxes and these taxes are a business ________ and a "________" between the price of a product and the cost of resources;

(2) high marginal tax rates reduce ________ to work, save, invest, and take risks; and

(3) increased government ________ of industry has increased its productivity;

b. the remedy for stagflation is a substantial (increase, decrease) ________ in taxes.

19. The program of the Reagan Administration ("Reaganomics") to reduce inflation and unemployment in the economy had four principal elements. These were

a. ________

b. ________

c. ________

d. ________

20. What three lessons have emerged from American macroeconomic experiences during the last fifteen to twenty years?

a. ________

b. ________

c. ________

■ PROBLEMS AND PROJECTS

1. On the next page is a traditional Phillips Curve.

* there is a trade-off between the two

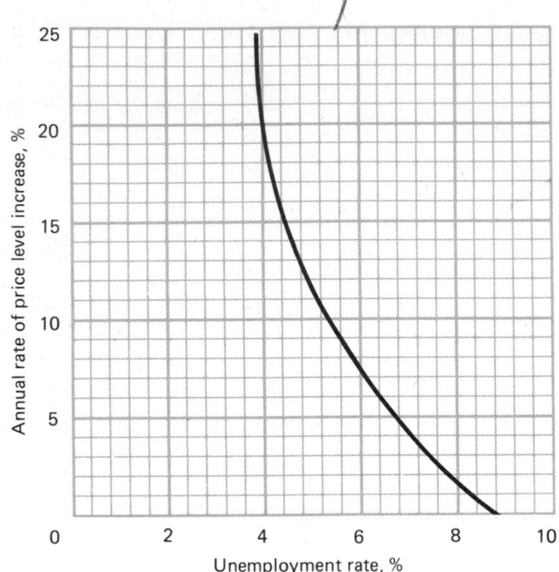

a. At full employment (a 4% unemployment rate) the price level would rise by 20 % each year.

b. If the price level were stable (increasing by 0% a year) the unemployment rate would be 9 %.

c. Which of the combinations along the Phillips Curve would you choose for the economy? ________

Why would you select this combination? ________

____

2. In columns (1) and (2) of the table below is a portion of an aggregate-supply schedule. Column (3) shows the number of full-time workers (in millions) that would have to be employed to produce each of the seven real national outputs (in billions) in the aggregate-supply schedule. The labor force is 80 million workers and the full-employment output of the economy is $________

a. If the aggregate-demand schedule were that shown by columns (1) and (4):

(1) The price level would be $________ and the real output would be $________

(2) the number of workers employed would be ________, the number of workers unemployed would be ________, and the unemployment *rate* would be ________ percent.

b. If aggregate demand were to increase to that shown in columns (1) and (5) and aggregate supply remained constant:

(1) the price level would rise to $________ and the real output would rise to $________

(2) employment would increase by ________ workers and the unemployment rate would fall to ________%.

(3) the price level has increased by and the rate of inflation has been ________%.

c. If aggregate demand were to decrease to that shown in columns (1) and (6) and aggregate supply remained constant:

(1) the price level would fall to $________ and the real output would fall to $________

(2) employment would decrease by ________

(1) Price level	(2) Real output produced	(3) Employment	(4) Real output purchased	(5) Real output purchased	(6) Real output purchased
$3	$ 800	69	$2300	$2600	$1900
4	1300	70	2200	2500	1800
5	1700	72	2100	2400	1700
6	2000	75	2000	2300	1600
7	2200	78	1900	2200	1500
8	2300	80	1800	2100	1400
9	2300	80	1700	2000	1300

workers and the unemployment rate would rise to ________________%.

(3) the price level has decreased and the rate of inflation has been (positive, negative) ________________

3. On the graph below are two aggregate-demand and two aggregate-supply curves. If aggregate demand is D_1, and aggregate supply is S_1, the equilibrium price level is ________________ and the equilibrium real output is ________________

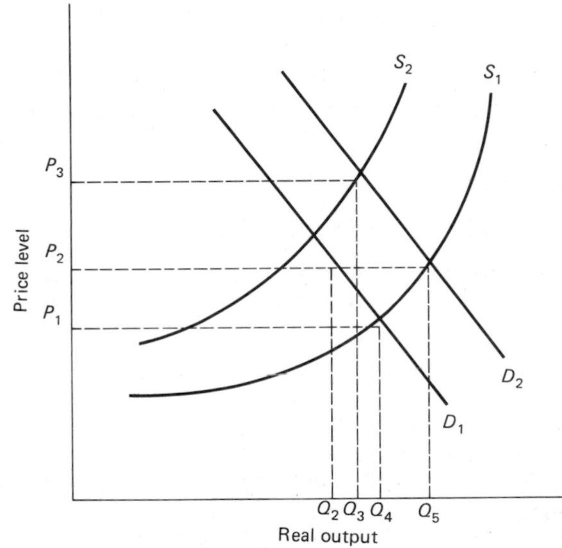

a. Suppose that to increase the real output of the economy and to reduce the unemployment rate the Federal government uses fiscal and monetary policies to increase aggregate demand from D_1 to D_2.

(1) If aggregate supply remains fixed at S_1,

(*a*) the price level will (rise, fall) ________________ to ________________;

(*b*) the output of the economy will ________________ to ________________; and

(*c*) the unemployment rate will ________________

(2) But, if aggregate supply were to decrease from S_1 to S_2 when the aggregate demand increases from D_1 to D_2,

(*a*) the price level will (rise, fall) ________________ to ________________;

(*b*) the output of the economy will ________________ to ________________; and

(*c*) the unemployment rate will ________________

b. Suppose that aggregate demand had increased from D_1 to D_2 while aggregate supply remained at S_1 and the price level had risen to P_2; and that to reduce inflation in the economy the Federal government had used fiscal and monetary policies to decrease aggregate demand from D_2 to D_1.

(1) If prices were *flexible* downward,

(*a*) the price level would fall from P_2 to ________________;

(*b*) the output of the economy would ________________ to ________________; and

(*c*) the unemployment rate would ________________

(2) But if prices were *inflexible* downward,

(*a*) the price level would remain at P_2;

(*b*) the output of the economy would ________________ to ________________; and

(*c*) the unemployment rate would ________________

(3) When prices are inflexible rather than flexible downward, the effects of a decrease in aggregate demand on

(*a*) the price level is (smaller, larger) ________________; and

(*b*) output and unemployment is ________________

4. Assume that the overall rate of increase in the productivity of labor in the economy is 4% per year.

a. The general level of wages in the economy can increase by ________________% a year without increasing unit labor costs and inducing cost-push inflation.

b. If the wage rate were increased by this percentage,

(1) In an industry in which the productivity of labor had increased 3%, labor costs per unit would (increase, decrease) ________________ by ________________%; and the application of the Kennedy-Johnson price guidepost would permit the price of the product produced by this industry to (rise, fall) ________________ by ________________%.

(2) In an industry in which the productivity of labor had increased by 6%, labor costs per unit would __________ by __________%; and the price guidepost would permit the price of the product to __________ by __________%.

(3) In an industry in which the productivity of labor had *decreased* by 2%, labor costs per unit would __________ by ______%; and the price guidepost would permit the price of the product to __________ by ______%.

■ SELF-TEST

Circle the T if the statement is true, the F if it is false.

1. In the Keynesian expenditures-output model the aggregate-supply curve has no intermediate range. T F

2. The Keynesian model is a reasonably satisfactory explanation of the macroeconomic behavior of the American economy between 1930 and 1970, but does not explain the stagflation of the 1970s and early 1980s. T F

3. Cost-push inflation is accompanied by increases in real output and employment. T F

4. It is usually not too difficult to determine whether the inflation experienced by an economy is demand-pull or cost-push inflation. T F

5. Cost-push inflation tends to be self-limiting. T F

6. When aggregate supply is constant, higher rates of inflation are accompanied by higher rates of unemployment. T F

7. According to the conventional Phillips Curve the rate of inflation increases as the level of unemployment decreases. T F

8. As the economy approaches full employment, some types of labor become fully employed before all of the labor force is fully employed. T F

9. Prices in the American economy tend to be flexible upward and inflexible downward. T F

10. Stagflation refers to a situation in which both the price level and the unemployment rate are rising. T F

11. The Phillips Curve seems to have shifted to the right during the 1970s and early 1980s. T F

12. Expectations of inflation induce workers to demand and their employers to pay them higher money wages. T F

13. When the nominal wage rate increases at a rate greater than the rate at which the productivity of labor increases, the unit labor cost will rise. T F

14. If the nominal wage rate increases by 8% and the productivity of labor remains constant, unit labor costs will rise by 8%. T F

15. Because of the negative slope of the Phillips Curve fiscal and monetary policies cannot be used to increase employment or to reduce the rate of inflation in the economy. T F

16. Accelerationists contend that when the price level rises the conventional downsloping Phillips Curve moves to the left. T F

17. Rational-expectations theorists maintain that workers believe expansionary monetary and fiscal policies will be inflationary and lower their real wages and that the reaction of workers to these expectations results in higher nominal wages, higher labor costs, and no change in employment in the economy. T F

18. Of the policies that might be employed to deal with stagflation, the market, wage-price, and supply-side policies are designed to move the Phillips Curve to the left. T F

19. Application of the antitrust laws has proved effective in the past in curbing the market power of big business; and so it is a promising technique for fighting stagflation. T F

20. Voluntary restraint by business and labor leaders is not apt to be effective in preventing price and wage increases because such restraint requires them to abandon their major goals. T F

21. The wage-price guideposts of the Kennedy-Johnson administrations for preventing cost-push inflation were to limit wage increases to the overall rate of increase in labor productivity in the economy. T F

22. The tax-based incomes policy discussed in the text would impose a 3% surtax on the personal incomes of workers who receive wage increases in excess of those granted to them by the wage guidepost. T F

23. Supply-side economists contend that Keynesian economics is unable to explain stagflation because costs and aggregate supply play an "active" role in the Keynesian model. **T F**

24. The tax "wedge" to which supply-side economists refer is the difference between the price of a product and the cost of the economic resources required to produce it. **T F**

25. If the economy were at point *A* on the Laffer Curve shown below, a decrease in tax rates would increase tax revenues. **T F**

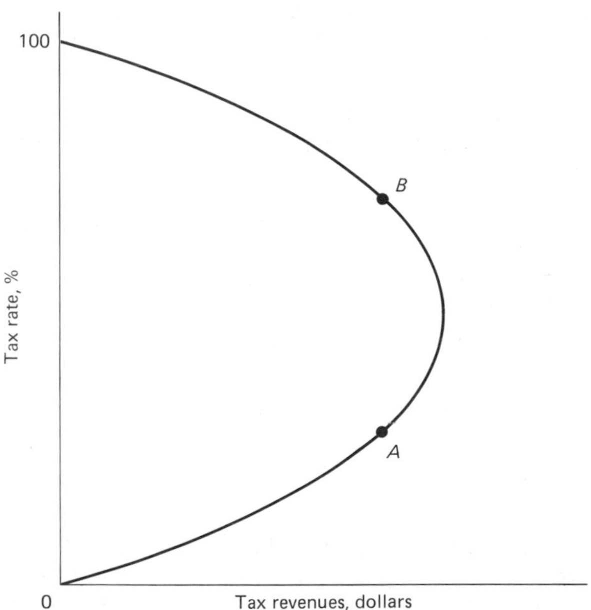

26. The supply-side economists believe that the economy is at a point such as point *B* on the Laffer Curve above, and that a substantial reduction in tax rates would both increase tax revenues and increase incentives to work, invest, innovate, and take risks. **T F**

Circle the letter that corresponds to the best answer.

1. In the Keynesian expenditures-output model it is impossible for the economy to experience (*a*) full employment; (*b*) inflation; (*c*) unemployment and inflation; (*d*) full employment and stable prices.

2. Demand-pull inflation is (*a*) the result of a decrease in aggregate demand; (*b*) accompanied by a decrease in real output and employment; (*c*) the result of the increased cost of producing goods and services; (*d*) may be accompanied by a decrease in the unemployment rate.

3. As long as aggregate supply remains constant and the economy operates along the intermediate range of the aggregate-supply curve, the greater the increase in aggregate demand (*a*) the greater is the increase in the price level; (*b*) the greater is the increase in the unemployment rate; (*c*) the smaller is the increase in real output; (*d*) the smaller is the increase in employment.

4. The conventional Phillips Curve (*a*) shows the inverse relation between the rate of increase in the price level and the unemployment rate; (*b*) makes it possible for the economy to achieve full employment and stable prices; (*c*) indicates that prices do not rise until full employment has been achieved; (*d*) slopes upward from left to right.

5. Labor-market adjustments do not eliminate bottleneck problems when there is less than full employment in the economy. Which of the following is *not* one of the reasons for these labor-market imbalances? (*a*) Unemployed workers often lack the skills or training needed for a new occupation; (*b*) the demand for workers in the markets in which there are labor shortages is inadequate; (*c*) there are artificial restrictions which prevent unemployed workers from filling the job openings; (*d*) unemployed workers do not know of the shortages of workers in other labor markets in the economy.

6. If inflation during periods of less than full employment is to be explained by market power, it must be assumed that: (*a*) only unions possess considerable market power; (*b*) only employers possess considerable market power; (*c*) both unions and employers possess considerable market power; (*d*) neither unions nor employers possess considerable market power.

7. The public policy dilemma illustrated by a Phillips Curve is the mutual inconsistency of: (*a*) more employment and price stability; (*b*) a higher unemployment rate and price stability; (*c*) inflation and more employment; (*d*) inflation and a lower unemployment rate.

8. Demand-management (monetary and fiscal) policies can be employed to (*a*) shift the Phillips Curve to the right; (*b*) shift the Phillips Curve to the left; (*c*) achieve full employment without inflation; (*d*) reduce the unemployment rate.

9. An increase in aggregate demand will increase the price level and decrease the unemployment rate; but if the increase in aggregate demand is accompanied by a decrease in aggregate supply (*a*) the increase in the price level will be smaller; (*b*) the decrease in the unemployment rate will be smaller; (*c*) the decrease in the unemployment rate will be larger; (*d*) the rate of inflation will be negative.

10. Which of the following was *not* one of the supply-side shocks to the American economy during the 1970s and early 1980s? (*a*) The imposition of wage and price controls; (*b*) the devaluation of the dollar; (*c*) the rise in the price charged by OPEC nations for oil; (*d*) worldwide agricultural shortfalls.

11. If the percentage change in the productivity of labor is 2% and the percentage change in nominal-wage rates is 5%, the percentage change in unit labor costs is (*a*) 1%; (*b*) 3%; (*c*) 7%; (*d*) 10%.

12. Suppose the overall rate of increase in the productivity of labor in the economy is 4%. If the productivity of labor in a particular industry has increased at a rate of only 3%, the Kennedy-Johnson wage-price guideposts would have allowed this industry (*a*) to increase both the wage rate and the price of its product by 3%; (*b*) to increase the wage rate by 3% and would have allowed no increase in price; (*c*) to increase the wage rate by 4% and would have allowed no increase in price; (*d*) to increase the wage rate by 4% and to increase price by about 1%.

13. A leftward shift in the aggregate-supply curve, aggregate demand remaining constant, will (*a*) decrease the price level; (*b*) decrease the unemployment rate; (*c*) increase real output; (*d*) increase both the price level and the unemployment rate.

14. A likely result of treating stagflation by stimulating aggregate demand with monetary and fiscal policies is (*a*) more inflation and less unemployment; (*b*) less inflation and more unemployment; (*c*) more inflation and more unemployment; (*d*) less inflation and unemployment.

15. A likely result of treating stagflation by restricting aggregate demand with monetary and fiscal policies is (*a*) a fall in the price level and the unemployment rate; (*b*) a rise in the price level and the unemployment rate; (*c*) no change in the price level and a fall in the unemployment rate; (*d*) no change in the price level and a rise in the unemployment rate.

16. In the view of the accelerationists, the long-run Phillips Curve is (*a*) horizontal; (*b*) vertical; (*c*) downsloping; (*d*) upsloping.

17. Accelerationists argue that if increases in nominal wage rates lag behind increases in the price level, when government attempts to reduce unemployment by using fiscal and monetary policies (*a*) employment and the price level rise in the long run; (*b*) employment remains constant and the price level rises in the short run; (*c*) employment rises and the price level remains constant in the short run; (*d*) employment remains constant and the price level rises in the long run.

18. The rational-expectations theorists contend that when government attempts to reduce unemployment by using fiscal and monetary policies (*a*) unemployment decreases temporarily and the price level rises; (*b*) unemployment decreases permanently and the price level rises; (*c*) unemployment decreases neither temporarily nor permanently and the price level rises; (*d*) unemployment decreases both temporarily and permanently and the price level falls.

19. Which of the following is *not* one of the *manpower* policies that might reduce stagflation? (*a*) Application of antimonopoly laws to labor unions; (*b*) removal of racial discrimination as an obstacle to employment; (*c*) improvement of the flow of job information between workers without jobs and employers with unfilled positions; (*d*) expansion of job training programs.

20. Which one of the following proposals for fighting stagflation is aimed more at demand-pull inflation than at cost-push inflation? (*a*) Restriction of aggregate expenditures; (*b*) restriction of the market power of labor unions; (*c*) restriction of the market power of business firms; (*d*) restriction by government of price and wage increases.

21. From the viewpoint of supply-side economists, stagflation is the result of excessive (*a*) taxes; (*b*) government regulation; (*c*) transfer payments; (*d*) all of the above.

22. Supply-side economists contend that the American system of taxes and transfer payments reduces incentives to (*a*) work; (*b*) save; (*c*) invest; (*d*) all of the above.

23. Which was *not* an element in the Reaganomics program for reducing stagflation in the American economy? (*a*) A reduction in defense expenditures; (*b*) a reduction in personal and corporate income tax rates; (*c*) a reduction in the regulation of private business firms; (*d*) a reduction in the rate of growth in the money supply.

24. Critics of the proposal of supply-side economists to reduce tax rates by a substantial percentage contend that decreased tax rates would (*a*) reduce aggregate demand and increase unemployment; (*b*) increase tax revenues; (*c*) have little effect on incentives; (*d*) all of the above.

25. During the 1980–1982 period the program of the Reagan administration reduced (*a*) unemployment; (*b*) the rate of inflation; (*c*) the Federal budget deficit; (*d*) all of the above.

26. Which of the following is *not* one of the economic lessons of the 1970s and early 1980s? (*a*) Both aggregate demand and aggregate supply affect the state of the macroeconomy; (*b*) expectations of inflation contribute to and make the control of inflation difficult; (*c*) American macroeconomic instability can often be traced to events outside of the U.S.; (*d*) central economic planning is the only means by which the economy's resources can be efficiently allocated and full employment without inflation achieved.

■ DISCUSSION QUESTIONS

1. Why does the Keynesian expenditures-output model imply that the economy may have either unemployment or inflation but will not experience unemployment and inflation simultaneously? What do Keynesians believe must be done if the economy is to realize full employment and stable prices simultaneously?

2. Use the aggregate demand-aggregate supply model to explain demand-pull and cost-push inflation and the differences between these two types of inflation.

3. What is a Phillips Curve? Explain how a Phillips Curve with a negative slope may be derived by holding aggregate supply constant and mentally increasing aggregate demand.

4. Explain what is meant by premature inflation and the two major causes of it.

5. What is the public policy dilemma illustrated by the Phillips Curve? Do demand-management (monetary and fiscal) policies enable the Federal government to move the curve or to move from one point to another point on the curve?

6. How do the "reversibility problem" and shifts in the aggregate-supply curve complicate the public policy dilemma imposed on the economy by the Phillips Curve?

7. Were the rates of inflation and of unemployment consistent with the Phillips Curve in the 1950s and 1960s? What do these two rates suggest about the curve in the 1970s and early 1980s?

8. What were the supply-side shocks to the American economy during the 1970s and early 1980s? How did these shocks affect aggregate supply and the Phillips Curve in the United States?

9. How do expectations of inflation and declines in the productivity of labor affect aggregate supply and the Phillips Curve?

10. When do increases in money-wage rates increase unit labor costs, decrease aggregate supply, and increase the price level in the economy?

11. What is stagflation? Why is it difficult to treat stagflation with demand-management policies?

12. What are the views of accelerationists on (*a*) the effects of expansionary monetary and fiscal policy on employment in the short run and the short-run Phillips Curve; and (*b*) the long-run Phillips Curve? How do they reach these conclusions?

13. How do rational-expectations theorists believe expansionary monetary and fiscal policy affects the price level and employment in the short run and in the long run? By what logic do they reach these conclusions and in what way do their conclusions differ from those of the accelerationists?

14. What are the two kinds of market policies that might be employed to shift the Phillips Curve to the left? Within each of these two categories, what specific things might be done to reduce the causes of premature inflation?

15. Explain (*a*) what is meant by wage-price policy; (*b*) why wage-price policy is often called incomes policy; and (*c*) the difference between wage-price guideposts and wage-price controls.

16. What (*a*) was the wage guidepost and (*b*) the price guidepost of the Kennedy-Johnson administrations? Why would adherence to these guideposts by labor and management have limited the rate of inflation?

17. What wages and prices were controlled during the Nixon Administration? Why did it seem necessary to control them?

18. State the cases *for* and *against* the use of wage-price (or incomes) policy to limit inflation. Build each case upon the three points around which the wage-price policy debate has centered.

19. How might a tax-based incomes policy be used to control increases in money-wage rates?

20. Why do supply-side economists believe Keynesian economics "does not come to grips with stagflation"? In the view of the supply-siders, what have been the three principal causes of stagflation in the United States?

21. What were the four major steps the Reagan administration proposed to increase employment and reduce inflation in the American economy?

22. Explain (*a*) the provisions of the Economic Recovery Tax Act of 1981 and (*b*) the Laffer Curve. Contrast the positions of the supply-side economists and Keynesians with respect to the act and the curve.

23. Criticize and defend the contention that Reaganomics has worked well to reduce stagflation in the United States.

24. What are the three economic lessons to be found in the macroeconomic events of the past fifteen or more years?

17
Money and banking

By and large, Chapter 17 is descriptive and factual. It contains only a brief explanation of how the financial system affects the operation of the economy. The purpose of this chapter is, however, to prepare you for a more detailed explanation (in Chapters 18 and 19).

Of special importance in this chapter are the many terms and definitions which will be new to you. These must be learned if the following two chapters and their analysis of how the financial system affects performance of the economy are to be understood. Chapter 17 also contains a factual description of the institutions which comprise the American financial system—the Board of Governors of the Federal Reserve System, the Federal Reserve Banks, the commercial banks, and the "thrifts"—and the functions of these four institutions.

You will do well to pay particular attention to the following. (1) What money is and the functions it performs, what types of money exist in the American economy and their relative importance, and how the three measures of the money supply (*M*1, *M*2, and *M*3) are defined; (2) what gives value to or "backs" American money; (3) why people want to have money in their possession and what determines how much money they want to have on hand at any time; (4) how the total demand for money and the money supply together determine the equilibrium rate of interest; and (5) the four principal institutions of the American financial system and their functions.

Several points are worth repeating here because so much depends upon their being fully understood. First, money is whatever performs the three functions of money, and in the United States money consists largely of the debts (promises to pay) of the Federal Reserve Banks and depository institutions. In the United States, this money is "backed" by the goods and services for which its owners can exchange it and not by gold.

Second, because money is used as a medium of exchange, consumers and business firms wish to have money on hand to use for transaction purposes; and the quantity of money they demand for this purpose is directly related to the size of the economy's money (or nominal) gross national product. This means that when either the price level or the real gross national product increases they will want to have more money on hand to use for transactions. But money is also used as a store of value: consumers and firms who own assets may choose to have some of their assets in the form of money (rather than in stocks, bonds, goods, or property). There is, therefore, also an asset demand for money. Holding money, however, imposes a cost on those who hold it. This cost is the interest they lose when they own money rather than (say) bonds. This means that people will demand less money for asset purposes when the rate of interest (the cost of holding money) is high and more when the rate of interest is low: the quantity of money demanded for this purpose is inversely related to the interest rate. The total demand for money is the sum of the transactions demand and the asset demand and, therefore, depends upon the money GNP and the rate of interest. This total demand and the money supply determine interest rates in the economy.

Third, the central bank in the United States is the twelve Federal Reserve Banks and the Board of Governors of the Federal Reserve System which oversees their operation. These banks, while privately owned by the commercial banks, are operated more or less as an agency of the Federal government not for profit, but primarily to regulate the nation's money supply in the best interests of the economy as a whole and secondarily to perform other services for the banks, the government, and the economy. They are able to perform their primary function because they are bankers' banks where depository institutions (commercial banks and the "thrifts") can deposit and borrow money. They do not deal directly with the public.

Fourth, these depository institutions accept deposits and make loans, but they also are literally able to create money by lending checkable deposits. Because they are able to do this, they have a strong influence on the size of the money supply and the value of money. The Federal Reserve Banks exist primarily to regulate the money supply and its value by influencing and controlling the amount of money depository institutions create.

■ CHECKLIST

When you have studied this chapter you should be able to:

☐ List the three functions of money; and explain the meaning of each function.

☐ Define the money supply, *M*1.

☐ Identify the four kinds of checkable deposits; and the four principal kinds of depository institutions.

☐ Explain the meaning of near-money and identify the principal near-monies; and then define *M*2 and *M*3.

☐ Present three reasons why near-monies are important.

☐ Explain why money in the American economy is debt; and whose debts paper money and checkable deposits are.

☐ Present three reasons why currency and checkable deposits are money and have value.

☐ Indicate the precise relationship between the value of money and the price level.

☐ Explain what is meant by stabilizing the value of money and enumerate the two devices government utilizes to try to stabilize its value.

☐ Identify the two demands for money and the determinant of each of these demands; and explain the relationship between each demand and its determinant.

☐ Explain what determines the equilibrium rate of interest; and how changes in the money GNP and in the money supply will affect this interest rate.

☐ Describe the structure of the American financial system.

☐ Explain why the Federal Reserve Banks are central, quasi-public, bankers' banks.

☐ Enumerate the five functions of the Federal Reserve System; explain the meaning of each of these functions; and indicate which is the most important.

■ CHAPTER OUTLINE

1. Money is whatever performs the three basic functions of money: a medium of exchange, a standard of value, and a store of value.

2. In the American economy money is whatever is generally used as a medium of exchange; and consists of the debts of the Federal government and of commercial banks and other financial institutions.

a. The narrowly defined money supply is called *M*1 and has two principal components.

(1) The smaller component is currency: coins which are token money and paper money largely in the form of Federal Reserve Notes.

(2) The larger and more important component is checkable deposits in commercial banks and savings institutions.

(3) These checkable deposits include demand deposits (checking accounts) and ATS accounts in commercial banks; and other deposits against which checks may be written (NOW accounts and share drafts) in such savings institutions as savings and loan associations, mutual savings banks, and credit unions.

(4) Currency and checkable deposits owned by the Federal government, commercial banks and savings institutions, and the Federal Reserve Banks are not, however, included in *M*1 or any of the more broadly defined money supplies.

b. *M*2 and *M*3 are the more broadly defined money supplies; and include not only the currency and checkable deposits in *M*1 but such near-monies as noncheckable savings deposits and time deposits in commercial banks and savings institutions.

c. The amount of these near-monies held by the public is important for at least three reasons.

d. Credit cards are not money but are a device by which the cardholders obtain a loan (credit) from the issuer of the card.

3. In the United States:

a. Money is the promise of a commercial bank, a savings (thrift) institution, or a Federal Reserve Bank to pay; but these debts cannot be redeemed for anything tangible.

b. Money has value only because people can exchange it for desirable goods and services.

c. The value of money is inversely related to the price level.

d. Money is "backed" by the confidence which the public has that the value of money will remain stable; and the

Federal government can use monetary and fiscal policy to keep the value of money relatively stable.

4. Business firms and households wish to hold and, therefore, demand money for two reasons.

a. Because they use money as a medium of exchange they have a transactions demand which is directly related to the money gross national product of the economy.

b. Because they also use money as a store of value they have an asset demand which is inversely related to the rate of interest.

c. Their total demand for money is the sum of the transactions and asset demands.

d. This total demand for money along with the supply of money determine the equilibrium interest rate in the money market of the economy.

5. The financial sector of the American economy has changed dramatically in recent years; and the Depository Institutions Deregulation and Monetary Control Act of 1980 narrowed the earlier differences between a commercial bank and the various thrift institutions.

a. But, despite the trend toward deregulation, the financial system remains centralized and regulated by government because the absence of centralization in the past led to an inappropriate supply of money, a multitude of different kinds of money, and a mismanagement of the money supply.

b. In the Federal Reserve System:

(1) The Board of Governors exercises control over the supply of money and the banking system.

(2) The Federal Reserve Banks are central, quasi-public, bankers' banks.

(3) Over 14,000 commercial banks exist in the American financial system; and some of them are state banks and some are national banks. But since 1980 the distinctions between state and national banks and between commercial banks and thrift institutions have all but been eliminated.

(4) The thrift institutions, like all commercial banks, are subject to the reserve requirements imposed by and may borrow from the Federal Reserve Banks; but they are also subject to the rules imposed upon them by other regulatory agencies. Both they and the commercial banks by performing the two essential functions of holding deposits and making loans expand the supply of money.

c. The Board of Governors and the Federal Reserve Banks perform five functions aimed at providing certain essential services, supervision of the member commercial banks, and the regulation of the supply of money.

■ IMPORTANT TERMS

Medium of exchange
Standard of value
Store of value
Money supply
***M*1**
Currency
Paper money
Checkable deposit
Commercial bank
Thrift (savings) institution
Token money
Intrinsic value
Face value
Federal Reserve Note
Checking account
Demand deposit
Savings and loan association
Mutual savings bank
Credit union
NOW account
Share draft account
ATS account
Near-Money
***M*2**
***M*3**
Noncheckable savings account
Time deposit
Legal tender
Value of money
Federal Deposit Insurance Corporation
Federal Savings and Loan Insurance Corporation
Transactions demand for money
Asset demand for money
Total demand for money
Money market
Depository Institutions Deregulation and Monetary Control Act
Depository institution
Board of Governors
Open Market Committee
Federal Advisory Committee
Federal Reserve Bank
Central bank
Quasi-public bank
Bankers' bank
Commercial bank
State bank
National bank
Member bank

■ FILL-IN QUESTIONS

1. Three functions of money are:

a. medium of exchange

b. standard of value

c. store of value

2. *M*1 is the sum of:

a. currency which consists of coins and paper money;

b. and (demand, time, checkable) Checkable deposits in (commercial banks, thrift institutions, depository institutions) depository institutions

c. not owned by depository institutions, the Fed. Reserve Banks, or the Federal government.

3. In addition to:

a. commercial banks, the principal depository institutions in the American economy are S&loan associations, Mutual savings banks, and credit unions.

b. demand deposits, checkable deposits include NOW and ATS accounts and share drafts.

4. In the American economy:

a. *M*2 is equal to *M*1 plus

(1) (checkable, noncheckable) noncheckable savings deposits

(2) and (small, large) small time deposits

b. *M*3 is equal to *M*2 plus (small, large) large time deposits

c. Large time deposits are mainly Certificates of deposits which have a face value of $100,000 or more

5. Near-money in the United States includes not only noncheckable savings and time deposits:

a. but such government securities as Treasury bills and U.S. government savings bonds

b. all of which can be easily converted into currency or checkable deposits without the risk of financial loss

6. List three reasons why the existence of near-money is important.

a. Greater the wealth, greater willingness to spend out of money incomes

b. conversion into monies (vice versa) affect stability of econ

c. ______

7. Money in the United States consists largely of the debts of thrift institutions and the Fed. Reserve Banks.

8. In the United States currency and checkable deposits:

a. (are, are not) are not "backed" by gold and silver;

b. are money because they are used as a medium of exchange, they are in some cases legal tender, and they are relatively (abundant, scarce) scarce

9. Money has value because it can be exchanged for goods & services and its value varies (directly, inversely) inversely with changes in the price level.

10. The total demand for money is the sum of:

a. the transactions demand which depends (directly, inversely) directly upon the GNP (money

b. and the asset demand which depends inversely upon the rate of interest

11. The total demand for money and the supply of money determine the equilibrium interest rate in the money market.

12. Two groups which help the Board of Governors of the Federal Reserve System to formulate its policies are Open Mkt. Committee and the Fed. Advisory Council

13. The three principal characteristics of the Federal Reserve Banks are:

a. central banks

b. quasi-public banks

c. bankers banks

14. If a bank is a bankers' bank it means that it accepts the deposits of and makes loans to (households, business firms, depository institutions, the public sector) depository institutions

deflation - means price level is down

inflation - price level is up

15. Both commercial banks and thrift institutions perform two essential functions for the economy: they hold the deposits of and make loans to the public; and in performing these functions they (increase, decrease) increase money supply.

16. The five major functions of the Federal Reserve Banks are:

a. hold deposits or reserves of comm banks & other depository institution

b. provide facilities for rapid collection of checks

c. act as fiscal agent for Fed gov't

d. supervise operations of member banks

e. regulate supply of money in terms of best interests of whole econ

The most important of the functions which the Federal Reserve Banks perform is that of regulating money supply

■ PROBLEMS AND PROJECTS

1. From the figures in the table below it can be concluded that:

	Billions of dollars
Small time deposits	1,630
Large time deposits	645
Checkable deposits	448
Noncheckable savings deposits	300
Currency	170

a. $M1$ is equal to the sum of $ 170 and $ 448; and totals $ 618 billion.

b. $M2$ is equal to $M1$ plus $ 300 and $ 1630; and totals $ ~~1930~~ 2548 billion.

c. $M3$ is equal to $M2$ plus $ 645 and totals $ 3,193 billion.

2. If the price level:

a. Fell by 20%, the value of money would rise by 25 %.

b. Rose by 10%, the value of money would fall by 9 %.

3. The total demand for money is equal to the transaction plus the asset demand for money.

a. Assume each dollar held for transaction purposes is spent (on the average) four times per year to buy final goods and services.

(1) This means that transaction demand for money will be equal to (what fraction or percent) 1/4 (25%) of the money GNP; and

(2) If the money GNP is $2000 billion, the transaction demand will be $ 500 billion.

b. The schedule below shows the number of dollars demanded for asset purposes at each rate of interest.

Rate of interest	Amount of money demanded (billions): For asset purposes	Total
16%	$ 20	$ 520
14	40	540
12	60	560
10	80	580
8	100	600
6	120	620
4	140	640

(1) Given the transactions demand for money in (*a*), complete the table.

(2) On the graph on the next page plot the *total* demand for money (D_m) at each rate of interest.

c. Assume the money supply (S_m) is $580 billion.

(1) Plot this money supply on the graph which you drew on page 152.

(2) Using either the graph or the table, the equilibrium rate of interest is 10 %.

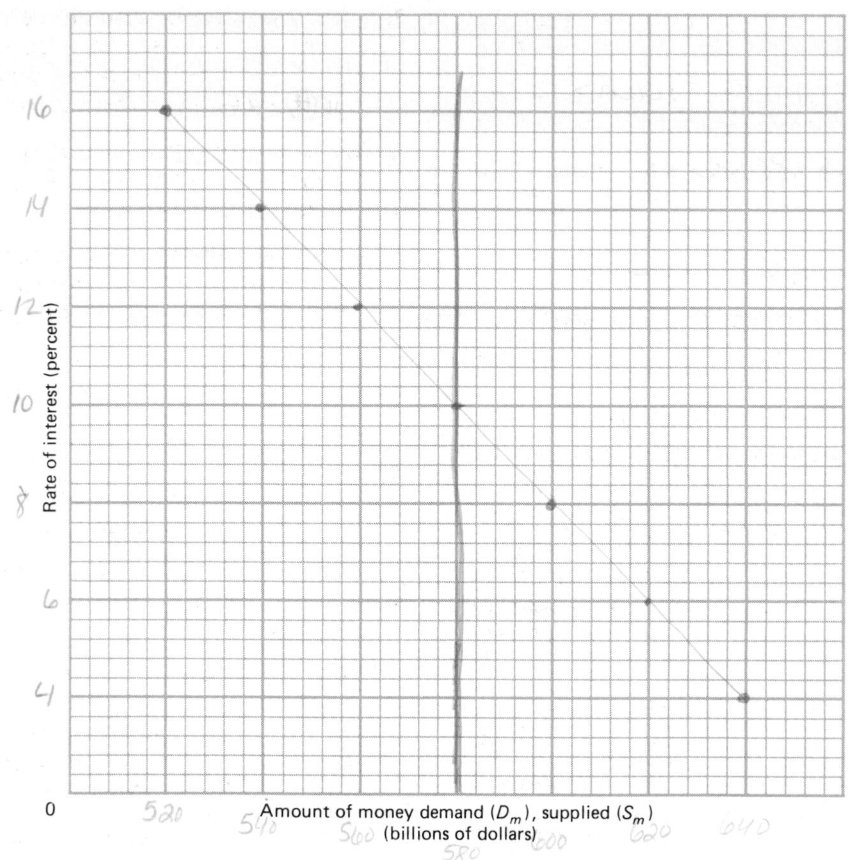

d. Should the money supply:

(1) increase to \$600 billion the equilibrium interest rate would (rise, fall) fall to 8 %.

(2) decrease to \$540 billion the equilibrium interest rate would rise to 14 %.

e. If the money GNP:

(1) increased by \$80 billion, the total demand for money would (increase, decrease) increase by \$ 20 billion at each rate of interest and the equilibrium rate of interest would (rise, fall) * rise by 2 %.

(2) decreased by \$120 billion, the total demand for money would fall by \$ 30 billion at each rate of interest and the equilibrium interest rate would * fall by 3 %.

■ SELF-TEST

Circle the T if the statement is true, the F if it is false.

1. The money supply designated *M*1 is the sum of currency and noncheckable deposits. T (F)

2. The currency component of *M*1 includes both coins and paper money. (T) F

3. If a coin is "token money," its face value is less than its intrinsic value. T (F)

4. Both commercial banks and thrift institutions accept checkable deposits. (T) F

5. The demand deposits of the Federal government at the Federal Reserve Banks are a component of *M*1. T (F)

6. *M*2 exceeds *M*1 by the amount of noncheckable savings and small time deposits. (T) F

7. A *small* time deposit is one that is less than $100,000. T F

8. *M*2 is less than *M*3 by the amount of small time deposits in depository institutions. T F

9. Economists and public officials are in general agreement on how to define the money supply in the United States. T F

10. A near-money is a medium of exchange. T F

11. The larger the volume of near-monies owned by consumers, the larger will be their average propensity to save. T F

12. Currency and checkable deposits are money because they are acceptable to sellers in exchange for goods and services. T F

13. If money is to have a fairly stable value, its supply must be limited relative to the demand for it. T F

14. There is a transactions demand for money because households and business firms use money as a store of value. T F

15. An increase in the price level would, *ceteris paribus*, increase the transactions demand for money. T F

16. An increase in the money GNP, other things remaining the same, will increase both the total demand for money and the equilibrium rate of interest in the economy. T F

17. The Board of Governors of the Federal Reserve System is appointed by the President of the United States and confirmed by the Senate. T F

18. The Federal Reserve Banks are owned and operated by the United States government. T F

19. Federal Reserve Banks are bankers' banks because they make loans to and accept deposits from depository institutions. T F

20. The most important function of the Federal Reserve Banks is the control of the size of the economy's money supply. T F

Circle the letter that corresponds to the best answer.

1. Which of the following is *not* one of the functions of money? (*a*) A factor of production; (*b*) a medium of exchange; (*c*) a store of value; (*d*) a standard of value.

2. Checkable deposits are (*a*) all deposits in commercial banks; (*b*) demand deposits in commercial banks; (*c*) deposits in thrift institutions on which checks may be written; (*d*) the sum of *b* and *c* above.

3. The largest element of the currency component of *M*1 is (*a*) coins; (*b*) United States Notes; (*c*) silver certificates; (*d*) Federal Reserve Notes.

4. Which of the following constitutes the largest element in the *M*1 money supply? (*a*) Currency; (*b*) Federal Reserve Notes; (*c*) time deposits; (*d*) checkable deposits.

5. Checkable deposits are money because they are (*a*) legal tender; (*b*) fiat money; (*c*) a medium of exchange; (*d*) token money.

6. Which of the following is *not* called a thrift institution? (*a*) A commercial bank; (*b*) a savings and loan association; (*c*) a credit union; (*d*) a mutual savings bank.

7. Which of the following is *not* a checkable deposit? (*a*) A NOW account; (*b*) a time deposit; (*c*) an ATS account; (*d*) a share draft.

8. The supply of money *M*1 consists almost entirely of the debts of (*a*) the Federal government; (*b*) the Federal Reserve Banks; (*c*) depository institutions; (*d*) the Federal Reserve Banks and depository institutions.

9. Which of the following is *not* a near-money? (*a*) A noncheckable savings account; (*b*) a time deposit; (*c*) a credit card; (*d*) a certificate of deposit.

10. Which of the following *best* describes the "backing" of money in the United States? (*a*) The gold bullion stored at Fort Knox, Kentucky; (*b*) the belief of holders of money that it can be exchanged for desirable goods and services; (*c*) the willingness of banks and the government to surrender something of value in exchange for money; (*d*) the faith and confidence of the public in the ability of government to pay its debts.

11. If the price level increases 20%, the value of money decreases (*a*) $14\frac{2}{7}$%; (*b*) $16\frac{2}{3}$%; (*c*) 20%; (*d*) 25%.

12. To keep the value of money fairly constant the Federal government (*a*) utilizes price and wage controls; (*b*) employs fiscal policy; (*c*) controls the money supply; (*d*) does both *b* and *c* above.

13. The total quantity of money demanded is (*a*) directly related to money GNP and the rate of interest; (*b*) directly related to money GNP and inversely related to the rate of interest; (*c*) inversely related to money GNP and directly related to the rate of interest; (*d*) inversely related to money GNP and the rate of interest.

14. There is an asset demand for money because money is (*a*) a medium of exchange; (*b*) a standard of value; (*c*) a store of value; (*d*) a standard of deferred payment.

15. If the dollars held for transactions purposes are, on the average, spent five times a year for final goods and services, then the quantity of money people will wish to hold for transactions is equal to (*a*) five times the money GNP; (*b*) 20% of the money GNP; (*c*) five divided by the money GNP; (*d*) 20% divided by the money GNP.

16. An increase in the rate of interest would increase (*a*) the opportunity cost of holding money; (*b*) the transactions demand for money; (*c*) the asset demand for money; (*d*) the prices of bonds.

17. Suppose the transactions demand for money is equal to 10% of the money GNP, the supply of money is $450 billion, and the asset demand for money is that shown in the table below. If the money GNP is $3,000 billion, the equilibrium interest rate is (*a*) 14%; (*b*) 13%; (*c*) 12%; (*d*) 11%.

Interest rate (%)	Asset demand (billions)
14	$100
13	150
12	200
11	250

18. Using the information in multiple-choice question 17, if the money GNP remains constant an increase in the money supply from $450 billion to $500 billion would cause the equilibrium interest rate to (*a*) rise to 14%; (*b*) fall to 11%; (*c*) remain unchanged; (*d*) fall to 12%.

19. Since the passage of the DIDMC Act in 1980, (*a*) both nonmember commercial banks and thrift institutions have been subject to the reserve requirements set by the Federal Banks; (*b*) the thrift institutions have been allowed to accept checkable deposits; (*c*) nonmember commercial banks and the thrifts have been allowed to borrow at the Federal Reserve Banks; (*d*) all of the above.

20. Both commercial banks and thrift institutions (*a*) accept the checkable deposits of the public; (*b*) make loans to the public; (*c*) expand the money supply; (*d*) do all of the above.

■ DISCUSSION QUESTIONS

1. How would you define money? What are the components of the *M*1 supply of money in the United States? Which of these components is the larger?

2. What is (*a*) a checkable deposit; (*b*) a noncheckable deposit; (*c*) a thrift (or savings) institution; (*d*) a depository institution?

3. What is a near-money? What are the more important near-monies in the American economy? Define *M*2 and *M*3 and explain why the existence of near-monies is important.

4. For what reasons are checkable deposits included in the money supply?

5. What "backs" the money used in the United States? What determines the value of money? Explain the relationship between the value of money and the price level.

6. What must government do if it is to stabilize the value of money?

7. What are the two reasons people wish to hold money? How are these two reasons related to the "functions" of money?

8. Explain the determinant of each of the two demands for money and how a change in the size of these determinants will affect the amount of money people wish to hold.

9. The rate of interest is a price. Of what good or service is it the price? Explain how demand and supply determine this price.

10. Outline the structure of the Federal Reserve System and explain the chief functions of each of the four parts of the system.

11. As briefly as possible outline the three characteristics of the Federal Reserve Banks and explain the meaning of these characteristics.

12. What are the chief functions which the Federal Reserve Banks perform? Explain briefly the meaning of each of these functions. Which of the chief functions is the most important?

18
How banks create money

Chapter 17 explained the institutional structure of banking in the United States today, the functions which banks and the other depository institutions and money perform, and the composition of the money supply. Chapter 18 explains how banks literally create money—checking account money—and the factors which determine and limit the money-creating ability of commercial banks. Even though the other depository institutions also create checkable deposits, this chapter focuses its attention on the commercial banks because they have and will continue to create a very large part of the total amount of money created by all depository institutions in the United States. But where the term *commercial bank* (or *bank*) appears it is legitimate to substitute depository *institution*; and it is permissible to substitute *checkable deposit* for *demand deposit* (or checking account).

The device (and a most convenient and simple device it is) employed to explain commercial banking operations and money creation is the balance sheet. All banking transactions affect this balance sheet, and the first step to understanding how money is created is to understand how various simple and typical transactions affect the commercial bank balance sheet.

In reading this chapter you must analyze for yourself the effect upon the balance sheet of each and every banking transaction discussed. The important items in the balance sheet are demand deposits and reserves, because demand deposits *are* money, and the ability of a bank to create new demand deposits is determined by the amount of reserves the bank has. Expansion of the money supply depends upon the possession by commercial banks of excess reserves. Excess reserves do not appear explicitly in the balance sheet but do appear there implicitly because excess reserves are the difference between the actual reserves and the required reserves of commercial banks.

Two cases—the single commercial bank and the banking system—are presented in order to help you build an understanding of banking and money creation. It is important here to understand that the money-creating potential of a single commercial bank differs in an important way from the money-creating potential of the entire banking system; it is equally important to understand how the money-creating ability of many single commercial banks is *multiplied* and results in the money-creating ability of the banking system as a whole.

Certain assumptions are used throughout most of the chapter to analyze money-creating ability; in certain instances these assumptions may not be completely realistic and may need to be modified. The chapter concludes with a discussion of how the earlier analysis must be modified—but not changed in its essentials—to take account of these slightly unrealistic assumptions.

■ CHECKLIST

When you have studied this chapter you should be able to:

☐ Recount the story of how goldsmiths came to issue paper money and became bankers who created money and held fractional reserves.

☐ Explain the effects of the deposit of currency in a checking account on the composition and size of the money supply.

☐ Compute a bank's required and excess reserves when you are given the needed balance-sheet figures.

☐ Explain why a commercial bank is required to maintain a reserve; and why this reserve is not sufficient to protect the depositors from losses.

☐ Indicate how the deposit of a check drawn on one commercial bank in a second commercial bank will affect the reserves and excess reserves of the two banks.

☐ Show what happens to the money supply when a commercial bank makes a loan (or buys securities); and what happens to the money supply when a loan is repaid (or a bank sells securities).

☐ Explain what happens to a commercial bank's reserves and demand deposits after it has made a loan, a check has been written on the newly created demand deposit, deposited in another commercial bank and cleared; and what happens to the reserves and demand deposits of the commercial bank in which the check was deposited.

☐ Describe what would happen to a commercial bank's reserves if it made loans (or bought securities) in an amount that exceeded its excess reserves.

☐ State the money-creating potential of a commercial bank (the amount of money a commercial bank can safely create by lending or buying securities).

☐ State the money-creating potential of the banking system; and explain how it is possible for the banking system to create an amount of money which is a multiple of its excess reserves when no individual commercial bank ever creates money in an amount greater than its excess reserve.

☐ Compute the size of the monetary multiplier and the money-creating potential of the banking system when you are provided with the necessary data.

☐ List the two leakages which reduce the money-creating potential of the banking system.

☐ Explain why the size of the money supply needs to be controlled.

CHAPTER OUTLINE

1. The balance sheet of the commercial bank is a statement of the assets, liabilities, and net worth (capital stock) of the bank at a specific time; and in the balance sheet the bank's assets equal its liabilities plus its net worth.

2. The history of the early goldsmiths illustrates how paper money came into being, how they became bankers when they began to make loans and issue money in excess of their gold holdings, and how the presently used fractional reserve system with its two significant characteristics was developed.

3. By examining the ways in which the balance sheet of the commercial bank is affected by various transactions, it is possible to understand how a single commercial bank in a multibank system can create money.

a. Once a commercial bank has been founded,

(1) by selling shares of stock and obtaining cash in return;

(2) and acquired the property and equipment needed to carry on the banking business;

(3) the deposit of cash in the bank does not affect the total money supply; it only changes its composition by substituting demand deposits for currency in circulation;

(4) three reserve concepts are vital to an understanding of the money-creating potential of a commercial bank:

(*a*) the *legal reserve deposit* (required reserve) which a bank *must* maintain at its Federal Reserve Bank (or as vault cash—which can be ignored) equals the reserve ratio multiplied by the deposit liabilities of the commercial bank;

(*b*) the *actual reserves* of a commercial bank are its deposits at the Federal Reserve Bank (plus the vault cash which is ignored);

(*c*) the *excess reserves* equal to the actual reserves less the required reserve;

(5) the writing of a check upon the bank and its deposit in a second bank results in a loss of reserves and deposits for the first and a gain in reserves and deposits for the second bank.

b. When a single commercial bank lends or buys securities it increases its own deposit liabilities and, therefore, the supply of money by the amount of the loan or security purchase. But the bank only lends or buys securities in an amount equal to its excess reserves because it fears the loss of reserves to other commercial banks in the economy.

c. An individual commercial bank balances its desire for profits (which result from the making of loans and the purchase of securities) with its desire for liquidity or safety (which it achieves by having excess reserves or vault cash).

4. The ability of a banking system composed of many individual commercial banks to lend and to create money is a multiple (greater than one) of its excess reserves; and is equal to the excess reserves of the banking system multiplied by the demand-deposit (or monetary) multiplier.

a. The banking system as a whole can do this even though no single commercial bank ever lends an amount greater than its excess reserve because the banking system, unlike a single commercial bank, does not lose reserves.

b. The monetary (or demand-deposit) multiplier is equal to the reciprocal of the required reserve ratio for demand deposits; and the maximum expansion of demand deposits is equal to the excess reserves in the banking system times the monetary multiplier.

c. The potential lending ability of the banking system may not be fully achieved if there are leakages because borrowers choose to have additional currency or bankers choose to have excess reserves.

d. If bankers lend as much as they are able during periods of prosperity and less than they are able during recessions, they add to the instability of the economy; and to reduce this instability the Federal Reserve Banks must control the size of the money supply.

■ IMPORTANT TERMS

Balance sheet

Fractional reserve system of banking

Vault cash (till money)

Legal (required) reserve (deposit)

Reserve ratio

Fractional reserve

Actual reserve

Excess reserve

Federal Deposit Insurance Corporation

The lending potential of an individual commercial bank

Commercial banking system

Monetary (demand-deposit) multiplier

The lending potential of the banking system

Leakage

■ FILL-IN QUESTIONS

1. The balance sheet of a commercial bank is a statement of the bank's assets, liabilites and not worth at some specific point in time.

2. The coins and paper money which a bank has in its possession are called vault cash or till money.

3. When a person deposits cash in a commercial bank and receives a demand deposit in return, the size of the money supply has (increased, decreased, not changed) not changed

4. The legal reserve deposit of a commercial bank (ignoring vault cash) must be kept at the Fed. Reserve Bank in its district and must equal (at least) its deposit liabilities multiplied by the reserve ratio

5. The excess reserves of a commercial bank equal its actual less its required

6. If commercial banks are allowed to accept (or create) deposits in excess of their reserves, the banking system is operating under a system of fractional reserves.

7. When a check is drawn upon bank X, deposited in bank Y, and cleared, the reserves of bank X are (increased, decreased, not changed) decreased and the reserves of bank Y are increased; deposits in bank X are decreased and deposits in bank Y are increased

8. A single commercial bank in a multibank system can safely make loans or buy government securities equal in amount to the excess reserves of that commercial bank.

9. When a commercial bank makes a new loan of $10,000, it (increases, decreases) increases the supply of money by $ 10,000

10. When a commercial bank sells a $2000 government bond to a securities dealer the supply of money (increases, decreases) ______ by $ ______

11. A bank ordinarily pursues two conflicting goals; they are ______ and ______

12. The banking system can make loans (or buy government securities) and create money in an amount equal to its excess reserves multiplied by the ______________

______________________________.

Its lending potential per dollar of excess reserves is greater than the lending potential of a single commercial bank because it does not lose ______________ to other banks.

13. The greater the reserve ratio is, the (larger smaller) ______________ is the monetary multiplier.

14. If the required reserve ratio is 16⅔ percent, the banking system is $6 million short of reserves, and the banking system is unable to increase its reserves, the banking system must ______________ the money supply by $ ______________

15. The money-creating potential of the commercial banking system is lessened by the withdrawal of ______________ from banks and by the decisions of bankers to keep ______________ reserves.

16. Commercial banks in the past:

a. have kept considerable excess reserves during periods of (prosperity, recession) ______________ ______________ and have kept few or no excess reserves during periods of ______________

b. and by behaving in this way have made the economy (more, less) ______________ unstable.

■ PROBLEMS AND PROJECTS

1. Below is the simplified balance sheet of a commercial bank. Assume that the figures given show the bank's assets and demand-deposit liabilities *prior to each of the following four transactions.* Draw up the balance sheet as it would appear after each of these transactions is completed and place the balance-sheet figures in the appropriate column. *Do not* use the figures you place in columns a, b, or c when you work the next part of the problem: start all parts of the problem with the printed figures.

		(a)	(b)	(c)	(d)
Assets:					
Cash	$100	$____	$____	$____	$____
Reserves	200	____	____	____	____
Loans	500	____	____	____	____
Securities	200	____	____	____	____
Liabilities and net worth:					
Demand deposits	900	____	____	____	____
Capital stock	100	100	100	100	100

a. A check for $50 is drawn by one of the depositors of the bank, given to a person who deposits it in another bank, and cleared (column a).

b. A depositor withdraws $50 in cash from the bank, and the bank restores its vault cash by obtaining $50 in additional cash from its Federal Reserve Bank (column b).

c. A check for $60 drawn on another bank is deposited in this bank and cleared (column c).

d. The bank sells $100 in government bonds to the Federal Reserve Bank in its district (column d).

2. At the top of the next page are five balance sheets for a single commercial bank (columns 1a–5a). The required reserve ratio is 20%.

a. Compute the required reserves (A); ignoring vault cash, the excess reserves* (B) of the bank; and the amount of new loans it can extend (C).

*If the bank is short of reserves and must reduce its loans or obtain additional reserves, show this by placing a minus sign in front of the amounts by which it is short of reserves.

	(1a)	(2a)	(3a)	(4a)	(5a)
Assets:					
Cash	$ 10	$ 20	$ 20	20	$ 15
Reserves	40	40	25	40	45
Loans	100	100	100	100	150
Securities	50	60	30	70	60
Liabilities and net worth:					
Demand deposits	175	200	150	180	220
Capital stock	25	20	25	50	50
A. Required reserve	$ 8	$ ___	$ ___	$ ___	$ ___
B. Excess reserve	32	___	___	___	___
C. New loans	32	___	___	___	___

b. Draw up for the individual bank the five balance sheets as they appear after the bank has made the new *loans* that it is capable of making (columns 1-5b).

	(1b)	(2b)	(3b)	(4b)	(5b)
Assets:					
Cash	$___	$___	$___	$___	$___
Reserves	___	___	___	___	___
Loans	___	___	___	___	___
Securities	___	___	___	___	___
Liabilities and net worth:					
Demand deposits	___	___	___	___	___
Capital stock	___	___	___	___	___

3. Following are several reserve ratios. Compute the monetary multiplier for each of the reserve ratios and enter the figures in column 2. In column 3 show the maximum amount by which a single commercial bank can increase its loans for each dollar's worth of excess reserves it possesses. In column 4 indicate the maximum amount by which the banking system can increase its leans for each dollar's worth of excess reserves in the system.

Money multiplier = $\left(\frac{1}{\text{res's ratio}}\right)$

(1)	(2)	(3)	(4)
12½%	___	$___	$___
16⅔%	___	___	___
20%	___	___	___
25%	___	___	___
30%	___	___	___
33⅓%	___	___	___

4. Shown on the next page is the simplified consolidated balance sheet for *all* commercial banks in the economy. Assume that the figures given show the bank's assets and liabilities *prior to each of the following three transactions;* and that the reserve ratio is 20%. *Do not* use the figures you placed in columns 2 and 4 when you begin parts *b* and *c* of the problem: start parts *a, b,* and *c* of the problem with the printed figures.

a. The public deposits $5 in cash in the banks and the banks send the $5 to the Federal Reserve, where it is added to their reserves. Fill in column 1. If the banking system extends the new loans it is capable of extending, show in column 2 the balance sheet as it would then appear.

b. The banking system sells $8 worth of securities to the Federal Reserve. Complete column 3. Assuming the system extends the maximum amount of credit of which it is capable, fill in column 4.

		(1)	(2)	(3)	(4)	(5)	(6)
Assets:							
Cash	$ 50	$50	$50	$___	$___	$___	$___
Reserves	100	105	105	___	___	___	___
Loans	200	200	220	___	___	___	___
Securities	200	200	220	___	___	___	___
Liabilities and net worth:							
Demand deposits	500	505	525	___	___	___	___
Capital stock	50	50	50	50	50	50	50
Loans from Federal Reserve	0	0	0	___	___	___	___
Excess reserves		4	0	___	___	___	___
Maximum possible expansion of the money supply		20	0	___	___	___	___

c. The Federal Reserve lends $10 to the commercial banks; complete column 5. Complete column 6 showing the condition of the banks after the maximum amount of new loans which the banks are capable of making is granted.

■ SELF-TEST

Circle the T if the statement is true, the F if it is false.

1. The balance sheet of a commercial bank shows the transactions in which the bank has engaged during a given period of time. T F

2. A commercial bank's assets plus its net worth equal the bank's liabilities. T F

3. Goldsmiths increased the money supply when they accepted deposits of gold and issued paper receipts to the depositors. T F

4. Roberta Lynn, the dancing star, deposits a $30,000 check in a commercial bank and receives a demand deposit in return; an hour later the Manfred Iron and Coal Company borrows $30,000 from the same bank. The money supply has increased $30,000 as a result of the two transactions. T F

5. A commercial bank may maintain its legal reserve either as a deposit in its Federal Reserve Bank or as government bonds in its own vault. T F

6. The legal reserve which a commercial bank maintains must equal at least its own deposit liabilities multiplied by the required reserve ratio. T F

7. The actual reserves of a commercial bank equal excess reserves plus required reserves. T F

8. The reserve of a commercial bank in the Federal Reserve Bank is an asset of the Federal Reserve Bank. T F

9. A check for $1000 drawn on bank X by a depositor and deposited in bank Y will increase the excess reserves of bank Y by $1000. T F

10. A single commercial bank can safely lend an amount equal to its excess reserves multiplied by the required reserve ratio. T F

11. When a borrower repays a loan of $500, either in cash or by check, the supply of money is reduced by $500. T F

12. The granting of a $5000 loan and the purchase of a $5000 government bond from a securities dealer by a commercial bank have the same effect on the money supply. T F

13. A commercial bank seeks both profits and liquidity; but these are conflicting goals. T F

14. If the banking system has $10 million in excess reserves and if the reserve ratio is 25%, it can increase its loans by $40 million. T F

15. While a single commercial bank can increase its loans only by an amount equal to its excess reserves, the entire banking system can increase its loans by an amount equal to its excess reserves multiplied by the reciprocal of the reserve ratio. **T F**

16. When borrowers from a commercial bank wish to have cash rather than demand deposits, the money-creating potential of the banking system is increased. **T F**

Circle the letter that corresponds to the best answer.

1. The goldsmiths became bankers when (*a*) they accepted deposits of gold for safe storage; (*b*) they issued receipts for the gold stored with them; (*c*) their receipts for deposited gold were used as paper money; (*d*) they issued paper money in excess of the amount of gold stored with them.

2. When cash is deposited in a demand-deposit account in a commercial bank there is (*a*) a decrease in the money supply; (*b*) an increase in the money supply; (*c*) no change in the composition of the money supply; (*d*) a change in the composition of the money supply.

3. A commercial bank has actual reserves of $9000 and deposit liabilities of $30,000; and the required reserve ratio is 20%. The excess reserves of the bank are (*a*) $3000; (*b*) $6000; (*c*) $7500; (*d*) $9000.

4. A commercial bank is required to have a deposit at its Federal Reserve Bank in order (*a*) to protect the deposits in the commercial bank against losses; (*b*) to provide the means by which checks drawn on the commercial bank and deposited in other commercial banks can be collected; (*c*) to add to the liquidity of the commercial bank and protect it against a "run" on the bank; (*d*) to provide the Board of Governors of the Federal Reserve System with a means of controlling the lending ability of the commercial bank.

5. A depositor places $750 in cash in a commercial bank, and the reserve ratio in 33⅓%; the bank sends the $750 to the Federal Reserve Bank. As a result, the *reserves* and the *excess reserves* of the bank have been increased, respectively, by (*a*) $750 and $250; (*b*) $750 and $500; (*c*) $750 and $750; (*d*) $500 and $500.

6. A commercial bank has no excess reserves, but then a depositor places $600 in cash in the bank, and the bank adds the $600 to its reserves by sending it to the Federal Reserve Bank. The commercial bank then lends $300 to a borrower. As a consequence of these transactions the size of the money supply has: (*a*) not been affected; (*b*) increased by $300; (*c*) increased by $600; (*d*) increased by $900.

7. A commercial bank has excess reserves of $500 and a required reserve ratio of 20%; it grants a loan of $1000 to a borrower. If the borrower writes a check for $1000 which is deposited in another commercial bank, the first bank will be short of reserves, after the check has been cleared, in the amount of: (*a*) $200; (*b*) $500; (*c*) $700; (*d*) $1000.

8. A commercial bank sells a $1000 government security to a securities dealer. The dealer pays for the bond in cash, which the bank adds to its vault cash. The money supply has: (*a*) not been affected; (*b*) decreased by $1000; (*c*) increased by $1000; (*d*) increased by $1000 multiplied by the reciprocal of the required reserve ratio.

9. A commercial bank has deposit liabilities of $100,000, reserves of $37,000, and a required reserve ratio of 25%. The amount by which a *single commercial bank* and the amount by which the *banking system* can increase loans are, respectively: (*a*) $12,000 and $48,000; (*b*) $17,000 and $68,000; (*c*) $12,000 and $60,000; (*d*) $17,000 and $85,000.

10. If the required reserve ratio were 12½% the value of the monetary multiplier would be (*a*) 5; (*b*) 6; (*c*) 7; (*d*) 8.

11. The commercial banking system has excess reserves of $700 and makes new loans of $2100 and is just meeting its reserve requirements. The required reserve ratio is: (*a*) 20%; (*b*) 25%; (*c*) 30%; (*d*) 33⅓%.

12. The commercial banking system, because of a recent change in the required reserve ratio from 20% to 30%, finds that it is $60 million short of reserves. If it is unable to obtain any additional reserves it must decrease the money supply by (*a*) $60 million; (*b*) $180 million; (*c*) $200 million; (*d*) $300 million.

13. Only one commercial bank in the banking system has an excess reserve, and its excess reserve is $100,000. This bank makes a new loan of $80,000 and keeps an excess reserve of $20,000. If the required reserve ratio for all banks is 20%, the potential expansion of the money supply is (*a*) $80,000; (*b*) $100,000; (*c*) $400,000; (*d*) $500,000.

14. The money-creating potential of the banking system is reduced when (*a*) bankers choose to have excess reserves; (*b*) borrowers choose to hold none of the funds they have borrowed in currency; (*c*) the Federal Reserve lowers the required reserve ratio; (*d*) bankers borrow from the Federal Reserve.

15. The excess reserves held by banks tend to (*a*) rise during periods of prosperity; (*b*) fall during periods of recession; (*c*) rise during periods of recession; (*d*) fall when interest rates in the economy fall.

16. Unless controlled, the money supply will (*a*) fall during periods of prosperity; (*b*) rise during periods of recession; (*c*) change in a procyclical fashion; (*d*) change in an anticyclical fashion.

■ DISCUSSION QUESTIONS

1. How did the early goldsmiths come to issue paper money and then become bankers? Explain the difference between a 100% and a fractional reserve system of banking and why the latter system is subject to "runs" and requires public regulation.

2. Commercial banks seek both profits and safety. Explain how the balance sheet of the commercial banks reflects the desires of bankers for income and for liquidity.

3. Do the reserves held by commercial banks satisfactorily protect the bank's depositors? Are the reserves of commercial banks needed? Explain your answers.

4. Explain why the granting of a loan by a commercial bank increases the supply of money. Why does the repayment of a loan decrease the supply of money?

5. The owner of a sporting goods store writes a check on his account in a Kent, Ohio, bank and sends it to one of his suppliers who deposits it in his bank in Cleveland, Ohio. How does the Cleveland bank obtain payment from the Kent bank? If the two banks were in Kent and New York City, how would one bank pay the other? How are the excess reserves of the two banks affected?

6. Why is a single commercial bank able to lend safely only an amount equal to its excess reserves?

7. No one commercial bank ever lends an amount greater than its excess reserve, but the banking system as a whole is able to extend loans and expand the money supply by an amount equal to the system's excess reserves multiplied by the reciprocal of the reserve ratio. Explain why this is possible and how the multiple expansion of deposits and money takes place.

8. On the basis of a given amount of excess reserves and a given reserve ratio, a certain expansion of the money supply may be possible. What are two reasons why the potential expansion of the money supply may not be fully achieved?

9. Why is there a "need for monetary control" in the American economy?

19
The Federal Reserve Banks and monetary policy

Chapter 19 is the third chapter dealing with money and banking. It explains how the Board of Governors of the Federal Reserve System and the Federal Reserve Banks affect output, income, employment, and the price level of the economy. Central-bank policies designed to affect these variables are called monetary policies, the goal of which is full employment without inflation.

You should have little difficulty with this chapter if you have understood the material in Chapter 18. In Chapter 19 attention should be concentrated on the following: (1) the cause-effect chain, as Keynesians see it, between monetary policy; commercial bank reserves and excess reserves; the supply of money; the rate of interest; and investment spending, aggregate demand, output, employment, and the price level; (2) the important items on the balance sheet of the Federal Reserve Banks; (3) the three major controls available to the Federal Reserve Banks, and how the employment of these controls can affect the reserves, excess reserves, the actual money supply, and the money-creating potential of the banking system; (4) the actions the Federal Reserve would take if it were pursuing a tight money policy to curb inflation, and the actions it would take if it were pursuing an easy money policy to prevent or eliminate depression; (5) the relative importance of the three major controls; and (6) the three minor selective controls which the Federal Reserve Banks use or have used to influence the economy.

In order to acquire a thorough knowledge of the manner in which each of the Federal Reserve transactions affects reserves, excess reserves, the actual money supply, and the potential money supply, you must study very carefully each of the sets of balance sheets which are used to explain these transactions. On these balance sheets the items to watch are again reserves and demand deposits! Be sure that you know why each of the balance sheet changes is made and are able, *on your own,* to make the appropriate balance-sheet entries to trace through the effects of any transaction.

Following the examination of "The Tools of Monetary Policy" Professor McConnell explains again how the demand for and the supply of money determine the interest rate (in the "money market"); how the interest rate determined there and the investment-demand schedule determine the level of planned investment in the economy; and how planned investment and the saving schedule together determine the equilibrium NNP. This restatement of the Keynesian theory makes it clear that the effect of a change in the money supply depends upon just how steep or flat the down sloping demand-for-money and investment-demand curves are. Professor McConnell also uses the aggregate-supply and the aggregate-demand curves to show you how changes in the money supply affect national output and the price level in the three stages along the aggregate-supply curve.

The strengths and shortcomings of monetary policy in reducing unemployment (and expanding national output) and in reducing inflation are examined in the next-to-last major section of the chapter. Here you will also encounter the dilemma faced by the Fed: it cannot simultaneously control both the money supply and the level of interest rates in the economy. The reason it can't will be explained for you.

The last section of Chapter 19 is a summary of Chapters 9 through 19. It will recall for you the main outline of the Keynesian theory of employment and the principal public policies that may be used to promote full employment without creating inflation. They will help you to see that the various principles discussed in the previous chapters are *not* separate theories but are, in fact, connected parts of the one Keynesian theory; and that the public policies discussed in earlier chapters are *not* really separate policies but are alternative means of achieving the goal of economic stabilization.

This one theory of employment and the alternative means of achieving this one goal are summarized for you in Figure 19-3. This is probably the single most important figure in the textbook.

■ CHECKLIST

When you have studied this chapter you should be able to:

☐ Explain, using the Keynesian cause-effect chain, the links between a change in the money supply and a change in the equilibrium NNP.

☐ List the important assets and liabilities of the Federal Reserve Banks.

☐ Identify the three tools of monetary policy; and explain how each may be employed by the Federal Reserve to expand and to contract the money supply.

☐ Prescribe the three specific monetary policies the Federal Reserve should utilize to reduce unemployment; and the three specific policies it should employ to reduce inflationary pressures in the economy.

☐ State which of the three monetary-policy tools is the most effective.

☐ Identify three selective controls; and explain how each is used to promote economic stability.

☐ Draw the demand-for-money and the supply-of-money curves and use them to show how a change in the supply of money will affect the interest rate; draw an investment-demand curve to explain the effects of changes in the interest rate on investment spending; and construct a leakages-injections graph to show the effects of a change in planned investment on the equilibrium NNP.

☐ State precisely how the steepness of the demand-for-money and of the investment-demand curves affects the impact of a change in the money supply on the equilibrium NNP.

☐ Use the aggregate-demand and aggregate-supply curves to show the effects of changes in the money supply on national output and the price level in the Keynesian, classical, and intermediate ranges.

☐ List three strengths and four shortcomings of monetary policy.

☐ State the target (or policy) dilemma confronted by the Fed; and explain why it faces this dilemma.

☐ Summarize the Keynesian theory of employment and the policies that may be utilized to promote a full-employment noninflationary NNP.

■ CHAPTER OUTLINE

1. The objective of monetary policy is full employment without inflation.

a. The Federal Reserve Banks according to the Keynesians can accomplish this objective by exercising control over the amount of excess reserves held by commercial banks and thereby influencing the size of the money supply, the rate of interest, and the level of aggregate expenditures.

b. Decreases (increases) in the rate of interest tend to increase (decrease) planned investment and, therefore, aggregate expenditures.

2. By examining the consolidated balance sheet and the principal assets and liabilities of the Federal Reserve Banks, an understanding of the ways in which the Federal Reserve can control and influence the reserves of commercial banks and the money supply can be obtained.

a. The principal assets of the Federal Reserve Banks (in order of size) are U.S. government securities and loans to commercial banks.

b. Their principal liabilities are Federal Reserve Notes, the reserve deposits of commercial banks and U.S. Treasury deposits.

3. The Federal Reserve Banks employ three principal tools (techniques or instruments) to control the reserves of banks and the size of the money supply.

a. The Federal Reserve can buy and sell government securities in the open market.

(1) Buying securities in the open market from either banks or the public increases the reserves of banks.

(2) Selling securities in the open market to either banks or the public decreases the reserves of banks.

b. It can raise or lower the reserve ratio.

(1) Raising the reserve ratio decreases the excess reserves of banks and the size of the monetary (demand-deposit) multiplier.

(2) Lowering the reserve ratio increases the excess reserves of banks and the size of the monetary multiplier.

c. And it can also lower the discount rate to encourage banks to borrow reserves from the Fed and raise it to discourage them from borrowing reserves from the Fed.

d. A tight (easy) money policy involves increasing (decreasing) the reserve ratio, selling (buying) bonds in the open market, and increasing (decreasing) the discount rate.

e. Open-market operations are the most effective device for controlling the money supply.

f. The Federal Reserve may also employ selective controls to affect the availability of credit; and these controls are the setting of margin requirements, the setting of the terms of credit available to purchasers of durable consumer goods, and moral suasion.

4. To restate the effects of monetary policy on the equilibrium NNP:

a. In the money market the demand-for and the supply-of-money curves determine the real interest rate; the investment-demand curve and this rate of interest determine planned investment; and planned investment along with the saving curve determine the equilibrium NNP.

b. And:

(1) The steeper the demand-for-money curve and the flatter the investment-demand curve the greater will be the effect on the equilibrium NNP of a change in the money supply.

(2) Changes in the equilibrium NNP that result from a change in the money supply will alter the demand for money and dampen the effect of the change in the money supply on the NNP.

c. Or, restated in terms of the aggregate demand-aggregate supply model: the flatter (steeper) the aggregate-supply curve is, the greater (smaller) is the effect of a change in the money supply on real national output and employment and the smaller (greater) is the effect on the price level.

5. Whether monetary policy is effective in promoting full employment without inflation is a debatable question because monetary policy has both strengths and shortcomings in fighting recession and inflation.

a. Its strengths are that it can be more quickly changed than fiscal policy; it is more politically acceptable than fiscal policy; and (some economists believe) it is the key determinant of economic activity and, therefore, more effective than fiscal policy.

b. Its weaknesses are that it is more effective in fighting inflation than it is in curbing recession; it can be offset by changes in the velocity of money; it is relatively ineffective in controlling cost-push inflation; and it may not have a significant impact on investment spending in the economy.

c. A most difficult problem for the Fed is its inability to control both the money supply and the level of interest rates at the same time.

(1) If the Fed's policy target is the stabilization of interest rates, an increase in the money GNP (and the resulting increase in the demand for money) will require it to increase the money supply; and if its policy target is the stabilization of the money supply, an increase in the money GNP (and the demand for money) will force interest rates upward.

(2) Controversy surrounds the issue of which of these two policy targets is preferable; and the Fed switched from stabilizing interest rates to stabilizing the money supply in October of 1979, and from stabilizing the money supply to a middle-of-the-road policy in October of 1982.

6. The income, employment, output, and prices of an economy are in Keynesian theory positively related to the level of aggregate expenditures which has three principal components.

a. These three components are consumption spending which depends upon the stable consumption schedule and the income of the economy; investment spending which is more unstable; and government spending which depends partly on the level of spending needed to achieve full employment and price stability.

b. To achieve economic stability, government employs both fiscal and monetary policy; but to be effective these two types of policy must be coordinated.

■ IMPORTANT TERMS

Monetary policy	**Moral suasion**
Quantitative control	**Margin requirement**
Open-market operations	**Money market**
Discount rate	**Feedback effects**
Easy money policy	**Velocity of money**
Tight money policy	**Cost-push inflation**
Selective control	

■ FILL-IN QUESTIONS

1. The objective of monetary policy in the United States is a ___FE noninflationary___ level of total output. Responsibility for these monetary policies rests with the ___Board of Gov.___ of the Federal Reserve System; and they are put into effect by the twelve Federal Reserve ___Banks___

2. To eliminate inflationary pressures in the economy Keynesians argue that the monetary authority should seek to (increase, decrease) decrease the reserves of commercial banks; this would tend to decrease the money supply and to increase the rate of interest; and this in turn would cause investment spending, aggregate expenditures, and NNP to decrease

3. The two important assets of the Federal Reserve Banks are securities and loans to comm. banks Their three major liabilities are res of comm. banks Treasury deposits and Fed. Reserve Notes

4. The three tools (or instruments) employed by the monetary authority to control the money supply are open-mkt system, changing reserve ratio, and changing discount rate

5. The Federal Reserve Banks buy and sell government securities in the open market in order to change the amount of new money commercial banks are able to create and the rate of interest in the economy.

6. If the Federal Reserve Banks were to sell $10 million in government bonds to the *public* and the reserve ratio were 25%, the supply of money would immediately be reduced by $10 mil., the reserves of commercial banks would be reduced by $10 mil., and the excess reserves of the banks would be reduced by $7.5 mil.. But if these bonds were sold to the commercial banks, the supply of money would immediately be reduced by $0, the reserves of the bank would be reduced by $10 mil, and the excess reserves of the banks would be reduced by $10 mil.

7. Changes in the reserve ratio affect the ability of commercial banks to create money in two ways: they affect the amount of excess reserves held by the commercial banks; and the size of the monetary multiplier

8. If the Federal Reserve Banks were to lower the discount rate commercial banks would tend to borrow (more, less) more from them; and this would (increase, decrease) increase their excess reserves.

9. To increase the supply of money, the Federal Reserve Banks should (raise, lower) lower the reserve ratio, (buy, sell) buy securities in the open market, and/or (increase, decrease) decrease the discount rate.

10. The most effective quantitative control is open-mkt. operations

11. The three selective controls are changes in margin requirement and in consumer credit and the use of moral suasion

12. Graphically, in an economy in which government neither purchases goods and services nor collects net taxes and which neither exports nor imports goods and services:

a. the equilibrium real interest rate is determined by the demand-for- and the supply-of- money curves;

b. this equilibrium interest rate and the Investment Demand curve determine the level of planned investment;

c. and the level of planned investment, using the leakages-injections approach, and the Savings curve determine the equilibrium NNP;

d. but when the supply-of-money curve increases (shifts to the right), the real interest rate will (increase, decrease) decrease, planned investment will increase, and the equilibrium NNP will increase

13. The effect of a $1 billion increase or decrease in the money supply upon the equilibrium NNP is greater the (flatter, steeper) steeper the demand-for-money curve and the flatter the investment-demand curve.

14. An increase in the money supply will shift the aggregate (supply, demand) demand curve to the (right, left) right

a. In the Keynesian (or depression) range along the aggregate-supply curve this increase in the money supply will have a (small, large) large effect on real national output and a small effect on the price level.

b. In the classical range along the aggregate supply curve this increase in the money supply will have a small effect on real national output and a large effect on the price level.

c. In the intermediate range along the aggregate- supply curve the effect of an increase in the money supply on the real national output is greater the (steeper, flatter) flatter the aggregate-supply curve, and the effect on the price level is greater the steeper the aggregate-supply curve.

15. The:

a. strengths of monetary policy are that it is more flexible, more politically acceptible, and (in the view of the monetarists) more effective than fiscal policy;

b. weaknesses of monetary policy are that it is more effective in curbing (recession, inflation) inflation than recession, can be ineffective if the velocity of money changes in the (same, opposite) opposite direction as the money supply, cannot be used to fight (demand-pull, cost-push) cost-push inflation, and will not be effective if changes in the interest rate have little or no effect on investment spending in the economy.

16. The target dilemma faced by the Fed is that it is (able, unable) unable to control both the money supply and the level of interest rates simultaneously.

a. If it is to stabilize the interest rate it must (increase, decrease) increase the money supply when the money GNP rises.

b. And if it stabilizes the money supply it must allow the interest rate to increase when the money GNP rises.

17. In the Keynesian theory the levels of output, employment, income, and prices depend on the level of aggregate expenditures which in turn depend (in a closed economy) upon the amounts of consumption, investment, and gov't spending in the economy.

18. Government seeks to bring about a full-employment noninflationary NNP by employing both fiscal and Monetary policies.

■ PROBLEMS AND PROJECTS

1. Assume that the consolidated balance sheet below is for all commercial banks. Assume also that the required reserve ratio is 25% and that cash is *not* a part of the commercial banks' legal reserve.

Assets		Liabilities	
Cash	$ 50	Demand Deposits	$400
Reserves	100	Loans from Federal Reserve	25
Loans	150	Net worth	75
Securities	200		
	$500		$500

a. To *increase* the supply of money by $100, the Federal Reserve Banks could *either:*

(1) (increase, decrease) decrease the reserve ratio to ________%;

(2) *or* (buy, sell) buy securities worth $________ in the open market.

b. To *reduce* the supply of money by $50, the Federal Reserve Banks could *either:*

(1) __________ the reserve ratio to __________%

(2) __________ securities worth $__________ in the open market.

2. Shown below are the consolidated balance sheets of the Federal Reserve and of the commercial banks. Assume that the reserve ratio for commercial banks is 25%, that cash is *not* a part of a bank's legal reserve, and that the figures in column 1 show the balance sheets of the Federal Reserve and the commercial banks *prior to each of the following five transactions.* Place the new balance-sheet figures in the appropriate columns and complete A, B, C, D, and E in these columns. *Do not* use the figures you place in columns (2) through (5) when you work the next part of the problem; start all parts of the problem with the printed figures in column (1).

a. The Federal Reserve Banks sell $3 in securities to the public which pays by check (column 2).

b. The Federal Reserve Banks buy $4 in securities from the commercial banks (column 3).

c. The Federal Reserve Banks lower the required reserve ratio for commercial banks to 20% (column 4).

d. The U.S. Treasury buys $5 worth of goods from American manufacturers and pays the manufacturers by checks drawn on its accounts at the Federal Reserve Banks (column 5).

e. Because the Federal Reserve Banks have raised the discount rate, commercial banks repay $6 which they owe to the Federal Reserve (column 6).

3. On the graph at the top of the next page is the demand-for-money curve which shows the amounts of money consumers and firms wish to hold at various rates of interest (when the money NNP in the economy is given).

	(1)	(2)	(3)	(4)	(5)	(6)
	Federal Reserve Banks					
Assets:						
Gold certificates	$ 25	$	$	$	$	$
Securities	30					
Loans to commercial banks	10					
Liabilities						
Reserves of commercial banks	50					
Treasury deposits	5					
Federal Reserve Notes	10					
	Commercial Banks					
Assets:						
Reserves	$ 50	$	$	$	$	$
Securities	70					
Loans	90					
Liabilities:						
Demand deposits	200					
Loans from Federal Reserve	10					
A. Required reserves						
B. Excess reserves						
C. How much has the money supply changed?						
D. How much *more* can the money supply change?						
E. What is the total of D and E?						

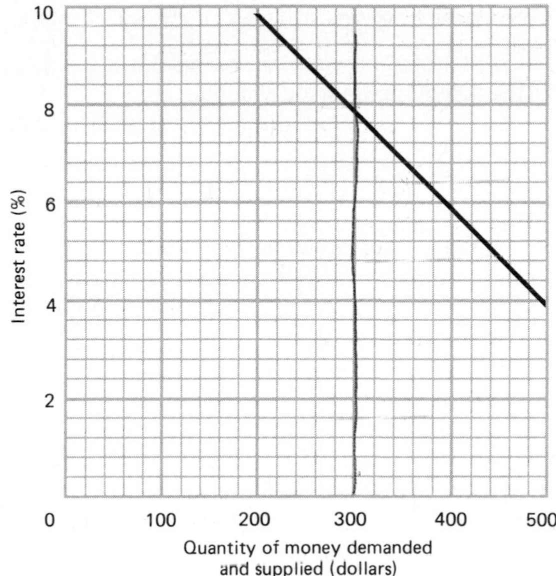

a. Suppose the supply of money is equal to $300.

(1) Draw on this graph the supply-of-money curve.

(2) The equilibrium rate of interest in the economy is 8 %.

b. On the next graph is an investment-demand curve which shows the amounts of planned investment at various rates of interest. Given your answer to (2) above, how much will investors plan to spend for capital goods? $ 20 mil

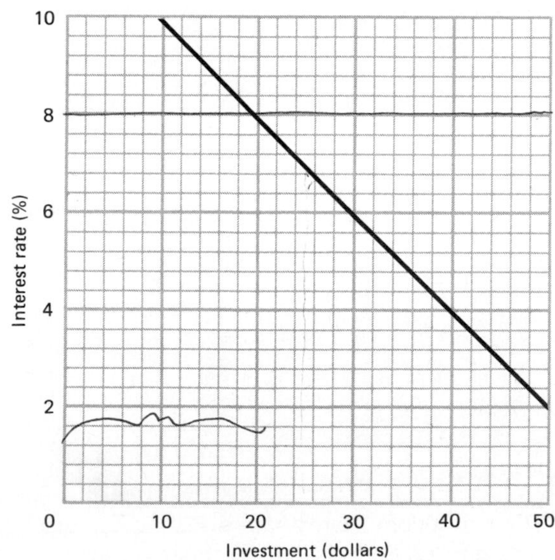

c. On the graph below is the saving curve in an economy in which the only leakage from the NNP is saving. (There are no taxes collected and no imports of goods and services.)

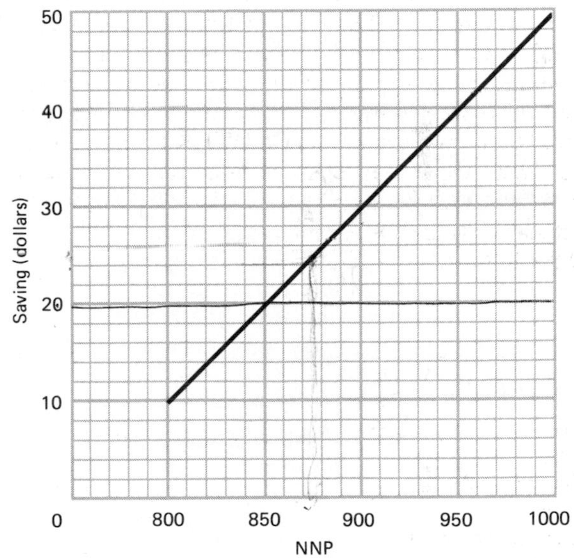

(1) On this graph plot the investment curve when planned investment is the amount given by you in your answer to (*b*) above.

(2) If the only injection into this economy is investment spending (that is, if there is no government spending for and no exports of goods and services), the equilibrium NNP will be $ 850

d. Assume the money supply increases to $400. On the first graph plot the new supply-of-money curve. The new:

(1) Equilibrium interest rate is 6 %;

(2) Level of planned investment is $ 30 ;

(3) Equilibrium NNP is $ 900

e. Suppose the full-employment noninflationary NNP in this economy is $875.

(1) At this NNP saving would be $ 25

(2) For this NNP to be the equilibrium NNP, investment would have to be equal to $________

(3) For investment to be at this level the rate of interest would have to be ________%.

(4) And for the interest rate to be at this level the supply of money would have to be equal to $________

f. In this economy:

(1) the marginal propensity to save is equal to ________ and the multiplier has, therefore, a value equal to ________;

(2) a one percentage point decrease in the interest rate will (increase, decrease) ________ planned investment by $________ and will, therefore, (increase, decrease) ________ the equilibrium NNP by $________;

(3) but for the interest rate to decrease by one percentage point the money supply must (increase, decrease) ________ by $________

4. Columns (1) and (2) of the table below are the aggregate-supply schedule. (The price level is a price index and real national output is measured in billions of dollars.)

(1) Price level	(2) Real national output	(3) AE_1	(4) AE_2	(5) AE_3	(6) AE_4	(7) AE_5	(8) AE_6
.30	$1500	$1600	$1700	$2070	$2400	$2920	$3020
.30	1600	1600	1700	2070	2400	2920	3020
.30	1700	1600	1700	2070	2400	2920	3020
.40	1790	1500	1600	1970	2300	2820	2920
.50	1870	1400	1500	1870	2200	2720	2820
.60	1940	1300	1400	1770	2100	2620	2720
.70	2000	1200	1300	1670	2000	2520	2620
.80	2050	1100	1200	1570	1900	2420	2520
.90	2090	1000	1100	1470	1800	2320	2420
1.00	2120	900	1000	1370	1700	2220	2320
1.10	2120	800	900	1270	1600	2120	2220
1.20	2120	700	800	1170	1500	2020	2120

a. The Keynesian range on this aggregate-supply schedule is from a real national output of zero to $________ billion.

b. The classical range on this aggregate-supply curve is at the real national output of $________ billion.

c. If the aggregate-demand schedule were that shown in columns (1) and (3) the equilibrium real national output would be $________ billion and the price level would be ________

d. If the aggregate-demand schedule increased from that shown in columns (1) and (3) to the one shown in columns (1) and (4) the equilibrium real national output would ________ and the price level would ________

e. If the aggregate-demand schedule increased from that shown in columns (1) and (5) to the one shown in columns (1) and (6) the equilibrium real national output would ________ and the price level would ________

f. And if the aggregate-demand schedule increased from that shown in columns (1) and (7) to the one shown in columns (1) and (8) the equilibrium real national output would ________ and the price level would ________

5. Columns (1) and (2) in the following table show the money supply and columns (3) and (4) show the demand for money. (Dollar figures are in billions and the interest rate is a percentage.)

(1) Supply of money	(2) Interest rate	(3) Demand for money	(4) Demand for money
$400	.08	$100	$200
400	.07	200	300
400	.06	300	400
400	.05	400	500
400	.04	500	600
400	.03	600	700
400	.02	700	800

a. The equilibrium interest rate is ________%.

b. Suppose the Fed wishes to stabilize the interest rate at this level; but the money GNP produced by the economy increases, and as a result the demand for money in the economy increases to that shown in columns (3) and (4). The Fed will have to (increase, decrease) ________ the supply of money to $________ billion.

c. But if the Fed stabilizes the supply of money at $400 billion and the money GNP increases to increase the demand for money to that shown in columns (3) and (4) the interest rate will (rise, fall) ________ to ________%.

d. If the Fed stabilizes the interest rate it must (increase, decrease) increase the supply of money when the money GNP rises and ________ it when the money GNP falls; and if it holds the supply of money constant the interest rate will (rise, fall) ________ when the money GNP increases and ________ when the money GNP decreases.

■ SELF-TEST

Circle the T if the statement is true, the F if it is false.

1. Consumer spending is more sensitive to changes in the rate of interest than is investment demand. T F

2. The securities owned by the Federal Reserve Banks are almost entirely U.S. government bonds. T F

3. If the Federal Reserve Banks buy $15 in government securities from the public in the open market, the effect will be to increase the excess reserves of commercial banks by $15. T F

4. When the Federal Reserve sells bonds in the open market, the price of these bonds falls. T F

5. A change in the reserve ratio will affect the multiple by which the banking system can create money, but it will not affect the actual or excess reserves of member banks. T F

6. If the reserve ratio is lowered, some required reserves are turned into excess reserves. T F

7. When commercial banks borrow from the Federal Reserve Banks they increase their excess reserves and their money-creating potential. T F

8. If the monetary authority wished to follow a tight money policy, it would seek to reduce the reserves of commercial banks. T F

9. An increase in the required reserve ratio tends to reduce the profits of banks. T F

10. The equilibrium rate of interest is found at the intersection of the demand-for-money and the supply-of-money curves. T F

11. An increase in the equilibrium NNP will shift the demand-for-money curve to the left and increase the equilibrium interest rate. T F

12. Monetary policy is more effective in fighting recession than it is in curbing inflation. T F

13. Unlike fiscal policy, monetary policy is an effective means of controlling cost-push inflation. T F

14. In an economy in which the NNP is either rising or falling the Fed is unable to control both the money supply and interest rates. T F

15. When the economy is at or near full employment an increase in the money supply tends to be inflationary. T F

16. It is generally agreed that fiscal policy is more effective than monetary policy in controlling the business cycle because fiscal policy is more flexible. T F

Circle the letter that corresponds to the best answer.

1. The agency directly responsible for monetary policy in the United States is: (*a*) the twelve Federal Reserve Banks; (*b*) the Board of Governors of the Federal Reserve System; (*c*) the Congress of the United States; (*d*) the U.S. Treasury.

2. In the Keynesian chain of cause and effect between changes in the excess reserves of commercial banks and the resulting changes in output and employment in the economy (*a*) an increase in excess reserves will decrease the money supply; (*b*) a decrease in the money supply will increase the rate of interest; (*c*) an increase in the rate of interest will increase aggregate expenditures; (*d*) an increase in aggregate expenditures will decrease output and employment.

3. Which of the following is most likely to be affected by changes in the rate of interest? (*a*) Consumer spending; (*b*) investment spending; (*c*) the spending of the Federal government; (*d*) the exports of the economy.

4. The largest single asset in the Federal Reserve Banks' consolidated balance sheet is (*a*) securities; (*b*) the reserves of commercial banks; (*c*) Federal Reserve Notes; (*d*) loans to commercial banks.

5. The largest single liability of the Federal Reserve Banks is (*a*) securities; (*b*) the reserves of commercial banks; (*c*) Federal Reserve Notes; (*d*) loans to commercial banks.

6. Assuming that the Federal Reserve Banks sell $20 million in government securities to commercial banks and the reserve ratio is 20%, then the effect will be: (*a*) to reduce the actual supply of money by $20 million; (*b*) to reduce the actual supply of money by $4 million; (*c*) to reduce the potential money supply by $20 million; (*d*) to reduce the potential money supply by $100 million.

7. Which of the following acts would *not* have the same general effect upon the economy as the other three? (*a*) The Federal Reserve Banks sell bonds in the open market; (*b*) The Federal Reserve increases the discount rate; (*c*) the Federal Reserve eases credit for the purchase of consumer durables; (*d*) the Federal Reserve raises the reserve ratio.

8. Which of the following is the most important control used by the Federal Reserve Banks to regulate the money supply? (*a*) Changing the reserve ratio; (*b*) open-market operations; (*c*) changing the discount rate; (*d*) changing the margin requirements.

9. Which of the following is *not* one of the selective controls which have been employed by the Federal Reserve? (*a*) Setting tariff rates; (*b*) moral suasion; (*c*) setting margin requirements; (*d*) setting credit terms for consumer durable goods.

10. A change in the money supply has the *least* effect on the equilibrium NNP when (*a*) both the demand-for-money and investment-demand curves are steep; (*b*) both the demand-for-money and investment-demand curves are flat; (*c*) the demand-for-money curve is flat and the investment-demand curve is steep; (*d*) the demand-for-money curve is steep and the investment-demand curve is flat.

11. An increase in the money supply will have little or no effect on the real national output and employment in (*a*) the Keynesian range on the aggregate-supply curve; (*b*) the intermediate range along the aggregate-supply curve; (*c*) the classical range on the aggregate-supply curve; (*d*) any of the three ranges on the aggregate-supply curve.

12. An increase in the money supply will have little or no effect on the price level in (*a*) the Keynesian range; (*b*) the intermediate range; (*c*) the classical range; (*d*) any of the three ranges.

13. An increase in the money supply is *least* effective in stimulating aggregate expenditures when the velocity of money (*a*) falls as the money supply increases; (*b*) remains constant; (*c*) rises as the money supply increases; (*d*) is equal to 5.

14. The Fed (*a*) can stabilize both the interest rate and the money supply; (*b*) cannot stabilize the interest rate; (*c*) cannot stabilize the money supply; (*d*) cannot stabilize both the interest rate and the money supply.

15. Between October of 1979 and October of 1982 the Fed attempted to (*a*) stabilize interest rates and allowed the money supply to fluctuate; (*b*) stabilize the money supply and allowed interest rates to fluctuate; (*c*) stabilize neither the money supply nor interest rates; (*d*) stabilize both the money supply and interest rates.

16. Which of the following are coordinated policies? (*a*) An increase in government expenditures and in the money supply; (*b*) a decrease in personal tax rates and in the money supply; (*c*) an increase in transfer payments and a decrease in the money supply; (*d*) an increase in corporate tax rates and in the money supply.

■ DISCUSSION QUESTIONS

1. Explain from a Keynesian viewpoint how the Board of Governors and the Federal Reserve Banks can influence income, output, employment, and the price level. In your explanation, employ the following concepts: reserves, excess reserves, the supply of money, the availability of bank credit, and the rate of interest.

2. Why are changes in the rate of interest more likely to affect investment spending than consumption and saving?

3. What are the important assets and liabilities of the Federal Reserve Banks?

4. Explain how the monetary-policy tools of the Federal Reserve Banks would be used to contract the supply of money. How would they be used to expand the supply of money?

5. What is the difference between the effects of the Federal Reserve's buying (selling) government securities in the open market from (to) commercial banks and from (to) the public?

6. Which of the monetary-policy tools available to the Federal Reserve is most effective? Why is it more effective than other tools?

7. How do the selective controls differ from general or quantitative controls? What are the principal selective controls? Explain how the Federal Reserve would use these controls in following a tight and an easy money policy.

8. Using the Keynesian theory and three graphs, explain what determines (*a*) the equilibrium interest rate; (*b*) planned investment; and (*c*) the equilibrium NNP. Now employ these three graphs to show the effects of a decrease in the money supply upon the equilibrium NNP.

9. Utilizing your answers to the question above, (*a*) what determines how large the effect of the decrease in the money supply on the equilibrium NNP will be; and (*b*) how would the change in the equilibrium NNP affect the demand-for-money curve, the interest rate, planned investment, and the NNP itself?

10. How does a change in the money supply affect the aggregate-demand curve? How will a change in the money supply and the resulting shift in the aggregate-demand curve affect the real national output and the price level in (*a*) the Keynesian range, (*b*) the classical range, and (*c*) the intermediate range along the aggregate-supply curve?

11. What are the strengths and shortcomings of monetary policy?

12. Why is monetary policy more effective in controlling inflation than in reducing unemployment?

13. What is the target (or policy) dilemma of the Fed? What target did the Fed set (*a*) before October of 1979; (*b*) between October of 1979 and October of 1981; and (*c*) after October of 1981?

14. Suppose the money GNP in the American economy is increasing or decreasing. Why is the Federal Reserve unable to keep both interest rates and the size of the money supply from changing?

15. Explain as briefly as possible what Keynesians believe determines the level of national output in the American economy.

16. Distinguish between fiscal and monetary policy and explain how we may use each of them to achieve reasonably full employment and relatively stable prices.

20
Alternative views: monetarism and rational expectations

Economics has always been an arena in which conflicting theories and policies opposed each other. This field of intellectual combat, in major engagements, has seen Adam Smith do battle with the defenders of a regulated economy. It witnessed the opposition of Karl Marx to the orthodox economics of his day. In more recent times it saw Keynes in conflict with the classical economists. Around the major engagements have been countless minor skirmishes between opposing viewpoints. Out of these major and minor confrontations have emerged not winners and losers but the advancement of economic theory and the improvement of economic policy.

Monetarism and (more recently) rational-expectations theory are the latest challengers to enter this intellectual arena. The opponent is the reigning champion, Keynesianism, which bested classical economics in the same arena during the 1940s. Monetarists and rational-expectations theorists wish to free the economy from what they see as the destabilizing effects of discretionary fiscal and monetary policies. They view the Keynesians as the proponents of government intervention and see themselves as the defenders of *laissez faire.*

Chapter 20 examines both monetarism and rational-expectations theory; but it directs most of its attention toward monetarism. But this chapter is more than a comparison of the attitudes of Keynesians and monetarists toward the role of government in the economy. And it is more than a comparison of the basic equations of the two schools of thought. The basic equation of the Keynesians and the equation of exchange of the monetarists say pretty much the same thing. The equation of exchange ($MV = PQ$) is another way of saying that the economy will produce the NNP which is equal to the aggregate quantity of goods and services demanded.

The issue is whether the income velocity of money—the V in the equation of exchange—is stable or unstable. If it is stable, as the monetarists contend, then the only kind of policy that can be used to control (to increase or decrease) money NNP is monetary policy; and fiscal policy cannot expand or contract money NNP. But if V is unstable, as the Keynesians argue, then fiscal policy is the only effective means and monetary policy is an ineffective means of controlling money NNP. The issue of whether V is stable or unstable becomes an issue of whether the size of the money supply matters very much or very little. Monetarists argue that the M in the equation of exchange is the only thing that matters and their Keynesian rivals contend that it doesn't matter very much.

The emphasis in Chapter 20 is on monetarism because earlier chapters have emphasized Keynesianism. You are not expected, however, to determine which of the two groups is correct. But you should see that monetarism is an alternative to Keynesianism; that the economic issue is the stability of V; and that the political issue is, therefore, whether monetary or fiscal policy is more effective.

Rational-expectations theorists take a more extreme position in the debate over the relative effectiveness of monetary and fiscal policies. Their position is that the economy tends to produce its full-employment output and that neither of the two types of policy can expand real output and employment in either the short run or the long run: the only effect on the economy of an expansionary monetary or fiscal policy is inflation. They are modern-day (or the new) classical economists who argue that neither the size of the money supply nor the fiscal policies of government has any effect on real output and employment. While this extreme position will be strange to those who have come to believe government can bring about full employment without inflation in the economy, advocates of the rational-expectations theory are careful to explain how they reach these conclusions; and you should be sure you understand the assumptions they make in order to reach their unusual conclusions before you dismiss their extreme position.

Out of the debate among Keynesians, monetarists, and rational-expectationists, as out of the confrontations of the past, will eventually come better economic theory and the policies that solve economic problems. In the meantime, you can adopt an eclectic position: neither the Keynesians, monetarists, nor rational-expectations theorists are entirely correct and neither of them is wholly wrong.

■ CHECKLIST

When you have studied this chapter you should be able to:

☐ Compare the positions of Keynesian and monetarist economists on the competitiveness of a capitalistic economy and its inherent stability and on the role government should play in stabilizing it.

☐ Write the equation of exchange and define each of the four terms in the equation.

☐ Show how the basic Keynesian equation is "translated" into the equation of exchange.

☐ Compare the monetarist and Keynesian views on the functions of money; on why households and firms demand money; and on what determines the quantity of money demanded.

☐ Explain why the monetarists believe money NNP is directly and predictably linked to *M*.

☐ Write a brief scenario which explains what monetarists believe will happen to change the money NNP and to *V* when *M* is increased.

☐ Construct a scenario which explains what Keynesians believe will happen to the interest rate and to *V* and money NNP if *M* is increased.

☐ Explain why Keynesians favor and monetarists reject the use of fiscal policy to stabilize the economy.

☐ State the monetary rule of the monetarists, and the two reasons why they propose a rule instead of discretionary monetary policy.

☐ Use the aggregate demand-aggregate supply models of the Keynesians and the monetarists to compare and contrast the effects of an expansionary monetary or fiscal policy on the real national output and the price level.

☐ State the two basic assumptions of the rational-expectations theory; and explain how the advocates of this theory believe firms, workers, and consumers react to the announcement of an expansionary monetary or fiscal policy to frustrate the achievement of the goal of the policy.

☐ Use aggregate demand and aggregate supply to show the effects of an expansionary monetary or fiscal policy on real output and the price level in the RET.

☐ Write a brief scenario to explain why rational-expectations theorists believe discretionary monetary and fiscal policies are procyclical; and state what type of government policy is advocated by these theorists.

☐ Present three criticisms of the RET.

■ CHAPTER OUTLINE

1. Monetarism and rational-expectations theory (RET) are alternatives to the Keynesian macroeconomic theory and policy recommendations; and while this chapter examines both of these alternatives, it stresses monetarism.

2. Keynesians and monetarists differ over the inherent stability of capitalistic economies and ideologically over the role government should play in the economy.

a. Keynesians believe that because many markets in a capitalistic economy are noncompetitive it is unstable, that government should intervene to stabilize the economy, and that fiscal policy is a more effective stabilizer than monetary policy.

b. Monetarists believe that because markets in a capitalistic economy are competitive the economy would be stable if it were not for government interference, that government intervention destabilizes the economy, and that government should not use either discretionary fiscal or monetary policy to try to stabilize it.

3. In the Keynesian model the equilibrium output of the economy is the output at which

$$C_a + I_n + G = \text{NNP}$$

a. In the monetarist model the basic equation is the equation of exchange,

$$MV = PQ$$

but because MV (total spending) $= C_a + I_n + G$ and $PQ =$ NNP, the equations are different ways of stating the same relationship.

b. While Keynesians assign a secondary role to money because they believe the links in the cause-effect chain of the previous chapter are loose ones, monetarists, believing V in the equation of exchange is constant, find that while a change in M may affect Q in the short run it will in the long run affect only P.

4. Whether *V* in the equation of exchange is stable or unstable is a critical question because if it is stable *PQ* is closely linked to *M;* and if it is unstable the link between *PQ* and *M* is loose and uncertain.

a. Reasoning that money is a medium of exchange and that the only demand for money is the transactions demand, monetarists conclude that the quantity of money demanded is a stable percentage of NNP (that NNP/*M* is constant); that an increase (a decrease) in *M* will leave firms and households with more (less) money than they wish to have; that they will, therefore, increase (decrease) spending for consumer and capital goods; and that this will cause the NNP and the amount of money they wish to hold for transactions purposes to rise (fall) until their demand for money is equal to *M* and NNP/*M* = *V.*

b. But Keynesians argue that consumers and business firms also have an asset demand for money; that this asset demand for money is inversely related to the rate of interest; and that an increase (a decrease) in *M* will decrease (increase) the interest rate, increase (decrease) the amount of money people wish to hold as an asset, lower (raise) *V,* and leave the effect on NNP uncertain.

c. Empirical evidence confirms neither the contention of the monetarists that *V* is stable nor the contention of the Keynesians that it is variable (or unstable).

5. Because their theories (their views on the stability of *V*) differ, Keynesians and monetarists disagree over the effectiveness of fiscal and monetary policies in stabilizing the economy.

a. Keynesians favor the use of fiscal policy to stabilize the economy because they believe it is a more powerful stabilizer; but the monetarists argue that the use of fiscal policy is both harmful and ineffective because of the crowding-out effect it has on investment expenditures in the economy.

b. Arguing that discretionary changes in *M* have produced monetary mismanagement and macroeconomic instability, the monetarists have proposed the monetary rule that *M* be increased at the same annual rate as the potential annual rate of increase in the real GNP.

c. In the aggregate demand–aggregate supply model the monetarists see an aggregate-supply curve that is very steep (or vertical) and in which an increase in aggregate demand has little (or no) effect on real national output and increases the price level by a relatively large amount; but the Keynesians see an aggregate-supply curve that is nearly flat (or horizontal) and in which an increase in aggregate demand has little (or no) effect on the price level and increases the real national output by a relatively large amount.

6. The RET, developed since the mid-1970s and called the new classical economics, is an alternative to Keynesian economics and to monetarism.

a. Economists who advocate the RET make two basic assumptions:

(1) business firms, consumers, and workers understand how the economy works so that they can anticipate the effect on the economy of an economic event or a change in economic policy, and use all available information to make decisions in a way to further their own self-interests; and

(2) all markets in the economy are so competitive that equilibrium prices and quantities quickly adjust to these events and changes in public policy.

b. From these assumptions the proponents of the RET conclude that the response of the public to the expected inflationary effect of an expansionary monetary (or fiscal) policy will cancel the intended effect on output and employment in the economy.

c. In an aggregate demand–aggregate supply model of the RET the aggregate supply curve is vertical; and any monetary or fiscal policy that increases or decreases aggregate demand affects only the price level, and has no effect on real output or employment, real wages, or real interest rates in either the short or the long run.

d. Rational-expectations theorists argue that discretionary monetary and fiscal policies are pro- (rather than counter-) cyclical; and would (like the monetarists) replace discretionary policies with rules.

e. The appeal of the RET comes from the inability of Keynesian economics to explain and to develop policies to correct stagflation, and from the long-sought connection between micro- and macroeconomics; but RET has been subjected to three basic criticisms.

(1) One criticism is that people are not so well informed on the workings of the economy and the effect of economic policy on it as the rational-expectations theorists assume.

(2) A second criticism is that many markets in the economy are not so competitive as assumed in the RET, and do not, therefore, adjust their prices as rapidly as assumed.

(3) And the third criticism is that monetary and fiscal policies have worked in the past to expand real output and employment in the economy.

f. The debate among Keynesians, monetarists, and rational-expectationists will continue into the future; and three concluding comments put this debate into perspective.

■ IMPORTANT TERMS

Keynesianism
Monetarism
Equation of exchange
Income (or circuit) velocity of money
Crowding-out effect
Monetary rule
Rational-expectations theory

■ FILL-IN QUESTIONS

1. Keynesians believe that capitalism is inherently (stable, unstable) ______________ because many of its markets are (competitive, noncompetitive) ______________, advocate (government intervention, laissez faire) ______________, and favor (monetary, fiscal) ______________ over ______________ policy.

2. Monetarists argue that capitalism is inherently ______________ because most of its markets are ______________, advocate ______________, and favor the use of (discretionary, nondiscretionary) ______________ (monetary, fiscal) ______________ policy.

3. The basic equation of the monetarists is ______________ = ______________

a. This equation is called the ______________

b. Indicate below what each of the four letters in this equation represents.

(1) *M:* ______________

(2) *V:* ______________

(3) *P:* ______________

(4) *Q:* ______________

4. The basic equation of the Keynesians is $C_a + I_n + G =$ NNP.

a. $C_a + I_n + G$ is ______________ and in the equation of exchange is equal to ______________

b. Money NNP is equal to ______________ in the equation of exchange.

5. Monetarists argue that

a. any increase in *M* will (increase, decrease) ______________ *PQ;*

b. in the *short run* any increase in *M* may (increase, decrease) ______________ both *P* and *Q;* but

c. in the *long run* any increase in *M* will (increase, decrease) ______________ only (*P, Q*) ______________

6. In the debate on the stability of *V:*

a. monetarists argue that money is used only as a ______________, that the only demand for money is the ______________ demand, that this demand is a fixed percentage of ______________ and that *V* is, therefore, ______________

b. Keynesians contend that money is also used as a ______________ and that there is also an ______________ demand for money, that this demand is inversely related to the ______________, and that *V* is, therefore, ______________

7. An increase in *M:*

a. to the monetarist's way of thinking will

(1) leave the public with (more, less) ______________ money than it wishes to have,

(2) induce the public to (increase, decrease) ______________ its spending for consumer and capital goods,

(3) which will result in a(n) ______________ in money NNP

(4) until the money NNP (or *MV*) is equal to ______________ times ______________

b. to the Keynesian's way of thinking it will

(1) result in a(n) ________________ in the rate of interest,

(2) which will ____________ the demand for money

(3) and ________________ V

(4) and the effect on money NNP will be ________________________

8. It is, in short, the view of the:

a. monetarists that V (in the equation of exchange) is stable and that there is a direct relationship between ________________ and ________________

b. Keynesians that V is (directly, inversely) __________ related to the interest rate; that the interest rate (increases, decreases) ____________ when M increases; and that, therefore, M and V are (directly, inversely) ________________ related to each other.

9. In the debate on the use of fiscal policy:

a. the Keynesians contend that the more effective tool for stabilizing the economy is (fiscal, monetary) ________________ policy; but

b. the monetarists reply that government borrowing to finance a budget deficit will (raise, lower) __________ the rate of interest and have a ________________ effect on investment spending.

10. Monetarists would have the supply of money increase at the same annual rate as the potential rate of growth of ________________ and this is a rate of from ________________ to ________________%.

11. Monetarists proposed the adoption of the "Monetary Rule" because they believe that discretionary monetary policy tends to (stabilize, destabilize) ____________ the economy.

12. In the:

a. Keynesian model of the economy the aggregate supply curve is relatively (steep, flat) ________________ and an increase in aggregate demand will have a relatively (large, small) ________________ effect on the price level and a relatively ________________ effect on the real national output.

b. monetarist model the aggregate supply curve is relatively ____________ and an increase in aggregate demand will have a relatively ____________ effect on price level and a relatively ____________ effect on real national output.

13. In the rational-expectations theory:

a. individuals correctly anticipate the effects of any economic event or a change in public policy on the economy and make decisions based on their anticipations to maximize their own ________________;

b. the markets in the economy are (noncompetitive, purely competitive) ________________ and prices in these markets are perfectly (inflexible, flexible) ________________; and as a result,

c. an expansionary monetary or fiscal policy will lead the public to expect (inflation, a recession) ________________ and they will react in a way that results in (an increase, a decrease, no change) ________________ in the real output of the economy and ________________ in the price level.

14. The aggregate supply curve in the RET is (vertical, horizontal) ____________ and a change in aggregate demand brings about a change in (the price level, the real output) ________________ and no change in ________________ of the economy.

15. Proponents of the RET:

a. contend that discretionary monetary and fiscal policies are (pro-, counter-) ________________ cyclical; and

b. like the monetarists, favor (policy rules, discretionary policy) ________________

16. The critics of the RET maintain that people are (less well, better) ________________ informed than assumed in the theory; markets are (more, less) ________________ competitive than assumed in the theory and prices are, therefore, (sticky, flexible) ________________; and monetary and fiscal policies have been employed in the past to (stabilize, destabilize) ______________ the economy and to expand its (real, nominal) ______________ output.

■ PROBLEMS AND PROJECTS

1. You must imagine that you are a monetarist in this problem and assume that V is constant and equal to 4. In the table below is the aggregate supply schedule: the real output Q which producers will offer for sale at seven different price levels P.

P	Q	PQ	MV
$1.00	100	$____	$____
2.00	110	____	____
3.00	120	____	____
4.00	130	____	____
5.00	140	____	____
6.00	150	____	____
7.00	160	____	____

a. Compute and enter in the table above the seven values of PQ.

b. Assume M is $90. Enter the values of MV on each of the seven lines in the table. The equilibrium

(1) money (or nominal) national output (PQ or MV) is $______________

(2) price level is $______________

(3) real national output (Q) is $______________

c. When M increases to $175, MV at each price level is $______________; and the equilibrium

(1) money (or nominal) national output is $______________

(2) price level is $______________

(3) real national output is $______________

2. In this problem you are a Keynesian. The left side of the following table shows the amounts of money firms and households wish to have for transactions at different levels of money NNP. The right side of the table shows the amounts of money they want to have as assets at different rates of interest.

a. Suppose the money NNP is $500, the interest is 7%, and the supply of money is $125.

Money NNP	Transactions demand	Interest rate	Asset demand
$ 500	$ 50	7.0%	$ 75
600	60	6.8	80
700	70	6.6	85
800	80	6.4	90
900	90	6.2	95
1000	100	6.0	100

(1) The amount of money demanded for transactions is $______________

(2) The amount of money demanded as an asset is $______________

(3) The total amount of money demanded for both purposes is $______________

(4) The amount of money firms and households wish to have is (greater than, less than, equal to) ______________ the amount of money they actually have.

(5) The velocity of money (equal to money NNP divided by the supply of money) is ______________

b. Assume the Federal Reserve Banks expand the supply of money to $160 by purchasing securities in the open market; and that as a result the rate of interest falls to 6% and the money NNP rises to $600.

(1) The amount of money demanded for transactions is now $______________ and the amount demanded as an asset is now $______________

(2) The total amount of money demanded is $______________ and the amount of money the public wishes to have is ______________ the amount of money they actually have.

(3) The velocity of money is ______________

c. Suppose the Federal government pursues an expansionary fiscal policy which raises the money NNP from \$600 to \$800 and the interest rate from 6% to 6.8%, and the money supply remains at \$160.

(1) The transactions demand for money is \$________________, the asset demand is \$________________, and the total demand is \$________________

(2) The velocity of money is ________________

d. The effect of the easy money policy was to (increase, decrease) ________________ the velocity of money and the effect of the expansionary fiscal policy was to ________________ it.

3. On the graph below are three aggregate-supply curves: S_1, S_2, and S_3.

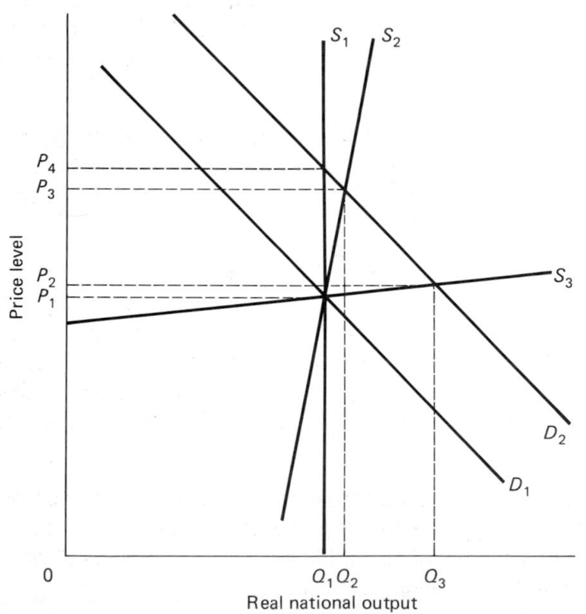

a. S_1 is the (Keynesian, classical, rational-expectations) ________________ supply curve, S_2 is the ________________ supply curve, and S_3 is the ________________ supply curve.

b. Regardless of which is the economy's supply curve, if the aggregate-demand curve is D_1, the equilibrium real national output is ________________ and the equilibrium price level is ________________

c. Should aggregate demand increase from D_1 to D_2 in the

(1) classical model the equilibrium real national output would (increase, decrease, remain constant) ________________ to (at) ________________ and the equilibrium price level would (increase, decrease, remain constant) ________________ to (at) ________________;

(2) Keynesian model the equilibrium real national output would ________________ to (at) ________________ and the equilibrium price level would ________________ to (at) ________________;

(3) rational-expectations model the equilibrium real national output would ________________ to (at) ________________ and the equilibrium price level would ________________ to (at) ________________

■ SELF-TEST

Circle the T if the statement is true, the F if it is false.

1. The chief exponent of the monetarist position is Milton Friedman. **T F**

2. The basic equations of the Keynesians and the monetarists are no more than two different ways of stating the same relationship. **T F**

3. Most monetarists believe that an increase in the money supply will have no effect on real output and employment in either the short run or the long run. **T F**

4. Keynesians contend that changes in the money supply will have little or no effect on the rate of interest. **T F**

5. Keynesians also maintain that relatively small changes in the interest rate have relatively large effects on investment spending. **T F**

6. Monetarists argue that *V* in the equation of exchange is stable and that a change in *M* will bring about a direct and proportional change in *P*. **T F**

7. In the monetarists' analysis the demand for money is directly related to money NNP. **T F**

8. From the monetarist viewpoint, the economy is in equilibrium when the amount of money firms and households want to hold is equal to the money supply. **T F**

9. Keynesians contend that the velocity of money is unstable. **T F**

10. In the Keynesians' analysis the demand for money is directly related to the rate of interest. **T F**

11. Keynesians argue that a decrease in the rate of interest will decrease the velocity of money. **T F**

12. Statistical evidence reveals that the velocity of money has remained almost constant from one year to the next. **T F**

13. An expansionary fiscal policy will, the Keynesians contend, decrease the velocity of money. **T F**

14. Monetarists conclude that discretionary monetary policy has resulted in macroeconomic instability. **T F**

15. Economists who have advanced the rational-expectations theory argue that discretionary fiscal and monetary policies have helped to stabilize the economy. **T F**

16. Most economists are proponents of the rational-expectations theory (the new classical economics). **T F**

Circle the letter that corresponds to the best answer.

1. Keynesians (*a*) believe capitalism is inherently stable; (*b*) believe the markets in a capitalistic economy are highly competitive; (*c*) argue against the use of discretionary monetary policy; (*d*) contend that government intervention in the economy is desirable.

2. Monetarists (*a*) argue for the use of discretionary monetary policy; (*b*) contend that government policies have reduced the stability of the economy; (*c*) believe a capitalistic economy is inherently unstable; (*d*) believe the markets in a capitalistic economy are largely noncompetitive.

3. Which of the following is *not* true? (*a*) *MV* is total spending; (*b*) *PQ* is the real NNP; (*c*) *PQ* is money NNP; (*d*) $MV = C_a + I_n + G$

4. If *V* in the equation of exchange is constant, an increase in *M* will necessarily increase (*a*) *P;* (*b*) *Q;* (*c*) both *P* and *Q;* (*d*) *P* times *Q.*

5. Monetarists contend that (*a*) the only demand for money is the transactions demand; (*b*) the only demand for money is the asset demand; (*c*) there is no transactions demand; (*d*) there is both a transactions and an asset demand for money.

6. From the monetarist viewpoint, an increase in the supply of money will (*a*) raise the rate of interest; (*b*) increase spending for consumer and capital goods; (*c*) increase the asset demand for money; (*d*) increase the demand for government securities.

7. Keynesians argue that (*a*) the only demand for money is the asset demand; (*b*) the only demand for money is the transactions demand; (*c*) there is no transactions demand; (*d*) there is both a transactions and an asset demand for money.

8. From the Keynesian viewpoint, an increase in supply of money will (*a*) raise the rate of interest; (*b*) decrease spending for consumer and capital goods; (*c*) increase the asset demand for money; (*d*) decrease the demand for government securities.

9. The crowding-out effect is the effect of borrowing funds to finance a government deficit on (*a*) imports into the economy; (*b*) the money supply; (*c*) investment spending; (*d*) consumer expenditures.

10. Keynesians contend that borrowing to finance a government deficit incurred in order to increase employment and output in the economy will (*a*) have little or no effect on the rate of interest; (*b*) have little or no effect on investment spending; (*c*) have a significant effect on *Q* in the equation of exchange; (*d*) have all of the above effects.

11. The rule suggested by the monetarists is that the money supply increase at the same rate as (*a*) the price level; (*b*) the real output of the economy; (*c*) the velocity of money; (*d*) none of the above.

12. In the classical model (*a*) the aggregate-supply curve is very steep and an increase in aggregate demand will have little or no effect on the price level; (*b*) the aggregate-supply curve is nearly flat and an increase in aggregate demand will have little or no effect on the price level; (*c*) the aggregate-supply curve is very steep and an increase in aggregate demand will have a large effect on the price level; (*d*) the aggregate-supply curve is nearly flat and an increase in aggregate demand will have a large effect on the price level.

13. In the Keynesian model (*a*) the aggregate-supply curve is very steep and an increase in aggregate demand will have a large effect on real national output; (*b*) the aggregate-supply curve is nearly flat and an increase in aggregate demand will have a large effect on real national output; (*c*) the aggregate-supply curve is very steep and an increase in aggregate demand will have little or no effect on real national output; (*d*) the aggregate-supply curve is nearly flat and an increase in aggregate demand will have little or no effect on real national output.

14. In the rational-expectations theory (*a*) individuals understand how the economy works and can correctly anticipate the effects of an event or a change in public policy on the economy; (*b*) the markets in the economy are purely competitive; (*c*) individuals to maximize their own self-interests respond to any expansionary fiscal or monetary policy in a way that prevents an increase in real output and fosters an increase in the price level; (*d*) all of the above are true.

15. In the model of the rational-expectations theorists an increase in aggregate demand will (*a*) increase the price level and have no effect on real national output; (*b*) increase real national output and have no effect on the price level; (*c*) increase both the price level and the real national output; (*d*) have none of the above effects.

16. To stabilize the economy rational-expectations theorists favor the use of (*a*) price controls; (*b*) discretionary fiscal policy; (*c*) discretionary monetary policy; (*d*) policy rules.

■ DISCUSSION QUESTIONS

1. How do the views of Keynesians and monetarists on the competitiveness of capitalistic economies, its stability, and the need for government intervention in the economy differ?

2. What is the basic equation of the Keynesians and the basic equation of the monetarists? Define all terms in both equations and explain how the Keynesian equation can be converted to the monetarist equation.

3. Why do Keynesians believe that monetary policy is an "uncertain, unreliable and weak stabilization tool as compared to fiscal policy"?

4. Explain how a change in M in the equation of exchange will, to the monetarist way of thinking, affect (*a*) P times Q, (*b*) P and Q in the short run, and (*c*) P and Q in the long run.

5. Explain the differences between the monetarist and Keynesian views on why firms and households demand money (or liquid balances); on what determines the demand for money; and the stability, therefore, of the velocity of money.

6. Suppose firms and households, because of an increase in the money supply, find themselves with more money than they wish to have. What do the monetarists believe they will do with this excess money? What effect will this have on the velocity of money and money NNP?

7. Suppose the supply of money increases. What do Keynesians believe will happen to the rate of interest, the amount of money firms and households will wish to hold, planned investment spending, and to the money NNP?

8. What empirical evidence is there to support the Keynesian contention that V is unstable or the monetarist contention that it is relatively stable?

9. Why do the Keynesians advocate and the monetarists reject the use of fiscal policy to stabilize the economy?

10. What is the monetary rule? Why do monetarists suggest this rule to replace discretionary monetary policy?

11. How do the aggregate demand–aggregate supply models of the Keynesians and monetarists differ? What effect will an expansionary monetary or fiscal policy have upon real national output and the price level in each of these models?

12. In as few words as possible, explain how and why rational-expectations theorists believe firms, workers, and consumers will respond to an expansionary monetary or fiscal policy; and how these responses make the policy ineffective and promote economic instability.

13. How will an expansionary monetary or fiscal policy affect real national output and the price level in the rational-expectations theorists' aggregate demand-aggregate supply model? Why does it have these effects?

14. What criticisms have been made of the RET by its opponents?

15. Why has the debate among Keynesians, monetarists, and rational-expectationists been "healthy"?

21
The economics of growth

This is the first of three chapters dealing with the important and controversial topic of economic growth. Chapter 21 presents the theory of growth; Chapter 22 examines the American economic growth record and the issues surrounding further growth in the United States; and Chapter 23 explains the special problems which underdeveloped nations encounter in their attempts to grow.

The purpose of Chapter 21 is to explain what makes economic growth possible. After briefly defining and pointing out the significance of growth, the text analyzes the six factors that make growth possible. The four *supply* factors increase the output potential of the economy. Whether the economy actually produces its full potential—that is, whether the economy has both full employment and full production—depends upon two other factors: the level of aggregate expenditures (the *demand* factor) and the efficiency with which the economy reallocates resources (the *allocative* factor).

The crucial thing to note about the supply factors is that when labor increases more rapidly than natural resources, or capital or both of these, the economy is subject to diminishing returns and eventually to decreasing output per worker and to a declining standard of living. This will breed the misery and poverty forecast by Malthus over 185 years ago. Diminishing returns can, however, be offset—and more than offset—by increasing the productivity of labor. The productivity of labor is improved by expanding the stock of capital, by technological progress, and by improvements in the *quality* of the labor force and of management. Diminishing returns have been *more* than offset by those nations which have experienced economic growth. The nations which have not experienced growth have found the force of diminishing returns too great for them: their improvements in technology, capital, and labor just barely offset the effect of diminishing returns.

Probably the most important principle or generalization developed in the chapter employs the theory of employment presented in Chapter 13. Here we discover that the maintenance of full employment in an economy whose productive capacity is increasing annually requires that investment increase annually to ensure sufficient aggregate expenditures for the expanding full-employment output. And because investment increases an economy's productive capacity, not only must investment increase from year to year, but it must also increase by increasing amounts to ensure the production of the full-employment output. You must be sure you understand the "why" of this principle, because it is fundamental to an understanding of full employment without inflation in a growing economy.

Actually, Chapter 21 contains very little that is really new. It uses a few of the ideas, terms, and theories found in earlier chapters to explain what makes an economy capable of growing (that is, what increases the size of its full-employment or capacity output) and what is necessary if it is actually to grow (that is, if it is to produce all which its expanding capacity allows). With careful reading you should have little or no trouble with Chapter 21, providing you have done a good job on the earlier chapters and providing you keep in mind the fundamental distinction between the supply factors and the demand and allocative factors.

■ CHECKLIST

When you have studied this chapter you should be able to:

☐ Distinguish between employment theory and growth economics.

☐ Define economic growth in two different ways.

☐ Explain why economic growth is important to any economy.

☐ Identify the four supply factors in economic growth.
☐ State the law of diminishing returns.
☐ State the Malthusian thesis and explain why Malthus reached this conclusion.
☐ Explain how the effects of diminishing returns on the standard of living can be offset or forestalled.
☐ Contrast the income-creating and capacity-creating effects of net investment.
☐ Calculate the full-employment rate of growth when you are supplied with the needed data; and explain why NNP must grow at this rate to maintain full employment.
☐ Outline the three types of economic policies that might be utilized to stimulate economic growth in the United States.

■ CHAPTER OUTLINE

1. While employment theory is concerned with the short run and an economy with a fixed productive capacity, growth economics deals with the long run and changes in productive capacity over time.

a. Economic growth means an increase in either the total or the per capita real output of an economy; and is measured in terms of the annual percentage rate of growth of either total or per capita real output.

b. Economic growth is important because it lessens the burden of scarcity: it provides the means of satisfying existing wants more fully and of fulfilling new wants.

c. One or two percentage point differences in the rate of growth result in substantial differences in annual increases in the economy's output.

2. Whether economic growth *can* occur depends upon four supply factors (or, said another way, upon the quantity of labor employed and the productivity of labor); and whether it will occur depends upon the demand factor and the allocative factor.

3. The classical model of economic growth analyzed the effects of population growth and diminishing returns upon total and per capita real output.

a. In an economy where the quantities of land and capital are relatively fixed, the law of diminishing returns operates so that increases in the quantity of labor employed eventually result in a decline in output per worker (the productivity of labor).

b. The optimum population is the population at which the output per worker (per capita output and income) is a maximum.

c. Because of diminishing returns and the tendency for population to increase, Malthus predicted widespread poverty as time passed.

4. But growth can occur and poverty can be avoided if diminishing returns are offset by the increases in the productivity of workers that are brought about by more capital, technological progress, and improvements in the quality of the labor force and management.

5. The amount the actual output of the economy increases depends not only upon the supply factors but also upon the demand factor.

a. To maintain full employment without inflation aggregate expenditures must grow at the same rate as the economy's productive capacity.

b. In the simple macroeconomic growth model the full-employment rate of growth equals the average propensity to save divided by the capital-output ratio; and achievement of the full-employment rate of growth requires that net investment grow at the same rate.

6. For economic growth to be possible, the economy must also be capable of reallocating its resources with reasonable speed and completeness.

7. To stimulate economic growth in the American economy Keynesians stress policies that would expand aggregate expenditures and constrain government spending and consumption; supply-side economists stress policies that would expand the economy's capacity output by increasing saving, investment, work effort, and risk taking; and others advocate the use of an industrial policy that would shape the structure and the composition of industry in the economy.

■ IMPORTANT TERMS

Economic growth
Supply factor
Demand factor
Allocative factor
Law of diminishing returns
Average product
Increasing returns
Optimum population
Labor productivity
Income-creating aspect of investment
Capacity-creating aspect of investment
Capital-output ratio
Full-employment rate of growth
Industrial policy

■ FILL-IN QUESTIONS

1. Employment theory assumes the productive capacity of the economy is (fixed, variable) ______________ while growth economics is concerned with an economy whose productive capacity (increases, remains constant) ______________ over time.

2. Economic growth can mean an increase in either the ______________ or the ______________ of an economy.

3. A rise in output per capita (increases, decreases) ______________ the standard of living and ______________ the burden of scarcity in the economy.

4. Assume an economy has a GNP of $3600 billion. If the growth rate is 5%, GNP will increase by $________ billion a year; but if the rate of growth is only 3%, the annual increase in GNP will be $________ billion. A two percentage point difference in the growth rate results in a $________ billion difference in the annual increase in GNP.

5. The four supply factors in economic growth are ______________, ______________, ______________, and ______________.
The other two growth factors are the ______________ factor and the ______________ factor.

6. The law of diminishing returns is that when additional equal quantities of labor are used with fixed quantities of other resources, (beyond some point) the ______________ per worker or the (total, average) ______________ product of labor will diminish.

7. The population size which results in the maximum output per worker (or the maximum average product of labor) is the ______________

8. Malthus predicted that because of diminishing returns and the tendency for the ______________ of an economy to increase, the standard of living would ______________

9. The tendency for the standard of living to fall as the population increases can be lessened or even overcome by increasing the ______________ of workers. The three principal means of doing this are to increase the stock of ______________, to improve ______________, and to improve the quality of ______________

10. In an economy increasing its productive capacity each year it is necessary that ______________ increase by the right amount each year if full employment is to be maintained.

11. Expenditures for new capital goods both increase ______________ and add to the ______________ of the economy; the amount by which investment expenditures expand the latter depends upon the volume of investment expenditures and the ______________

12. To have the economic growth which the supply and demand factors make possible, an economy must also be able to ______________ its resources from one use to another.

13. To stimulate economic growth in the United States:
a. Keynesians stress the (supply, demand) ______________ side of growth, favor (high, low) ______________ interest rates to expand ______________ spending, and would use fiscal policies to (expand, contract) ______________ government spending and consumption.

b. Supply-side economists stress policies that would stimulate ________, ________, ________ and entrepreneurial ________ to expand (aggregate expenditures, capacity output) ________

c. Others stress policies that would shape the ________ and ________ of American industry and are called ________ policy.

■ PROBLEMS AND PROJECTS

1. If between 1983 and 1984:

a. the real GNP increased from $3200 billion to $3488 billion it increased at a rate of ______%;

b. the real GNP per capita increased from $13,600 to $14,688 it increased at a rate of ______%.

2. The table below shows the total production of an economy as the quantity of labor employed increases. The quantities of all other resources employed are constant.

Units of labor	Total production	Average product of labor
0	0	
1	80	______
2	200	______
3	330	______
4	400	______
5	450	______
6	480	______
7	490	______
8	480	______

a. Compute the average products of labor and enter them in the table.

b. There are increasing returns from the first through the ________ unit of labor and decreasing returns from the ________ through the eighth unit.

c. The optimum population in this economy would be ________ units of labor because with this many units of labor the (total, average) ________ output of labor is a maximum.

3. Column 1 of the next table lists the various quantities of labor an economy might employ. Columns 2 and 3 show total production and the average product of labor for each quantity of labor, respectively.

(1) Quantity of labor	(2) Total production	(3) Average product of labor	(4) New total product-tion	(5) New average product of labor
0	0		0	
1	80	80	100	______
2	200	100	220	______
3	330	110	360	______
4	400	100	500	______
5	450	90	600	______
6	480	80	660	______
7	490	70	700	______
8	480	60	720	______

a. Assume the economy has and employs 4 units of labor. The average product of labor is ________

b. Now suppose that a rise in the productivity of workers increases the figures shown in column 2 to those in column 4. Compute the new average products of labor and enter them in column 5.

c. If the economy continued to employ 4 units of labor, the average productivity of labor would have increased by ______%.

d. As a result of this increase in productivity the optimum population for this economy has (increased, decreased) ________ from 3 to ________ units of labor.

e. If, while the productivity of workers increased, the

number of units of labor this economy had, and employed, increased from 4 to:

(1) 5, the average product of labor would have (increased, decreased) ________ from 100 to ________

(2) 7, the average product of labor would have ________

(3) 8, the average product of labor would have ________

4. Assume that in an economy in which aggregate expenditures contain only consumption and net investment components the average propensity to consume is 0.80, that in year 1 the economy's equilibrium real output (NNP) is its full employment of $1000, and that the supply factors make it possible for the full-employment real output to increase at a rate of 10% per year.

a. Complete the table at the bottom of the page by computing:

(1) the full-employment output in year 2 and in year 3.

(2) the amounts that would be spent for consumption and saved if the economy produced its full-employment output in year 2 and in year 3.

(3) the amounts that would have to be invested and aggregate expenditures in years 2 and 3 if the equilibrium output of the economy is to equal its full-employment output. (Investment will have to be equal to the saving done when the economy produces a full-employment output; and $C + I$ must equal the full-employment output.)

b. Examination of the completed table reveals that to maintain full employment in an economy in which the average propensity to save is a constant and in which the full-employment output is growing at the rate of 10% annually:

(1) aggregate expenditures must grow at a rate of ________% per year; and

(2) net investment must grow at an annual rate of ________%.

c. Further examination of the completed table shows that when the:

(1) average propensity to consume is constant and equal to 0.8, the *marginal* propensity to consume is equal to ________

(2) average propensity to save is constant and equal to 0.2, the *marginal* propensity to save is equal to ________

d. Employing your knowledge of the multiplier, had net investment increased by 5% from $200 to $210 between year 1 and year 2, the equilibrium output of the economy would have increased from $1000 to $ ________

(1) This is a ________% increase in NNP.

(2) The equilibrium NNP is (greater than, less than, equal to) ________ the full-employment output of the economy.

(3) In year 2 there will be (recession, inflation) ________ in the economy.

e. Still employing the multiplier, if net investment increased by 15% from $200 to $230 between year 1 and year 2, the equilibrium output of the economy would have tried to increase from $1000 to $ ________

(1) This equilibrium output is (greater than, less than, equal to) ________ the full-employment output and (can, cannot) ________ actually be produced.

	Full-employment				
Year	Output (NNP)	Consumption	Saving	Investment	Aggregate expenditures ($C + I$)
1	$1000	$800	$200	$200	$1000
2	____	____	____	____	____
3	____	____	____	____	____

(2) There will in year 2 be ______________ in the economy.

f. Still further examination of the completed table reveals that for the economy to grow at any given rate—such as 10%—the *amount* that net investment must increase (increases, decreases, remains constant) ____________

____

5. This problem is much like problem 4 above; but it is a little more difficult because it does not ignore the capacity-creating aspect of investment as problem 4 did.

Assume in an economy in which the only two components of aggregate spending are consumption and net investment that the average propensity to consume is 0.7, the capital-output ratio is 3, and in year 1 the economy is producing a full-employment output of $900.

a. In the table below compute the amount of saving that would be done in year 1 if the economy produced its full-employment output and the amount of investment that would be needed if the economy were to produce an equilibrium output equal to its full-employment output; and enter these two figures in the table.

b. Now compute the increase in full-employment output between year 1 and year 2 that results from the investment undertaken in year 1. (*Hint:* Divide the investment in year 1 by the capital-output ratio.)

c. Add the increase in full-employment output that results from the investment in year 1 to the full-employment output of year 1 to find the full-employment output of year 2; and calculate the amount of saving that would be done at full employment in year 2, the amount of investment needed to bring about full-employment, and the increase in the full-employment output between year 2 and year 3.

d. Find the full-employment output and saving in year 3; the necessary amount of investment in year 3; the increase in full-employment output between year 3 and year 4.

e. This economy's full-employment rate of growth is 10% and:

(1) will be achieved if ______________________ grows at a rate of 10%

(2) can be computed by dividing the economy's ______________________________ by the ______________________________

f. Were the economy's average propensity to save 0.1 and its capital-output ratio 4 its full-employment rate of growth would be equal to ________%.

■ SELF-TEST

Circle the T if the statement is true, the F if it is false.

1. Growth economics concern an economy in which productive capacity is not fixed. **T F**

2. The better of the two definitions of economic growth is an increase in the per capita real output of the economy. **T F**

3. Suppose two economies both have GNPs of $500 billion. If the GNPs grow at annual rates of 3% in the first and 5% in the second economy, the difference in their amounts of growth in one year is $10 billion. **T F**

4. The demand factor in economic growth refers to the ability of the economy to expand its production as the demand for products grows. **T F**

5. The allocative factor in economic growth refers to the ability of the economy to move resources from one use to another as the productive capacity of the economy grows. **T F**

Year	Full-employment Output (NNP)	Full-employment Saving	Full-employment Investment	Increase in full-employment output
1	$900	$_____	$_____	$_____
2	_____	_____	_____	_____
3	_____	_____	_____	_____

6. Diminishing returns for labor are the eventual result of increasing the employment of labor by percentages larger than the employment of other resources is increased. **T F**

7. The effect of diminishing returns to labor upon the standard of living is overcome whenever the average productivity of labor is increased. **T F**

8. Malthus predicted that diminishing returns and increases in the size of the population would cause the standard of living to fall to the subsistence level. **T F**

9. If the volume of investment expands more rapidly than is necessary to keep the full-employment output of the economy expanding at the rate which the supply factors allow, the result will be unemployment. **T F**

10. Other things being constant, the productive capacity of an economy will increase by an amount equal to net investment multiplied by the capital-output ratio. **T F**

11. One of the requirements for allocative efficiency is the reasonably rapid and complete employment of the new workers in the labor force. **T F**

12. Supply-side economists favor increasing taxes to stimulate saving, investment, and economic growth in the economy. **T F**

Circle the letter that corresponds to the best answer.

1. Which of the following is *not* one of the benefits of economic growth to a society? (*a*) Everyone enjoys a greater real income; (*b*) the standard of living in that society increases; (*c*) the burden of scarcity decreases; (*d*) the society is better able to satisfy new wants.

2. If the real output of an economy were to increase from \$2000 billion to \$2100 billion in one year the rate of growth of real output during that year would be (*a*) 0.5%; (*b*) 5%; (*c*) 10%; (*d*) 50%.

3. Suppose an economy has a real GNP of \$700 billion and an annual growth rate of 5%. Over a *two*-year period real GNP will increase by: (*a*) \$14 billion; (*b*) \$35 billion; (*c*) \$70 billion; (*d*) \$71¾ billion.

4. If the production possibilities curve of an economy moves from *AB* to *CD* on the following graph, and the economy changes the combination of goods it produces from *X* to *Y*, there has been: (*a*) improvement in both the supply and the other growth factors; (*b*) an improvement in only the supply factor; (*c*) an improvement in only the demand and allocative growth factors; (*d*) an improvement in the level of total employment in the economy.

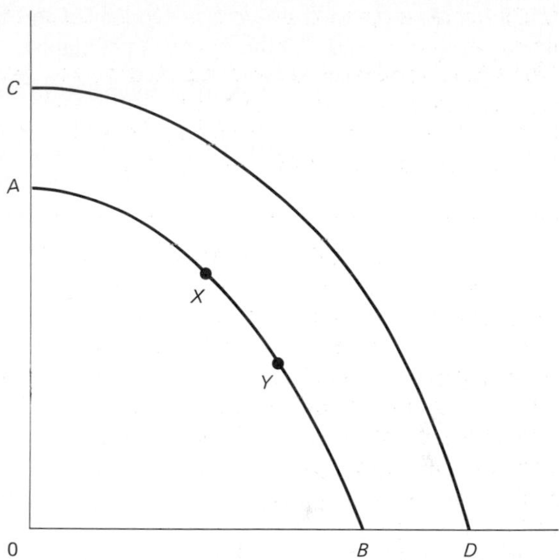

5. Which of the following is *not* a supply factor in economic growth? (*a*) An expansion in purchasing power; (*b*) an increase in the economy's stock of capital goods; (*c*) more natural resources; (*d*) technological progress.

6. Using the data given in the table below, the average product of 4 units of labor is (*a*) 70; (*b*) 60; (*c*) 50; (*d*) 40.

Units of labor	Total production
0	0
1	50
2	110
3	160
4	200
5	230
6	250
7	260
8	265

7. The law of diminishing returns is that as increased quantities of one resource are added to fixed quantities of other resources there will eventually be a decrease in: (*a*) total production; (*b*) the average product of the resource which is increased; (*c*) the average product of the resources which are fixed; (*d*) the optimum population.

8. The "optimum population" of an economy is: (*a*) the largest population the resources of that economy are capable of supporting; (*b*) the level of population which enables the economy to produce the largest possible output; (*c*) the level of poulation which enables the economy to produce the largest possible output per person; (*d*) the level of population which results in the greatest amount of natural resources and capital equipment per person in the economy.

9. Which of the following will *not* usually increase the average product of labor? (*a*) Technological improvements; (*b*) an expanded labor force; (*c*) an increase in the amount of capital per worker; (*d*) better-educated workers.

10. If an economy is to maintain a constant *rate* of economic growth, assuming that the average propensity to consume is constant: (*a*) the volume of investment spending must increase at a more rapid rate; (*b*) the volume of investment spending must increase at the same rate; (*c*) the volume of investment spending need only remain constant; (*d*) the volume of investment spending must increase by the same amount that the output of the economy increases.

11. The rate at which the full-employment ouput of an economy grows is greater (*a*) the greater are its APC and capital-output ratio; (*b*) the greater is its APC and the smaller is its capital-output ratio; (*c*) the smaller is its APC and the greater is its capital-output ratio; (*d*) the smaller are its APC and capital-output ratio.

12. To stimulate economic growth Keynesians favor (*a*) an easy-money policy; (*b*) constraints on government spending; (*c*) constraints on consumption spending; (*d*) all of the above.

■ DISCUSSIONS QUESTIONS

1. How does growth economics differ from the theory of employment (or the theory of national income determination)?

2. What is meant by economic growth? Why should the citizens of the United States be concerned with economic growth?

3. What are the six basic ingredients of economic growth? What is the essential difference between the supply factors and the other two factors? Is there any relationship between the strength of the supply factors and the strength of the demand factor?

4. State the law of diminishing returns. What is the cause of diminishing returns?

5. What is an optimum population? Why is this concept important?

6. What predictions did Malthus make for the economic future of mankind? On what bases did he make this prediction?

7. What can be done to offset or overcome the tendency for the productivity of labor and the standard of living to decline as the employment of labor and the population increase?

8. Explain why an increasing level of aggregate expenditures is necessary in an economy whose productive capacity is increasing if full employment is to be maintained. Why does the maintenance of full employment in a growing economy in which the average propensity to save is constant require that investment increase at the same rate as the full-employment output?

9. What determines (*a*) how much the investment of one year will increase the full-employment of the economy; (*b*) the full-employment rate of growth in an economy? What two events would bring about an increase in the full-employment rate of growth?

10. What is meant by allocative efficiency? Why is this kind of efficiency important if there is to be economic growth?

11. What (*a*) policies do Keynesians advocate to stimulate economic growth; (*b*) policies do supply-side economists favor to stimulate economic growth; (*c*) is meant by "industrial policy"?

22
Economic growth: facts and issues

Chapter 22 is the second of the three chapters concerned with economic growth. It is concerned primarily with economic growth in the United States. In Chapter 23 you will look at economic growth in the underdeveloped nations of the world.

Using the two definitions of growth found in Chapter 21, Chapter 22 begins by describing how much and how fast the American economy has grown. That it has grown is fairly obvious. The net result of this growth is that Americans now enjoy a high standard of living.

Why has the United States grown economically? First, because the American population and the size of its labor force have grown. Second and more important, the productivity of the labor force in the United States has increased. The increase in the productivity of labor is the result of technological advances; the expansion of the stock of capital goods in the American economy; the improved education and training of its labor force; economies of scale; the reallocation of resources; the generous quantities of natural resources with which the American economy was endowed; and its social, cultural, and political environment. (Note, however, that the regulations of government tend to slow the rates at which the productivity of labor and the output of the economy grow.) But in addition to the increases in the ability of the economy to produce goods and services made possible by the supply and allocative factors, aggregate expenditures have expanded sufficiently (though unsteadily) to bring about most of the actual growth made possible by the increases in the quantity and the productivity of labor.

In the last ten or fifteen years, however, the rate at which the productivity of labor in the United States increased was dramatically less than it had been in earlier years. This slowdown has had a number of consequences and a number of causes for the American economy. None of the consequences is, however, good; and they add to the problems that we face. You should be sure you understand the causes because the solutions to problems require elimination of the causes.

The latter part of Chapter 22 asks two important questions. Whether further economic growth is *desirable* in the already affluent American economy is the first of these questions. The controversy over whether growth should be a social goal with a high priority in the United States has, of course, two sides to it. The case in defense of and the case against growth are both considered. You will have to decide for yourself which case is the stronger and whether the social benefits from growth are worth the costs.

The second question is whether further economic growth in the world is *possible*. Here the author looks at the dismal predictions of the Club of Rome. The Club of Rome is an informal group of all kinds of people from all over the world who first met in that city in 1968 and later commissioned a team of professors from the Massachusetts Institute of Technology to prepare a report on the "Predicament of Mankind." Their report, a book entitled *The Limits to Growth,* aroused a storm of controversy throughout the world. Their prediction was that the way things are going throughout the world today, not only will world growth end within the next 100 years but population and the standard of living will also suddenly decline or collapse. More optimistically, the critics of the Doomsday model, in the last section of the chapter, point out that there are good reasons to be suspicious of these dismal predictions. The end of the world may not be at hand.

■ CHECKLIST

When you have studied this chapter you should be able to:

☐ Describe the growth record of the American economy since 1940 and its rates of economic growth since World World II.

☐ State the two fundamental means by which an economy can increase its real GNP and the relative importance of these two means of increasing the real GNP in the United States since 1929.

☐ Enumerate the several sources of the growth of the productivity of labor in the United States since 1929; and state their relative importance in the growth of its real national income.

☐ Identify the chief detriment to the increase in labor productivity; and state by how much it and other factors have slowed the growth of real national income in the United States since 1929.

☐ Explain why the actual rate of growth in the United States has been less than its potential rate of growth and why it has been unstable.

☐ Enumerate the five principal causes and the three principal consequences of the slowdown in the rate at which labor productivity has increased in the United States since the mid-1960s.

☐ Present the case against further economic growth in the United States.

☐ Defend further economic growth.

☐ Outline the assumptions and conclusions of the Doomsday models.

☐ Criticize the assumptions of the Doomsday models and explain how the feedback mechanisms and technological progress might work to prevent the collapse of the economy.

■ CHAPTER OUTLINE

1. Over the last fifty-five or so years the growth record of the American economy has been impressive; but American growth in recent years has been slower than in many of the developed nations.

2. An economy can increase its real output by increasing the quantity of labor employed, by increasing the productivity of labor, or by doing both of these things.

3. Denison estimates that between 1929 and 1982 the real national income in the United States grew at an average annual rate of 2.9%.

a. Two-thirds of this growth was the result of the increased productivity of labor, and one-third of it was the result of the increased quantity of labor employed in the economy.

b. During this period the American population and its labor force expanded; and despite decreases in the length of the workweek and birthrates, the increased participation of women in the labor force and the growth of its population continue to expand the size of the labor force by two million workers a year.

c. Technological advance is combining given amounts of resources in new ways that result in a larger output; and during the 1929–1982 period it accounted for 28% of the increase in real national income.

d. Saving and investment have expanded the American economy's stock of capital; increased the quantity of tools, equipment, and machinery with which each worker has to work; and accounted for 19% of the increase in real national income between 1929 and 1982.

e. Increased investment in human capital (in the training and education of workers) expands the productivity of workers; and accounted for 14% of the 1929–1982 increase in real national income.

f. Economies of scale and the improved allocation of resources also expand the productivity of workers; and in the American economy 9% and 8%, respectively, of the increase in real national income between 1929 and 1982 can be attributed to them.

g. But such detriments (or deterrents) to the growth of productivity as the government regulation of industry, of pollution, and of worker health and safety divert investment away from productivity-increasing additions to capital; and they accounted for a negative 9% of the increased real national income in the 1929–1982 period.

h. Such difficult-to-quantify factors as its general abundance of natural resources and social-cultural-political environment have also contributed to economic growth in the United States.

i. While actual growth in real national income during the 1929–1982 period averaged 2.9% a year, it would have been (an estimated) 3.2% a year if aggregate demand had not at times fallen below its full-employment levels.

j. Increases in the productivity of labor have been more important than increases in the quantity of labor employed in expanding real national income in the American economy; but these increases in productivity cannot be taken for granted, are not automatic, and are the results of the changes in the economy described above.

4. Since the mid-1960s the annual rates of increase in the productivity of labor in the United States have decreased substantially.

a. The significance of this slowdown is that

(1) it decreases the rates at which real wage rates and the standard of living can rise;

(2) it contributes to rising unit labor costs and to inflation in the American economy; and

(3) it leads to higher prices for American goods in world markets and the loss of these markets to American producers.

b. The suggested causes of this decrease in the rate at which the productivity of labor has increased include

(1) the smaller proportion of the GNP spent for investment and a change in the composition of this investment spending;

(2) a decline in the stock of capital per worker;

(3) a fall in the quality (training and experience) of the American labor force;

(4) a slowdown (as reflected in expenditures for R and D) in technological progress; and

(5) the adversarial relationship between workers and managers in the American system of industrial relations.

c. There is some evidence to indicate that the decline in the rate of productivity increases may have ended because of changes in the factors which depressed it.

5. Americans today debate whether economic growth is or is not desirable.

a. Those opposed to rapid economic growth contend that

(1) it pollutes the environment;

(2) it is not needed to resolve domestic problems;

(3) it makes people more anxious and insecure; and

(4) while providing more goods and services, it does not result in a better life.

b. Those in favor of growth argue that

(1) it results in a higher standard of living and lessens the burden of scarcity;

(2) it is not the cause of pollution;

(3) it is the easiest way to bring about a more equitable distribution of income; and

(4) ending or slowing growth will not improve the quality of life.

6. The Doomsday models not only forecast an end to economic growth but also predict sudden collapses in the world's population and its capacity to produce goods and services.

7. Critics of the Doomsday models argue that the forecasters have:

a. made unrealistic assumptions;

b. assumed the stock of natural resources is fixed;

c. made inadequate allowances for such feedback mechanisms as the price system and changes in human behavioral patterns; and

d. underestimated future technological progress.

■ IMPORTANT TERMS

Labor productivity
Productivity slowdown
Infrastructure
R and D
Club of Rome
Doomsday model
Feedback mechanism

■ FILL-IN QUESTIONS

1. In the United States since 1940 the real GNP has increased almost __________-fold and the real per capita GNP has increased almost __________ times.

2. Since 1950 the rates of growth in real GNP and per capita GNP have, on the average, been __________% and __________%, respectively.

3. The real GNP of any economy in any year is equal to the __________ of labor employed *multiplied* by the __________ of labor.

a. The former is measured by the number of (workers, hours of labor) __________ employed.

b. The latter is equal to the real GNP per __________ per __________

4. The quantity of labor employed in the economy in any year depends on the size of the employed __________ force and the __________ __________ of the average workweek. The size element depends upon the size of the working-age __________ and the labor-force __________ rate.

5. Between 1929 and 1982 the real national income of the United States grew at an average annual rate of ______%. Of this growth, ______/3 was the result of increases in the quantity of ____________ employed and ______/3 was the result of increases in the ____________ of ____________

6. In addition to (increases, decreases) ____________ in the quantity of labor employed, the growth of the American economy between 1929 and 1982 can be attributed to ____________ in the productivity of labor which resulted from:

a. technological ____________;

b. increases in the quantity of ____________ employed and in the quantity employed per ____________;

c. the improved ____________ and ____________ of workers;

d. economies of ____________; and

e. the improved ____________ of resources.

7. An increase in the stock of capital of a nation is the result of saving and ________. In the United States the stock of capital has historically grown (more, less) ____________ rapidly than the quantity of labor employed.

8. Technological progress means that we learn how to employ given quantities of resources to obtain greater ____________; and, more often than not, this progress requires ____________ in new machinery and equipment.

9. The principal detriment to growth of real national income in the 1929–1982 period seems to have been government ____________ which diverted (consumption, investment) ____________ spending away from uses that would have increased the ____________ of labor.

10. Two other factors that have led to economic growth in the United States are its abundant ____________ resources and its social-cultural-political ____________

11. When aggregate expenditures do not increase so much as the productive capacity of the economy increases, the result is a(n) (inflationary, recessionary) ____________ gap and a (faster, slower) ____________ rate of economic growth.

12. The annual rates of increase in the productivity of labor, between the middle 1960s and 1982, have (risen, fallen, remained constant) ____________

____

a. This has resulted in a (rise, fall) ____________ in the rates at which the standard of ____________ and the (money, real) ____________ wages of labor have increased, in a (rise, fall) ____________ in unit labor costs and (inflation, deflation) ____________ in the United States, and the loss of international markets to (American, foreign) ____________ producers of goods and services.

b. Its causes have been the (rise, fall) ____________ in investment spending as a percentage of GNP and changes in the composition of (consumption, investment) ____________ spending, the (rise, fall) ____________ in the amount of ____________ available per worker, the (improvement, deterioration) ____________ of the quality of the labor force, a slower rate of ____________ progress, and the adversarial relationship between ____________ and ____________ in the United States.

c. Since about 1982 the rate of increase in the productivity of labor in the United States has been constant or has (increased, decreased) ____________

13. Influential economists arguing against the need for growth in the United States believe that growth ____________ the environment, does not lead to the solution of ____________, breeds ____________ and ____,

and does not result in the ________________________

14. Those who favor growth for the American economy argue that it is the basic way to raise the standard of ________________ and lessen the ________________ dilemma, that economic growth does not necessarily result in ____________________, that growth is the only practical way of obtaining a more ____________________ distribution of ____________________, and that limiting growth will not bring about ____________________

15. The Doomsday models:

a. are based on current and projected trends in world ______________, ______________, ______________, ______________, and ______________

b. predict that within the next ____________ years there will be a sudden collapse in the world's ______________ and ______________

16. The criticisms of the Doomsday models are that the models employ ________________ assumptions, underestimate future ________________ progress, and make inadequate allowance for ____________________ mechanisms.

■ PROBLEMS AND PROJECTS

1. Suppose the real GNP and the population of an economy in seven different years were those shown in the next table.

a. How large would the real per capita GNP of the economy be in each of the other six years? Put your figures in the table.

b. What would have been the size of the optimum population of this economy? ____________________

c. What was the *amount* of growth in real GNP between year 1 and year 2? $____________________

d. What was the *rate* of growth in real GNP between year 3 and year 4? ____________________%

Year	Population, millions	Real GNP, billions of dollars	Per capita real GNP
1	30	$ 9	$ 300
2	60	24	______
3	90	45	______
4	120	66	______
5	150	90	______
6	180	99	______
7	210	105	______

2. The table below shows the quantity of labor (measured in hours) and the productivity of labor (measured in real GNP per hour) in a hypothetical economy in three different years.

Year	Quantity of labor	Productivity of labor	Real GNP
1	1000	$100	$______
2	1000	105	______
3	1100	105	______

a. Compute the economy's real GNP in each of the three years and enter them in the table.

b. Between years 1 and 2, the quantity of labor remained constant; but

(1) the productivity of labor increased by ____________ percent; and

(2) as a consequence, real GNP increased by ____________ percent.

c. Between years 2 and 3, the productivity of labor remained constant; but

(1) the quantity of labor increased by ____________ percent; and

(2) as a consequence, real GNP increased by ____________ percent.

d. Between years 1 and 3

(1) real GNP increased by ________________%; and

(2) this rate of increase is approximately equal to the sum of the rates of increase in the ______________ and the ______________ of labor.

■ SELF-TEST

Circle the T if the statement is true, the F if it is false.

1. Real GNP has tended to increase more rapidly than real per capita GNP in the United States. **T F**

2. Growth and rates-of-growth estimates generally attempt to take account of changes in the quality of goods produced and in the amount of leisure members of the economy enjoy. **T F**

3. The real GNP of an economy in any year is equal to its input of labor divided by the productivity of labor. **T F**

4. Increased labor productivity has been more important than increased labor inputs in the growth of the American economy since 1929. **T F**

5. Since 1929 improved technology has accounted for about 28% of the increase in labor productivity in the United States. **T F**

6. More often than not technological progress requires the economy to invest in new machinery and equipment. **T F**

7. The single most important source of the growth of labor productivity in the United States since 1929 has been the increase in the size of the American labor force. **T F**

8. The United States today invests a larger percentage of its GNP in capital than most of the other industrially advanced nations. **T F**

9. The regulation of industry, the pollution of the environment, and the health and safety of workers by government tends to reduce the rate at which labor productivity grows. **T F**

10. The availability of natural resources in the United States has been a significant factor in the growth of the American economy. **T F**

11. The American social, cultural, and political environment has, in general, worked to slow the economic growth of the United States. **T F**

12. Increases in labor productivity can, at least in the American economy, be taken pretty much for granted because the rate of increase has been nearly constant for well over half a century. **T F**

13. Between the mid-1960s and 1982 the productivity of labor in the United States fell. **T F**

14. The adversarial nature of industrial relations between managers and their employees in the United States tends to slow the rate at which the productivity of labor increases. **T F**

15. The Club of Rome model predicts that if present trends continue the world's population and its per capita outputs of industrial products and food will decline before the year 2100. **T F**

Circle the letter that corresponds to the best answer.

1. Since 1940 real GNP in the United States has increased about (*a*) twofold; (*b*) threefold; (*c*) fourfold; (*d*) fivefold.

2. Between 1870 and 1969 the total output of the American economy increased at an average *annual* rate of about: (*a*) ½ of 1%; (*b*) 2%; (*c*) 3½%; (*d*) 5%.

3. Total output per capita in the United States between 1870 and 1969 increased at an average annual rate of about: (*a*) 1%; (*b*) 2%; (*c*) 3%; (*d*) 4%.

4. Denison estimates that between 1929 and 1982 the real national income of the United States grew at an annual rate of (*a*) 2.1%; (*b*) 2.9%; (*c*) 3.3%; (*d*) 3.9%.

5. About what fraction of the growth in the real national income of the United States since 1929 has been due to increases in the quantity of labor employed? (*a*) ¼; (*b*) ⅓; (*c*) ½; (*d*) ⅔.

6. The factor accounting for the greatest increase in the productivity of labor in the United States between 1929 and 1982 was (*a*) economies of scale; (*b*) technological advance; (*c*) the improved education and training of the labor force; (*d*) the expanded quantity of capital.

7. The population and labor force of the United States were in 1982, respectively, about (*a*) 122 and 49 million;

(*b*) 110 and 49 million; (*c*) 232 and 122 million; (*d*) 232 and 110 million.

8. Approximately what percentages of the labor force have completed high school and four years of college? (*a*) 45% and 8%; (*b*) 44% and 13%; (*c*) 60% and 8%; (*d*) 75% and 20%.

9. Which of the following is *not* one of the consequences when aggregate expenditures increase by less than the productive capacity of the economy? (*a*) Inflation; (*b*) a GNP gap; (*c*) a slower rate of economic growth; (*d*) unemployed labor.

10. During the 1948–1962 period the productivity of labor in the United States increased at an average annual rate of (*a*) 2.1%; (*b*) 2.9%; (*c*) 3.3%; (*d*) 3.9%.

11. The decline in the rate at which the productivity of labor has increased since the mid-1960s can be attributed to a number of causes. Which of the following is *not* one of these causes? (*a*) The decrease in the relative prices of American goods in world markets; (*b*) the decrease in the quality of the American labor force; (*c*) the decrease in the capital-labor ratio; (*d*) the decrease in the rate of technological progress

12. The decline in the rate at which the productivity of labor has increased since the mid-1960s in the United States has brought about (*a*) a fall in the relative prices of American goods in world markets; (*b*) a fall in the standard of living in the United States; (*c*) rising unit labor costs and inflation in the United States; (*d*) all of the above.

13. Which of the following is *not* a part of the case against economic growth? (*a*) Growth produces pollution; (*b*) growth impedes the increased production of consumer goods; (*c*) growth prevents the attainment of a better life; (*d*) growth is not needed to provide us with the means of solving domestic social problems.

14. Which of the following is *not* a part of the case in defense of economic growth? (*a*) Growth lessens the unlimited wants–scarce resources problem; (*b*) growth lessens the extent of anxiety and insecurity; (*c*) growth need not be accompanied by the pollution of the environment; (*d*) growth is the only practical way to reduce poverty.

15. Which is *not* one of the criticisms leveled against the Doomsday models? (*a*) The assumptions are less plausible than other assumptions that might have been made; (*b*) future technological progress has been underestimated; (*c*) feedback mechanisms have been neglected; (*d*) the extent of world poverty has been overstated.

■ DISCUSSION QUESTIONS

1. What has been the growth record of the American economy since 1940 and since 1870? Compare recent American growth rates with those in other nations.

2. What is the relationship between the real GNP produced in any year and the quantity of labor employed and labor productivity?

3. In what units are the quantity of labor and the productivity of labor measured? What (*a*) are the two principal determinants of the quantity of the labor input; (*b*) determines the size of the labor force?

4. What have been the sources of the growth of the real national income in the United States since 1929? What has tended to slow the increase in labor productivity and in real national income?

5. What changes have occurred in the size of the American population and labor force since 1929? What factor has slowed the rate of growth of the former and what factor has speeded the growth of the latter?

6. What is the relationship between investment and the stock of capital? By how much has capital per worker expanded since 1869? What is the connection between increases in the capital stock and the rate of economic growth?

7. What is technological advance and why are technological advance and capital formation closely related processes?

8. What is meant by and, therefore, tends to increase the "quality" of labor. How is this quality usually measured?

9. What are the economic consequences if aggregate expenditures increase more than the productive capacity of the economy increases? If aggregate demand increases less than productive capacity increases?

10. By how much did the annual increases in the productivity of labor decline in the United States between the mid-1960s and 1982? What have been (*a*) the causes and (*b*) the consequences of this decline?

11. What arguments can be presented on both sides of the question of whether growth in the United States is desirable?

12. What are the assumptions and conclusions of the Club of Rome models?

13. What have the critics had to say about the Doomsday models and the predictions made by the forecasters who use these models?

23
Growth and the underdeveloped nations

Chapter 23 is the third of the three chapters concerned with economic growth. Chapter 21 dealt with the theory of growth; and Chapter 22 examined the record and problems of economic growth in the United States.

This chapter looks at the problem of raising the standard of living faced by the underdeveloped nations of the world. Economic growth both in these underdeveloped nations and in the developed or the advanced nations requires that the nation's resources and technological knowledge be expanded. Application of this principle in the underdeveloped nations, however, faces a set of obstacles quite different from those that limit economic growth in the United States. The emphasis in this chapter is on the obstacles to economic growth in the poor and underdeveloped nations of the world. You should concentrate your attention on these obstacles. You will then understand why increasing the quantity and quality of resources and improving technology is especially difficult in the world's underdeveloped nations.

The existence of these special obstacles does not mean that increases in the living standards of the underdeveloped nations are impossible. What it does mean is that the underdeveloped nations are going to have to do things that did not need to be done in the United States (or in the other developed nations) in order to grow. Governments of the poor countries will have to take an active role in promoting growth. Population increases are going to have to be limited. And dramatic changes in social practices and institutions will be required. If these things are not done it will not be possible to eliminate or reduce the obstacles to growth.

No matter how successful the underdeveloped nations are in eliminating these obstacles they probably will still not be able to grow very rapidly without the help of the developed nations. There seem to be at least two reasons why the developed nations will offer the less developed ones some amount of assistance. The citizens of the more advanced nations feel some moral obligation to aid the less fortunate peoples of the world; and they may feel it is in their own self-interest to aid the poor of the world.

Underdeveloped nations have (on the whole) grown during the past thirty years; but the rate at which they have grown has been about the same as that at which the developed nations have grown. This has meant (because the GNPs per capita in the former nations were initially so much smaller) that the gap between the two groups has widened over this period of time. For this and other reasons nations in the Third World have become increasingly dissatisfied with their relationships with the more advanced nations; and they have argued for the establishment of a New International Economic Order. Here you should look at these relationships from the viewpoint of the Third World nations that are not oil exporters. To understand the proposals they have made you must understand why they feel their relationships with the developed nations benefit mostly the developed and largely hurt the underdeveloped nations.

The question that remains to be answered is the one posed in the final section of this chapter. Will the poor nations increase their standards of living by substantial amounts in the future? What appears to be the best available answer—no one can really see into the future—is well expressed by the term "cautious optimism." Many of the underdeveloped nations will raise their living standards substantially *if* they do the many things that have to be done. The terrible *if!* Can these things be done?

On this note of uncertainty we conclude the topic of economic growth and the study of macroeconomics; and turn to microeconomics and to supply and demand.

■ CHECKLIST

When you have studied this chapter you should be able to:

☐ Distinguish between developed, semideveloped, and underdeveloped nations, and locate the former and latter nations geographically.

☐ Identify the Third World nations; describe the population and output of the Third World nations; and explain why the gap between the standards of living of the Third World and the developed has widened over the past thirty years.

☐ Enumerate the human implications of the poverty in the underdeveloped nations.

☐ Identify the four factors which make growth in real GNP possible.

☐ Identify the three specific problems related to human resources that plague the underdeveloped nations; and the five problems population growth creates in these nations.

☐ Contrast the traditional and the more recent views of unemployment in the underdeveloped countries.

☐ Present three reasons for the emphasis on capital formation in the underdeveloped nations; and explain the obstacles to saving and the obstacles to investment in these nations.

☐ Explain why transferring the technologies used in the advanced nations to the underdeveloped ones may not be a realistic method of improving the technology of the latter nations.

☐ Provide an explanation of the relationship among investment, the capital-output ratio, the rate of growth in real GNP, in population, and in the standard of living.

☐ Enumerate several of the sociocultural and institutional factors which inhibit growth in the underdeveloped nations.

☐ Explain why poverty in the poor nations is a vicious circle.

☐ List five reasons why governments in the underdeveloped nations will have to play a crucial role if the vicious circle is to be broken.

☐ Identify the three ways in which the developed nations may help the underdeveloped nations to grow economically.

☐ State the six proposals made by Third World nations that would, if implemented, result in a New International Economic Order; and the arguments made by them in support of these proposals.

☐ Write three scenarios describing the future of the Third World.

■ CHAPTER OUTLINE

1. The underdeveloped nations of the world comprise two-thirds of the world's population.

a. Most of the countries of Asia, Africa, and South America are underdeveloped, and all of them have one common characteristic—poverty (that is, a low per capita income or standard of living).

b. The world's nations can be divided into the industrially advanced market economies, the centrally planned economies, and the Third World countries; and it is the last which are underdeveloped (or semideveloped), contain one-half the world's population, produce only one-seventh of the world's output. Despite equal rates of growth in per capita output over the past thirty years, the gap between the per capita outputs of rich and poor nations has widened.

c. While all Third World nations have low standards of living they are different in many ways and have experienced different rates of growth.

d. Compared with the developed nations, the underdeveloped or Third World nations have lower life expectancies, more disease, less food per person and more malnutrition, less schooling and literacy, and fewer nonhuman sources of energy.

e. Because of an increasing disparity between the standards of living in the developed and the underdeveloped nations and because many of the underdeveloped nations became politically independent only after World War II, these nations are discontented and determined to raise their standards of living.

f. The economic and social environment of the underdeveloped nations is vastly different from that in which the United States found itself when it began its development; consequently, the underdeveloped nations cannot develop merely by following the examples of the United States and other advanced nations.

2. Economic development requires that the quantity and quality of economic resources be increased and that technological knowledge be expanded; but there are many special obstacles to such a program in the underdeveloped nations.

a. Many (but not all) underdeveloped nations possess inadequate natural resources and this limits their ability to develop.

b. Many underdeveloped nations are overpopulated, are plagued by unemployment, and have poor quality labor forces.

c. Usually very short of capital goods, underdeveloped nations find it difficult to accumulate capital because of their low saving potentials and the absence of investors and incentives to invest.

d. Technological knowledge is primitive in underdeveloped nations, and they might adopt the technologies employed in the advanced nations; but the technologies of the advanced nations are not appropriate to the resource-endowments of the underdeveloped nations, and they will have to develop their own technologies.

e. In addition, a nation must have a strong will to develop and alter its own social, cultural, and institutional environment to grow economically.

3. In summary, underdeveloped nations save little and, therefore, invest little in real and human capital because they are poor; and because they do not invest, their outputs per capita remain low and they remain poor. Even if this vicious circle were to be broken, a rapid increase in population would leave the standard of living unchanged.

4. It is probable that the governments of these nations will have to play a major role by sponsoring and directing many of the early development plans if the obstacles to growth are to be overcome.

5. The advanced nations of the world can in a number of ways help the poor nations to develop.

a. They can lower the barriers which prevent the underdeveloped nations from selling their products in the developed nations.

b. The flow of private capital from the advanced nations helps the underdeveloped nations increase their productive capacities and per capita outputs.

c. Loans and grants from governments and international organizations also enable the underdeveloped nations to accumulate capital.

6. Because they have not grown so rapidly as they had hoped and are dissatisfied with their relationships with industrially advanced nations, Third World countries during the past decade or so have urged the creation of a New International Economic Order which would involve six basic changes.

7. No one can now predict whether the Third World nations will in the future grow or stagnate; but at least three scenarios can be written to forecast the courses of events during the next thirty or so years.

■ IMPORTANT TERMS

Underdeveloped nation
Third World
Investment in human capital
Domestic capital formation
Nonfinancial (in-kind) investment
Basic social capital
Capital-saving technological advance
Capital-using technological advance
The will to develop
World Bank
Neocolonialism
Green revolution
New International Economic Order (NIEO)
Preferential tariff treatment
Stabilization fund
Terms of trade

■ FILL-IN QUESTIONS

1. The common characteristic of underdeveloped nations is ______

2. The underdeveloped nations are found chiefly in the following areas of the world:

______,

______,

and ______;
and they account for approximately (one-third, one-half, two-thirds) ______ of the world's population.

3. The nations of the world can be divided into the industrially advanced countries with either market or centrally planned economies and the ______ countries. In these latter countries are found ______% of the world's population but only ______% of the world output of goods and services; and the annual rate of growth of output per capita is ________%.

4. To grow, every economy must increase its supplies of ____________________, ____________________, and ____________________ or improve its ____________________

5. Which resource is *least* easily increased in most underdeveloped nations? ____________________ ____________________

6. Three characteristics of the human resources in most underdeveloped nations are:

a. ____________________

b. ____________________

c. ____________________

7. The per capita standard of living = ____________________ divided by ____________________ and social unrest = ____________________ minus ____________________

8. If the process of capital accumulation is "cumulative," investment increases the (population, output, natural resources) ________ of the economy and this in turn makes it possible for the economy to save more and to ____________ more in capital goods.

9. Domestic capital accumulation requires that a nation save and invest. The former is difficult in underdeveloped nations because of a low ____________ and the latter is difficult because of a lack of ____________ and of ____________ to invest.

10. Nonfinancial (or in-kind) investment involves the transfer of surplus labor from (agriculture, industry) ____________ to the improvement of agricultural facilities or the construction of basic (private, social) ____________ capital.

11. The technologies used in the advanced industrial nations might be borrowed by and used in the underdeveloped nations; but

a. the technologies used in the advanced nations are based upon a labor force that is (skilled, unskilled) ____________, labor that is relatively (abundant, scarce) ____________, and capital that is relatively ____________, and their technologies tend to be (labor, capital)-____________ using; while

b. the technologies required in the underdeveloped countries must be based on a labor force that is ____________, labor that is relatively ____________, and capital that is relatively ____________, and their technologies need to be ____________-using.

12. If technological advances make it possible to replace a worn-out plow, costing $10 when new, with a new $5 plow, the technological advance is capital (saving, using) ____________________

13. The "will to develop" in underdeveloped nations involves a willingness to change the ____________ and ____________ arrangements of the nation.

14. In most underdeveloped nations saving is small because the ____________ per capita is small. Because saving is small, ____________ in real and human capital is also small. And for this reason the ______ of labor and ______ per capita remain small.

15. List five reasons why the role of government in fostering economic development will need to be large in the underdeveloped nations, especially during the early stages of development:

a. ____________________

b. ____________________

c. ____________________

d. ______________________________

e. ______________________________

16. The three major ways in which the United States can assist economic development in the underdeveloped nations are ______________________________

______________________________,

______________________________,

and ______________________________

17. In pressing for the establishment of a New International Economic Order the Third World nations have argued (among other things) that:

a. because Third World nations had no part in their formation and because they are "stacked" against them, there should be a change in the __________ by which international trade, finance, and investment are conducted;

b. the advanced nations, to deprive Third World nations of their export markets, have erected barriers to ______________________ and the Third World nations should be accorded preferential ____________________

c. the dealings of the Third World nations with corporations in the advanced nations have led to the greater part of the benefits from the ____________________ of their natural resources going to others and to the increased ____________________ of Third World nations on world markets;

d. there has been, as a result of the higher prices charged for manufactured goods by corporations in the advanced nations, a shift against them in the ____________________ of ____________________ and that these might be improved by the establishment of ________________ funds and by ________________

e. except for the oil-exporting countries of the Third World, the size of their ______________________________ abroad has increased and these should either be ____________________ or ____________________

f. the foreign aid which they have received has been ______________________ and should be increased to ______________% of the GNP of the advanced nations, have no ________________ attached to it, and should be provided on a long-term and ______________ basis.

18. No one can forecast the future course of events in the Third World nations; but at least three scenarios can be written.

a. In the most optimistic scenario real GNP grows at a rate of 5 to 6% a year; and there is little or no growth in the ______________ and an improved ______________

b. In a second scenario groups of underdeveloped nations form (common markets, cartels) ______________ to raise the prices of the (manufactured goods, raw materials) ________________ they export.

c. And in the third scenario the poor nations acquire nuclear capabilities and engage in wars of (redistribution, national liberation) ________________ with the rich nations.

■ PROBLEMS AND PROJECTS

1. Suppose that the real GNP per capita in the average advanced industrialized nation is \$8000 per year and in the average underdeveloped nation is \$500 per year.

a. The gap between their standards of living is \$________________ per year.

b. If GNP per capita were to grow at a rate of 5% during a year in both the advanced and the underdeveloped nations:

(1) the standard of living in the advanced nations would rise to \$________________ a year;

(2) the standard of living in the underdeveloped nations would rise to \$__________ a year; and

(3) the gap between their standards of living would (narrow, widen) ______________________________ to \$________________ a year.

2. While economic conditions are not identical in all underdeveloped nations, there are certain conditions common to or typical of most of them. In the spaces after each of the following characteristics, indicate briefly the nature of this characteristic in most underdeveloped nations.

a. Standard of living (per capita income). ________

b. Average life expectancy. ________

c. Extent of unemployment. ________

d. Literacy. ________

e. Technology. ________

f. Percentage of the population engaged in agriculture. ________

g. Size of the population relative to the land and capital available. ________

h. The birth and death rates. ________

i. Quality of the labor force. ________

j. Amount of capital equipment relative to the labor force. ________

k. Level of saving. ________

l. Incentive to invest. ________

m. Amount of basic social capital. ________

n. Extent of industrialization. ________

o. Size and quality of the entrepreneurial class and the supervisory class. ________

p. Per capita public expenditures for education and per capita energy consumption. ________

q. Per capita consumption of food. ________

r. Disease and malnutrition. ________

3. Suppose that it takes a minimum of 5 units of food to keep a person alive for a year, that the population can double itself every 10 years, and that the food supply can increase every 10 years by an amount equal to what it was in the beginning (year 0).

a. Assume that both the population and the food supply grow at these rates. Complete the following table by computing the size of the population and the food supply in years 10 through 60.

Year	Food supply	Population
0	200	20
10	____	____
20	____	____
30	____	____
40	____	____
50	____	____
60	____	____

b. What happens to the relationship between the food supply and the population in the 30th year? ________

c. What would actually prevent the population from growing at this rate following the 30th year? ________

d. Assuming that the actual population growth in the years following the 30th does not outrun the food supply, what would be the size of the population in:

(1) Year 40: ________

(2) Year 50: ________

(3) Year 60: ________

e. Explain why the standard of living failed to increase in the years following the 30th even though the food supply increased by 75% between years 30 and 60. ________

■ SELF-TEST

Circle the T if the statement is true, the F if it is false.

1. Among the nations of the world with poulations greater than one million persons the United States had the highest per capita income in 1980. **T F**

2. The difference between the per capita incomes in the underdeveloped nations and the per capita incomes in the developed nations has decreased over the past years. **T F**

3. The rates of growth in GNP per capita in Third World nations are all approximately 3% a year. **T F**

4. Economic growth in the underdeveloped nations can be accelerated by adopting the policies which history shows led to the rapid growth of the American economy. **T F**

5. Economic growth in both advanced and underdeveloped nations requires using resources more efficiently or increasing the supplies of these resources. **T F**

6. It is impossible to achieve a high standard of living with a small supply of natural resources. **T F**

7. Nations with large populations are overpopulated. **T F**

8. The chief factor preventing the elimination of unemployment in the underdeveloped nations is the small number of job openings available in the cities. **T F**

9. Saving in the underdeveloped nations is a smaller percentage of national output than in the more advanced industrial nations, and this is the chief reason total saving in the underdeveloped nations is small. **T F**

10. Before private investment can be increased in underdeveloped nations it is necessary to reduce the amount of investment in basic social capital. **T F**

11. Technological advances in the underdeveloped nations will be made rapidly because they do not require pushing forward the frontiers of technological knowledge and the technologies used in the advanced nations can be easily transferred to the underdeveloped ones. **T F**

12. When technological advances are capital-saving it is possible for an economy to increase its productivity without any *net* investment in capital goods. **T F**

13. The policies of the governments of underdeveloped nations have often tended to reduce the incentives of foreigners to invest in the underdeveloped nations. **T F**

14. Underdeveloped nations will not need foreign aid if the developed nations will reduce tariffs and import quotas on the goods which the underdeveloped nations export. **T F**

15. An increase in the output and employment of the United States works to the advantage of the underdeveloped nations because it provides the underdeveloped nations with larger markets for their exports. **T F**

16. Foreign aid from the United States to the underdeveloped nations has consistently exceeded 1% of its GNP. **T F**

17. Many in the Third World nations believe that the public and private aid extended by the developed to the underdeveloped nations is designed to increase profits in the former and to exploit the latter nations. **T F**

18. Were a fund to be established to stabilize the price of a commodity such as copper, the fund would be used to purchase the commodity when its price fell. **T F**

19. Preferential tariff treatment for Third World nations means that the developed nations would set their tariffs on commodities imported from underdeveloped nations below those established for the same commodities imported from developed nations. **T F**

20. One of the proposals associated with the establishment of a New International Economic Order is that the aid from the developed to the Third World nations be automatic, have no "strings" attached to it, and equal at least 1% of the GNPs of the advanced nations. **T F**

Circle the letter that corresponds to the best answer.

1. Which of the following is the most underdeveloped nation? (*a*) U.S.S.R.; (*b*) Israel; (*c*) Canada; (*d*) India.

2. Which of the following is a Third World nation? (*a*) The People's Republic of China; (*b*) Canada; (*c*) Belgium; (*d*) Egypt.

3. When the rate of growth in per capita GNP is greater in the underdeveloped than in the developed nations the gap between their standards of living (*a*) will decrease; (*b*) will increase; (*c*) will remain unchanged; (*d*) may do any of the above.

4. Which of the following is high in the underdeveloped nations? (*a*) Life expectancy; (*b*) infant mortality; (*c*) literacy; (*d*) per capita energy consumption.

5. In the "equation" for social unrest, (*a*) social unrest = the standard of living − aspirations; (*b*) social unrest = real GNP ÷ population; (*c*) social unrest = real GNP per capita − the standard of living; (*d*) social unrest = aspirations − the standard of living.

6. Which of the following is the most serious obstacle to economic growth in underdeveloped nations? (*a*) The supply of natural resources; (*b*) the size and quality of the labor force; (*c*) the supply of capital equipment; (*d*) technological knowledge.

7. An increase in the total output of consumer goods in an underdeveloped nation may not increase the average standard of living because (*a*) of diminishing returns; (*b*) it may provoke an increase in the population; (*c*) of disguised unemployment; (*d*) the quality of the labor force is so poor.

8. Which of the following best describes the unemployment found in the underdeveloped nations? (*a*) The result of cyclical fluctuations in aggregate demand; (*b*) the agricultural workers who have migrated from rural to urban areas and failed to find employment in the cities; (*c*) the workers in excess of the optimum population; (*d*) workers whose productivity is subject to diminishing returns.

9. Which of the following is *not* a reason for placing special emphasis on capital accumulation in underdeveloped nations? (*a*) The inflexible supply of arable land; (*b*) the low productivity of workers; (*c*) the low marginal contribution of capital equipment; (*d*) the possibility that capital accumulation will be "cumulative."

10. Which of the following is *not* a factor limiting saving in underdeveloped nations? (*a*) The output of the economy is too low to permit a large volume of saving; (*b*) those who do save do not make their saving available to their own economies; (*c*) the highly unequal distribution of income; (*d*) the low marginal contribution of capital equipment to production.

11. Which of the following is *not* an obstacle to capital formation (investment) in underdeveloped nations? (*a*) The absence of strong incentives to invest; (*b*) the lack of basic social capital; (*c*) the absence of a large entrepreneurial class; (*d*) the lack of capital-saving changes in technology.

12. Which of the following is an example of basic social capital? (*a*) A steel plant; (*b*) an electric power plant; (*c*) a farm; (*d*) a deposit in a financial institution.

13. Which of the following seems to be the *most* needed and widespread institutional change required of underdeveloped nations? (*a*) Adoption of birth control; (*b*) development of strong labor unions; (*c*) increase in the nation's basic social capital; (*d*) land reform.

14. Suppose the average propensity to save in an underdeveloped nation is .09 and that the capital-output ratio is 3. At what rate can total real output increase? (*a*) 2.7%; (*b*) 3.0%; (*c*) 3.3%; (*d*) 3.9%.

15. Assume the total real output of an underdeveloped economy increases from $100 billion to $115.5 billion while its population expands from 200 million to 210 million people. Real income per capita has, as a result, increased by (*a*) $50; (*b*) $100; (*c*) $150; (*d*) $200.

16. The role of government in the early stages of economic development will probably be a major one for several reasons. Which one of the following is *not* one of these reasons? (*a*) Only government can provide a larger amount of the needed basic social capital; (*b*) the absence of private entrepreneurs to accumulate capital and take risks; (*c*) the necessity of creating *new* money to finance capital accumulation; (*d*) the slowness and uncertainty of the price system in fostering development.

17. The terms of trade for a nation exporting tin worsen whenever (*a*) the price of tin rises; (*b*) the price of tin falls; (*c*) the price of tin rises and the prices of imported goods decline; (*d*) the price of tin falls and the prices of imported goods rise.

18. Which one of the following is *not* one of the proposals included in the New International Economic Order for which Third World nations have argued? (*a*) A change in the rules by which international financial institutions are governed; (*b*) the elimination of OPEC; (*c*) the renegotiation and cancellation of the debts of Third World nations to the developed nations; (*d*) abandonment of the neo-colonial policies of the developed nations.

19. The long-term external debt of the Third World nations that do not export oil is currently about (*a*) $300 billion; (*b*) $450 billion; (*c*) $625 billion; (*d*) $970 billion.

20. During the remainder of this and in the next century the underdeveloped nations will (*a*) increase their standards of living; (*b*) form cartels to control the supplies of raw materials and bring about a redistribution of wealth and income in the world; (*c*) obtain nuclear capabilities and (threaten to) wage war to force the developed nations to share their wealth and income with them; (*d*) do one or more or none of the above.

■ DISCUSSION QUESTIONS

1. What nations of the world can be called "developed"? Which can be classified as "semideveloped"? Where are the "underdeveloped" nations of the world found?

2. Compare the incomes (per capita) and rates of growth in the developed and Third World nations. What are the "human implications" of the poverty found in the latter nations? (Use the socioeconomic indicators found in Table 23-2 of the text to contrast the quality of life in the developed and underdeveloped nations.)

3. What events increased the desire of the underdeveloped nations to improve their standard of living? Why should social unrest increase in the underdeveloped nations even though their standards of living have been increasing?

4. Why is advice to the underdeveloped nations to follow the example of the United States inappropriate and unrealistic?

5. What must any nation, developed or underdeveloped, do if it is to increase its standard of living? Answer in terms of the production possibilities curve concept.

6. What obstacles do the human resources of underdeveloped nations place in the path of economic development? What is the difference between the traditional view and the more recent view of the unemployment problem in the underdeveloped nations?

7. What reasons exist for placing special emphasis on capital accumulation as a means of promoting economic growth in underdeveloped nations?

8. Why is domestic capital accumulation difficult in underdeveloped nations? Answer in terms of both the saving side and the investment side of capital accumulation. How does a lack of basic social capital inhibit investment in underdeveloped nations?

9. In addition to the obstacles which limit domestic investment, what other obstacles tend to limit the flow of foreign capital into underdeveloped nations?

10. How might the underdeveloped nations improve their technology without engaging in slow and expensive research? Why might this be an inappropriate method of improving the technology used in the underdeveloped nations?

11. What is meant by the "will to develop"? How is it related to social and institutional change in underdeveloped nations?

12. Explain the "vicious circle" of poverty found in the underdeveloped nations. How does population growth make an escape from this vicious circle difficult?

13. Why is the role of government expected to be a major one in the early phases of development in underdeveloped nations?

14. How can the United States help underdeveloped nations? What types of aid can be offered?

15. How is it possible for the United States to assist underdeveloped nations without spending a penny on "foreign aid"? Is this type of aid sufficient to ensure rapid and substantial development in the underdeveloped nations?

16. Discuss the World Bank in terms of its purposes, characteristics, sources of funds, promotion of private capital flows, and success. What are its affiliates and their purposes?

17. Explain the principal proposals which constitute the program of the Third World nations for the establishment of a New International Economic Order. Explain the arguments made by the Third World to support each of these proposals.

18. Write the three scenarios which might plausibly forecast the future of the Third World nations.

24
Demand, supply, and elasticity: some applications

In this chapter the text shifts from the study of *macro*economics to the study of *micro*economics; from an analysis of national output and the price level to analysis of the outputs and prices of firms and industries; and from an examination of the economy as a whole to an examination of the parts of the economy. In addition, the central question to be answered is no longer what will be the level of resource employment, but how are resources allocated among different products, by whom and by what methods will these products be produced, and how will the income generated in their production be distributed among the owners of various resources.

You learned in earlier chapters that the price system is the method used by the American economy to answer these three Fundamental Questions; and you found that in a competitive market demand and supply determine the price and the quantity of the good or service bought and sold in that market.

Chapter 24 begins with a review of demand and supply, but before you start to read Chapter 24 you are urged—you would be commanded if this were possible—to read and study Chapter 4 again. It is absolutely necessary that you have mastered Chapter 4 if the new material in this chapter is to be understood and digested.

As might be guessed, Chapter 24 is, in a sense, a continuation of Chapter 4. In the earlier part of the book it was necessary for you to have only an elementary knowledge of supply and demand. Now the economic principles, problems, and policies to be studied require a more detailed examination and analysis of supply and demand principles. Of particular importance and value in studying much of the material found in the remainder of the text is the concept of elasticity to which the major portion of Chapter 24 is devoted.

With respect to the concept of elasticity of demand, it is essential for you to understand (1) what elasticity measures; (2) how the price-elasticity formula is applied to measure the elasticity of demand; (3) the difference between elastic, inelastic, and unitary elastic demand; (4) how total revenue varies in each of these three cases; and (5) the meaning of perfect elasticity and perfect inelasticity.

When you have become thoroughly acquainted with the elasticity of demand concept, you will find you have very little trouble understanding the elasticity of *supply* and that the transition requires no more than the substitution of the words "quantity supplied" for the words "quantity demanded." Here attention should be concentrated upon the meaning of elasticity of supply, its measurement, and its principal determinant.

In the final section of the chapter two topics are discussed. The first of these topics is price ceilings and supports. You should note that these ceilings and supports prevent supply and demand from determining the equilibrium price of a commodity and from determining the quantity of the commodity which will be bought and sold in the market. The consequences will be shortages or surpluses of the commodity.

The incidence of a sales or excise tax is the second topic. Incidence means "who ends up paying the tax." The most important thing you will learn is that the elasticities of demand *and* of supply determine how much of the tax will be paid by buyers and how much of it will be paid by sellers. You should be especially careful to learn and to understand how the two elasticities affect the incidence of a tax.

Demand and supply and elasticity are the foundation of the next ten chapters in the text. If you will master these topics now you will be able to understand the material in these chapters.

■ CHECKLIST

When you have studied this chapter you should be able to:

☐ Define demand and state the *law of demand.*

☐ Define supply and state the *law of supply.*

☐ Determine the equilibrium price and the equilibrium quantity.

☐ Predict the effect of changes in demand and/or supply on the equilibrium price and quantity.

☐ Define the price elasticity of demand and compute the coefficient of elasticity when you are given the demand data.

☐ Explain the meaning of elastic, inelastic, and unitary elastic demand; and apply the total-revenue test to determine whether demand is elastic, inelastic, or unitary elastic.

☐ List the four major determinants of the price elasticity of demand; and explain how each of them affects elasticity.

☐ Define the price elasticity of supply; compute the coefficient of the elasticity of supply from data; and explain how time affects the elasticity of supply.

☐ Explain the economic consequences of price supports and price ceilings.

☐ State the relationship between the price elasticities of demand and supply and the incidence of an excise tax.

■ CHAPTER OUTLINE

1. It is necessary to review the analysis of supply and demand and the concepts found in Chapter 4 before studying this chapter.

2. Price elasticity of demand is a measure of the sensitivity of quantity demanded to changes in the price of a product; and when quantity demanded is relatively sensitive (insensitive) to a price change demand is said to be elastic (inelastic).

a. The exact degree of elasticity can be measured by using a formula to compute the elasticity coefficient.

(1) The changes in quantity demanded and in price are measured in percentages so that the elasticity coefficient is not affected by the choice of units employed to measure price and quantity.

(2) Because price and quantity demanded are inversely related to each other the price elasticity of demand coefficient is a negative number; but economists ignore the minus sign in front of the coefficient and focus their attention on its absolute value.

(3) Demand is elastic (inelastic, unit elastic) when the percentage change in quantity is greater than (less than, equal to) the percentage change in price and the elasticity coefficient is greater than (less than, equal to) 1.

b. In measuring the percentage changes in quantity and in price the average of the two quantities and the average of the two prices are used as the reference points.

c. The way in which total revenue changes (increases, decreases, or remains constant) when price changes is a test of the elasticity of demand for a product.

d. It is important to note that the elasticity of demand:

(1) is not the same at all prices and that demand is typically elastic at higher and inelastic at lower prices;

(2) cannot be judged from the slope of the demand curve.

e. The price elasticity of demand for a product depends upon the number of good substitutes the product has, its relative importance in the consumer's budget, whether it is a necessity or a luxury, and the period of time under consideration.

f. Price elasticity of demand is of practical importance in matters of public policy and in the setting of prices by the individual business firm.

g. Price elasticity of supply is a measure of the sensitivity of quantity supplied to changes in the price of the product; while there is no total-revenue test, the formula used to measure elasticity of demand can also be used to measure elasticity of supply. The elasticity of supply depends primarily upon the amount of time sellers have to adjust to a price change.

3. Supply and demand analysis and the elasticity concepts have many important applications.

a. Legal price ceilings and price supports prevent price from performing its rationing function.

(1) A price ceiling results in a shortage of the commodity; may bring about formal rationing by government and a black market; and causes a misallocation of resources.

(2) A price support creates a surplus of the commodity; and may induce government to undertake measures either to increase the demand for or to decrease the supply of the commodity.

b. The price elasticities of demand and supply determine the incidence of a sales or excise tax.

(1) The imposition of such a tax on a commodity decreases the supply of the commodity and increases its

price. The amount of the price increase is the portion of the tax paid by the buyer; the seller pays the rest.

(2) The price elasticities of demand and supply affect the portions paid by buyers and sellers.

(*a*) The more elastic (inelastic) the demand for the commodity, the greater (smaller) is the portion paid by the seller.

(*b*) The more elastic (inelastic) the supply of the commodity, the greater (smaller) is the portion paid by the buyer.

(3) In addition to these conclusions, it is possible to discover who benefits from the subsidization of the production of a product and how taxes and subsidies may be used to improve the allocation of resources whenever spillover costs or benefits are present.

■ IMPORTANT TERMS

Review
Demand
Supply
Law of demand
Law of supply
Equilibrium price
Equilibrium quantity
Competition (competitive market)
Rationing function of prices
Change in demand
Change in supply
Change in quantity demanded
Change in quantity supplied
New
Price elasticity of demand
Elastic demand
Inelastic demand
Total-revenue test
Elasticity coefficient
Elasticity formula
Unitary elasticity
Perfect inelasticity of demand
Perfect elasticity of demand
Perfect elasticity of supply
Elastic supply
Inelastic supply
Market period
Short run
Long run
Increasing-cost industry
Constant-cost industry
Price ceiling
Price support
Tax incidence

Note: Before answering the Fill-in, Self-test, and Discussion questions and working out the Problems and Projects, you should return to Chapter 4 in this study guide and review the important terms, answer the questions, and rework the problems.

■ FILL-IN QUESTIONS

1. The efficient use of an economy's available resources requires that these resources be ____________ employed and that they be ____________ among alternative uses in an efficient way.

a. The present chapter begins the study of the (latter, former) ____________ aspect of the efficient use of resources and the study of (macro-, micro-) ____________ economics.

b. This requires an analysis of the ____________ system and how individual ____________ are determined in various kinds of markets in the economy.

2. If a relatively large change in price results in a relatively small change in quantity demanded, demand is ____________; if a relatively small change in price results in a relatively large change in quantity demanded, demand is ____________

3. If a change in price causes no change in quantity demanded, demand is perfectly (elastic, inelastic) ____________ and the demand curve is (horizontal, vertical) ____________; if an extremely small change in price results in an extremely large change in quantity demanded, demand is ____________ and the demand curve is ____________

4. If the price of a commodity declines,

a. When demand is inelastic the loss of revenue due to the lower price is ____________ the gain in revenue due to the greater quantity demanded.

b. When demand is elastic the loss of revenue due to the lower price is ____________ the gain in revenue due to the greater quantity demanded.

c. When demand is of unitary elasticity the loss of revenue due to the lower price is ____________ the gain in revenue due to the greater quantity demanded.

5. If demand is elastic, price and total revenue are (directly, inversely) ____________ related; if demand is inelastic, they are ____________ related.

6. Complete the summary table below.

If demand is	The elasticity coefficient is	If price rises, total revenue will	If price falls, total revenue will
Elastic	> than 1	fall	rise
Inelastic	< than 1	rise	fall
Of unitary elasticity	____	____	____

7. List four determinants of the price elasticity of demand:

a. Substitute goods

b. Luxury vs. necessity

c. Proportion of income

d. Time

8. The most important factor affecting the price elasticity of supply is time which a seller has to respond to a price Δ

9. If the demand and supply schedules for a certain product are those given in the table, answer the following questions.

Quantity demanded	Price	Quantity supplied
12,000	$10	18,000
13,000	9	17,000
14,000	8	16,000
15,000	7	15,000
16,000	6	14,000
17,000	5	13,000
18,000	4	12,000

a. The equilibrium price of the product is $ 7 and the equilibrium quantity is 15,000

b. If the government imposes a price ceiling of $5 on this product, there would be a (shortage, surplus) shortage of 4,000 units.

c. If the government supports a price of $8, there would be a surplus of 2,000 units.

10. Price ceilings imposed by the United States government have usually occurred during war periods, result in shortage of the commodities, and require that the government institute ~~subsidies~~ rationing

11. The two most common examples of government-imposed minimum prices are minimum wage, ____ and ag price supports

12. A minimum price imposed by the government on a commodity causes a surplus of the commodity and requires that the government either ____ or ____ to eliminate this.

13. Price ceilings and price supports prevent prices from performing their rationing function.

14. When a sales or excise tax is levied on a commodity, the amount of the tax borne by buyers of the commodity is equal to the amt the price of the commodity rises as a result of the tax

The incidence of such a tax depends on the price elasticity of demand and of supply.

a. The buyer's portion of the tax is larger the (more, less) less elastic the demand and the more elastic the supply.

b. The seller's portion of the tax is larger the more elastic the demand and the less elastic the supply.

■ **PROBLEMS AND PROJECTS**

1. In the following table, using the demand data given, complete the table by computing total revenue at each of the seven prices and the six price elasticity coefficients between each of the seven prices, and indicate whether demand is elastic, inelastic, or of unitary elasticity between each of the seven prices.

Price	Quantity demanded	Total revenue	Elasticity coefficient	Character of demand
$1.00	300	$ 300		
			2.71	E
.90	400	360		
			1.89	E
.80	500	400		
			1.36	E
.70	600	420		
			1.0[illegible]	UE
.60	700	420		
			.73[illegible]	I
.50	800	400		
			.53	I
.40	900	360		

2. Using the supply data in the schedule shown below, complete the table by computing the six price elasticity of supply coefficients between each of the seven prices, and indicate whether supply is elastic, or of unitary elasticity.

Price	Quantity supplied	Elasticity coefficient	Character of supply
$1.00	800		
		1.27	E
.90	700		
		1.30	E
.80	600		
		1.36	E
.70	500		
		1.45	E
.60	400		
		1.57	E
.50	300		
		1.8	E
.40	200		

3. On the following graph are three different supply curves (S_1, S_2, and S_3) for a product bought and sold in a competitive market.

a. The supply curve for the:

(1) market period is the one labeled ____________

(2) short run is the one labeled ____________

(3) long run is the one labeled ____________

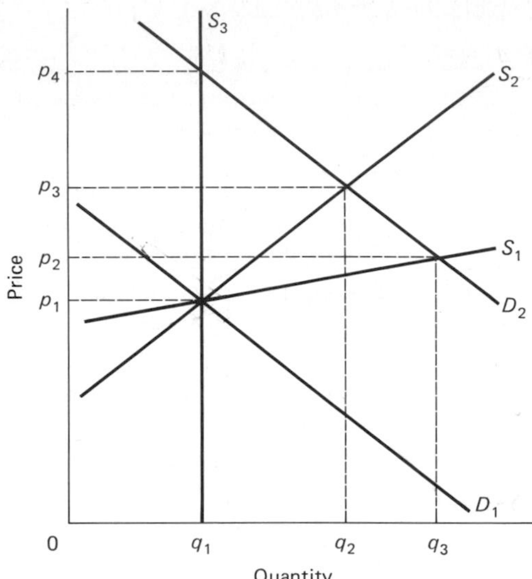

b. No matter what the period of time under consideration, if the demand for the product were D_1, the equilibrium price of the product would be P_1 and the equilibrium quantity would be Q_1

c. Were demand to increase D_1 to D_2:

(1) in the market period the equilibrium price would increase to ____________ and the equilibrium quantity would ____________

(2) in the short run the price of the product would increase to ____________ and the quantity would increase to ____________

(3) in the long run the price of the product would be ____________ and the quantity would be ____________

d. The longer the period of time allowed to sellers to adjust their outputs the (more, less) more elastic is the supply of the product.

e. The more elastic the supply of a product, the (greater, less) less is the effect on equilibrium price and the greater is the effect on equilibrium quantity of an increase in demand.

Quantity demanded (pounds)	Price (per pound)	Before-tax quantity supplied (pounds)	After-tax quantity supplied (pounds)
150	$4.60	900	______
200	4.40	800	______
250	4.20	700	______
300	4.00	600	______
350	3.80	500	______
400	3.60	400	______
450	3.40	300	0
500	3.20	200	0
550	3.00	100	0

4. In the table above are the demand and supply schedules for copra in the New Hebrides Islands.

a. Before a tax is imposed on copra, its equilibrium price is $______

b. The government of New Hebrides now imposes an excise tax of $.60 per pound on copra. Complete the after-tax supply schedule in the right-hand column of the table.

c. After the imposition of the tax, the equilibrium price of copra is $______

d. Of the $.60 tax, the amount borne by

(1) the buyer is $______ or ______%

(2) the seller is $______ or ______%

5. Two graphs follow.

a. On the graph in the next column draw a perfectly elastic demand curve and a normal upsloping supply curve for a commodity.

(1) Now impose an excise tax on the commodity, and draw the new supply curve that would result.

(2) As a consequence of the tax, the price of the commodity has ______

(3) It can be concluded that when demand is perfectly elastic, the buyer bears ______ of the tax and the seller bears ______ of the tax.

(4) Thus the *more* elastic the demand, the ______

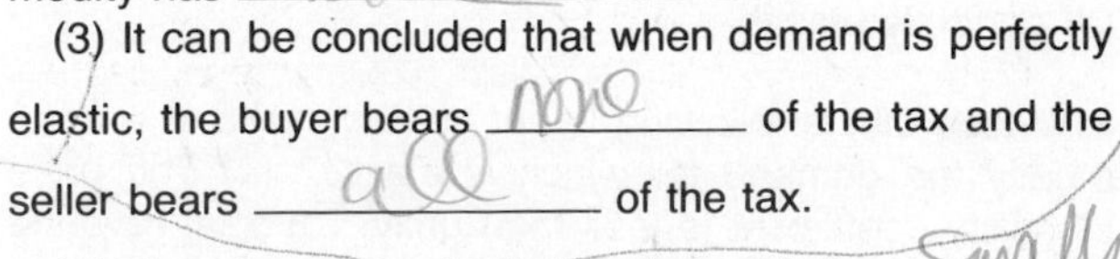

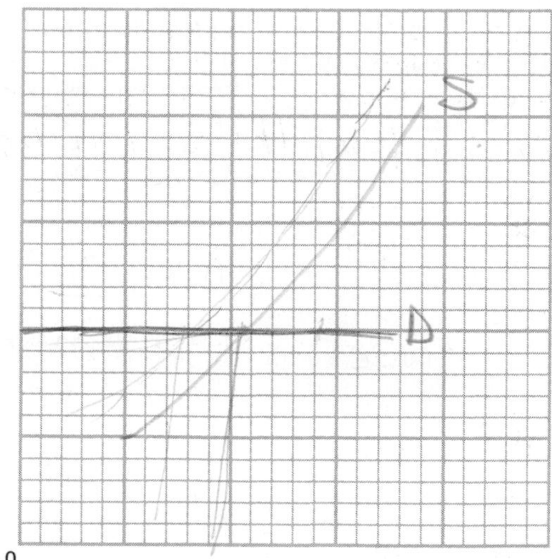

is the portion of the tax borne by the buyer and the ______ is the portion borne by the seller.

(5) But the *less* elastic the demand, the ______ is the portion borne by the buyer and the ______ is the portion borne by the seller.

b. On the graph on the next page draw a perfectly elastic supply curve and a normal downsloping demand curve.

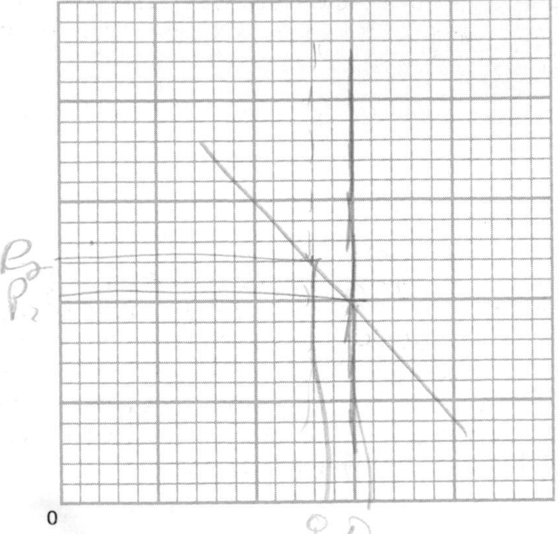

(1) Again impose an excise tax on the commodity and draw the new supply curve.

(2) As a result of the tax, the price of the commodity has ____________________

(3) From this it can be concluded that when supply is perfectly elastic, the buyer bears ____________ of the tax and the seller bears ____________ of the tax.

(4) Thus the *more* elastic the supply, the ____________ is the portion of the tax borne by the buyer and the ____________ is the portion borne by the seller.

(5) But the *less* elastic the supply, the ____________ is the portion borne by the buyer and the ____________ is the portion borne by the seller.

■ SELF-TEST

Circle the T if the statement is true, the F if it is false.

1. If the relative change in price is greater than the relative change in quantity demanded, the price elasticity coefficient is greater than one. **T F**

2. Total revenue will not change when price changes if the price elasticity of demand is unitary. **T F**

3. Demand tends to be inelastic at higher prices and elastic at lower prices. **T F**

4. Price elasticity of demand and the slope of the demand curve are two different things. **T F**

5. The demand for most agricultural products is inelastic. Consequently, an increase in supply will reduce the total income of producers of agricultural products. **T F**

6. If an increase in product price results in no change in the quantity supplied, supply is perfectly elastic. **T F**

7. If the government imposes a price ceiling above what would be the free-market price of a commodity, a shortage of the commodity will develop. **T F**

8. A state government seeking to increase its excise-tax revenues is more likely to increase the tax rate on restaurant meals than on automobile tires. **T F**

9. When an excise tax is placed on a product bought and sold in a competitive market, the portion of the tax borne by the seller equals the amount of the tax less the rise in the price of the product due to the tax. **T F**

10. The more elastic the demand for a good, the greater will be the portion of an excise tax on the good borne by the seller. **T F**

Circle the letter that corresponds to the best answer.

1. If when the price of a product rises from \$1.50 to \$2, the quantity demanded of the product decreases from 1000 to 900, the price elasticity of demand coefficient is: (*a*) 3.00; (*b*) 2.71; (*c*) 0.37; (*d*) 0.33.

2. If a 1% fall in the price of a commodity causes the quantity demanded of the commodity to increase 2%, demand is: (*a*) inelastic; (*b*) elastic; (*c*) of unitary elasticity; (*d*) perfectly elastic.

3. Which of the following is *not* characteristic of a commodity the demand for which is elastic? (*a*) The price elasticity coefficient is less than unity; (*b*) total revenue decreases if price rises; (*c*) buyers are relatively sensitive to price changes; (*d*) the relative change in quantity is greater than the relative change in price.

4. Which of the following is *not* characteristic of a good the demand for which is inelastic? (*a*) There are a large number of good substitutes for the good; (*b*) the buyer spends a small percentage of his total income on the good; (*c*) the good is regarded by consumers as a necessity; (*d*) the period of time for which demand is given is very short.

5. If a 5% fall in the price of a commodity causes quantity supplied to decrease by 8%, supply is: (*a*) inelastic; (*b*) of unitary elasticity; (*c*) elastic; (*d*) perfectly inelastic.

6. If supply is inelastic and demand decreases, the total revenue of sellers will: (*a*) increase; (*b*) decrease; (*c*) decrease only if demand is elastic; (*d*) increase only if demand is inelastic.

7. The chief determinant of the price elasticity of supply of a product is: (*a*) the number of good substitutes the product has; (*b*) the length of time sellers have to adjust to a change in price; (*c*) whether the product is a luxury or a necessity; (*d*) whether the product is a durable or a nondurable good.

8. If the government sets a minimum price for a commodity and this minimum price is less than the equilibrium price of the commodity, the result will be: (*a*) a shortage of the commodity; (*b*) a surplus of the commodity; (*c*) neither a shortage nor a surplus of the commodity; (*d*) an increase in total receipts from the sale of the commodity if demand is inelastic.

9. In a competitive market the portion of an excise tax borne by a buyer is equal to: (*a*) the amount the price of the product rises as a result of the tax; (*b*) the amount of the tax; (*c*) the amount of the tax less the amount the price of the product rises as a result of the tax; (*d*) the amount of the tax plus the amount the price of the product rises as a result of the tax.

10. Which of the following statements is correct? (*a*) The more elastic the supply, the greater the portion of an excise tax borne by the seller; (*b*) the more elastic the demand, the greater the portion of an excise tax borne by the seller; (*c*) the more inelastic the supply, the greater the portion of an excise tax borne by the buyer; (*d*) the more inelastic the demand, the greater the portion of an excise tax borne by the seller.

■ DISCUSSION QUESTIONS

1. Define and explain the price elasticity of demand concept in terms of each of the following: (*a*) the relative sensitiveness of quantity demanded to changes in price; (*b*) the behavior of total revenue when price changes; (*c*) the elasticity coefficient; (*d*) the relationship between the relative (percentage) change in quantity demanded and the relative (percentage) change in price.

2. What is meant by perfectly elastic demand? By perfectly inelastic demand? What does the demand curve look like when demand is perfectly elastic and when it is perfectly inelastic?

3. In computing the price elasticity coefficient, it usually makes a considerable difference whether the higher price and lower quantity or the lower price and higher quantity are used as a point of reference. What have economists done to eliminate the confusion which would arise if the price elasticity of demand coefficient varied and depended upon whether a price rise or fall were being considered?

4. When the price of a commodity declines, the quantity demanded of it increases. When demand is elastic, total revenue is greater at the lower price; but when demand is inelastic, total revenue is smaller. Explain why total revenue will sometimes increase and why it will sometimes decrease.

5. Demand seldom has the same elasticity at all prices. What is the relationship between the price of most commodities and the price elasticity of demand for them?

6. What is the relationship, if there is a relationship, between the price elasticity of demand and the slope of the demand curve?

7. What are the factors which together determine the price elasticity of demand for a product?

8. Of what practical importance is the price elasticity of demand? Cite examples of its importance to business firms, workers, farmers, and governments.

show how this works w/ graph

9. Explain what determines the price elasticity of supply of an economic good or service.

10. Why does the government from time to time impose price ceilings and minimum prices on certain goods and services? What are the consequences of these ceilings and minimums if they are not set at the price which would prevail in the free market?

11. Explain the effect which the imposition of an excise tax has upon the supply of a commodity bought and sold in a competitive market. How do you find what part of the tax is passed on to the buyer and what part is borne by the seller? What determines the division of the tax between buyer and seller?

12. What is the relationship between the price elasticity of demand for a commodity and the portion of an excise tax on a commodity borne by the buyer and by the seller? What is the relationship between the price elasticity of supply and the incidence of the tax?

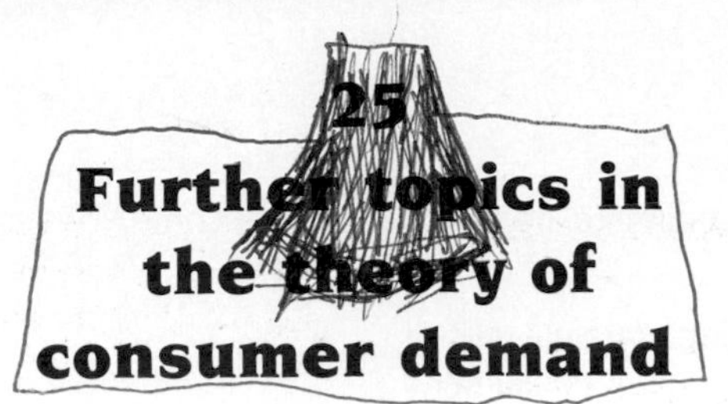

In earlier chapters it has been pointed out that consumers typically buy more of a product as its price decreases and less of it as its price increases. Chapter 25 looks behind this law of demand to explain why consumers behave this way. Two explanations are presented. One, developed in terms of the income effect and the substitution effect, is a general and simple explanation. The other, developed in terms of the concept of marginal utility, is a more detailed explanation and is more difficult to understand. (A third explanation employs indifference curves to explain consumer demand; is a newer and in many ways a better explanation of consumer behavior; and is found in the appendix to this chapter.)

The marginal-utility explanation requires that you first understand the concepts and assumptions upon which this theory of consumer behavior rests, and second, do some rigorous reasoning using these concepts and assumptions. It is an exercise in logic, but be sure that you follow the reasoning. To aid you, several problems are provided so that you can work things out for yourself.

Of course no one believes that consumers actually perform these mental gymnastics before they spend their incomes or make a purchase. But the marginal-utility approach to consumer behavior is studied because consumers behave "as if" they made their purchases on the basis of very fine calculations. Thus, this approach explains what we do in fact observe, and makes it possible for us to predict with a good deal of precision how consumers will react to changes in their incomes and in the prices of products.

The consumption of any good or service requires that the consumer use scarce and valuable time. The final section of the chapter will show you how the value of the time required for the consumption of a product can be put into the marginal-utility theory; and what the implications of this modification of the theory are.

■ CHECKLIST

When you have studied this chapter you should be able to:

☐ Define and distinguish between the income and the substitution effects of a price change; and use the two effects to explain why a consumer will buy more (less) of a commodity when its price falls (rises).

☐ Define marginal utility; and state the law of diminishing marginal utility.

☐ List the four assumptions made in the theory of consumer behavior.

☐ State the utility-maximizing rule.

☐ Use the utility-maximizing rule to determine how a consumer would spend his fixed income when you are given the utility and price data.

☐ Derive a consumer's demand for a product from utility, income, and price data.

☐ Explain how the value of time is incorporated into the theory of consumer behavior; and several of the implications of this modification of the theory.

■ CHAPTER OUTLINE

1. The law of consumer demand can be explained by employing either the income-effect and substitution-effect concepts, or the concept of marginal utility.

a. Consumers buy more of a commodity when its price falls because their money income will go further (the income effect) and because the commodity is now less expensive relative to other commodities (the substitution effect).

b. The essential assumption made in the alternative explanation is that the more the consumer buys of any commodity, the smaller becomes the marginal (extra) utility obtained from it.

2. The assumption (or law) of diminishing marginal utility is the basis of the theory that explains how a consumer will spend his or her income.

a. The typical consumer, it is assumed, is rational, knows his or her marginal-utility schedules for the various goods available, has a limited money income to spend, and must pay a price to acquire each of the goods which yield utility.

b. Given these assumptions, the consumer maximizes the total utility obtained when the marginal utility of the last dollar spent on a commodity is the same for all commodities.

c. Algebraically, total utility is a maximum when the marginal utility of the last unit of a commodity purchased divided by its price is the same for all commodities.

3. To find a consumer's demand for a product the utility-maximizing rule is applied to determine the amount of the product the consumer will purchase at different prices, income, and tastes and the prices of other products remaining constant.

4. The marginal-utility theory includes the fact that consumption takes time and time is a scarce resource.

a. The full price of any consumer good or service is equal to its market price plus the value of time taken to consume it (the income the consumer could have earned had he used that time for work).

b. The inclusion of the value of consumption time in theory of consumer behavior has several significant implications.

■ IMPORTANT TERMS

Income effect	**Law of diminishing marginal utility**
Substitution effect	**Rational**
Utility	**Budget restraint**
Marginal utility	**Utility-maximizing rule**

■ FILL-IN QUESTIONS

1. A fall in the price of a product tends to (increase, decrease) ______________ the *real* income of a consumer, and a rise in its prices tends to ______________ real income. This is called the ______________ effect.

2. When the price of a product increases, the product becomes relatively (more, less) ______________ expensive than it was and the prices of other products become relatively (higher, lower) ______________ than they were; the consumer will, therefore, buy (less, more) ______________ of the product in question and ______________ of the other products. This is called the ______________ effect.

3. The law of diminishing marginal utility is that marginal utility will (increase, decrease) ______________ as a consumer increases the quantity of a particular commodity consumed.

4. The marginal-utility theory of consumer behavior assumes that the consumer is ______________ and has certain ______________ for various goods.

5. A consumer cannot buy all he or she wishes of every good and service because income is ______________ and goods and services have ______________; these two facts are called the ______________

6. When the consumer is maximizing the utility which his income will obtain for him, the ______________ is the same for all the products he buys.

7. If the marginal utility of the last dollar spent on one product is greater than the marginal utility of the last dollar spent on another product, the consumer should (increase, decrease) ______________ her purchases of the first and ______________ her purchases of the second product.

8. Assume there are only two products, X and Y, a consumer can purchase with a fixed income. The consumer is maximizing utility algebraically when:

(a) ______________ *(c)* ______________

______________ = ______________

(b) ______________ *(d)* ______________

9. In deriving a consumer's demand for a particular product the two factors (other than the tastes of the consumer) which are held constant are:

a. ______

b. ______

10. The consumption of any product requires ______

a. This is a valuable economic resource because it is ______

b. Its value is equal to ______

c. And the full price to the consumer of any product is, therefore, ______ plus ______

■ PROBLEMS AND PROJECTS

1. Suppose that when the price of bread is a dollar per loaf, the Robertson family buys six loaves of bread in a week.

a. When the price of bread falls to 80 cents, the Robertson family will increase its bread consumption to seven loaves.

(1) Measured in terms of bread, the fall in the price of bread will ______ their real income by ______ loaves. (*Hint:* How many loaves of bread *could* they now buy without changing the amount they spend on bread?)

(2) Is the Robertsons' demand for bread elastic or inelastic? ______

b. When the price of bread rises from a dollar to $1.20 per loaf, the Robertson family will decrease its bread consumption to four loaves.

(1) Measured in terms of bread, this rise in the price of bread will ______ their real income by ______ loaf.

(2) Is the Robertsons' demand for bread elastic or inelastic? ______

2. Assume that Palmer finds only three goods, A, B, and C, are for sale; and that the amounts of utility which their consumption will yield him are as shown in the table at the bottom of the page. Compute the marginal utilities for successive units of A, B, and C and enter them in the appropriate columns.

3. Using the marginal-utility data for goods A, B, and C which you obtained in problem 2, assume that the prices of A, B, and C are $5, $1, and $4, respectively, and that Palmer has an income of $37 to spend.

a. Complete the table at the top of the next page by computing the *marginal utility per dollar* for successive units of A, B, and C.

b. Palmer would *not* buy 4 units of A, 1 unit of B, and 4 units of C because ______

c. Palmer would *not* buy 6 units of A, 7 units of B, and 4 units of C because ______

Good A			Good B			Good C		
Quantity	Utility	Marginal utility	Quantity	Utility	Marginal utility	Quantity	Utility	Marginal utility
1	21	______	1	7	______	1	23	______
2	41	______	2	13	______	2	40	______
3	59	______	3	18	______	3	52	______
4	74	______	4	22	______	4	60	______
5	85	______	5	25	______	5	65	______
6	91	______	6	27	______	6	68	______
7	91	______	7	28.2	______	7	70	______

Good A		Good B		Good C	
Quantity	Marginal utility per dollar	Quantity	Marginal utility per dollar	Quantity	Marginal utility per dollar
1	______	1	______	1	______
2	______	2	______	2	______
3	______	3	______	3	______
4	______	4	______	4	______
5	______	5	______	5	______
6	______	6	______	6	______
7	______	7	______	7	______

d. When Palmer is maximizing his utility he will buy: (1) ______ units of A, (2) ______ units of B, (3) ______ units of C; his total utility will be ______ and the marginal utility of the last dollar spent on each good will be ______

e. If Palmer's income increased by $1, he would spend it on good ____, assuming he can buy fractions of a unit of a good, because ______

4. Ms. Thompson has an income of $36 to spend each week. The only two goods she is interested in purchasing are D and E. The marginal-utility schedules for these two goods are shown in the table below.

The price of E does not change from week to week and is $4. The marginal utility per dollar from E is also shown in the table.

But the price of D varies from one week to the next. The marginal utility per dollar from D when the price of D is $6, $4, $3, $2, and $1.50 is shown in the table.

a. Complete the table below to show how much of D Ms. Thompson will buy each week at each of the five possible prices of D.

Price of D	Quantity of D demanded
$6.00	____
4.00	____
3.00	____
2.00	____
1.50	____

b. What is the table you completed in *a* above called?

______

	Good D						Good E	
Quantity	MU	MU/$6	MU/$4	MU/$3	MU/$2	MU/$1.50	MU	MU/$4
1	45	7.5	11.25	15	22.5	30	40	10
2	30	5	7.5	10	15	20	36	9
3	20	3.33	5	6.67	10	13.33	32	8
4	15	2.5	3.75	5	7.5	10	28	7
5	12	2	3	4	6	8	24	6
6	10	1.67	2.5	3.33	5	6.67	20	5
7	9	1.5	2.25	3	4.5	6	16	4
8	7.5	1.25	1.88	2.5	3.75	5	12	3

5. Assume that a consumer can purchase only two goods. These two goods are *R* (recreation) and *M* (material goods). The market price of *R* is \$2 and the market price of *M* is \$1. The consumer spends all her income in such a way that the marginal utility of the last unit of *R* she buys is 12 and the marginal utility of the last unit of *M* she buys is 6.

a. If we ignore the time it takes to consume *R* and *M*, is the consumer maximizing the total utility she obtains from the two goods? ______

b. Suppose it takes 4 hours to consume each unit of *R* and 1 hour to consume each unit of *M*; and the consumer can earn \$2 an hour when she works.

(1) The full price of a unit of *R* is \$______

(2) The full price of a unit of *M* is \$______

c. If we take into account the full price of each of the commodities, is the consumer maximizing her total utility? ______ How do you know this? ______

d. If the consumer is not maximizing her utility, should she increase her consumption of *R* or of *M*? ______ Why should she do this? ______

e. Will she use more or less of her time for consuming *R*? ______

■ SELF-TEST

Circle the T if the statement is true, the F if it is false.

1. An increase in the real income of a consumer will result from an increase in the price of a product which the consumer is buying. **T F**

2. Utility and usefulness are not synonymous. **T F**

3. All consumers are subject to the budget restraint. **T F**

4. When the consumer is maximizing his total utility, the marginal utilities of the last unit of every product he buys are identical. **T F**

5. Because utility cannot actually be measured, the marginal-utility theory cannot really explain how consumers will behave. **T F**

6. To find a consumer's demand for a product, the price of the product is varied while his tastes and income and the prices of other products remain unchanged. **T F**

7. A consumer can earn \$10 an hour when he works. It takes 2 hours to consume a product. The value of the time required for the consumption of the product is \$5. **T F**

Circle the letter that corresponds to the best answer.

1. The reason the substitution effect works to encourage a consumer to buy more of a product when its price decreases is (*a*) the real income of the consumer has been increased; (*b*) the real income of the consumer has been decreased; (*c*) the product is now relatively less expensive than it was; (*d*) other products are now relatively less expensive than they were.

2. Which of the following best expresses the law of diminishing marginal utility? (*a*) The more a person consumes of a product, the smaller becomes the utility which he receives from its consumption; (*b*) the more a person consumes of a product, the smaller becomes the additional utility which he receives as a result of consuming an additional unit of the product; (*c*) the less a person consumes of a product, the smaller becomes the utility which he receives from its consumption; (*d*) the less a person consumes of a product, the smaller becomes the additional utility which he receives as a result of consuming an additional unit of the product.

3. Which of the following is *not* an essential assumption of the marginal-utility theory of consumer behavior? (*a*) The consumer has a small income; (*b*) the consumer is rational; (*c*) goods and services are not free; (*d*) goods and services yield decreasing amounts of marginal utility as the consumer buys more of them.

4. Assume a consumer has the marginal-utility schedules for goods X and Y given in the table below, that the prices

Good X		Good Y	
Quantity	MU	Quantity	MU
1	8	1	10
2	7	2	8
3	6	3	6
4	5	4	4
5	4	5	3
6	3	6	2
7	2	7	1

of X and Y are $1 and $2, respectively, and that the income of the consumer is $9. When the consumer is maximizing the total utility he receives, he will buy (*a*) 7X and 1Y; (*b*) 5X and 2Y; (*c*) 3X and 3Y; (*d*) 1X and 4Y.

5. When the consumer in multiple-choice question 4 above purchases the combination of X and Y that maximizes his total utility, his utility is (*a*) 36; (*b*) 45; (*c*) 48; (*d*) 52.

6. Suppose that the prices of A and B are $3 and $2, respectively, that the consumer is spending his entire income and buying 4 units of A and 6 units of B, and that the marginal utility of both the 4th unit of A and the 6th unit of B is 6. It can be concluded that (*a*) the consumer is in equilibrium; (*b*) the consumer should buy more of A and less of B; (*c*) the consumer should buy less of A and more of B; (*d*) the consumer should buy less of both A and B.

7. The full price of a product to a consumer is (*a*) its market price; (*b*) its market price plus the value of its consumption time; (*c*) its market price less the value of its consumption time; (*d*) the value of its consumption time less its market price.

■ DISCUSSION QUESTIONS

1. Explain, employing the income-effect and substitution-effect concepts, the reasons consumers buy more of a product at a lower price than at a higher price, and vice versa.

2. Why is utility a "subjective concept"? How does the subjective nature of utility limit the practical usefulness of the marginal-utility theory of consumer behavior?

3. What essential assumptions are made about consumers and the nature of goods and services in developing the marginal-utility theory of consumer behavior? What is meant by "budget restraint"?

4. When is the consumer in equilibrium and maximizing his total utility? Explain why any deviation from this equilibrium will decrease the consumer's total utility.

5. Using the marginal-utility theory of consumer behavior, explain how an individual's demand schedule for a particular consumer good can be obtained. Why does a demand schedule obtained in this fashion almost invariably result in an inverse or negative relationship between price and quantity demanded?

6. Explain how a consumer might determine the value of his or her time. How does the value of time affect the full price the consumer pays for a good or service?

7. What does taking time into account explain that the traditional approach to consumer behavior does not explain?

APPENDIX TO CHAPTER 25
Indifference Curve Analysis

This brief appendix contains the third explanation or approach to the theory of consumer behavior. In it you are introduced first to the budget line and then to the indifference curve. These two geometrical concepts are next combined to explain when a consumer is purchasing the combination of two products that maximizes the total utility obtainable with his or her income. The last step is to vary the price of one of the products to find the consumer's demand (schedule or curve) for the product.

■ CHECKLIST

When you have studied this appendix you should be able to:

☐ Define the budget line; and state how to measure its slope and what determines its location.

☐ Define an indifference curve; and state the two characteristics of an individual indifference curve.

☐ Explain what an indifference map is; and determine which indifference curves on a map bring a consumer more and less total utility.

☐ State, employing the indifference curve approach, which combination of two products maximizes the total utility of a consumer; and why this is the utility-maximizing combination.

☐ Explain how to use the indifference curve approach to derive a consumer's demand for a particular product.

☐ Contrast the assumptions regarding the measurability of utility made in the marginal-utility and the indifference curve approaches to consumer behavior.

■ APPENDIX OUTLINE

1. A budget line shows graphically the different combinations of two products a consumer can purchase with a particular money income; and it has a negative slope.

a. An increase (decrease) in the money income of the consumer will shift the budget line to the right (left) without affecting its slope.

b. An increase (decrease) in the prices of both products shifts it to the left (right); but an increase (decrease) in the price of the product the quantity of which is measured horizontally (the price of the other product remaining constant) pivots the budget line around a fixed point on the vertical axis in a clockwise (counterclockwise) direction.

2. An indifference curve shows graphically the different combinations of two products which bring a consumer the same total utility.

a. An indifference curve is downsloping; if utility is to remain the same when the quantity of one product increases the quantity of the other product must decrease.

b. An indifference curve is also convex to the origin; the more a consumer has of one product the smaller is the quantity of a second product he is willing to give up to obtain an additional unit of the first product.

c. The consumer has an indifference curve for every level of total utility; and the nearer (farther) a curve is to (from) the origin in this indifference map the smaller (larger) is the utility of the combinations on that curve.

3. The consumer is in equilibrium and purchasing the combination of two products that brings the maximum utility to him where the budget line is tangent to an indifference curve.

4. In the marginal-utility approach to consumer behavior it is assumed that utility is measurable; but in the indifference curve approach it need only be assumed that a consumer can say whether a combination of products has more, less, or the same amount of utility as another combination.

5. The demand (schedule or curve) for one of the products is derived by varying the price of that product and shifting the budget line, holding the price of the other product and the consumer's income constant, and finding the quantity of the product the consumer will purchase at each price when in equilibrium.

■ IMPORTANT TERMS

Budget line
Indifference curve
Marginal rate of substitution
Indifference map
Equilibrium position

■ FILL-IN QUESTIONS

1. A budget line shows the various combinations of two products that can be purchased with a given ______________; and, when quantities of X are measured horizontally and quantities of Y vertically, it has a slope equal to the ratio of ______________ to the ______________

2. When:

a. a consumer's income increases the budget line moves to the (right, left) ______________

b. quantities of E are measured horizontally and quantities of F vertically, an increase in the price of E will fan the budget line (outward, inward) ______________ around a fixed point on the ______________ axis.

3. An indifference curve shows the various combinations of two products that give a consumer the same ______________

a. An indifference curve slopes (upward, downward) ______________ and the slope of an indifference curve is equal to the marginal ______________ of ______________.

b. It is (concave, convex) ______________ to the origin.

4. The more a consumer has of one product, the (greater, smaller) ______________ is the quantity of a second product he or she will give up to obtain an additional unit of the first product: as a result the marginal rate of substitution of the first for the second product (increases, decreases) ______________ as a consumer moves from left to right (or downward) along an indifference curve.

5. The farther from the origin an indifference curve lies, the (greater, smaller) ______________ is the total utility obtained from the combinations of products on that curve.

6. A consumer obtains the greatest obtainable total utility or satisfaction when he or she purchases that combination of two products at which his or her budget line is ______________. At this point the marginal rate of substitution is equal to ______________

7. Were a consumer to purchase a combination of two products which lies on her budget line and at which her budget line is steeper than the indifference curve intersecting that point, she could increase her satisfaction by trading (down, up) ______________ her budget line.

8. The marginal-utility approach to consumer behavior requires that we assume utility (is, is not) __________ numerically measurable; and the indifference curve approach (does, does not) ______________ require we make this assumption.

9. When quantities of product X are measured along the horizontal axis, a decrease in the price of X:

a. fans the budget line (inward, outward) __________ and to the (right, left) ______________;

b. puts the consumer, when in equilibrium, on a (higher, lower) ______________ indifference curve;

c. and normally induces the consumer to purchase (more, less) ______________ of product X.

10. Using indifference curves and different budget lines to determine how much of a particular product an individual consumer will purchase at different prices makes it possible to derive that consumer's ______________ curve or schedule for that product.

■ PROBLEMS AND PROJECTS

1. In the next column are the schedules for three indifference curves.

a. Measure quantities of A along the horizontal axis (from 0 to 9) and quantities of B along the vertical axis (from 0 to 45) on the graph at the top of the next page.

(1) Plot the 8 combinations of A and B from indifference schedule 1 and draw through the 8 points a curve which is in no place a straight line. Label this curve IC 1.

(2) Do the same for the 9 points in indifference schedule 2 and label it IC 2.

(3) Repeat the process for the 10 points in indifference schedule 3 and label the curve IC 3.

Indifference schedule 1		Indifference schedule 2		Indifference schedule 3	
A	B	A	B	A	B
0	28	0	36	0	45
1	21	1	28	1	36
2	15	2	21	2	28
3	10	3	15	3	21
4	6	4	10	4	15
5	3	5	6	5	10
6	1	6	3	6	6
7	0	7	1	7	3
		8	0	8	1
				9	0

b. Assume the price of A is $12, the price of B is $2.40, and a consumer has an income of $72.

(1) Complete the table below to show the quantities of A and B this consumer is able to purchase.

A	B
0	___
1	___
2	___
3	___
4	___
5	___
6	___

(2) Plot this budget line on the graph you completed in part *a* (above).

(3) This budget line has a slope equal to ______________

c. To obtain the greatest satisfaction or utility from his income of $72 this consumer will:

(1) purchase ________ units of A and ________ of B;

(2) and spend $________ on A and $________ on B.

2. Shown at the bottom of the next page is a graph with three indifference curves and three budget lines. This consumer has an income of $100 and the price of D remains constant at $5.

a. When the price of C is $10 the consumer's budget line is BL 1 and the consumer:

(1) purchases ____________ C and ____________ D;

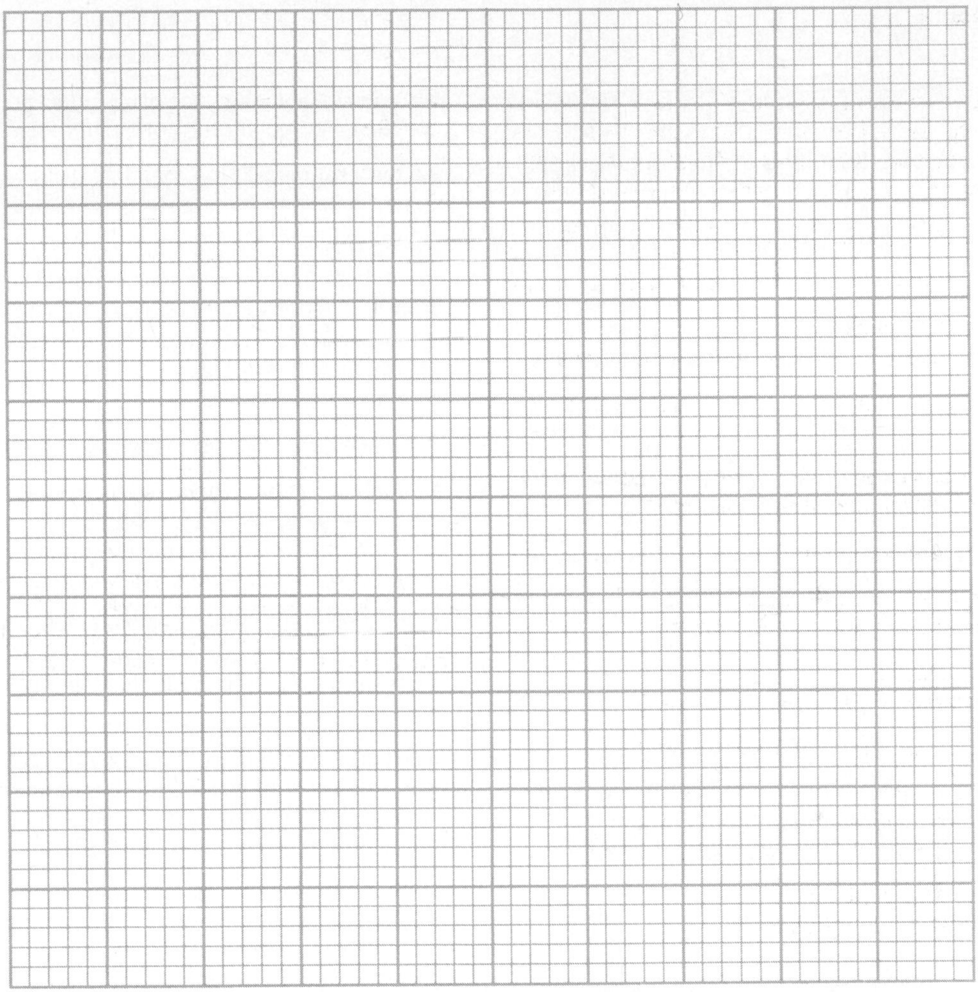

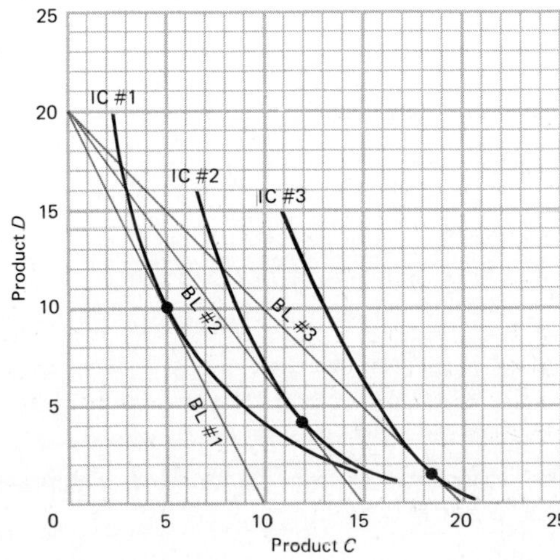

(2) and spends $________ on C and $________ on D.

b. If the price of C is $6⅔ the budget line is BL 2 and the consumer:

(1) purchases ____________ C and ____________ D;

(2) and spends $________ for C and $________ for D.

c. And when the price of C is $5 the consumer has budget line BL 3 and:

(1) buys ____________ C and ____________ D; and

(2) spends $________ on C and $________ on D.

d. On the graph on the next page plot the quantities of C demanded at the three prices.

e. Between $10 and $5 this consumer's demand for C is (elastic, inelastic) ____________ and for him products C and D are (substitutes, complements) ____________

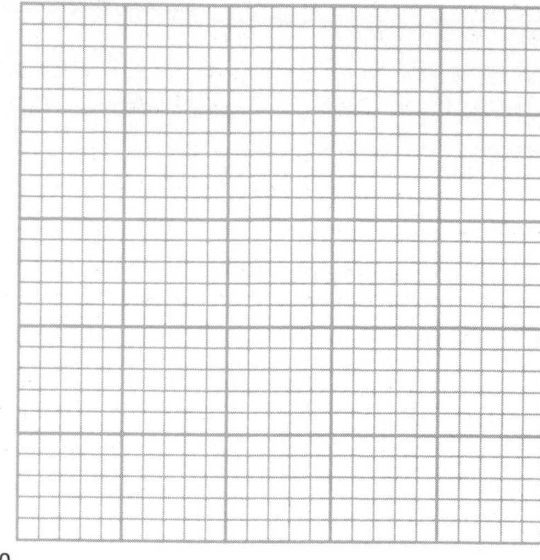

■ SELF-TEST

Circle the T if the statement is true, the F if it is false.

1. The slope of the budget line when quantities of F are measured horizontally and quantities of G vertically is equal to the price of G divided by the price of F. **T F**

2. An increase in the money income of a consumer shifts the budget line to the right. **T F**

3. The closer to the origin an indifference curve lies the smaller is the total utility a consumer obtains from the combinations of products on that indifference curve. **T F**

4. If a consumer moves from one combination (or point) on an indifference curve to another combination (or point) on the same curve the total utility obtained by the consumer does not change. **T F**

5. A consumer maximizes total utility when he or she purchases the combination of the two products at which his or her budget line crosses an indifference curve. **T F**

6. A consumer is unable to purchase any of the combinations of two products which lie below (or to the left) of the consumer's budget line. **T F**

7. An indifference curve is concave to the origin. **T F**

8. A decrease in the price of a product normally enables a consumer to reach a higher indifference curve. **T F**

9. It is assumed in the marginal-utility approach to consumer behavior that utility is numerically measurable. **T F**

10. In both the marginal-utility and indifference curve approaches to consumer behavior it is assumed that a consumer is able to say whether the total utility obtained from combination A is greater than, equal to, or less than the total utility obtained from combination B. **T F**

Circle the letter that corresponds to the best answer.

1. Suppose a consumer has an income of $8, the price of R is $1, and the price of S is $0.50. Which of the following combinations is on the consumer's budget line? (*a*) 8R and 1S; (*b*) 7R and 1S; (*c*) 6R and 6S; (*d*) 5R and 6S.

2. If a consumer has an income of $100, the price of U is $10, and the price of V is $20, the maximum quantity of U the consumer is able to purchase is (*a*) 5; (*b*) 10; (*c*) 20; (*d*) 30.

3. When the income of a consumer is $20, the price of T is $5, the price of Z is $2, and the quantity of T is measured horizontally, the slope of the budget line is (*a*) ⅖; (*b*) 2½; (*c*) 4; (*d*) 10.

4. An indifference curve is a curve which shows the different combinations of two products that (*a*) give a consumer equal marginal utilities; (*b*) give a consumer equal total utilities; (*c*) cost a consumer equal amounts; (*d*) have the same prices.

5. In the schedule for an indifference curve below, how much of G is the consumer willing to give up to obtain the third unit of H? (*a*) 3; (*b*) 4; (*c*) 5; (*d*) 6.

Quantity of G	Quantity of H
18	1
12	2
7	3
3	4
0	5

Use the following diagram to answer multiple-choice questions 6 and 7.

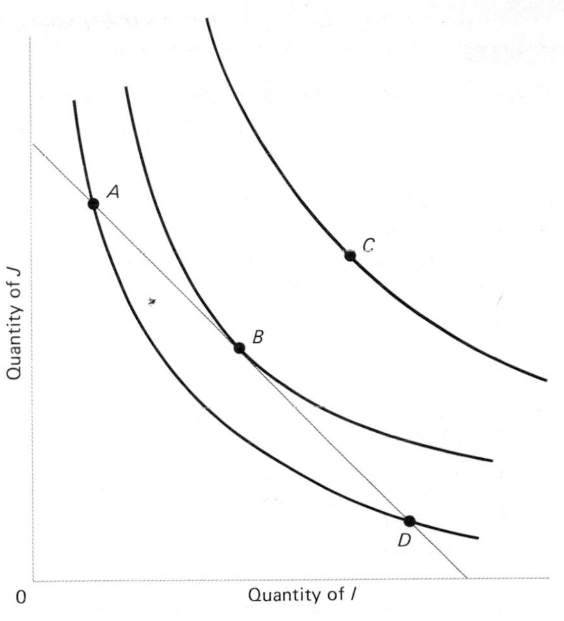

6. Which combination of I and J will the consumer purchase? (*a*) A; (*b*) B; (*c*) C; (*d*) D.

7. Suppose the price of I increases. The budget line will fan (*a*) inward around a point of the J axis; (*b*) outward around a point on the J axis; (*c*) inward around a point on the I axis; (*d*) outward around a point on the I axis.

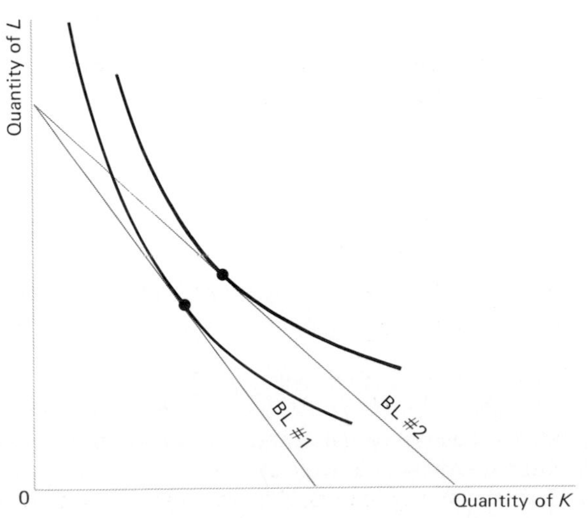

8. To derive the demand for product K the price of K is varied. Held constant is (*a*) the money income of the consumer; (*b*) the price of another product L; (*c*) thecon-sumer's preferences; (*d*) all of the above.

Use the diagram at the bottom of the previous column to answer multiple-choice questions 9 and 10.

9. If the budget line shifts from BL 1 to BL 2 it is because (*a*) the price of K has increased; (*b*) the price of K has decreased; (*c*) the price of L has increased (*d*) the price of L has decreased.

10. When the budget line shifts from BL 2 to BL 1 the consumer will (*a*) buy more of K and L; (*b*) buy less of K and L; (*c*) buy more of K and less of L; (*d*) buy less of K and more of L.

■ DISCUSSION QUESTIONS

1. Explain why the slope of the budget line is negative; and why the slope of an indifference curve is negative and convex to the origin.

2. How will each of the following events affect the budget line? (*a*) A decrease in the money income of the consumer; (*b*) an increase in the prices of both products; (*c*) a decrease in the price of one of the products.

3. Explain why the budget line can be called "objective" and an indifference curve "subjective."

4. Suppose a consumer purchases a combination of two products that is on his or her budget line but the budget line is not tangent to an indifference curve at that point. Of which product should the consumer buy more and of which should he or she buy less? Why?

5. Explain how the indifference map of a consumer and the budget line are utilized to derive the consumer's demand for one of the products. In deriving demand, what is varied and what is held constant?

6. What is the "important difference between the marginal utility theory and the indifference curve theory of consumer demand"?

26
The costs of production

In previous chapters the factors which influence the demand for a product purchased by consumers were examined in some detail. Chapter 26 turns to the other side of the market and begins the investigation of the forces which determine the amount of a particular product a business firm will produce and the price it will charge for that product. In addition to the demand for the product, the factors that determine the output of a firm and the price of the product are the costs of producing the product *and* the structure of the market in which the product is sold. In the next four chapters you will learn how costs and demand determine price and output in four different kinds of market structures: pure competition, pure monopoly, monopolistic competition, and oligopoly.

Chapter 26 is an examination of the way in which the costs of the firm change as the output of the firm changes. This chapter is extremely important if the four chapters which follow it are to be understood. For this reason it is necessary for you to master the material dealing with the costs of the firm.

You will probably find that you have some difficulty with the new terms and concepts. Particular attention, therefore, should be given to them. These new terms and concepts are used in the explanation of the costs of the firm and will be used over and over again in later chapters. If you will try to learn them in the order in which you encounter them you will have little difficulty because the later terms build on the earlier ones.

After the new terms and concepts are well fixed in your mind, understanding the generalizations made about the relationships between cost and output will be much simpler. Here the important things to note are (1) that the statements made about the behavior of costs are *generalizations* (they do not apply to any particular firm or enterprise, but are more or less applicable to every business firm); and (2) that the generalizations made about the relationships between particular types of cost and the output of the firm are fairly precise generalizations. When attempting to learn these generalizations, you will find it worthwhile to draw rough graphs (with cost on the vertical and output on the horizontal axis) which describe the cost relationships. Try it especially with the following types of costs: *short-run* fixed, variable, total, average fixed, average variable, average total, and marginal costs; and *long-term* average cost.

One last cue: In addition to learning *how* the costs of the firm vary as its output varies, be sure to understand *why* the costs vary the way they do. In this connection note that the behavior of short-run costs is the result of the law of diminishing returns and that the behavior of long-run costs is the consequence of economies and diseconomies of scale.

■ CHECKLIST

When you have studied this chapter you should be able to:

☐ Define economic cost and distinguish between an explicit and an implicit cost.

☐ Explain the difference between normal profit and economic profit and why the former is a cost and the latter is not a cost.

☐ State the law of diminishing returns.

☐ Compute marginal and average product when you are given the necessary data; and explain the relationship between marginal and average product.

☐ Explain the difference between a fixed cost and a variable cost; and between average cost and marginal cost.

☐ Compute and graph average fixed cost, average variable cost, average total cost, and marginal cost when you are given total-cost data.
☐ State the relationship between average product and average variable cost and between marginal product and marginal cost.
☐ Explain the difference between the short run and the long run; and between short-run costs and long-run costs.
☐ State why the long-run average cost curve is expected to be U-shaped; and list the causes of the economies and the diseconomies of scale.
☐ Indicate the relationship between long-run average costs and the structure and competitiveness of an industry.

■ CHAPTER OUTLINE

1. Because resources are scarce and may be employed to produce many different products, the economic cost of using resources to produce any one of these products is an opportunity cost: the amount of other products that cannot be produced

a. In money terms, the costs of employing resources to produce a product are also an opportunity cost: the payments a firm must make to the owners of resources to attract these resources away from their best alternative opportunities for earning incomes; and these costs may be either explicit or implicit.

b. Normal profit is an implicit cost and is the minimum payment that entrepreneurs must receive for performing the entrepreneurial functions for the firm.

c. Economic, or pure, profit is the revenue a firm receives in excess of all its explicit and implicit economic (opportunity) costs. (The firm's accounting profit is its revenue less only its *explicit* costs.

d. The firm's economic costs vary as the firm's output varies; and the way in which costs vary with output depends upon whether the firm is able to make short-run or long-run changes in the amounts of resources it employs. The firm's plant is a fixed resource in the short run and a variable resource in the long run.

2. In the short run the firm cannot change the size of its plant and can vary its output only by changing the quantities of the variable resources it employs.

a. The law of diminishing returns determines the manner in which the costs of the firm change as it changes its output in the short run.

b. The total short-run costs of a firm are the sum of its fixed and variable costs. As output increases:

(1) the fixed costs do not change;

(2) the variable costs increase at first at a decreasing and then at an increasing rate;

(3) and total costs at first increase at a decreasing and then at an increasing rate.

c. Average fixed, variable, and total costs are equal, respectively, to the firm's fixed, variable, and total costs divided by the output of the firm. As output increases:

(1) average fixed cost decreases;

(2) average variable cost at first decreases and then increases;

(3) and average total cost also decreases at first and then increases.

d. Marginal cost is the extra cost incurred in producing one additional unit of output.

(1) Because the marginal product of the variable resource increases and then decreases (as more of the variable resource is employed to increase output), marginal cost decreases and then increases as output increases.

(2) At the output at which average variable cost is a minimum, average variable cost and marginal cost are equal; and at the output at which average total cost is a minimum, average total cost and marginal cost are equal.

3. In the long run all the resources employed by the firm are variable resources, and all its costs, therefore, are variable costs.

a. As the firm expands its output by increasing the size of its plant, average cost tends to fall at first because of the economies of large-scale production; but as this expansion continues, sooner or later, average cost begins to rise because of the diseconomies of large-scale production.

b. The economies and diseconomies encountered in the production of different goods are important factors influencing the structure and competitiveness of various industries.

■ IMPORTANT TERMS

Economic cost	**Economic (pure) profit**
Opportunity cost	**Short run**
Explicit cost	**Long run**
Implicit cost	**Law of diminishing returns**
Normal profit	**Total product**

Marginal product
Average product
Fixed resource
Variable resource
Fixed cost
Variable cost
Total cost
Average fixed cost
Average variable cost
Average (total) cost
Marginal cost
Economies of (large) scale
Diseconomies of (large) scale
Constant returns to scale
Minimum efficient scale (MES)
Natural monopoly

■ FILL-IN QUESTIONS

1. The cost of producing a particular product is the quantity of ________ products that cannot be produced. The value or worth of any resource is what it can earn in its best alternative use and is called the (out-of-pocket, opportunity) ________ cost of that resource.

2. The money cost of producing a product is the amount of money the firm must pay to resource owners to ________ these resources away from alternative employments in the economy; and these costs may be either ________ or ________ costs.

3. Normal profit is a cost because it is the payment which the firm must make to obtain the services of the ________

a. Economic profit is not a cost and is equal to the firm's total ________ less its total ________

b. Accounting profit is equal to the firm's total revenue less its (explicit, implicit) ________ costs.

4. In the short run the firm can change its output by changing the quantity of the (fixed, variable) ________ resources it employs; but it cannot change the quantity of the ________ resources. This means that the firm's plant capacity is fixed in the (short, long) ________ run and variable in the ________ run.

5. The law of diminishing returns is that as successive units of a (fixed, variable) ________ resource are added to a ________ resource beyond some point the (total, marginal) ________ product of the former resource will decrease.

6. When the marginal product of any input:

a. exceeds its average product the average product is (rising, falling) ________;

b. is less than its average product the average product is ________;

c. is equal to its average product the average product is a (minimum, maximum) ________.

7. On the graph below sketch the way in which the average product and the marginal product of a resource change as the firm increases its employment of that resource.

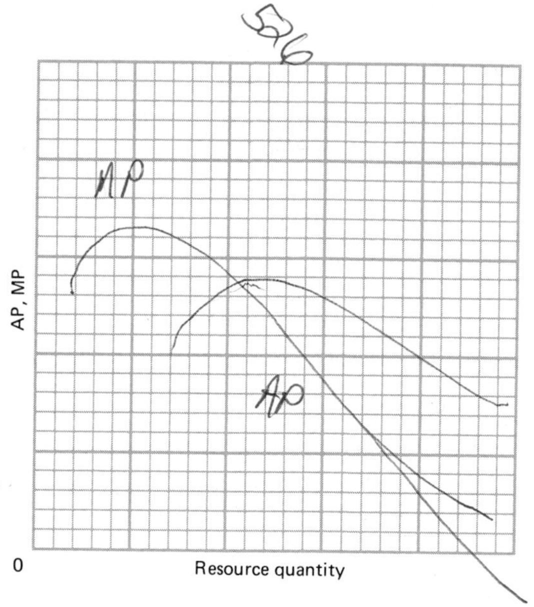

AP, MP

0 Resource quantity

8. The short-run costs of a firm are either ________ costs or ________ costs, but in the long run all costs are ________ costs.

9. On the graph (page 231, top) sketch the manner in which fixed cost, variable cost, and total cost change as the output the firm produces in the short run changes.

10. The law of diminishing returns causes a firm's ________ cost, ________ cost, and ________ cost to decrease at first and then to increase as the output of the firm increases.

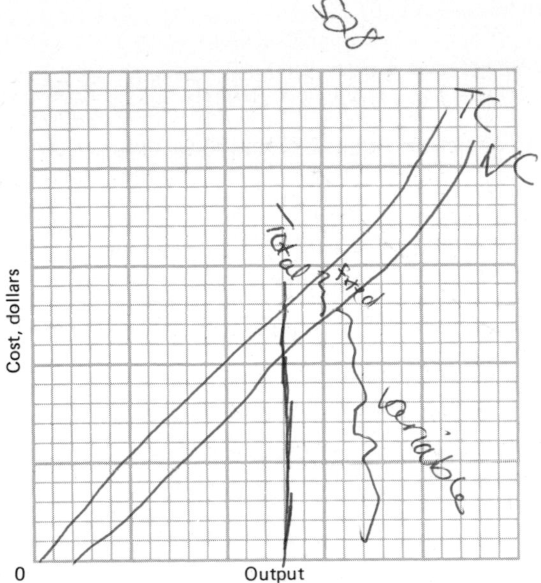

Sketch these three cost curves on the graph below in such a way that their proper relationship to each other is shown.

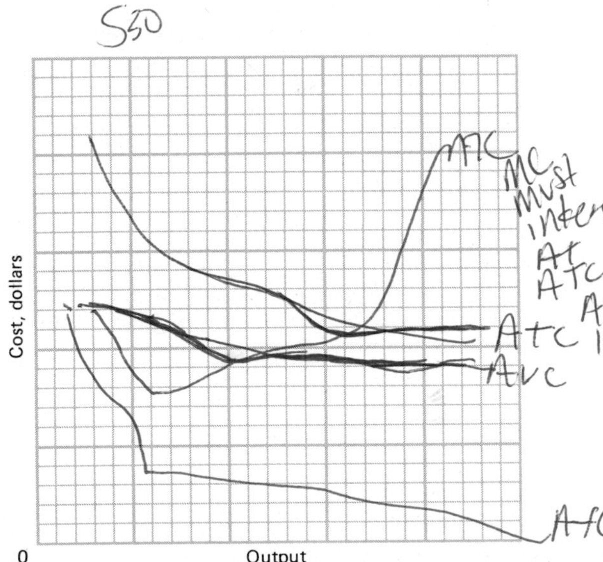

11. Marginal cost is the increase in either ________ cost or ________ which occurs when the firm increases its output by one unit.

12. If marginal cost is less than average variable cost, average variable cost will be (rising, falling, constant) ________ but if average variable cost is less than marginal cost, average variable cost will be ________

13. Assume that labor is the only variable input in the short run and that the wage rate paid to labor is constant.

a. When the marginal product of labor is rising, the marginal cost of producing a product is (rising, falling) ________

b. When the average variable cost of producing a product is falling, the average product of labor is ________

c. At the output at which marginal cost is a minimum, the marginal product of labor is a (minimum, maximum) ________

d. At the output at which the average product of labor is a maximum, the average variable cost of producing the product is a ________

e. At the output at which average variable cost is a minimum:

(1) average variable cost and ________ cost are ________

(2) average product and ________ product are ________

14. The long-run average cost of producing a product is equal to the lowest of the short-run costs of producing that product after the firm has had all the time it requires to make the appropriate adjustments in the size of its ________

15. Below are the short-run average-cost curves of producing a product with three different sizes of plants, plant 1, plant 2, and plant 3. Draw the firm's long-run average-cost curve on this graph.

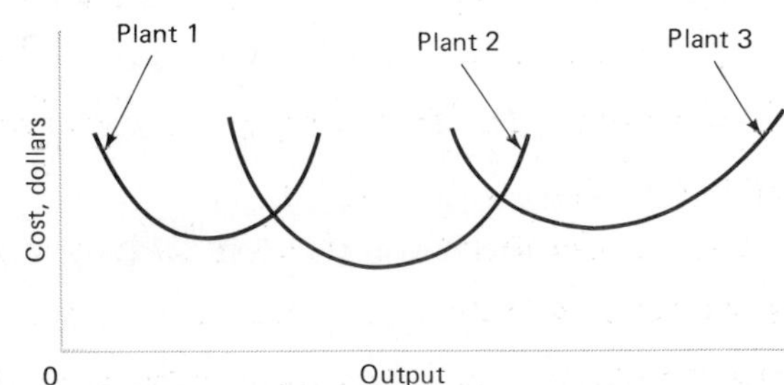

16. List below four important types of economy of large scale:

a. ____________________

b. ____________________

c. ____________________

d. ____________________

17. The factor which gives rise to diseconomies of large scale is ____________

18. Economies and diseconomies of scale are significant in the American economy because they affect the ____________ and the ____________ of the firms in a particular industry.

■ PROBLEMS AND PROJECTS

1. The table at the top of the next column shows the total production of a firm as the quantity of labor employed increases. The quantities of all other resources employed are constant.

a. Compute the marginal products of the first through the eighth unit of labor and enter them in the table.

b. There are increasing returns to labor from the first through the third unit of labor and decreasing returns from the fourth through the eighth unit.

c. When total production is increasing, marginal product is (positive, negative) positive and when total production is decreasing, marginal product is negative

d. Now compute the average products of the various quantities of labor and enter them in the table.

Units of labor	Total production	Marginal product of labor	Average product of labor
0	0		0
1	80	80	80
2	200	120	100
3	330	130	110
4	400	70	100
5	450	50	90
6	480	30	80
7	490	10	70
8	480	−10	60

Quantity of labor employed	Total output	Marginal product of labor	Average product of labor	Total labor cost	Marginal cost	Average variable cost
0	0	—	—	$0	—	—
1	5	5	5	____	$____	$____
2	11	6	5½	____	____	____
3	18	7	6	____	____	____
4	24	6	6	____	____	____
5	29	5	5⅘	____	____	____
6	33	4	5½	____	____	____
7	36	3	5⅐	____	____	____
8	38	2	4¾	____	____	____
9	39	1	4⅓	____	____	____
10	39	0	3⁹⁄₁₀	____		____

2. Assume that a firm has a plant of fixed size and that it can vary its output only by varying the amount of labor it employs. The table at the bottom of the previous page shows the relationships between the amount of labor employed, the output of the firm, the marginal product of labor, and the average product of labor.

a. Assume each unit of labor costs the firm $10. Compute the total cost of labor for each quantity of labor the firm might employ, and enter these figures in the table.

b. Now determine the marginal cost of the firm's product as the firm increases its output. Divide the *increase* in total labor cost by the *increase in total output* to find the marginal cost. Enter these figures in the table.

c. When the marginal product of labor:

(1) Increases, the marginal cost of the firm's product (increases, decreases) ______

(2) Decreases, the marginal cost of the firm's product ______

d. If labor is the only variable input, the total labor cost and total variable cost are equal. Find the average variable cost of the firm's product (by dividing the total labor cost by total output) and enter these figures in the table.

e. When the average product of labor:

(1) Increases, the average variable cost (increases, decreases) ______

(2) Decreases, the average variable cost ______

3. In the table at the bottom of this page you will find a schedule of a firm's fixed cost and variable cost.

a. Complete the table by computing total cost, average fixed cost, average total cost, and marginal cost.

b. On the first graph on page 234 plot and label fixed cost, variable cost, and total cost.

c. On the second graph on page 234 plot average fixed cost, average variable cost, average total cost, and marginal cost; label the four curves.

4. On page 235 are the short-run average-total-cost schedules for three plants of different size which a firm might build to produce its product. Assume that these are the only possible sizes of plants which the firm might build.

Output	Fixed cost	Variable cost	Total cost	Average fixed cost	Average variable cost	Average total cost	Marginal cost
$ 0	$200	$ 0	$ 200				
1	200	50	250	$200	$50.00	$250.00	$ 50
2	200	90	290	100	45.00	145	40
3	200	120	320	66.67	40.00	106.67	30
4	200	160	360	50	40.00	90	40
5	200	220	420	40	44.00	84.	60
6	200	300	500	33.34	50.00	83.34	80
7	200	400	600	28.57	57.14	85.71	100
8	200	520	720	25	65.00	90.	120
9	200	670	870	22.22	74.44	96.66	150
10	200	900	1100	20	90.00	110.00	230

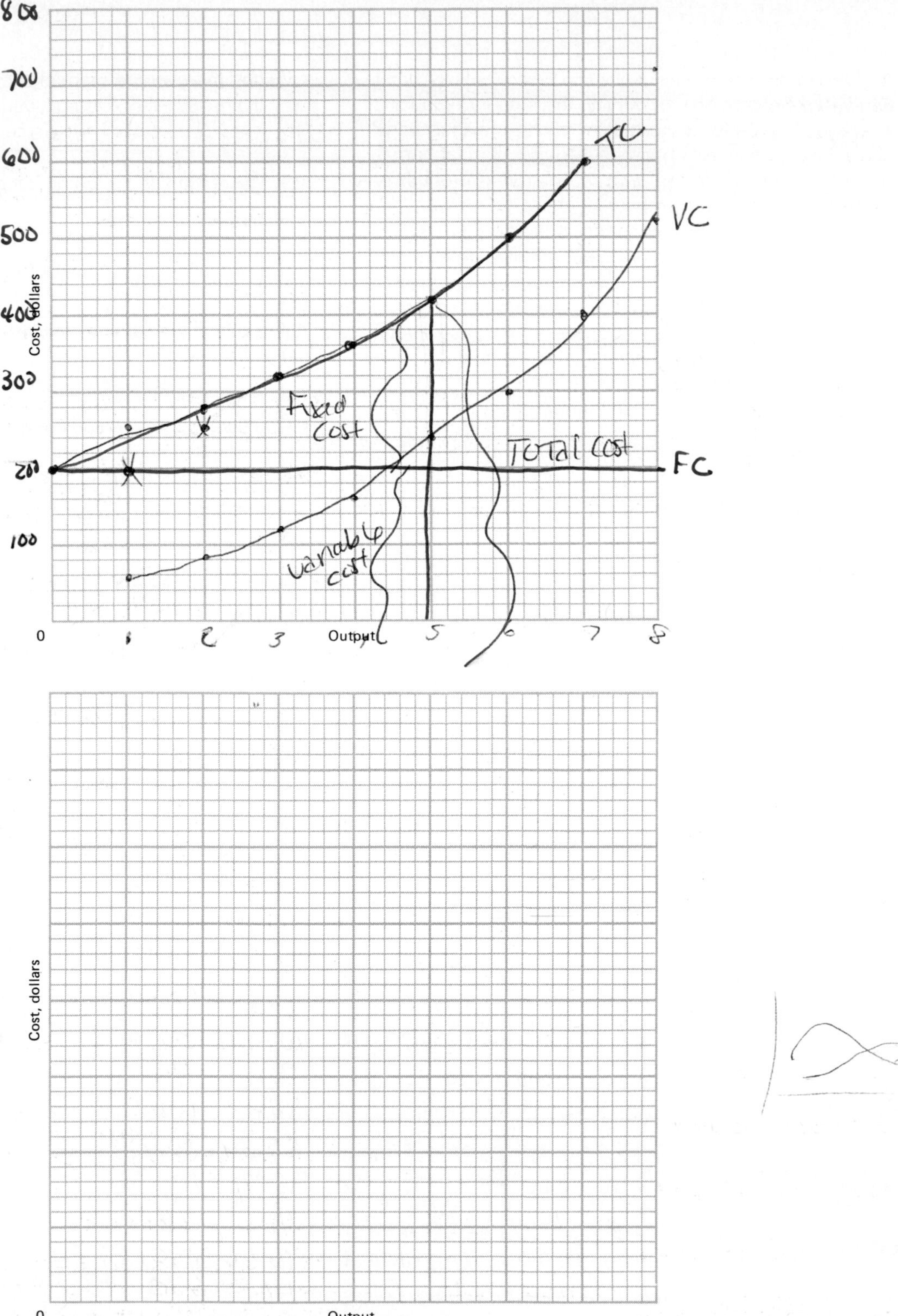
Cost, dollars
0
Output
TC
VC
FC
Fixed cost
Total cost
Variable cost
Cost, dollars
0
Output

Plant size A		Plant size B		Plant size C	
Output	ATC	Output	ATC	Output	ATC
10	$ 7	10	$17	10	$53
20	6	20	13	20	44
30	5	30	9	30	35
40	4	40	6	40	27
50	5	50	4	50	20
60	7	60	3	60	14
70	10	70	4	70	11
80	14	80	5	80	8
90	19	90	7	90	6
100	25	100	10	100	5
110	32	110	16	110	7
120	40	120	25	120	10

a. Complete the *long-run* average-cost schedule for the firm in the table below.

Output	Average cost
10	$______
20	______
30	______
40	______
50	______
60	______
70	______
80	______
90	______
100	______
110	______
120	______

b. For outputs between:

(1) ____________ and ____________, the firm should build plant A.

(2) ____________ and ____________, the firm should build plant B.

(3) ____________ and ____________, the firm should build plant C.

■ SELF-TEST

Circle the T if the statement is true, the F if it is false.

1. The economic costs of a firm are the payments it must make to resource owners to attract their resources from alternative employments. **T F**

2. Economic or pure profit is an explicit cost, while normal profit is an implicit cost. **T F**

3. In the short run the size (or capacity) of a firm's plant is fixed. **T F**

4. The resources employed by a firm are all variable in the long run and all fixed in the short run. **T F**

5. The law of diminishing returns is that as successive amounts of a variable resource are added to a fixed resource, beyond some point total output will diminish. **T F**

6. When average product is falling, marginal product is greater than average product. **T F**

7. When marginal product is negative, total production (or output) is decreasing. **T F**

8. The larger the output of a firm, the smaller is the fixed cost of the firm. **T F**

9. If the fixed cost of a firm increases from one year to the next (because the premium it must pay for the insurance on the buildings it owns has been increased) while its variable-cost schedule remains unchanged, its marginal cost-schedule will also remain unchanged. **T F**

10. Marginal cost is equal to average variable cost at the output at which average variable cost is a minimum. **T F**

11. When the marginal product of a variable resource increases, the marginal cost of producing the product will decrease; and when marginal product decreases, marginal cost will increase. **T F**

12. One of the explanations of why the long-run average-cost curve of a firm rises after some level of output has been reached is the law of diminishing returns. **T F**

13. A firm can avoid the diseconomies of large scale by becoming a multiplant firm. **T F**

14. If a firm has constant returns to scale in the long run the total costs of producing its product do not change when it expands or contracts its output. **T F**

15. Many firms appear to be larger than is necessary for them to achieve the minimum efficient scale. **T F**

Circle the letter that corresponds to the best answer.

1. Normal profit is defined as the cost of obtaining the services of (*a*) management; (*b*) entrepreneurs; (*c*) capital; (*d*) land.

2. The revenues of a firm less its explicit costs are defined as the firm's (*a*) normal profit; (*b*) accounting profit; (*c*) economic profit; (*d*) economic rent.

3. Which of the following is most likely to be a long-run adjustment for a firm which manufactures jet fighter planes on an assembly-line basis? (*a*) An increase in the amount of steel the firm buys; (*b*) a reduction in the number of "shifts" of workers from three to two; (*c*) a changeover from the production of one type of jet fighter to the production of a later-model jet fighter; (*d*) a changeover from the production of jet fighters to the production of sports cars.

4. Assume that the only variable resource is labor and that as the amount of labor employed by a firm increases, the output of the firm increases in the way shown in the table below. The marginal product of the fourth unit of labor is (*a*) 3 units of output; (*b*) 3¾ units of output; (*c*) 4 units of output; (*d*) 15 units of output.

Amount of labor	Amount of output
1	3
2	8
3	12
4	15
5	17
6	18

5. Employing the schedule in the question above, when the firm hires four units of labor the average product of labor is (*a*) 3 units of output; (*b*) 3¾ units of output; (*c*) 4 units of output; (*d*) 15 units of output.

6. Because the average product of a variable resource initially increases and later decreases as a firm increases its output (*a*) average variable cost decreases at first and then increases; (*b*) average fixed cost declines as the output of the firm expands; (*c*) variable cost at first increases by increasing amounts and then increases by decreasing amounts; (*d*) marginal cost at first increases and then decreases.

7. Because the marginal product of a resource at first increases and then decreases as the output of the firm increases: (*a*) average fixed cost declines as the output of the firm increases; (*b*) average variable cost at first increases and then decreases; (*c*) variable cost at first increases by increasing amounts and then increases by decreasing amounts; (*d*) total cost at first increases by decreasing amounts and then increases by increasing amounts.

For questions 8, 9, and 10 use the data given in the table below. The fixed cost of the firm is $500 and the firm's variable cost is indicated in the table.

Output	Variable cost
1	$ 200
2	360
3	500
4	700
5	1,000
6	1,800

8. The average variable cost of the firm when 4 units of output are produced is: (*a*) $175; (*b*) $200; (*c*) $300; (*d*) $700.

9. The average total cost of the firm when 4 units of output are being produced is: (*a*) $175; (*b*) $200; (*c*) $300; (*d*) $700.

10. The marginal cost of the sixth unit of output is: (*a*) $200; (*b*) $300; (*c*) $700; (*d*) $800.

11. Marginal cost and average variable cost are equal at the output at which (*a*) marginal cost is a minimum; (*b*) marginal product is a maximum; (*c*) average product is a maximum; (*d*) average variable cost is a maximum.

12. In the following table three short-run cost schedules are given for three plants of different sizes which a firm might build in the long run. What is the *long-run* average cost of producing 40 units of output? (*a*) $7; (*b*) $8; (*c*) $9; (*d*) $10.

Plant 1		Plant 2		Plant 3	
Output	ATC	Output	ATC	Output	ATC
10	$10	10	$15	10	$20
20	9	20	10	20	15
30	8	30	7	30	10
40	9	40	10	40	8
50	10	50	14	50	9

13. Using the data given for question 10, at what output is long-run average cost a minimum? (*a*) 20; (*b*) 30; (*c*) 40; (*d*) 50.

14. Which of the following is *not* a factor which results in economies of scale? (*a*) More efficient utilization of the firm's plant; (*b*) increased specialization in the use of labor; (*c*) greater specialization in the management of the firm; (*d*) utilization of more efficient equipment.

15. The long-run average costs of producing a particular product are one of the factors that determine (*a*) the competition among the firms producing the product; (*b*) the number of firms in the industry producing the product; (*c*) the size of each of the firms in the industry producing the product; (*d*) all of the above.

■ DISCUSSION QUESTIONS

1. Explain the meaning of the opportunity cost of producing a product and the difference between an explicit and an implicit cost. How would you determine the implicit money cost of a resource?

2. What is the difference between normal and economic profit? Why is the former an economic cost? How do you define accounting profit?

3. What type of adjustments can a firm make in the long run that it cannot make in the short run? What adjustments can it make in the short run? How long is the short run?

4. Why is the distinction between the short run and the long run important?

5. State precisely the law of diminishing returns. Exactly what is it that diminishes, and why does it diminish?

6. Distinguish between a fixed cost and a variable cost. Why are short-run total costs partly fixed and partly variable costs, and why are long-run costs entirely variable?

7. Why do short-run variable costs increase at first by decreasing amounts and later increase by increasing amounts? How does the behavior of short-run variable costs influence the behavior of short-run total costs?

8. Describe the way in which short-run average fixed cost, average variable cost, average total cost, and marginal cost vary as the output of the firm increases.

9. What is the connection between marginal product and marginal cost and between average product and average variable cost? How will marginal cost behave as marginal product decreases and increases? How will average variable cost change as average product rises and falls?

10. What is the precise relationship between marginal cost and minimum average variable cost and between marginal cost and minimum average total cost? Why are these relationships necessarily true?

11. What does the long-run average-cost curve of a firm show? What relationship is there between long-run average cost and the short-run average-total-cost schedules of the different-sized plants which a firm might build?

12. Why is the long-run average-cost curve of a firm U-shaped?

13. What is meant by an economy of large scale? What are some of the more important types of such an economy?

14. What is meant by and what causes diseconomies of large scale?

15. Why are the economies and diseconomies of scale of great significance, and how do they influence the size of firms in an industry and the number of firms in an industry?

27
Price and output determination: pure competition

Chapter 27 is the first of four chapters which bring together the demand for a product and the production costs studied in Chapter 26. Each of the four chapters combines demand and production costs in a *different* market structure; and analyzes and draws conclusions for that particular kind of product market. The questions which are analyzed and for which *both short-run* and *long-run* answers are sought are the following. Given the costs of the firm, what output will it produce; what will be the market price of the product; what will be the output of the entire industry; what will be the profit received by the firm; and what relationships will exist between price, average total cost, and marginal cost.

In addition to finding the answers to these questions you should learn *why* the questions are answered the way they are in each of the market models and in what way the answers obtained in one model *differ* from those obtained in the other models.

Actually, the answers are obtained by applying logic to different sets of assumptions. It is important, therefore, to note specifically how the assumptions made in one model differ from those of other models. Each model assumes that every firm is guided in making its decisions solely by the desire to maximize its profits, and that the costs of the firm are not materially affected by the type of market in which it *sells* its output. The important differences in the models which account for the differing answers involve (1) such characteristics of the market as the number of sellers, the ease of entry into and exodus from the industry, and the kind of product (standardized or differentiated) produced; and (2) the way in which the *individual firm* sees the demand for its product.

Chapter 27 begins by describing the three major characteristics of each of the four basic types of market models. From this point on it focuses its attention entirely on the purely competitive model. There are several good reasons for studying pure competition. Not the least of these reasons is that in the long run, pure competition—subject to certain exceptions—results in an ideal or perfect allocation of resources. After obtaining the answers to the questions listed in the first paragraph above, the author returns at the end of the chapter to explain in what sense competitive resource allocation is ideal and in what cases it may be less than ideal. In Chapters 28 and 29, which concern monopoly and monopolistic competition, respectively, it will be found that in these market situations resource allocation is less than ideal. You, therefore, should pay special attention in Chapter 27 to what is meant by an ideal allocation of resources and why perfect competition results in this perfect allocation.

■ CHECKLIST

When you have studied this chapter you should be able to:

☐ List the three major characteristics of each of the four basic market models.

☐ Explain why a purely competitive firm is a "price-taker" and the way in which it sees the demand for its product and the marginal revenue from the sale of an additional unit of its product.

☐ Compute average, total, and marginal revenue when you are given the demand schedule faced by a purely competitive firm.

☐ Use both the total revenue-total cost and the marginal revenue-marginal cost approaches to determine the output the purely competitive firm will produce in the short run; and explain *why* the firm will produce this output.

☐ Explain how to find the *firm's* short-run supply curve; and construct its short-run supply schedule when you are given its short-run cost schedules.

☐ Explain how to find the *industry's* short-run supply curve (or schedule).
☐ Determine the price at which the product will sell, the output of the industry, and the output of the individual firm in the short run.
☐ Determine the price that will be charged and the output of the individual firm and of the industry when the industry is in long-run equilibrium; and explain how the entry and exit of firms assure this result.
☐ Define a constant-cost and an increasing-cost industry; and explain how to obtain the long-run industry supply curve in both of these industries.
☐ Explain the significance of $P = AC = MC$; and distinguish between productive and allocative efficiency.
☐ Identify the several possible shortcomings of a purely competitive price system.

■ CHAPTER OUTLINE

1. The price a firm charges for the good or service it produces and its output of that product depend not only on the demand for and the cost of producing it but on the character (or structure) or the market (industry) in which it sells the product.

2. The models of the markets in which firms sell their products are pure competition, pure monopoly, monopolistic competition, and oligopoly; and these four models are defined in terms of the number of firms in the industry, whether the product they sell is standardized or differentiated, and how easy it is for new firms to enter the industry.

3. This chapter examines pure competition in which a large number of independent firms, no one of which is able by itself to influence market price, sell a standardized product in a market which firms are free to enter and to leave in the long run. Although pure competition is rare in practice, there are at least three good reasons for studying this "laboratory case."

4. A firm selling its product in a purely competitive industry cannot influence the price at which the product sells; and is a price taker.

a. The demand for its product is, therefore, perfectly elastic.

b. Average revenue (or price) and marginal revenue are equal and constant at the fixed market price; and total revenue increases at a constant rate as the firm increases its output.

c. The demand (average revenue) and marginal revenue curves faced by the firm are horizontal and identical at the market price; and the total revenue curve has a constant positive slope.

5. There are two complementary approaches to the analysis of the output that the purely competitive firm will produce in the short run.

a. Employing the total-revenue–total-cost approach, the firm will produce the output at which total economic profit is the greatest or total loss is the least, provided that the loss is less than the firm's fixed costs (that is, provided that total revenue is greater than total variable cost). If the firm's loss is greater than its fixed cost, it will lessen its loss by producing no output.

b. Employing the marginal-revenue–marginal-cost approach, the firm will produce the output at which marginal revenue (or price) and marginal cost are equal, provided price is greater than average variable cost. If price is less than average variable cost, the firm will shut down to minimize its loss. The short-run supply curve of the individual firm is that part of its short-run marginal-cost curve which is above average variable cost.

c. Table 27-8 in the text summarizes the principles which the competitive firm follows when it decides what output to produce in the short run.

d. The short-run supply curve of the industry (which is the sum of the supply curves of the individual firms) and the total demand for the product determine the short-run equilibrium price and equilibrium output of the industry; and the firms in the industry may be either prosperous or unprosperous in the short run.

6. In the long run the price of a product produced under conditions of pure competition will equal the minimum average total cost, and firms in the industry will neither have economic profits nor suffer losses.

a. If economic profits are being received in the industry during the short run, firms will enter the industry in the long run (attracted by the profits), increase total supply, and thereby force price down to the minimum average total cost.

b. If losses are being suffered in the industry during the short run, firms will leave the industry in the long run (seeking to avoid losses), reduce total supply, and thereby force price up to the minimum average total cost.

c. If an industry is a constant-cost industry, the entry of new firms will not affect the average-total-cost schedules or curves of firms in the industry. An increase in demand, therefore, will result in no increase in the long-run equilibrium price, and the industry will be able to supply larger outputs at a constant price.

d. If an industry is an increasing-cost industry, the entry of new firms will raise the average-total-cost schedules or curves of firms in the industry. An increase in demand, therefore, will result in an increase in the long-run equilibrium price, and the industry will supply larger quantities only at higher prices.

7. In the long run, each purely competitive firm is compelled by competition to produce that output at which price (or marginal revenue), average cost, and marginal cost are equal and average cost is a minimum.

a. An economy in which all industries were purely competitive would use its resources efficiently.

(1) Goods are efficiently produced when the average total cost of producing them is a minimum; and buyers benefit most from this efficiency when they are charged a price just equal to minimum average total cost.

(2) Resources are efficiently allocated when goods are produced in such quantities that the total satisfaction obtained from the economy's resources is a maximum; or when the price of each good is equal to its marginal cost.

b. Even in a purely competitive economy, the allocation of resources may not, for at least four reasons, be the most efficient.

■ IMPORTANT TERMS

Pure competition
Pure monopoly
Monopolistic competition
Oligopoly
Imperfect competition
Price-taker
Total revenue
Average revenue
Marginal revenue
Total-receipts–total-cost approach
Marginal-revenue–marginal-cost approach
The profit-maximizing case
Break-even point
The loss-minimizing case
The close-down case
MR = MC rule
***P* = MC rule**
The firm's short-run supply curve (schedule)
The competitive industry's short-run supply curve (schedule)
Short-run competitive equilibrium
Long-run competitive equilibrium
Constant-cost industry
Increasing-cost industry
Long-run supply
Productive efficiency
Allocative efficiency

■ FILL-IN QUESTIONS

1. The four market models examined in this and the next three chapters:

a. are ____________________, ____________________, ____________________, and ____________________;

b. differ in terms of the __________ of firms in the industry, whether the product is __________ or __________, and how easy or difficult it is for new firms to __________ the industry.

2. What are the four specific conditions which characterize pure competition?

a. ____________________

b. ____________________

c. ____________________

d. ____________________

3. The individual firm in a purely competitive industry is a price-(maker, taker) __________; and finds that the demand for its product is perfectly (elastic, inelastic) __________ and that marginal revenue is (less than, greater than, equal to) __________ the price of the product.

4. Economic profit is equal to ____________________

5. The two approaches which may be used to determine the most profitable output for any firm are the __________ approach and __________ approach.

6. A firm should produce in the short run only if it can obtain a __________ or suffer a loss which is no greater than its ____________________
Provided it produces any output at all:

a. It will produce that output at which its profit is a (maximum, minimum) ________ or its loss is a ________

b. Or, said another way, the output at which marginal ________ and marginal ________ are equal.

7. A firm will produce at a loss in the short run if the price which it receives is greater than its average (fixed, variable, total) ________ cost.

8. In the short run the individual firm's supply curve is ________; the short-run market supply curve is ________

9. The short-run equilibrium price for a product produced by a purely competitive industry is the price at which ________ and ________ are equal; the equilibrium quantity is ________

10. In a purely competitive industry in the short run the number of firms in the industry and the sizes of their plants are (fixed, variable) ________; but in the long run they are ________

11. When a purely competitive industry is in long-run equilibrium the price which the firm is paid for its product is equal not only to marginal revenue but to long-run ________ cost and to long-run ________ cost; and long-run average cost is a (maximum, minimum, neither) ________

12. Firms tend to enter industry in the long run if ________ and leave it if ________

13. If the entry of new firms into an industry tends to raise the costs of all firms in the industry, the industry is said to be a(n) (constant-, increasing-, decreasing-) ________ cost industry; and its long-run supply curve is (horizontal, downsloping, upsloping) ________

14. If an economy is to make the best use of its scarce resources it is necessary that it achieve both ________ and ________ efficiency.

15. The purely competitive economy achieves productive efficiency in the long run because price and ________ cost are equal and the latter is a (maximum, minimum) ________

16. In the long run the purely competitive economy is allocatively efficient because price and ________ cost are equal.

17. List four reasons why resource allocation in a purely competitive economy may be less than efficient.

a. ________

b. ________

c. ________

d. ________

■ PROBLEMS AND PROJECTS

1. Employing the following set of terms, complete the table at the top of the next page by inserting the appropriate letter or letters in the blanks.

a. one
b. few
c. many
d. a very large number
e. standardized
f. differentiated
g. some
h. considerable
i. very easy
j. blocked
k. fairly easy
l. fairly difficult
m. none
n. unique

Market characteristics	Pure competition	Pure monopoly	Monopolistic competition	Oligopoly
	Market mode			
Number of firms	a very large #	one	many	few
Type of product	standardized	unique	differentiated	either
Control over price	none	considerable	some	considerable
Conditions of entry	very easy	blocked	fairly easy	fairly difficult
Nonprice competition	none			

2. Below is the demand schedule facing the individual firm.

average revenue = price

Price	Quantity demanded	Average revenue	Total revenue	Marginal revenue
$10	0	$ 0	$ 0	
				$ 10
10	1	10	10	
				10
10	2	20	20	
				10
10	3	10	30	
				10
10	4	10	40	
				10
10	5	10	50	
				10
10	6	10	60	

a. Complete the table by computing average revenue, total revenue, and marginal revenue.

b. Is this firm operating in a market which is purely competitive? yes How can you tell? price = marginal revenue

c. On the graph on page 243 plot the demand schedule, average revenue, total revenue, and marginal revenue; label each of these curves. (*Note:* Plot marginal revenue at ½, 1½, 2½, etc., units of output rather than 1, 2, 3, etc.)

d. The coefficient of the price elasticity of demand is the same between every pair of quantities demanded. How much is it? ________

e. What relationship exists between average revenue and marginal revenue? Equal

3. Assume that a purely competitive firm has the schedule of costs given in the table below.

a. Complete the table on the next page to show the total revenue and total profit of the firm at each level of output the firm might produce. Assume market prices of $55, $120, and $200.

Output	TFC	TVC	TC	AFC	AVC	ATC	MC	π
0	$300	$ 0	$ 300					
1	300	100	400	$300	$100	$400	$100	250
2	300	150	450	150	75	225	50	750
3	300	210	510	100	70	170	60	1140
4	300	290	590	75	73	148	80	1410
5	300	400	700	60	80	140	110	1550
6	300	540	840	50	90	140	140	1560
7	300	720	1,020	43	103	146	180	1380
8	300	950	1,250	38	119	156	230	910
9	300	1,240	1,540	33	138	171	290	100
10	300	1,600	1,900	30	160	190	360	

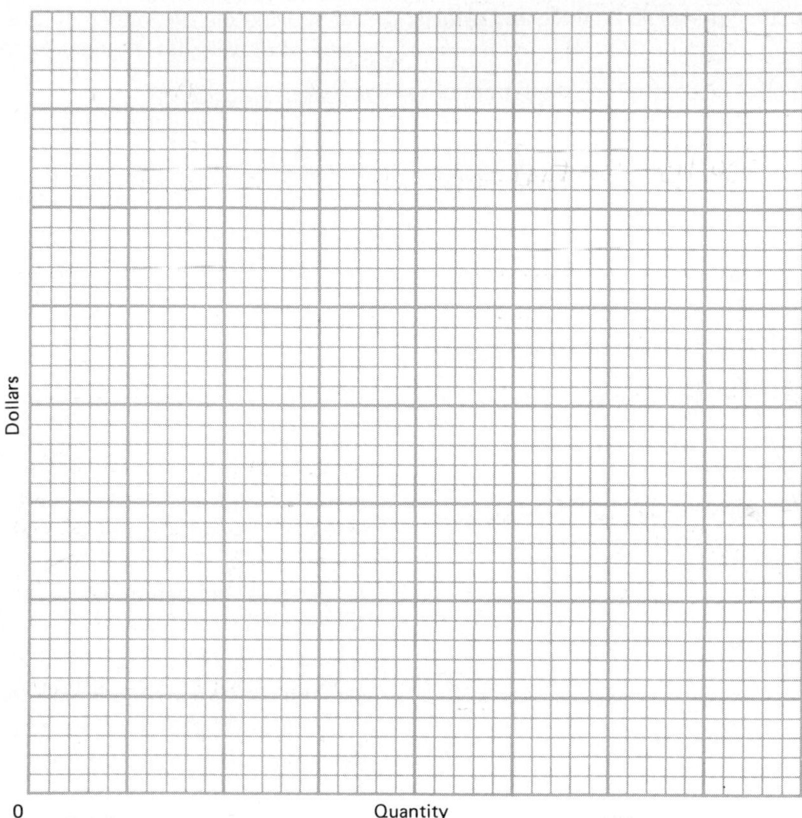

TR−TC = π

Output	Market price = $55		Market price = $120		Market price = $200	
	Revenue	Profit	Revenue	Profit	Revenue	Profit
0	$ 0	$ −300	$____	$____	$____	$____
1	55	−345	____	____	____	____
2	110	____	____	____	____	____
3	____	____	____	____	____	____
4	____	____	____	____	____	____
5	____	____	____	____	____	____
6	____	____	____	____	____	____
7	____	____	____	____	____	____
8	____	____	____	____	____	____
9	____	____	____	____	____	____
10	____	____	____	____	____	____

b. Indicate what output the firm would produce and what its profits would be at a:

(1) Price of $55: output of __________ and profit of __________

(2) Price of $120: output of __________ and profit of __________

(3) Price of $200: output of __________ and profit of __________

c. Complete the supply schedule of a firm in the table below and indicate what the profit of the firm will be at each price.

Price	Quantity supplied	Profit
$360	______	$______
290	______	______
230	______	______
180	______	______
140	______	______
110	______	______
80	______	______
60	______	______

d. If there are 100 firms in the industry and all have the same cost schedule:

(1) Complete the market supply schedule in the next table.

Quantity demanded	Price	Quantity supplied
400	$360	______
500	290	______
600	230	______
700	180	______
800	140	______
900	110	______
1,000	80	______

(2) Using the demand schedule given in (1):

(*a*) what will the market price of the product be? $__________;

(*b*) what quantity will the individual firm produce? __________;

(*c*) how large will the firm's profit be? $__________;

(*d*) will firms tend to enter or leave the industry in the long run? __________ Why? __________

4. If the total costs assumed for the individual firm in problem 3 were long-run total costs and if the industry were a constant-cost industry:

a. What would be the market price of the product in the long run? $__________

b. What output would each firm produce when the industry was in long-run equilibrium? __________

c. Approximately how many firms would there be in the industry in the long run, given the present demand for the product? __________

d. If the following were the market demand schedule for the product, how many firms would there be in the long run in the industry? __________

Price	Quantity demanded
$360	500
290	600
230	700
180	800
140	900
110	1,000
80	1,100

e. On the following graph draw a long-run supply curve of

(1) a constant-cost industry

(2) an increasing-cost industry

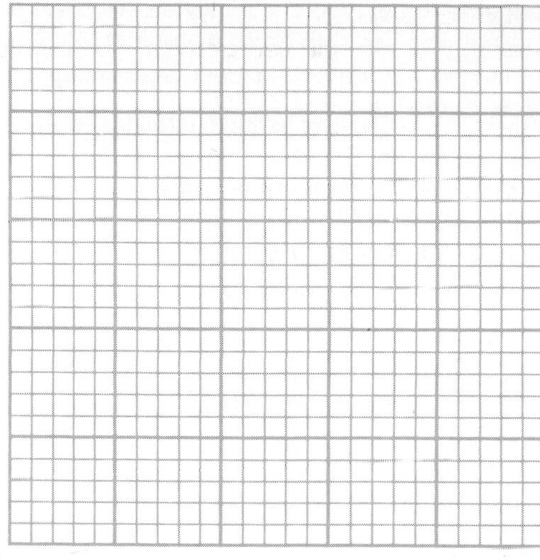

■ SELF-TEST

Circle the T if the statement is true, the F if it is false.

1. The structures of the markets in which business firms sell their products in the American economy are all pretty much the same. T F

2. A large number of sellers does not necessarily mean that the industry is purely competitive. T F

3. Only in a purely competitive industry do individual firms have no control over the price of their product. T F

4. Imperfectly competitive markets are defined as all markets except those which are purely competitive. T F

5. One of the reasons for studying the pure competition model is that many industries are almost purely competitive. T F

6. The purely competitive firm views an average-revenue schedule which is identical to its marginal-revenue schedule. T F

7. A purely competitive firm will produce in the short run the output at which marginal cost and marginal revenue are equal provided that the price of the product is greater than its average variable cost of production. T F

8. If a purely competitive firm is producing an output less than its profit-maximizing output, marginal revenue is greater than marginal cost at that output. T F

9. The short-run supply curve of a purely competitive firm tends to slope upward from left to right because of the law of diminishing returns. T F

10. A firm wishing to maximize its profits will always produce that output at which marginal costs and marginal revenue are equal. T F

11. When firms in a purely competitive industry are earning profits which are less than normal, the supply of the product will tend to decrease in the long run. T F

12. Given the short-run costs of firms in a purely competitive industry, the profits of these firms depend solely upon the level of the total demand for the product. T F

13. Pure competition, if it could be achieved in all industries in the economy, would result in the most efficient allocation of resources. T F

14. Under conditions of pure competition firms are forced to employ the most efficient production methods available to them if they are to earn no more than normal profits. T F

15. The marginal costs of producing a product are society's measure of the marginal worth of alternative products. T F

16. There is no scientific basis for determining which distribution of total money income results in the greatest satisfaction of wants in the economy. T F

Circle the letter that corresponds to the best answer.

1. Which of the following is *not* one of the four models of the markets (industries) in which American business firms sell their products? (*a*) Pure competition; (*b*) monopoly; (*c*) monopolistic competition; (*d*) oligopsony.

2. The four models of the markets (industries) in which business firms sell their products differ in terms of (*a*) the number of firms in the industry; (*b*) how easy or difficult it is for new firms to enter the industry; (*c*) whether the product is standardized or differentiated; (*d*) all of the above.

3. Which of the following is *not* characteristic of pure competition? (*a*) Large number of sellers; (*b*) differentiated product; (*c*) easy entry; (*d*) no advertising.

4. If the product produced by an industry is standardized, the market structure can be: (*a*) pure competition or monopolistic competition; (*b*) pure competition or oligopoly; (*c*) monopolistic competition or oligopoly; (*d*) pure competition, monopolistic competition, or oligopoly.

5. Into which of the following industries is entry least difficult? (*a*) Pure competition; (*b*) pure monopoly; (*c*) monopolistic competition; (*d*) oligopoly.

6. Which of the following industries comes *closest* to being purely competitive? (*a*) Wheat; (*b*) shoes; (*c*) retailing; (*d*) farm implements.

7. In which of the following market models is the individual seller of a product a "price-taker"? (*a*) Pure competition; (*b*) pure monopoly; (*c*) monopolistic competition; (*d*) oligopoly.

8. In a purely competitive industry: (*a*) each of the existing firms will engage in various forms of nonprice competition; (*b*) new firms are free to enter and existing firms are able to leave the industry in the short run; (*c*) individual firms do not have a "price policy"; (*d*) each of the firms produces a differentiated (nonstandardized) product.

9. The demand schedule or curve confronted by the individual purely competitive firm is: (*a*) perfectly inelastic; (*b*) inelastic but not perfectly inelastic; (*c*) perfectly elastic; (*d*) elastic but not perfectly elastic.

10. A firm will be willing to produce at a loss in the short run if: (*a*) the loss is no greater than its total fixed costs; (*b*) the loss is no greater than its average fixed costs; (*c*) the loss is no greater than its total variable costs; (*d*) the loss is no greater than its average variable cost.

11. The individual firm's short-run supply curve is that part of its marginal-cost curve lying above its: (*a*) average-total-cost curve; (*b*) average-variable-cost curve; (*c*) average-fixed-cost curve; (*d*) average-revenue curve.

12. If a single purely competitive firm's most profitable output in the short run were an output at which it was neither receiving a profit nor suffering a loss, one of the following would *not* be true. Which one? (*a*) Marginal cost and average total cost are equal; (*b*) marginal cost and average variable cost are equal; (*c*) marginal cost and marginal revenue are equal; (*d*) marginal cost and average revenue are equal.

13. Which one of the following statements is true of a purely competitive industry in short-run equilibrium? (*a*) Price is equal to average total cost; (*b*) total quantity demanded is equal to total quantity supplied; (*c*) profits in the industry are equal to zero; (*d*) output is equal to the output at which average total cost is a minimum.

14. When a purely competitive industry is in long-run equilibrium, one of the following statements is *not* true. Which one? (*a*) Firms in the industry are earning normal profits; (*b*) price and long-run average total cost are equal to each other; (*c*) long-run marginal cost is at its minimum level; (*d*) long-run marginal cost is equal to marginal revenue.

15. Increasing-cost industries find that their costs rise as a consequence of an increased demand for the product because of: (*a*) the diseconomies of scale; (*b*) diminishing returns; (*c*) higher resource prices; (*d*) a decreased supply of the product.

16. Which one of the following is *most likely* to be a constant-cost industry? (*a*) Agricultural and extractive industries; (*b*) an industry in the early stages of its development; (*c*) an industry which employs a significant portion of the total supply of some resource; (*d*) the steel and oil industries.

17. It is contended that which of the following triple identities results in the most efficient use of resources? (*a*) $P = AC = MC$; (*b*) $P = AR = MR$; (*c*) $P = MR = MC$; (*d*) $AC = MC = MR$.

18. An economy is producing the goods most wanted by society when, for each and every good, its; (*a*) price and average cost are equal; (*b*) price and marginal cost are equal; (*c*) marginal revenue and marginal cost are equal; (*d*) price and marginal revenue are equal.

19. The operation of a competitive price system accurately measures (*a*) both spillover costs and spillover benefits; (*b*) spillover costs but not spillover benefits; (*c*) spillover benefits but not spillover costs; (*d*) neither spillover costs nor spillover benefits.

■ DISCUSSION QUESTIONS

1. What are the four market models (or situations) which economists employ and what are the major characteristics of each type of market?

2. If pure competition is so rare in practice, why are students of economics asked to study it?

3. Explain how the firm in a purely competitive industry sees the demand for the product it produces in terms of (*a*) the price elasticity of demand; (*b*) the relation of average to marginal revenue; and (*c*) the behavior of total, average, and marginal revenues as the output of the firm increases.

4. Why is a firm willing to produce at a loss in the short run if the loss is no greater than the fixed costs of the firm?

5. Explain how the short-run supply of an individual firm and of the purely competitive industry are determined.

6. What determines the equilibrium price and output of a purely competitive industry in the short run? Will economic profits in the industry be positive or negative?

7. Why do the MC = MR rule and MC = *P* rule mean the same thing under conditions of pure competition?

8. What are the important distinctions between the short run and the long run and between equilibrium in the short run and in the long run in a competitive industry?

9. When is the purely competitive industry in long-run equilibrium? What forces the purely competitive firm into this position?

10. What is a constant-cost industry? What is an increasing-cost industry? Under what economic conditions is each likely to be found? What will be the nature of the long-run supply curve in each of these industries?

11. When has an economy achieved the most efficient use of its scarce resources? What two kinds of efficiency are necessary if the economy is to make the most efficient use of its resources?

12. Why is it said that a purely competitive economy is an efficient economy?

13. What did Adam Smith mean when he said that self-interest and competition bring about results which are in the best interest of the economy as a whole without government regulation or interference?

14. Even if an economy is purely competitive, the allocation of resources may not be ideal. Why?

15. Does pure competition *always* promote both the use of the most efficient technological methods of production and the development of better methods?

28
Price and output determination: pure monopoly

Chapter 28 is the second of the four chapters which deal with specific market models and is concerned with what economists call pure monopoly. Like pure competition, pure monopoly is rarely found in the American economy. But there are industries which are close to being pure monopolies and these industries produce over 5% of the GNP; and an understanding of pure monopoly is helpful in understanding the more realistic situation of oligopoly.

It is only possible for pure monopoly, approximations of pure monopoly, and oligopoly to exist if firms are prevented in some way from entering an industry in the long run. Anything which tends to prevent entry is referred to as a "barrier to entry." The second part of Chapter 28 is devoted to a description of the more important types of barriers to entry. Remember that barriers to entry not only make it possible for monopoly to exist in the economy but also explain why so many markets are oligopolies (which you will study in Chapter 30).

Like the preceding chapter, this chapter tries to answer certain questions about the firm. These are: what output will the firm produce; what price will it charge; what will be the profit received by the firm; and what will be the relationship between price and average cost and between price and marginal cost? In answering these questions for the monopoly firm and in comparing pure competition and pure monopoly note the following.

1. Both the competitive and monopoly firm try to maximize profits by producing that output at which marginal cost and marginal revenue are equal.
2. The individual competitor sees a perfectly elastic demand for its product at the going market price because it is but one of many firms in the industry; but the monopolist sees a market demand schedule which is less than perfectly elastic because the monopolist *is* the industry. The former, therefore, has *only* an output policy and is a price taker; but the latter is able to determine the price at which it will sell its product and is a price maker.
3. When demand is perfectly elastic, price is equal to marginal revenue and is constant; but when demand is less than perfectly elastic, marginal revenue is less than price and both decrease as the output of the firm increases.
4. Because entry is blocked in the long run, firms cannot enter a monopolistic industry to compete away profits as they can under conditions of pure competition.

In addition to determining the price the monopolist will charge, the quantity of its product it will produce, and the size of its profits, Chapter 28 has three other goals. It examines the economic effects of monopoly by comparing it with pure competition. Chapter 28 also explains what is meant by price discrimination, the conditions which must prevail if a monopolist is to engage in price discrimination, and the two economic consequences of discrimination. The final section of Chapter 28 introduces you to the problem a government agency faces when it must determine the maximum price a public utility will be allowed to charge for its product.

■ CHECKLIST

When you have studied this chapter you should be able to:

☐ Define pure monopoly.

☐ List the six barriers to entry and explain how each of them would prevent or deter the entry of new firms into an industry.

☐ Describe the demand curve or schedule for the product produced by a pure monopolist.

□ Define marginal revenue and compute marginal revenue when you are given the demand for the monopolist's product.

□ Explain the relationship between the price the monopolist charges and the marginal revenue from the sale of an additional unit of product and between the monopolist's demand and marginal revenue schedules (curves).

□ State the principle which explains what output the monopolist will produce and the price that will be set; and determine this output and price when you are given the demand and cost data.

□ Describe the effects of pure monopoly on the price of the product, the quantity of the product produced, and the allocation of the economy's resources.

□ Explain how and why significant economies of scale and X-inefficiency are apt to affect the costs of purely competitive and monopolistic firms.

□ Define technological progress (or dynamic efficiency) and compare technological progress in the competitive and monopolistic models.

□ Describe the effects of monopoly on the distribution of income in the economy.

□ Define price discrimination, list the three conditions which must exist before there can be price discrimination, and explain the two economic consequences of price discrimination.

□ Identify for the regulated monopoly (a public utility) the socially optimum and the fair-return price; and explain the dilemma which the regulatory agency encounters.

■ CHAPTER OUTLINE

1. Pure monopoly is a market situation in which a single firm sells a product for which there are no close substitutes. While it is rare in practice, the study of monopoly provides an understanding of firms which are "almost" monopolies and is useful in understanding monopolistic competition and oligopoly.

2. Pure monopoly (and oligopoly) can exist in the long run only if potential competitors find there are barriers which prevent their entry into the industry. There are at least six types of entry barriers; but they are seldom perfect in preventing the entry of new firms, and efficient production may, in some cases, require that firms be prevented from entering an industry.

3. The pure monopolist employs the cost and demand data to determine the most profitable output and the price to charge.

a. Unlike the pure competitor, the monopolist has a price policy. Because it is the sole supplier, the price charged will determine the amount of the product sold (or the amount produced will determine the price at which it can be sold). Consequently, price is greater than marginal revenue (and both decrease as the output of the monopolist increases); and the firm is a price maker.

b. Monopoly power in the sale of a product does not necessarily affect the prices the monopolist pays or the costs of production.

c. The monopolist produces that output at which marginal cost and marginal revenue are equal; and charges the price at which this profit-maximizing output can be sold.

d. It is not true that a monopolist charges as high a price as is possible, and it is not true that profit per unit is as large as it might be; and a monopoly may not be profitable at all.

4. The existence of pure monopoly has significant effects on the economy as a whole.

a. Because it produces smaller outputs and charges higher prices than would result under conditions of pure competition and because price is greater than both average total and marginal cost, monopoly misallocates resources (results in neither productive nor allocative efficiency).

b. A monopolist may, however, have lower or higher average costs than a pure competitor producing the same product would have.

(1) If there are economies of scale in the production of the product the monopolist is able to produce the good or service at a lower long-run average cost than a large number of small pure competitors could produce it.

(2) But if a monopolist is more susceptible to X-inefficiency than a purely competitive firm its long-run average costs at every level of output are higher than what those of a purely competitive firm would be.

c. A monopolist may also be more or less efficient over time than pure competitors in developing new lower-cost techniques of producing existing products and in developing new products.

d. Monopoly contributes to income inequality in the economy.

5. To increase profits a pure monopolist may engage in price discrimination by charging different prices to different buyers of the same product (when the price differences do not represent differences in the costs of producing the product).

a. To discriminate the seller must have some monopoly power; be capable of separating buyers into groups which have different price elasticities of demand; and be able to prevent the resale of the product.

b. The seller charges each group the highest price that group would be willing to pay for the product rather than go without it. Discrimination increases not only the profits but also the output of the monopolist.

c. Price discrimination is common in the American economy.

6. The prices charged by monopolists are often regulated by governments to reduce the misallocation of resources.

a. A ceiling price determined by the intersection of the marginal-cost and demand schedules is the socially optimum price and improves the allocation of resources.

b. This ceiling may force the firm to produce at a loss; and so government may set the ceiling at a level determined by the intersection of the average-cost and demand schedules to allow the monopolist a fair return.

c. The dilemma of regulation is that the socially optimum price may cause losses for the monopolist, and that a fair-return price results in a less efficient allocation of resources.

■ IMPORTANT TERMS

Pure monopoly	**X-inefficiency**
Barrier to entry	**Dynamic efficiency**
Natural monopoly	**Price discrimination**
Tying agreement	**Socially optimum price**
Unfair competition	**Fair-return price**
The economies of being established	**Dilemma of regulation**

■ FILL-IN QUESTIONS

1. Pure monopoly is an industry in which a single firm is the sole producer of a product for which there are no (substitutes, close substitutes) ______________ and into which entry in the long run is (easy, difficult, blocked) ______________

2. What are the six most important types of barrier to entry?

a. ______________

b. ______________

c. ______________

d. ______________

e. ______________

f. ______________

3. If there are substantial economies of scale in the production of a product, a small-scale firm will find it difficult to enter into and survive in an industry because its average costs will be (greater, less) ______________ than those of established firms; and a firm will find it difficult to start out on a large scale because it will be nearly impossible to acquire the needed (labor, money capital) ______________

4. Public utility companies tend to be ______________ ______________ monopolies, and they receive their franchises from and are ______________ by governments.

5. The demand schedule confronting the pure monopolist is ______________ perfectly elastic; this means that marginal revenue is (greater, less) ______________ than average revenue (or price) and that both marginal revenue and average revenue (increase, decrease) ______________ as output increases.

6. When the profits of a monopolist are a maximum ______________ and ______________ are equal; and price (or average revenue) is (greater, less) ______________ than marginal cost.

7. Three common fallacies about pure monopoly are that:

a. It charges the ______________ price.

b. Its average (or per unit) profit is ______________ ______________

c. It always receives a ______________

8. The output produced by a monopolist is inefficiently *produced* because the average total cost of producing the product is not ________________ and resources are not efficiently *allocated* because ________________ is not equal to ________________

9. Resources can be said to be more efficiently allocated by pure competition than by pure monopoly only if the purely competitive firm and the monopoly have the same ________________ and they will not be the same if the monopolist:

a. by virtue of being a large firm enjoys economies of ________________ not available to a pure competitor; or

b. is more susceptible to ________________ than pure competitors.

10. Monopolists are more dynamically efficient than pure competitors if they improve the ________________ of producing existing products (and thereby lower the ________________ of producing them) and develop new ________________ over time more rapidly than pure competitors.

11. Monopoly seems to result in a greater inequality in the distribution of income because the owners of monopolies are largely in the (upper, middle, lower) ________________ income groups.

12. There is price discrimination whenever a product is sold at different ________________ and these differences are not equal to the differences in the ________________ of producing the product.

13. Price discrimination is possible only when the following three conditions are found.

a. ________________

b. ________________

c. ________________

14. The two economic consequences of a monopolist's engagement in price discrimination are a(n) (increase, decrease) ________________ in the profits and a(n) ________________ in the output of the monopolist.

15. The misallocation of resources that results from monopoly can be *eliminated* if a ceiling price for the monopolist's product is set equal to ________________; such a price is, however, usually less than ________________

16. If a regulated monopolist is allowed to earn a fair return, the ceiling price for the product is set equal to ________________; such a price reduces but does not eliminate the ________________ of resources caused by monopoly.

■ PROBLEMS AND PROJECTS

1. The demand schedule for the product produced by a monopolist is given in the next table.

Price	Quantity demanded	Total revenue	Marginal revenue
$700	0	$____	
			$____
650	1	____	
			____
600	2	____	
			____
550	3	____	
			____
500	4	____	
			____
450	5	____	
			____
400	6	____	
			____
350	7	____	
			____
300	8	____	
			____
250	9	____	
			____
200	10	____	

a. Complete the table by computing total revenue at each of the eleven prices and the ten marginal-revenue figures.

b. Regardless of the cost of producing this product the monopolist will never produce an output greater than 7 because beyond 7 units the demand for the product is ______________

c. Using the table of costs given in problem 3 of Chapter 27:

(1) What output will the monopolist produce? ______________

(2) What price will the monopolist charge? $______________

(3) What total profit will the monopolist receive? $______________

d. Assume this monopolist is able to engage in price discrimination and to sell each unit of the product at a price equal to the maximum price the buyer of that unit of the product would be willing to pay.

(1) Complete the table below by computing total revenue at each of the eleven quantities and the marginal revenue this discriminating monopolist obtains from each additional unit sold.

Quantity demanded	Price	Total revenue	Marginal revenue
0	$700	$____	
1	650	____	$____
2	600	____	____
3	550	____	____
4	500	____	____
5	450	____	____
6	400	____	____
7	350	____	____
8	300	____	____
9	250	____	____
10	200	____	____

(2) From the table it can be seen that the marginal revenue which the discriminating monopolist obtains from the sale of an additional unit is equal to the ______________

(3) Using the same table of costs, the discriminating monopolist would produce ______________ units of the product, charge the buyer of the last unit of product produced a price of $______________, and obtain a total economic profit of $______________

(4) If the pure monopolist is able to engage in price discrimination its profits will be (larger, smaller, the same) ______________ and it will produce an output that is (larger, smaller, the same) ______________

2. In the table below are cost and demand data for a pure monopolist.

Quantity demanded	Price	Marginal revenue	Average cost	Marginal cost
0	$17.50			
1	16.00	$16.00	$24.00	$24.00
2	14.50	13.00	15.00	6.00
3	13.00	10.00	11.67	5.00
4	11.50	7.00	10.50	7.00
5	10.00	4.00	10.00	8.00
6	8.50	1.00	9.75	8.50
7	7.00	−2.00	9.64	9.00
8	5.50	−5.00	9.34	9.25
9	4.00	−8.00	9.36	9.50

a. An unregulated monopolist would produce ______________ units of a product, sell it at a price of $______________, and receive a total profit of $______________

b. If this monopolist were regulated and the maximum price it could charge were set equal to marginal cost, it would produce ______________ units of a product, sell it at a price of $______________, and receive a total profit of $______________. Such regulation would either ______________ the firm or require that the regulating government ______________ the firm.

c. If the monopolist were not regulated and were allowed to engage in price discrimination by charging the maximum price it could obtain for each unit sold it would produce 6 units (because the marginal revenue from the

6th unit and the marginal cost of the 6th unit would both be $8.50). Its total revenue would be $__________, its total costs would be $__________, and its total profit would be $__________.

d. If the monopolist were regulated and allowed to charge a fair-return price, it would produce __________ units of a product, charge a price of $__________, and receive a profit of $__________

e. From which situation—*a, b,* or *d*—does the most efficient allocation of resources result? __________ From which situation does the least efficient allocation result? __________ In practice, government would probably select situation __________

■ SELF-TEST

Circle the T if the statement is true, the F if it is false.

1. The pure monopolist produces a product for which there are no substitutes. **T F**

2. The weaker the barriers to entry into an industry, the more competition there will be in the industry, other things being equal. **T F**

3. Monopoly is always undesirable unless it is regulated by the government. **T F**

4. The monopolist can increase the sale of its product if he charges a lower price. **T F**

5. As a monopolist increases its output, it finds that its total revenue at first decreases, and that after some output level is reached, its total revenue begins to increase. **T F**

6. A purely competitive firm is a price-taker but a monopolist is a price-maker. **T F**

7. A monopolist will not voluntarily sell at a price at which the demand for its product is inelastic. **T F**

8. The monopolist determines the profit-maximizing output by producing that output at which marginal cost and marginal revenue are equal and sets the product price equal to marginal cost and marginal revenue at that output. **T F**

9. The monopolist maximizing total profit is also producing that output at which per unit (or average) profit is a maximum. **T F**

10. Resources are misallocated by monopoly because price is not equal to marginal cost. **T F**

11. When there are substantial economies of scale in the production of a product, the monopolist may charge a price that is lower than the price that would prevail if the product were produced by a purely competitive industry. **T F**

12. The purely competitive firm is more likely to be affected by X-inefficiency than a monopolist. **T F**

13. Economists are agreed that monopolies are less dynamically efficient than competitive firms. **T F**

14. In a society in which technology is not changing and the economies of scale can be employed by both pure competitors and monopolists, the purely competitive firm will use the more efficient methods of production. **T F**

15. One of the economic effects of monopoly is less income inequality. **T F**

16. The dilemma of monopoly regulation is that the production by a monopolist of an output that causes no misallocation of resources may force the monopolist to suffer an economic loss. **T F**

Circle the letter that corresponds to the best answer.

1. Which of the following is the *best* example of a pure monopoly? (*a*) Your neighborhood grocer; (*b*) the telephone company in your community; (*c*) the manufacturer of a particular brand of toothpaste; (*d*) the only airline furnishing passenger service between two major cities.

2. Which of the following is *not* an important characteristic of a natural monopoly? (*a*) Substantial economies of scale are available; (*b*) very heavy fixed costs; (*c*) it is a public utility; (*d*) competition is impractical and/or would be very expensive for the consumer.

3. Monopoly can probably exist over a long period of time only if: (*a*) it is based on the control of raw materials; (*b*) it controls the patents on the product; (*c*) cut-throat competition is employed to eliminate rivals; (*d*) government assists the monopoly and prevents the establishment of rival firms.

4. Which of the following is *not* true with respect to the demand data confronting a monopolist? (*a*) Marginal revenue is greater than average revenue; (*b*) marginal revenue decreases as average revenue decreases; (*c*) demand is less than perfectly elastic; (*d*) average revenue (or price) decreases as the output of the firm increases.

5. Assume the cost and demand data for a pure monopolist are those given in the table below. How many units of output will the firm produce? (*a*) 1; (*b*) 2; (*c*) 3; (*d*) 4.

Output	Total cost	Price
0	$ 500	$1,000
1	520	600
2	580	500
3	700	400
4	1,000	300
5	1,500	200

6. The monopolist in question 5 above would set its price at (*a*) $120; (*b*) $200; (*c*) 233; (*d*) $400.

7. When the monopolist is maximizing total profits *or* minimizing losses; (*a*) total revenue is greater than total cost; (*b*) average revenue is greater than average total cost; (*c*) average revenue is greater than marginal cost; (*d*) average total cost is less than marginal cost.

8. A monopolist does not *produce* the product as efficiently as is possible because: (*a*) the average total cost of producing it is not a minimum; (*b*) the marginal cost of producing the last unit is less than its price; (*c*) it is earning a profit; (*d*) average revenue is greater than the cost of producing an extra unit of output.

9. X-inefficiency means that a firm fails to (*a*) produce an output at the lowest average cost possible; (*b*) produce an output at the lowest total cost possible; (*c*) employ resources in their least-cost combination to produce an output; (*d*) do all of the above.

10. Dynamic efficiency refers to (*a*) the achievement of economies of scale in producing products; (*b*) the development over time of more efficient (less costly) techniques of producing products and the improvement of these products; (*c*) the avoidance of X-inefficiency; (*d*) the avoidance of allocative inefficiency.

11. Over time monopoly *may* result in greater technological improvement than would be forthcoming under conditions of pure competition for several reasons. Which of the following is *not* one of these reasons? (*a*) Technological advance will lower the costs and enhance the profits of the monopolist, and these increased profits will not have to be shared with rivals; (*b*) technological advance will act as a barrier to entry and thus allow the monopolist to continue to be a monopolist; (*c*) technological advance requires research and experimentation, and the monopolist is in a position to finance them out of profits; (*d*) technological advance is apt to make existing capital equipment obsolete, and the monopolist can reduce costs by speeding up the rate at which its capital becomes obsolete.

12. Which of the following is *not* one of the conditions which must be realized before a seller finds price discrimination is workable? (*a*) The buyer must be unable to resell the product; (*b*) the product must be a service; (*c*) the seller must have some degree of monopoly power; (*d*) the seller must be able to segment the market.

13. If a monopolist engages in price discrimination rather than charging all buyers the same price its (*a*) profits and its output are greater; (*b*) profits and its output are smaller; (*c*) profits are greater and its output is smaller; (*d*) profits are smaller and its output is greater.

14. Look at the demand data in question 5 above. If the monopolist could sell each unit of the product at the maximum price the buyer of that unit would be willing to pay for it and if the monopolist sold 4 units, total revenue would be (*a*) $1200; (*b*) $1800; (*c*) $2000; (*d*) $2800.

15. If the monopolist for whom cost and demand data are given in question 5 above were forced to produce the socially optimum output by the imposition of a ceiling price, the ceiling price would have to be: (*a*) $200; (*b*) $300; (*c*) $400; (*d*) $500.

16. A monopolist who is limited by the imposition of a ceiling price to a fair return sells the product at a price equal to: (*a*) average total cost; (*b*) average variable cost; (*c*) marginal cost; (*d*) average fixed cost.

■ DISCUSSION QUESTIONS

1. What is pure monopoly? Why is it studied if it is so rare in practice?

2. What is meant by a barrier to entry? What kinds of such barriers are there? How important are they in pure competition, pure monopoly, monopolistic competition, and oligopoly?

3. Why are the economies of scale a barrier to entry?

4. Why are most natural monopolies also public utilities? What does government hope to achieve by granting exclusive franchises to and regulating such natural monopolies?

5. What advantage does the going, established firm have over the new, immature firm in an industry?

6. Compare the pure monopolist and the individual pure competitor with respect to: (*a*) the demand schedule; (*b*) the marginal-revenue schedule; (*c*) the relationship between marginal revenue and average revenue; (*d*) price policy; (*e*) the ability to administer (or set) price.

7. Explain why marginal revenue is always less than average revenue when demand is less than perfectly elastic.

8. Suppose a pure monopolist discovered it was producing and selling an output at which the demand for its product was inelastic. Explain why a decrease in its output would increase its economic profits.

9. What output will the monopolist produce? What price will it charge?

10. Why does the monopolist not charge the highest possible price for the product? Why does the monopolist not set the price for the product in such a way that average profit is a maximum? Why are some monopolies unprofitable?

11. In what sense is resource allocation and production more efficient under conditions of pure competition than under monopoly conditions?

12. What are the two complications that may result in a monopolist having lower or higher average costs than a competitive firm? How do each of these complications affect the average costs of a monopolist and what evidence is there to support the belief that these two complications lower or raise the average costs of a monopolist?

13. Does monopoly, when compared with pure competition, result in more or less dynamic efficiency (technological progress)? What are the arguments on *both* sides of this question? What evidence is there to support the two views?

14. How does monopoly allegedly affect the distribution of income in the economy and why does monopoly seemingly have this effect on income distribution in the American economy?

15. What is meant by price discrimination and what conditions must be realized before it is workable? Explain how a monopolist who discriminates would determine what price to charge for each unit of the product sold (or to charge each group of buyers) and how discrimination would affect the profits and the output of the monopolist.

16. How do public utility regulatory agencies attempt to eliminate the misallocation of resources that results from monopoly? Explain the dilemma that almost invariably confronts the agency in this endeavor; and explain why a fair-return price only reduces but does not eliminate misallocation.

29
Price and output determination: monopolistic competition

Chapter 29 is the third of the four chapters which deal with specific market situations. As its name implies, monopolistic competition is a blend of pure competition and pure monopoly; and one of the reasons for studying those relatively unrealistic market situations was to prepare you for this realistic study of monopolistic competition. It must be pointed out that monopolistic competition is not a realistic description of all markets; but the study of it will help you to understand the many markets which are nearly monopolistically competitive. It will also help you to understand why oligopoly is prevalent in the American economy and how oligopoly differs from monopolistic competition.

The first task is to learn exactly what is meant by monopolistic competition. Next you should examine the demand curve which the monopolistically competitive firm sees for its product and note how and why it differs from the demand curves faced by the purely competitive firm and by the monopolist. In this connection it is also important to understand that as the individual firm changes the character of the product it produces or changes the extent to which it promotes the sale of its product, both the costs of the firm and the demand for its product will change. A firm confronts a different demand curve every time it alters its product or its promotion of the product.

With the product and promotional campaign of the firm *given,* the price-output analysis of the monopolistic competitor is relatively simple. In the short run this analysis is identical with the analysis of the price-output decision of the pure monopolist in the short run. It is only in the long run that the competitive element makes itself apparent: The entry (or exit) of firms forces the price the firm charges down (up) *toward* the level of average cost. This price is not equal either to *minimum* average cost or to marginal cost; and consequently monopolistic competition, on these two scores, can be said to be less efficient than pure competition.

A relatively large part of Chapter 29 is devoted to a discussion of nonprice competition. This is done for very good reasons. In monopolistically competitive industries a part of the competitive effort of individual firms is given over to product differentiation, product development, and product advertising. Each firm has three things to manipulate—price, product, and advertising—in trying to maximize its profits. While monopolistic competition may not be so economically efficient as pure competition in terms of a *given* product and the promotion of it, when all the economic effects—good and bad—of differentiation, development, and advertising are considered this shortcoming may or may not be offset. Whether it is actually offset is an unanswerable question. If Chapter 29 has one central idea it is this. Monopolistic competition cannot be compared with pure competition solely on the basis of prices charged at any given moment of time; it must also be judged in terms of whether it results in better products, in a wider variety of products, in better-informed consumers, in lower-priced radio and television programs, magazines, and newspapers, and other redeeming features.

In short, the study of monopolistic competition is a realistic study and for that reason it is a difficult study. Many factors have to be considered in explaining how such a group of firms behaves and in appraising the efficiency with which such an industry allocates scarce resources.

■ CHECKLIST

When you have studied this chapter you should be able to:

☐ List the characteristics of monopolistic competition.

☐ Determine the output of and the price charged by a monopolistic competitor (producing a given product and engaged in a given amount of sales promotion) in the short run when you are given the cost and demand data.

☐ Explain why the price charged by a monopolistic competitor (producing a given product and engaged in a given amount of sales promotion) will in the long run tend to equal average cost.

☐ Identify the "wastes of monopolistic competition" and explain why product differentiation may "offset" these wastes.

☐ Enumerate the three principal types of nonprice competition.

☐ Present the major arguments in the cases for and against advertising.

■ CHAPTER OUTLINE

1. A monopolistically competitive industry is one in which a fairly large number of independent firms produces differentiated products, in which both price and various forms of nonprice competition occur, and into which entry is relatively easy in the long run. Many American industries approximate monopolistic competition.

2. Assume that the products the firms in the industry produce and the amounts of promotional activity in which they engage are given.

a. The demand curve confronting each firm will be highly but not perfectly elastic because each firm has many competitors who produce close but not perfect substitutes for the product it produces.

b. In the short run the individual firm will produce the output at which marginal cost and marginal revenue are equal and charge the price at which that output can be sold; either profits or losses may result in the short run.

c. In the long run the entry and exodus of firms will *tend* to change the demand for the product of the individual firm in such a way that profits are eliminated (price and average costs are made equal to each other).

3. Monopolistic competition among firms producing a *given* product and engaged in a *given* amount of promotional activity results in less economic efficiency and more waste than does pure competition. Although the average cost of each firm is equal in the long run to its price, the industry does not realize allocative efficiency (because output is smaller than the output at which marginal cost and price are equal); and it does not realize productive efficiency (because the output is smaller than the output at which average cost is a minimum).

4. In addition to setting its price and output so that its profit is maximized, each individual firm also attempts to differentiate its product and to promote (advertise) it in order to increase the firm's profit; these additional activities give rise to nonprice competition among firms.

a. Product differentiation and product development, as devices which firms employ in the hope of increasing their profit, may offset the wastes of monopolistic competition to the extent that they result in a wider variety and better quality of products for consumers.

b. Whether the advertising of differentiated products results in economic waste or in greater economic efficiency is debatable; there are good arguments on both sides of this question and there is no clear answer to it.

c. Empirical evidence on the economic effects of advertising shows that it leads to less competition and a misallocation of resources in some cases and to more competition and lower prices in other cases.

d. The monopolistically competitive firm tries to adjust its price, its product, and its promotion of the product so that the amount by which the firm's total revenue exceeds the total cost of producing and promoting its product is a maximum.

■ IMPORTANT TERMS

Monopolistic competition
Product differentiation
Nonprice competition
Wastes of monopolistic competition

■ FILL-IN QUESTIONS

1. In a monopolistically competitive market a (few, relatively large number of) ________________ producers sell (standardized, differentiated) ________________ products; these producers (do, do not) ________________ collude; and they engage in both ________________ and ________________ competition. In the long run entry into the industry is (difficult, fairly easy) ________________

2. Because monopolistically competitive firms sell differentiated products each firm has (no, limited, complete) ____________ control over the price of its product and there is ____________ between the firms.

3. Given the product being produced and the extent to which that product is being promoted, in the *short run:*

a. The demand curve confronting the monopolistically competitive firm will be (more, less) ____________ elastic than that facing a monopolist and ____________ elastic than that facing a pure competitor.

b. The elasticity of this demand curve will depend upon ____________ and ____________

c. The firm will produce the output at which ____________ and ____________ are equal.

4. In the long run, the *entry* of new firms into a monopolistically competitive industry will (expand, reduce) ____________ the demand for the product produced by each firm in the industry and (increase, decrease) ____________ the elasticity of that demand.

5. In the long run, *given* the product and the amount of product promotion, the price charged by the individual firm will tend to equal ____________, its economic profits will tend to equal ____________ ____________, and its average cost will be ____________ than the minimum average cost of producing and promoting the product.

6. Given the product and the extent of product promotion, monopolistic competition is wasteful because ____________ ____________ and because ____________

7. In the long run, the monopolistic competitor cannot protect and increase profits by varying the product's price or output, but it can try to protect and increase profits by ____________ and ____________

8. Product differentiation and product development tend to result in the consumer being offered a wider ____________ of goods at any given time and an improved ____________ of goods over a period of time.

9. The different case studies of the economic effects of advertising indicate that in the U.S. it is (competitive, anticompetitive, both) ____________ ____________

10. In attempting to maximize his profits the monopolistic competitor will vary the price, the ____________, and the ____________ of the product until the firm feels no further change in these three variables will result in greater profit.

■ PROBLEMS AND PROJECTS

1. Listed below are several industries. Indicate in the space after each whether you believe it is monopolistically competitive (MC) or not monopolistically competitive (N). If you indicate the latter, explain why you think the industry is not a monopolistically competitive one.

a. The production of automobiles in the United States. ____________

b. The retail distribution of automobiles in the United States. ____________ ____________

c. Grocery supermarkets in a city of 500,000 people. ____________ ____________

d. The retail sale of gasoline in a city of 500,000 people. ____________ ____________

e. The production of low-priced shoes in the United States. ______________________

____

f. The mail-order sale of men's clothes.

____

____

2. Assume that the short-run cost and demand data given in the table below confront a monopolistic competitor selling a given product and engaged in a given amount of product promotion.

Output	Total cost	Marginal cost	Quantity demanded	Price	Marginal revenue
0	$ 50		0	$120	
1	80	$____	1	110	$____
2	90	____	2	100	____
3	110	____	3	90	____
4	140	____	4	80	____
5	180	____	5	70	____
6	230	____	6	60	____
7	290	____	7	50	____
8	360	____	8	40	____
9	440	____	9	30	____
10	530	____	10	20	____

a. Compute the marginal cost and marginal revenue of each unit of output and enter these figures in the table.

b. In the short run the firm will (1) produce ________ units of output, (2) sell its product at a price of $________________, and (3) have a total economic profit of $________________

c. In the long run, (1) the demand for the firm's product will ________________, (2) until the price of the product equals ________________ and (3) the total economic profits of the firm are ________________

■ SELF-TEST

Circle the T if the statement is true, the F if it is false.

1. Monopolistic competitors have no control over the price of their products. **T F**

2. The publisher of McConnell's *Economics* and this *Study Guide* is a monopolistic competitor. **T F**

3. The smaller the number of firms in an industry and the greater the extent of product differentiation, the greater will be the elasticity of the individual seller's demand curve. **T F**

4. One reason why monopolistic competition is wasteful, given the products the firms produce and the extent to which they promote them, is that the average cost of producing the product is greater than the minimum average cost at which the product could be produced. **T F**

5. The wider the range of differentiated products offered to consumers by a monopolistically competitive industry the less excess capacity there will be in that industry. **T F**

6. A firm will improve the quality of its product only if it expects that the additional revenue which it will receive will be greater than the extra costs involved. **T F**

7. If advertising expenditures fluctuate directly (or positively) with total spending in the economy, they will be countercyclical and lead to greater stability in employment and the price level. **T F**

8. Those who contend that advertising contributes to the growth of monopoly in the economy argue that the advertising by established firms creates barriers to the entry of new firms into an industry. **T F**

9. There tends to be rather general agreement among both critics and defenders of advertising that advertising increases the average cost of producing and promoting the product. **T F**

10. Empirical evidence clearly indicates that advertising reduces competition and leads to a misallocation of the economy's resources. **T F**

Circle the letter that corresponds to the best answer.

1. Which of the following is *not* characteristic of monopolistic competition? (*a*) Product differentiation; (*b*) a relatively large number of firms; (*c*) a feeling of interdependence among the firms; (*d*) relatively easy entry in the long run.

2. Given the following short-run demand and cost schedules for a monopolistic competitor what output will the firm produce? (*a*) 2; (*b*) 3; (*c*) 4; (*d*) 5.

Price	Quantity demanded	Total cost	Output
$10	1	$14	1
9	2	17	2
8	3	22	3
7	4	29	4
6	5	38	5
5	6	49	6

3. Assuming the short-run demand and cost data in question 2 above, *in the long run* the number of firms in the industry; (*a*) will be less than in the short run; (*b*) will be the same as in the short run; (*c*) will be greater than in the short run; (*d*) cannot be determined from the available information.

4. In the short run a monopolistically competitive firm (*a*) obtains an economic profit; (*b*) breaks even; (*c*) suffers an economic loss; (*d*) may have an economic profit or loss or break even.

5. Given the product the firm is producing and the extent to which the firm is promoting it, *in the long run* (*a*) the firm will produce that output at which marginal cost and price are equal; (*b*) the elasticity of demand for the firm's product will be less than it was in the short run; (*c*) the number of firms in the industry will be greater than it was in the short run; (*d*) the economic profits being earned by the firms in the industry will tend to equal zero.

6. Which of the following is *not* one of the features of monopolistic competition which may offset the wastes associated with such a market structure? (*a*) A wider variety of products is offered to consumers; (*b*) much advertising is self-canceling; (*c*) the quality of products improves over time; (*d*) consumers are better informed of the availability and prices of products.

7. If an industry is to be economically efficient it is necessary that (*a*) price equal average cost; (*b*) price equal marginal cost; (*c*) average cost equal marginal cost; (*d*) all of the above.

8. Were a monopolistically competitive industry in long-run equilibrium a firm in that industry might be able to increase its economic profits by (*a*) increasing the price of its product; (*b*) increasing the amounts it spends to advertise its product; (*c*) decreasing the price of its product; (*d*) decreasing the output of its product.

9. Which of the following can be fairly concluded with respect to the economic effects of advertising? (*a*) Advertising helps to maintain a high level of aggregate demand in the economy; (*b*) consumers benefit less from advertising expenditures than they do from expenditures for product development; (*c*) advertising in the American economy leads almost invariably to higher product prices; (*d*) lower unit costs and lower prices result when a firm advertises because advertising increases the size of the firm's market and promotes economies of scale.

10. In seeking to maximize its profits the three variables which the monopolistically competitive firm must consider are (*a*) price, product, and promotion; (*b*) price, publicity, and product; (*c*) price, product, and publicity; (*d*) product, publicity, and promotion.

DISCUSSION QUESTIONS

1. What are the chief characteristics of a monopolistic competitive market? In what sense is there competition and in what sense is there monopoly in such a market?

2. What is meant by product differentiation? By what methods can products be differentiated? How does product differentiation affect the kind of competition in, and inject an element of monopoly into, markets?

3. Comment on the elasticity of the demand curve faced by the monopolistically competitive firm in the short run. Assume that the firm is producing a given product and is engaged in a given amount of promotional activity. What two factors determine just how elastic that demand curve will be?

4. What output will the monopolistic competitor produce in the short run, and what price will it charge for its product? What determines whether the firm will earn profits or suffer losses in the short run?

5. In the long run what level of economic profits will the individual monopolistically competitive firm *tend* to receive? Why is this just a tendency? What forces economic profits toward this level, and why will the firm produce a long-run output which is smaller than the most "efficient" output? (Again assume, in answering this question, that the firm is producing a given product and selling it with a given amount of promotional activity.)

6. In what two senses is monopolistic competition wasteful or a misallocation of resources?

7. What methods, other than price cutting, can an individual monopolistic competitor employ to attempt to protect and increase its economic profits in the long run?

8. To what extent and how do product differentiation and product development offset the "wastes" associated with monopolistic competition?

9. Does advertising result in a waste of resources, or does it promote a more efficient utilization of resources? What arguments can be presented to support the contention that it is wasteful and detrimental, and what claims are made to support the view that it is beneficial to the economy? What empirical evidence is there?

10. When is a monopolistic competitor in long-run equilibrium not only with respect to the price it is charging but also with respect to the product it is producing and the extent to which it is promoting its product?

30
Price and output determination: oligopoly

This last of the four chapters dealing with specific market situations is in a way the most difficult. Oligopoly is one of those areas of economic study where economists have found it impossible to reach definite conclusions. Under conditions of pure competition, pure monopoly, and monopolistic competition fairly precise conclusions regarding market prices and the outputs of individual firms are reached; but such conclusions are not easily drawn from an analysis of oligopoly. This is why the study of oligopoly is difficult—the generalizations are few in number—and this is unfortunate but also unavoidable.

Oligopoly is probably the most realistic market situation which you will examine, and many economists believe it is the type of market most prevalent—or at least, most important—in the American economy. Because it is so realistic its study is all the more difficult. Chapter 30 is little more than an introduction to this very complex market situation. There are, however, certain things you can and should learn about it.

What oligopoly *is* is fairly simple to understand. The consequences of "fewness" and "mutual interdependence" are not quite so easy to grasp, but they are of the greatest importance. For these reasons you should make every attempt to learn exactly *what is meant* by mutual interdependence and *why it exists* in an oligopoly. If you can do this, you will be well on the road to understanding why specific and definite conclusions cannot be reached concerning market prices and the outputs of individual firms. You will also see why oligopolists are loath to engage in price competition and why they frequently resort to collusion to set prices and to nonprice competition to determine market shares.

Because oligopoly includes a number of different (though similar) market structures, Chapter 30 has analyzed four variants of oligopoly for you. The kinked demand curve model is the first of these variants. It explains why, in the absence of collusion, oligopolists will not raise or lower their prices even when their costs change. But the kinked demand curve does not explain what price oligopolists will set; it only explains why price, once set, will be relatively inflexible. To set price oligopolists often resort to some form of collusion.

Cartels and gentlemen's agreements are the most overt forms of collusion and this second variant of oligopoly is analyzed for you. The third variant is the tacit collusion which is to be found when price leadership exists. Cost-plus pricing is the final variant of oligopoly discussed in Chapter 30.

Whether oligopoly is socially efficient (and, therefore, desirable) is a debatable question. Both the traditional and Schumpeter-Galbraith viewpoints are presented; and the question of whether large firms lead to rapid technological progress is examined by looking at the sources of major inventions.

In the final section of the chapter the American automobile industry is examined to illustrate a real-world oligopoly in action. Here you will see that three firms dominated an industry characterized by high barriers to entry, price-leadership, and nonprice competition in the three decades following World War II. But you will also discover that the American automobile industry, like the Old Gray Mare, "ain't what she used to be." It has fallen on hard times. And while the depressed condition of the industry has many causes, events outside the United

States—higher oil prices and increased foreign exports—have played a leading role in changing, perhaps forever, the market structure of this oligopoly.

■ CHECKLIST

When you have studied this chapter you should be able to:

☐ Define oligopoly and distinguish between homogeneous and differentiated oligopolies.

☐ Identify the three most significant causes of oligopoly and explain how each of these tends to result in oligopolistic industries.

☐ Explain why it is difficult to predict what price will be charged and what output will be produced by an oligopolist.

☐ Employ the kinked demand curve to explain why oligopoly prices tend to be inflexible.

☐ State the three principal advantages of collusion to oligopolists, at least three forms which such collusion may take, and five obstacles to this collusion.

☐ Explain what price colluding oligopolists with identical cost and demand curves and producing a homogeneous product would set and what output each would produce.

☐ Describe how a firm (such as General Motors) employs cost-plus pricing to determine the prices it will charge for its products.

☐ Explain the role played by nonprice competition in oligopolistic industries, the three principal forms of such competition, and two reasons why oligopolists emphasize nonprice competition.

☐ Compare the Schumpeter-Galbraith view with the traditional view of oligopoly; and explain whether the empirical evidence does or does not support the former viewpoint.

☐ Describe the American automobile industry in terms of the number of sellers and their market shares, the height and kinds of barriers to entry, the method employed to set prices, the types of nonprice competition, the level of profits, and the rate of technological progress; and explain how foreign competition and recession have changed the industry in recent years.

■ CHAPTER OUTLINE

1. Oligopoly is frequently encountered in the American economy.

a. It is composed of a few firms which sell either a standardized or a differentiated product; and the concentration ratio, despite its several shortcomings, is a measure of the extent to which "fewness" prevails in a particular industry.

b. The existence of an oligopoly is usually the result of economies of scale, other barriers to entry, and the advantages of merger.

c. The firms in the industry are mutually interdependent because they are few in number.

2. The economic analysis of oligopoly is difficult for two reasons: the term "oligopoly" actually covers many different market situations; and the individual oligopolist, because of the uncertainty which accompanies mutual interdependence, is seldom able to estimate its own demand curve. Important characteristics of oligopoly are inflexible prices and simultaneous price changes.

3. An examination of four oligopoly models will help to explain the pricing practices of oligopolists.

a. In the kinked demand curve model oligopolists do not collude.

(1) Each firm believes that when it lowers its price its rivals will lower their prices; and when it increases its price its rivals will not increase their prices.

(2) The firm is, therefore, reluctant to change its price for fear of decreasing its profits.

(3) But this model has at least two shortcomings.

b. The uncertainties and disadvantages of noncollusive oligopoly may induce firms to collude.

(1) Firms that collude tend to set their prices and joint output at the same level at which a pure monopolist would set them.

(2) The method of collusion employed by the firms may be one of several forms which include the cartel and the gentlemen's agreement.

(3) At least five obstacles make it difficult for firms to collude.

c. Price leadership is the third model and a frequent form of tacit collusion in which one firm initiates price changes and the other firms in the industry follow its lead.

d. In the cost-plus pricing model a firm determines its price by adding a percentage markup to its average cost of production.

4. Oligopolistic firms avoid price competition but engage in nonprice competition to determine each firm's market share (sales).

5. To compare the efficiency of an oligopolist with that of a pure competitor is difficult.

a. It has been traditional to believe that oligopoly has

much the same result as monopoly; but Schumpeter and Galbraith believe that oligopoly is needed if there is to be rapid technological progress (dynamic efficiency).

b. While the evidence is not conclusive, it appears that most of the important inventions have not been made by large firms; and the structure of the industry may not affect its technological progress.

6. The automobile industry in the United States is an example of an oligopoly in which are found a few large firms and significant barriers to entry; price leadership; styling competition among the sellers; and significant competition from foreign producers.

■ IMPORTANT TERMS

Oligopoly	**Price war**
Fewness	**Collusive oligopoly**
Homogeneous oligopoly	**Cartel**
Differentiated oligopoly	**Gentlemen's agreement**
Concentration ratio	**Price leadership**
Interindustry competition	**Cost-plus pricing**
Mutual interdependence	**Traditional view (of oligopoly)**
Noncollusive oligopoly	**Schumpeter-Galbraith view (of oligopoly)**
Kinked demand curve	

■ FILL-IN QUESTIONS

1. In an oligopoly a ______ firms produce either a ______ or a ______ product, and entry into such an industry is ______

2. The three major underlying causes of oligopoly are ______, ______, and ______

3. Because oligopoly consists of a small number of firms, they are necessarily ______; this means that when setting the price of its product each producer must consider ______; the monopolist does not face this problem because it has ______ rivals; and the pure and monopolistic competitor do not face it because each has ______ rivals.

4. Formal economic analysis cannot be easily used to explain the prices and outputs of oligopolists because oligopoly is in fact (one, a small number of, many) ______ specific market situation(s); and when firms are mutually interdependent each firm is (certain, uncertain) ______ about how its rivals will react when it changes the price of its product.

5. Oligopoly prices tend to be (flexible, inflexible) ______ and oligopolists tend to change their prices (independently, simultaneously) ______

6. The kinked demand curve which the individual noncolluding oligopolist sees for its product is highly (elastic, inelastic) ______ at prices above the current or going price and tends to be only slightly ______ or ______ below that price.

7. The kinked demand curve for a noncolluding oligopolist is drawn on the assumption that if the oligopolist raises its price its rivals will ______ and if it lowers its price its rivals will ______

8. Because the oligopolist who confronts a kinked demand curve finds that there is a ______ in its marginal-revenue curve, small changes in the marginal-cost curve do not change the ______

9. When oligopolists collude, the prices they set and their combined output tend to be the same as would be set (in a purely competitive industry) ______

10. A cartel is a formal agreement among sellers in which the price and the total output of the product and each seller's share of the market are specified.

11. A gentlemen's agreement is (a formal, an informal) informal agreement on prices; each firm's share of the market is determined by ingenuity of seller as reflected in nonprice comp.

12. Five obstacles to collusion among oligopolists are:

a. ability to achieve concessions & compromises

b. # of firms

c. cheating—price cutting for business

d. recession

e. legal obstacles—anti-trust

13. When one firm in an oligopoly is almost always the first to change its price and the other firms change their prices after it has changed its price there is a type of (overt, tacit) tacit collusion called price leadership

14. When a firm employs a cost-plus formula to determine the price it will charge for a product it adds a percentage mark-up to the average cost of producing the product.

15. There tends to be very little (price, nonprice) price competition among oligopolists and a great deal of nonprice competition which they use to determine each firm's share of the mkt

The two reasons for the emphasis on this kind of competition are:

a. price cuts are so easily matched

b. oligopolists have financial res's

16. The traditional view of oligopoly is that it results in (lower, higher) higher prices and profits, lower outputs, and a rate of technological progress that is (slower, faster) slower than would be found if the industry were more competitive.

17. In the Schumpeter-Galbraith view of oligopoly:

a. Only oligopolists have both the means and the incentive to be technologically progressive;

b. Over time oligopolists will bring about a more rapid rate of product improvement, lower costs and prices, and perhaps greater output and employment than the same industry competitively organized.

18. The empirical evidence seems to indicate that the large oligopolists (have, have not) have not been the major source of technological progress in the United States.

■ PROBLEMS AND PROJECTS

1. The kinked demand schedule which an oligopolist believes confronts the firm is given in the table below.

Price	Quantity demanded	Total revenue	Marginal revenue
$2.90	100	$290	
2.80	200	560	$2.70
2.70	300	810	2.50
2.60	400	1040	2.30
2.50	500	1250	2.10
2.40	525	1260	.40
2.30	550	1265	.20
2.20	575	1265	0
2.10	600	1260	-.20

a. Compute the oligopolist's total revenue at each of the nine prices, and enter these figures in the table.

b. Also compute marginal revenue between the nine prices and enter these figures in the table.

c. What is the current, or going, price for the oligopolist's product? $2.50 How much is it selling? 500

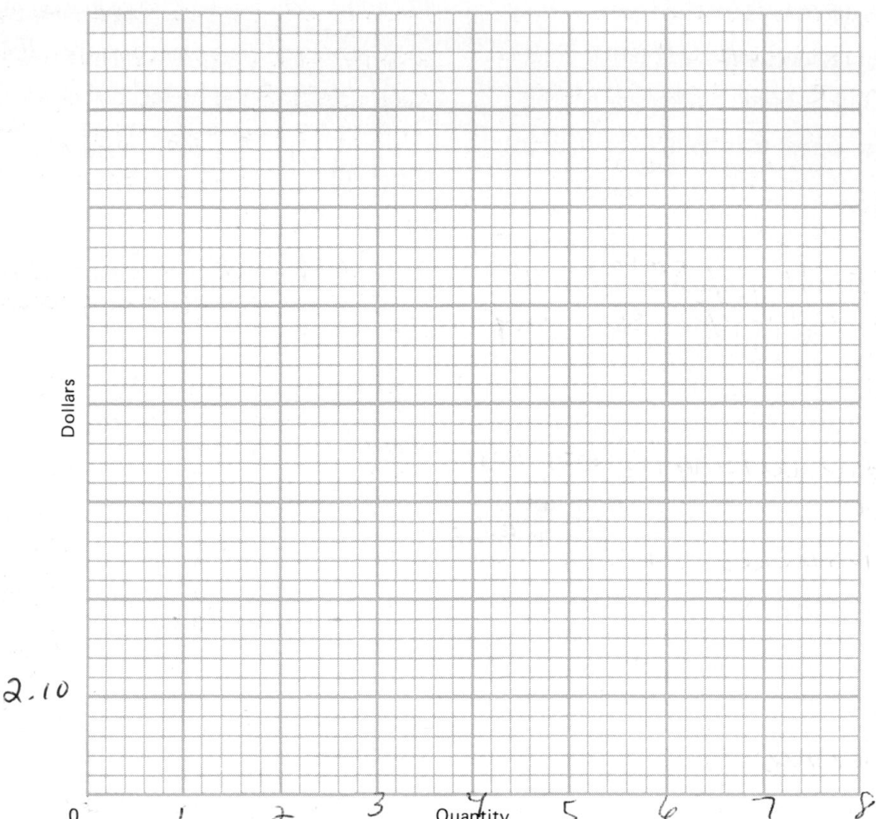

d. On the graph above plot the oligopolist's demand curve and marginal-revenue curve. Connect the demand points and the marginal-revenue points with as straight a line as possible. (*Be sure* to plot the marginal-revenue figures at the average of the two quantities involved, that is, at 150, 250, 350, 450, 512½, 537½, 562½, and 587½.)

e. Assume that the marginal-cost schedule of the oligopolist is given in columns (1) and (2) of the table in the next column. Plot the marginal-cost curve on the graph on which demand and marginal revenue were plotted.

(1) Given demand and marginal cost, what price should the oligopolist charge to maximize profits? $________ How many units of product will it sell at this price? ________________

(2) If the marginal-cost schedule changed from that shown in columns (1) and (2) to that shown in columns (1) and (3), what price should it charge? $________

(1) Output	(2) MC	(3) MC′	(4) MC″
150	$1.40	$1.90	$.40
250	1.30	1.80	.30
350	1.40	1.90	.40
450	1.50	2.00	.50
512½	1.60	2.10	.60
537½	1.70	2.20	.70
562½	1.80	2.30	.80
587½	1.90	2.40	.90

What level of output will it produce? ________ How have profits changed as a result of the change in costs? ________

Plot the new marginal-cost curve on the graph.

(3) If the marginal-cost curve schedule changed from that shown in columns (1) and (2) to that shown in col-

umns (1) and (4), what price should it charge? $______

What level of output will it produce? ______

How have profits changed as a result of the change in costs? ______

Plot the new marginal-cost curve on the graph.

2. An oligopoly producing a homogeneous product is composed of three firms. Assume that these three firms have identical cost schedules. Assume also that if any one of these firms sets a price for the product, the other two firms charge the same price. As long as they all charge the same price they will share the market equally; and the quantity demanded of each will be the same.

Below is the total-cost schedule of one of these firms and the demand schedule that confronts it when the other firms charge the same price as this firm.

a. Complete the marginal-cost and marginal-revenue schedules facing the firm. MC=MR

b. What price would this firm set if it wished to maximize its profits? 90

c. How much would:

(1) It sell at this price? 5

(2) Its profits be at this price? $280

d. What would be the industry's:

(1) Total output at this price? 15

(2) Joint profits at this price? $840

e. Is there any other price this firm can set, assuming that the other two firms charge the same price, which would result in a greater joint profit for them? no

If so, what is that price? $______

f. If these three firms colluded in order to maximize their joint profit, what price would they charge? $90

π = TR − TC
450 − 170

Output	Total cost	Marginal cost	Price	Quantity demanded		Marginal revenue
0	$ 0		$140	0		
1	30	$ 30	130	1	130	$ 130
2	50	20	120	2	240	110
3	80	30	110	3	330	90
4	120	40	100	4	400	70
5	170	50	90	5	450	50
6	230	60	80	6	480	30
7	300	70	70	7	490	10
8	380	80	60	8	480	−10

3. A firm producing automobiles has $4 billion invested in capital and its average total cost schedule is shown below.

Output (cars per year)	Average total cost
1,100,000	$14,000
1,200,000	$10,000
1,300,000	$8,000
1,400,000	$7,000
1,500,000	$6,500
1,600,000	$6,250
1,700,000	$6,600
1,800,000	$7,200

a. If the objective of the firm is to have an annual return *after* taxes equal to 10% of its invested capital it must earn $400 million after taxes each year.

b. To earn this amount after taxes when its earnings are taxed at a 50% rate it must earn $__________ *before* taxes.

c. When the firm estimates that its most likely annual output (its "standard volume") is 1,500,000 automobiles:

(1) to achieve its objective of a 10% after-tax return on its investment it must earn $________ per automobile. (*Hint:* Divide the required return before taxes by its annual output.)

(2) to earn this amount per automobile it must set the price of an automobile at $________

(3) the markup is approximately ______ %.

■ SELF-TEST

Circle the T if the statement is true, the F if it is false.

1. The products produced by the firms in an oligopolistic industry may be either homogeneous (standardized) or differentiated. **T F**

2. Concentration ratios are low in those industries which are oligopolies. **T F**

3. The uncertainty which exists in oligopolies is the uncertainty faced by each firm on how its rivals will react if it changes its price. **T F**

4. The kinked demand curve is an economic tool which can be used to explain how the current market price of a product is determined. **T F**

5. A cartel is usually a written agreement among firms which sets the price of the product and determines each firm's share of the market. **T F**

6. The practice of price leadership is almost always based on a formal written or oral agreement. **T F**

7. An oligopolist utilizing a cost-plus pricing formula typically adds a percentage markup to what its unit cost would be if it operated at full capacity. **T F**

8. Price competition between firms is an important characteristic of oligopoly. **T F**

9. Nonprice competition is the typical method of determining each oligopolist's share of the total market. **T F**

10. It is often argued that oligopolists typically possess both the means and the incentives to technological progress, and that the means are the substantial profits received by them. **T F**

11. Almost all the important technological advances in the United States between 1880 and 1965 can be attributed to the research and development activities of large business firms. **T F**

12. The American automobile industry is a fairly good example of a differentiated oligopoly. **T F**

Circle the letter that corresponds to the best answer.

1. The number of firms in an oligopolistic industry is (*a*) one; (*b*) a few; (*c*) many; (*d*) very many.

2. Concentration ratios take into account (*a*) interindustry competition; (*b*) import competition; (*c*) the existence of separate local markets for products; (*d*) none of the above.

3. Which of the following does *not* contribute to the existence of oligopoly? (*a*) The economies of large-scale production; (*b*) the gains in profits that result from mergers; (*c*) high barriers to entry into an industry; (*d*) standardized products.

4. Mutual interdependence is only characteristic of (*a*) pure and monopolistic competition; (*b*) monopolistic competition and oligopoly; (*c*) pure competition and oligopoly; (*d*) oligopoly.

5. Mutual interdependence means that: (*a*) each firm produces a product similar but not identical to the products produced by its rivals; (*b*) each firm produces a product identical to the products produced by its rivals; (*c*) each firm must consider the reactions of its rivals when it determines its price policy; (*d*) each firm faces a perfectly elastic demand for its product.

6. The prices of products produced by oligopolies tend to be (*a*) relatively flexible and when firms change prices they are apt to change them at the same time; (*b*) relatively inflexible and when firms change prices they are not apt to change them at the same time; (*c*) relatively inflexible and when firms change prices they are apt to change them at the same time; (*d*) relatively flexible and when firms change prices they are not apt to change them at the same time.

7. The demand curve confronting an oligopolist tends to be: (*a*) elastic; (*b*) of unitary elasticity; (*c*) inelastic; (*d*) one which depends upon the prices charged by his rivals.

8. If an individual oligopolist's demand curve is "kinked," it is necessarily: (*a*) inelastic below the going price; (*b*) inelastic above the going price; (*c*) elastic above the going price; (*d*) of unitary elasticity at the going price.

9. Below is the demand schedule confronting an oligopolist. Which one of the eight prices seems to be the "going" price of the product produced by the firm? (*a*) $4.50; (*b*) $4; (*c*) $3.50; (*d*) $3.

Price	Quantity demanded
$5.00	10
4.50	20
4.00	30
3.50	40
3.00	42
2.50	44
2.00	46
1.00	48

10. Which of the following is *not* a means of colluding? (*a*) A cartel; (*b*) a kinked demand curve, (*c*) a gentlemen's agreement; (*d*) price leadership.

11. Oligopolists tend to collude because collusive control over the price they charge permits them to (*a*) increase their profits; (*b*) decrease their uncertainties; (*c*) deter the entry of new firms into their industry; (*d*) do all of the above.

12. When oligopolists collude the results are generally: (*a*) greater output and higher price; (*b*) greater output and lower price; (*c*) smaller output and lower price; (*d*) smaller output and higher price.

13. Which of the following constitutes an obstacle to collusion among oligopolists? (*a*) A general business recession; (*b*) a small number of firms in the industry; (*c*) a homogeneous product; (*d*) the patent laws.

14. It is the belief of Schumpeter and Galbraith that an industry organized oligopolistically when compared with the same industry organized competitively would over time (*a*) foster more rapid improvement in the quality of the good or service produced; (*b*) bring about a greater reduction in the average cost of producing the product; (*c*) lower the price of the product by a larger percentage; (*d*) all of the above.

■ DISCUSSION QUESTIONS

1. What are the essential characteristics of an oligopoly? How does it differ from monopolistic competition?

2. Explain how the concentration ratio in a particular industry is computed. What is the relationship between this ratio and fewness?

3. What are the shortcomings of the concentration ratio as a measure of the extent of competition in an industry?

4. What are the underlying causes of oligopoly?

5. What do "mutual interdependence" and "uncertainty" mean with respect to oligopoly? Why are they special characteristics of oligopoly?

6. Why is it difficult to employ formal economic analysis to explain the prices charged by and the outputs of oligopolists?

7. Explain what the kinked demand curve is, its most important characteristics, the assumptions upon which it is based, and the kind of marginal-revenue curve to which it gives rise. How can the kinked demand curve be used to explain why oligopoly prices are relatively inflexible? Under what conditions will oligopolists acting independently raise or lower their prices even though their demand curves may be kinked?

8. Why do oligopolists find it advantageous to collude? What are the obstacles to collusion?

9. Suppose a few firms produce a homogeneous product, have identical cost curves, and charge the same price. How will the price they set, their combined output of the product, and their joint profit compare with what would be found in the same industry if it were a pure monopoly with several plants?

10. Explain (*a*) a cartel; (*b*) a gentlemen's agreement; (*c*) price leadership, and (*d*) cost-plus pricing.

11. Why do oligopolists engage in little price competition and in extensive nonprice competition?

12. Contrast the Schumpeter-Galbraith view on the dynamic economic efficiency of oligopoly with the traditional view.

13. What does the empirical evidence have to say about sources of technological progress in the United States?

14. Using the following criteria, describe the American automobile industry. (1) Number of firms and their market shares; (2) the barriers to entry; (3) the means used to establish the prices of automobiles; (4) the role of nonprice competition; (5) profits; and (6) technological progress.

15. Explain the causes of and the effects of foreign competition on the American automobile industry during the past ten or so years. How has competition in the market for automobiles in the United States been affected?

31
Production and the demand for economic resources

Chapter 31 is the first of a group of three chapters which examine the markets for resources. Resource markets are markets in which employers of resources and the owners of these resources determine the prices at which resources will be employed and the quantities of these resources that will be hired. (These resources—you should recall—are labor, land, capital, and entrepreneurial ability. The prices of resources have particular names. The price paid for labor is called a wage, the price paid for the use of land is rent, the price paid for the use of capital is interest, and the price paid for entrepreneurial ability is profit.)

The employers of resources are business firms who use resources to produce their products. When the number of employers and the number of owners of a resource are large the market for that resource is a competitive market; and—as you already know—the demand for and the supply of that resource will determine its price and the total quantity of it that will be employed. Chapter 31 begins the examination of resource markets by looking at the business firm and the demand (or employer) side of the resource market. The material in this chapter is *not* an explanation of what determines the demand for a *particular* resource; but it is an explanation of what determines the demand for *any* resource. In Chapters 32 and 33 the other sides of the resource markets and particular resources are examined in detail.

The list of important terms for Chapter 31 is relatively short, but included in the list are two very important concepts—marginal revenue product and marginal resource cost—which you must grasp if you are to understand how much of a resource a firm will hire. These two concepts are similar to but not identical with the marginal-revenue and marginal-cost concepts employed in the study of product markets and in the explanation of how large an output a firm will produce. Marginal revenue and marginal cost are, respectively, the change in the firm's total revenue and the change in the firm's total cost when it produces and sells an additional unit of *output;* marginal revenue product and marginal resource cost are, respectively, the change in the firm's total revenue and the change in the firm's total cost when it hires an additional unit of an *input.* (*Note:* The two new concepts deal with changes in revenue and costs as a consequence of hiring more of a *resource*.)

When a firm wishes to maximize its profits, it produces that *output* at which marginal revenue and marginal cost are equal. But how much of each resource does it hire if it wishes to maximize its profits? It hires that amount of each *resource* at which the marginal revenue product and the marginal resource cost of that resource are equal. And a firm that employs the amount of each resource that maximizes its profits *also* produces the output that maximizes its profits. (If you doubt this statement, see footnote number 16 in the text.)

There is another similarity between the output and the input markets insofar as the firm is concerned. You will recall that the competitive firm's *supply* curve is a portion of its *marginal-cost* curve. The competitive firm's *demand* curve for a resource is a portion of its *marginal-revenue-product* curve. Just as cost is the important determinant of supply, the revenue derived from the use of a resource is the important factor determining the demand for that resource.

■ CHECKLIST

When you have studied this chapter you should be able to:

☐ Present four reasons for studying resource pricing.
☐ Define marginal revenue product.

■ Determine the marginal revenue product schedule of a resource used to produce a product which is sold in a purely competitive market when you are given the relevant data.

□ Find the marginal revenue product schedule of a resource used to produce a product which is sold in an imperfectly competitive market when you are given the necessary data.

□ Define marginal resource cost.

□ State the principle employed by a profit-maximizing firm to determine how much of a resource it will employ; and, when you are given data, apply this principle to find the quantity of a resource a firm will hire.

□ Explain why the marginal revenue product schedule of a resource is the firm's demand for the resource.

□ List the three factors which would change a firm's demand for a resource; and predict the effect of an increase or decrease in each of these factors upon the demand of a firm for a resource.

□ Enumerate the four determinants of the price elasticity of demand for a resource; and state precisely how a change in each of these four determinants would affect the price elasticity of demand for a resource.

□ State the rule employed by a firm to determine the least-cost combination of resources; and utilize this rule to find the least-cost combination when you are given the needed data.

□ State the rule employed by a profit-maximizing firm to determine how much of each of several resources to employ; and, when you are given the necessary data, apply this rule to find the quantity of each resource the firm will hire.

□ Explain what is meant by the "marginal productivity theory of income distribution"; the reason it is said to result in "a fair and equitable distribution of income"; and the two major criticisms of this theory.

■ CHAPTER OUTLINE

1. The study of what determines the prices of resources is important because resource prices influence the size of individual incomes and the distribution of income; allocate scarce resources; affect the way in which firms combine resources to produce their products; and raise ethical questions about the distribution of income.

2. Economists generally agree upon the basic principles of resource pricing, but the complexities of different resources markets make these principles difficult to apply.

3. The demand for a single resource depends upon (or is derived from) the demand for the goods and services it can produce.

a. Because resource demand is a derived demand, the demand for a single resource depends upon the marginal productivity of the resource and the market price of the good or service it is used to produce.

b. Marginal revenue product combines these two factors—the marginal physical product of a resource and the market price of the product it produces—into a single useful tool.

c. A firm will hire a resource up to the quantity at which the marginal revenue product of the resource is equal to its marginal resource cost. MRP= MRC

d. The firm's marginal-revenue-product schedule for a resource is that firm's demand schedule for the resource.

e. If a firm sells its output in an imperfectly competitive market, the more the firm sells the lower becomes the price of the product. This causes the firm's marginal-revenue-product (resource demand) schedule to be less elastic than it would be if the firm sold its output in a purely competitive market.

f. The market (or total) demand for a resource is the sum of the demand schedules of all firms employing the resource.

4. Changes in the demand for the product being produced, changes in the productivity of the resource, and changes in the prices of other resources will tend to change the demand for a resource.

a. A change in the demand for a product produced by a resource such as labor will change the demand of a firm for labor in the same direction.

b. A change in the productivity of a resource such as labor will change the demand of a firm for the resource in the same direction.

c. A change in the price of a

(1) *substitute* resource will change the demand for a resource such as labor in the same direction if the substitution effect outweighs the output effect, and in the opposite direction if the output effect outweighs the substitution effect;

(2) *complementary* resource will change the demand for a resource such as labor in the opposite direction.

5. The elasticity of the demand for a particular resource depends upon the rate at which the marginal physical product of that resource declines, the extent to which other resources can be substituted for the particular resource, the elasticity of demand for the product being produced, and the ratio of the cost of the resource to the total costs of the firm.

6. Firms typically employ more than one resource in producing a product.

a. The firm employing resources in perfectly competitive markets is hiring resources in the least-cost combination when the ratio of the marginal physical product of a resource to its price is the same for all the resources the firm hires.

b. The firm is hiring resources in the most profitable combination if it hires resources in a competitive market when the marginal revenue product of each resource is equal to the price of that resource.

c. A numerical example illustrates the least-cost and profit-maximizing rules for a firm that employs resources in perfectly competitive markets.

d. If the firm employs resources in imperfectly competitive markets it is hiring resources in the least-cost combination when the ratio of the marginal physical product of a resource to its marginal resource cost is the same for all resources; and it is hiring resources in the most profitable combination when the marginal revenue product of each resource is equal to its marginal resource cost.

7. The marginal productivity theory of income distribution seems to result in an equitable distribution of income because each unit of a resource receives a payment equal to its marginal contribution to the firm's revenue; but the theory has at least two serious faults.

a. The distribution of income will be unequal because resources are unequally distributed among individuals in the economy.

b. The income of those who supply resources will not be based on their marginal productivities if there is monopsony or monopoly in the resource markets of the economy.

■ IMPORTANT TERMS

Derived demand
Marginal revenue product
Marginal resource cost
MRP = MRC rule
Substitution effect
Output effect
Least-cost rule (combination)
Profit-maximizing rule (combination)
Marginal productivity theory of income distribution

■ FILL-IN QUESTIONS

1. Resource prices allocate ________________ and are one of the factors that determine the (incomes, costs) ________________ of households and the ________________ of business firms.

2. The demand for a resource is a ________ demand and depends upon the ________________ of the resource and the ________________ of the product produced from the resource.

3. A firm will find it profitable to hire units of a resource up to the quantity at which the ________________ ________________ and the ________________ of the resource are equal; and if the firm hires the resource in a purely competitive market, the ________________ and the ________________ of the resource will be equal.

4. A firm's demand schedule for a resource is the firm's ________________ schedule for that resource because both indicate the quantities of the resource the firm will employ at various resource ________________.

5. A producer that sells its product in an imperfectly competitive market finds that the more of a resource it hires, the (higher, lower) ____________ becomes the price at which it can sell its product. As a consequence, the marginal-revenue-product (or demand) schedule for the resource is (more, less) ____________ elastic than it would be if the output were sold in a purely competitive market.

6. The market demand curve for a resource is obtained by ____

7. The demand for a resource will change if the demand for the ________________ changes, if the ________________ of the resource changes, or if the ________________ of other resources change.

8. In the space to the right of each of the following, indicate whether the change would tend to increase (+) or decrease (−) a firm's demand for a particular resource.

a. An increase in the demand for the firm's product. ________

b. A decrease in the amounts of all other resources the firm employs. ________

c. An increase in the productivity of the resource. ________

d. An increase in the price of a substitute resource when the output effect is greater than the substitution effect. ________

e. A decrease in the price of a complementary resource. ________

9. The output of the firm being constant, a decrease in the price of resource A will induce the firm to hire (more, less) ________ of resource A and ________ of other resources; this is called the ________ effect. But if the decrease in the price of A results in lower total costs and an increase in output, the firm may hire ________ of both resources; this is called the ________ effect.

10. Four determinants of the price elasticity of demand for a resource are the rate at which the ________ of the resource decreases, the ease with which other resources can be ________ for it, the ________ of demand for the product which it is used to produce, and the ________

11. Suppose a firm employs resources in purely competitive markets. If the firm wishes to produce any given amount of its product in the least costly way, the ratio of the ________ of each resource to its ________ must be the same for all resources.

12. A firm that hires resources in purely competitive markets is employing the combination of resources which will result in maximum profits for the firm when the ________ of every resource is equal to its ________

13. When the marginal revenue product of a resource is equal to the price of that resource, the marginal revenue product of the resource divided by its price is equal to ________

14. Assume that a firm employs resources in imperfectly competitive markets. The firm is:

a. Employing the combination of resources that enables it to produce any given output in the least costly way when the ________ of every resource divided by its ________ is the same for all resources.

b. Employing the combination of resources that maximizes its profits when the ________ of every resource is equal to its ________ (or when the ________ of each resource divided by its ________ is equal to ________).

15. In the marginal productivity theory the distribution of income is an equitable one because each unit of each resource is paid an amount equal to its ________.

■ PROBLEMS AND PROJECTS

1. The table following shows the total production a firm will be able to obtain if it employs varying amounts of resource A while the amounts of the other resources the firm employs remain constant.

Quantity of resource A employed	Total product	Marginal physical product of A	Total revenue	Marginal revenue product of A
0	0		$ 0	
1	12	12	18	$ 18
2	22	10	33	15
3	30	8	45	12
4	36	6	54	9
5	40	4	60	6
6	42	2	63	3
7	43	1	64.50	1.50

a. Compute the marginal physical product of each of the seven units of resource A and enter these figures in the table

b. Assume the product the firm produces sells in the market for $1.50 per unit. Compute the total revenue of the firm at each of the eight levels of output and the marginal revenue product of each of the seven units of resource A. Enter these figures in the table.

c. On the basis of your computations complete the firm's demand schedule for resource A by indicating in the table below how many units of resource A the firm would employ at the given prices.

MRC = MRP

Price of A	Quantity of A demanded
$21.00	0
18.00	1
15.00	2
12.00	3
9.00	4
6.00	5
3.00	6
1.50	7

2. In the table at the top of page 276 are the marginal-physical-product data for resource B. Assume that the quantities of other resources employed by the firm remain constant.

a. Compute the total product (output) of the firm for each of the seven quantities of resource B employed and enter these figures in the table.

b. Assume that the firm sells its output in an imperfectly competitive market and that the prices at which it can sell its product are those given in the table. Compute and enter in the table:

(1) Total revenue for each of the seven quantities of B employed.

(2) The marginal revenue product of each of the seven units of resource B.

c. How many units of B would the firm employ if the market price of B were:

(1) $25: 0

(2) $20: 1

(3) $15: 2

(4) $9: 3

(5) $5: 4

(6) $1: 4

3. In the table at the bottom of page 276 are the marginal-physical and marginal-revenue-product schedules for resource C and resource D. Both resources are variable and

Quantity of resource B employed	Marginal physical product of B	Total product	Product price	Total revenue	Marginal revenue product of B
0		0		$0.00	
1	22	____	$1.00	____	$____
2	21	____	.90	____	____
3	19	____	.80	____	____
4	16	____	.70	____	____
5	12	____	.60	____	____
6	7	____	.50	____	____
7	1	____	.40	____	____

are employed in purely competitive markets. The price of C is $2 and the price of D is $3.

a. The least-cost combination of C and D that would enable the firm to produce:

(1) 64 units of its product is ____ C and ____ D.

(2) 99 units of its product is ____ C and ____ D.

b. The profit-maximizing combination of C and D is ____ C and ____ D.

c. When the firm employs the profit-maximizing combination of C and D, it is also employing C and D in the least-cost combination because ____ equals ____

d. Examination of the figures in the table reveals that the firm sells its product in a ____ competitive market at a price of $____

e. Employing the profit-maximizing combination of C and D, the firm's:

(1) Total output is ____

(2) Total revenue is $____

(3) Total cost is $____

(4) Total profit is $____

■ SELF-TEST

Circle the T if the statement is true, the F if it is false.

1. In the resource markets of the economy resources are demanded by business firms and supplied by households. T F

Quantity of resource C employed	Marginal physical product of C	Marginal revenue product of C	Quantity of resource D employed	Marginal physical product of D	Marginal revenue product of D
1	10	$5.00	1	21	$10.50
2	8	4.00	2	18	9.00
3	6	3.00	3	15	7.50
4	5	2.50	4	12	6.00
5	4	2.00	5	9	4.50
6	3	1.50	6	6	3.00
7	2	1.00	7	3	1.50

2. The prices of resources are an important factor in the determination of the supply of a product. T F

3. A resource which is highly productive will always be in great demand. T F

4. A firm's demand schedule for a resource is the firm's marginal-revenue-product schedule for the resource. T F

5. A producer's demand schedule for a resource will be more elastic if the firm sells its product in a purely competitive market than it would be if it sold the product in an imperfectly competitive market. T F

6. The market demand for a particular resource is the sum of the individual demands of all firms that employ that resource. T F

7. When two resources are substitutes for each other both the substitution effect and the output effect of a decrease in the price of one of these resources operate to increase the quantity of the other resource employed by the firm. T F

8. The output effect of an increase in the price of a resource is to increase the quantity demanded of that resource. T F

9. If two resources are complementary, an increase in the price of one of them will reduce the demand for the other. T F

10. An increase in the price of a resource will cause the demand for the resource to decrease. T F

Use the following information as the basis for answering questions 11 and 12. The marginal revenue product and price of resource A are $12 and a constant $2, respectively; and the marginal revenue product and price of resource B are $25 and a constant $5, respectively. The firm sells its product at a constant price of $1.

11. The firm should decrease the amount of A and increase the amount of B it employs if it wishes to decrease its total cost without affecting its total output. T F

12. If the firm wishes to maximize its profits, it should increase its employment of both A and B until their marginal revenue products fall to $2 and $5, respectively. T F

13. When a firm hires a resource in an imperfectly competitive market it finds that the price of the resource is greater than its marginal resource cost. T F

14. As long as the markets in an economy are competitive the marginal productivity theory of income distribution results in an equal distribution of the economy's income among its households. T F

15. The marginal productivity theory of income distribution results in an equitable distribution only if resource markets are perfectly competitive. T F

Circle the letter that corresponds to the best answer.

1. The prices paid for resources affect (*a*) the money incomes of households in the economy; (*b*) the allocation of resources among different firms and industries in the economy; (*c*) the quantities of different resources employed to produce a particular product; (*d*) all of the above.

2. The study of the pricing of resources tends to be complex because: (*a*) supply and demand do not determine resource prices; (*b*) economists do not agree on the basic principles of resource pricing; (*c*) the basic principles of resource pricing must be varied and adjusted when applied to particular resource markets; (*d*) resource pricing is essentially an ethical question.

3. The demand for a resource is *derived* from (*a*) the marginal productivity of the resource and price of the good or service produced from it; (*b*) the marginal productivity of the resource and the price of the resource; (*c*) the price of the resource and the price of the good or service produced from it; (*d*) the price of the resource and the quantity of the resource demanded.

4. As a firm that sells its product in an imperfectly competitive market increases the quantity of a resource it employs, the marginal revenue product of that resource falls because (*a*) the price paid by the firm for the resource falls; (*b*) the marginal physical product of the resource falls; (*c*) the price at which the firm sells its product falls; (*d*) both the marginal physical product and the price at which the firm sells its product fall.

Use the following total-product and marginal-physical-product schedules for a resource to answer questions 5, 6, and 7. Assume that the quantities of other resources the firm employs remain constant.

Units of resource	Total product	MPP
1	8	8
2	14	6
3	18	4
4	21	3
5	23	2

5. If the product the firm produces sells for a constant $3 per unit, the marginal revenue product of the 4th unit of the resource is (*a*) $3; (*b*) $6; (*c*) $9; (*d*) 12.

6. If the firm's product sells for a constant $3 per unit and the price of the resource is a constant $15, the firm will employ how many units of the resource? (*a*) 2; (*b*) 3; (*c*) 4; (*d*) 5.

7. If the firm can sell 14 units of output at a price of $1 per unit and 18 units of output at a price of $0.90 per unit, the marginal revenue product of the 3rd unit of the resource is (*a*) $4; (*b*) $3.60; (*c*) $2.20; (*d*) $0.40.

8. Which of the following would increase a firm's demand for a particular resource? (*a*) An increase in the prices of complementary resources used by the firm; (*b*) a decrease in the demand for the firm's product; (*c*) an increase in the productivity of the resource; (*d*) a decrease in the price of the particular resource.

9. In finding the substitution effect of a change in the price of a particular resource which of the following is assumed to be constant? (*a*) The total output of the firm; (*b*) the total expenditures of the firm; (*c*) the employment of all other resources; (*d*) the MPPs of all resources.

10. Suppose resource A and resource B are substitutes and the price of A increases. If the output effect is greater than the substitution effect, (*a*) the quantity of A employed by the firm will increase and the quantity of B employed will decrease; (*b*) the quantity of both A and B employed by the firm will decrease; (*c*) the quantity of both A and B employed will decrease; (*d*) the quantity of A employed will decrease and the quantity of B employed will increase.

11. Which of the following would result in an increase in the elasticity of demand for a particular resource? (*a*) An increase in the rate at which the marginal physical product of that resource declines; (*b*) a decrease in the elasticity of demand for the product which the resource helps to produce; (*c*) an increase in the percentage of the firm's total costs accounted for by the resource; (*d*) a decrease in the number of other resources which are good substitutes for the particular resource.

12. A firm is allocating its expenditure for resources in a way that will result in the least total cost of producing any given output when: (*a*) the amount the firm spends on each resource is the same; (*b*) the marginal revenue product of each resource is the same; (*c*) the marginal physical product of each resource is the same; (*d*) the marginal physical product per dollar spent on the last unit of each resource is the same.

13. A firm that hires resources in competitive markets is *not necessarily* maximizing its profits when: (*a*) the marginal revenue product of every resource is equal to 1; (*b*) the marginal revenue product of every resource is equal to its price; (*c*) the ratio of the marginal revenue product of every resource to its price is equal to 1; (*d*) the ratio of the price of every resource to its marginal revenue product is equal to 1.

14. If a firm employs resources in imperfectly competitive markets, to maximize its profits the marginal revenue product of each resource must equal: (*a*) its marginal physical product; (*b*) its marginal resource cost; (*c*) its price; (*d*) one.

15. In the marginal productivity theory of income distribution when all markets are purely competitive, each unit of each resource receives a money payment equal to (*a*) its marginal physical product; (*b*) its marginal revenue product; (*c*) the needs of the resource-owner; (*d*) the payments received by each of the units of the other resources in the economy.

■ DISCUSSION QUESTIONS

1. Why is it important to study resource pricing?

2. Why is resource demand a derived demand, and upon what two factors does the strength of this derived demand depend?

3. Explain why firms that wish to maximize their profits follow the MRP = MRC rule.

4. What constitutes a firm's demand schedule for a resource? Why? What determines the total, or market, demand for a resource?

5. Why is the demand schedule for a resource less elastic when the firm sells its product in an imperfectly competitive market than when it sells it in a purely competitive market?

6. Explain what will cause the demand for a resource to increase and what will cause it to decrease.

7. Explain the difference between the "substitution effect" and the "output effect."

8. What determines the elasticity of the demand for a resource? Explain the exact relationship between each of these four determinants and elasticity.

9. Assuming a firm employs resources in purely competitive markets, when is it spending money on resources in such a way that it can produce a given output for the least total cost?

10. When is a firm that employs resources in purely competitive markets utilizing these resources in amounts that will maximize the profits of the firm?

11. Were a firm to employ resources in *imperfectly* competitive markets, what would your answers to questions 9 and 10 be?

12. What *is* the marginal productivity theory of income distribution? What ethical proposition must be accepted if this distribution is to be fair and equitable? What are the two major shortcomings of the theory?

32
The pricing and employment of resources: wage determination

The preceding chapter of the text defined marginal revenue product and marginal resource cost. It also explained what determines the demand for *any* resource. Chapter 32 builds upon these explanations and applies them to the study of a particular resource, labor, and the wage rate, the price paid for labor.

But as you learned in Chapters 27 through 30, it requires more than an understanding of supply and demand to explain the price of a product and the output of a firm and an industry. An understanding of the competitiveness of the market in which the product is sold is also required. It was for this reason that purely competitive, monopolistic, monopolistically competitive, and oligopolistic markets were examined in detail. The same is true of labor markets. The competitiveness of labor markets must be examined if the factors which determine wage rates and the quantity of labor employed are to be understood.

Following comments on the meanings of certain terms, the general level of wages, and the reasons for the high and increasing general wage level in the United States, Chapter 32 explains how wage rates are determined in particular types of labor markets. Six kinds of labor markets are studied: (1) the competitive market in which the number of employers is large and labor is nonunionized; (2) the monopsony market in which a single employer hires labor under competitive (nonunion) conditions; (3) a market in which a union controls the supply of labor, the number of employers is large, and the union attempts to increase the total demand for labor; (4) a similar market in which the union attempts to reduce the total supply of labor; (5) another similar market in which the union attempts to obtain a wage rate that is above the competitive-equilibrium level by threatening to strike; and (6) the bilateral monopoly market, in which a single employer faces a labor supply controlled by a single union.

It is, of course, important for you to learn the characteristics of and the differences between each of these labor markets. It is also important that you study each of them carefully to see *how* the characteristics of the market affect the wage rate that will be paid in these markets. In the first two types of market the wage rate which will be paid is quite definite, and here you should learn exactly what level of wages and employment will prevail.

When unions control the supply of labor, wage and employment levels are less definite. If the demand for labor is competitive, the wage rate and the amount of employment will depend upon how successful the union is in increasing the demand for labor, in restricting the supply of labor, or in setting a wage rate which employers will accept. If there is but a single employer, wages and employment will fall within certain limits; exactly where they occur within these limits will depend upon the bargaining strength of the union and of the firm. You should, however, know what the limits are.

The sections explaining wages in particular labor markets are the more important parts of the chapter. But the sections which examine the effects of minimum wage laws on employment and wage rates, the reasons why different workers receive different wage rates, and the effect of investment in human capital are also important. You should, therefore, pay attention to (1) the case against, the case for, and the real-world effects of the minimum wage; (2) the several causes of wage differentials; and (3) the theory of human capital and the criticisms of that theory.

■ CHECKLIST

When you have studied this chapter you should be able to:

☐ Define wages (or the wage rate); and distinguish between money and real wages.

☐ List the several factors which have led to the high and rising general level of real wages in the United States.

☐ Explain, using graphs, what determines the wage rate and the level of employment in competitive labor markets and in monopsonistic labor markets; and be able, when given numerical data, to find the equilibrium wage rate and employment level in each of these models.

☐ List three techniques labor unions use to increase the demand for labor.

☐ Enumerate the devices used by the labor movement and by craft unions to decrease the supply of labor; and explain the effects of these devices upon wage rates and the employment of labor.

☐ Explain, using a graph, how the organization of workers by an industrial union in a previously competitive labor market would affect the wage rate and employment level.

☐ Use a graph to explain why the equilibrium wage rate and employment level is indeterminate when a labor market is a bilateral monopoly; and to predict the range within which the wage rate will be found.

☐ Present the case for and the case against a legally established minimum wage.

☐ List the three major factors which explain why wage differentials exist.

☐ Define investment in human capital; explain the cause-effect chain in the theory of human capital; and criticize this theory.

■ CHAPTER OUTLINE

1. A wage (or the wage rate) is the price paid per unit of time for any type of labor and can be measured either in money or in real terms. Earnings are equal to the wage multiplied by the amount of time worked.

2. The general (or average) level of real wages in the United States is among the highest in the world because the demand for labor in the United States has been great relative to the supply of labor.

a. The demand for labor in the United States has been strong because labor has been highly productive; and it has been highly productive for several major reasons.

b. The real hourly wage rate and output per hour of labor are closely and directly related to each other; and real income per worker can increase only at the same rate as output per worker.

c. The increases in the demand for labor that have resulted from the increased productivity of labor over time have been greater than the increases in the supply of labor in the United States; and as a result the real wage rate in the United States has increased in the long run.

3. The wage rate received by a specific type of labor depends upon the demand for and the supply of that labor and upon the competitiveness of the market in which that type of labor is hired.

a. In a purely competitive and nonunionized labor market the total demand for and the total supply of labor determine the wage rate; from the point of view of the individual firm the supply of labor is perfectly elastic at this wage rate (that is, the marginal labor cost is equal to the wage rate) and the firm will hire the amount of labor at which the marginal revenue product of labor is equal to its marginal labor cost.

b. In a monopsonistic and nonunionized labor market the firm's marginal labor costs are greater than the wage rates it must pay to obtain various amounts of labor; and it hires the amount of labor at which marginal labor cost and the marginal revenue product of labor are equal. Both the wage rate and the level of employment are less than they would be under purely competitive conditions.

c. In labor markets in which labor unions represent workers, the unions attempt to raise wage rates by

(1) increasing the demand for labor by increasing the demands for the products produced by the union workers, by increasing the productivity of these workers, and by increasing the prices of resources which are substitutes for the labor provided by the members of the union;

(2) reducing the supply of labor; or

(3) imposing upon employers wage rates in excess of the equilibrium wage rate which would prevail in a purely competitive market.

d. Labor unions are aware that actions taken by them to increase wage rates may also increase the unemployment of their members and may, therefore, limit their demands for higher wages; but the unemployment effect of higher wages is lessened by increases in and a relatively inelastic demand for labor.

e. In a labor market characterized by bilateral monopoly, the wage rate depends, within certain limits, on the relative bargaining power of the union and of the employer.

f. Whether minimum wage laws reduce poverty is a debatable question; but the evidence suggests that while they increase the incomes of employed workers they also reduce the number of workers employed.

4. Not all labor receives the same wage. Wage differentials exist because

a. the labor force consists of noncompeting groups;
b. jobs vary in difficulty and attractiveness; and
c. laborers are not perfectly mobile.

5. Some economists have argued that differences in the earnings of workers are to a large extent the result of differences in the amounts invested in human capital.

a. An investment in human capital increases the productivity of workers; and is the amount spent to improve the education, health, and mobility of workers.

b. Like the investments a business firm makes in such real capital as a machine, a worker decides to invest in human capital if the discounted value of the additional lifetime earnings that result from the investment are greater than the cost of the investment.

c. The human capital theory explains not only wage differentials and the rising level of real wages the United States has experienced historically, but other phenomena which would otherwise be mysteries.

d. But critics of the theory have questioned the effectiveness of investments in human capital in raising the productivity and incomes of the investors and in reducing poverty and income inequality.

■ IMPORTANT TERMS

Wage (rate)
Earnings
Money wage (rate)
Real wage (rate)
Marginal resource (labor) cost
Competitive labor market
Monopsony
Oligopsony
Exclusive unionism
Craft union
Occupational licensure
Inclusive unionism
Industrial union
Bilateral monopoly
Minimum wage
Wage differential
Noncompeting groups
Equalizing differences
Immobility
Theory of human capital
Human capital investment

■ FILL-IN QUESTIONS

1. A wage rate is the price paid for labor per unit of time________ and the earnings of labor are equal to the wage________ multiplied by time________; money wages are an amount of money, while real wages are the G&S the money wages will buy.________

2. The general level of wages is higher in the United States than in most foreign countries because:

a. The demand for labor in the U.S. is (strong, weak) strong________ relative to the supply of labor;

b. American labor tends to be highly productive, among other reasons, because it has relatively large amounts of capital equipment and ~~technology~~ natural res's________ with which to work and employs a generally superior technology________ to produce goods and because of the high quality________ of the American labor force.

3. In a competitive labor market:

a. the supply curve slopes upward from left to right because it is necessary for employers to pay higher wages________ to attract workers from alternative employment________

b. the demand is the sum of the demand (MRP) schedules________ of all firms hiring this type of labor;

c. the wage rate will equal the rate at which the total Q of L demanded________ and the total Q of L supplied________ are equal.

4. Insofar as an individual firm hiring labor in a competitive market is concerned, the supply of labor is perfectly elastic because the individual firm is unable to affect the wagerate it must pay.

5. The individual employer who hires labor in a competitive market hires that quantity of labor at which the MRP of labor is equal to the MRC or the wage rate

6. A monopsonist employing labor in a market which is competitive on the supply side will hire that amount of labor at which MRP ~~MLC~~ and MLC are equal. And because the marginal labor cost is (greater, less) greater than the wage rate in such a market the employer will pay a wage rate which is less than both the MRP of labor and the marginal labor cost

7. When compared with a competitive labor market, a market dominated by a monopsonist results in (higher, lower) lower wage rates and in (more, less) less employment.

8. The basic objective of labor unions is to raise wage rates; they attempt to accomplish this goal either by increasing the demand for labor, restricting the supply of labor, or imposing above-equil wage rates on employers.

9. Craft unions typically try to increase wages by restricting supply of labor while industrial unions try to increase wages by imposing above-equil wage rates

a. If they are successful, employment in the craft or industry is (decreased, increased, not affected) decreased

b. This effect on the employment of their members may lead unions to (increase, decrease) decrease their wage demands.

c. But unions will not worry too much about the effect on employment of higher wage rates if the economy is (growing, expanding, stationary) growing or if the demand for labor is relatively (elastic, inelastic) inelastic

10. Labor unions can increase the demand for the services of their members by increasing the demand for products they produces, by increasing the productivity of their members, and by increasing the prices of resources which are substitutes for the services supplied by their members.

11. In a labor market which is a bilateral monopoly, the monopsonist will not pay a wage greater than MRP of labor; the union will ask for some wage greater than the comp & monop equil wage Within these limits the wage rate will depend on bargaining strength of each

12. The imposition of effective minimum wage rates, ignoring any shock effects, in:

a. competitive labor markets is to (increase, decrease) increase the wage rate and to decrease employment.

b. monopsonistic labor markets is to increase the wage rate and to increase employment.

c. the economy as a whole seems to have been to increase the wage rate and to decrease employment.

13. Actual wage rates received by different workers tend to differ because workers are not homogeneous, because jobs differ in attractiveness, and because labor markets are imperfect

14. The total labor force is composed of a number of noncompeting groups of workers.

Within each of these groups some workers receive higher wages than others, and these wage differentials are called equalizing differences

15. Workers performing identical jobs often receive different wages; these differences are due to ____ immobilities of three basic types: geographical, sociological, and institutional

16. Investment according to the theory of human capital:

a. consists of expenditures for education heatth, ____, and Mobility

b. increases the productivity and wage rates of workers;

c. explains a good part of the increases in the level of real wages in the United States;

d. and accounts for the existence of noncompeting groups and differences in the wages and incomes among groups.

■ PROBLEMS AND PROJECTS

1. Suppose a single firm has for a particular type of labor the marginal revenue product schedule given in the following table.

Number of units of labor	MRP of labor
1	$15
2	14
3	13
4	12
5	11
6	10
7	9
8	8

a. Assume there are 100 firms with the same marginal-revenue-product schedules for this particular type of labor. Compute the total or market demand for this labor by completing column 1 in the table below.

(1) Quantity of labor demanded	(2) Wage rate	(3) Quantity of labor supplied
100	$15	850
200	14	800
300	13	750
400	12	700
500	11	650
600	10	600
700	9	550
800	8	500

b. Using the supply schedule for labor given in columns 2 and 3:

(1) What will be the equilibrium wage rate? $10.00

(2) What will be the total amount of labor hired in the market? 600

c. The individual firm will:

(1) have a marginal labor cost of $10.00

(2) employ 6 units of labor.

(3) pay a wage of $10.00

d. On the following graph plot the market demand and supply curves for labor and indicate the equilibrium wage rate and the total quantity of labor employed.

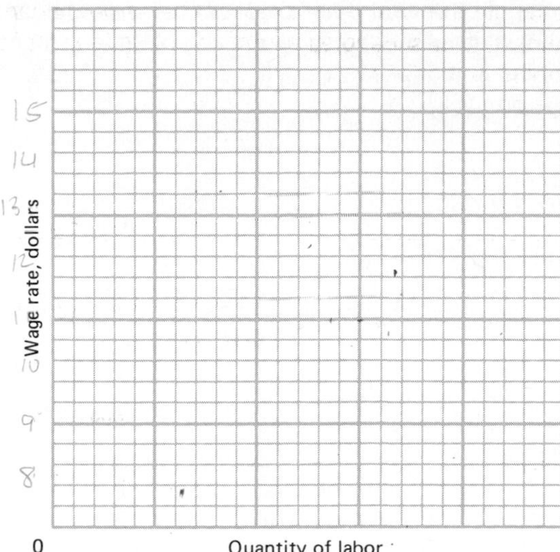

e. On the graph below plot the individual firm's demand curve for labor, the supply curve for labor, and the marginal-labor-cost curve which confronts the individual firm; and indicate the quantity of labor the firm will hire and the wage it will pay.

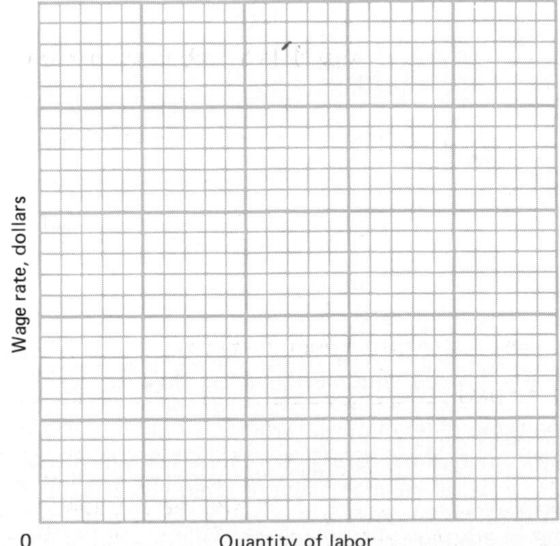

f. The imposition of a $12 minimum wage rate would change the total amount of labor hired in this market to ______________

2. In the table below assume a monopsonist has the marginal-revenue-product schedule for a particular type of labor given in columns 1 and 2 and that the supply schedule for labor is that given in columns 1 and 3.

(1) Number of labor units	(2) MRP of labor	(3) Wage rate	(4) Total labor cost	(5) Marginal labor cost
0		$ 2	$______	
1	$36	4	______	$______
2	32	6	______	______
3	28	8	______	______
4	24	10	______	______
5	20	12	______	______
6	16	14	______	______
7	12	16	______	______
8	8	18	______	______

a. Compute the firm's total labor costs at each level of employment and the marginal labor cost of each unit of labor, and enter these figures in columns 4 and 5.

b. The firm will:

(1) hire ______________ units of labor.

(2) pay a wage of $______________

(3) have a marginal revenue product for labor of $______________ for the last unit of labor employed.

c. Plot the marginal revenue product of labor, the supply curve for labor, and the marginal-labor-cost curve on the following graph and indicate the quantity of labor the firm will employ and the wage it will pay.

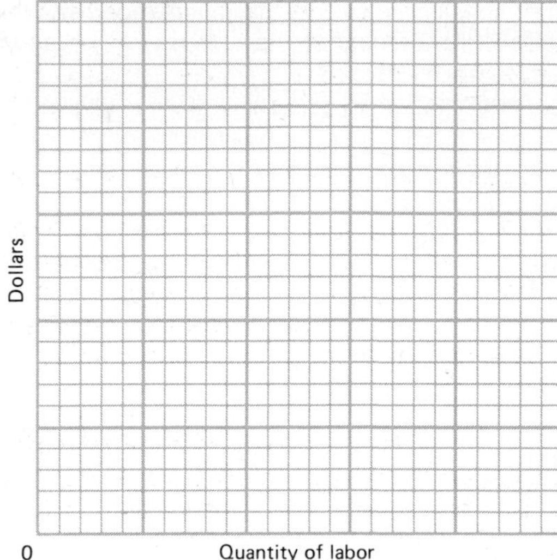

d. If this firm hired labor in a competitive labor market, it would hire at least ____________ units and pay a wage of at least $____________

3. Assume that the employees of the monopsonist in problem 2 organize a strong industrial union. The union demands a wage rate of $16 for its members, and the monopsonist decides to pay this wage because a strike would be too costly.

a. In the table below compute the supply schedule for labor which now confronts the monopsonist by completing column 2.

(1) Number of labor units	(2) Wage rate	(3) Total labor cost	(4) Marginal labor cost
1	$______	$______	$______
2	______	______	______
3	______	______	______
4	______	______	______
5	______	______	______
6	______	______	______
7	______	______	______
8	______	______	______

b. Compute the total labor cost and the marginal labor cost at each level of employment, and enter these figures in columns 3 and 4.

c. The firm will:

(1) hire ____________ units of labor.

(2) pay a wage of $____________

(3) pay total wages of $____________

d. As a result of unionization the wage rate has ____________, the level of employment has ____________, and the earnings of labor have ____________

e. On the graph below plot the firm's marginal revenue product of labor schedule, the labor supply schedule, and the marginal-labor-cost schedule. Indicate also the wage rate the firm will pay and the number of workers it will hire.

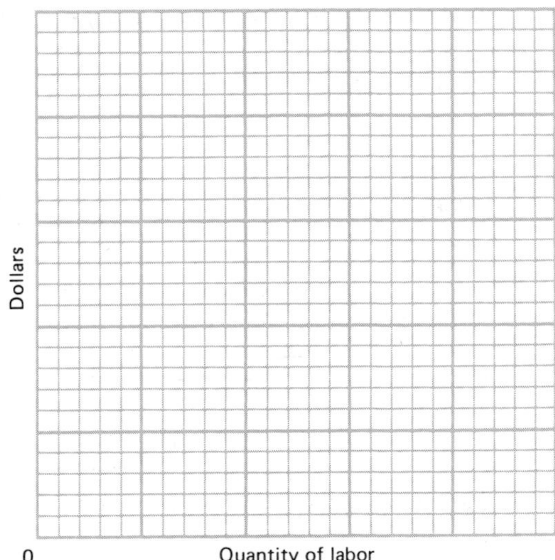

■ SELF TEST

Circle the T if the statement is true, the F if it is false.

1. The general level of real wages is higher in the United States than in many foreign countries because the supply of labor is large relative to the demand for it. **T F**

2. The average real income per worker and the average real output per worker in an economy are two names for the same thing. **T F**

3. If an individual firm employs labor in a competitive market, it finds that its marginal labor cost is equal to the wage rate in that market. T F

4. Given a competitive employer's demand for labor, the lower the wage it must pay the more workers it will hire. T F

5. Both monopsonists and firms hiring labor in competitive markets hire labor up to the quantity at which the marginal revenue product of labor and marginal labor cost are equal. T F

6. Restricting the supply of labor is a means of increasing wage rates more commonly used by craft unions than by industrial unions. T F

7. Occupational licensure has been one of the principal means employed by the Federal government to increase the number of blacks and Hispanics in certain skilled occupations and trades. T F

8. The imposition of an above-equilibrium wage rate will cause employment to fall off more when the demand for labor is inelastic than it will when the demand is elastic. T F

9. Union members are paid wage rates which on the average are greater by 10% or more than the wage rates paid to nonunion members. T F

10. The actions of both exclusive and inclusive unions that raise the wage rates paid to them by competitive employers of labor also cause, other things remaining constant, an increase in the employment of their members. T F

11. If a labor market is competitive, the imposition of an effective minimum wage will increase the wage rate paid and decrease employment in that market. T F

12. When an effective minimum wage is imposed upon a monopsonist the wage rate paid by the firm will increase and the number of workers employed by it may also increase. T F

13. An increase in the minimum wage rate in the American economy tends to increase the unemployment of teenagers and of others in low-wage occupations. T F

14. Actual wage rates received in different labor markets tend to differ because the demands for particular types of labor relative to their supplies differ. T F

15. "Ben Robbins is a skilled artisan of a particular type, is unable to obtain membership in the union representing that group of artisans, and is, therefore, unable to practice his trade." This is an example of labor immobility. T F

Circle the letter that corresponds to the best answer.

1. Real wages would decline if the: (*a*) prices of goods and services rose more rapidly than money-wage rates; (*b*) prices of goods and services rose less rapidly than money-wage rates; (*c*) prices of goods and services and wage rates both rose; (*d*) prices of goods and services and wage rates both fell.

2. Which of the following has *not* led to the generally high productivity of American workers? (*a*) The high level of real wage rates in the United States; (*b*) the superior quality of the American labor force; (*c*) the advanced technology utilized in American industries; (*d*) the large quantity of capital available to assist the average worker in the United States.

3. Between 1889 and 1969 output per hour of labor and real hourly wage rates increased in the United States at an average annual rate of (*a*) 2.4%; (*b*) 2.0%; (*c*) 1.6%; (*d*) 1.2%.

4. The individual firm which hires labor under competitive conditions faces a supply curve for labor which: (*a*) is perfectly inelastic; (*b*) is of unitary elasticity; (*c*) is perfectly elastic; (*d*) slopes upward from left to right.

5. A monopsonist pays a wage rate which is: (*a*) greater than the marginal revenue product of labor; (*b*) equal to the marginal revenue product of labor; (*c*) equal to the firm's marginal labor cost; (*d*) less than the marginal revenue product of labor.

6. Compared with a competitive labor market, a monopsonistic market will result in: (*a*) higher wage rates and a higher level of employment; (*b*) higher wage rates and a lower level of employment; (*c*) lower wage rates and a higher level of employment; (*d*) lower wage rates and a lower level of employment.

7. Higher wage rates and a higher level of employment are the usual consequences of: (*a*) inclusive unionism; (*b*) exclusive unionism; (*c*) an above-equilibrium wage rate; (*d*) an increase in the productivity of labor.

8. Which of the following would *not* increase the demand for a particular type of labor? (*a*) An increase in the productivity of that type of labor; (*b*) an increase in the prices of those resources which are substitutes for that type of labor; (*c*) an increase in the prices of those resources which are complements to that type of labor; (*d*) an increase in the demand for the products produced by that type of labor.

9. Industrial unions typically attempt to increase wage rates by: (*a*) imposing an above-equilibrium wage rate upon employers; (*b*) increasing the demand for labor; (*c*) decreasing the supply of labor; (*d*) forming a bilateral monopoly.

Use the data in the table below to answer multiple-choice questions 10, 11, and 12.

Wage rate	Quantity of labor supplied	Marginal labor cost	Marginal revenue product of labor
$10	0	—	$18
11	100	$11	17
12	200	13	16
13	300	15	15
14	400	17	14
15	500	19	13
16	600	21	12

10. If the firm employing labor were a monopsonist the wage rate and the quantity of labor employed would be, respectively, (*a*) $14 and 300; (*b*) $13 and 400; (*c*) $14 and 400; (*d*) $13 and 300.

11. But if the market for this labor were competitive the wage rate and the quantity of labor employed would be, respectively, (*a*) $14 and 300; (*b*) $13 and 400; (*c*) $14 and 400; (*d*) $13 and 300.

12. If the firm employing labor were a monopsonist and the workers were represented by an industrial union, the wage rate would be (*a*) between $13 and $14; (*b*) between $13 and $15; (*c*) between $14 and $15; (*d*) below $13 or above $15.

13. The fact that a baseball player receives a wage of $800,000 a year can *best* be explained in terms of: (*a*) noncompeting labor groups; (*b*) equalizing differences; (*c*) labor immobility; (*d*) imperfections in the labor market.

14. The fact that unskilled construction workers receive higher wages than gas-station attendants is *best* explained in terms of: (*a*) noncompeting labor groups; (*b*) equalizing differences; (*c*) labor immobility; (*d*) imperfections in the labor market.

15. Which of the following is *not* true? (*a*) investment in human capital, according to the proponents of the human-capital theory, increases the productivity of workers; (*b*) expenditures for health, education, and mobility are investments in human capital; (*c*) whether to invest in real capital is a decision similar to the decision whether to invest in human capital; (*d*) differences in the amounts invested in human capital, human-capital theorists argue, explain the equalizing differences in wage rates.

■ DISCUSSION QUESTIONS

1. Why is the general level of real wages higher in the United States than in most foreign nations? Why has the level of real wages continued to increase even though the supply of labor has continually increased?

2. Explain why the productivity of the American labor force increased in the past to its present high level.

3. In the competitive model what determines the market demand for labor and the wage rate? What kind of supply situation do all firms as a group confront? What kind of supply situation does the individual firm confront? Why?

4. In the monopsony model what determines employment and the wage rate? What kind of supply situation does the monopsonist face? Why? How does the wage rate paid and the level of employment compare with what would result if the market were competitive?

5. In what sense is a worker who is hired by a monopsonist "exploited" and one who is employed in a competitive labor market "justly" rewarded? Why do monopsonists wish to restrict employment?

6. When supply is less than perfectly elastic, marginal labor cost is greater than the wage rate. Why?

7. What basic methods do labor unions employ to try to increase the wages received by their members? If these methods are successful in raising wages, what effect do they have upon employment?

8. What three methods might labor employ to increase the demand for labor? If these methods are successful, what effects do they have upon wage rates and employment?

9. When labor unions attempt to restrict the supply of labor to increase wage rates, what devices do they employ to do this for the economy as a whole and what means do they use to restrict the supply of a given type of worker?

10. How do industrial unions attempt to increase wage rates, and what effect does this method of increasing wages have upon employment in the industry affected?

11. Both exclusive and inclusive unions are able to raise the wage rates received by their members. Why might unions limit or temper their demands for higher wages? What two factors determine the extent to which they will or will not reduce their demands for higher wages?

12. What is bilateral monopoly? What determines wage rates in a labor market of this type?

13. What is the effect of minimum wage laws upon wage rates and employment in (*a*) competitive labor markets; (*b*) monopsony labor markets; (*c*) the economy as a whole?

14. How (*a*) do the wage rates paid to union members differ from those paid to nonunion employees; (*b*) do minimum wage rates affect the employment of workers in high- and low-wage occupations?

15. Why are the wage rates received by workers in different occupations, by workers in the same occupations, and by workers in different localities different?

16. Explain what is meant by investment in human capital and why the decision to invest in human capital is like the decision to invest in real capital. What, according to the proponents of the human-capital theory, is the effect of investment in human capital upon the productivity, the wage rate, and the income of workers?

17. Using the theory of human capital, explain (*a*) geographic differences in wage rates; (*b*) why younger people are more mobile; (*c*) why a society tends to educate younger rather than older people; and (*d*) the historic rise in real wages in the American economy.

18. Outline the argument of the critics of the theory of human capital and the important public-policy issue which their criticism raises.

33
The pricing and employment of resources: rent, interest, and profits

Chapter 33 concludes the study of the prices of resources by examining rent, interest, and profits. Compared with the study of wage rates in Chapter 32, each of the first three major sections in Chapter 33 is considerably briefer and a good deal simpler. You might do well to treat these sections as if they were actually three minichapters.

There is nothing especially difficult about Chapter 33. By now you should understand that the marginal revenue product of a resource determines the demand for that resource and that this understanding can be applied to the demand for land and capital. It will be on the supply side of the land market that you will encounter whatever difficulties there are. The supply of land is unique because it is perfectly *inelastic:* changes in rent do not change the quantity of land which will be supplied. Demand, given the quantity of land available, is thus the sole determinant of rent. Of course land varies in productivity and can be used for different purposes, but these are merely the factors which explain why the rent on all land is not the same.

Capital, as the economist defines it, means capital goods. Is the rate of interest, then, the price paid for the use of capital goods? No, not quite. Capital is not one kind of good; it is many different kinds. In order to be able to talk about the price paid for the use of capital goods there must be a simple way of adding up different kinds of capital goods. The simple way is to measure the quantity of capital goods in terms of money. The rate of interest is, then, the price paid for the use of money (or of financial capital). It is the demand for and the supply of money that determine the rate of interest in the economy. Business firms and households wish to hold—that is, demand—money for two principal reasons. Like the demand for any other good or service, the greater the price of using money (the interest rate) the smaller is the amount of money firms and households will wish to hold. And like other *normal* goods and services, the greater the economy's income (GNP) the greater will be the demand for money.

On the supply side, the Federal Reserve Banks, the monetary authority in the American economy, determine how much money will be available. At any time the supply of money is a fixed quantity. This means that the quantity of money available does not rise or fall as a result of changes in the interest rate; and the supply of money is said to be perfectly inelastic. It is this perfectly inelastic supply and the demand for money that determine the equilibrium interest rate. Like other commodities a change in either the supply of or the demand for money will cause this equilibrium interest rate to change.

This theory of interest will be familiar to you if you have previously studied Chapters 12, 17, and 19 in the macroeconomic-principles parts of the text; but you may wish to review the relevant parts of those chapters. If you have not yet studied these chapters you should probably examine them. Footnote number 3 in Chapter 33 of the text tells you which sections of these three chapters should be read by you.

When it comes to profits, supply and demand analysis fails the economist. Profits are not merely a wage for a particular type of labor; rather they are rewards for taking risks and the gains of the monopolist. Such things as "the quantity of risk taken" or "the quantity of effort required to establish a monopoly" simply can't be measured; consequently it is impossible to talk about the demand for or the supply of them. Nevertheless, profits are important in the economy. They are largely rewards for doing things that have to be done if the economy is to allocate resources efficiently and to progress and develop; they are the lure or the bait which makes people willing to take the risks that result in efficiency and progress.

The final section of Chapter 33 answers two questions about the American economy. What part of the national income goes to workers and what part goes to capitalists—those who provide the economy with land, capital goods, and entrepreneurial ability? And have the shares going to workers and to capitalists changed in the past eighty or so years? The student may be surprised to learn that the lion's share—about 80%—of the national income goes to workers today and went to workers at the beginning of the century; and that capitalists today and in 1900 got about 20%. There is, in short, no evidence to support the belief that workers get less and capitalists more or the opposite belief that workers obtain a greater part and capitalists a smaller part of the national income today than they did three-quarters of a century ago in the United States.

■ CHECKLIST

When you have studied this chapter you should be able to:

☐ Define economic rent and explain what determines the amount of economic rent paid.

☐ Explain why economic rent is a surplus (or unearned income); and state the means Henry George and the socialists would use to recover this surplus.

☐ Explain why the owners of land do not all receive the same economic rent; and why, if economic rent is a surplus, a firm must pay rent.

☐ Define the interest rate and explain why interest rates differ.

☐ Identify the two demands for money and explain what determines the amount of money that will be demanded for each of these two purposes.

☐ Explain what the equilibrium rate of interest in the economy will be when the monetary authority has determined the supply (or stock) of money.

☐ State how much money (or financial capital) an individual business firm will tend to borrow at the equilibrium interest rate.

☐ Distinguish between the nominal and the real interest rate; and explain how the latter is related to the former.

☐ Explain how the real interest rate affects investment spending and the equilibrium NNP; and the allocation of capital goods among firms (the composition of the production of real capital).

☐ Define economic profit and distinguish between economic profit, normal profit, and business profit.

☐ Explain why profits are received by some firms and the functions of profits in the American economy.

☐ State the current relative size of labor's and of capital's share of the national income and describe what has happened to these shares in the U.S. economy since 1900.

■ CHAPTER OUTLINE

1. Economic rent is the price paid for the use of land or natural resources whose supply is perfectly inelastic.

a. Demand is the active determinant of economic rent because changes in the level of economic rent do not change the quantity of land supplied; and economic rent is, therefore, a payment which in the aggregate need not be paid to ensure that the land will be available.

b. Some people have argued that land rents are unearned incomes, and that either land should be nationalized or rents should be taxed away; and the single tax advocated by Henry George would have no effect on resource allocation in the economy.

(1) Critics have pointed out three disadvantages of such a tax.

(2) But there is a renewed interest in taxing land values to improve the equity and efficiency of local tax systems.

c. Economic rents on different types of land vary because land differs in its productivity.

d. Land has alternative uses; and rent is a cost to a firm because it must pay rent to lure land away from alternative employments.

2. The interest rate is the price paid for the use of money.

a. While it is convenient to speak as if there were but a single interest rate there are actually a number of different rates of interest.

b. The transaction demand for money is directly related to the level of money GNP and the asset demand is inversely related to the rate of interest; and these two demands along with the supply of money (controlled by the monetary authority) determine the equilibrium rate of interest.

(1) The quantity of real capital demanded in the economy and the quantities of real and financial capital demanded by individual firms is inversely related to the equilibrium interest rate.

(2) But it is the real interest rate (the nominal interest rate less the rate of inflation) that determines the quantities of capital demanded.

c. The interest rate plays two roles.

(1) Because of the inverse relationship between the interest rate and total investment, the level of the interest rate affects the total output of capital goods and the equilibrium NNP of an economy.

(2) The interest rate rations (allocates) financial and real capital among competing firms and determines the composition of the total output of capital goods.

3. Economic profit is what remains of the firm's revenues after all its explicit and implicit opportunity costs have been deducted.

a. Profit is a payment for entrepreneurial ability, which involves combining and directing the use of resources in an uncertain and innovating world.

b. Profits are

(1) rewards for assuming the risks in an economy in which the future is uncertain and subject to change;

(2) rewards for assuming the risks and uncertainties inherent in innovation; and

(3) surpluses which business firms obtain from the exploitation of monopoly power.

c. The expectation of profits motivates business firms to innovate, and profits (and losses) guide business firms to produce products and to use resources in the way desired by society.

4. National income data for the American economy indicate the following.

a. In the period 1982–1984 wages and salaries were 75% of the national income, but using a broader definition of labor income (wages and salaries plus proprietors' income—which is mostly a payment for labor), labor's share was about 80% and capital's share (rent, interest, and corporate profits) was about 20% of national income.

b. Since the years 1900–1909 wages and salaries have increased from 55 to about 75%.

(1) But labor's share, employing the broader definition of labor income, has remained at about 80% and capital's share at about 20% of the national income because of the structural changes which occurred in the American economy.

(2) The growth of labor unions in the United States does not explain the increases in the wages and salaries received by workers.

(3) The pursuit-and-escape theory may explain the stability of labor's and capital's shares of the national income.

■ IMPORTANT TERMS

Economic rent
Incentive function
Single-tax movement
Truth in Lending Act
The (*or* pure) rate of interest
The theory of interest
Transaction demand (for money)
Asset demand (for money)
Nominal (money) interest rate
Real interest rate
Normal profit
Economic (pure) profit
Static economy
Insurable risk
Uninsurable risk
Pursuit-and-escape theory

■ FILL-IN QUESTIONS

1. Rent is the price paid for the use of ______ and ______ and their total supply is ______

2. The active determinant of rent is (demand, supply) ______ and the passive determinant is ______ . Because rent does *not* perform a(n) (rationing, incentive) ______ function economists consider it to be a ______

3. Socialists argue that land rents are (earned, unearned) ______ incomes and that land should be ______ so that these incomes can be used for the good of society as a whole. Proponents of the ______ argue that economic rent could be completely taxed away without affecting the amount of land available for productive purposes.

4. Rents on different pieces of land are not the same because ______ . And while rent from the viewpoint of the economy as a whole is a surplus, rent is a cost to ______ users of land which must be paid because land has ____________

5. Interest is the price paid for the use of ____________; and interest rates on different loans tend to differ because of differences in ____________, ____________, and ____________, and because of ____________

6. There are two components in the demand for money.

a. The ____________ demand is directly related to the ____________

b. And the ____________ demand is inversely related to the ____________

7. In the American economy:

a. At any moment the money supply is an amount determined by ____________

b. The equilibrium interest rate is the rate at which the ____________ is equal to ____________

8. Were the Federal Reserve Banks to increase the money supply, the equilibrium rate of interest would (increase, decrease) ____________ and investment spending would ____________. As a result the equilibrium NNP would ____________

9. As far as the individual business firm is concerned:

a. The supply of financial and real capital at the equilibrium rate of interest is perfectly (elastic, inelastic) ____________

b. The profit-maximizing amount of financial and real capital to employ in producing goods and services is the amount at which the ____________ and the ____________ are equal.

10. The (nominal, real) ____________ interest rate is equal to the ____________ interest rate minus the rate of ____________; and it is the ____________ interest rate that is crucial in determining how much business firms will invest.

11. In the American economy the interest rate is an "____________ price"; but it performs two important functions. It helps to determine how much ____________ will occur in the economy and then ____________ it among various firms and industries.

12. Normal profits are a payment for the resource called (land, labor, capital, entrepreneurial ability) ____________ and this resource performs four functions: It combines the other ____________ to produce goods and services, makes (routine, nonroutine) ____________ decisions for the firm, (invents, innovates) ____________ new products and production processes, and bears the economic (costs, risks, criticisms) ____________ associated with the other three functions.

13. When the future is ____________, businesses necessarily assume risks, some of which are ____________ and some of which are ____________. The risks which businesses cannot avoid arise either because the ____________ is changing or because the firm itself deliberately engages in ____________

14. Profits:

a. Are important in the American economy because the expectation of profits stimulates firms to innovate, and the more innovation there is, the higher will be the levels of ____________, ____________, and ____________ in the economy;

b. and losses promote the efficient ____________ of resources in the economy unless the profits are the result of (competition, monopoly) ____________

15. Defining labor income broadly to include both wages and salaries and proprietors' income:

a. Labor's share of the national income is today about 80 %;

b. The capitalists' share is the sum of rent, interest, corporate π, and ______; and is today about 20 % of the national income;

c. Since the beginning of the twentieth century:

(1) Labor's share has (increased, decreased, remained constant) remained constant

(2) Capital's share has remained constant

16. The pursuit-and-escape theory suggests that:

a. when laborers increase their money wages they are in pursuit of the profits of business firms;

b. businesses escape by raising productivity and product prices;

c. and that as a result labor's share of national Y remains constant.

■ PROBLEMS AND PROJECTS

1. Assume that the quantity of a certain type of land available is 300,000 acres and the demand for this land is that given in the table below.

Pure land rent, per acre	Land demanded, acres
$350	100,000
300	200,000
250	300,000
200	400,000
150	500,000
100	600,000
50	700,000

a. The pure rent on this land will be $______

b. The total quantity of land rented will be ______ acres.

c. On the graph below plot the supply and demand curves for this land and indicate the pure rent for land and the quantity of land rented.

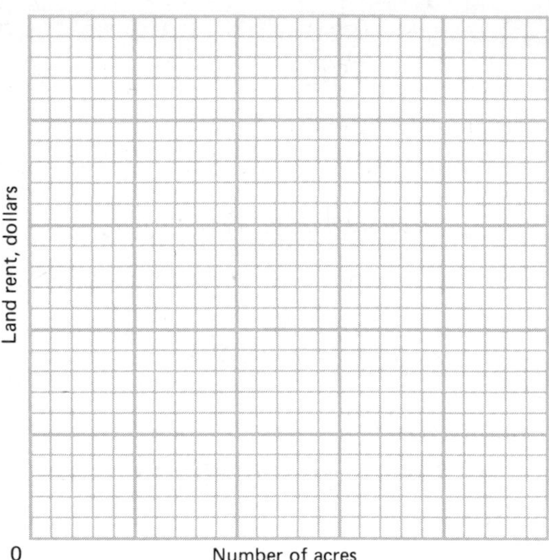

d. If landowners were taxed at a rate of $250 per acre for their land, the pure rent on this land after taxes would be $______ but the number of acres rented would be ______

2. The schedule below shows the asset demand for money.

Interest rate	Asset demand for money
8%	$ 60
7%	80
6%	100
5%	120
4%	140
3%	160
2%	180

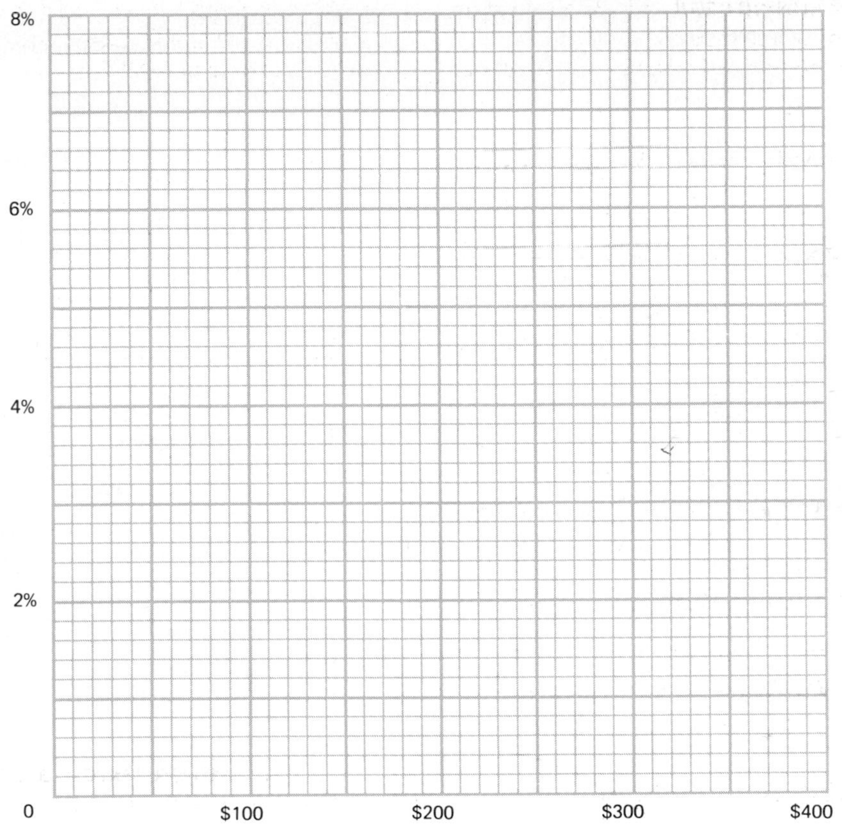

a. Plot this schedule on the graph above. (The interest rate is measured along the vertical axis and the demand for money is measured along the horizontal axis.)

b. Below is a schedule which shows the transactions demand for money. Suppose the GNP is $850.

GNP	Transactions demand for money
$ 750	$160
800	170
850	180
900	190
950	200
1000	210
1050	220

(1) The transactions demand for money is $________

(2) Plot this demand for money on the graph. (The curve will be a vertical line.)

c. In the table at the top of the next page show the total transactions and asset demand for money at each of the seven interest rates when the GNP is $850; and plot this demand for money on the graph.

d. Suppose the money supply is a fixed amount and equal to $280.

(1) Plot the money supply curve on the graph above. (It will be a vertical line.)

(2) Enter the supply of money at each of the seven interest rates in the next column in the table.

(3) Using either the money demand and supply curves or schedules, the equilibrium interest rate when GNP is $850 is ________________%.

Interest rate	Demand for money	Supply of money
8%	$______	$______
7%	______	______
6%	______	______
5%	______	______
4%	______	______
3%	______	______
2%	______	______

e. If a firm had the marginal revenue product of capital schedule (a demand for capital) given in the table below, it would at the equilibrium rate of interest wish to employ $______________ of financial and real capital.

Quantity of capital	Marginal revenue product of capital
$100,000	8%
200,000	7
300,000	6
400,000	5
500,000	4
600,000	3
700,000	2

f. Suppose the GNP remains at $850.

(1) If the money supply were to increase to $300:

(*a*) the rate of interest would (rise, fall) __________ to __________%;

(*b*) and the firm in *e* (above) would (increase, decrease) __________ the amount of capital it wishes to employ to $__________

(2) if the money supply were to decrease to $240:

(*a*) the rate of interest would ______________________________

(*b*) and the firm in *e* (above) would ______________________________

3. What would the

a. real rate of interest be if the nominal interest rate were 14% and the annual rate of inflation were 8%? __________%

b. the nominal rate of interest be if the real interest rate were 4% and the annual rate of inflation were 6%? __________%

4. The table below shows estimated wages and salaries, proprietors' income, corporate profits, interest, rent, and the national income of the United States in 1985.

Wages and salaries	$2373 billion
Proprietors' income	242 billion
Corporate profits	299 billion
Interest	288 billion
Rent	14 billion
National income	3216 billion

a. Wages and salaries were __________% of the national income.

b. Labor's share of the national income was __________% and capital's share was __________%.

■ SELF-TEST

Circle the T if the statement is true, the F if it is false.

1. Rent is the price paid for the use of land and other property resources. **T F**

2. Rent is a surplus because it does not perform an incentive function. **T F**

3. Rent is unique because it is not determined by demand and supply. **T F**

4. The renewed interest in land taxation is the result of the Federal government's search for additional revenue with which to balance its budget. **T F**

5. Money is an economic resource and the interest rate is the price paid for this resource. **T F**

6. The transactions demand for money is directly related to the level of money GNP. **T F**

7. The asset demand for money is inversely related to the interest rate. T F

8. A decrease in the money supply would tend to increase the interest rate and to decrease investment spending and the equilibrium NNP. T F

9. It is the nominal rather than the real interest rate that determines the amounts invested by business firms in additional capital. T F

10. A normal profit is the minimum payment the entrepreneur must expect to receive to induce him or her to provide a firm with entrepreneurial ability. T F

11. If the economists' definition of profits were used, total profits in the economy would be greater than they would be if the accountants' definition were used. T F

12. The expectation of profits is the basic motive for innovation, while actual profits and losses aid in the efficient allocation of resources. T F

13. The increasing importance of the corporation in the American economy is a part of the explanation of why wages and salaries have increased as shares of the national income. T F

14. The growth of labor unions is the main cause of the expansion of wages and salaries as a share of the national income. T F

15. Over the past seventy-five years there has been a shift from labor-intensive to capital- and land-intensive production. T F

Circle the letter that corresponds to the best answer.

1. The supply of land is: (*a*) perfectly inelastic; (*b*) of unitary elasticity; (*c*) perfectly elastic; (*d*) elastic but not perfectly elastic.

2. Which of the following is *not* characteristic of the tax proposed by Henry George? (*a*) It would be equal to 100 percent of all land rent; (*b*) it would be the only tax levied by government; (*c*) it would not affect the supply of land; (*d*) it would reduce rents paid by the amount of the tax.

3. A single tax on land in the United States would (*a*) bring in tax revenues sufficient to finance all current government spending; (*b*) be impractical because it is difficult to distinguish between payments for the use of land and those for the use of capital; (*c*) tax all "unearned" incomes in the economy at a rate of 100%; (*d*) be or do all of the above.

4. Which of the following is *not* true? (*a*) The greater the demand for land, the greater will be the economic rent paid for the use of land; (*b*) the "windfall profits" tax on the increases in the profits of petroleum producers which have resulted from the rise in oil prices is a good example of a tax on economic rent; (*c*) individual users of land have to pay a rent to its owners because that land has alternative uses; (*d*) the less productive a particular piece of land is, the greater will be the rent its owner is able to earn from it.

5. The smaller the *rate* of interest on a loan: (*a*) the greater the risk involved; (*b*) the shorter the length of the loan; (*c*) the smaller the amount of the loan; (*d*) the greater the imperfections in the money market.

6. If the nominal interest rate were 10% and the annual rate of inflation were 4%, the real interest rate would be (*a*) 14%; (*b*) 6%; (*c*) 2½%; (*d*) −6%.

7. Changes in the rate of interest do *not:* (*a*) affect the total amount of investment in the economy; (*b*) affect the amount of investment occurring in particular industries; (*c*) guarantee that the demand for and the supply of money will be equal; (*d*) guarantee that there will be full employment in the economy.

8. The profit-maximizing amount of financial and real capital an individual firm would employ is the amount at which the interest rate is equal to the (*a*) marginal revenue product of capital; (*b*) marginal physical product of capital; (*c*) marginal cost of capital; (*d*) marginal resource cost of capital.

9. If the annual rate of interest were 18% and the rate of profit a firm expects to earn annually by building a new plant were 20%, the firm would (*a*) not build the new plant; (*b*) build the new plant; (*c*) have to toss a coin to decide whether to build the new plant; (*d*) not be able to determine from these figures whether to build the plant.

10. Which of the following is an economic cost? (*a*) Business profit; (*b*) normal profit; (*c*) economic profit; (d) windfall profit.

11. Which of the following would *not* be a function of the entrepreneur? (*a*) The introduction of a new product on the market; (*b*) the making of decisions in a static economy; (*c*) the incurring of unavoidable risks; (*d*) the combination and direction of resources in an uncertain environment.

12. Business firms obtain profits because (*a*) not all risks are insurable; (*b*) not all markets are competitive; (*c*) the economy is dynamic; (*d*) of all of these.

13. The monopolist who obtains an economic profit is able to do so because: (*a*) he is an innovator; (*b*) all his risks are insurable; (*c*) uncertainty has been reduced to the minimum; (*d*) most of his decisions are nonroutine.

14. Since around 1900: (*a*) capital's share of national income has increased; (*b*) labor's share has increased; (*c*) labor's share has decreased; (*d*) capital's share has been almost constant.

15. In the pursuit-and-escape theory (*a*) labor attempts by obtaining higher wages to reduce the profits of business firms; (*b*) business firms prevent decreases in their profits by increasing the productivity of labor; (*c*) business firms prevent decreases in their profits by increasing the prices they charge consumers; (*d*) all of the above occur.

■ DISCUSSION QUESTIONS

1. Explain what determines the economic rent paid for the use of land. What is unique about the supply of land?

2. Why is land rent a "surplus"? What economic difficulties would be encountered if the government adopted Henry George's single tax proposal as a means of confiscating this surplus? What arguments are used to support the renewed interest in the heavy taxation of land values?

3. Even though land rent is an economic surplus it is also an economic cost for the individual user of land. Why and how can it be both an economic surplus and an economic cost?

4. What is the interest rate? What is the difference between the nominal and real interest rate, and why is the real interest rate the determinant of investment spending by individual firms in the economy?

5. Why are there actually many different rates in the economy at any given time?

6. Explain what determines (*a*) the amount of money firms and households wish to hold for transaction purposes; (*b*) the amount they wish to have for asset purposes; (*c*) the amount of money available for these purposes; and (*d*) the equilibrium rate of interest.

7. How would a change in the money supply affect (*a*) the interest rate; (*b*) investment spending; and (*c*) the equilibrium NNP?

8. What two important functions does the rate of interest perform in the economy?

9. What are profits? For what resource are they a payment, and what tasks does this resource perform?

10. Why would there be no economic profits in a purely competitive static economy?

11. "The risks which an entrepreneur assumes arise because of uncertainties which are external to the firm and because of uncertainties which are developed by the initiative of the firm itself." Explain.

12. What two important functions do profits or the expectation of profits perform in the economy? How does monopoly impede the effective performance of these functions?

13. Monopoly results in profits and reduces uncertainty. Is it possible that monopolists may undertake more innovation as a result? Why?

14. What part of the American national income is wages and salaries and what part is labor income? Why do your answers to these two questions differ? What part of the national income is the income of capitalists? What kinds of income are capitalist income?

15. What have been the historical trends in the shares of national income that are wages and salaries, labor income, and capitalist income? What changes in the American economy can account for these trends?

16. Explain (*a*) why the growth of labor unions is not a good explanation of the expanding share of the national income going for wages and salaries; (*b*) the pursuit-and-escape theory.

34
General equilibrium: the price system and its operation

Chapter 34 provides a conclusion to the previous ten chapters and ties together many of the things you have already learned about microeconomics. By this time you have read a large amount of material concerning the operation of supply and demand in product and resource markets and under different market conditions. You may have lost sight of the fact—emphasized in Chapter 5—that the American economy is a *system* of markets and prices. This means that *all* prices and *all* markets are linked together.

The chief purpose of Chapter 34 is to help you understand why and how these markets are linked together, connected, and interrelated. The theory which explains the relationships between different markets and different prices is called *general* equilibrium analysis. (By way of contrast, the theory which explains a single product or resource market and the price of the one good or service bought and sold in that market is called *partial* equilibrium analysis.) An understanding of general equilibrium is necessary in order to understand how the price system as a whole operates to allocate its scarce resources.

The author employs three approaches to enable the student to grasp the essentials and the importance of general equilibrium analysis. He first illustrates general equilibrium by examining the effects of an increase in the demand for automobiles. Then, using graphs and curves, he explains in more detail the effects of an increase in the demand for a hypothetical product X accompanied by a decrease in the demand for product Y. Both of these explanations include not only the short- and long-run effects upon the products involved but also the effects upon the markets in which the producers employ resources, upon the markets for complementary and substitute products, upon the markets in which the resources used to produce these other products are employed, and upon the distribution of income in the economy. Finally, to help you understand the interrelationships between the different sectors of the economy, the author employs an input-output table.

Having examined these market and price interrelationships, you should next note this. Given the distribution of income among consumers, and subject to several important exceptions, a price system in which all markets are purely competitive will bring about an ideal allocation of the economy's resources. It will maximize the satisfaction of consumer wants and thereby maximize economic welfare in the economy. The American economy, of course, is *not* made up of purely competitive markets. And because of these imperfectly competitive markets, the allocation of resources is actually less than ideal and economic welfare is somewhat less than a maximum.

In addition—and these are important exceptions—even a purely competitive price system does not allocate resources to allow for the spillover costs and the spillover benefits of the products it produces; and it does not produce social goods in sufficient quantities. Hence government seems to be needed (remember the fourth economic function of government in Chapter 6) to adjust output for spillover costs and benefits and to provide society with social goods.

A price system that allocates resources ideally does not necessarily distribute its total output (or income) in accordance with our ethical standards. Economists don't and probably never will know which of the many possible distributions of income is ideal. But according to society's notions of what is right and wrong (just and unjust), it is wrong to have highly unequal distributions of incomes, or incomes below a certain minimum level. Hence the third economic function of government: the redistribution of income and wealth.

Chapter 34 ends by reemphasizing the importance of general equilibrium analysis. Interrelations between markets and prices do exist, and they can be extremely important in tracing through the economy the *total effect* of an economic policy or the *full consequences* of changes in consumers' tastes, the availability of resources (oil, for example), and technology. At the conclusion of this chapter you should be ready to examine several of the trouble spots in the operation of the price system and in the way in which we allocate our scarce resources. These trouble spots are examined in the next six chapters which make up Part 6 of the text.

■ CHECKLIST

When you have studied this chapter you should be able to:

☐ Distinguish between partial and general equilibrium analysis.

☐ Identify the four concepts which underlie the demand and supply curves in the product and resource markets of the economy.

☐ Explain, using graphs if you wish, both the immediate and secondary effects of a change in tastes, technology, or the availability of resources upon equilibrium prices and quantities in the product and resource markets; and upon the distribution of income in the economy.

☐ List the three reasons why a purely competitive price system tends to produce the goods and services which maximize consumer welfare.

☐ State the two ways in which the real world differs from a purely competitive price system; and explain the effect of these two imperfections upon allocative efficiency.

☐ Present two reasons why, given the distribution of income, even a purely competitive economy would not allocate resources so effectively as possible.

☐ Explain why economists are unable to determine which distribution of income is the best.

☐ Specify what is shown along the left side, along the top, and in each of the boxes of an input-output table.

☐ Find the effects, when you are given an input-output table, of a change in the output of one industry upon the outputs of other industries in the economy.

■ CHAPTER OUTLINE

1. Partial equilibrium analysis is the study of equilibrium prices and quantities in the specific product and resource markets which form the price-market system. General equilibrium analysis is the study of the interrelations among these markets.

2. Any change in tastes, in the supply of resources, or in technology will not only have an immediate effect upon equilibrium price and quantity in a specific market, but will also have secondary effects in other markets and upon other equilibrium prices and quantities.

3. To understand the effects of an increase in consumer demand for product X accompanied by a decrease in consumer demand for product Y, imagine that the industry producing X uses only type A labor and that the industry producing Y uses only type B labor.

a. Assume also that the demand curve for each product has a negative slope because of diminishing marginal utility and the supply curve has a positive slope because of increasing marginal cost; and assume that the demand curve for each type of labor has a negative slope because of diminishing marginal product and the supply curve has a positive slope because of the work-leisure preferences of workers.

b. Beginning with all markets in long-run equilibrium, the short-run effects are an increased (decreased) output and price and economic profits (losses) in industry X (Y), an increased (decreased) derived demand for type A (type B) labor, and increased (decreased) wage rates and employment for type A (type B) labor.

c. The long-run adjustments are the entry (exit) of firms in industry X (Y); an increase (decrease) in the supply of X (Y); a higher (lower) price than existed initially in industry X (Y), assuming increasing-cost industries; an increase (decrease) in the supply of A (B); and higher (lower) wage rates for A (B) than initially existed.

d. In addition to these adjustments there will also be:

(1) An increase (decrease) in the demand for and the prices and outputs of products which are substitutes (complements) for X or complements (substitutes) for Y; and an increased (decreased) demand for the resources used to produce those products whose outputs increase (decrease).

(2) An increase (decrease) in the demand for the other resources used along with A (B).

(3) A redistribution of income from workers and entrepreneurs in industry Y to those in industry X.

4. Given the distribution of consumer income, purely competitive product and resource markets result in an allocation of an economy's resources and the output of

goods and services that is
a. allocatively efficient;
b. productively efficient; and
c. maximizes the satisfaction of wants.

5. To the extent that product and resource markets in the real world are imperfectly competitive, the satisfaction of wants will be less than a maximum, and adjustments to changes will be less complete and slower. But this may be offset by more rapid technological progress and a greater variety of products.

6. For two reasons, even an economy in which all markets are perfectly competitive may not allocate resources efficiently.
a. The price system does not take spillover costs and spillover benefits into account and does not automatically produce social goods.
b. The price system may not distribute the economy's income ideally or optimally.

7. The input-output table indicates the specific relationships that exist among the outputs of the various sectors of the economy.
a. The outputs of each sector are the inputs of the other sectors; and the inputs of each sector are the outputs of the other sectors.
b. Because of this interdependence, any change in the output of one sector will alter the outputs of the other sectors.

8. General equilibrium analysis is important because it provides a wider understanding of the effects of any economic change or policy upon the economy.
a. Real-world examples illustrate the importance of general equilibrium analysis.
b. And input-output analysis is used for economic forecasting and, in underdeveloped nations and the U.S.S.R., for economic planning.

■ IMPORTANT TERMS

Price system
Partial equilibrium analysis
General equilibrium analysis
Input-output analysis
Input-output table

■ FILL-IN QUESTIONS

1. Partial equilibrium analysis is concerned with prices and outputs in ___particular___ markets in the economy, and general equilibrium analysis is concerned with the ___interrelationships___ among markets and prices.

2. General equilibrium exists in an economy where there is ___equilibrium___ in all the ___product___ and ___resource___ markets in the economy.

3. A change in the demand for product Z will affect not only the equilibrium price and quantity of product Z but may also affect the equilibrium price and quantity of:
a. ___res's used for Z___
b. ___other products w/ same res'___
c. ___subs or comp. for Z___
d. ________________

4. The economic changes or disturbances which may result not only in "big splashes" but also in little waves and ripples are of three basic types: changes in ________, changes in ________________, and changes in ________________

5. When studying the markets for products and for resources, we assume that the demand curves slope ________________ and the supply curves slope ________________
a. The slope of the demand curve for:
(1) Products is due to ________________
(2) Resources is due to ________________
b. The slope of the supply curve for:
(1) Products is due to ________________
(2) Labor is due to ________________

6. Assume the demand for consumer good P increases while the demand for consumer good Q decreases. In the short run:
a. The price and output of P will (increase, decrease)

__________ and the price and output of Q will __________

b. Profits in industry __________ will increase and profits in industry __________ will decrease.

c. If the only resource used in industry P is type C labor and the only resource used in industry Q is type D labor, the demand for C will (increase, decrease) __________ and the demand for D will __________

d. Wage rates and the quantity of labor employed in the market for __________ will increase while those in the market for __________ will decrease.

7. Using the same assumptions made in 6 above, if the two industries are increasing-cost industries, the increase in the demand for P along with the decrease in the demand for Q will in the long run:

a. Cause firms to enter industry __________ and to leave industry __________

b. Cause the supply of P to (increase, decrease) __________ and the supply of Q to __________

c. Bring about a(n) __________ in the price of P and a(n) __________ in the price of Q.

d. Increase the supply of type __________ labor and decrease the supply of type __________ labor.

e. __________ the employment of type C labor and __________ the employment of type D labor.

8. Still using the assumptions made in 6 and 7 above, the increase in the price of P and the decrease in the price of Q will:

a. Increase the demand for products which are (substitutes, complements) __________ for P and decrease the demand for __________

b. (Increase, Decrease) __________ the demand for those resources used along with type C labor and __________ the demand for those resources used along with type D labor.

c. Redistribute income from workers and entrepreneurs in industry __________ to those in industry __________

9. Given the distribution of income, purely competitive product and resource markets bring about the production of a combination of goods and services which maximizes the __________ of the consumers of the economy because:

a. The price of each good or service is equal to its __________

b. The average cost of producing each product is a __________ and each firm employs the resources required to produce its product in the __________ combination.

c. The marginal utility of the last dollar spent by a consumer on each good or service is __________ for all goods and services.

10. Product and resource markets in the real world are actually __________ competitive. As a result the allocation of resources is less than __________ and adjustments to changes in tastes, technology, and the availability of resources are __________ and __________

11. Two potential offsets to imperfectly competitive markets are more rapid __________ and greater __________

12. The ability of a purely competitive price system to allocate resources efficiently is open to question for two reasons.

a. It fails to take into account the __________ __________ and the __________ of the goods and services produced and it neglects or ignores the production of ____________ goods.

b. It does not necessarily result in an ideal ____________ of income.

13. Listed down the left side of an input-output table are the ____________ sectors of the economy and listed across the top of the table are the ____________ sectors. The output of any sector is a(n) ____________ of other sectors; and the inputs of any sector are the ____________ of other sectors.

14. Assuming constant returns to scale, if industry X sells 30% of its product to industry Y and if industry Y increases its production by 25%, then industry X will have to increase its production by ____________%.

15. An understanding of general equilibrium analysis is important if one is to evaluate the overall ____________ ____________ of the economy, to understand the specific economic ____________ it faces, and to formulate good economic ____________ to solve them.

■ PROBLEMS AND PROJECTS

1. Below are three types of economic change which can occur in the economy. In the spaces allotted following each change, indicate what you think the effect will be—increase (+), decrease (−), no change (0), or an indeterminate change (?)—on demand or supply, price, and output or employment in the markets affected by the initial change.

No answers to this problem will be found in the "Answers" section because the answer to each question depends upon such things as whether the short run or the long run is considered, whether the industry is an increasing- or constant-cost industry, and whether you consider only the "immediate-secondary effect" of the initial change. The purpose of this exercise is to get you to *attempt* to trace through the economy the full effect of an initial change and to see the extent and complexity of price-market interrelations.

a. Decrease in the demand for consumer good X but no *initial* change in the demand for other consumer goods.

(1) Effect on the price of and the quantity of good X produced. ________

(2) Effect on the demand for, the price of, and the output of goods which are substitutes for good X. ________

(3) Effect on the demand for, the price of, and the output of goods which are complements for good X. ________

(4) Effect on the demand for, the price of, and the employment of resources used in the production of good X. ________

(5) Effect on the supply of, the price of, and the output of goods which employ the same resources used in the production of good X. ________

(6) Effect on the demand for, the price of, and the employment of resources which are substitutes for the resources used to produce good X. ________

b. Decrease in the supply of resource Y.

(1) Effect on the price of and the employment of resource Y. ________

(2) Effect on the supply of, the price of, and the output of goods which employ resource Y in the production process. ________

(3) Effect on the demand for, the price of, and the employment of resources which are complementary to resource Y. ________

(4) Effect on the demand for, the price of, and the output of those goods which are substitutes for the goods produced with resource Y. ________

(5) Effect on the demand for, the price of, and the output of those goods which are complements for goods produced with resource Y. ________

(6) Effect on the demand for, the price of, and the employment of resources which are substitutes for resource Y.

c. Improvement in the technology of producing good Z. ________

(1) Effect on the supply of, the price of, and the output of good Z. ________

(2) Effect on the demand for, the price of, and the output of goods which are substitutes for good Z. ______

(3) Effect on the demand for, the price of, and the output of goods which are complements for good Z. ______

(4) Effect on the demand for, the price of, and the employment of resources used to produce good Z. ______

(5) Effect on the supply of, the price of, and the output of those goods which also employ the resources used to produce good Z. ______

2. Below is an incomplete input-output table for an economy with five sectors. All the figures in the table are physical units rather than dollars.

Producing sectors	Using sectors A	B	C	D	E	Total outputs
A	100	150	75	—	25	425
B	30	20	70	80	200	—
C	10	60	—	20	20	110
D	205	35	40	10	—	300
E	—	140	60	35	80	390

a. Complete the table by computing (by addition or subtraction) the missing input-output figures.

b. Assume that sector B wishes to expand its output by 100 units. By what percentage does sector B wish to expand its output? ______%

c. Assuming constant returns to scale in all sectors of the economy, by how many *units* will each of the following sectors of the economy have to expand its output if sector B is to expand its output by 100 units?

(1) Sector A: ______

(2) Sector C: ______

(3) Sector D: ______

(4) Sector E: ______

d. By what *percentage* will each of these sectors have to expand its output?

(1) Sector A: ______%

(2) Sector C: ______%

(3) Sector D: ______%

(4) Sector E: ______%

e. What further adjustments in the outputs of the various sectors of the economy will follow those given in (*c*) and (*d*) above?

______

______

■ SELF-TEST

Circle the T if the statement is true, the F if it is false.

1. General equilibrium analysis is the same thing as macroeconomics. **T F**

2. The study of the effect of an increase in the demand for product C, other things remaining equal, upon the price and the output of product C is an example of partial equilibrium analysis. **T F**

3. The supply curve for a product slopes upward in the short run because of the diminishing marginal productivity of variable resources. **T F**

Use the following data for the next three questions below and for multiple-choice questions 6 and 7. Initially there is general equilibrium, and then the demand for consumer good W increases and the demand for consumer good Z decreases. Both industries are increasing-cost industries in the long run. Industry W employs only type G labor, and Z employs only type H labor.

4. In the short run, price, output, and profits will increase in industry Z and decrease in industry W. **T F**

5. In the long run, the quantity of type G labor employed will increase and the quantity of type H labor employed will decrease. **T F**

6. Income will be redistributed from workers and entrepreneurs in industry Z to those in industry W. **T F**

7. Given the distribution of income in the economy, purely competitive product and resource markets lead to the production of a collection of products which maximizes the satisfaction of consumer wants. **T F**

8. In the real world, product and resource markets tend to be purely competitive. **T F**

9. When there are spillover benefits from the consumption of a product bought and sold in a purely competitive market resources are overallocated to the production of that product. **T F**

10. A change in the distribution of income in the economy will change the way the economy allocates its scarce resources. **T F**

11. A purely competitive price system results in an ideal or optimal distribution of income. **T F**

12. General equilibrium analysis gives a broader picture of the economic consequences of economic changes and economic policies than partial equilibrium analysis even though some of these consequences turn out to be insignificant. **T F**

Circle the letter that corresponds to the best answer.

1. The price system produces approximately what percentage of the output and employs about what percentage of the resources of the American economy? (*a*) 70%; (*b*) 80%; (*c*) 90%; (*d*) 100%.

2. The downward slope of the demand curve for a product is the result of: (*a*) diminishing marginal utility; (*b*) diminishing marginal productivity; (*c*) increasing marginal cost; (*d*) the work-leisure preferences of workers.

3. The upward slope of the supply curve of labor is the result of: (*a*) diminishing marginal utility; (*b*) diminishing marginal productivity; (*c*) increasing marginal cost; (*d*) the work-leisure preferences of workers.

4. If the demand for consumer good A increased, which one of the following would *not* be a possible consequence? (*a*) Increase in the price of A; (*b*) increase in the demand for resources used to produce A; (*c*) increase in the supply of those goods which are substitutes for A; (*d*) increase in the prices of other goods which employ the same resources used to produce A.

5. If the supply of resource B increased, which one of the following would *not* be a possible consequence? (*a*) Decrease in the price of B; (*b*) decrease in the demand for those goods produced from B; (*c*) decrease in the demand for those resources which are substitutes for resource B; (*d*) decrease in the demand for those goods which are substitutes for the goods produced with resource B.

Use the data preceding true-false question 4 to answer the following two questions.

6. When the new long-run general equilibrium is reached: (*a*) the wage rate for type G labor will be higher than it was originally; (*b*) the wage rate for type G labor will be lower than it was originally; (*c*) wage rates in both labor markets will be the same as they were originally; (*d*) it is impossible to tell what will have happened to wage rates.

7. As a result of the changes in the demands for W and Z: (*a*) the demand for products which are substitutes for Z will have increased; (*b*) the demand for products which are complements for W will have increased; (*c*) the demand for products which are substitutes for Z will have decreased; (*d*) the demand for products which are complements for Z will have decreased.

8. Which of the following is *not* the result of purely competitive product and resource markets? (*a*) The distribution of income among consumers maximizes the satisfaction of wants in the economy; (*b*) the average cost of producing each product is a minimum; (*c*) the price of each product is equal to its marginal cost; (*d*) the marginal utility of every product divided by its price is the same for all products purchased by an individual consumer.

9. All but one of the following is the result of imperfectly competitive product and resource markets. Which one? (*a*) Resources are allocated less efficiently than under purely competitive conditions; (*b*) the price system is less responsive to changes in tastes, technology, and the availability of resources than a purely competitive price system; (*c*) there is a smaller variety of products than in a purely competitive system; (*d*) monopoly drives prices above and monopsony drives them below their competitive levels.

10. Which of the following is a disadvantage of a purely competitive price system? (*a*) Underallocates resources to those products whose production entails a spillover cost; (*b*) overallocates resources to those products whose consumption entails spillover benefits; (*c*) underallocates resources to the production of social goods and services; (*d*) fails to distribute income optimally.

Use the following input-output table to answer questions 11 and 12 below.

Producing sectors	Using sectors					Total outputs
	A	B	C	D	E	
A	20	15	35	25	60	155
B	45	55	90	10	20	220
C	40	15	80	10	5	150
D	65	10	25	20	40	160
E	100	75	80	45	10	310

11. If sector C were to decrease its output by 50 units, and assuming constant returns to scale in all sectors, the *initial* impact on sector B would be a decrease in its output of: (*a*) 5 units; (*b*) 13$\frac{6}{7}$ units; (*c*) 26$\frac{2}{3}$ units; (*d*) 30 units.

12. If sector C is to increase its output by 50 units, and assuming constant returns to sector, E's output will have to increase initially by: (*a*) 8.6%; (*b*) 19.4%; (*c*) 20%; (*d*) 37.5%.

■ DISCUSSION QUESTIONS

1. Explain the difference between partial equilibrium and general equilibrium analysis.

2. Why is general equilibrium analysis so important?

3. Suppose the demand for television sets decreases at the same time that the demand for airline travel increases. What would be (*a*) the short-run effects of these changes in the markets for television sets and airline travel and in the markets for television-set production workers and airline workers; (*b*) the long-run effects in these markets; (*c*) the long-run effects in the markets for complementary and substitute products and in the markets for other resources; and (*d*) the effect upon the distribution of income?

4. Imagine that the availability of iron ore used to produce steel increased or the technology of steel making improved. What would be the short- and long-run effects upon (*a*) the steel industry; (*b*) steelworkers; (*c*) the automobile industry; (*d*) the aluminum industry; (*e*) the machine tool industry; and (*f*) the coal industry?

5. Why is a purely competitive price system "conducive to an efficient allocation of resources"?

6. When a price system is less than purely competitive, what are the economic consequences?

7. What costs, benefits, and goods does even a purely competitive price system neglect or ignore? What are the economic results of this neglect?

8. What is meant by an ideal or optimal distribution of income? Why can't economists determine—even theoretically—what the optimal distribution of income is?

9. Explain precisely what an input-output table is and the kind of information it contains.

10. In addition to indicating the interrelationships between the various sectors of the economy, an input-output table can be used for what other purposes?

35
Antitrust and regulation

This is the first of six chapters which deal with specific trouble spots in the American economy and is one of the two chapters which concern the monopoly problem. Chapter 35 examines the monopoly problem in output markets, and Chapter 39 examines the monopoly problem in labor markets. It should be noted that the term "monopoly" as used here does *not* mean pure or absolute monopoly; it means, instead, control of a large percentage of the total supply by one or a few suppliers. Actually there is no such thing as pure monopoly.

Whether big business and industrial monopolies are a real threat to efficient resource allocation and technological progress in the United States is certainly a debatable question. It is a question that will be argued from time to time by the American people and their representatives in Congress. Chapter 35 does not attempt to answer the question. It is important, however, for you to see that it is a debatable question and to see that there are good and plausible arguments on both sides of the question.

A part of Chapter 35 is devoted to an examination of the ways in which the Federal government has attempted to prevent the formation of business monopolies and to limit the use of monopoly power. In this section you will find a discussion of a number of Federal laws, and the question which a student almost always raises is, "Am I expected to know these laws?" The answer is yes, you should have a general knowledge of these laws. Another question which students often raise with respect to these laws is, "What good is there in knowing them anyhow?" In examining any important current problem it is important to know how the problem arose, what steps have already been taken to solve it, how successful the attempts were, and why the problem is still not solved. A more general answer to the same question is that an informed citizenry is necessary if a democracy is to solve its problems. And most of these laws continue in force and are enforced; many of you will work for business firms which are subject to their provisions.

After looking at the case for and the defense of big business and at the antitrust laws enacted by the Federal government, Chapter 35 presents the two major issues that have arisen in the interpretation of the antitrust laws; asks how effective these laws have been; and observes that the Federal government has in several ways promoted and fostered monopoly and restricted competition in the United States.

But in addition to restricting and to fostering monopoly, the Federal government has also undertaken to regulate, beginning with the railroads in 1887, industries that appeared to be natural monopolies. This regulation by agencies and commissions has, however, at least three serious problems of which you should be aware. One of these problems is that some of the regulated industries may not be natural monopolies at all and would be competitive industries if they were left unregulated. From this problem comes the legal cartel theory of regulation: many industries desire to be regulated so that competition among the firms in the industry will be reduced and the profits of these firms increased. A consequence of the problems encountered in regulating industries has been the trend in recent years to deregulate a few of the industries previously regulated by agencies or commissions. One of the industries which has been deregulated in the United States is the airline industry; and the case of the airlines is examined in a section of the text. Here you will see that despite the predictions of the critics of deregulation, deregulation has been beneficial for consumers and the economy.

Beginning in the early 1960s a host of new agencies and commissions began to engage in regulation which is different from the regulation of the prices charged by and the services offered by specific industries, and its critics contend that the economy is now overregulated to such an extent that, on balance, this new regulation has been harmful to the economy.

Antitrust and regulation, you should conclude when you have finished this chapter, is a trouble spot in the economy because important questions and issues remain to be answered and how we answer them will affect how well or poorly the economy will perform and how good or bad our lives will be in the future.

■ CHECKLIST

When you have studied this chapter you should be able to:

☐ Explain how the term monopoly is used in this chapter.

☐ Set forth the case against monopoly.

☐ Present the defense of monopoly.

☐ Outline the major provisions of each of the following:
- Sherman Act
- Clayton Act
- Federal Trade Commission Act
- Wheeler-Lea Act
- Celler-Kefauver Act

☐ Contrast the behavioral and structural approaches to the enforcement of the antitrust laws (to judging the competitiveness of a particular industry); and explain why defining the market in which a particular firm sells its product is an important issue in the interpretation of the antitrust laws.

☐ Relate how the antitrust laws have been applied to existing market structures, the different types of mergers, and price-fixing.

☐ List three groups which have been exempted from the provisions of the antitrust laws and two laws or policies of the Federal government which tend to restrict competition and promote monopoly in the United States.

☐ Define a natural monopoly; and explain how the theory of natural monopoly was applied to American railroads in 1887.

☐ State the three problems that have been encountered in the economic regulation of industries by agencies and commissions.

☐ Distinguish between the public interest and legal cartel theories of regulation.

☐ Describe the principal economic effects of the deregulation of the airline industry in the United States; and compare these effects with the effects predicted by the critics of deregulation.

☐ Contrast industrial (or economic) regulation with social regulation; and state the principal concerns and the three distinguishing features of the latter.

☐ Present the case against social regulation made by its critics; and state the three implications of overregulation.

■ CHAPTER OUTLINE

1. The term "monopoly," as used in this chapter, means a situation in which a small number of firms control all or a substantial percentage of the total output of a major industry. Business firms may be large in either an absolute or a relative sense, and in many cases they are large in both senses. Chapter 35 is concerned with firms large in both senses.

2. Whether business monopoly is beneficial or detrimental to the American economy is debatable. A case can be made against business monopoly; but business monopoly can also be defended.

a. Many argue that monopoly results in a misallocation of resources; is not needed for firms to achieve the economics of mass production and does not lead to technological progress; contributes to income inequality in the economy; and is politically dangerous.

b. But others argue that business monopoly is often faced by interindustry and foreign competition; that large firms are necessary if they are to achieve the economies of scale in producing goods and services; and that monopolistic industries promote a high rate of technological progress.

3. Government policies toward business monopoly have not been clear and consistent; legislation and policy, however, have for the most part been aimed at restricting monopoly and promoting competition.

a. Following the Civil War, the expansion of the American economy brought with it the creation of trusts (or business monopolies) in many industries; and the fear of the trusts resulted in the enactment of antitrust legislation.

b. The Sherman Antitrust Act of 1890 was the first antitrust legislation and made monopolization and restraint of trade crimes.

c. In 1914 the Clayton Antitrust Act outlawed a number of specific techniques by which monopolies had been created.

d. During the same year Congress passed the Federal Trade Commission Act which established the Federal Trade Commission to investigate unfair practices that might lead to the development of monopoly power; and in 1938 amended this act by passing the Wheeler-Lea Act to prohibit deceptive practices (including false and misleading advertising and misrepresentation of products).

e. And in 1950 passage of the Celler-Kefauver Act plugged a loophole in the Clayton Act and prohibited mergers that might lead to a substantial reduction in competition.

4. The effectiveness of the antitrust laws in preventing monopoly and maintaining competition has depended upon the zeal with which the Federal government has enforced the laws and upon the interpretation of these laws by the Federal courts; and two major issues have arisen in the interpretation of the antitrust laws.

a. The first of these issues is whether an industry should be judged on the basis of monopolistic structure or on the basis of monopolistic behavior; and this issue has resulted in controversy and in two different approaches to the application of the antitrust laws.

b. The second issue is whether to define the market in which firms sell their products narrowly or broadly.

c. Whether the antitrust laws have been effective is a difficult question to answer; but the application of the laws to existing market structures, to the three types of mergers, and to price-fixing has ranged from lenient to strict.

5. Government in the United States has also restricted competition by exempting labor unions, agricultural cooperatives, and (at the local and state levels) certain occupational groups from the provisions of the antitrust laws; by granting monopoly power to the producers of patented goods; and by imposing tariffs and other barriers to international trade to protect American producers from foreign competition.

6. In addition to the enactment of the antitrust laws, government has undertaken to regulate natural monopolies.

a. If a single producer can provide a good or service at a lower average cost (because of economies of scale) than several producers and competition is, therefore, not economical, a natural monopoly exists; and government may either produce the good or service or (following the public interest theory) regulate private producers of the product for the benefit of the public.

b. The first Federal regulatory agency was the Interstate Commerce Commission which, following the passage of the Interstate Commerce Commission Act in 1887, began to regulate the rates and services of railroads.

c. The effectiveness of the regulation of business firms by regulatory agencies has been criticized for three principal reasons.

(1) Regulation, it is argued, increases costs and leads to an inefficient allocation of resources and higher prices.

(2) The regulatory agencies, it is also contended, have been "captured" by the regulated industries and protect them rather than the public.

(3) And some of the regulated industries, it can be argued, are not natural monopolies and would be competitive if they were not regulated.

d. The legal cartel theory of regulation is that potentially competitive industries want and support the regulation of their industries in order to increase the profits of the firms in the industries by limiting competition among them.

7. The three criticisms of the regulation of industries and the legal cartel theory of regulation led during the 1970s and 1980s to the deregulation of a number of industries in the United States; and the deregulation of the airlines is a case study of the effects of deregulation on air fares, on air services, on competition in the industry, and on the firms and workers in the industry.

8. Beginning in the early 1960s a "new" social regulation developed rapidly and resulted in the creation of additional regulatory agencies.

a. This regulation differed in several ways from the older regulation of specific industries and aimed to improve the quality of life in the United States.

b. While the objectives of the new regulation are desirable, the costs to the economy are high; and critics argue that the marginal costs of this regulation exceed its marginal benefits and it is, therefore, inefficient.

c. This overregulation, they argue, is inflationary, slows the rate of innovation, and lessens competition.

d. The defenders of the new regulation contend that it is needed to fight serious and neglected problems and that the social benefits will over time exceed the costs.

e. The current policy of the Reagan administration is to reduce regulation in order to increase the production of the economy.

■ IMPORTANT TERMS

Monopoly
Big business
Interindustry competition
Regulatory agency
Sherman Act
Clayton Act
Tying agreement
Interlocking directorate
Federal Trade Commission Act
Federal Trade Commission

Cease-and-desist order
Wheeler-Lea Act
Celler-Kefauver Act
Horizontal merger
Vertical merger
Conglomerate merger
U.S. Steel case
Rule of reason
Alcoa case
DuPont cellophane case
Patent laws
Natural monopoly
Public utility
Interstate Commerce Commission Act
Interstate Commerce Commission
Public interest theory of regulation
Legal cartel theory of regulation
Industrial (economic) regulation
Social regulation

p. 705

■ FILL-IN QUESTIONS

1. As used in this chapter, monopoly means that (one firm, a few firms) ~~one~~ fews firms control(s) all or a substantial portion of the output of a major industry; and this chapter is concerned with firms that are large (absolutely, relatively, both absolutely and relatively) both relatively & absolutely

2. Those who argue the case against business monopoly assert that it results in a misallocation of resources, (slows, speeds) slows the rate of technological progress, contributes to the unequal distribution of income, and creates political dangers in the United States.

3. Those who defend business monopoly contend that their power is limited by interindustry and Foreign competition, that large firms are necessary to achieve economies of Scale, ________, and that the large firms are conducive to a rapid rate of tech progress

4. Federal legislation and policies have mostly attempted to maintain (competition, monopoly) ~~Mo~~ competition, but at times they have fostered the development of Monopoly

5. The Sherman Act of 1890 made it illegal to Mopolize -ize or to restrain trade between the states or between nations.

6. The Clayton Act of 1914 prohibited such practices as price discrimination, acquisition of the ~~tying~~ stocks of competing corporations, tying contracts, and interlocking directorates.

7. The Federal Trade Commission was set up under the act of that name in 1914 to investigate unfair competitive practices, hold public hearings on such complaints, and to issue cease & desist orders.

8. The Wheeler-Lea Act had the effect of prohibiting false and misleading advertising.

9. The Celler Kefauver Act banned the acquisition of the *assets* of one firm by another, and the Clayton Antitrust Act prohibited the acquisition of the *stock* of one firm by another when the result would be reduced competition.

10. The two basic issues in applying the antitrust laws are whether the extent of business monopoly in a particular industry should be judged on the basis of that industry's behavior or its structure; and whether the size of the market in which a firm sells its product should be defined narrowly or broadly.

a. The courts judged the steel industry on the basis of its behavior in 1920 when they applied the rule of reason in the U.S. Steel case; but used the other method of judging an industry in 1945 in the Alcoa case.

b. In 1956 they ruled that although Du Pont sold nearly all the Cellophane produced in the United States it did not dominate the market for flexible packaging materials

11. The Federal government promotes the growth of monopoly and restricts competition when it exempts certain industries or practices from the provisions of the anti-trust laws.

a. Federal legislation has exempted labor unions and ag co-operatives.

b. The patent laws have the effect of granting inventors legal monopolies on their products; and tariffs and other barriers to trade shelter American producers from foreign competition.

12. When a single firm is able to supply the entire market at a lower average cost than a number of competing firms, there is a natural monopoly. In the United States many of these monopolies are controlled by regulatory Commissions or agencies

13. The first Federal regulatory law was the Interstate Commerce Comm. Act of 1887 which established a commission to regulate the ________________

14. The three major criticisms of regulation of industries by an agency or commission are:

a. The regulated firms have no incentive to reduce their ________________s because the commission will then require them to lower their prices; and, because the prices they are allowed to charge are based on the value of their capital equipment, firms tend to make uneconomical substitutions of (labor, capital) ________________ for ________________

b. The regulatory commission has been "captured" or is controlled by ________________

c. Regulation has been applied to industries which are not ________________ monopolies and which in the absence of regulation would be ________________.

15. The public interest theory of regulation assumes that the objective of regulating an industry is to protect society from abuses of ________________ power; but an alternative theory assumes that the firms wish to be regulated because it enables them to form, and the commission helps them to create, a profitable and legal ________________

16. The basic reason for the "new" social regulation and the creation and growth of the new regulatory agencies has been the desire to improve the (quantity, quality) ________________ of life in the United States.

a. It is concerned with the ________________ under which goods and services are produced, the impact of their production upon ________________, and the physical ________________ of the goods.

b. And it differs in several ways from the "old" regulation which is labeled ________________ or ________________ regulation.

17. Critics of the "new" social regulation contend:

a. its marginal costs are (greater, less) ________________ than its marginal benefits; and

b. that its results are (recession, inflation) ________________, a (slower, more rapid) ________________ rate of innovation, and (more, less) ________________ competition in the economy.

18. The Reagan administration appears committed to (more, less, the same amount of) ________________ regulation of the economy.

■ PROBLEMS AND PROJECTS

Below is a list of Federal laws. Following this list is a series of provisions found in Federal laws. Match each of the laws with the appropriate provision by placing the appropriate capital letter after each of the provisions.

A. Sherman Act
B. Clayton Act
C. Federal Trade Commission Act
D. Wheeler-Lea Act
E. Celler-Kefauver Act
F. Interstate Commerce Commission Act

a. Established a commission to investigate and prevent unfair methods of competition. ____

b. Established a commission to regulate the railroads, their rates, and their services. ____

c. Made monopoly and restraint of trade illegal and criminal. ____

d. Prohibited the acquisition of the assets of a firm by another firm when such an acquisition will lessen competition. ____

e. Had the effect of prohibiting false and misleading advertising and the misrepresentation of products. ____

f. Clarified the Sherman Act and outlawed specific techniques or devices used to create monopolies and restrain trade. ____

2. Indicate with the letter L for *leniently* (or permissively) and the letter S for *strictly* how the antitrust laws tend to be applied to each of the following.

a. Vertical mergers in which each of the merging firms sells 10% or more of the total output of its industry ____

b. Price fixing ____

c. Conglomerate mergers ____

d. Existing market structures in which no firm sells 60% or more of the total output of its industry ____

e. Horizontal mergers in which the merged firms would sell 10% or more of the total output of their industry and no one of the firms is on the verge of bankruptcy ____

f. Horizontal mergers in which the merged firms would sell 10% or more of the total output of their industry and one of the firms is on the verge of bankruptcy ____

■ SELF-TEST

Circle the T if the statement is true, the F if it is false.

1. The term "monopoly" in this chapter is taken to mean a situation in which a single firm produces a unique product and entry into the industry is blocked. **T F**

2. It is clear that on balance, business monopoly is detrimental to the functioning of the American economy. **T F**

3. Those who defend business monopolies contend that they are technologically more progressive than smaller firms. **T F**

4. The Federal government has consistently passed legislation and pursued policies designed to maintain competition. **T F**

5. Business monopolies and "trusts" developed in the American economy during the two decades preceding the American Civil War. **T F**

6. The courts in 1920 applied the rule of reason to the U.S. Steel Corporation and decided that the corporation possessed monopoly power and had unreasonably restrained trade. **T F**

7. Those who believe an industry should be judged on the basis of its structure contend that any industry with a monopolistic structure must behave like a monopolist. **T F**

8. The market for DuPont's product was broadly defined by the courts in the DuPont Cellophane case of 1956. **T F**

9. The Reagan administration has committed itself to a more vigorous enforcement of the antitrust laws. **T F**

10. The current policy of those responsible for the administration of the antitrust laws is to apply these laws to and to punish those firms that obtain large shares of a market by being more efficient competitors. **T F**

11. A natural monopoly exists when the *minimum* average cost of producing a good or service of one firm is less than the *minimum* average cost of any other firm. **T F**

12. Public ownership rather than public regulation has been the primary means utilized in the United States to ensure that the behavior of natural monopolists is socially acceptable. **T F**

13. The rationale underlying the public interest theory of regulation of natural monopolies is to allow the consumers of their goods or services to benefit from the economies of scale and to prevent the abuse of the market power of the monopolist by allowing it to charge a price no greater than the marginal cost of producing the good or service. **T F**

14. Regulated firms, because the prices they are allowed to charge are set to enable them to earn a "fair" return over their costs, have a strong incentive to reduce their costs. **T F**

15. While painful for the firms and the workers in the industry, the deregulation of airlines in the United States has been generally beneficial to consumers of airline services. **T F**

16. Those who favor the "new" social regulation believe that it is needed in order to improve the quality of life in the United States. **T F**

17. Critics of the "new" social regulation argue that it has resulted in the overregulation of the economy and that its marginal costs exceed its marginal benefits. **T F**

18. The relief of regulated industries is one of the economic policies of the Reagan administration. **T F**

Circle the letter that corresponds to the best answer.

1. "Big business" in this chapter refers to which one of the following? (*a*) Firms that are absolutely large; (*b*) firms that are relatively large; (*c*) firms that are either absolutely or relatively large; (*d*) firms that are both absolutely and relatively large.

2. Which of the following is *not* a part of the case *against* business monopoly? (*a*) Monopolists are larger than they need to be to benefit from economies of scale; (*b*) monopolists earn economic profits which they use for research and technological development; (*c*) monopoly leads to the misallocation of resources; (*d*) monopoly leads to greater income inequality.

3. An essential part of the defense of business monopoly is that the power of big business is limited by (*a*) interindustry competition; (*b*) foreign competition; (*c*) potential competition from new firms in the industry; (*d*) all of the above.

4. Which one of the following laws stated that contracts and conspiracies in restraint of trade, monopolies, attempts to monopolize, and conspiracies to monopolize are illegal? (*a*) Sherman Act; (*b*) Clayton Act; (*c*) Federal Trade Commission Act; (*d*) Wheeler-Lea Act.

5. Which one of the following acts specifically outlawed tying contracts and interlocking directorates? (*a*) Sherman Act; (*b*) Clayton Act; (*c*) Federal Trade Commission Act; (*d*) Wheeler-Lea Act.

6. Which one of the following acts has given the Federal Trade Commission the task of preventing false and misleading advertising and the misrepresentation of products? (*a*) Sherman Act; (*b*) Clayton Act; (*c*) Federal Trade Commission Act; (*d*) Wheeler-Lea Act.

7. Which of the following acts banned the acquisition of the assets of a firm by a competing firm when the acquisition would tend to reduce competition? (*a*) The Celler-Kefauver Act; (*b*) the Wheeler-Lea Act; (*c*) the Clayton Act; (*d*) the Federal Trade Commission Act.

8. Toward which of the following has the application of the antitrust laws been the most lenient in recent years? (*a*) Conglomerate mergers; (*b*) horizontal mergers; (*c*) vertical mergers; (*d*) price fixing.

9. Toward which of the following has the application of the antitrust laws been the most strict in recent years? (*a*) Existing market structures; (*b*) conglomerate mergers; (*c*) mergers in which one of the firms is on the verge of bankruptcy; (*d*) price fixing.

10. Which of the following does *not* restrict competition in the American economy? (*a*) The exemption of labor unions and agricultural cooperatives from the antitrust laws; (*b*) protective tariffs and other barriers to international trade; (*c*) the difficulties many new firms encounter in obtaining charters that allow them to become corporations; (*d*) American patent laws.

11. Which one of the following was *not* characteristic of the Interstate Commerce Act of 1887? (*a*) It was based on the supposition that competition was uneconomic in the railroad industry; (*b*) transportation was deemed essential to many individuals, firms, and industries; (*c*) it substituted government management and operation of the railroads for private management and operation; (*d*) the Interstate Commerce Commission was established to regulate railroad rates and services.

12. Those who oppose the regulation of industry by regulatory agencies contend that (*a*) many of the regulated industries are not natural monopolies; (*b*) the regulatory agencies have been "captured" by the firms they are supposed to regulate; (*c*) regulation results in higher costs and reduced efficiency in the production of the good or service produced by the regulated industry; (*d*) all of the above are true.

13. The legal cartel theory of regulating natural monopolies (*a*) would allow the forces of demand and supply to determine the rates (prices) of the good or service; (*b*) would attempt to protect the public from abuses of monopoly power; (*c*) assumes that the regulated industry wishes to be regulated and government officials provide the regulation in return for public support; (*d*) assumes that both the demand for and supply of the good or service produced by the regulated industry are perfectly inelastic.

14. Critics of the deregulation of industry argue that (among other things) deregulation will lead to (*a*) higher prices for the products produced by the industry; (*b*) the monopolization of the industry by a few large firms; (*c*) a decline in the quantity or the quality of the product produced by the industry; (*d*) all of the above.

15. Deregulation of airlines in the United States has so far resulted in (*a*) higher air fares; (*b*) the monopolization of the airline industry by two large firms; (*c*) a reduction in the availability of air services in the smaller communities; (*d*) lower wage rates for airline employees.

16. Which of the following is *not* a concern of the "new" social regulation? (*a*) The prices charged for goods; (*b*) the physical characteristics of goods produced; (*c*) the conditions under which goods are manufactured; (*d*) the impact upon society of the production of goods.

17. Which of the following is *not* engaged in the "new" social regulation? (*a*) The Environmental Protection Agency; (*b*) the Interstate Commerce Commission; (*c*) the Equal Employment Opportunity Commission; (*d*) the Occupational Safety and Health Administration.

18. Which of the following is *not* one of the criticisms levied against the "new" social regulation by its opponents? (*a*) It contributes to inflation; (*b*) it will require too long a time for it to achieve its objectives; (*c*) it will slow the rate of innovation in the economy; (*d*) it is anticompetitive.

■ DISCUSSION QUESTIONS

1. Explain the difference between the way the term "monopoly" is used in this chapter and the way it is used in Chapter 28. How can "big business" be defined? How is the expression used in this chapter?

2. What are the chief arguments in the case against business monopoly? In what two ways is the term *unprogressive* used in these arguments?

3. What are the chief arguments advanced in defense of business monopoly?

4. What are the historical background to and the main provisions of the Sherman Act?

5. The Clayton Act and the Federal Trade Commission Act amended or elaborated the provisions of the Sherman Act, and both aimed at preventing rather than punishing monopoly. What were the chief provisions of each of these acts, and how did they attempt to prevent monopoly? In what two ways is the FTC Act important?

6. What loophole in the Clayton Act was plugged by the Celler-Kefauver Act in 1950 and how did it alter the coverage of the antitrust laws with respect to mergers?

7. Contrast the two different approaches to the application of the antitrust laws that are illustrated by the decisions of the courts in the U.S. Steel and Alcoa cases.

8. Why is defining the market an important issue in the application of the antitrust laws? How did the courts define the market in the case brought against DuPont for monopolizing the market for Cellophane.

9. How are the antitrust laws applied today to (*a*) existing market structures; (*b*) horizontal mergers; (*c*) vertical mergers; (*d*) conglomerate mergers; and (*e*) price fixing?

10. In what ways has the Federal government restricted competition and fostered monopoly in the American economy?

11. What is a natural monopoly and what are the two alternative ways that can be used to ensure that it behaves in a socially acceptable fashion?

12. Why was the Interstate Commerce Commission Act passed in 1887 to regulate American railroads?

13. Explain the three major criticisms levied against public interest regulation as it is practiced by commissions and agencies in the United States.

14. What is the legal cartel theory of regulation? Contrast it with the public interest theory of regulation.

15. Why have a number of industries in the American economy been deregulated recently? What did the proponents and the critics of deregulation predict would be the economic effects of deregulation? How has deregulation affected the airline industry?

16. How does the new social regulation differ from the older industrial (or economic) regulation? What is the objective of this type of regulation, its three principal concerns, and its three distinguishing features?

17. The critics of the new social regulation argue that it has resulted in overregulation of the economy. What does this mean and, if there is overregulation, what are its more important implications?

18. State the policy of the Reagan administration toward (*a*) the enforcement of the antitrust laws and (*b*) the regulation of the economy.

36
Rural economics: the farm problem

Probably no economic problem has aroused public interest to the extent and for the number of years that the farm problem has. It has concerned not only those directly engaged in agriculture or living and working in rural areas but also every American consumer and taxpayer. Other problems seem to come and go; the farm problem seems always to have been with us; and the problems of farmers have become acute in the decade of the 1980s.

Chapter 36 is devoted exclusively to an examination of the farm problem—the second of the six specific trouble spots studied in this part of the book. The chapter opens with a brief history of the experiences of American farmers. The *symptoms* of the farm problem are declining farm prices, declining farm incomes, farm incomes which are low relative to the incomes of nonfarm families, and a highly unequal distribution of farm income among farm families.

The symptoms of the farm problem, however, are not the same thing as the *causes* of the farm problem. If the problem is to be solved, it is necessary to understand what has occasioned the straits in which agriculture finds itself. In fact, as the author points out, the failure to solve the problem has been brought about by the failure to understand and treat its causes. Actually there are two farm problems, a long-run problem and a short-run problem. Each problem has its own particular causes, and the chapter deals with each of the two problems in turn.

The long-run problem is that farm incomes have declined over the years and are low relative to nonfarm incomes; and the short-run problem is that farm prices and incomes have fluctuated sharply from year to year. To understand the causes of each of these problems you will have to make use of the concept of inelastic demand and to employ your knowledge of how demand and supply determine price in a competitive market. The effort which you put into the study of these tools in previous chapters will now pay a dividend; understanding the causes of a real-world problem and the policies designed to solve the problem.

The agricultural policies of the Federal government have been directed at enhancing and stabilizing farm incomes by supporting farm prices. In connection with the support of farm prices you are introduced to the concept of parity. Once you understand parity and recognize that the parity price has in the past been above what the competitive price would have been you will come to some important conclusions. Consumers paid higher prices for and consumed smaller quantities of the various farm products; and at the prices supported by the Federal government there were surpluses of these products. The Federal government bought these surpluses to keep the price above the competitive market price. The purchases of the surpluses were financed by American taxpayers.

To eliminate these surpluses, government looked for ways to increase the demand for or to decrease the supply of these commodities. Programs to increase demand and decrease supply were put into effect, but they failed to eliminate the annual surpluses. Agriculture in the United States had a problem which these farm policies, for reasons explained in the text, did not solve.

In the early 1970s an economic boom came to American agriculture. Congress enacted a new farm program designed to reduce the extent of government involvement in agriculture and to replace supported prices with target prices.

Target prices are explained in the text. Here you will also find a comparison of the economic consequences of target prices with those of supported prices. Observe that they are alike in two respects: both result in the same income for farmers and in a misallocation of resources.

Out of over 50 years of attempts by the Federal government to enhance and stabilize farm prices and farm incomes has come the widespread realization that the agricultural policies of government to achieve these objectives have (to a large extent) been failures. With this realization have come two additional observations. First, the macroeconomic policies of the Federal government which affect interest rates in the economy have a significant impact on the fortunes and well-being of the agricultural sector of the economy. Interest rates have an important effect on the costs of farmers and their ability to export farm commodities. Second, it may be futile to try to enhance farm incomes in an economy in which the basic problem is too many farmers; and it may be better to allow farm prices and farm incomes to drift downward toward their long-run equilibrium levels in a free market. This would accelerate the movement of farmers out of agriculture and improve the allocation of the economy's resources. But to prevent unstable farm prices and farm incomes, the Federal government should try to stabilize farm prices in the short run as they move toward their long-run free-market (or competitive) levels. This could be accomplished by the proposed free-market stabilization policy examined in the text.

The final section surveys what the pessimists and the optimists say about the possibility of worldwide shortages of agricultural products (that is, food) in the next century. The question is one of feast or famine during the years in which you will live the greater part of your life.

■ CHECKLIST

When you have studied this chapter you should be able to:

☐ Outline briefly the economic history of American agriculture during the twentieth century.

☐ Compare per capita farm and nonfarm income and rural and nonrural poverty; and describe the three different groups within the farm sector and the diversity of income among these three groups.

☐ Identify both the long-run and the short-run farm problem; and explain the four causes of the former and the cause of the latter problem.

☐ Explain why the long-run farm problem is the result of a misallocation of resources in a growing economy.

☐ Enumerate the several arguments which are made in support of Federal assistance to agriculture.

☐ Explain the meaning of parity in both real and money terms and define the parity ratio.

☐ Explain how the farm policies of the Federal government tried to increase farm prices and incomes; and the effect and the costs to the consumer and the taxpayer of these policies.

☐ Describe the means by which the Federal government attempted to restrict the supply and bolster the demand for farm products.

☐ Explain what a target price is and how it differs from a supported price; and how large a cash subsidy ("deficiency payment") a farmer would receive from the Federal government.

☐ Compare the price-support and the target-price programs with respect to the incomes received by farmers, the quantities received by and the prices paid by consumers, the costs to taxpayers, and the allocation of resources in the economy.

☐ Present five major criticisms of American farm policy.

☐ Explain how the macroeconomic policies of the Federal government affect the costs and the export sales of farmers.

☐ Describe the market-oriented income stabilization proposal; contrast it with a policy aimed at the enhancement of farm incomes; explain how the Federal government would stabilize farm prices; and enumerate the four advantages its proponents feel this approach to agricultural policy would have.

☐ List the contentions of the pessimists and of the optimists on the issue of whether the world will be able to feed itself by the beginning of the next century.

■ CHAPTER OUTLINE

1. A history of American agriculture in the twentieth century makes it clear that agricultural prices and farm incomes have fluctuated with changes in foreign and domestic demand and with changes in supply resulting from improvements in agricultural technology.

2. The evidence also makes it clear that farmers are, on the average, poorer than people not engaged in agriculture (and that poverty among farm families is more common than among nonfarm families); that there is a great diversity of incomes among farmers (who, based on their annual sales and incomes, can be divided into three groups); and that this diversity among farmers makes it difficult to devise farm policies to benefit farmers.

3. The farm problem is both a long-run and a short-run problem: the long-run problem is the tendency for farm prices and incomes to lag behind the upward trend of prices and incomes in the rest of the economy; and the short-run problem is the frequent sharp changes in the incomes of farmers from one year to the next.

a. The causes of the long-run (low farm-income) problem are the inelastic demand for farm products, the large increases in the supply of these products relative to the modest increases in the demand for them, and the relative immobility of agricultural resources.

b. The causes of the short-run (income-instability) problem are the inelastic demand for farm products, fluctuations in the output of agricultural products, fluctuations in the domestic demand, and the unstable foreign demand which result in relatively large changes in agricultural prices and farm incomes.

c. The long-run problem is, therefore, the result of four factors; and the short-run problem is the result of inelastic demand and changes in the demand for and the supply of farm products.

d. Another explanation of the long-run problem is that as the American economy grew and improved its agricultural technology, it reallocated too small an amount of its resources away from agriculture and into the nonagricultural sectors of the economy.

4. Those who have represented the farmer have claimed that the farmer has a right to special assistance from the Federal government. In addition to several other arguments it is claimed that:

a. farmers have made it possible for the American economy to have more food and fiber at relatively lower prices and that the cost of this progress has been borne (in the form of lower relative incomes) by farmers; and

b. farmers have no control over the prices they receive (because they sell their products in competitive markets) but the prices they pay are controlled (by oligopolists who sell in noncompetitive markets).

5. Farmers since the 1930s have been able to obtain various forms of public aid; but the primary purpose of the Federal government has been to enhance and to stabilize farm prices and incomes.

a. The cornerstone of Federal policy to raise farm prices is the concept of parity (or the parity price) which would give the farmer year after year the same real income per unit of output.

b. Historically farm policy supported farm prices at some percentage of the parity price. But because the supported price was almost always above the market price, government had to support the price by purchasing and accumulating surpluses of agricultural products; and while farmers gained from this policy, consumers lost; and to reduce the annual and accumulated surpluses, government attempted

(1) to reduce the output (or supply) of farm products by acreage-allotment, acreage-reserve, and (more recently) payment-in-kind programs; and

(2) to expand the demand for farm products by finding new uses for farm products, expanding domestic demand, and increasing the foreign demand for agricultural commodities.

c. In the 1970s the Federal government shifted from price supports to target prices to aid farmers and to avoid the accumulation of surplus farm commodities. The target price is the guaranteed minimum price of a farm product; and if the market price of the product falls below its target price the Federal government pays the farmer the difference between the target and market prices multiplied by the number of units of the product produced by the farmer.

d. Comparing price-support and target-price programs reveals that (so long as the target and the support prices are the same) the total income of farmers is the same; but with a target-price program consumers obtain a larger quantity of the product at a lower price (and, therefore, spend less for it because demand is inelastic), the subsidies paid to farmers by government (the costs to taxpayers) are greater, and there are no costs of storing surpluses for the government. Both programs, however, result in a misallocation of resources in the economy.

6. By the 1980s it had become apparent that the farm program was not working well and that the goals and techniques of farm policy needed to be changed.

a. Agricultural policy in the United States has been subjected to at least five major criticisms.

(1) It has confused the symptoms and causes of the problem and failed to move resources out of agriculture.

(2) The major benefits of the program were not directed toward the low-income farmers.

(3) The various farm programs of the Federal government have often operated to offset (or contradict) each other.

(4) Farm policy has also been less effective in achieving its goal of enhancing farm incomes because interest rates in the economy have risen and the international value of the dollar has fallen.

(5) And the costs of the farm programs to the Federal government have soared dramatically in the last few years.

b. Such nonfarm macroeconomic policies of the Federal

government as those affecting interest rates in the United States, the international value of the dollar, and the ability of farmers to sell their products in foreign markets have become increasingly important (even critical) to the well-being of American agriculture.

c. One suggested new approach to agricultural policy would have the Federal government shift from the goal of enhancing to the goal of stabilizing farm incomes (by having it support farm prices and accumulate surpluses when market prices fall below and sell from these surpluses when market prices rise above the long-run trend of prices in the free market); and proponents of this market-oriented income approach believe it would have at least four advantages.

7. While the American economy has persistently found itself with agricultural surpluses, most of the rest of the world has been plagued by chronic shortages; and the question of whether the world as a whole in the future will be able to feed itself can be answered either pessimistically or optimistically.

■ IMPORTANT TERMS

Farm problem
Long-run farm problem
Short-run farm problem
Agricultural Adjustment Act of 1933
Parity concept
Parity ratio
Price support
Acreage-allotment program
Acreage-reserve (soil bank) program
Payment-in-kind (PIK)
Public Law 480
Food for Peace program
Target price
Market-oriented income stabilization

■ FILL-IN QUESTIONS

1. What was the economic condition—prosperity or depression—of American agriculture in each of the following periods?

a. 1894 to 1914 ___P___

b. 1914 to 1919 ___P___

c. 1921 to 1940 ___D___

d. 1940s ___P___

e. 1950s and 1960s ___P___

f. 1970s ___P___

g. 1980s ___D___

2. The per capita farm income tends to be (greater, less) ___less___ than per capita nonfarm income; and the incomes of the three different groups within the farm sector of the economy are (similar, diverse) diverse

a. The farms with annual receipts of $100,000 or more from farming are (12, 16, 71) ___12___% of all farms and receive (12, 19, 68) ___68___ ______% of the total annual receipts from farming.

b. Farms with annual receipts of less than $40,000 are ___71___% of all farms and receive ___12___% of the total annual receipts from farming.

c. And the farms with annual receipts between $40,000 and $100,000 are ___16___% of all farms and receive ___19___% of the total annual receipts from farming.

3. The long-run farm problem is farm prices and incomes that (run ahead of, lag behind) ___lag behind___ the trends of prices and incomes in the rest of the economy; and the short-run problem is the (stability, instability) ___instability___ of farm prices and incomes from one year to the next.

4. The basic causes of the long-run farm problem are the (elastic, inelastic) ___inelastic___ demand for agricultural products, increases in supply which have been (greater, less) ___greater___ than the increases in demand, and the relative (mobility, immobility) ___immobility___ of agricultural resources.

5. The demand for farm products tends to be inelastic because farm products have few good ___substitutes___

6. The supply of farm commodities has increased rapidly since about the time of World War I because of ___technological___ progress.

7. The demand for agricultural products in the United States has not increased so rapidly as the supply of these products because the population of the U.S. has not ____________________ and because as the income of Americans has increased their expenditures for farm products have increased (more, less) ____________ than proportionally.

8. The price system has failed to reallocate farmers into occupations earning higher incomes because as resources, farmers, their land, and their capital are highly ____________.

9. The basic cause of the short-run farm problem is the ____________ demand for agricultural commodities. This contributes to unstable farm prices and incomes in two ways. Relatively (large, small) ____________ changes in the output of farm products result in relatively ____________ changes in farm prices and incomes; and relatively ____________ changes in demand result in relatively ____________ changes in prices and incomes.

10. As the American economy has grown and improved its agricultural technology, it has failed to reallocate ____________ from ____________ to ____________ sectors of the economy.

11. Two reasons advanced to support the farmers' claim to assistance from the government are the contentions that the farmer:

a. Has borne too large a share of the cost of ____________ in the U.S.

b. Sells the commodities produced in (competitive, noncompetitive) ____________ markets and is, therefore, (able, unable) ____________ to control the prices of these commodities.

12. Since the 1930s the farm policy in the United States has been designed to ____________ and to ____________ farm prices and farm incomes.

13. If farmers were to receive a parity price for a product, year after year a given output would enable them to acquire a (fixed, increased) ____________ amount of goods and services.

14. If the government supports farm prices at an above-equilibrium level, the result will be (shortages, surpluses) ____________ which the government must ____________ in order to maintain prices at their support level.

a. Farmers benefit from this price-support program because it increases their ____________

b. But consumers are hurt by it because they must pay higher ____________ and higher ____________

15. To bring the equilibrium level of prices in the market up to their support level, government has attempted to (increase, decrease) ____________ the demand for and to ____________ the supply of farm products.

16. Three programs employed by the government to reduce agricultural production were the acreage-____________, the acreage-____________, and the payment-____________ programs. To increase demand it has attempted to find new ____________ ____________ for agricultural commodities, to increase domestic ____________, and to ____________ more to foreign countries.

17. In the 1970s during the boom in the exportation of farm commodities the Federal government shifted from the use of support prices to the use of ____________ prices to enable the government to avoid the accumulation of stocks of ____________ farm commodities.

18. Were the market price of a certain farm product to fall below the target price of the product:

a. the Federal government would make a cash payment to farmers equal to the difference between ____________ ____________ for every unit of the product sold by them;

b. the *total* income of farmers would equal this cash payment *plus* ______

c. when compared with a support price that is equal to the target price,

(1) the total income of farmers will be (more, less, the same) ______

(2) the total expenditures of consumers for this product will be ______ because the demand for farm products is (elastic, inelastic, unitary elastic) ______

(3) the cash payments made by the Federal government to farmers will be (greater than, smaller than, the same as) ______ the cost to the government of a price-support program;

(4) the cost to taxpayers of storing government surpluses will be ______

(5) and (like, unlike) ______ a price-support program results in an (over-, under-, optimum) ______ allocation of resources to the production of this product.

19. After over 50 years of experience with programs designed to enhance and stabilize the incomes of farmers there is sufficient evidence to suggest that these programs (do, do not) ______ work well.

a. The various farm programs have failed to ______ resources, have largely benefited farmers with (high, low) ______ incomes, have produced conflicts and ______, have been (increasingly, decreasingly) ______ effective in achieving their goals, and have become (more, less) ______ expensive.

b. The evidence also suggests that the (microeconomic, macroeconomic) ______ policies of the Federal government are crucial to the well-being of farmers because these policies affect ______ rates in the economy. These rates affect

(1) the costs to farmers of carrying the ______ they have incurred; and

(2) the international value of the ______ which is one determinant of the quantities of farm commodities farmers are able to ______

20. The market-oriented income stabilization policy:

a. would have the Federal government (buy, sell) ______ agricultural commodities when their market prices fell below and ______ agricultural commodities when their market prices rose above their long-run trends of prices; and

b. would, its proponents contend, (expand, contract) ______ government involvement in agriculture, improve the ______ of resources in the long run, reduce the costs of the farm programs to ______, and stimulate the ______ of agricultural commodities.

■ **PROBLEMS AND PROJECTS**

1. The following table gives the index of prices farmers paid in three different years. The price farmers received in year 1, the base year, for a certain agricultural product was $3.50 per bushel.

a. Compute the parity price of the product in years 2 and 3 and enter them in the table.

Year	Index of prices paid	Parity price	Price received	Parity ratio
1	100	$3.50	$3.50	100%
2	120	____	3.78	___%
3	200	____	5.25	___%

b. The prices received for the product in each year are also shown in the table. Complete the table by computing the parity *ratio* in years 2 and 3. *(Hint:* It is *not* necessary to construct an index of prices received in order to compute the parity ratio. This ratio can be computed by dividing the price received by the parity price.)

2. In columns 1 and 2 in the following table is a demand schedule for agricultural product X.

(1) Price	(2) Bushels of X demanded	(3) Bushels of X demanded
$2.00	600	580
1.80	620	600
1.60	640	620
1.40	660	640
1.20	680	660
1.00	700	680
.80	720	700
.60	740	720

a. Is demand elastic or inelastic in the price range given? ______

b. If the amount of X produced should increase from 600 to 700 bushels, the income of producers of X would ______ from $______ to $______; an increase of ______% in the amount of X produced would cause income to ______ by ______%.

c. If the amount of X produced were 700 bushels and the demand for X decreased from that shown in columns 1 and 2 to that shown in columns 1 and 3, the price of X would ______ from $______ to $______; the income of farmers would ______ from $______ to $______

d. Assume that the government supports a price of $1.80, that the demand for X is that shown in columns 1 and 2, and that farmers grow 720 bushels of X.

(1) At the supported price there will be a surplus of ______ bushels of X.

(2) If the government buys this surplus at the support price the cost to the taxpayers of purchasing the surplus is $______

(3) The total income of the farmers producing product X when they receive the support price of $1.80 per bushel for their entire crop of 720 bushels is $______

(4) Had farmers to sell the crop of 720 bushels at the free-market price, the price of X would be only $______ per bushel; and the total income of these farmers would be $______

(5) The gain to farmers producing X from the price-support program is, therefore, $______

(6) In addition to the cost to taxpayers of purchasing the surplus, consumers pay a price that is $______ greater than the free-market price and receive a quantity of X that is ______ bushels less than they would have received in a free market.

3. The demand schedule for agricultural product Y is given in columns 1 and 2 of the following table.

(1) Price	(2) Bales of Y demanded	(3) Bales of Y demanded
$5.00	40,000	41,000
4.75	40,200	41,200
4.50	40,400	41,400
4.25	40,600	41,600
4.00	40,800	41,800
3.75	41,000	42,000
3.50	41,200	42,200

a. If farmers were persuaded by the government to reduce the size of their crop from 41,000 to 40,000 bales, the income of farmers would ______ from $______ to $______

b. If the crop remained constant at 41,000 bales and the demand for Y increased to that shown in columns 1 and 3, the income of farmers would ______ from $______ to $______

4. The demand and supply schedules for agricultural product Z are shown below.

Pounds of Z demanded	Price	Pounds of Z supplied
850	$1.30	1150
900	1.20	1100
950	1.10	1050
1000	1.00	1000
1050	.90	950
1100	.80	900
1150	70	850

a. The Federal government considers supporting the price of Z at $1.30 a pound. At this price:

(1) the quantity demanded is ________________ pounds, the quantity supplied is ________________ pounds, and the surplus is ________________ pounds;

(2) buyers spend $________________ for Z, the Federal government spends $________________ to purchase the surplus of Z, and the total income of the farmers who produce Z is ________________

b. As an alternative to the price-support program the government considers a target-price program with the target price set at $1.30 a pound.

(1) Knowing that they are going to receive at least $1.30 a pound for Z, farmers will produce ________________ pounds of Z and when they sell this quantity of Z to demanders the market price of Z is $________________ a pound.

(2) At this market price the buyers of Z will spend $________________ for Z. The difference between the target price and the market price is $__________ a pound; and the government will make a total cash payment of $________________ to the producers of Z. The total income of the producers of Z from both buyers and the government is $__________

c. Regardless of whether government supports the price of Z at $1.30 a pound or sets a target price of $1.30 a pound, the total income of the farmers who produce Z is $________________. But if the government selects the target-price program:

(1) the cost of the program to the government is (more, less) ________________ than the cost of the price-support program by $________________

(2) the buyers of Z obtain ________________ pounds more of Z, pay a price which is $__________ lower, and spend $________________ less on Z.

5. Suppose the demand for sow jowls during a certain period of time was that shown in the next table; and the Federal government wished to stabilize the price of sow jowls at $.70 a pound.

Price (per pound)	Quantity demanded (pounds)
$1.00	1000
.90	1020
.80	1040
.70	1060
.60	1080
.50	1100
.40	1120

a. If the output of sow jowls were 1100 pounds during that period of time, the market price of sow jowls would be $________________ and the Federal government would (buy, sell) ________________ (how many) ________________ pounds of sow jowls.

b. But if the output were 1000 pounds during that period of time, the market price of sow jowls would be $________________ and the Federal government would __________ (how many) __________ pounds of sow jowls.

■ SELF-TEST

Circle the T if the statement is true, the F if it is false.

1. Per capita nonfarm income is greater than per capita farm income. **T F**

2. A greater percentage of nonfarm families live in poverty than farm families. **T F**

3. The diversity in farm incomes refers to the fact that a small percentage of the farms receive a large percentage of total farm income and a large percentage of the farms receive a small percentage of total farm income. **T F**

4. The diversity in the incomes of farm families simplifies the problem of formulating farm policies to enhance and stabilize farm prices and incomes. **T F**

5. The long-run farm problem is that the incomes of farmers have been low relative to incomes in the economy as a whole. **T F**

6. Most of the recent technological advances in agriculture have been initiated by farmers. **T F**

7. The supply of agricultural products has tended to increase more rapidly than the demand for these products in the United States. T F

8. The size of the farm population of the United States has declined at a more rapid rate than the rate at which agriculture's share of national income has declined. T F

9. The size of the farm population in the United States has declined in both relative and absolute terms since about 1935. T F

10. The quantities of agricultural commodities produced tend to be fairly *insensitive* to changes in agricultural prices because a large percentage of farmers' total costs are variable. T F

11. The short-run farm problem is the sharp year-to-year fluctuations in farm prices and farm incomes that frequently occur. T F

12. The rate at which resources have been shifted from agriculture to the nonagricultural sectors of the American economy has been less than the rate which technological progress made possible. T F

13. The major aim of agricultural policy in the United States has been to enhance and stabilize farm prices and farm incomes. T F

14. Were the index of prices paid 500 percent higher and the price received by farmers 400 greater than in the base year, the parity ratio would be 125 percent. T F

15. Application of the parity concept to farm prices causes farm prices to decline and results in agricultural surpluses. T F

16. When government supports farm prices at above-equilibrium levels it can reduce the annual surpluses of agricultural commodities either by increasing the supply or by decreasing the demand for them. T F

17. The acreage-allotment, acreage-reserve, and the payment-in-kind programs were designed to decrease the supply of farm products. T F

18. Restricting the number of acres which farmers employ to grow agricultural products has not been a very successful method of reducing surpluses because farmers tend to cultivate their land more intensively when the acreage is reduced. T F

19. Look at the diagram preceding multiple-choice question 15. If the demand for the product is inelastic OQ_3CP_1 is greater than OQ_1BP_3. T F

20. A target price is a minimum price which the Federal government guarantees farmers will receive for a farm product by making a deficiency payment equal to the market price less the target price of the product to farmers for every unit of the product they produce. T F

21. A market-oriented income stabilization policy would shift the goal of farm policy from enhancing to stabilizing farm incomes. T F

22. Tight money and large Federal deficits are beneficial to the well-being of the agricultural sector of the American economy. T F

Circle the letter that corresponds to the best answer.

1. Which one of the following periods has little or nothing in common with the other three insofar as the economic condition of American agriculture in the period is concerned? (*a*) 1900 to 1914; (*b*) 1914 to 1919; (*c*) 1921 to 1940; (*d*) 1940 to 1950.

2. The 12% of the 2.4 million American farms that have annual sales in excess of $100,000 per farm receive what percentage of the total receipts from farming? (*a*) 12%; (*b*) 19%; (*c*) 33%; (*d*) 68%.

3. The 71% of the 2.4 million American farms that have annual sales (or receipts) less than $40,000 per farm receive what percentage of the total receipts from farming in the United States? (*a*) 12%; (*b*) 19%; (*c*) 33%; (*d*) 68%.

4. Which of the following is *not* characteristic of American agriculture? (*a*) Farmers sell their products in highly competitive markets; (*b*) farmers buy in markets which are largely noncompetitive; (*c*) the demand for agricultural products tends to be inelastic; (*d*) agricultural resources tend to be highly mobile.

5. If both the demand for and the supply of a product increase, (*a*) the quantity of the product bought and sold will increase; (*b*) the quantity of the product bought and sold will decrease; (*c*) the price of the product will increase; (*d*) the price of the product will decrease.

6. Which one of the following is *not* a reason why the increases in the demand for agricultural commodities have been relatively small? (*a*) The population of the United States has not increased so rapidly as the productivity of agriculture; (*b*) the increased per capita incomes of American consumers have resulted in less than proportionate increases in their expenditures for farm products; (c) the demand for agricultural products is inelastic; (d) the standard of living in the United States is well above the level of bare subsistence.

7. The price system has failed to solve the problem of low farm incomes because: (a) the demand for agricultural products is relatively inelastic; (b) the supply of agricultural products is relatively elastic; (c) agricultural products have relatively few good substitutes; (d) agricultural resources are relatively immobile.

8. If the demand for agricultural products is inelastic, a relatively small increase in supply will result in: (a) a relatively small increase in farm prices and incomes; (b) a relatively small decrease in farm prices and a relatively large increase in farm incomes; (c) a relatively large decrease in farm prices and incomes; (d) a relatively large increase in farm prices and a relatively small decrease in farm incomes.

9. The year-to-year instability of farm prices and farm incomes is the result of fluctuations in (a) the outputs of farmers; (b) the domestic demand for farm products; (c) the foreign demand for agricultural commodities; (d) all of the above.

10. Which of the following is *not* one of the arguments used in support of public aid for agriculture in the United States? (a) Farmers have had to bear a disproportionate part of the cost of economic progress; (b) farmers are subject to hazards to which other industries are not subject; (c) farmers sell their products in highly competitive markets; (d) farmers are more affected by competition from foreign producers than other parts of the economy.

11. Farm parity means that (a) the real income of the farmer remains constant; (b) a given output will furnish the farmer with a constant amount of real income; (c) the purchasing power of the farmer's money income remains constant; (d) the money income of the farmer will buy a constant amount of goods and services.

12. If the price of a certain farm product were \$.75 in the base period when the index of prices paid by farmers was 90, and if the present index of prices paid by the farmers is 150, then the parity price of the farm product today is: (a) \$.90; (b) \$1.12½; (c) \$1.25; (d) \$1.50.

13. The necessary consequences of the government's supporting farm prices at an above-equilibrium level is: (a) a surplus of agricultural products; (b) increased consumption of agricultural products; (c) reduced production of agricultural products; (d) the dumping of agricultural products.

14. Another consequence of having government support farm prices at an above-equilibrium level is that consumers pay higher prices for farm products and (a) consume more of these products and pay higher taxes; (b) consume less of these products and pay higher taxes; (c) consume more of these products and pay lower taxes; (d) consume less of these products and pay lower taxes.

Use the diagram below to answer multiple-choice questions 15 through 17. *D* is the demand for and *S* is the supply of a certain farm product.

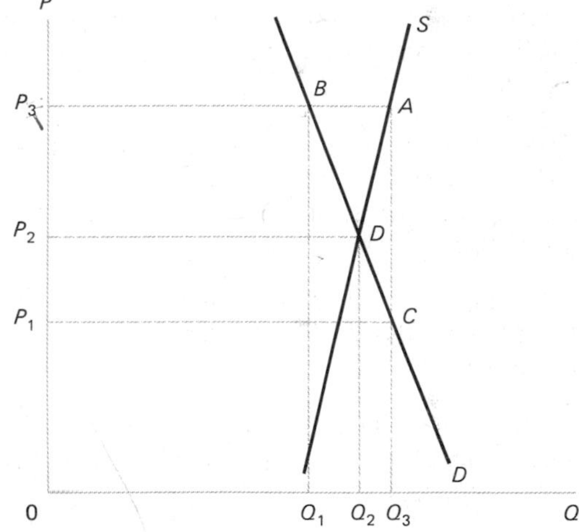

15. If the Federal government supported the price of this product at P_3, the total amount it would have to spend to purchase the surplus of the product would be (a) OQ_3AP_3; (b) Q_1Q_3AB; (c) P_1CAP_3; (d) OQ_1BP_3.

16. If the target price of the product were P_3, the total "deficiency payments" made by the Federal government to producers of the product would be (a) OQ_3AP_3; (b) Q_1Q_3AB; (c) P_1CAP_3; (d) OQ_1DP_3.

17. Regardless of whether the Federal government supports the price of the product at P_3 or sets the target-price at P_3, the total income of producers of the product will be (a) OQ_3AP_3; (b) OQ_1BP_3; (c) OQ_3CP_1; (d) OQ_2DP_2.

18. If the support price and the target price of a certain farm product were the same, the replacement of a price-support program by a target-price program would (a) increase the market price of the product; (b) increase the subsidy payments made by government to farmers; (*c*) increase the expenditures made by consumers of the product; (*d*) increase the incomes of farmers.

19. Which one of the following is *not* a reason why the farm program has been generally unsuccessful in accomplishing its aims? (*a*) The farm programs have not eliminated the basic cause of the problem; (*b*) restricting agricultural output increases farm prices but reduces farm income when demand is inelastic; (*c*) the farm program has become increasingly more costly and less effective; (*d*) the principal beneficiaries of government aid have been farmers with high, not low, incomes.

20. The nonfarm, macroeconomic policies of the Federal government most critical to the well-being of the agricultural sector of the economy are those that affect (*a*) interest rates in the economy; (*b*) the international value of the dollar; (*c*) the accessibility of foreign markets to farmers; (*d*) all of the above.

21. The goal of a market-oriented income stabilization policy would be (*a*) to prevent farm prices and incomes from falling in the long run; (*b*) to prevent sharp fluctuations in farm prices and incomes from one year to the next; (*c*) to increase farm prices and incomes in the long run; (*d*) to prevent both sharp year-to-year fluctuations and falling long-run farm prices and incomes.

22. In a market-oriented income stabilization policy the Federal government would (*a*) sell surplus farm commodities when their prices fall below their long-run trend of prices; (*b*) buy surplus farm commodities when their prices rise above their long-run trend of prices; (*c*) sell surplus farm commodities when their prices rise above their long-run trend; (*d*) buy surplus farm commodities when their market prices fall.

23. Which of the following is *not* one of the advantages its proponents see in a market-oriented income stabilization policy? (*a*) An expansion in the employment of resources in the agricultural sector of the economy; (*b*) an expansion in the exports of the agricultural sector of the economy; (*c*) a reduction in the costs to taxpayers of the farm program; (*d*) a reduction in government involvement in agriculture

■ DISCUSSION QUESTIONS

1. What was the economic condition of American agriculture: (*a*) prior to World War I; (*b*) during World War I; (*c*) from 1920 to 1940; (*d*) during World War II; (*e*) between 1950 and 1970? Explain the fundamental causes of the condition of agriculture in each of these periods.

2. Comment on (*a*) the size of farm incomes relative to nonfarm incomes; (*b*) the trend of farm incomes relative to nonfarm incomes; (*c*) the diversity in the incomes of farmers among the three groups examined in the text.

3. What is the long-run farm problem and its specific causes? What is the short-run farm problem and its causes?

4. Why does the demand for agricultural products tend to be inelastic?

5. What have been the specific causes of the large increases in the supply of agricultural products since World War I?

6. Why has the demand for agricultural products failed to increase at the same rate as the supply of these products?

7. Explain why the farm population tends to be relatively immobile. If farmers were more mobile, how would the price system reallocate their labor away from agriculture and into more prosperous occupations?

8. Explain why the inelastic nature of the demand for and the supply of agricultural products results in prices and incomes which change by large amounts as a consequence of small changes in either demand or supply.

9. Why do agricultural interests claim that farmers have a special right to aid from the Federal government?

10. What is meant by "the farm program"? What particular aspect of the farm problem has traditionally received the major attention of farmers and their representatives in Congress?

11. Explain the concept of parity and the parity ratio?

12. Why is the result of government-supported prices invariably a surplus of farm commodities? How do supported prices affect consumers and farmers?

13. What programs has the government used to try to restrict farm production? Why have these programs been relatively unsuccessful in limiting agricultural production?

14. How has the Federal government tried to increase the demand for farm products?

15. Explain what a target price is and how large a deficiency payment farmers would receive if the target price were greater than the market price.

16. Assuming the support price and the target price of a farm product would be the same, compare the price-support and target-price programs with respect to each of the following. (*a*) The total income received by farmers; (*b*) the total expenditures made by the consumers of the product; (*c*) the subsidy costs to taxpayers; (*d*) the storage costs of surpluses; and (*e*) the allocation of resources in the economy.

17. Why has farm policy not been successful in preventing falling farm prices and incomes, surpluses, and the disparity in farm incomes?

18. Why and in what ways have the nonfarm policies of the Federal government been critical to the well-being of the farm sector? What monetary and fiscal policies are harmful and beneficial to farmers?

19. Explain (*a*) how the market-oriented income stabilization policy would shift the emphasis from enhancing to stabilizing farm prices and incomes; (*b*) how the Federal government would stabilize farm prices and incomes if it adopted this policy; and (*c*) what advantages the proponents of this policy believe it would have.

20. What are the arguments of the pessimists and of the optimists on the issue of whether the world will be able to feed itself in the next century?

37
Urban economics: the problems of the cities

The farmers whose economic problems were examined in the last chapter have tilled the soil since before the beginning of recorded history. Cities and the problems of city living are nearly as old. Cities have been plagued by crowded conditions, crime, disease, poverty, and pollution for as long as cities have existed. Like the problems of the farmers, the problems of the cities are not entirely new. What makes the problems of the cities especially important in the United States today is the statistic that over three-fourths of the American population now reside in cities. (By way of contrast, only about one-twentieth of the population is engaged in farming.)

While the problems of cities may not be completely new, some of these problems have become more pressing than ever before. Other city problems are new and did not exist in the large cities of early recorded history. It is not possible in a single chapter to examine all the contemporary problems confronting American cities. The author, therefore, focuses his attention on the more crucial of these problems, their causes, and their potential solutions.

Economics is not the only discipline interested in the development of cities and in their problems. Other social scientists and natural and physical scientists are concerned and contribute to the analysis of these problems and to their solutions. This is to say that city problems and solutions go well beyond economics. But economics is an essential part of the explanation of the development of cities, their current plight, and the steps necessary to the improvement of city living. And this is the subject matter of this chapter: the economic aspects of urban problems.

The organization of Chapter 37 is relatively simple. Professor McConnell first explains the economic reasons cities emerge and grow by examining the economies of agglomeration. But as cities grow larger the disadvantages of agglomeration eventually appear. Then deglomerative forces lead firms and families to the suburbs where they can enjoy the benefits of urban life without having to contend with its increasing problems. With this flight to suburbia comes political fragmentation and an economic imbalance between the central city and the suburbs. This historical development is the source of many of our current urban problems. The three problems given special attention by the author are the ghetto, transportation, and pollution. Each is examined in some detail and the possible solutions to each problem are considered. The final section of the chapter looks at the financial and institutional changes which may have to be made before any improvement in city living is possible. These changes include the political consideration of the fragmented local governments and the employment of new methods of financing metropolitan governments.

The problem of the inadequate income of many of those who live in cities, especially in the ghettos, is not examined in great detail in this chapter. Poverty and the economics of inequality in the American economy is the trouble spot examined in Chapter 38.

■ CHECKLIST

When you have studied this chapter you should be able to:

☐ Define the economies of agglomeration and identify four principal agglomerative economies.

☐ Define a deglomerative force and identify the two kinds of deglomerative forces.

☐ Explain the advantage firms and households obtain and the disadvantages which they avoid by moving to the suburbs; and identify the two main consequences of this flight to suburbia.

☐ Explain what is meant by political fragmentation; and the economic imbalance and the cumulative decline that have resulted from the decline of the central city and suburban growth.

☐ Enumerate the circumstances which have given rise to central-city ghettos; and identify three means by which poverty in the ghettos might be reduced.

☐ State four causes of urban blight; and explain why the policies designed to reduce it have failed.

☐ Explain why an efficient transportation system is required in the larger cities; why the use of the automobile has increased and mass-transit systems have deteriorated; and the potential short-run and long-run solutions to the urban transportation problem.

☐ Describe, using the materials-balance approach, the four causes of the pollution problem and three potential solutions to the problem.

☐ Determine, when given the necessary data, the price (emission fee) a government agency should charge for pollution rights.

☐ List the institutional and fiscal changes which are prerequisites to a solution to urban problems; and the three potential solutions to the larger fiscal problem of local governments.

■ CHAPTER OUTLINE

1. Today over three-fourths of the American population live in urban areas.

2. Economic forces have led to the development and expansion of cities.

a. Firms can lower the cost of transporting resources and products by locating near their markets and other firms.

b. The increased productivity of agriculture has reduced the number of workers in farming. These excess workers have been drawn to cities where, because of the economies of agglomeration, business firms and jobs are located.

c. Only the large populations of urban centers have a demand for the amenities of life that is sufficient to warrant their production; and, as a result, consumers in cities find a wider variety of products available.

d. Deglomerative forces, sooner or later, limit the growth of central cities and the concentration of firms, and lead to the expansion of suburbs and to business decentralization.

3. To reap the advantages of urban life and to avoid its disadvantages, firms and households have moved to the suburbs. This flight to suburbia and the resulting suburban sprawl have had at least two important consequences.

a. A large number of separate political units surround the central city.

b. Wealth and income have increased in the suburbs and decreased in the central city; and the central city has experienced a decline in its tax base while its problems and need for public revenue have expanded.

4. A problem characteristic of large cities is the central city ghetto of low income, nonwhite, inadequately housed, and poorly educated inhabitants.

a. The poverty of the ghetto can be reduced by providing more and better jobs, income maintenance, and better education and training for those who live there.

b. The deterioration of the physical environment of the ghetto (urban blight) has a number of causes; and the policies adopted by government have failed to prevent and reverse it.

5. The flight to the suburbs has led to a locational mismatch of jobs and the labor force, automobile congestion and pollution, and the need for a more efficient transportation system.

6. The improvement of urban transportation requires solutions to both a short-run and a long-run problem.

a. To utilize the existing transport facilities more effectively entails the adoption of user charges and peak pricing policies.

b. To build a better transport system entails the development of public mass-transit systems.

7. Because of their high concentrations of population, industry, and automobiles, urban areas have a pollution problem.

a. The dimensions of the problem are well known and the long-run consequences are potentially disastrous.

b. The cause of the pollution problem is the materials imbalance between the wastes that result from production and consumption and the ability of the environment to reabsorb these wastes.

c. To reduce pollution requires that the costs of pollution be made private instead of social costs (be transferred from society to the polluter); and this may be accomplished by legislated standards, levying special taxes on polluters, or by creating a market for pollution rights.

8. Solutions to the various urban problems require that

sufficient financial resources be allocated and that certain institutional changes be made.

a. Consolidation of the many political units would increase the efficiency of decision making and improve equity by putting the needs and the resources within the same governmental unit.

b. To obtain sufficient resources to deal with urban problems may also require Federal revenue sharing, the shifting of some of the burden to the Federal government, and a restructuring of the property tax.

■ IMPORTANT TERMS

Economies of agglomeration
Internal economies of scale
External economies of scale
Infrastructure
Deglomerative forces
Urban sprawl
Political fragmentation
User charge
Peak pricing
Materials balance approach
Emission fees
Market for pollution rights
Black capitalism
Comprehensive Employment and Training Act of 1973 (CETA)

■ FILL-IN QUESTIONS

1. About ________ million people and ________% of the American population live in cities today.

2. Deciding *where* to produce goods and services is a part of the decision of (what, how, for whom) ________ ________ to produce. The *where* decision is an important one because there are ________ costs involved in moving ________ to the firm and in moving the finished products to ________.

3. Before cities can develop agriculture must be able to produce ________ food and fiber so that ________ is available to produce nonagricultural goods and services.

4. The economies of agglomeration refer to the lower production and marketing costs which firms realize when they locate ________ each other and their markets. Four such economies are:

a. ________

b. ________

c. ________

d. ________

5. The deglomerative forces include all those forces which result in (lower, higher) ________ production costs. Some of these are internal to the firm; but others are ________ to the firm, are shifted to ________ and are called ________ costs.

6. The flight of people and firms to the suburbs enables them to obtain the (advantages, disadvantages) ________ ________ of a metropolitan area and to avoid its ________

The chief consequences of this movement have been political ________ and an economic (balance, imbalance) ________ between the central city and the suburbs.

7. The movement of the higher-income families and the wealthier firms to new political units in suburbia has:

a. eroded the (excise, property) ________ tax base and brought about increases in tax (collections, rates) ________ in the central city;

b. left behind a central city of poor families, many of whom are (small, large) ________ and on welfare, living in (densely, sparsely) ________ ________ populated areas for which the cost of providing social facilities and services is (low, high) ________

8. The central city ghetto has developed in major American cities because:

a. the more prosperous and better ________ ________ whites have moved to the ________ and left behind obsolete ________ *b.* their places have been taken by poorly ______________________, unskilled, and ______________ -income blacks.

c. job opportunities for the ghetto inhabitants have shifted from the ______________ to the ______________; and access to these opportunities has been limited by the deterioration of the ______________ system and by racial ______________

9. To alleviate poverty in the ghettos requires that their residents be provided with more and better ______________, improved ______________ and ______________; and that a program of income ______________ be instituted.

10. Among the causes of urban blight are the exodus of families and firms from the central city and the resulting spillover costs; the property-tax ______________; ______________ against blacks and other minorities; and rent ______________

11. Flight to the suburbs has also resulted in:

a. a locational mismatch because the ______________ of those who live in suburbia are in the central city and of those who live in the central city are in suburbia;

b. the need for a more efficient ______________ system;

c. expanded use of the ______________, traffic ______________, and air ______________

d. the construction of still more ______________, the development of more distant ______________, and still more ______________ and ______________

e. the general deterioration of the ______________ systems of the cities.

12. It has been suggested that

a. to relieve highway congestion there be a ______________ on drivers and that ______________ policies should be used on highways and mass-transit systems;

b. in the long run it will be necessary to rebuild the ______________ in urban areas.

13. The materials balance approach to pollution is that the weight of the residual ______________ produced by society has come to exceed the ability of ______________ to ______________ them. This imbalance is the result of increases in the nation's ______________ and ______________, changes in ______________ and the absence of economic ______________ to refrain from pollution.

14. The institutional and financial prerequisites to the solution of urban problems are political ______________ and an increase in the ______________ of urban governments.

15. Political consolidation will result in more efficient ______________ making and reduce the disparity between ______________ and ______________ within urban areas.

16. The larger financial problem of urban areas will be reduced by political consolidation, Federal revenue ______________, the shifting of some of the financial burden of cities to ______________, and by overhauling the property tax so that ______________ is taxed more heavily and ______________ less heavily.

■ PROBLEMS AND PROJECTS

1. Describe conditions in the central city ghetto by placing one or more of the adjectives in the list below after each of the following indicators of well-being.

high	crowded
low	grossly inadequate
inadequate	deteriorated
old	deplorable
poor	

a. Schools: __________

b. Mortality rates: __________

c. Income levels: __________

d. Medical care: __________

e. Housing: __________

f. Crime rates: __________

g. Sanitation: __________

h. Disease incidence: __________

2. Below is a table showing the average number of motor vehicles traveling each mile of highway in a hypothetical metropolitan area and the estimated cost to society of each vehicle-mile traveled during various periods of the day. Compute the total cost per mile of highway in each of the seven periods of the day.

Period of the day	Vehicles per highway-mile	Cost per vehicle-mile	Total cost
7am–9am	500	$ .60	$______
9am–12n	150	.10	______
12n–2pm	200	.15	______
2pm–4pm	100	.10	______
4pm–6pm	600	.85	______
6pm–10pm	200	.15	______
10pm–7am	50	.10	______

a. In every twenty-four hour period the total number of vehicles traveling each mile of highway is __________ and the total cost for each mile of highway traveled is $__________

b. The average cost to society for a vehicle to travel one mile is $__________

c. Assuming that the number of vehicles per highway-mile is not affected by the imposition of a user charge and that the user charge is the same during all periods, the user charge that would enable society to recover the full cost of the highway system would be $__________ per vehicle-mile.

d. Imagine now that the imposition of this user charge results in the following change in vehicular traffic during the various periods of the day. The cost per vehicle-mile remains the same in each period; and the total cost in each period is shown in the table below.

Period of the day	Vehicles per highway-mile	Total cost	Total revenue
7am–9am	450	$270.00	$______
9am–12n	135	13.50	______
12n–2pm	180	27.00	______
2pm–4pm	90	9.00	______
4pm–6pm	540	459.00	______
6pm–10pm	180	27.00	______
10pm–7am	45	4.50	______

(1) The total cost per day of each mile of highway is $__________

(2) Compute the total revenue in each period when a 50 cents per mile user charge is made. The total revenue per day on each mile of highway is $__________

(3) In what two periods are the revenues received less than the cost in that period? __________ and __________

e. If it is desired to reduce the number of vehicles per mile of highway in these two periods to 400, and if each 1 cent increase in the user charge decreases the number of vehicles per mile by 10 vehicles, the user charge in the:

(1) 7am–9am period should be increased to ______ cents per mile

(2) 4pm–6pm period should be increased to ______ cents per mile

3. Assume the atmosphere of Cuyahoga County, Ohio (the Cleveland metropolitan area) is able to reabsorb 1500 tons of pollutants per year. The schedule on the next page shows the price polluters would be willing to pay for the right to dispose of 1 ton of pollutants per year and the total quantity of pollutants they would wish to dispose of at each price.

Price (per ton of pollutant rights)	Total quantity of pollutant rights demanded (tons)
$ 0	4,000
1,000	3,500
2,000	3,000
3,000	2,500
4,000	2,000
5,000	1,500
6,000	1,000
7,000	500

a. If there were no emission fee, polluters would put ________________ tons of pollutants in the air each year; and this quantity of pollutants would exceed the ability of nature to reabsorb them by ________________ tons.

b. To reduce pollution to the capacity of the atmosphere to recycle pollutants, an emission fee of $________________ per ton should be set.

c. Were this emission fee set, the total emission fees set would be $________________

d. Were the quantity of pollution rights demanded at each price to increase by 500 tons, the emission fee could be increased by $________________ and total emission fees collected would increase by $________________

■ SELF-TEST

Circle the T if the statement is true, the F if it is false.

1. About 180 million Americans live in cities. **T F**

2. Since 1900 the percentage of the American population living in central cities has increased. **T F**

3. External economies of scale shift a firm's average-cost curve downward. **T F**

4. A deglomerative force increases the cost of producing a product and may be either internal or external to the firm. **T F**

5. The flight to the suburbs has involved the migration of families but has not resulted in the movement of business firms. **T F**

6. Political fragmentation refers to the control of both the central city and most of the suburbs around it by a single metropolitan government. **T F**

7. The flight to the surburbs has brought about a general improvement in the public mass-transit systems of cities. **T F**

8. Black capitalism entails the development in ghetto areas of business firms which are owned and operated by blacks. **T F**

9. It has been estimated that improved employment opportunities for its residents will eliminate 90% of the ghetto poverty. **T F**

10. CETA provides grants to state and local governments to help them provide manpower training programs. **T F**

11. Tax rates tend to be higher in the suburbs than in central cities. **T F**

12. Rent controls tend to reduce the shortage of housing in urban areas. **T F**

13. The programs and subsidies of the Federal government have, by and large, failed to reduce or even to prevent the spread of urban blight. **T F**

14. When an urban bus company utilizes a peak-pricing system the fares it charges riders are higher during rush hours than at other times of the day. **T F**

15. The long-run solution to the urban transportation problem will require the expansion and improvement of mass-transit systems. **T F**

16. Pollution is caused almost exclusively by profit-seeking business firms. **T F**

17. An effective antipollution policy requires that the social costs of pollution be turned into private costs. **T F**

18. Because in any period of time and in any region the quantity of pollutants that can be absorbed by nature is fixed, the supply of pollutant rights will be perfectly elastic. **T F**

19. The *equity* grounds for political consolidation are that it will put the resources and the needs within the same political jurisdiction. **T F**

20. The "larger fiscal problem" refers to the inability of urban governments, even if there were political consolidation, to find sufficient tax revenues to cover their costs. **T F**

Circle the letter that corresponds to the best answer.

1. About what percentage of the American population lives in cities? (*a*) 85%; (*b*) 80%; (*c*) 75%; (*d*) 70%.

2. Deciding where to produce a product is a part of the decision a firm makes when it decides (*a*) what to produce; (*b*) how much to produce; (*c*) how to produce; (*d*) for whom to produce.

3. Which of the following will result in an internal economy of scale for firm A? (*a*) The growth of the market for firm A's product; (*b*) the development of other firms who are able to perform specialized services for firm A; (*c*) the expansion and improvement of the infrastructure; (*d*) the improvement of the transportation facilities used by firm A.

4. The flight to the suburbs has had all but one of the following consequences. Which one? (*a*) Political consolidation; (*b*) an economic imbalance between the central city and the suburbs; (*c*) an erosion of the property-tax base in the central city; (*d*) a mismatch between the location of the labor force and the location of job opportunities.

5. Which of the following is *not* characteristic of the economic imbalance between the central city and its suburbs? (*a*) The more prosperous citizens and firms are in the suburbs and the less prosperous ones are in the central city; (*b*) the cost of public services *per citizen* is higher in the suburbs than in the central city; (*c*) the tax base shrinks in the central city and grows in the suburbs; (*d*) tax rates increase in the central city.

6. Which of the following has probably been the *most* important cause of the emergence of black ghettos? (*a*) Racial discrimination; (*b*) the flight to the suburbs; (*c*) the deterioration of public mass-transit systems; (d) high crime rates in the central cities.

7. The unemployment rate among blacks is (*a*) less than; (*b*) about the same as; (*c*) double; (*d*) triple the rate for whites.

8. Which one of the following is *not* true? (*a*) Mortgage subsidies of one kind or another have been more helpful to high- and middle-income groups than to low-income groups; (*b*) urban-renewal projects have increased the supply of housing for low-income families; (*c*) some low-income families have been helped by public-housing and rent-subsidy programs; (*d*) some housing programs have been inadequately financed.

9. Which of the following is *not* generally considered to be a step that would lead to the solution of the urban transportation problem? (*a*) The imposition of user charges on the highway system; (*b*) following a peak-pricing policy on the public mass-transit systems; (*c*) the reconstruction and expansion of the mass-transit systems; (*d*) the construction of more and the expansion of existing highways to connect the central city with the suburbs.

10. User charges imposed on those who drive on urban freeways would tend to (*a*) relieve congestion on the freeways; (*b*) discourage the use of public transportation facilities; (*c*) reduce the funds available for the expansion of the freeway system; (*d*) do all of the above.

11. Which of the following has *not* contributed to the pollution problem in the United States? (*a*) Increasing population density; (*b*) rising gasoline prices; (*c*) an expanding standard of living; (*d*) the rise in the use of leaded gasoline.

12. Which of the following would do little or nothing to reduce pollution? (*a*) Create a market for pollution rights; (*b*) charge polluters an emission fee; (*c*) enact legislation that prohibits pollution and fines polluters; (*d*) redesign and reconstruct the infrastructure.

13. An emission fee levied against polluters will tend to (*a*) encourage the use of pollution-abatement equipment; (*b*) decrease pollution; (*c*) reduce the revenues of governments that levy the fee; (*d*) externalize the internal costs of pollution.

14. An increase in the demand for pollution rights will (*a*) increase both the quantity of pollutants discharged and the market price of pollution rights; (*b*) increase the quantity discharged and have no effect on the market price; (*c*) have no effect on the quantity discharged and increase the market price; (*d*) have no effect on either the quantity discharged or the market price.

15. Which one of the following is *not* an argument on grounds of *efficiency* for political consolidation? (*a*) There are economies of scale that result from consolidation; (*b*) within the same political jurisdiction a citizen will be able to choose the community with the levels of taxation and public services the citizen finds most attractive; (*c*) there are from the public goods and services produced in a small political unit spillover benefits which accrue to residents in other political units and these goods and services are, therefore, underproduced; (*d*) the quality of public goods and services is increased without any increase in total costs by consolidation.

16. Which of the following would do little by itself to solve the problems of the central city? (*a*) Political consolidation; (*b*) increased use of local income taxes; (*c*) Federal revenue sharing with the cities; (*d*) reduced taxation of buildings.

17. One of the proposed solutions to the larger fiscal problem of city governments is to shift some of the financial responsibility for these governments (*a*) back to the cities, themselves; (*b*) onto their suburbs; (*c*) to county and regional governments; (*d*) to the Federal and state governments.

18. The suggestion to overhaul the property tax system has been made (*a*) because the property tax is proportional; (*b*) to reduce land values; (*c*) as an incentive for the construction and improvement of buildings; (*d*) to increase the supply of land.

■ DISCUSSION QUESTIONS

1. Explain why firms must decide where to produce and why they tend to agglomerate.

2. What is the difference between an internal and an external economy? What are the principal economies which induce firms to locate near other firms?

3. What is a deglomerative force? What are the principal deglomerative forces internal to the firm? What deglomerative forces are external to the firm?

4. Explain the reasons for the flight of families and business firms to the suburbs. What families and kinds of firms have remained in the central city?

5. Explain in detail the two most important consequences of the flight to suburbia.

6. Explain why ghettos developed in central cities and describe living conditions in and the characteristics of the typical ghetto. What can be done to alleviate ghetto poverty?

7. What are the chief causes of urban blight? What steps has the Federal government taken to reduce it and why have these programs failed to help low-income families in the central city and to arrest the spread of the blight?

8. What are the causes of the urban transportation problem and what might be done to improve the urban transportation system in (*a*) the short run and (*b*) the long run?

9. Employing the materials balance approach, explain the causes of the pollution problem. What are the three major policies that might be adopted to reduce pollution and what problems would be encountered in applying these policies?

10. What are the institutional and financial prerequisites to the solution of urban problems? Why are these changes necessary and how might they be accomplished?

38
Income distribution: inequality, poverty, and discrimination

Chapter 38 examines the fourth of the so-called trouble spots in the American economy: the unequal distribution of the total income of the economy among its families, the poverty of many of these families, and the economic discrimination that is a major factor leading to the unequal distribution and to poverty.

The things which you should learn from this chapter are found in the checklist below. In addition, the following ideas have an important bearing on the discussion of inequality and poverty. First, you will recall from Chapter 6 that one of the functions of government in the American economy is to modify the economic results which a *pure* price-market system would yield: it is the price-market system and the institutions of capitalism which bring about an unequal distribution of income, and government in the United States has worked to reduce—but not eliminate—this unequal distribution.

Second, the critics of the price-market system (see Chapter 5) have attacked the system because it has unequally distributed income. But American capitalism has replied by repairing many of its faults. It is for this reason that the Socialist party and other groups advocating drastically different economic systems have met with little success in the United States.

Third, the single most effective method of reducing the importance of income inequality and the extent of poverty in the United States has been the maintenance of full employment and an expanding average standard of living. Other programs have aided in the achievement of this goal, but the best cure has been the high and increasing output of the American economy.

Fourth, very few people advocate an absolutely equal distribution of income; the question to be decided is not one of inequality or equality, but of how much or how little inequality there should be. The question can be looked at either ethically or economically, and the economist has nothing to offer on the ethical question but his own personal value judgment. From the economic point of view it is the task of the economist to observe that less income inequality may result in a smaller national output and a lower employment rate. This is "the big trade-off" confronting the economy and it requires that the people of the United States make a choice. The pros and cons of the income-inequality issue represent no more than different opinions on the degree to which we should reduce our economic efficiency (total output and employment) in order to reduce income inequality.

Finally, while poverty is caused by many forces, it is essentially an economic problem. Any attack on poverty will have to be basically an economic attack. There are reasons why the problem of poverty may not be solved in the United States; but one of these reasons is not that the American economy cannot afford to abolish poverty. The costs of poverty far outweigh the costs of eliminating it; and surely a rich nation can afford what it costs to provide the necessities of life for all of its citizens.

■ CHECKLIST

When you have studied this chapter you should be able to:

☐ Present data from the textbook to support the conclusion that there is considerable income inequality in the United States.

☐ Report what has happened to the distribution of income in the United States since1929 and since 1947.

☐ State what is measured on each axis when a Lorenz curve is used to describe the degree of income inequality; and what area measures the extent of income inequality.

☐ Explain the two ways in which Census Bureau data on income inequality have been adjusted; and what the adjusted data reveal about the degree of and the trends in income equality in the United States.

☐ Describe the effects of taxes and of transfer payments on the extent of inequality in the distribution of income and poverty in the American economy.

☐ Enumerate six causes of an unequal distribution of income.

☐ State the case *for* and the case *against* income equality; and then explain the trade-off between equality and efficiency that is at the heart of the debate over how much income inequality is desirable.

☐ Use current government standards to define poverty and to describe the extent of poverty in the United States; enumerate the groups in which poverty is concentrated; and explain why poverty tends to be invisible.

☐ List four kinds of discrimination; and explain how much this discrimination costs the United States each year.

☐ Use the crowding model to explain why women and blacks receive lower wages and why the labor resources of the economy are more efficiently allocated when occupational discrimination is eliminated.

☐ State the comparable worth doctrine and three objections to using it to set wages for women.

☐ List a few of the nondiscriminatory factors that have resulted in women receiving lower incomes than men.

☐ Contrast social insurance with public assistance (welfare); and enumerate the three programs in the former and the four programs in the latter category.

☐ Explain how a negative income tax (NIT) might be employed to reduce poverty and the two crucial elements in any NIT plan.

☐ List the three goals of any NIT plan and explain why it is impossible to devise a program in which these three objectives do not conflict.

■ CHAPTER OUTLINE

1. There is considerable income inequality in the American economy.

a. The extent of the inequality can be seen by examining a personal-distribution-of-income table.

b. Since 1929 the real incomes received by all income classes have increased; and between 1929 and 1947 the relative distribution of personal income changed to reduce income inequality. But since 1947 the relative distribution has been almost constant.

c. The Lorenz curve is a geometric device for portraying the extent of inequality in any group at any time, for comparing the extent of inequality among different groups, and for contrasting the extent of inequality at different times.

2. The data published annually by the Bureau of the Census may overstate the extent of income inequality in the United States.

a. By broadening the concept of income to include in-kind transfers, education provided by government, and capital gains, and by subtracting Federal personal income and payroll taxes, Browning concluded that inequality in the distribution of income is less than assumed and has lessened with the passage of time.

b. By looking at earnings over a lifetime rather than in a single year Paglin found that there is less income inequality than census data indicate and that income equality has lessened since World War II.

3. The tax system and the transfer payments of government in the United States significantly reduce the extent of income inequality and of poverty in the American economy.

4. The impersonal price system does not necessarily result in a distribution of income which society deems just; at least six specific factors explain why income inequality exists.

5. The important question which society must answer is not whether there will or will not be income inequality but what is the best amount of inequality.

a. Those who argue for equality contend that it leads to the maximum satisfaction of consumer wants (utility) in the economy.

b. But those who argue for inequality contend that equality would reduce the incentives to work, save, invest, and take risks; and that these incentives are needed if the economy is to be efficient: to produce as large an output (and income) as it is possible for it to produce from its available resources.

c. In the United States there is a trade-off between economic equality and economic efficiency. A more nearly equal distribution of income results in less economic efficiency (a smaller national output) and greater economic efficiency leads to a more unequal distribution of income. The debate over the right amount of inequality depends, therefore, upon how much output society is willing to sacrifice to reduce income inequality.

6. Aside from inequality in the distribution of income, there is great concern today with the problem of poverty in the United States.

a. Using the generally accepted definition of poverty, about 14% of the people in the American economy live in poverty; and these poor tend to be concentrated among certain kinds of families.

b. Poverty in the United States tends to be invisible because it is obscured by the general affluence of the economy as a whole and hidden from the eyes of the remainder of society.

7. The greater incidence of poverty among blacks, Hispanics, and women is in part the result of discrimination.

a. This discrimination is found in the wage, employment, human-capital, and occupational discrimination to which these groups are subject.

b. Women and blacks have been subjected to occupational discrimination which has crowded them into a small number of occupations in which the supply of workers is large relative to the demand for them and wage rates and incomes are, therefore, lower; and the crowding model illustrates these effects and the effects of the elimination of this discrimination.

c. The costs of this discrimination to the economy are estimated at 4% of the GNP.

d. It is necessary to add to the examination of income inequality, poverty, and discrimination in the United States that

(1) the comparable worth doctrine has been suggested as a further method of reducing occupational discrimination against women; and while this suggestion has been subjected to several criticisms, it will be an important public-policy issue in the future; and

(2) the differences between the incomes of men and women and between those of whites and nonwhites are not all due to discrimination and are instead due to nondiscriminatory factors.

8. The income-maintenance system of the United States is intended to reduce poverty and includes both social insurance and public assistance (welfare) programs.

a. OASDI ("social security") and Medicare are the principal social insurance programs and are financed by taxes levied on employers and employees.

b. The unemployment insurance programs maintained by the states and financed by taxes on employers are also a part of the social insurance program of the United States.

c. The public assistance programs include SSI, AFDC, food stamps, and Medicaid.

d. The social security (or welfare) system has been criticized in recent years; and its critics argue that it is costly to administer, is inequitable, and impairs incentives to work.

9. A new approach to income maintenance would employ a negative income tax (NIT) to subsidize families whose incomes are below a certain level.

a. In any NIT plan a family would be guaranteed a minimum income and the subsidy to a family would decrease as its earned income increases. But a comparison of three alternative plans reveals that the guaranteed income, the (benefit-loss) rate at which the subsidy declines as earned income increases, and the (break-even) income at which the subsidy is no longer paid may differ.

b. The comparison of the plans also indicates there is a conflict among the goals of taking families out of poverty, maintaining incentives to work, and keeping the costs of the plan at a reasonable level; and that a trade-off among the three goals is necessary because no one plan can achieve all three goals.

■ IMPORTANT TERMS

Income inequality
Lorenz curve
In-kind transfer
Optimal distribution of income
Equality vs. efficiency (the big) trade-off
Poverty
Wage discrimination
Employment discrimination
Human-capital discrimination
Occupational discrimination
Crowding model of occupational discrimination
Comparable worth doctrine
Income-maintenance system
Social security programs
Public assistance (welfare) programs
Old age, survivors, and disability insurance (OASDI)
Medicare
Unemployment insurance (compensation)
Supplemental security income (SSI)
Aid to families with dependent children (AFDC)
Food stamp program
Medicaid
Negative income tax (NIT)
Guaranteed income
Benefit-loss rate
Break-even income

■ FILL-IN QUESTIONS

1. It can fairly be said that the extent of income inequality in the United States is ____________

a. The percentage of total personal income received by the highest quintile has since 1929 (increased, decreased) ____________ and the percentage received by the lowest two quintiles has ____________; and these changes can fairly be said to have been (slight, significant) ____________.

b. But since the close of World War II the distribution of personal income in the United States (has, has not) ____________ changed significantly.

2. Income inequality can be portrayed graphically by drawing a (Laffer, marginal utility, Lorenz) ____________ curve.

a. When such a curve is plotted, the cumulative percentage of (income, families) ____________ is measured along the horizontal and the cumulative percentage of ____________ is measured along the vertical axis.

b. The curve which would show a completely (perfectly) equal distribution of income is a diagonal line which would run from the (lower, upper) ____________ left to the ____________ right corner of the graph.

c. The extent or degree of income inequality is measured by the area which lies between the ____________ and the ____________

3. Two major criticisms of the census data on the distribution of income in the United States are that the income concept used in the census is too (narrow, broad) ____________ and that the income-accounting period is too (short, long) ____________. When the data are adjusted to take account of these two criticisms the distribution of income is (more, less) ____________ unequal and over time the inequality has become (greater, smaller) ____________

4. The tax system and the transfer programs in the American economy significantly (reduce, expand) ____________ the degree of inequality in the distribution of income.

5. The important factors which explain (or cause) income inequality are differences in ____________; in ____________ and ____________; in job ____________ and risk; in the ownership of ____________; in market ____________; and in luck, connections, misfortune, and discrimination.

6. Those who argue for the:

a. equal distribution of income contend that it results in the maximization of total (income, utility) ____________ in the economy;

b. unequal distribution of income believe it results in a greater total (income, utility) ____________

7. The so-called "big trade-off" is between economic ____________ and economic ____________. This means that:

a. less income inequality leads to a (greater, smaller) ____________ total output; and

b. a larger total output requires (more, less) ____________ income inequality.

8. Using the more or less official definition of poverty,

a. The poor includes any family of four with less than $____________ and any individual with less than $____________ a year to spend.

b. Approximately ____________% of the population and about ____________ million people are poor.

9. Poverty tends to be concentrated:

a. among the (young, elderly) ____________

b. among (whites, blacks and Hispanics) ____________

c. in families headed by ____________

10. In the affluent American economy much of its poverty is ____________

11. The four principal kinds of economic discrimination are:

a. wage

b. employment

c. human-capital

d. occupational

This discrimination against blacks costs the economy an amount equal to 4 % of its present total output or more than $ 160 billion a year.

12. The occupational discrimination that pushes women and blacks into a small number of occupations in which the supply of labor is large relative to the demand for it is explained by the crowding model.

a. Because supply is large relative to demand, wages and incomes in these occupations are (high, low) [low circled]

b. The reduction or elimination of this occupational discrimination would result in a (more, less) more efficient allocation of the labor resources of the economy, and a(n) (expansion, contraction) expansion in the national income and output.

13. The income-maintenance system in the United States consists of social insurance programs and public assistance programs.

a. In the first category of programs are

(1) OASDI "social sec"

and medi- care ; and

(2) unemployment compensation.

b. In the second category are

(1) (use initials) SSI and AFDC ;

(2) the food-stamp program; and

(3) medi- caid

c. Critics of the income-maintenance system often refer to "the welfare mess" and point to its three *ins*: they contend that it is administratively *in-*efficient, is *in-*equidable, and impairs work *in-*centives

14. The two critical elements of any negative income tax plan are a guranteed income below which family incomes would not be allowed to fall and a benefit - loss rate which specifies the rate at which the subsidy would be reduced if earned income increases.

15. The three goals of any negative income tax plan:

a. are to get families out of poverty, provide incentives to work, and ensure the costs of the program are reasonable;

b. are (complementary, conflicting) conflicting

■ PROBLEMS AND PROJECTS

1. The distribution of personal income among families in a hypothetical economy is shown in the table on the next page.

a. Complete the table by computing:

(1) The percentage of all families in each income class and all lower classes; enter these figures in column 4.

(2) The percentage of total income received by each income class and all lower classes; enter these figures in column 5.

b. From the distribution of income data in columns 4 and 5 it can be seen that:

(1) Consumer units with less than $10,000 a year income constitute the lowest ________% of all families and receive ________% of the total income.

(2) Families with incomes of $25,000 a year or more constitute the highest ________% of all families and receive ________% of the total income.

c. Use the figures you entered in columns 4 and 5 to draw a Lorenz curve on the graph on page 341. (Plot the seven points and the zero-zero point and connect them with a smooth curve.)

(1) On the same graph draw a diagonal line which would indicate complete equality in the distribution of income.

(2) Shade the area of the graph that shows the degree of income inequality.

(1) Personal income class	(2) Percentage of all families in this class	(3) Percentage of total income received by this class	(4) Percentage of all families in this and all lower classes	(5) Percentage of total income received by this and all lower classes
Under $5,000	18	4	______	______
5,000-9,999	12	6	______	______
10,000-14,999	14	12	______	______
15,000-19,999	17	14	______	______
20,000-24,999	19	15	______	______
25,000-49,999	11	20	______	______
50,000 and over	9	29	______	______

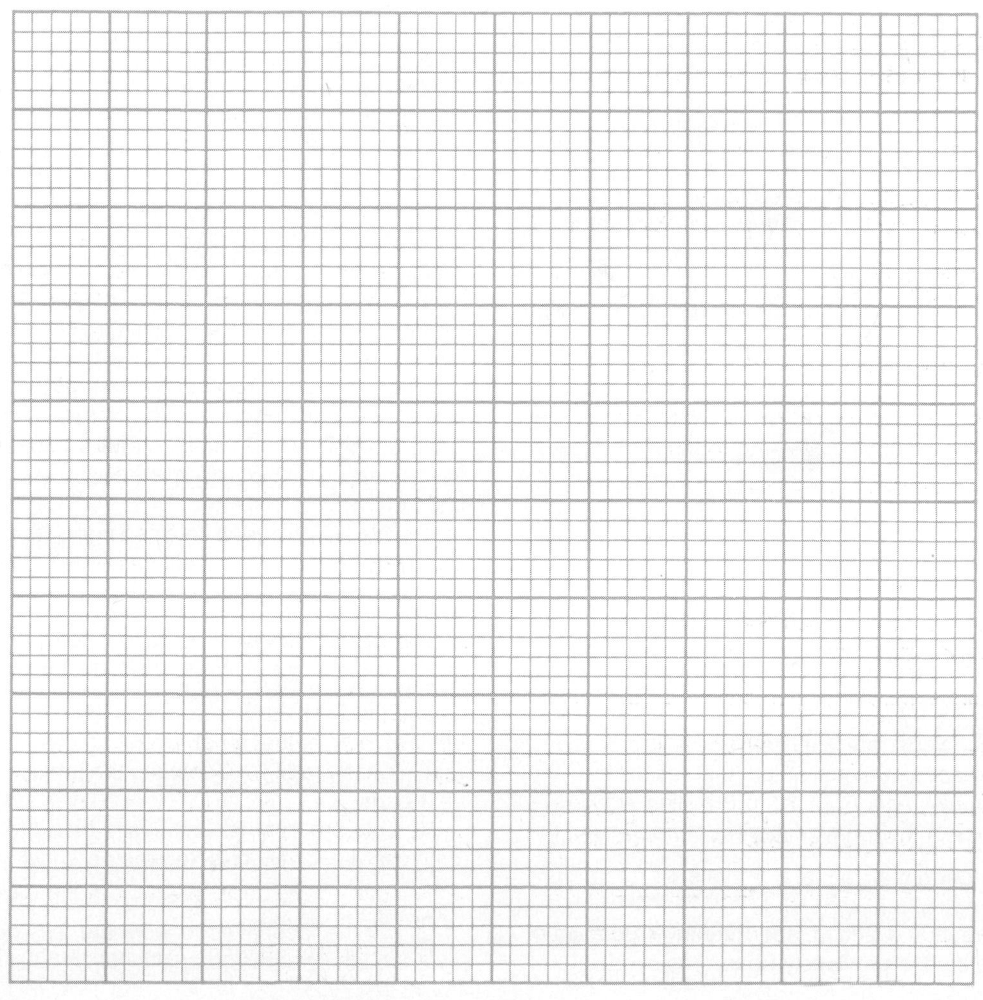

2. Suppose there are only three labor markets in the economy and each of these markets is perfectly competitive. The table below contains the demand (or marginal-revenue-product) schedule for labor in *each* of these three markets.

Wage rate (marginal revenue product of labor per hour)	Quantity of labor (millions per hour)
$11	4
10	5
9	6
8	7
7	8
6	9
5	10
4	11
3	12

a. Assume there are 24 million homogeneous workers in the economy and that one-half of these workers are male and one-half are female.

(1) If the 12 million female workers can be employed only in labor market Z, for all of them to find employment the hourly wage rate must be $______

(2) If of the 12 million male workers, 6 million are employed in labor market X and 6 million are employed in labor market Y, the hourly wage rate in labor markets X and Y will be $______

b. Imagine now that the impediment to the employment of females in labor markets X and Y is removed; and that as a result (and because the demand and marginal revenue product of labor is the same in all three markets) 8 million workers find employment in each labor market.

(1) In labor market Z (in which only females had previously been employed):

(*a*) the hourly wage rate will rise to $______

(*b*) the *decrease* in national output that results from the decrease in employment from 12 to 8 million workers is equal to the loss of the marginal revenue products of the workers no longer employed; and it totals $______ million.

(2) In labor market X and in labor market Y (in each of which only males had previously been employed):

(*a*) the hourly wage rate will fall to $______

(*b*) the *increase* in national output that results from the increase in employment from 6 to 8 million workers is equal to the marginal revenue products of the additional workers employed; and the gain in *each* of these markets is $______ million and the total gain in the two markets is $______

(3) the *net* gain to society from the reallocation of female workers is $______ million.

3. The table below contains different possible earned incomes for a family of a certain size.

Earned income	NIT subsidy	Total income
$ 0	$5,000	$5,000
5,000	______	______
10,000	______	______
15,000	______	______
20,000	______	______
25,000	______	______

a. Assume that $5,000 is the guaranteed income for a family of this size and that the benefit-loss rate is 20%. Enter the NIT subsidy and the total income at each of the five remaining earned-income levels. (*Hint:* 20% of $5,000 is $1,000.)

(1) This NIT program retains strong incentives to work because whenever the family earns an additional $5,000 its total income increases by $______

(2) But this program is costly because the family receives a subsidy until its earned income, the break-even income, is $______

b. To reduce the break-even income the benefit-loss rate is raised to 50%. Complete the table at the top of the next page.

(1) This program is less costly than the previous one because the family only receives a subsidy until it earns the break-even income of $______;

(2) but the incentives to work are less because whenever the family earns ad additional $5,000 its total income increases by only $______

Earned income	NIT subsidy	Total income
$ 0	$5,000	$5,000
2,500	______	______
5,000	______	______
7,500	______	______
10,000	______	______

c. Both of the previous two NIT programs guaranteed an income of only $5,000. Assume that that guaranteed income is raised to $7,500 and the benefit-loss rate is kept at 50%. Complete the table below.

Earned income	NIT subsidy	Total income
$ 0	$7,500	$7,500
3,000	______	______
6,000	______	______
9,000	______	______
12,000	______	______
15,000	______	______

(1) This program is more costly than the previous one because the break-even income has risen to $______

(2) The incentives to earn additional income are no better in this program than in the previous one. But to improve these incentives by reducing the benefit-loss rate to 40% would raise the break-even income to (divide the guaranteed income by the benefit-loss rate $______

d. To summarize:

(1) given the guaranteed income, the lower the benefit-loss rate the (greater, less) ______ are the incentives to earn additional income and the (greater, less) ______ is the break-even income and the cost of the NIT program;

(2) and given the benefit-loss rate, the greater the guaranteed income, the (greater, less) ______ is the break-even income and the cost of the program;

(3) but to reduce the break-even income and the cost of the program requires either a(n) (increase, decrease) ______ in the benefit-loss rate or a(n) ______ in the guaranteed income.

■ SELF-TEST

Circle the T if the statement is true, the F if it is false.

1. According to the author of the text, there is considerable income inequality in the United States. **T F**

2. Since 1929 the percentage of total personal income received by families in the highest income quintile has decreased. **T F**

3. In drawing a Lorenz curve the percentage of families in each income class is measured along the horizontal axis and the percentage of the total income received by those families is measured on the vertical axis. **T F**

4. After the adjustments made by Edgar Browning in the Census Bureau data, the distribution of personal income in the United States is less unequal, and there is a trend over time toward less inequality. **T F**

5. Adjustments for differences in the ages of receivers of income seem to make the distribution of personal income in the United States more unequal. **T F**

6. The distribution of income in the United States *after* taxes and transfers are taken into account is less unequal than it is before they are taken into account. **T F**

7. Those who favor equality in the distribution of income contend that equality will lead to stronger incentives to work, save, invest, and take risks and to a greater national output and income. **T F**

8. In the trade off between equality and economic efficiency, an increase in efficiency requires a decrease in inequality. **T F**

9. Using the semiofficial definition of poverty, about 14% of the population of the United States is poor. **T F**

10. The cost of discrimination against blacks in the United States is equal to approximately 4% of the national output. **T F**

11. The difference between the average earnings of full-time female and male workers is only partly the result of occupational discrimination. T F

12. OASDI, Medicare, and unemployment compensation are public assistance (or welfare) programs. T F

13. Those who have been critical of the American system of income maintenance contend that the welfare system impairs incentives to work. T F

14. In a NIT program, the benefit-loss rate is the rate at which subsidy benefits decrease as the earned income of a family increases. T F

15. The lower the benefit-loss rate the smaller are the incentives to earn additional income. T F

Circle the letter that corresponds to the best answer.

1. Approximately what percentage of all American families have personal incomes of over $25,000 annually? (*a*) 25%; (*b*) 30%; (*c*) 35%; (*d*) 40%.

2. Approximately what percentage of all American families have personal incomes of less than $10,000 a year? (*a*) 5%; (*b*) 10%; (*c*) 15%; (*d*) 20%.

3. Which of the following would be evidence of a decrease in income inequality in the United States? (*a*) A decrease in the percentage of total personal income received by the lowest quintile; (*b*) an increase in the percentage of total personal income received by the highest quintile; (*c*) an increase in the percentage of total personal income received by the four lowest quintiles; (*d*) a decrease in the percentage of total personal income received by the four lowest quintiles.

4. When a Lorenz curve has been drawn, the degree of income inequality in an economy is measured by (*a*) the slope of the diagonal that runs from the southwest to the northeast corner of the diagram; (*b*) the slope of the Lorenz curve; (*c*) the area between the Lorenz curve and the axes of the graph; (*d*) the area between the Lorenz curve and the southwest-northeast diagonal.

5. In the post-World War II period there has been: (*a*) a significant decrease in the percentage of total personal income received by the highest quintile; (*b*) a significant increase in the percentage of total personal income received by the lowest quintile; (*c*) a significant increase in the percentage of total personal income received by the middle three quintiles; (*d*) no significant change in the percentage of total personal income received by any of the five quintiles.

6. Which of the following is *not* one of the causes of the unequal distribution of income in the United States? (*a*) The unequal distribution of property; (*b*) in-kind transfers; (*c*) the inability of the poor to invest in human capital; (*d*) luck and the unequal distribution of misfortune.

7. Suppose that Ms. Anne obtains 5 units of utility from the last dollar of income received by her and that Mr. Charles obtains 8 units of utility from the last dollar of his income. Those who favor an equal distribution of income would (*a*) advocate redistributing income from Charles to Anne; (*b*) advocate redistributing income from Anne to Charles; (*c*) be content with this distribution of income between Anne and Charles; (*d*) argue that any redistribution of income between them would increase total utility.

8. Poverty does not have a precise definition, but the officially accepted definition of "poor" is any family of four and any individual with less to spend annually, respectively, than (approximately) (*a*) $10,600 and $5,278; (*b*) $9,000 and $4,500; (*c*) $10,600 and $5,300; (*d*) $5,300 and $2,700.

9. Poverty in the United States is *not* concentrated among (*a*) families headed by women; (*b*) blacks and Hispanics; (*c*) the elderly; (*d*) children under 6 years of age.

10. The average weekly earnings of full-time female workers is about what percentage of the average annual earnings of full-time male employees? (*a*) 60%; (*b*) 75%; (*c*) 90%; (*d*) 95%.

11. Which of the following is *not* one of the four dimensions of economic discrimination? (*a*) Wage discrimination; (*b*) racial and sexual discrimination; (*c*) occupational discrimination; (*d*) human-capital discrimination.

12. The crowding of women and minorities into certain occupations (*a*) is the result of occupational discrimination; (*b*) results in the misallocation of resources; (*c*) explains the lower wage rates in the crowded occupations; (*d*) all of the above.

13. Which of the following is a part of the American income-maintenance system? (*a*) Public housing; (*b*) agricultural subsidies; (*c*) unemployment insurance; (*d*) minimum-wage laws.

14. Which of the following is designed to provide a nationwide minimum income for the aged, the blind, and the disabled? (*a*) OASDI; (*b*) SSI; (*c*) AFDC; (*d*) ABD.

15. A negative income tax would (*a*) reduce incentives to work; (*b*) fail to eliminate poverty; (*c*) be too costly; (*d*) result in at least one but not necessarily all of the above.

■ DISCUSSION QUESTIONS

1. How much income inequality is there in the American economy? Cite figures to support your conclusion. What causes income inequality in American capitalism?

2. Has the distribution of income changed in the United States during the past 50 to 55 years? If it has, in what way, to what extent, and why has it changed? Has income distribution changed in the past 40 or so years?

3. What is measured along each of the two axes when a Lorenz curve is drawn? (*a*) If the distribution of income were completely equal, what would the Lorenz curve look like? (*b*) If one family received all of the income of the economy, what would the Lorenz curve look like? (*c*) After the Lorenz curve for an economy has been drawn, how is the degree of income inequality in that economy measured?

4. How does the Bureau of the Census measure income in its published data on the distribution of income in the United States? What are the two major criticisms of these data?

5. How did (*a*) Edgar Browning and (*b*) Morton Paglin adjust the census data on the distribution of income? What do their adjusted figures reveal about the distribution of income in the United States?

6. What effect do taxes and transfers have upon the distribution of income in the United States? How much of this change in the distribution of income is the result of the transfer payments made by government?

7. State the case for an equal distribution of income and the case for an unequal distribution. What would be traded for what in the "big trade-off"?

8. What is the currently accepted and more or less official definition of poverty? How many people and what percentage of the American population are poor if we use this definition of poverty?

9. What characteristics—other than the small amounts of money they have to spend—do the greatest concentrations of the poor families of the nation *tend* to have?

10. Why does poverty in the United States tend to be invisible or hidden?

11. What is meant by economic discrimination and what are the four major types of such discrimination? How does this discrimination affect the earnings of blacks (and other minorities) and women relative to the earnings of white men in the United States?

12. If labor markets were competitive, what would be the effect of reducing or eliminating occupational discrimination in these labor markets upon the wage rates received by men and women and upon the national output?

13. What (*a*) are the comparable worth doctrine and the objections to it; and (*b*) are the factors other than discrimination that lead to differences in the earnings of men and women in the United States.

14. Explain the difference between social insurance and public assistance (or welfare). List and briefly describe the three social insurance and the four public assistance programs that constitute the income-maintenance system of the United States.

15. Explain how poverty and the unequal distribution of income would be reduced by a negative income tax. Be sure to include in your explanation definitions of guaranteed income, the benefit-loss rate, and break-even income.

16. What are the three goals or objectives of any NIT plan? Explain why there is a conflict among these objectives—why all three goals cannot be achieved simultaneously.

39
Labor unions and their economic impact

Another trouble spot in the American economy is the area called labor-management relations. It is almost always in the news for one reason or another—strikes, new legislation, wage increases, employee "give-backs," union demands, and charges and countercharges by both employers and unions.

The labor union is an important institution in American capitalism. But labor unions did not always occupy the position in the economy that they now do. The first part of Chapter 39 is devoted to a historical review of their development in the United States and is separated into three periods. The important thing for you to see is that the growth and power of unions in each of these periods clearly depended upon the rights and recognition given to them by Federal law. At first the law repressed them, then it encouraged them, and finally it has sought to curb and control their greatly increased power.

Until 1955 the labor movement in the United States was divided into those unions affiliated with the AFL and those affiliated with the CIO. But in 1955 the labor movement was united when the AFL and CIO merged. Since then, however, unionism in the American economy has declined: the percentage of the labor force organized in unions has declined; and in more recent years the number of union members has decreased. The second major section of Chapter 39 examines three possible hypotheses which separately or together might explain this decline in unionism in the U.S.

In Chapter 32 you learned how unions directly and indirectly seek to influence wage rates. The impact of the union upon its own membership, upon employers, and upon the rest of the economy is more than just a matter of wages, however. The third major section of Chapter 39 examines the contents usually found in a contract between a union and an employer. The purpose of this examination is to give you some idea of the goals which unions seek and other issues over which employers and employees bargain and upon which they must reach an agreement. Another extremely important idea which you will find in the section is this: Labor-management relations mean more than the periodic signing of a contract; they also mean the day-to-day working relations between the union and the employer and the new problems and issues not specifically settled in the contract which must be resolved under the general provisions of that contract.

The fourth and final section of the chapter examines the economic effects or impact of unions on the economy. Unions affect the economy in four principal ways: they affect the wage rates of their members relative to the wage rates of nonunionized workers; the productivity of labor and, therefore, the efficiency with which the economy uses its resources; the inequality with which the earnings of labor are distributed among workers; and the rate of inflation in the economy. Just how unions affect these four economic variables is, to a large extent, uncertain and debatable. The author of the text presents you with both sides of the issues, however, and draws whatever conclusions can be obtained from the empirical evidence.

■ CHECKLIST

When you have studied this chapter you should be able to:

☐ Describe the attitudes and behavior of the courts and business toward labor unions during the repression phase.

☐ Identify the three fundamental ideas of Samuel Gompers.

□ Explain how the Norris-LaGuardia Act and the Wagner Act contributed to the revival and rapid growth of the labor movement during the encouragement phase.

□ Contrast the beliefs of John L. Lewis and the founders of the CIO with those of the leaders of the AFL during the 1930s.

□ Identify the four headings into which the provisions of the Taft-Hartley Act can be put; and outline the provisions of the Landrum-Griffin Act.

□ State the extent to which unionism in the United States has declined over the past 30 years; and present three hypotheses to explain this decline.

□ Enumerate and explain the contents of the four basic areas of a collective-bargaining agreement.

□ Describe the effects unions have on the wages of their members, on the wages of unorganized (nonunion) workers, and on the average level of real wages in the American economy; and state the size of the wage advantage of unionized workers.

□ List the three ways in which unions might have a negative impact and the three ways in which they might have a positive impact on efficiency in the economy; and explain in detail how the unionization of a particular labor market leads to the misallocation of labor and a decline in the national output.

□ Identify the way in which unions increase and the two ways in which they decrease the inequality with which the earnings of labor are distributed.

□ Contrast the causes of inflation in the demand-pull and cost-push models and then identify the sources of persistent inflation in the American economy.

■ CHAPTER OUTLINE

1. The history of labor unions in the United States can be divided into three periods or phases.

a. During the repression phase, between 1790 and 1930, the growth of unions was severely limited by the judicial application of the criminal conspiracy doctrine and by the refusal of many firms to recognize and bargain with unions; but between 1886 and 1930 the AFL, following the union philosophy of Samuel Gompers, was able to organize many crafts and expand its membership.

b. Between 1930 and 1947, the encouragement phase, labor union membership grew rapidly, encouraged by prolabor legislation; and the CIO was formed to unionize industrial workers.

c. In the intervention phase from 1947 onward, government regulation and control of labor-management relations increased with the passage of the Taft-Hartley and Landrum-Griffin Acts.

2. The merger of the AFL and the CIO in 1955 reunited the American labor movement, but since then membership in unions as a percentage of the labor force has declined; and there are three complementary explanations of the relative decline in union membership.

a. The structural-change explanation (or hypothesis) is that a number of changes in the structure of the economy and of the labor force have occurred and these changes have not been favorable to the expansion of union membership.

b. The substitution hypothesis is that many of the benefits once provided to union members by their unions are now provided to them by government and this reduces the attractiveness of union membership.

c. The managerial-opposition hypothesis is that the opposition of management to unions has increased and become more aggressive in recent years, and the legal and illegal tactics employed by management against unions have decreased union membership.

3. Collective bargaining between labor and management results in collective-bargaining (or work) agreements between them.

a. This bargaining and the resulting agreements are more often than not the result of compromise; strikes and violence are actually quite rare.

b. The work agreements reached take many different forms; but the agreement between the employer and the union usually covers four basic areas: union status and managerial prerogatives, wages and hours, seniority and the control of job opportunities, and the grievance procedure.

c. Collective bargaining is, however, more than the periodic negotiation of an agreement; it also involves union and workers' security and day-to-day labor-management relations in an economy which is continually changing.

4. Labor unions may increase wage rates, increase or decrease economic efficiency, make the distribution of income more or less unequal, and contribute to inflation.

a. While unions have increased the wages of their members relative to the wages of nonunion members, they have had little or no effect on the average level of real wages in the economy.

b. Whether unions result in more or less efficiency and

an increase or a decrease in the productivity of labor in the economy is a question with two sides.

(1) The negative view is that they decrease efficiency by their featherbedding and work rules, by engaging in strikes, and by fostering a misallocation of labor resources.

(2) The positive view is that they increase efficiency by having a shock effect on the performance of management, by reducing worker turnover, and by the informal transfer of skills from the more- to the less-skilled workers fostered by the seniority system.

(3) The empirical evidence shows that unions have increased labor productivity in some industries and decreased it in other industries; but this evidence has not led to any general conclusion on the effect of unionization on the productivity of labor in the economy.

c. There is also no agreement on the effect of unions on the distribution of earnings among workers.

(1) Some economists argue that unions increase earnings and reduce employment in the labor markets which are unionized; but this increases the supply of labor and lowers earnings in the labor markets which are not unionized: the result is an increase in the inequality with which earnings are distributed.

(2) Other economists observe that unions try to obtain equal wage rates for all workers performing the same jobs both within a single firm and among different firms; and that the effect is to decrease the inequality with which earnings are distributed.

d. Whether unions generate wage-push inflation is a controversial issue.

(1) In the demand-pull model of inflation increases in wage rates are a result (or the effect) of an increase in aggregate demand and not the cause of inflation; but in the wage-push model of inflation union-imposed increases in wage rates greater than the increases in the productivity of labor lead to higher price levels in the economy.

(2) Most experts would agree that inflation in the past has been the result of increases in aggregate demand or of supply-side shocks and has not been the result of increases in wage rates; but unions do perpetuate and make it more difficult to control inflation.

■ IMPORTANT TERMS

Criminal-conspiracy doctrine
Injunction
Discriminatory discharge
Blacklisting
Lockout
Yellow-dog contract
Company union
Business unionism
American Federation of Labor
Norris-LaGuardia Act
Wagner (National Labor Relations) Act
National Labor Relations Board
Congress of Industrial Organizations
Taft-Hartley (Labor-Management Relations) Act
Landrum-Griffin (Labor-Management Reporting and Disclosure) Act
Structural-change hypothesis
Substitution hypothesis
Managerial-opposition hypothesis
Jurisdictional strike
Sympathy strike
Secondary boycott
Featherbedding
Closed shop
Reopening clause
Union shop
Open shop
Nonunion shop
Right-to-work law
Managerial prerogatives
Cost-of-living adjustment (COLA)
Grievance procedure
Seniority
Fringe benefit
Collective voice
Exit mechanism
Voice mechanism

Two terms for review:

Craft unionism
Industrial unionism

■ FILL-IN QUESTIONS

1. About ______ million workers belong to labor unions in the United States. This is approximately what percentage of the civilian labor force? ______

2. During the repression phase of labor union history, union growth was slow because of the hostility of the ______ toward labor unions and the reluctance of American businesses to ______ and ______ with labor unions.

3. Unions were limited in their growth between 1790 and 1930 by courts which applied the ______ doctrine to labor unions and issued ______ to prevent strikes, picketing, and boycotts.

4. Employers used the following nonjudicial means of retarding the growth of labor unions in the repression

phase: ______________________________,
______________________________,
______________________________,
______________________________,
______________________________,
______________________________,
and ______________________________

5. The philosophy of the AFL under the leadership of Samuel Gompers was ______________________________
______________, ______________,
and ______________________________

6. In the encouragement phase of labor union history, unions grew as a consequence of such favorable legislation as the ______________________________
and ______________________________
Acts; and the (AFL, CIO) ______________, based on the principle of (craft, industrial) ______________ unionism, was formed to organize (skilled, both skilled and unskilled) ______________ workers in a particular industry or group of related industries.

7. The National Labor Relations Act of 1935 guaranteed the "twin rights" of labor; the right to ______________
and the right to ______________; in addition it established the ______________ Board and listed a number of unfair labor practices by (management, unions) ______________________________

8. Three important events that occurred in the history of labor unions after 1946 were the passage of the
______________ and ______________
Acts and the ______________ of the AFL and the CIO.

9. Since the merger of the AFL and CIO in 1955 union membership as a percentage of the labor force has (increased, decreased, remained constant) ______________
______________ and the number of unionized workers has
____

10. The three complementary hypotheses which can be used to explain the changes in the size of the union membership are the ______________, ______________,
and the ______________________________ hypotheses.

11. A typical work agreement between a union and an employer covers the following four basic areas:

a. ______________________________

b. ______________________________

c. ______________________________

d. ______________________________

12. Collective bargaining between management and labor unions is concerned (only, not only) ______________ with wage rates, is a (periodic, continuous) ______________ process, and takes place in a (static, dynamic) ______________ climate (economy).

13. Unionization of workers in the American economy has tended to (increase, decrease, have no effect on) ______________ the wage rates of union members, to ______________ the wage rates of nonunion workers, and to ______________ the average level of real wage rates received by all workers.

14. Unions have a

a. negative effect on productivity and efficiency in the economy to the extent that they

(1) engage in ______________ and impose ______________ rules on their employers,

(2) engage in ______________ against their employers, or

(3) impose (above-, below-) ______________ equilibrium wage rates on employers that lead to the ______________ of labor resources;

b. positive effect on productivity and efficiency in the economy to the extent that

(1) the wage increases they obtain have a ________ effect that induces employers to substitute (labor, capital) ________ for ________ and to hasten their search for technologies that (increase, decrease) ________ the costs of production,

(2) they (increase, decrease) ________ labor turnover, or

(3) the ________ system results in the (formal, informal) ________ training of (younger, older) ________ by ________ employees.

15. Unionization has the effect of:

a. increasing the inequality with which labor earnings are distributed when it displaces workers from (high, low) ________ -wage employment in (unionized, nonunionized) ________ labor markets to ________ -wage employment in ________ labor markets;

b. decreasing the inequality with which labor earnings are distributed if it results in a wage rate for a particular job that is (the same, different) ________ within the firm and is ________ among firms.

16. In the:

a. demand-pull model of inflation increases in wage rates are the (result, cause) ________ of inflation; and in the cost-push model of inflation increases in wage rates in excess of increases in the productivity of labor are the ________ of inflation;

b. American economy the major episodes of rapid inflation have been the result of expansions in aggregate (demand, supply) ________ or shocks on the ________ side.

c. United States the existence of labor unions (perpetuates, decelerates) ________ existing inflation and makes it (more, less) ________ difficult for government to control inflation because they enter into (short-, long-) ________ term contracts with their employers.

■ PROBLEMS AND PROJECTS

1. Below is a list of frequently employed terms, and following the terms is a series of identifying phrases. Match the term with the phrase by placing the appropriate letter after each of the phrases. *Note:* All the terms will not be needed.

A. Injunction
B. Blacklisting
C. Lockout
D. Yellow-dog contract
E. Company union
F. Business union
G. Jurisdictional strike
H. Sympathy strike
I. Secondary boycott
J. Featherbedding
K. Closed shop
L. Union shop
M. Open shop
N. Nonunion shop
O. Checkoff
P. Craft union
Q. Industrial union

1. A worker must be a member of the union before he is eligible for employment. ________
2. A worker agrees when employed not to join a union. ________
3. A union open to all workers employed by a given firm or in a given industry. ________
4. A union organized and encouraged by an employer to prevent the formation of a union which might make "unreasonable" demands. ________
5. The refusal of a labor union to buy or to work with the products produced by another union or group of nonunion workers. ________
6. A dispute between two unions over whose members are to perform a certain job. ________
7. A court order which forbids a person or group of persons to perform some act. ________
8. The closing of the place of employment by the employer as a means of preventing the formation of a union. ________
9. Concern of unions with better pay, hours, and working

conditions rather than with plans for social and economic reform. _______

10. Payment of workers for work not actually performed. _______

2. Next is a list of provisions found in four important pieces of labor legislation. Identify the act in which the provision is found by putting either (N) for the Norris-LaGuardia Act, (W) for the Wagner Act, (T) for the Taft-Hartley Act, or (L) for the Landrum-Griffin Act in the space following each provision.

a. Specified that contracts between a union and an employer must contain a termination or reopening clause. _______

b. Established a board to investigate unfair labor practices and to conduct elections among workers. _______

c. Guaranteed to workers the right to organize unions to bargain collectively. _______

d. Declared that yellow-dog contracts were unenforceable and limited the use of injunctions against unions. _______

e. Regulated union elections and finances and guaranteed certain rights to union members in their dealings with the union and its officers. _______

f. Outlawed the closed shop, jurisdictional and certain sympathy strikes, secondary boycotts, and featherbedding. _______

g. Provided a procedure whereby strikes affecting the health and safety of the nation might be delayed. _______

h. Outlawed company unions, antiunion discrimination in hiring and discharging workers, and interfering with the rights of workers to form unions. _______

3. Suppose there are two identical labor markets in the economy. The supply of workers and the demand for workers in each of these markets are shown in the table in the next column.

a. In each of the two labor markets the equilibrium wage rate in a competitive labor market would be $__________ and employment would be __________ workers.

Quantity of labor demanded	Wage rate (MRP of labor)	Quantity of labor supplied
10	$100	70
20	90	60
30	80	50
40	70	40
50	60	30
60	50	20
70	40	10

b. Now suppose that in the first of these labor markets workers form a union and the union imposes an above-equilibrium wage rate of $90 on employers.

(1) Employment in the unionized labor market will (rise, fall) __________ to __________ workers; and

(2) the output produced by workers employed by the firms in the unionized labor market will (expand, contract) __________ by $__________

c. If the workers displaced by the unionization of the first labor market all enter and find employment in the second labor market which remains nonunionized and competitive,

(1) the wage rate in the second labor market will (rise, fall) __________ to __________

(2) the output produced by the workers employed by firms in the second labor market will (expand, contract) __________ by $__________

d. While the total employment of labor in the two labor markets has remained constant, the total output produced by the employers in the two labor markets has (expanded, contracted) __________ by $__________

■ SELF-TEST

Circle the T if the statement is true, the F if it is false.

1. An injunction is a court order which declares that combinations of workers to raise wages are illegal. **T F**

2. Blacklisting was a device employed by early labor unions to cut off a firm's labor supply. **T F**

3. The CIO was based on the principle of industrial unionism while the AFL was operated on the craft union philosophy. **T F**

4. The Taft-Hartley Act lists a number of unfair labor practices on the part of management. **T F**

5. Under the provisions of the Labor-Management Relations Act of 1947 yellow-dog contracts and featherbedding are prohibited. **T F**

6. The merger of the AFL and CIO in 1945 was one of the main causes of a feeling that labor unions had become too powerful that led to the enactment of the Taft-Hartley Act in 1947. **T F**

7. Union membership has increased in every year since the end of World War II. **T F**

8. Strikes precede nearly 25 percent of the contracts negotiated by labor unions and management. **T F**

9. Collective bargaining between labor and management means no more than deciding upon the wage rates employees will receive during the life of the contract. **T F**

10. The four-points criteria employed by unions in arguing for higher wages can also be used by management to resist higher wages and to argue for decreased wages. **T F**

11. Seniority means that the worker with the longest continuous employment by a firm is the last to be laid off and the first to be recalled from a layoff. **T F**

12. The wages of union members exceed the wages of nonunion members on the average by more than 40%. **T F**

13. Strikes in the American economy result in fairly little lost work time and reductions in total output. **T F**

14. The imposition of an above-equilibrium wage rate in a particular labor market tends to reduce the employment of labor in that market. **T F**

15. The loss of output in the American economy that is the result of increases in wage rates imposed by unions on employers is relatively large. **T F**

16. Reduced labor turnover tends to decrease the productivity of labor. **T F**

17. The seniority system, its advocates argue, expands the informal training of less-skilled, younger workers and improves the productivity of a firm's work force. **T F**

18. It is generally agreed that unions decrease the productivity of labor in the American economy. **T F**

19. Freeman and Medoff conclude that unionization, on balance, increases income inequality by about 3%. **T F**

20. In the demand-pull model of inflation increased wage rates are the result of increases in aggregate demand that increase the demand for labor in the economy. **T F**

Circle the letter that corresponds to the best answer.

1. About what percentage of all civilian workers are members of unions? (*a*) 15%; (*b*) 18%; (*c*) 24%; (*d*) 27%.

2. Which of the following would *not* be used by a firm to prevent the organization of a genuine union among its employees? (*a*) Lockout; (*b*) featherbedding; (*c*) company union; (*d*) yellow-dog contract.

3. Which one of the following was an essential part of Samuel Gompers' union philosophy? (*a*) Industrial unionism; (*b*) support of the Democratic Party at the polls; (*c*) establishment of producer cooperatives operated by labor and management; (*d*) business unionism.

4. The Norris-La Guardia Act outlawed: (*a*) yellow-dog contracts; (*b*) the closed shop; (*c*) company unions; (*d*) blacklisting.

5. The Wagner Act outlawed: (*a*) company unions; (*b*) the closed shop; (*c*) featherbedding; (*d*) injunctions against unions.

6. The Taft-Hartley Act outlawed: (*a*) the nonunion shop; (*b*) the open shop; (*c*) the union shop; (*d*) the closed shop.

7. Which one of the following is *not* a provision of the Landrum-Griffin Act? (*a*) Allows a worker to sue his union if the union denies the member certain rights; (*b*) unions are prohibited from making political contributions in elections for Federal offices; (*c*) requires regularly scheduled union elections and the use of secret ballots; (*d*) guarantees union members the right to attend union meetings, to vote and to participate in the meeting, and to nominate union officers.

8. Which one of the following is *not* presently an unfair practice? (*a*) The refusal of either unions or companies to bargain in good faith; (*b*) the coercion of employees by unions to join and by companies not to join unions; (*c*) the practices of company and business unionism; (*d*) both jurisdictional strikes and secondary bycotts.

9. The decline in union membership in the United States in recent years can be explained by the (*a*) managerial-growth hypothesis; (*b*) structural-change hypothesis; (*c*) relative-income hypothesis; (*d*) complementary-expansion hypothesis.

10. If workers at the time they are hired have a choice of joining the union and paying dues or of not joining the union and paying no dues, there exists: (*a*) a union shop; (*b*) an open shop; (*c*) a nonunion shop; (*d*) a closed shop.

11. Unionization has tended to (*a*) increase the wages of union workers and decrease the wages of nonunion workers; (*b*) increase the wages of nonunion workers and decrease the wages of union workers; (*c*) increase the wages of both union and nonunion workers; (*d*) increase the average level of real wages in the economy.

12. Which of the following tends to decrease (to have a negative effect on) productivity and efficiency in the economy? (*a*) Reduced labor turnover; (*b*) featherbedding and union-imposed work rules; (*c*) the seniority system; (*d*) the shock effect of higher union-imposed wage rates.

13. The higher wages imposed on employers in a unionized labor market tend to result in (*a*) lower wage rates in nonunionized labor markets and a decline in national output; (*b*) lower wage rates in nonunionized labor markets and an expansion in national output; (*c*) higher wage rates in nonunionized labor markets and a decline in national output; (*d*) higher wage rates in nonunionized labor markets and an expansion in national output.

14. The reallocation of labor from employment where its MRP is $50,000 to employment where its MRP is $40,000 will (*a*) increase the output of the economy by $10,000; (*b*) increase the output of the economy by $90,000; (*c*) decrease the output of the economy by $10,000; (*d*) decrease the output of the economy by $90,000.

15. Which of the following tends to increase (have a positive effect on) productivity and efficiency in the economy? (*a*) Reduced labor turnover; (*b*) featherbedding and union-imposed work rules; (*c*) strikes; (*d*) the unionization of a particular labor market.

16. A wage increase imposed by unions on employers has a shock effect if it induces employers to (*a*) accelerate the substitution of capital for labor; (*b*) hasten their search for productivity-increasing technologies; (*c*) speed their employment of productive techniques that reduce their costs; (*d*) do any or all of the above.

17. Unions tend to reduce labor turnover by providing workers with all but one of the following. Which one? (*a*) An exit mechanism; (*b*) a voice mechanism; (*c*) a collective voice; (*d*) a wage advantage.

18. The effect of union-imposed wage increases in the unionized labor markets of the economy is to (*a*) decrease inequality in the distribution of labor earnings; (*b*) leave unchanged the distribution of labor earnings; (*c*) increase inequality in the distribution of labor earnings; (*d*) destabilize the distribution of earnings between unionized and nonunionized workers.

19. In the wage-push model of inflation, increases in money-wage rates that exceed increases in the productivity of labor (*a*) increase aggregate supply and the price level in the economy; (*b*) increase aggregate supply and decrease the price level in the economy; (*c*) decrease aggregate supply and the price level in the economy; (*d*) decrease aggregate supply and increase the price level in the economy.

20. Most of the sustained and rapid inflation in the United States has *not* been the result of (*a*) increases in aggregate demand; (*b*) supply-side shocks; (*c*) increases in the money supply; (*d*) increases in money-wage rates.

■ DISCUSSION QUESTIONS

1. What are the three phases in the history of labor unions in the United States? What was the law with respect to unions, what was the extent of unionization, and what were the principal events in each of these periods?

2. How were the courts able to retard the growth of unions between 1790 and 1930? How did employers attempt to limit union growth?

3. Explain the union philosophy of Samuel Gompers.

4. What were the chief provisions of the Norris-La Guardia Act and the Wagner Act?

5. Explain how the principles of the CIO differed from those on which the AFL was based.

6. Contrast the philosophy and policy embodied in the Wagner Act with that found in the Taft-Hartley Act.

7. What are the four main sections of the Taft-Hartley Act? What specific practices are outlawed by the act and what specific things are required of unions, union officers, and bargaining agreements?

8. Explain the major provisions of the Landrum-Griffin Act.

9. What evidence is there that the labor movement in the United States has declined? What are three possible causes of this decline?

10. What are the four basic areas usually covered in the collective-bargaining agreement between management and labor?

11. What are the four arguments employed by labor (management) in demanding (resisting) higher wages? Why are these arguments "two-edged"?

12. How large is the union wage advantage in the United States? How has the unionization of many labor markets affected the average level of real wages in the American economy?

13. By what basic means do unions have a positive and a negative effect on economic efficiency in the economy? What appears to have been the overall effect of unions on economic efficiency in the American economy?

14. What effect does the unionization of a particular labor market have upon (*a*) the wage rate in that market, (*b*) the wage rates in other labor markets, and (*c*) the total output of the economy?

15. Explain how unions (*a*) reduce labor turnover and (*b*) improve the skills of younger workers.

16. How and in what ways do unions affect (*a*) the distribution of earnings among workers and (*b*) the price level (the rate of inflation)?

40
The radical critique: the economics of dissent

Chapter 40 is the last of the six chapters concerned with the "Current Economic Problems" of the American economy. Unlike the first five chapters in this part of the text, Chapter 40 does not examine a particular trouble spot (such as monopoly, agriculture, the cities, poverty, etc.). Instead it asks if American capitalism is one big trouble spot or problem.

Those who see American capitalism as a giant sore spot are called radical economists, the New Left, or neo-Marxists. Their viewpoint is labeled the radical critique, radical economics, or the economics of dissent. It is their contention that modern capitalism, based on private property, the corporation, and the profit motive, is such a bad system that it ought to be abolished and replaced with a system of socialism. What they recommend is essentially an updated or modern version of Marxian economics. Karl Marx argued that capitalism had brought about the tremendous rise in the standard of living in Western Europe; but that capitalism would eventually destroy itself. Its success, he believed, would lead to economic conditions which in turn would lead to the collapse of capitalism, revolution, and the coming of socialism. Chapter 40 begins, therefore, with a detailed examination of the radical economists' Marxian heritage and with an analysis of the New Left's historical predecessor, the Old Left.

From the Old Left the author turns to an explanation of the two fundamental differences between orthodox economics—the kind of economics accepted by almost all economists, including the author of the text—and radical economics. These two differences are differences in approach or methodology. Orthodox economists, the radical economists argue, don't see what is really going on in the world around them. They either have their eyes closed or are rather simpleminded; and see harmony where there is actually conflict. Moreover, orthodox economists, the New Left contends, have too narrow a viewpoint. They look only at economic matters and disregard the other aspects of modern society; and within economics they devote their efforts to nitpicking while ignoring real and important economic problems.

The most important section of Chapter 40 is a summary of the way in which the radical economists view American capitalism. They see the economy dominated by a relatively few large monopoly corporations in league with the state (that is, the Federal government) and out to exploit workers and consumers. This exploitation leads to inequality in the distribution of income and wealth, alienation (which you should be sure to define), an economy which irrationally and wastefully uses its resources, and imperialism which exploits underdeveloped nations. The radical economists agree that they don't like what they see in the American economy; and that what is needed is socialism. They don't agree at all on just what socialism is—on what a better economic system would be like.

The chapter concludes with a rebuttal by the orthodox economists. Their critique of radical economics has four parts. The first three parts add up to an attack on the objectivity of the radical economists. They are blinded by their preconceptions and ignore any facts that weaken their case. The fourth part is the most devastating in the view of most of their critics. They don't present any of the details of the better economic system which is to replace the capitalism which they detest. Rejecting both the market system and a bureaucratic government, they don't tell us how they are going to allocate scarce resources to satisfy the unlimited wants of society. The histories of France and Russia suggest that revolution and the elimination of an old system do not always bring about the introduction of a better system. And many, like Hamlet, would

> . . . rather bear those ills we have
> Than fly to others we know not of . . .

■ CHECKLIST

When you have studied this chapter you should be able to:

☐ Use the following six categories to explain, from the viewpoint of Marx and the Old Left, the development and eventual collapse of capitalism:

- the class struggle
- private property and the exploitation of labor
- capital accumulation and its consequences
- the increasing degradation of the working class
- monopoly capitalism and imperialism
- revolution and socialism

☐ Contrast the positions of the orthodox and the radical economists in the "harmony or conflict" controversy.

☐ Explain why the radical economists believe orthodox economics is plagued by "disciplinary narrowness."

☐ Outline the eight main features in the radical conception of capitalism.

☐ Enumerate the three characteristics found in every socialist (radical) vision of a new society.

☐ Present the four arguments offered by orthodox economists to rebut the contentions of the radical economists.

■ CHAPTER OUTLINE

1. Radical economists reject the orthodox explanation of the operation of capitalism and its analysis of the problems of a capitalistic society.

2. The radical explanation of capitalism builds upon the work of Karl Marx who examined the development of capitalism and concluded that capitalism would eventually collapse.

a. Marx argued that as capitalist economies expanded the factory system, improved technology, and increased material well-being, one class of people (capitalists) struggled with another class (workers) to take some of the workers' output from them.

b. The capitalists, fortified by the institution of private property, control the machinery and equipment (the capital) needed to produce goods; and driven by their desire for profits (surplus value), they employ their superior bargaining power to exploit workers and pay them subsistence wages which are less than the value of their production.

c. Competition forces capitalists to reinvest their profits in more and better capital; and this capital accumulation not only expands the national output but also results in technological unemployment, in a growing industrial Reserve Army, and in a declining rate of profit.

d. These events operate to provide workers with a mere subsistence wage; to ever-increasing unemployment; and, in trying to prevent the profit rate from falling, to still further exploitation of workers.

e. Competition among capitalists in an atmosphere of falling profits and growing unemployment, Marx contended, would lead to the monopolization of industry by a few capitalists; and eventually, searching for cheap foreign labor and foreign markets for their products, to imperialism.

f. The ultimate result of the workings of capitalism is revolution by the workers, the overthrow of capitalism, and the establishment of a socialist state without classes.

3. There are, in the opinion of radical economists, two fundamental shortcomings in orthodox economics.

a. Orthodox economists see a harmony and the reconciliation of opposing interests in capitalism; but radical economists see an irreconcilable conflict between capitalists (and the government which they dominate) and the rest of society.

b. Orthodox economists, say the radical economists, focus their attention only on the economic aspects of society, ignore the noneconomic aspects of modern capitalism, and fail to understand the real problems of society.

4. The radical economists have a modern version of Marx and see American capitalism in this light.

a. A small group of huge, multiproduct, multinational, monopolistic corporations dominates the American economy.

b. These corporate giants also dominate government and

(1) prevent the control of monopoly,

(2) obtain subsidies from tax revenues, and

(3) have government create markets for them.

c. The expansion of capitalism and of the corporate giants requires the expansion of markets and output; and creates new problems while it fails to solve old problems.

d. The first of these problems is the exploitation of workers that is explained by three basic defects in the marginal productivity theory of income distribution of orthodox economists.

(1) The markets for products and labor are not competitive but monopolies and monopsonies.

(2) Workers are unable to obtain wage rates equal to their potential marginal revenue products because they cannot develop their natural abilities and society discriminates among workers on the basis of race or sex.

(3) Owners of real capital obtain the income produced not by them but by their capital.

e. The second problem is the unequal distribution of income and wealth which the radical economists see to be the result of

(1) the unearned incomes received by owners of capital and the economic and political powers that accompany these incomes; and

(2) the existence of dual labor markets.

f. Alienation, or the absence of decision-making power and the inability of individuals to control their lives, is a third problem.

g. A fourth problem is the irrational and wasteful use of resources to produce goods which do not fulfill consumer needs.

h. The last problem is the exploitation of the less developed nations of the world and is the result of imperialism.

i. Radical economists, while agreeing that the socialism which should replace capitalism ought to be based on private profits and ought to be decent, human, and democratic, cannot agree on the exact nature of the new society.

5. In reply to the radical economists, orthodox economists contend:

a. that this radical conception of capitalism is not consistent with reality;

b. that radical economics is nonobjective because it ignores facts and interprets all events in terms of its conception of capitalism;

c. that the problems of American capitalism cannot all be the result of ideology because other economies with different ideological bases have the same problems;

d. and that the radical economists have not explained the kind of system with which they would replace modern capitalism.

■ IMPORTANT TERMS

Radical economics
Marxian economics
Old Left
Class struggle
Bourgeois
Proletariat
Surplus value
Law of capitalist accumulation
Industrial Reserve Army
Monopoly capitalism
Imperialism
Dictatorship of the proletariat
New Left
Exploitation
Dual labor market
Alienation
Participatory socialism

■ FILL-IN QUESTIONS

1. Man, according to Marx, is engaged in a perpetual struggle with ______________ to obtain material wealth.

a. Simultaneously, some people attempt to improve their own material well-being by wresting output from ________________ people.

b. And under the capitalistic system this latter struggle is the struggle of capitalists (or the ________________ ________________) against workers (or the ________________).

2. Because of the institution of private ______________, capitalists control the machinery and equipment necessary to produce goods and services; and workers are dependent upon the capitalists for ______________; and the capitalists are driven by their desire for profits (or ________________) to exploit workers by paying them a ________________ which is less than the ________________ of their output.

3. The accumulation of capital means that capitalists are forced by (government, workers, competition) ______________ to invest their ______________ in additional and superior machinery and equipment; and capital accumulation results in an expansion of the ________________ output, the substitution of capital for ________________, and a decline in the rate of ________________.

4. In an effort to offset the decline in the profit rate capitalists will increase the (wages, exploitation) __________ of the working class.

5. As capitalism continues to develop:

a. Marx reasoned that unemployment and falling profits

would lead to (the monopolization of, increasing competition in) ______________ industry.

b. Lenin reasoned that the final state of this development would be (socialism, democracy, imperialism) ______________

6. Exploitation and unemployment would, Marx predicted, eventually result in a ______________ by the working class, the establishment of a dictatorship of the ______________, the socialization of ______________, the abolition of the ______________ class, and finally in the formation of a ______________ society.

7. The radical economists find two major methodological deficiencies in the orthodox approach to economics and believe:

a. the orthodox economists have an incorrect perception of reality and see (conflict, harmony) ______________ where there is actually ______________

b. orthodox economics as a discipline is too (narrow, broad) ______________, is too remote from the real problems of society, and fails to recognize the importance of (economic, religious, political) ______________ power in capitalistic societies.

8. In the radical conception of capitalism:

a. the economy is dominated by ______________ corporations which also dominate the ______________, depend upon finding new ______________ for their ever-increasing production, and exploit both ______________ and ______________;

b. capitalism brings about income (equality, inequality) ______________, the alienation of individuals, the irrational use of society's resources, and ______________ beyond the economy's national boundaries;

c. these evils can be eliminated only by replacing capitalism with ______________

9. What are the three ways in which government is alleged by the radical economists to cater to the large corporations?

a. ______________

b. ______________

c. ______________

10. Orthodox economists argue that the wage rate of workers will equal their ______________; and that all resources will receive a reward (or income) in proportion to their contribution to the production of the ______________. But the radical economists challenge this theory by arguing:

a. that these conclusions are true only when markets in the economy are ______________;

b. capital goods were created in the past by ______________;

c. and while capital goods are productive, the capitalist is not productive and his income from the ownership of capital is (earned, unearned) ______________

11. Radical economists contend that the causes of inequality in the distribution of income and wealth in the United States are:

a. the capitalistic institutions which include (public, private) ______________ property and both economic and political (power, democracy, morality) ______________

b. the existence of ______________ labor markets and the payment of high wages in the (primary, secondary) ______________ labor market and the payment of low wages in the ______________ labor market.

12. Alienation:

a. means that individuals have little control over their ______________ and are remote from the ______________-making process;

b. is primarily the result, in the view of radical economists, of the dominance and size of ______________________

13. It is the view of radical economists that capitalism uses its resources irrationally and engages in wasteful production.

a. The primary cause of this is the capitalist's pursuit of ______________________

b. And some of the results are the deterioration of the ______________, the creation of wants, unnecessary (consumer, military, investment) ______________ spending, and ______________ activities throughout the world.

14. The radical economists advocate the replacement of capitalism with some variety of ______________; and agree that the new society should be ______________, decent, and human, and that there should be no private ______________

15. The orthodox economists rebut the radical critique of capitalism by arguing that radical economics has an invalid perception of (ideology, reality) ______________ and is not (objective, subjective) ______________, that not all of the problems of the American economy are the result of capitalism's (ideology, ideals) ______________, and that the radical economists offer no viable or attainable ______________ for the present economic system.

■ PROBLEMS AND PROJECTS

1. Suppose the subsistence wage for a worker is 4 units of output per day; and that the total daily output that can be produced by from 0 to 7 workers is shown in the next table.

Number of workers	Output	Marginal product
0	0	—
1	8	______
2	15	______
3	21	______
4	26	______
5	30	______
6	33	______
7	35	______

a. Compute the daily marginal product of each worker and enter them in the table.

b. If a capitalist can employ as many workers as he wishes at the subsistence wage, to maximize his profits he will employ ______________ workers per day.

c. The total wages paid to workers each day will be ______________

d. The daily output of the capitalist is ______________ and his daily surplus value is ______________

e. Were the capitalist to employ this number of workers, in order to obtain no surplus value he would have to pay each worker a daily wage of ______________

f. The daily exploitation of each worker is, therefore, ______________

2. In the table on the next page is a Marxian picture of what happens in a capitalistic economy as it develops.

a. In addition to the economy's gross national product the table also shows its capital consumption allowances (CCA) in each of the three years. Compute and enter into the table the economy's net national product for each year.

b. Workers in this economy always receive a subsistence wage of 4 in each year. Find total employment in each year by dividing the wages paid in that year by the subsistence wage; and enter these employment figures into the table.

c. Marx defined surplus value as all of the NNP not paid to workers as wages. Compute the surplus value in the

Year	GNP	CCA	NNP	Wages	Employ-ment	Surplus value	CCA plus wages	Rate of profit
1	500	100	______	280	______	______	______	______
2	504	110	______	276	______	______	______	______
3	509	120.4	______	272	______	______	______	______

economy in each year; and enter these surplus values in the table.

d. Marx defined the rate of profit to be equal to surplus value divided by the sum of capital consumption allowances and wages.

(1) Compute capital consumption allowances plus wages in each year; enter these into the table.

(2) Now compute the rate of profit in each year.

e. As the economy develops:

(1) Employment (increases, decreases, remains constant) ______________; and, therefore, unemployment ______________

(2) The rate of profit ______________

■ SELF-TEST

Circle the T if the statement is true, the F if it is false.

1. Among radical economists there is very little difference in their viewpoints. **T F**

2. Surplus value equals the value of the daily output of workers less their daily wage. **T F**

3. Capitalists, according to Marx, are able to exploit workers because the capitalists have monopoly control of the machinery and equipment needed to produce goods in an industrial society. **T F**

4. Marx argued that in a capitalistic society the demand for consumer goods would increase more rapidly than the economy's capacity to produce them and that unemployment would result. **T F**

5. In Marx's view the increasing degradation of the working class was the direct result of their tendency to have too many children. **T F**

6. Marx's *Capital* contained a clear and detailed picture of the society that would emerge after the overthrow of capitalism by a revolution of the working class. **T F**

7. Radical economists contend that the solution to the problems of capitalistic societies requires an end to the private ownership of capital goods and the abolition of the market system as the decision-making device for society. **T F**

8. Orthodox economists tend to emphasize the conflicts and the radical economists tend to stress the harmony found in modern capitalistic economies. **T F**

9. The modern and radical conception of capitalism is an extended and updated version of Marx's ideas. **T F**

10. Capitalism has reached a stage in the United States in which, according to radical economists, monopoly corporations dominate the economy. **T F**

11. Radical economists argue that because labor markets are not competitive workers receive a wage which is greater than their marginal revenue product. **T F**

12. Capitalistic institutions, in the opinion of radical economists, create and maintain most of the income inequality found in the United States. **T F**

13. Orthodox and radical economists agree that the primary function of education in modern capitalistic economies is to increase the technical skills of workers. **T F**

14. Alienation refers to the increase in the proportion of the working class that is either foreign born or from a minority group. **T F**

15. The radical economists argue that capitalism uses its resources to produce little needed goods and services and fails to produce goods and services which are most needed. **T F**

16. From the radical viewpoint, two basic causes of the irrational use of resources in capitalistic societies are the pursuit of profits and pollution. **T F**

17. The radical economists agree on almost all the particulars of the socialism with which they would replace capitalism. **T F**

18. Most radical economists reject both the price-market system and government bureaucracy as a means of allocating scarce resources. **T F**

19. The orthodox economists concede that only capitalistic societies are monopolistic, militaristic, and imperialistic; but argue that the abolition of private property and the profit motive will not solve these problems. **T F**

20. In their rebuttal of the radical economists' critique of capitalism, orthodox economists argue that radical economists ignore any facts that do not support their conclusions. **T F**

Circle the letter that corresponds to the best answer.

1. In the man-against-man struggle found in capitalistic societies, Marx envisioned the exploitation (*a*) of the bourgeois by capitalists; (*b*) of the proletariat by the bourgeois; (*c*) of workers by the proletariat; (*d*) of the bourgeois by the proletariat.

2. The institution which Marx believed made it possible for one class to exploit another in a capitalistic economy was (*a*) the use of money; (*b*) the use of capital goods; (*c*) the corporation; (*d*) private property.

3. Which of the following was *not* a consequence of capital accumulation in Marx's analysis of capitalism? (*a*) An increase in the profit rate; (*b*) an increase in unemployment; (*c*) an increase in national output; (*d*) an increase in the misery of the working class.

4. Marx argued that the development of capitalism would eventually result in (*a*) imperialism; (*b*) prolonged inflation; (*c*) a decline in the number of capitalists; (*d*) a rise in the real wages of workers.

5. Imperialism, according to Lenin, results from (*a*) the search of capitalists for cheap foreign labor; (*b*) the inability of capitalists to sell all of their output at home; (*c*) higher profit rates in less developed nations; (*d*) all of the above.

6. Which of the following is the process through which Marx predicted capitalism would be replaced by socialism? (*a*) Revolution; (*b*) evolution; (*c*) unionization; (*d*) liberalization.

7. The socialism which would replace capitalism would have all but one of the following characteristics. Which one? (*a*) The dictatorship of the proletariat; (*b*) the abolition of the capitalist class; (*c*) the sale of the capitalist's machinery and equipment to the proletariat; (*d*) the establishment of a classless society.

8. The radical economists contend that orthodox economics (*a*) is too broad a discipline to come to grips with real-world problems; (*b*) is overly concerned with the power of large corporations; (*c*) devotes too much of its attention to the study of conflict; (*d*) fails to recognize the political character of the modern corporation.

9. Which of the following, in the view of the radical economists, is *not* a consequence of capitalism in the United States? (*a*) Alienation; (*b*) anarchism; (*c*) inequality; (*d*) imperialism.

10. In the radical conception of American capitalism (*a*) the state dominates and controls the large corporations; (*b*) the presence in the economy of a large number of small businesses results in wasteful competition; (*c*) government employs progressive personal and corporate income taxes to subsidize greedy workers; (*d*) military spending by government provides markets for large corporations.

11. Capitalists, the radical economists contend, are able to exploit the working class because of (*a*) their monopsony position in labor markets; (*b*) their monopoly position in product markets; (*c*) the institution of private property; (*d*) all of the above.

12. The radical economists contend that (*a*) neither capital goods nor capitalists are productive; (*b*) capital goods are and capitalists are not productive; (*c*) capitalists are and capital goods are not productive; (*d*) both capital goods and capitalists are productive.

13. Which of the following, in the view of radical economists, is *not* a major factor in producing inequality in the distribution of income and in the ownership of wealth in the United States? (*a*) Weak inheritance taxes; (*b*) tax loopholes; (*c*) foreign competition; (*d*) the system of higher education.

14. In the primary labor market (*a*) wages are low and employment is unstable; (*b*) wages are low and employment is stable; (*c*) wages are high and employment is unstable; (*d*) wages are high and employment is stable.

15. Of the following, which is neither a cause nor a result of alienation? (*a*) The large size of corporate employers; (*b*) the unionization of workers; (*c*) the inability of individuals to influence business decisions; (*d*) assembly-line production.

16. Radical economists argue that the failure of the underdeveloped nations to grow (to expand their outputs of goods and services) is the result of their (*a*) overpopulation; (*b*) social systems; (*c*) shortages of natural resources; (*d*) inability to produce sufficient incomes to enable them to invest in capital goods.

17. The new society advocated by all radical economists is (*a*) socialism; (*b*) anarchy; (*c*) communism; (*d*) reformed price-market system.

18. The radical critique of capitalism is, in the opinion of orthodox economists, (*a*) scientific; (*b*) immoral; (*c*) valid; (*d*) ideological.

■ DISCUSSION QUESTIONS

1. Looking back into history Marx saw men engaged in two kinds of struggle. What were these two struggles?

2. Who, according to Marx, were the protagonists of the man-against-man struggle in a capitalistic society?

3. Why, in Marx's explanation of capitalism, are capitalists able to exploit workers? What does "exploit" mean?

4. What does capital accumulation mean? What forced Marx's capitalist to accumulate and what were the consequences of this accumulation?

5. Why did Marx believe that the working class would become increasingly more miserable?

6. What made Marx conclude that capitalistic development would lead to the monopolization of industry by a relatively few capitalists?

7. What is imperialism? Why did Lenin conclude that the development of capitalism would eventually lead to imperialism?

8. What did Marx envision as the causes and the results of the workers' revolution?

9. Explain the two methodological deficiencies which radical economists find in orthodox economics.

10. What evidence is there to suggest that a few large monopolistic corporations dominate the American economy? In what ways does the state allegedly cater to these corporations?

11. What, according to the radical economists, are the major problems that result from corporate capitalism?

12. Explain (*a*) the orthodox economist's theory of income distribution; and (*b*) the faults which the radical economists see in this theory.

13. In the view of the radical economists, how does the capitalistic system lead to inequality in the distribution of income and in the ownership of wealth? Why, in their view, are these causes "cumulative and self-reinforcing"?

14. Compare the economic conditions found in the primary labor market with those found in the secondary labor market. What historical reasons can be presented to explain the evolution of these dual labor markets?

15. What is alienation and what do the radical economists see as the causes of alienation in the United States?

16. Why do the radical economists argue that capitalistic production is irrational and its use of resources wasteful?

17. What are the three ways in which imperialism, if one accepts the views of radical economists, serves as an obstacle to the economic development of the poor nations of the world. According to John G. Gurley (quoted in the text), what forms has American imperialism taken in the last thirty years and what has been the aim of these imperialistic activities?

18. What kind of new society do the radicals envision or advocate? What are the different economic systems they recommend as replacements for capitalism?

19. How do the orthodox economists rebut the radical economists' critique of American capitalism?

20. What evidence is there to suggest that radical economists (*a*) have invalid perceptions of reality; (*b*) are not objective; and (*c*) overemphasize the significance of ideology?

41
International trade: comparative advantage and protectionism

This is the first of three chapters dealing with international trade and finance. International trade is a subject with which most people have little firsthand experience. For this reason many of the terms, concepts, and ideas encountered in these chapters will be unfamiliar and may not be readily grasped. However, most of this material is fairly simple if you will take some pains to examine it. The ideas and concepts employed are new, but they are not especially complex or difficult.

At the beginning it is essential to recognize that international trade is important to the United States. Exports from and imports into the American economy are $350 and $332 billion a year. The United States *absolutely* is the greatest exporting and importing nation in the world. In *relative* terms, other nations have exports and imports which are larger percentages of their GNPs. They may export and import more than 35 percent of GNP, while the United States exports and imports only about 11% of GNP. It is equally important for you to understand from the beginning that international trade differs from the trade that goes on within nations. Different nations use different monies, not just one money; resources are less mobile internationally than they are *intra*nationally; and nations place more political restrictions on international trade than they do on intranational trade.

But while foreign trade differs from domestic trade, nations trade for the same basic reason that people within a nation trade: to take advantage of the benefits of specialization. Nations specialize in and export those goods and services in the production of which they have a comparative advantage. A comparative advantage means that the opportunity cost of producing a particular good or service is lower in that nation than in another nation. These nations will avoid the production of and import the goods and services in the production of which other nations have a comparative advantage. In this way all nations are able to obtain products which are produced as inexpensively as possible. Put another way, when nations specialize in those products in which they have a comparative advantage, the world as a whole can obtain more goods and services from its resources; and each of the nations of the world can enjoy a standard of living higher than it would have if it did not specialize and export and import.

But regardless of the advantages of specialization and trade among nations, people in the United States and throughout the world have for well over 200 years debated whether free trade or protection was the better policy for their nation. Economists took part in this debate and, with few exceptions, argued for free trade and against protection. Those who favor free trade contend that free trade benefits both the nation and the world as a whole. "Free traders" argue that tariffs, import quotas, and other barriers to international trade prevent or reduce specialization and decrease both a nation's and the world's production and standard of living.

But nations have and continue to erect barriers to trade with other nations. The questions upon which the latter part of this chapter focuses attention are (1) what motivates nations to impose tariffs and to limit the quantities of goods imported from abroad; (2) what effects do protection have upon a nation's own prosperity and upon the prosperity of the world; and (3) what kinds of arguments do those who favor protection employ to support their position—on what grounds do they base their contention that their nation will benefit from the erection of barriers which reduce imports from foreign nations.

The chapter's final major section is a brief review of American policy toward trade barriers since 1934. That year began a series of gradual but substantial tariff-rate reductions which have continued almost up to the present year. Despite this progress in decreasing the barriers to trade with other nations, protectionism is not dead. Advocates of protection are alive—though not quite well—and the causes and costs of this rebirth of protectionism in the United States conclude the chapter.

Whether free trade or protection will be the policy of the United States in the years to come may well depend upon whether you understand that free trade helps everyone and that protection helps no one but the selfish.

■ CHECKLIST

When you have studied this chapter you should be able to:

☐ Explain the importance of international trade to the American economy in terms of the volume of this trade and American dependence on it and list the major exports and imports of the United States.

☐ Identify three features of international trade which distinguish it from the trade that takes place within a nation.

☐ State the two economic circumstances which make it desirable for nations to specialize and trade.

☐ Compute, when you are given the necessary figures, the costs of producing two commodities in two countries; determine which nation has the comparative advantage in the production of each commodity; calculate the range in which the terms of trade will be found; and explain the gains to each nation and to the world from specialization and trade.

☐ Restate the case for free trade.

☐ Identify the four principal types of artificial barriers to international trade and the motive for erecting these barriers.

☐ Explain the economic effects of a protective tariff on resource allocation, the price of the commodity, the total production of the commodity, and the outputs of foreign and domestic producers of the commodity.

☐ Enumerate the arguments used to support the case for protection and find the weakness in each of these arguments.

☐ List the major provisions of the Reciprocal Trade Agreements Act of 1934 and of the General Agreement on Tariffs and Trade of 1947; and explain why the former was a sharp change in the trade policy of the United States.

☐ Identify the four major goals of the European Economic Community (the Common Market).

☐ Identify the interrelated factors that explain the rebirth of protectionism in the United States; present examples of this rebirth; and state the costs of increased protection to the consumers of the United States relative to its benefits.

■ CHAPTER OUTLINE

1. Trade among nations is large enough and unique enough to warrant special attention.

a. While the relative importance of international trade to the United States is less than it is to other nations,

(1) this country's imports and exports are about 9 and 11% of its GNP, about $370 and $445 billion a year, respectively, and the United States is the largest trading nation in the world;

(2) the American economy depends on this trade for important raw materials and markets for its finished goods;

(3) the United States imports more from the rest of the world as a whole, Japan, and the OPEC nations than it exports to them, and most American trade is with other developed nations; and

(4) changes in the net exports (exports minus imports) have a multiplier effect on American output, employment, and prices.

b. International trade has three characteristics that distinguish it from domestic trade: resources are less mobile, the nations use different currencies (or money), and the trade is subjected to more political restrictions.

2. Specialization and trade among nations is advantageous because the world's resources are not evenly distributed and the efficient production of different commodities necessitates different methods and combinations of resources.

3. A simple hypothetical example explains comparative advantage and the gains from trade.

a. Suppose the world is composed of only two nations, each of which is capable of producing two different commodities and in which the production possibilities curves are different straight lines (whose cost ratios are constant but different).

b. With different cost ratios, each nation will have a comparative (cost) advantage in the production of one of the two commodities; and if the world is to use its resources economically each nation must specialize in the commodity in the production of which it has a comparative advantage.

c. The ratio at which one product is traded for another—the terms of trade—lies between the cost ratios of the two nations.

d. Each nation gains from this trade because specialization permits a greater total output from the same resources and a better allocation of the world's resources.

e. If cost ratios in the two nations are not constant, specialization may not be complete.

f. The basic argument for free trade among nations is that it leads to a better allocation of resources and a higher standard of living in the world; but it also increases competition and deters monopoly in these nations.

4. Nations, however, retard international trade by erecting artificial barriers; and tariffs, import quotas, a variety of nontariff barriers, and voluntary export restrictions are the principal barriers to trade.

a. Special interest groups within nations benefit from protection and persuade their nations to erect trade barriers; but the costs to consumers of this protection exceed the benefits to the economy.

b. The imposition of a tariff on a good imported from abroad has both direct and indirect effects on an economy.

(1) The tariff increases the domestic price of the good, reduces its domestic consumption, expands its domestic production, decreases foreign production, and transfers income from domestic consumers to government.

(2) It also reduces the income of foreign producers and the ability of foreign nations to purchase goods and services in the nation imposing the tariff, causes the contraction of relatively efficient industries in that nation, decreases world trade, and lowers the real output of goods and services.

5. The arguments for protection are military self-sufficiency, increasing the domestic employment of labor, diversification to stabilize the economy, the support of infant industries, and shielding the economy from the competition of cheap foreign labor; while most of these arguments are fallacious or based on half-truths, at least two of them warrant the protection of certain industries under certain conditions; and historical evidence suggests free trade promotes and protectionism deters prosperity and economic growth in the world.

6. Until 1934 the United States steadily increased tariff rates to protect private-interest groups.

a. Since the passage of the Reciprocal Trade Agreements Act, tariff rates have been substantially reduced; and many nations, including the United States, signed the General Agreement on Tariffs and Trade in an attempt to eliminate trade barriers.

b. The European Common Market sought the economic integration of Western Europe; and the Common Market nations have achieved considerable integration and have increased their growth rates; but their success has created problems for nonmember nations.

c. In recent years pressures for protection from goods produced abroad have reemerged in the United States.

(1) There are several interrelated causes of these pressures for protection.

(2) And the United States has in a number of ways restricted imports into the economy.

(3) But the costs to consumers in the United States of protection are high (and exceed its benefits); and protection is similar to a regressive tax because it redistributes income from the lowest to the highest income groups.

■ IMPORTANT TERMS

Closed economy
Open economy
Labor- (land-, capital-) intensive commodity
Cost ratio
Comparative advantage
Specialization
Terms of trade
Trading possibilities line
Tariff
Revenue tariff
Protective tariff
Import quota
Nontariff barriers (NTBs)
Voluntary export restrictions (VERs)
Reciprocal Trade Agreements Act of 1934
Most-favored-nation clause
General Agreement on Tariffs and Trade (GATT)
Economic integration
European Common Market (European Economic Community)

■ FILL-IN QUESTIONS

1. The imports and exports of the United States amount to about ________ % of the economy's GNP.

2. Special attention is devoted to international trade because resources are (more, less) ________ mobile between nations than within a nation; because each nation employs a different ________; and because international trade is subject to a (greater, smaller) ________ number of political interferences and controls than domestic trade.

3. Nations tend to trade among themselves because the

distribution of economic resources among them is (even, uneven) uneven and because the efficient production of various goods and services necessitates (the same, different) different technologies or combinations of resources.

4. The nations of the world tend to specialize in those goods in the production of which they have a comparative advantage to export those goods, and to import those goods in the production of which they do not have a " "

5. If the cost ratio in country X is 4 Panama hats equal 1 pound of bananas, while in country Y, 3 Panama hats equal 1 pound of bananas:

a. In country X hats are relatively (expensive, inexpensive) inexpensive and bananas relatively expensive

b. In country Y hats are relatively expensive and bananas relatively inexpensive

c. X has a comparative advantage and should specialize in the production of hats and Y has a comparative advantage and should specialize in the production of bananas

d. When X and Y specialize and trade, the terms of trade will be somewhere between 3 and 4 hats for each pound of bananas; and will depend upon world demand & supply for hats & bananas

e. When the actual terms of trade turn out to be 3½ hats for 1 pound of bananas, the cost of obtaining:

(1) 1 Panama hat has been decreased from 1/3 to 2/7 pounds of bananas in Y.

(2) 1 pound of bananas has been decreased from 4 to 3½ Panama hats in X.

f. This international specialization will not be complete if the cost of producing either good (increases, decreases, remains constant) increases as a nation produces more of it.

6. The basic argument for free trade is that it results in a better allocation of resources and a higher standard of living.

7. The barriers to international trade include tariffs, import quotas, the non tariff barriers, and voluntary export restrictions.

8. Nations erect barriers to international trade to benefit the economic positions of special interest groups even though these barriers (increase, decrease) decrease economic efficiency and trade among nations, and the benefits to a nation are (greater, less) less than the costs to it.

9. When the United States imposes a tariff on a good which is imported from abroad:

a. the price of that good in the United States will (increase, decrease) increase

b. the total purchases of the good in the United States will decrease

c. the output of:

(1) American producers of the good will increase ____

(2) foreign producers will decrease

d. the ability of foreigners to buy goods and services in the United States will decrease and, as a result, output and employment in American industries that sell goods and services abroad will decrease

10. List the five arguments which protectionists employ to justify trade barriers.

a. military self-sufficiency

b. infant industry

c. increase domestic employment

d. diversification for stability

e. cheap foreign labor

The only two arguments containing any reasonable justification for protection are the military self-suf. argument and the infant industry argument.

11. Until 1930 the trend of tariff rates in the United States was (upward, downward) upward ; but since the passage of the Reciprocal Trade Agreements Act in 1934 the trend has been downward. This act empowered the President to lower tariff rates by up to 50 % in return for a reduction in foreign restrictions on American goods and incorporated most-favored-nation clauses in American trade agreements.

12. The three main principles set down in the General Agreement on Tariffs and Trade are:

a. equal, nondiscriminatory treatment

b. reduce tariffs by multilateral negotiations

c. elimination of import quotas

13. The specific aims of the European Common Market were the abolition of tariffs & import quotas on all products traded among 13 nations among member nations, the establishment of common tariffs on goods imported from outside Common Mkt. nations, the free movement of capital and labor among member nations, and common policies with respect to other matters.

14. What are five interrelated factors which have resulted in the recent resurgence of pressures for the protection of American industries?

a. ______________________

b. ______________________

c. ______________________

d. ______________________

e. ______________________

15. The costs of protecting American producers from foreign competition are equal to the rise in the __________ American consumers have to pay for the protected goods.

a. These costs are (greater, less) __________ than the benefits to American producers.

b. The costs of protection were borne mostly by those consumers in the (highest, lowest) __________ income group.

■ PROBLEMS AND PROJECTS

1. Shown below are the production possibilities curves for two nations: the United States and Chile. Suppose these two nations do not currently engage in international trade or specialization, and suppose that points *A* and *a* show the combinations of wheat and copper they now produce and consume.

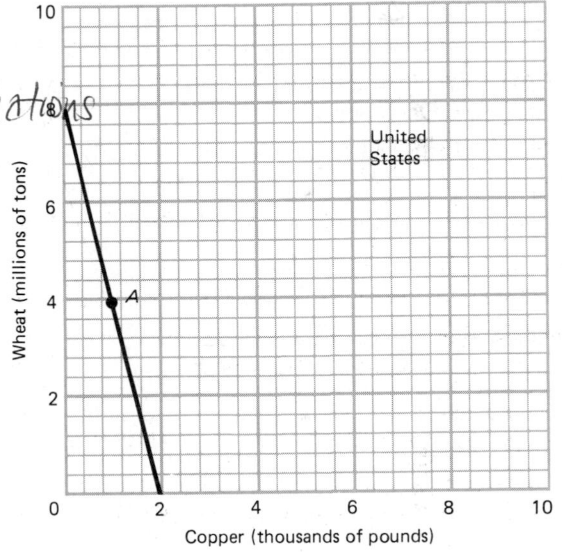

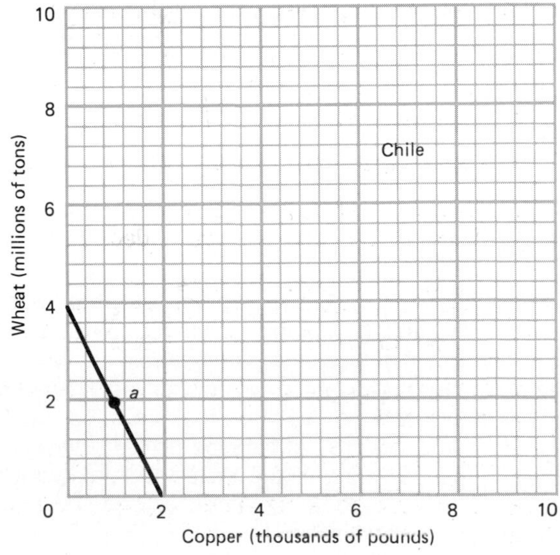

a. The straightness of the two curves indicates that the cost ratios in the two nations are (changing, constant) ___Constant___

b. Examination of the two curves reveals that the cost ratio in:

(1) The United States is ___8___ million tons of wheat for ___2___ thousand pounds of copper.

(2) Chile is ___4___ million tons of wheat for ___2___ thousand pounds of copper.

c. If these two nations were to specialize and trade wheat for copper,

(1) The United States would specialize in the production of wheat because ____________________

(2) Chile would specialize in the production of copper because ____________________

d. The terms of trade, if specialization and trade occur, will be greater than 2 and less than 4 million tons of wheat for 1 thousand pounds of copper because ____________________

e. Assume the terms of trade turn out to be 3 million tons of wheat for 1 thousand pounds of copper. Draw in the trading possibilities curve for the United States and Chile.

f. With these trading possibilities curves, suppose the United States decides to consume 5 million tons of wheat and 1 thousand pounds of copper while Chile decides to consume 3 million tons of wheat and 1 thousand pounds of copper. The gains from trade to:

(1) The United States are ___1___ million tons of wheat and ___0___ thousand pounds of copper.

(2) Chile are ___1___ million tons of wheat and ___0___ thousand pounds of copper.

2. The following table shows the quantities of woolen gloves demanded (*D*) in the United States at several different prices (*P*). Also shown in the table are the quantities of woolen gloves that would be supplied by American producers (S_a) and the quantities that would be supplied by foreign producers (S_f) at the nine different prices.

a. Compute and enter in the table the total quantities that would be supplied (S_t) by American and foreign producers at each of the prices.

P	D	S_a	S_f	S_t	S'_f	S'_t
$2.60	450	275	475	____	____	____
2.40	500	250	450	____	____	____
2.20	550	225	425	____	____	____
2.00	600	200	400	____	____	____
1.80	650	175	375	____	____	____
1.60	700	150	350	____	____	____
1.40	750	125	325	____	____	____
1.20	800	0	300	____	____	____
1.00	850	0	0	____	____	____

b. If the market for woolen gloves in the United States is a competitive one the equilibrium price for woolen gloves is $________ and the equilibrium quantity is ________

c. Suppose now that the United States government imposes an 80 cent ($0.80) per pair of gloves tariff on all gloves imported into the United States from abroad. Compute and enter into the table the quantities that would be supplied (S'_f) by foreign producers at the nine different prices. (*Hint:* If foreign producers were willing to supply 300 pairs at a price of $1.20 when there was no tariff they are now willing to supply 300 pairs at $2.00, the $0.80 per pair tariff plus the $1.20 they will receive for themselves. The quantities supplied at each of the other prices may be found in a similar fashion.)

d. Compute and enter into the table the total quantities that would be supplied (S'_t) by American and foreign producers at each of the nine prices.

e. As a result of the imposition of the tariff the equilibrium price has risen to $________ and the equilibrium quantity has fallen to ________

f. The number of pairs sold by:

(1) American producers has (increased, decreased) ________ by ________

(2) foreign producers has (increased, decreased) ________ by ________

g. The total revenues (after the payment of the tariff) of:

(1) American producers—who do *not* pay the tariff—have (increased, decreased) ________ by $________

(2) foreign producers—who *do* pay the tariff—have (increased, decreased) ________ by $________

h. The total amount spent by American buyers of woolen gloves has __________ by $__________

i. The tariff revenue of the United States government has __________ by $__________

j. The total number of dollars earned by foreigners has __________ by $__________; and, as a result, the total foreign demand for goods and services produced in the United States will __________ by $__________

■ SELF-TEST

Circle the T if the statement is true, the F if it is false.

1. Since 1970 the dollar volume of U.S. imports has increased and the dollar volume of its exports has decreased. T F

2. The American economy's share of world trade has decreased since 1947. T F

3. The United States exports and imports goods and services with a dollar value greater than any other nation in the world. T F

Use the following production possibilities to answer questions 4, 5, and 6 below and to answer multiple-choice questions 8 and 9.

NEPAL PRODUCTION POSSIBILITIES TABLE

	Production alternatives					
Product	A	B	C	D	E	F
Yak fat	0	4	8	12	16	20
Camel hides	40	32	24	16	8	0

KASHMIR PRODUCTION POSSIBILITIES TABLE

	Production alternatives					
Product	A	B	C	D	E	F
Yak fat	0	3	6	9	12	15
Camel hides	60	48	36	24	12	0

4. In Kashmir the cost of 1 camel hide is 3 units of yak fat. T F

5. Nepal has a comparative advantage in producing camel hides. T F

6. With specialization and trade, the trading possibilities curves of both nations would move to the right of their production possibilities curves. T F

7. Increasing production costs tend to prevent specialization among trading nations from being complete. T F

8. Trade among nations tends to bring about a more efficient use of the world's resources and a greater world output of goods and services. T F

9. Free trade among nations tends to increase monopoly and lessen competition in these nations. T F

10. A tariff on coffee in the United States is an example of a protective tariff. T F

11. The imposition of a tariff on a good imported from abroad will raise the price of the good and lower the quantity of it bought and sold. T F

12. To advocate tariffs which would protect domestic producers of goods and materials essential to national defense is to substitute a political-military objective for the economic objectives of efficiently allocating resources. T F

13. An increase in a nation's imports will, other things remaining constant, expand aggregate expenditures, real output, and employment in that nation. T F

14. One crop economies may be able to make themselves more stable and diversified by imposing tariffs on goods imported from abroad; but these tariffs are apt also to lower the standard of living in these economies. T F

15. The only argument for tariffs that has, in the appropriate circumstances, any economic justification is the increase-domestic-employment argument. T F

16. If the United States concludes a tariff agreement with and lowers the tariff rates on goods imported from another nation and that trade agreement contains a most-favored-nation clause, the lower tariff rates are then charged on those goods when they are imported from (most) other nations in the world. T F

17. The members of the European Economic Community have had rapid economic growth since they formed the Common Market in 1958. **T F**

18. The economic integration of nations creates larger markets for firms within the nations that integrate and makes it possible for these firms and their customers to benefit from the economies of large-scale (mass) production. **T F**

19. The formation of the European Economic Community (Common Market) has made it more difficult for American firms to compete with firms located within the Community for customers there. **T F**

20. The cost of protecting American firms and employees from foreign competition is the rise in the prices of products produced in the United States, and this cost almost always exceeds its benefits. **T F**

Circle the letter that corresponds to the best answer.

1. In 1985 the imports of the United States amounted to approximately what percentage of the United States' GNP? (*a*) 5%; (*b*) 7%; (*c*) 9%; (*d*) 4%.

2. To which of the following does the largest percentage of the U.S. exports of merchandise go? (*a*) Western Europe; (*b*) Canada; (*c*) Japan; (*d*) the OPEC nations.

3. From which does the largest percentage of the U.S. imports of merchandise come? (*a*) Western Europe; (*b*) Canada; (*c*) Japan; (*d*) the OPEC nations.

4. Which of the following is *not* true? (*a*) The greater part of the export-import trade in merchandise is with the underdeveloped nations; (*b*) the U.S. imports more merchandise from the OPEC nations than it exports to them; (*c*) the U.S. imports more merchandise from Japan than it exports to them; (*d*) the merchandise imports of the U.S. exceed its exports of merchandise.

5. In recent years the total exports and imports of goods and services of the U.S. have been between (*a*) $100 and $200 billion; (*b*) $200 and $300 billion; (*c*) $300 and $400 billion; (*d*) $400 and $500 billion.

6. International trade is a special and separate area of economic study because (*a*) international trade involves the movement of goods over greater distances than trade within a nation; (*b*) resources are more mobile internationally than domestically; (*c*) countries engaged in international trade use different monies; (*d*) international trade is based on comparative advantage.

7. Nations would not need to engage in trade if: (*a*) all products were produced from the same combinations of resources; (*b*) world resources were evenly distributed among nations; (*c*) world resources were perfectly mobile; (*d*) all of the above.

Use the tables preceding true-false question 4 to answer the following two questions:

8. If Nepal and Kashmir engage in trade, the terms of trade will be: (*a*) between 2 and 4 camel hides for 1 unit of yak fat; (*b*) between ⅓ and ½ units of yak fat for 1 camel hide; (*c*) between 3 and 4 units of yak fat for 1 camel hide; (*d*) between 2 and 4 units of yak fat for 1 camel hide.

9. If Nepal and Kashmir, in the absence of trade between them, both produced combination C, the gains from trade would be: (*a*) 6 units of yak fat; (*b*) 8 units of yak fat; (*c*) 6 units of yak fat and 8 camel hides; (*d*) 8 units of yak fat and 6 camel hides.

10. Which one of the following is characteristic of tariffs? (*a*) They prevent the importation of goods from abroad; (*b*) they specify the maximum amounts of specific commodities which may be imported during a given period of time; (*c*) they often protect domestic producers from foreign competition; (*d*) they enable nations to reduce their exports and increase their imports during periods of depression.

11. The motive for the erection by a nation of barriers to the importation of goods and services from abroad is to (*a*) improve economic efficiency in that nation; (*b*) protect and benefit special interest groups in that nation; (*c*) reduce the prices of the goods and services produced in that nation; (*d*) expand the export of goods and services to foreign nations.

12. When a tariff is imposed on a good imported from abroad (*a*) the demand for the good increases; (*b*) the demand for the good decreases; (*c*) the supply of the good increases; (*d*) the supply of the good decreases.

13. Tariffs lead to (*a*) the contraction of relatively efficient industries; (*b*) an overallocation of resources to relatively efficient industries; (*c*) an increase in the foreign demand for domestically produced goods; (*d*) an underallocation of resources to relatively inefficient industries.

14. Which one of the following arguments for protection is the least fallacious and most pertinent in the United States today? (*a*) The military self-sufficiency argument; (*b*) the increase-domestic-employment argument; (*c*) the cheap foreign labor argument; (*d*) the infant-industry argument.

15. Which of the following is the likely result of the United States employing tariffs to protect its high wages and standard of living from cheap foreign labor? (*a*) An increase in U.S. exports; (*b*) a rise in the American real NNP; (*c*) a decrease in the average productivity of American workers; (*d*) a decrease in the quantity of labor employed by industries producing the goods on which tariffs have been levied.

16. Which of the following is a likely result of imposing tariffs to increase domestic employment? (*a*) A short-run increase in domestic employment; (*b*) retaliatory increases in the tariff rates of foreign nations; (*c*) a long-run decline in exports; (*d*) all of the above.

17. The infant-industry argument for tariffs (*a*) is especially pertinent to the advanced industrial nations; (*b*) generally results in tariffs that are removed after the infant industry has matured; (*c*) makes it rather easy to determine which infant industries will become mature industries with comparative advantages in producing their goods; (*d*) might better be replaced by an argument for outright subsidies for infant industries.

18. Which one of the following specifically empowered the President of the United States to reduce its tariff rates up to 50% if other nations would reduce their tariffs on American goods? (*a*) The Underwood Act of 1913; (*b*) the Hawley-Smoot Act of 1930; (*c*) the Trade Agreements Act of 1934; (*d*) the General Agreement on Tariffs and Trade of 1947.

19. Which of the following is *not* characteristic of the General Agreement on Tariffs and Trade? Nations signing the agreement were committed to (*a*) the elimination of import quotas; (*b*) the reciprocal reduction of tariffs by negotiation; (*c*) the nondiscriminatory treatment of all trading nations; (*d*) the establishment of a world customs union.

20. The European Common Market (*a*) is designed to eliminate tariffs and import quotas among its members; (*b*) aims to allow the eventual free movement of capital and labor within the member nations; (*c*) imposes common tariffs on goods imported into the member nations from outside the Common Market area; (*d*) does all of the above.

21. Pressures for the protection of American industries have increased in recent years because of (*a*) previous decreases in the barriers to trade; (*b*) recession and unemployment in the United States; (*c*) increased competition from imported products; (*d*) all of the above.

■ DISCUSSION QUESTIONS

1. In relative and absolute terms, how large is the volume of the international trade of the United States? What has happened to these figures over the past twenty or so years?

2. What are the principal exports and imports of the American economy? What commodities used in the economy come almost entirely from abroad and what American industries sell large percentages of their outputs abroad?

3. Which nations are the principal "trading partners" of the United States? How much of this trade is with the developed and how much of it is with the underdeveloped nations of the world?

4. Are the American economy's exports of merchandise to the following greater or less than its imports of merchandise from them? (*a*) Japan, (*b*) the OPEC nations, and (*c*) the rest of the world.

5. In what ways is international trade different from the trade which takes place within a nation?

6. Why do nations specialize in certain products and export their surplus production of these goods at the same time that they are importing other goods? Why do they not use the resources employed to produce the surpluses which they export to produce the goods which they import?

7. What two facts—one dealing with the distribution of the world's resources and the other related to the technology of producing different products—are the basis for trade among nations?

8. Explain (*a*) the theory or principle of comparative advantage; (*b*) what is meant by and what determines the terms of trade; and (*c*) the gains from trade.

9. What is the "case for free trade"?

10. What motivates nations to erect barriers to the importation of goods from abroad and what types of barriers do they erect?

11. Suppose the United States were to increase the tariff on automobiles imported from West Germany (and other foreign countries). What would be the effect of this tariff-rate increase on (*a*) the price of automobiles in the United States; (*b*) the total number of cars sold in the United States during a year; (*c*) the number of cars produced by and employment in the West German automobile industry; (*d*) production by and employment in the American automobile industry; (*e*) West German income obtained by selling cars in the United States; (*f*) the West German demand for goods produced in the U.S.; (*g*) the production of and employment in those American industries which now export goods to West Germany; (*h*) the standards of living in the U.S. and in West Germany; (*i*) the allocation of resources in the American economy; and (*j*) the allocation of the world's resources?

12. What is the "case for protection"? How valid and pertinent to the United States is each of the basic arguments for protection?

13. What was the tariff policy of the United States: (*a*) between 1790 and 1930; (*b*) since 1934? Explain the basic provisions of the Reciprocal Trade Agreements Act. How has the United States cooperated with other nations since 1945 to reduce trade barriers?

14. What were the three cardinal principles contained in the General Agreement on Tariffs and Trade?

15. What were the four main goals of the European Economic Community? How does the achievement of these goals bring about an increased standard of living within the Community? What problems and what benefits does the success of the EEC create for the United States?

16. Why have the pressures for the protection of American firms and workers increased in the last few years? What (*a*) are several examples of this increased protection; and (*b*) are the costs to the American economy of protection?

42
Exchange rates and the balance of payments

In the last chapter you learned *why* nations engage in international trade and *why* they erect barriers to trade with other nations. In Chapter 42 you will learn *how* nations using different monies (or currencies) are able to trade with each other. The means they employ to overcome the difficulties that result from the use of different monies is fairly simple. When the residents of a nation (its consumers, business firms, or governments) wish to buy goods or services or real or financial assets from, make loans or gifts to, or pay interest and dividends to the residents of other nations they *buy* some of the money used in that nation. They pay for the foreign money with some of their own money. In other words, they *exchange* their own money for foreign money. And when the residents of a nation sell goods or services or real or financial assets to, receive loans or gifts from, or are paid dividends or interest by the residents of foreign nations and obtain foreign money they *sell* this foreign money—often called foreign exchange—in return for some of their own money. That is, they *exchange* foreign money for their own money. The markets in which one money is sold and is paid for with another money are called foreign exchange markets. The price that is paid (in one money) for a unit of another money is called the foreign exchange rate (or the rate of exchange). And like most prices, the foreign exchange rate for any foreign currency is determined by the demand for and the supply of that foreign currency.

As you know from Chapter 41, nations buy and sell large quantities of goods and services across national boundaries. But the residents of these nations also buy and sell such financial assets as stocks and bonds and such real assets as land and capital goods in other nations; and the governments and individuals in one nation make gifts (remittances) in other nations. At the end of a year, nations summarize their foreign transactions with the rest of the world. This summary is called the nation's international balance of payments: a record of how it obtained foreign money during the year and what it did with this foreign money. Of course, all foreign money obtained was used for some purpose—it did not evaporate—and consequently the balance of payments *always* balances. The international balance of payments is an extremely important and useful device for understanding the amounts and kinds of international transactions in which the residents of a nation engage. But it also enables us to understand the meaning of a balance of payments imbalance (a deficit or a surplus), the causes of these imbalances, and how to deal with them.

Probably the most difficult section of this chapter is concerned with balance of payments deficits and surpluses. A balance of payments deficit (surplus) is found when the receipts of foreign money are less (greater) than the payments of foreign money and the nation must reduce (expand) its official reserves to make the balance of payments balance. You should pay particular attention to the way in which a system of *flexible* exchange rates and the way in which a system of *fixed* exchange rates will correct balance of payments deficits and surpluses; and the advantages and disadvantages of these two alternative methods of eliminating imbalances.

As examples of these two types of exchange rate systems you will find in the final section of the chapter an examination of the gold standard, of the Bretton Woods system, and of the managed floating exchange rate system. In the first two systems exchange rates are fixed; and in the third system exchange rates are fixed in the short run (to obtain the advantages of fixed exchange rates) and flexible in the long run (to enable nations to correct balance of payments deficits and surpluses).

One last word for you. This chapter is filled with new terms. Some of these are just special words used in international economies to mean things with which you are already familiar. Be very sure you learn what all of the new terms mean. It will simplify your comprehension of this chapter and enable you to understand more readily the foreign trade "crisis" of the United States and its macroeconomic difficulties examined in the next chapter.

■ CHECKLIST

When you have studied this chapter you should be able to:

☐ Explain how American exports create a demand for dollars and generate a supply of foreign exchange; and how American imports create a demand for foreign exchange and generate a supply of dollars.

☐ Define each of the five balances found in a nation's international balance of payments; and distinguish between a deficit and a surplus in each of these five balances.

☐ Explain the relationship between the current and capital account balances; and between the balance of payments and changes in the official reserves of a nation.

☐ Provide an explanation of how flexible (floating) exchange rates function to eliminate payments deficits and surpluses; and enumerate the three disadvantages of this method of correcting imbalances.

☐ Identify the five principal determinants of the demand for and supply of a particular foreign money; and explain how a change in each of these determinants would affect the rate of exchange for that foreign money.

☐ Enumerate the four means by which a nation may fix (or "peg") foreign exchange rates.

☐ Explain how a nation with a payments deficit might employ its international reserves to prevent a rise in foreign exchange rates.

☐ Describe how a nation with a payments deficit might use fiscal and monetary policies, trade policies, and exchange controls to eliminate the deficit.

☐ List the three conditions which a nation had to fulfill if it was to be on the gold standard; explain how gold flows operated to reduce payments deficits and surpluses; and identify its two advantages and its two basic drawbacks.

☐ Explain how the Bretton Woods system stabilized exchange rates and attempted to provide for orderly changes in exchange rates to eliminate payments imbalances.

☐ Define the international monetary reserves of nations in the Bretton Woods system; explain why the United States had to incur balance of payments deficits to expand these reserves; and describe the dilemma this created for the United States.

☐ Describe how the United States severed the link between gold and the international value of the dollar in 1971 that led to the floating of the dollar and brought to an end the old Bretton Woods system.

☐ Explain what is meant by a system of managed floating exchange rates; and enumerate its two alleged virtues and its three alleged shortcomings.

☐ Contrast the adjustments necessary to correct payments deficits and surpluses when exchange rates are flexible and when they are fixed.

■ CHAPTER OUTLINE

1. Trade between two nations differs from domestic trade because the nations use different monies; but this problem is resolved by the existence of foreign-exchange markets in which the money used by one nation can be purchased and paid for with the money of the other nation.

a. American exports create a demand for dollars and generate a supply of foreign money in the foreign-exchange markets; increase the money supply in the United States and decrease foreign money supplies; and earn monies that can be used to pay for American imports.

b. American imports create a supply of dollars and generate a demand for foreign money in foreign-exchange markets; decrease the money supply in the United States and increase foreign money supplies; and use monies obtained by exporting.

2. The international balance of payments for a nation is an annual record of all its transactions with the other nations in the world; and it records all the payments received from and made to the rest of the world.

a. The current-account section of a nation's international balance of payments records its trade in currently produced goods and services; and within this section:

(1) the trade balance of the nation is equal to its exports of goods (merchandise) less its imports of goods (merchandise), and the nation has a trade surplus (deficit) if the exports are greater (less) than the imports;

(2) the balance on goods and services is equal to its exports of goods and services less its imports of goods and services; and

(3) the balance on the current account is equal to its balance on goods and services plus its net investment income (dividends and interest) from other nations and its net private and public transfers to other nations, and this balance may be either a surplus or a deficit.

b. The capital-account section of a nation's international balance of payments records its sales of real and financial assets (which earn it foreign money) and its purchases of real and financial assets (which use up foreign money), and the nation has a capital-account surplus (deficit) if its sales are greater (less) than its purchases of real and financial assets.

c. The current and capital accounts in a nation's international balance of payments are interrelated: a nation with a current-account deficit can finance the deficit by borrowing or selling assets abroad (with a capital-account surplus) and a nation with a current-account surplus can lend or buy assets abroad (incur a capital-account deficit).

d. The official reserves of a nation are the foreign currencies (monies) owned by its central bank: these reserves a nation uses to finance a net deficit on its current and capital accounts, and these reserves increase when a nation has a net surplus on its current and capital accounts; and in this way the nation's total outpayments and inpayments are made to equal each other (to balance).

e. A nation is said to have a balance-of-payments surplus (deficit) when the current and capital account balance is positive (negative) and its official reserves increase (decrease).

f. The merchandise or trade deficit of a nation implies its producers are losing their competitiveness in foreign markets, but is beneficial to consumers in that nation who receive more goods (imports) from abroad than they must pay for (export); and a balance-of-payments deficit is undesirable to the extent that the nation's official reserves are limited and require the nation to take painful macroeconomic adjustments to correct it.

3. The kinds of adjustments a nation with a balance-of-payments deficit or surplus must make to correct the imbalance depends upon whether exchange rates are flexible (floating) or fixed.

a. If foreign exchange rates float freely the demand for and the supply of foreign exchange determine foreign exchange rates; and the exchange rate for any foreign money is the rate at which the quantity of that money demanded is equal to the quantity of it supplied.

(1) A change in the demand for or supply of a foreign money will cause the exchange rate for that money to rise or fall; and when there is a rise (fall) in the price paid in dollars for a foreign money it is said that the dollar has depreciated (appreciated) and that the foreign money has appreciated (depreciated).

A HELPFUL HINT

The application of the terms *depreciate* and *appreciate* to foreign exchange confuses many students. Here are some hints that will help reduce the confusion.

First:

- depreciate means decrease; and appreciate means increase.

Second: what decreases when Country A's currency depreciates and increases when its currency appreciates is

- the quantity of Country B's currency that can be purchased for *one unit* of Country A's currency.

Third: when the exchange rate for B's currency:

- *rises* the quantity of B's currency that can be purchased for one unit of A's currency *decreases* (just as a rise in the price of cigars decreases the number of cigars that can be bought for a dollar) and A's currency has *depreciated;*
- *falls* the quantity of B's currency that can be purchased for one unit of A's currency *increases* (just as a fall in the price of cigars increases the number of cigars that can be bought for a dollar) and A's currency has *appreciated.*

---

(2) Changes in the demand for or supply of a foreign currency are largely the result of changes in tastes, relative income changes, relative price changes, changes in relative real interest rates, and speculation.

(3) When a nation has a payments deficit (surplus), foreign exchange rates will rise (fall); this will make foreign goods and services more (less) expensive, decrease (increase) imports, make a nation's goods and services less (more) expensive for foreigners to buy, increase (decrease) its exports; and these adjustments in foreign exchange rates and in imports and exports correct the nation's payments deficit (surplus).

(4) But flexible exchange rates increase the uncertainties faced by exporters, importers, and investors (and reduce international trade); change the terms of trade;

and destabilize economies (by creating inflation of unemployment).

b. When nations fix (or "peg") foreign exchange rates, the governments of these nations must intervene in the foreign exchange markets to prevent shortages and surpluses of foreign monies.

(1) One way for a nation to stabilize foreign exchange rates is for its government to sell (buy) a foreign money in exchange for its own money (or gold) when there is a shortage (surplus) of the foreign money.

(2) A nation with a payments deficit might also discourage imports by imposing tariffs, import quotas, and special taxes; and encourage exports by subsidizing them.

(3) To eliminate a payments deficit a nation might require exporters who earn foreign exchange to sell it to the government; and the government would then ration the available foreign exchange among importers and make the value of imports equal to the value of exports.

(4) Another way for a nation to stabilize foreign exchange rates is to employ fiscal and monetary policies to reduce its national income and price level and to raise interest rates relative to those in other nations; and, thereby, reduce the demand for and increase the supply of the different foreign monies.

4. The nations of the world in their recent history have employed three different exchange rate systems.

a. Between 1879 and 1934 (with the exception of the World War I years) the operation of the gold standard kept foreign exchange rates relatively stable.

(1) A nation was on the gold standard when it:

(a) defined its monetary unit in terms of a certain quantity of gold;

(b) maintained a fixed relationship between its stock of gold and its money supply; and

(c) allowed gold to be exported and imported without restrictions.

(2) Foreign exchange rates between nations on the gold standard would fluctuate only within a narrow range (determined by the cost of packing, insuring, and shipping gold from country to country); and if a foreign exchange rate rose (fell) to the upper (lower) limit of the range gold would flow out of (into) a nation.

(3) But if a nation has a balance-of-payments deficit (surplus) and gold flowed out of (into) the country, its money supply would decrease (increase); this would raise (lower) interest rates and reduce (expand) aggregate demand, national output, employment, and prices in that country; and the balance-of-payments deficit (surplus) would be eliminated.

(4) The gold standard resulted in nearly stable foreign-exchange rates (which by reducing uncertainty stimulated international trade), and automatically corrected balance-of-payments deficits and surpluses; but it required that nations accept such unpleasant adjustments as recession and inflation to eliminate their balance-of-payments deficits and surpluses, and it could operate only so long as nations with deficits did not run out of gold.

(5) During the worldwide Great Depression of the 1930s nations felt that remaining on the gold standard threatened their recoveries from the Depression, and the devaluations of their currencies (to expand exports and reduce imports) led to the breakdown and abandonment of the gold standard.

b. From the end of World War II until 1971 the Bretton Woods system, committed to the adjustable-peg system of exchange rates and managed by the International Monetary Fund (IMF), kept foreign-exchange rates relatively stable.

(1) The adjustable-peg system required the United States to sell gold to other member nations at a fixed price and the other members of the IMF to define their monetary units in terms of either gold or dollars (which established fixed exchange rates among the currencies of all member nations); and for the other member nations to keep the exchange rates for their currencies from rising by selling foreign currencies, selling gold, or borrowing on a short-term basis from the IMF.

(2) The system also provided for orderly changes in exchange rates to correct a fundamental imbalance (persistent and sizable balance-of-payments deficits) by allowing a nation to devalue its currency (increase its defined gold or dollar equivalent).

(3) The other nations of the world used gold and dollars as their international monetary reserves in the Bretton Woods system: for these reserves to grow the United States had to continue to have balance-of-payments deficits, but to continue the convertibility of dollars into gold it had to reduce the deficits; and, faced with this dilemma, the United States in 1971 suspended the convertibility of the dollar, brought an end to the Bretton Woods system of fixed exchange rates, and allowed the exchange rates for the dollar and the other currencies to float.

c. Exchange rates today are managed by individual nations to avoid short-term fluctuations and allowed to float in the long term to correct balance-of-payments deficits and surpluses; and this new system of managed floating exchange rates is favored by some and criticized by others.

(1) Its proponents contend that this system has not led to any decrease in world trade and it has enabled the world to adjust to severe economic shocks.

(2) Its critics argue that it has resulted in volatile exchange rates and has not reduced balance-of-payments deficits and surpluses; that it reinforces inflationary pressures in a nation; and that it is a "nonsystem" that a nation may employ to achieve its own domestic economic goals.

■ IMPORTANT TERMS

Financing exports and imports
Foreign exchange market
Export transaction
Import transaction
Rate of exchange (foreign exchange rate)
International balance of payments
Current account
Trade balance
Trade surplus
Trade deficit
Balance on goods and services
Balance on current account
Net investment income
Net transfers
Capital account
Capital inflow
Capital outflow
Balance on the capital account
Current account deficit
Current account surplus
Capital account deficit
Capital account surplus
Official reserves
Balance of payments deficit
Balance of payments surplus
Flexible (floating) exchange rate
Fixed exchange rate
Exchange rate (currency) depreciation
Exchange rate (currency) appreciation
Exchange control
Gold standard
Gold flow
Gold export point
Gold import point
Devaluation
Bretton Woods system
Adjustable pegs
International Monetary Fund
International monetary reserves
Managed floating exchange rate

■ FILL-IN QUESTIONS

1. The rate of exchange for the French franc is the number of (francs, dollars) ____ which an American must pay to obtain one (franc, dollar) ____

2. When the rate of exchange for the Saudi Arabian riyal is 30 American cents, the rate of exchange for the American dollar is ____ riyals.

3. American:

a. exports create a (demand for, supply of) ____ foreign money, generate a ____ dollars, (increase, decrease) ____ the money supply in the United States, and ____ money supplies abroad;

b. imports create a ____ foreign money, generate a ____ dollars, ____ the money supply in the United States, and ____ money supplies abroad.

4. In addition to the demand for foreign currency by American firms that wish to import goods from foreign countries, Americans also demand foreign money to purchase ____ and ____ services abroad and to pay ____ and ____ on foreign investments in the United States.

5. The balance of payments of a nation records all payments its residents make to and receive from residents in ____

a. Any transaction that *earns* foreign exchange for that nation is a (debit, credit) ____ and is shown with a (+, −) ____ sign.

b. A transaction that *uses up* foreign exchange is a ____ and is shown with a ____ sign.

6. When a nation has a:

a. balance of trade deficit its exports are (greater, less) ____ than its imports of ____,

b. balance-on-goods-and-services surplus its exports are greater than its imports of goods and services;
c. current-account deficit its balance on goods and services plus its net investment income and net remittances is (positive, negative) negative.

7. The capital account records the capital inflows and capital outflows of a nation.
a. The capital inflows are the expenditures made (in that nation, abroad) in that nation by residents of (that nation, other nations) other nations; and the capital outflows are the expenditures made in other nations by residents of that nation for real and financial assets.
b. A nation has a capital-account surplus when its capital-account inflows are (greater, less) greater than its outflows.

8. A nation:
a. may finance a current-account deficit by (buying, selling) selling assets or by (borrowing, lending) borrowing abroad; and
b. may use a capital-account surplus to (buy, sell) buy assets or to (borrow, lend) lend abroad.

9. The official reserves of a nation are the quantities of (foreign monies, its own money) __________ owned by its central bank. If that nation has
a. a deficit on the current and capital accounts its official reserves (increase, decrease) decrease;
b. a surplus on the current and capital accounts its official reserves increase;
c. either a current and capital account deficit or surplus, the sum of the current and capital balances and the increases or decreases in its official reserves total zero

10. A country has a balance-of-payments deficit if the sum of its current and capital accounts balance is (positive, negative) negative and its official reserves (increase, decrease) decrease; and a payments surplus when the sum of its current and capital accounts balance is positive and its official reserves increase

11. If foreign exchange rates float freely and a nation has a balance of payments *deficit:*
a. that nation's money in the foreign exchange markets will (appreciate, depreciate) and foreign monies will ~~depreciate~~ appreciate
b. as a result of these changes in foreign exchange rates, the nation's imports will (increase, decrease) decrease, its exports will increase, and the size of its deficit will decrease

12. What effect (depreciation or appreciation) would each of the following have upon the French franc in the foreign exchange market (*ceteris paribus*)?
a. The increased preference in the United States for domestic wines over wines produced in France: D
b. A rise in the national income of the United States: A
c. An increase in the price level in France: D
d. A rise in real interest rates in the United States: D
e. The belief of speculators in France that the dollar will appreciate in the foreign exchange market: D

13. There are three disadvantages of freely floating foreign exchange rates: The risks and uncertainties associated with flexible rates tend to (expand, diminish) __________ trade between nations; when a nation's currency depreciates, its terms of trade with other nations are (worsened, bettered) worsened; and fluctuating exports and imports can destabilize an economy and result in recession or in inflation in that economy.

14. To fix or "peg" the rate of exchange for the West German mark when:

a. the exchange rate for the mark is rising, the United States would (buy, sell) sell ______ marks in exchange for dollars;

b. the exchange rate for the mark is falling, the United States would buy ______ marks in exchange for dollars.

15. A nation with a balance of payments deficit:

a. might attempt to eliminate the deficit by (taxing, subsidizing) taxing ______ imports or by subsidizing ______ exports;

b. might employ exchange controls and ration foreign exchange among those who wish to (export, import) import ______ goods and services and require all those who export ______ goods and services to sell the foreign exchange they earn to the govt ______

16. If the United States has a payments deficit with Japan and the exchange rate for the Japanese yen is rising, the United States might employ (expansionary, contractionary) contractionary ______ fiscal and monetary policies to reduce the demand for the yen; but this would bring about (inflation, recession) recession ______ in the United States.

17. A nation is on the gold standard when it defines its money in terms of gold ______, maintains a fixed relationship between its money ______ supply and gold stock ______, and allows gold to be freely exported ______ from and imported ______ into the nation.

18. When the nations of the world were on the gold standard

a. exchange rates were relatively (stable, unstable) stable ______,

b. but when a nation had a payments deficit:

(1) gold flowed (into, out of) out of ______ the nation;

(2) its money supply and price level (increased, decreased) decreased ______ and its interest rates rose ______;

(3) its payments deficit (rose, fell) fell ______ and it experienced (inflation, recession) recession ______

19. The Bretton Woods system was established to bring about (flexible, fixed) fixed ______ exchange rates; and, to accomplish this, it employed the adjustable-peg ______ system of exchange rates. Under the Bretton Woods system:

a. a member nation defined its monetary unit in terms of gold ______ or dollars ______;

b. each member nation stabilized the exchange rate for its currency and prevented it from rising by (buying, selling) buying ______ foreign currency which it obtained from its exchange-stabilization ______ fund, by (buying, selling) selling ______ gold, or by (borrowing from, lending to) borrowing from ______ the International Monetary Fund;

c. a nation with a deeply rooted payments deficit could (devalue, revalue) devalue ______ its currency;

d. international monetary reserves included both gold ______ and $$ ______;

e. it was hoped that exchange rates in the short run would be (stable, flexible) stable ______ enough to promote international trade and in the long run would be flexible ______ enough to correct balance of payments imbalances.

20. The role of the dollar as a component of international monetary reserves produced a dilemma:

a. For these reserves to grow the United States had to incur balance of payments (surpluses, deficits) deficits ______

b. This resulted in an increase in the foreign holding of American dollars and in a decrease in the American reserves (stock) of gold ______.

c. The ability of the United States to convert dollars into gold and the willingness of foreigners to hold dollars (because they were "as good as gold"), therefore (increased, decreased) decreased

d. For the dollar to remain an acceptable international monetary reserve the U.S. payments deficits had to be (eliminated, continued) eliminated; but for international monetary reserves to grow the U.S. payments deficits had to be continued

21. The United States completed the destruction of the Bretton Woods system in 1971 when it suspended the convertibility of dollars into gold and allowed the value of the dollar to be determined by market forces (S & D). Since then the international monetary system has moved from exchange rates which (for all practical purposes) were (fixed, floating) Fixed to exchange rates which are Floating

22. The system of exchange rates which has developed since 1971 has been labeled a system of managed float exchange rates. This means that individual nations will:

a. in the short term buy and sell foreign exchange to keep exchange rates Stable

b. in the long term allow exchange rates to rise or fall to correct payments imbalances

■ PROBLEMS AND PROJECTS

1. Assume an American exporter sells $3 million worth of wheat to an importer in Colombia. If the rate of exchange for the Colombian peso is $0.02 (two cents), the wheat has a total value of 150 million pesos.

a. There are two ways the importer in Colombia may pay for the wheat. It might write a check for 150 million pesos drawn on its bank in Bogota and send it to the American exporter.

(1) The American exporter would then sell the check to its bank in New Orleans and its demand deposit there would increase by $__________ million.

(2) This New Orleans bank now sells the check for 150 million pesos to a correspondent bank (an American commercial bank that keeps an account in the Bogota bank).

(*a*) The New Orleans bank's account in the correspondent bank increases by __________ million (dollars, pesos) __________; and

(*b*) the correspondent bank's account in the Bogota bank increases by __________ million (pesos, dollars) __________

b. The second way for the importer to pay for the wheat is to buy from its bank in Bogota a draft on an American bank for $3 million, pay for this draft by writing a check for 150 million pesos drawn on the Bogota bank, and send the draft to the American exporter.

(1) The American exporter would then deposit the draft in its account in the New Orleans bank and its demand deposit account there would increase by $__________ million.

(2) The New Orleans bank collects the amount of the draft from the American bank on which it is drawn through the Federal Reserve Banks.

(*a*) Its account at the Fed increases by $__________ million; and

(*b*) the account of the bank on which the draft was drawn decreases by $__________ million.

c. Regardless of the way employed by the Colombian importer to pay for the wheat:

(1) The export of the wheat created a (demand for, supply of) __________ dollars and a __________ pesos

(2) The number of dollars owned by the American exporter has (increased, decreased) __________ and the number of pesos owned by the Colombian importer has __________

2. The table on page 381 contains hypothetical international balance of payments data for the United States. All figures are in billions.

a. Compute with the appropriate sign (+ or −) and enter in the table the six missing items.

b. The United States had a payments (deficit, surplus) __________ of $__________

Current account		
(1) U.S. merchandise exports	$+150	
(2) U.S. merchandise imports	−200	
(3) Balance of trade		____
(4) U.S. exports of services	+75	
(5) U.S. imports of services	−60	
(6) Balance on goods and services		____
(7) Net investment income	+12	
(8) Net transfers	−7	
(9) Balance on current account		____
Capital account		
(10) Capital inflows to the U.S.	+80	
(11) Capital outflows from the U.S.	−55	
(12) Balance on capital account		____
(13) Current and capital account balance		____
(14) Official reserves		____
		0

3. Following are the supply and demand schedules for the British pound.

Quantity of pounds supplied	Price $	Quantity of pounds demanded
400	5.00	100
360	4.50	200
300	4.00	300
286	3.50	400
267	3.00	500
240	2.50	620
200	2.00	788

a. If the exchange rates are flexible:

(1) What will be the rate of exchange for the pound? $________

(2) What will be the rate of exchange for the dollar? £________

(3) How many pounds will be purchased in the market? ________

(4) How many dollars will be purchased in the market? ________

b. If the government of the United States wished to fix or "peg" the price of the pound at $5.00 it would have to (buy, sell) ________ (how many) ________ pounds for $________

c. And if the British government wished to fix the price of the dollar at £⅖ it would have to (buy, sell) ________ (how many) ________ pounds for $________

■ SELF-TEST

Circle the T if the statement is true, the F if it is false.

1. The importation of goods and services by Americans from abroad creates a supply of dollars in the foreign exchange market. T F

2. American exports expand foreign money supplies and reduce the supply of money in the United States. T F

3. The international balance of payments of the United States records all the payments its residents receive from and make to the residents of foreign nations. T F

4. Exports are a debit item and are shown with a plus sign (+) and imports are a credit item and are shown with a minus sign (−) in the international balance of payments of a nation. T F

5. The United States had a balance of trade deficit in 1984. T F

6. The balance on goods and services of the United States in 1984 was positive (a surplus). T F

7. In 1984 the United States had positive net investment income and negative net transfers from the rest of the world. T F

8. In 1984 there was a net capital outflow from the United States and the United States had a capital-account deficit. T F

9. The United States would have a balance of payments surplus if the balance on its current and capital accounts were positive. T F

10. Any nation with a balance of payments deficit must reduce its official reserves. T F

11. The sum of a nation's current-account balance, its capital-account balance, and the change in its official reserves in any year is always equal to zero. **T F**

12. A large trade deficit in Brazil is harmful to consumers in Brazil. **T F**

13. If a nation has a balance of payments deficit and exchange rates are flexible, the price of that nation's money in the foreign exchange markets will fall and this will reduce its imports and increase its exports. **T F**

14. The expectations of speculators in the United States that the exchange rate for the Japanese yen will fall in the future will increase the supply of yen in the foreign exchange market and decrease the exchange rate for the yen. **T F**

15. Were the United States' terms of trade with Nigeria to worsen, Nigeria would obtain a greater quantity of American goods and services for every barrel of oil it exported to the United States. **T F**

16. If a nation wishes to fix (or "peg") the foreign exchange rate for the Swiss franc, it must buy Swiss francs with its own currency when the rate of exchange for the Swiss franc rises. **T F**

17. If exchange rates are stable and a nation has a payments surplus, prices and money incomes in that nation will tend to rise. **T F**

18. A nation using exchange controls to eliminate a payments surplus might depreciate its currency. **T F**

19. If country A defined its money as worth 100 grains of gold and country B defined its money as worth 20 grains of gold, then, ignoring packing, insuring, and shipping charges, 5 units of country A's money would be worth 1 unit of country B's money. **T F**

20. When nations were on the gold standard, foreign exchange rates fluctuated only within limits determined by the cost of moving gold from one nation to another. **T F**

21. If a nation maintains an exchange stabilization fund it would purchase its own money with gold or foreign monies when the value of its money falls in foreign exchange markets. **T F**

22. In the Bretton Woods system a nation could not devalue its currency by more than 10% without the permission of the International Fund. **T F**

23. In the Bretton Woods system a nation with persistent balance of payments surpluses had an undervalued currency and should have increased the pegged value of its currency. **T F**

24. Because the world's stock of gold did not grow very rapidly it became necessary for the United States to have payments deficits if international monetary reserves were to increase. **T F**

25. One of the basic shortcomings of the Bretton Woods system was its inability to bring about the changes in exchange rates needed to correct persistent payments deficits and surpluses. **T F**

26. Another basic shortcoming of the Bretton Woods system was its failure to maintain stable foreign exchange rates. **T F**

27. The United States shattered the Bretton Woods system in August 1971 by raising tariff rates on nearly all the goods it imported by an average of 40%. **T F**

28. Using the managed floating system of exchange rates, a nation with a persistent balance of payments surplus should allow the value of its currency in foreign exchange markets to decrease. **T F**

Circle the letter that corresponds to the best answer.

1. If an American could buy £25,000 for $100,000, the rate of exchange for the pound would be: (*a*) $40; (*b*) $25; (*c*) $4; (*d*) $.25.

2. American residents demand foreign currencies in order (*a*) to pay for goods and services imported from foreign countries; (*b*) to receive interest payments and dividends on their investments outside the United States; (*c*) to make real and financial investments in foreign nations; (*d*) to do all of the above.

3. A nation's balance of trade is equal to its (*a*) exports less its imports of merchandise (goods); (*b*) exports less its imports of goods and services; (*c*) exports less its imports of goods and services plus its net investment income and transfers; (*d*) exports less its imports of goods, services, and capital.

4. A nation's balance on the current account is equal to its (*a*) exports less its imports of merchandise (goods); (*b*) exports less its imports of goods and services; (*c*) exports less its imports of goods and services plus its net investment income and transfers; (*d*) exports less its imports of goods, services, and capital.

5. The net investment income of the United States in its international balance of payments is (*a*) the interest income it receives from foreign residents; (*b*) the dividends it receives from foreign residents; (*c*) the interest payments and dividends it receives from foreign residents; (*d*) the interest payments, dividends, and transfers it receives from foreign residents.

6. Capital flows into the United States include the purchase by foreign residents of (*a*) a factory building owned by Americans; (*b*) shares of stock owned by Americans; (*c*) bonds owned by Americans; (*d*) all of the above.

7. An American current account deficit may be financed by (*a*) borrowing abroad; (*b*) selling real assets to foreigners; (*c*) selling financial assets to foreigners; (*d*) doing any of the above.

8. The official reserves of the United States are (*a*) the stock of gold owned by the Federal government; (*b*) the foreign currencies owned by the Federal Reserve Banks; (*c*) the money supply of the United States; (*d*) all of the above.

9. A nation may be able to correct or eliminate a persistent (long-term) balance of payments deficit by (*a*) lowering the barriers on imported goods; (*b*) reducing the international value of its currency; (*c*) expanding its national income; (*d*) reducing its official reserves.

10. If exchange rates float freely the exchange rate for any currency is determined by (*a*) the demand for it; (*b*) the supply of it; (*c*) the demand for and the supply of it; (*d*) the official reserves that "back" it.

11. If a nation had a balance of payments surplus and exchange rates floated freely, (*a*) the foreign exchange rate for its currency would rise, its exports would increase, and its imports would decrease; (*b*) the foreign exchange rate for its currency would rise, its exports would decrease, and its imports would increase; (*c*) the foreign exchange rate for its currency would fall, its exports would increase, and its imports would decrease; (*d*) the foreign exchange rate for its currency would fall, its exports would decrease, and its imports would increase.

12. Assuming exchange rates are flexible, which of the following should increase the dollar price of the Swedish krona? (*a*) A rate of inflation greater in Sweden than in the United States; (*b*) real interest-rate increases greater in Sweden than in the United States; (*c*) national-income increases greater in Sweden than in the United States; (*d*) the increased preference of Swedes for American over Swedish automobiles.

13. Which of the following would be one of the results associated with the use of freely floating foreign exchange rates to correct a nation's balance of payments surplus? (*a*) The nation's terms of trade with other nations would be worsened; (*b*) importers in the nation who had made contracts for the future delivery of goods would find that they had to pay a higher price than expected for the goods; (*c*) if the nation were at full employment the decrease in exports and the increase in imports would be inflationary; (*d*) exporters in the nation would find their sales abroad had decreased.

14. When exchange rates are fixed and a nation at full employment has a payments surplus, the result in that nation will be: (*a*) a declining price level; (*b*) falling money income; (*c*) inflation; (*d*) rising real income.

15. The use of exchange controls to eliminate a nation's balance of payments deficit results in: (*a*) decreasing the nation's imports; (*b*) decreasing the nation's exports; (*c*) decreasing the nation's price level; (*d*) decreasing the nation's income.

16. A nation with a balance of payments surplus might attempt to eliminate this surplus by employing: (*a*) import quotas; (*b*) higher tariffs; (*c*) subsidies on items which the nation exports; (*d*) none of the above.

17. Which one of the following conditions did a nation *not* have to fulfill if it was to be one under the gold standard? (*a*) Use only gold as a medium of exchange; (*b*) maintain a fixed relationship between its gold stock and its money supply; (*c*) allow gold to be freely exported from and imported into the nation; (*d*) define its monetary unit in terms of a fixed quantity of gold.

18. If the nations of the world were on the gold standard and one nation has a balance of payments surplus: (*a*) foreign exchange rates in that nation would rise toward the gold import point; (*b*) gold would tend to be imported into that country; (*c*) the level of prices in that country would tend to fall; (*d*) employment and output in that country would tend to fall.

19. Under the gold standard a nation with a balance of payments deficit would experience all but one of the following. Which one? (*a*) Gold would flow out of the nation; (*b*) the nation's money supply would contract; (*c*) interest rates in the nation would fall; (*d*) real national output, employment, and prices in the nation would decline.

20. Which of the following was the principal disadvantage of the gold standard? (*a*) Unstable foreign exchange rates; (*b*) persistent payments imbalances; (*c*) the uncertainties and decreased trade that resulted from the depreciation of gold; (*d*) the domestic macroeconomic adjustments experienced by a nation with a payments deficit or surplus.

21. All but one of the following were elements in the adjustable-peg system of foreign exchange rates. Which one? (*a*) Each nation defined its monetary unit in terms of gold or dollars; (*b*) nations bought and sold their own currencies to stabilize exchange rates; (*c*) nations were allowed to devalue their currencies when faced with persistent payments deficits; (*d*) the deposit by all nations of their international reserves with the IMF.

22. Which one of the following was *not* characteristic of the International Monetary Fund in the Bretton Woods system? (*a*) Made short-term loans to member nations with balance of payments deficits; (*b*) tried to maintain relatively stable exchange rates; (*c*) required member nations to maintain exchange stabilization funds; (*d*) extended long-term loans to underdeveloped nations for the purpose of increasing their productive capacities.

23. The objective of the adjustable-peg system was exchange rates which were (*a*) adjustable in the short run and fixed in the long run; (*b*) adjustable in both the short and long run; (*c*) fixed in both the short and long run; (*d*) fixed in the short run; adjustable in the long run.

24. Which of the following is the best definition of international monetary reserves in the Bretton Woods system? (*a*) Gold; (*b*) dollars; (*c*) gold and dollars; (*d*) gold, dollars, and British pounds.

25. The dilemma created by the U.S. payments deficits was that (*a*) to maintain the status of the dollar as an acceptable international monetary reserve the deficit had to be reduced and to increase these reserves the deficits had to be continued; (*b*) to maintain the status of the dollar the deficit had to be continued and to increase reserves the deficit had to be eliminated; (*c*) to maintain the status of the dollar the deficit had to be increased and to expand reserves the deficit had to be reduced; (*d*) to maintain the status of the dollar the deficit had to be reduced and to expand reserves the deficit had to be reduced.

26. "Floating" the dollar means (*a*) the value of the dollar is determined by the demand for and the supply of the dollar; (*b*) the dollar price of gold has been increased; (*c*) the price of the dollar has been allowed to crawl upward at the rate of one-fourth of 1% a month; (*d*) the IMF decreased the value of the dollar by 10%.

27. A system of managed floating exchange rates (*a*) allows nations to stabilize exchange rates in the short term; (*b*) requires nations to stabilize exchange rates in the long term; (*c*) entails stable exchange rates in both the short and long term; (*d*) none of the above.

28. Floating exchange rates (*a*) tend to correct payments imbalances; (*b*) reduce the uncertainties and risks associated with international trade; (*c*) increase the world's need for international monetary reserves; (*d*) tend to expand the volume of world trade.

■ DISCUSSION QUESTIONS

1. What is foreign exchange and the foreign exchange rate? Who are the demanders and suppliers of a particular foreign exchange, say, the French franc? Why is a buyer (demander) in the foreign exchange markets always a seller (supplier) also.

2. What is meant when it is said that "a nation's exports pay for its imports"? Do nations pay for all their imports with exports?

3. What is an international balance of payments? What are the principal sections in a nation's international balance of payments and what are the principal "balances" to be found in it?

4. How can a nation finance a current account deficit and what can it do with a current account surplus? How does a nation finance a balance of payments deficit and what does it do with a balance of payments surplus?

5. Is it good or bad for a nation to have a balance of payments deficit or surplus?

6. What types of events cause the exchange rate for a foreign currency to appreciate or to depreciate? How will each of these events affect the exchange rate for a foreign money and for a nation's own money?

7. How can freely floating foreign exchange rates eliminate balance of payments deficits and surpluses? What are the problems associated with this method of correcting payments imbalances?

8. How may a nation employ its international monetary reserves to fix or "peg" foreign exchange rates? Be precise. How does a nation obtain or acquire these monetary reserves?

9. What kinds of trade controls may nations with payments deficits employ to eliminate their deficits?

10. How can foreign exchange controls be used to restore international equilibrium? Why do such exchange controls necessarily involve the rationing of foreign exchange? What effect do these controls have upon prices, output, and employment in nations that use them?

11. If foreign exchange rates are fixed, what kind of domestic macroeconomic adjustments are required to eliminate a payments deficit? To eliminate a payments surplus?

12. When was a nation on the gold standard? How did the international gold standard correct payments imbalances? What were the disadvantages of this method of eliminating payments deficits and surpluses?

13. Why does the operation of the international gold standard ensure relatively stable foreign exchange rates, that is, rates which fluctuate only within very narrow limits? What are limits and what are the advantages of stable exchange rates?

14. What is the "critical difference" between the adjustments necessary to correct payments deficits and surpluses under the gold standard and those necessary when exchange rates are flexible? How did this difference lead to the demise of the gold standard during the 1930s?

15. Explain (*a*) why the International Monetary Fund was established and what the objectives of the adjustable-peg (or Bretton Woods) system were; (*b*) what the adjustable-peg system was and the basic means it employed to stabilize exchange rates in the short run; and (*c*) when and how the system was to adjust exchange rates in the long run.

16. What did nations use as international monetary reserves under the Bretton Woods system? Why was the dollar used by nations as an international money and how could they acquire additional dollars?

17. Explain the dilemma created by the need for expanding international monetary reserves and for maintaining the status of the dollar.

18. Why and how did the United States shatter the Bretton Woods system in 1971? If the international value of the dollar is no longer determined by the amount of gold for which it can be exchanged, what does determine its value?

19. Explain what is meant by a managed floating system of foreign exchange rates. When are exchange rates managed and when are they allowed to float?

20. Explain the arguments of the proponents and the critics of the managed floating system.

43
International economic issues

Chapter 43 is the third of the three chapters that deal with international trade and finance. It builds on the two previous chapters, and examines three important international problems of the American economy in the 1980s.

The first of these problems has been labeled the foreign-trade crisis of the United States. The problem is that during the early 1980s the United States has imported goods and services with a dollar-and-cents value greater than the value of the goods and services it has exported; and it has incurred very large current-account deficits in these years. It has been able to do this only by increasing its debts to (by borrowing from) the rest of the world; and by 1985 it owed more to foreigners than they owed to people in the United States. The primary (though not the only) cause of this crisis is the high international value of (exchange rate for) the American dollar. The high exchange rate for the dollar means, as you learned in Chapter 42, that the exchange rates for foreign currencies are low. The low exchange rates for other currencies and the high exchange rate for the dollar has expanded American imports, contracted American exports, and produced the foreign-trade crisis in the United States.

The relatively high exchange rate for the dollar is the result of real interest rates which are higher in the United States than in the rest of the world. Real interest rates are higher in the American economy than in the rest of the world because the large budget deficits of the Federal government have forced it to borrow in the American money market; and these high interest rates in the United States have increased the attractiveness to foreigners of financial investment (buying bonds or lending) in the U.S., increased the foreign demand for dollars in the foreign exchange markets, and driven the price of the dollar upward in these markets.

The excess of its imports over its exports has had important effects on the American economy: while slowing the rate of inflation in the United States, it has increased the unemployment of labor and prevented the United States from producing as large a real output as it is capable of producing. The undesirable effects on the American economy have led to the search for economic policies to increase exports relative to imports and to expand employment and output in the United States. It is clear that the budget deficit of the Federal government must be reduced if real interest rates in the United States are to fall, the attractiveness of foreign financial investment in the U.S. and the foreign demand for the dollar are to diminish, the exchange rate for the dollar is to decline, American exports are to rise, American imports are to fall, and American employment and output are to expand.

The achievement of these results takes you to the second of the three international problems of the United States examined in this chapter. The domestic or internal goal of the American economy (full employment without inflation) may conflict or may be compatible with its international or external goal (equal exports and imports). The problem for the United States in the 1980s is that the expansion of its output and employment conflicts with the reduction of its international trade deficit: to expand output and employment requires an expansionary fiscal policy and an easy monetary policy. But the former will increase the budget deficit of the Federal government, increase Federal borrowing in the American money market, raise nominal and real interest rates there, increase the attractiveness of foreign financial investment in the United States and the demand for the dollar, raise the international value of the dollar, and increase American imports and decrease American exports. The expansion of the American economy, in short, also expands the trade deficit of the United States.

The second section of Chapter 43 contains an important general conclusion: the things a nation must do to promote full employment and stable prices are not always the things it has to do to achieve a zero balance of trade. The author explains when the policies that will eliminate unemployment or inflation are consistent and when they are inconsistent with the policies that will eliminate a trade surplus or deficit. You must be sure to understand when domestic policies conflict with and when they reinforce a nation's international economic policies. This general conclusion is extended and modified by three observations made at the end of the second section of the chapter.

The third and final section of the chapter examines the third of the three international economic issues: the effects of the migration of workers from a poor nation (such as Mexico) to a rich nation (such as the United States) upon wage rates, output and employment, and business incomes in the two nations. The method employed to find the effects of this immigration is to analyze the consequences of the changes in supply of labor in the labor markets of the two nations. The conclusions drawn by using supply and demand are definite and you should be sure you understand them. These conclusions, however, are only approximations of reality. The real world is more complicated than a supply-and-demand model. Be sure you understand the four complications which Professor McConnell introduces toward the end of this section and how these complications modify the conclusions obtained by using supply and demand.

The next chapter concludes the text and the study of international economics by examining what is probably the most important other economy in the world, the economy of the U.S.S.R.

■ CHECKLIST

When you have studied this chapter you should be able to:

☐ Define the American international-trade crisis.

☐ Enumerate and explain the causes of this crisis; and describe the effects of the crisis on output and employment and prices in the United States and on the indebtedness of Americans to foreigners.

☐ State what policy is needed to eliminate the foreign-trade crisis of the United States.

☐ Identify the assumed domestic (or internal) and international (or external) goals of the American economy; and state which goal is assumed to have the higher priority.

☐ State when a nation's policies to reduce unemployment (or to reduce inflationary pressures) are compatible with and when they are in conflict with the policies it might utilize to eliminate trade surpluses or deficits.

☐ List three things a nation might do to reduce the conflicts between the domestic and international goals of the economy.

☐ Recount briefly the history of immigration into the United States and the estimates of the number of legal and illegal immigrants entering the U.S. in recent years.

☐ Use a supply-and-demand model to explain the effects of the migration of workers from a poor to a rich nation on wage rates, output, and business incomes in the two nations.

☐ Explain how the four complicating factors modify the effects of migration on the two economies.

☐ Describe the three principal provisions of the Simpson-Mazzoli bill and the three major criticisms of these provisions.

■ CHAPTER OUTLINE

1. The United States faces an international-trade crisis in the 1980s: its exports have grown slowly but its imports have grown rapidly; and its merchandise and current-account deficits have expanded by increasing amounts since 1980.

a. These deficits have had three major causes.

(1) Large Federal-budget deficits, a tighter monetary policy, and lower rates of inflation in the United States than in the rest of the world caused high real interest rates in the United States; and the international value of the dollar rose after 1980 to increase American imports and to slow the increase in its exports.

(2) The more rapid recovery of the American economy from the 1980–1982 recession increased its imports by large amounts; and the less rapid recovery of the rest of the world increased American exports by only small amounts.

(3) American exports to the underdeveloped nations fell and its imports from them rose because they used restrictive monetary and fiscal policies and devalued their currencies to cope with their international debts to the developed nations.

b. The trade deficits of the United States have lowered real output and employment, restrained inflation, lessened the prices of imported goods in the United States, and increased the indebtedness of Americans to foreigners; have had the opposite effects on its industrialized trading partners; and have created additional problems for underdeveloped nations with dollar-denominated debts.

c. To deal with these problems the international value of the dollar must be reduced by lowering real interest rates in the United States; and this requires a decline in the Federal-budget deficits.

2. The international goals of a nation complicate and may conflict with its use of monetary and fiscal policy to achieve domestic goals.

a. It is assumed that foreign exchange rates are fixed; and that

(1) the goal of the economy domestically (or internally) is full employment without inflation, and this is its primary goal; and

(2) the goal of the economy internationally (or externally) is a current account balance of zero.

b. The policies designed to achieve full employment without inflation affect the current-account balance (because the imports of a nation are directly related to its national income); and policies designed to reach a zero current-account balance affect employment and the price level in the nation.

(1) The use of restrictive monetary and fiscal policies to retard inflation is *compatible* with a reduction in a current-account deficit.

(2) But the use of expansionary monetary and fiscal policies to reduce unemployment *conflicts* with a reduction in a current-account deficit.

(3) And the use of restrictive policies to retard inflation *conflicts* with a reduction in a current-account surplus.

(4) While expansionary policies to reduce unemployment are *compatible* with a reduction in a current-account surplus.

c. The conflicts between the domestic and international goals of a nation in (2) and (3) above may lead to the use of other policies.

(1) The imposition of tariffs and the devaluation of its currency may reduce a nation's current-account deficit and expand its output and employment; but these policies are apt to induce retaliation and to be ineffective.

(2) If foreign exchange rates are flexible the depreciation of a nation's currency may also reduce its current-account deficit by increasing its exports and decreasing its imports, and expanding its output and employment.

(3) And when exchange rates are flexible, an expansionary (easy) monetary policy will be more effective than fiscal policy in reducing unemployment *and* a current-account deficit because it lowers interest rates and the international value of its currency, expands its exports, and reduces its imports.

3. The immigration of workers into the United States is a controversial issue because this international movement of labor has economic effects on the American economy.

a. Largely unimpeded until World War I but then curtailed by law until liberalized after World War II, annual entry into the United States now consists of (approximately 500,000) legal and (500,000 to 1 million) illegal immigrants.

b. In a simple model, the movement of workers from one economy into another economy lowers the average level of wage rates, expands the national output, and increases business incomes in the latter economy; has the opposite effects in the former economy; and increases output in the world.

c. These conclusions must, however, be modified to take into account the costs of migration, remittances and backflows, the levels of employment in the two economies, and the effects on tax revenues and government spending in the economy receiving the immigrants.

d. In addition to its economic effects, immigration raises several noneconomic issues in the United States; and Congress in 1984 considered (but did not pass) the Simpson-Mazzoli bill which would have overhauled its immigration laws.

■ IMPORTANT TERMS

Foreign-trade crisis
Domestic (internal) economic goal
International (external) economic goal
Legal immigrant
Illegal immigrant
Remittances
Backflows
Simpson-Mazzoli bill

■ FILL-IN QUESTIONS

1. The crisis in the foreign trade of the United States is the (increases, decreases) increases in the size of the American merchandise and current-account (surpluses, deficits) ________________ during the 1980s which were brought about by the sharp increases in its (exports, imports) ______ and the small increases in its ______

2. The three causes of this trade crisis are

a. the (strong, weak) ______ dollar,

b. the (slow, rapid) ______ growth of the American economy, and

c. the (expanded, reduced) ______ exports of the United States to underdeveloped nations.

3. The rise in the international value of the dollar after 1980

a. made American goods (more, less) ______ expensive and foreign goods ______ expensive, (increased, decreased) ______ American exports, and ______ American imports;

b. was the result of relatively (high, low) ______ real interest rates in the United States caused by large Federal-budget (surpluses, deficits) ______, a (tight, easy) ______ monetary policy, and relatively (high, low) ______ rates of inflation in the United States.

4. American:

a. imports increased sharply in the 1980s because its national income (rose, fell) ______

b. exports to many underdeveloped nations declined because their foreign debt problem forced them to apply (expansionary, restrictive) ______ monetary and fiscal policies to their economies and to (revalue, devalue) ______ their currencies in order to expand their (exports, imports) ______ and reduce their ______

5. The effects of the American foreign-trade crisis have been to (expand, contract) ______ real national output and employment in the United States, to (speed, slow) ______ its rate of inflation, to (raise, lower) ______ the prices of goods it imported, and to (increase, decrease) ______ American indebtedness to foreigners. It has also changed the United States from a net (creditor, debtor) ______ to a net ______ nation.

6. To lower the international value of the dollar requires a (rise, fall) ______ in real interest rates in the United States which in turn necessitates a(n) (expansion, contraction) ______ in the budget deficit of the Federal government.

7. It is assumed that

a. the domestic (or internal) goal of the United States is ______

b. the international (or external) goal of the United States is ______

c. its primary goal is its (domestic, international) ______ goal.

8. The domestic policy which would:

a. reduce inflation (conflicts, is compatible) ______ with the policies needed to eliminate a trade *surplus;*

b. reduce unemployment ______ with the policies required to eliminate a trade *deficit.*

9. The conflicts between the domestic and international goals of the United States can be reduced by

a. changing its ______ on imported goods and the international value of its ______

b. allowing the exchange rates for its currency to ______

c. employing expansionary (monetary, fiscal) ______ policy to reduce unemployment and a current-account deficit.

10. During the 1970s and early 1980s the number of legal immigrants to the U.S. was about ______ a year and the number of illegal immigrants in recent years is estimated to be about ______ a year.

11. The movement of workers from a poor nation to a rich nation tends:

a. in the rich nation to (increase, decrease) ______

the national output, to decrease wage rates, and to increase business incomes;

b. in the poor nation to decrease national output, to increase wage rates, and to decrease business incomes; and

c. in the world to increase the real output of goods and services.

12. List the four complications that may modify the conclusions reached in question 11 above.

a. ______

b. ______

c. ______

d. ______

■ PROBLEMS AND PROJECTS

1. Assume:

a. the American economy has fully employed its labor force, is experiencing inflation, and has a current-account *deficit.*

(1) to reduce the inflationary pressures in the economy requires a(n) (expansionary, contractionary) ______ fiscal policy or a(n) (tight, easy) ______ monetary policy;

(2) if these measures are successful in curbing inflation without reducing employment, the economy's:

(*a*) exports will tend to (increase, decrease) ______

(*b*) imports will tend to ______

(*c*) the trade deficit of the American economy will tend to (increase, decrease) ______

(3) the measures undertaken to reduce inflation in the United States worked to (reduce, widen) ______ the trade deficits;

(4) but if the economy had begun with a trade *surplus* the fiscal and monetary measures taken to fight inflation would have (widened, narrowed) ______ the trade surplus.

b. the American economy has a relatively large portion (say 10%) of its labor force unemployed, is experiencing a recession, and has a current-account *deficit.*

(1) to reduce unemployment and increase the economy's real output requires a(n) ______ fiscal policy or a(n) ______ monetary policy;

(2) if these measures are successful in expanding employment and output in the economy:

(*a*) exports will tend to ______

(*b*) imports will tend to ______

(*c*) the trade deficit of the American economy will tend to ______

(3) the measures undertaken to reduce unemployment in the United States worked to (reduce, widen) ______ the trade deficit;

(4) but if the economy had begun with a payments *surplus* the fiscal and monetary policies employed to fight recession would have (widened, narrowed) ______ the surplus.

2. In the tables on the next page are the demands for labor and the levels of national output that can be produced at each level of employment in two countries.

a. If there were full employment in both countries and if:

(1) the labor force in Country A were 110, the wage rate in Country A would be $______

(2) the labor force in Country B were 40, the wage rate in Country B would be $______

b. With these labor forces and wage rates:

(1) total wages paid in A would be $______ and the incomes of businesses (capitalists) in A would be $______. (*Hint:* Subtract the total wages paid from the real output.)

(2) total wages paid in B would be $______ and business incomes in B would be $______

c. Assume the difference between the wage rates in the two countries induces 5 workers to migrate from B to A. So long as both countries maintain full employment,

Country A

Wage rate	Quantity of labor demanded	Real output
$20	95	$1900
18	100	1990
16	105	2070
14	110	2140
12	115	2200
10	120	2250
8	125	2290

Country B

Wage rate	Quantity of labor demanded	Real output
$20	10	$200
18	15	290
16	20	370
14	25	440
12	30	500
10	35	550
8	40	590

(1) the wage rate in A would (rise, fall) ____________ to $__________;

(2) and the wage rate in B would ________________ to $__________

d. The movement of workers from B to A would

(1) (increase, decrease) ________ the output of A by $__________;

(2) ________ the output of B by $________

(3) ________ their combined (and the world's) output by $________

e. This movement of workers from B to A also (increased, decreased) ____________________ business incomes in A by $____________ and ____________ business incomes in B by $_____

■ SELF-TEST

Circle the T if the statement is true, the F if it is false.

1. The foreign-trade crisis experienced by the American economy in the 1980s was characterized by sharp increases in American exports and slight increases in American imports. T F

2. The principal reason for the strong dollar in the early 1980s was the high real interest rates in the United States. T F

3. High real interest rates in the United States increased the attractiveness of financial investment in the United States to foreigners and the foreign demand for American dollars. T F

4. The rapid growth of the American economy lessened its foreign-trade crisis because its exports are directly related to its national income. T F

5. The strong international value of the dollar has imposed special hardships on American firms dependent on export markets and those that compete with imported goods. T F

6. The negative net exports of the United States have increased the indebtedness of Americans to foreigners. T F

7. In 1985 the status of the United States was changed from net-debtor to net-creditor nation. T F

8. During the years in which they were incurred the trade deficits the United States reduced its standard of living. T F

9. The external (or international) goal of the United States can be reasonably assumed to have a higher priority than its internal (or domestic) goal. T F

10. As the incomes of Americans rise they buy more goods and services produced in the United States and more goods and services produced abroad. T F

11. The policies used by a country to eliminate unemployment are compatible with the elimination of that country's current-account deficit. T F

12. The policies used by a country to reduce inflation conflict with the elimination of a current-account surplus. T F

13. Tariff reductions and the revaluation of its currency would (if there were no retaliation) enable a nation to reduce both its rate of inflation and a current-account surplus. T F

14. A fall in the exchange rate for a nation's currency tends to increase its exports and to decrease its imports. T F

15. A rise in the exchange rate for its currency will help to lessen a nation's unemployment and to reduce its current-account deficit. T F

16. An expansionary fiscal policy tends to increase interest rates in the economy. T F

17. An easy monetary policy is more effective in reducing unemployment and a current-account deficit than an expansionary fiscal policy. T F

18. The total number of legal and illegal immigrants entering the United States in recent years may be as large as one and one-half million annually. T F

19. The movement of workers from low- to high-average-income nations tends to increase the world's real output of goods and services. T F

20. Remittances to their families in Mexico from Mexican workers who have migrated to the United States expands the gain in the national output of the United States and expands the loss of national output in Mexico. T F

Circle the letter that corresponds to the best answer.

1. The foreign-trade crisis of the United States is the (*a*) increases in its merchandise and current-account surpluses; (*b*) decreases in its merchandise and current-account surpluses; (*c*) increases in its merchandise and current-account deficits; (*d*) decreases in its merchandise and current-account deficits.

2. Which of the following is *not* one of the causes of the growth of American trade deficits during the 1980s? (*a*) The strong dollar; (*b*) the rapid growth of the American economy; (*c*) the reduced imports of heavily indebted underdeveloped nations from the United States; (*d*) the high rate of inflation experienced by the American economy relative to rates in other nations.

3. High real interest rates in the United States during the 1980s were the result of all but one of the following. Which one? (*a*) The budget deficits of the Federal government; (*b*) the low demand of foreign investors for the dollar; (*c*) the tight money policy of the Federal Reserve Banks; (*d*) the relatively low rate of inflation in the United States.

4. The external debt problems of underdeveloped nations forced many of them to apply (*a*) restrictive monetary and fiscal policies and to devalue their currencies; (*b*) restrictive monetary and fiscal policies and to revalue their currencies; (*c*) expansionary monetary and fiscal policies and to devalue their currencies; (*d*) expansionary monetary and fiscal policies and to revalue their currencies.

5. The negative net exports of the United States in recent years have (*a*) decreased real national output and employment in the United States; (*b*) lessened its rate of inflation; (*c*) lowered the prices of imported goods; (*d*) done all of the above.

6. A rise in the international value of the dollar (*a*) increases the effective price of oil imported by underdeveloped nations from OPEC; (*b*) decreases the real value of the dollar debts of underdeveloped nations; (*c*) increases the international value of other currencies; (*d*) does all of the above.

7. The large trade deficits of the United States can be reduced by (*a*) an expansionary fiscal policy; (*b*) a contractionary (tight) monetary policy; (*c*) a reduction in the international value of the dollar; (*d*) higher real interest rates in the United States.

8. A reduction in the Federal-budget deficits will (*a*) increase the demand for funds and interest rates in the United States; (*b*) increase the demand for funds and decrease interest rates in the United States; (*c*) decrease the demand for funds and interest rates in the United States; (*d*) decrease the demand for funds and increase interest rates in the United States.

9. A fall in the international value of the dollar will (*a*) decrease the exports and imports of the United States; (*b*) decrease the exports and increase the imports of the United States; (*c*) increase the exports and imports of the United States; (*d*) increase the exports and decrease the imports of the United States.

10. The domestic (or internal) goal of the American economy is (*a*) full employment; (*b*) a relatively stable price level; (*c*) full employment with little or no inflation; (*d*) a zero current-account balance.

11. The international (or external) goal of the United States is (*a*) full employment with little or no inflation; (*b*) a current-account surplus; (*c*) a current-account deficit; (*d*) a zero current-account balance.

12. Which of the following policies are compatible? (*a*) Those designed to eliminate inflation and a current-account deficit; (*b*) those utilized to eliminate unemployment and a trade surplus; (*c*) both of the above; (*d*) neither of the above.

13. Which of the following policies conflict? (*a*) Those designed to reduce unemployment and a trade deficit; (*b*) those designed to reduce inflation and a trade surplus; (*c*) both of the above; (*d*) neither of the above.

14. Which of the following would (if there were no retaliation) enable a nation to reduce both unemployment and a current-account deficit? (*a*) A reduction in its tariffs and the devaluation of its currency; (*b*) a reduction in its tariffs and the revaluation of its currency; (*c*) an increase in its tariffs and the devaluation of its currency; (*d*) an increase in its tariffs and the revaluation of its currency.

15. An easy money policy will (*a*) expand output and employment and increase interest rates in the economy; (*b*) expand output and employment and decrease interest rates in the economy; (*c*) contract output and employment and increase interest rates in the economy; (*d*) contract output and employment and decrease interest rates in the economy.

16. Legal immigration into the United States was sharply curtailed (*a*) prior to World War I; (*b*) during the 1920s and 1930s; (*c*) after World War II; (*d*) by the Simpson-Mazzoli Act of 1984.

17. If there is full employment in both nations, the effect of the migration of workers from a poor to a rich nation is to increase (*a*) the average wage rate in the rich nation; (*b*) the output in the rich nation; (*c*) business incomes in the poor nation; (*d*) the total wages received by workers in the poor nation.

18. Which of the following would increase the gains realized in the world from the migration of workers? (*a*) The explicit and implicit costs of migration; (*b*) the remittances of workers to their native countries; (*c*) the migration of unemployed workers to nations in which they find employment; (*d*) the migration of employed workers to nations in which the taxes they pay are less than the welfare benefits they receive.

DISCUSSION QUESTIONS

1. What was the foreign-trade crisis of the United States during the 1980s? What were (*a*) its causes and (*b*) its effects on the American economy?

2. How do the large budget deficits of the Federal government result in a strong American dollar? Trace the cause-and-effect chain of economic events.

3. What policy is needed to ease the trade crisis of the United States and how would such a policy affect output and employment in the United States?

4. What domestic and international goals is the American economy assumed to have? Which of these goals is assumed to have the higher priority?

5. Explain when (and why) the policies employed by a nation to reduce unemployment of inflation conflict and when (and why) they are compatible with the elimination of trade deficits or surpluses?

6. What might a nation do to lessen the incompatibility of its domestic and international economic goals?

7. Construct a supply-and-demand model to explain the effects of the migration of labor from a poor to a rich nation on the average wage rate, output, and business income in the two nations. What is the effect of this migration on the real output of the world?

8. What four complications make it necessary to modify the conclusions you reached in question 7? Explain how each of these complications alters your conclusions.

9. How do the types of workers who immigrate and economic conditions in the economy to which they migrate change the benefits from immigration to the nation into which workers migrate?

10. What were the chief provisions of the Simpson-Mazzoli bill. What have been the charges levied against these provisions by the critics of the bill?

44
The economy of the Soviet Union

During the first few years following the Russian Revolution in 1917 many people in the United States were convinced that the economic system of the Soviet Union was unworkable and that it would sooner or later break down—proof that Marx, Lenin, and Stalin were unrealistic dreamers—and that the reconversion of their economy to a free enterprise, price-market system would follow. Slowly it dawned upon these people that the breakdown would not occur and, on the contrary, the Soviet economy was becoming more workable and more productive, and that Soviet Russia was becoming a very strong nation. In part this early belief that Soviet Russia would collapse was based on prejudice—they wanted it to collapse in order to prove to themselves that the system called capitalism was both the only feasible system of economic organization and an almost perfectly operated system—and in part it was based on ignorance of the institutions and methods employed by Russian communism.

The aim of Chapter 44 is to dispel some of the ignorance surrounding Soviet institutions and methods and by doing so eliminate the basis for much of the unwarranted prejudice against the Soviet *economic system.* (Chapter 44, of course, does not try to convince you that the United States should adopt the Soviet economic system, or to persuade you that the Russian way of life is morally, politically, or socially preferable.)

To accomplish its aim the chapter first examines the ideology and the two institutions of the Soviet economy which are remarkably different from anything found in American capitalism and which are the framework of the Russian economy. Within this framework the Fundamental Economic Problems are solved through central economic planning. Central economic planning has no counterpart in the United States, and it is to further central economic planning that the Soviet institutional framework is maintained. The better part of the chapter is devoted to explaining what central planning is and how it is employed in the U.S.S.R. to obtain answers to the Fundamental Economic Problems.

If you learn anything from this chapter you ought to learn that the Soviet *economy* is the source of its political and military strength and that the performance and growth of the Soviet and American economic systems (and the social and political institutions that accompany them) are watched throughout the world by people who will be inclined to adopt the economic and political and social system which promises them the best prospect of improving their own material well-being. In addition, you should be aware that it is not a question of "Will the Soviet system work?" but of how well it works.

There is great strength in the Soviet Union because the government is able to compel the economy to do pretty much as it wishes. The large and almost continuous increases in Soviet output are mostly the result of central economic planning and the direction of the economy toward the achievement of these plans by central authority. It is both the strength and weakness of the American economy that it lacks this central direction. But there seems to have been trouble in the Soviet Union in recent years. While it has grown at a dramatic rate and become a major industrial power over the last seventy years, its growth rate and the increases in the productivity of its labor force have slowed since the late 1960s. The reasons for these slowdowns you will find explained in the text. You will also find that Marshall Goldman predicts the slowdown of Soviet economic growth will shortly lead to a crisis there; and Professor McConnell explains why Goldman believes a crisis is on the horizon there.

■ CHECKLIST

When you have studied this chapter you should be able to:

☐ Outline the ideology underlying the command economy of the U.S.S.R.

☐ Identify the two outstanding institutions of the Soviet economy; and the ways in which the freedoms of consumers and workers are limited.

☐ Define central economic planning; and explain the difference between the Five-year Plan and the One-year Plans of the Soviet economy.

☐ List and explain the five techniques used in the Soviet planning system to achieve coordination.

☐ Explain how *Gosbank* helps *Gosplan* to achieve the objectives of the economic plan.

☐ Describe the incentive system employed in the U.S.S.R.

☐ Explain what determines the prices producers pay for inputs and receive for final products in the Soviet Union; and contrast the role of profits and losses and the significance of input prices in the U.S.S.R. and a market economy.

☐ Explain how the prices of consumer goods are determined in the Soviet economy and the function these prices perform.

☐ Compare the GNPs and the growth rates of the Soviet and American economies.

☐ Enumerate the five factors which have produced rapid growth in the past and four factors which have slowed recent growth in the U.S.S.R.

☐ Present four reasons why the rate at which the productivity of labor increases has fallen in the Soviet economy in recent years.

☐ List the two major accomplishments and the two major shortcomings of the Soviet system.

☐ Outline the crisis which Marshall Goldman argues will be reached in the Soviet Union within the next few years.

■ CHAPTER OUTLINE

1. The U.S.S.R. is a command economy which is better understood by examining its ideology and institutions.

a. Seen by its government as a dictatorship of the proletariat (or working class), the Soviet economy is based on an ideology of a classless society in which there is no private property and workers are not, therefore, exploited by capitalists who pay workers a subsistence wage that is less than the value of their production (in which there is no surplus value).

b. There are two major economic institutions in the Soviet Union.

(1) The state owns most of the property resources and little property is privately owned.

(2) Government uses central economic planning (rather than a price-market system) to allocate resources.

(3) In addition to these two institutions, consumers and workers have limited freedom of choice.

(a) Government, instead of consumer demand, determines the volume and composition of the production of consumer goods.

(b) Government control over education and wage rates determines the composition of the labor force and allocates it among alternative uses.

2. Central planning is used in the Soviet Union to answer the Five Fundamental Economic Questions.

a. Government in the U.S.S.R. sets forth the goals of the economy in its Five-year and its One-year Plans.

b. The basic problem encountered in planning for an entire economy is the difficulty of coordinating the many interdependent segments of the economy and the avoidance of the chain reaction that would result from a bottleneck in any one of these segments.

c. To coordinate its different sectors the Soviet economy establishes material balances, plans by negotiation, employs the priority principle, draws upon inventories to offset bottlenecks, and utilizes the "second economy."

d. To achieve the objectives of central planning the Soviet government relies upon such control agencies as *Gosplan,* other planning groups, and especially upon *Gosbank.*

e. To motivate economic units to fulfill the plan the U.S.S.R. employs monetary incentives, nonmonetary incentives, and admonitions to work.

f. Prices in the Soviet economy are established by the state and are used to promote the achievement of the plans.

(1) Producer prices are used to measure the efficiency of production.

(2) Consumer goods prices are employed to ration goods and services.

3. By engaging in central planning the government of the Soviet Union has sought to industrialize its economy and to achieve rapid economic growth.

a. It is today one of the world's leading industrial nations and its growth rate has been greater than that of the United States; but its GNP is only about 60% of that of the United States.

b. The sources of past growth in the Soviet Union were its large endowment of natural resources, its totalitarian government, its surplus farm labor, its adoption of the superior technologies developed in Western nations, and its virtual elimination of cyclical unemployment.

c. But at least four factors have slowed the Soviet growth rate in the past fifteen or so years.

(1) Their military expenditures divert resources from uses that would lead to greater growth.

(2) Their labor force has failed to expand as rapidly as it had during the 1970s and a shortage of labor has developed.

(3) Their inefficient agricultural sector has not expanded its output at a rate that would make greater overall growth possible.

(4) And the productivity of Soviet labor (which is only about 40% as productive as American workers) has grown at a low and declining rate because of the depletion of its natural resources, the lack of incentives for innovation and technological advance, poor worker discipline, and a planning system that may now be obsolete.

4. Any evaluation of the Soviet system requires an examination of its principal accomplishments and shortcomings.

a. Its major accomplishments have been the great improvements in education and its complete system of social insurance.

b. The shortcomings are the small increases in the consumers' standard of living and the general absence of personal freedom.

5. Marshall Goldman has suggested that because of a number of pressing problems which cannot be solved under a system of central planning the Soviet economy may be headed for a crisis in the near future; and that the Soviet government faces a dilemma: either reform the system and set off uncontrollable political and economic forces or renege on the "social contract" with its citizens that the system would reward them with an abundance in the future and allow morale, growth, and productivity to deteriorate.

■ IMPORTANT TERMS

Labor theory of value
Surplus value
State ownership
Central economic planning
Five-year Plan
Gosplan
One-year Plan
Material balances
Priority principle
"Second economy"
Gosbank
"Control by the ruble"
Turnover tax

■ FILL-IN QUESTIONS

1. The ideology of the Soviet economy is that:

a. the value of any commodity is determined by the amount of ____________ required to produce it;

b. in capitalistic economies where capital is (privately, publicly) ____________ owned capitalists exploit workers by paying them a wage that is equal to the ____________ wage and obtain ____________ value at their expense; and

c. in a communist economy capital and other property will be ____________ owned, society will be ____________ less, and it will be governed by the Communist Party as a dictatorship of the ____________

2. The two institutions of the U.S.S.R. which are in sharp contrast with private property and the price-market system in the American economy are the ownership by the ____________ of property resources and ____________ planning.

3. In the Soviet union,

a. the volume and the composition of the production of consumer goods is determined by (consumer demand, government) ____________;

b. the composition and allocation of the labor force is determined by government which controls the ________ system and ____________ rates.

4. The goals or objectives of the Soviet economy are set by the ____________ (which means they are set by the ____________ Party).

5. The two most important plans made in the Soviet economy are the ____________________-year and the ______________-year Plans.

6. The basic planning problem in the Soviet Union is the ______________ of the various sectors of the economy. The failure of any one of these sectors to produce its planned output results in a ______________ which has a ______________ reaction throughout the remainder of the economy.

7. To coordinate the various segments of the economy the Soviet government ______________ or matches the quantities of ______________ demanded and supplied; plans by ______________; and when bottlenecks appear it applies the ______________ principle and draws upon its ______________.
The achievement of the plans for the economy are also aided by the illegal activities in the "______________ ______________"

8. The agency primarily responsible for the construction of the economic plan in the Soviet Union is (*Gosplan, Gosbank*) ______________ and the agency primarily responsible for ensuring that the provisions of the plan are enforced is ______________

9. Production in the Soviet Union is motivated by ______________ incentives, by ______________ incentives, and by admonitions to ______________

10. In the U.S.S.R. prices are used as an accounting device for assessing the productive ______________ of plants and industries and as a means of ______________ products among consumers.

11. If a plant or industry in the United States were profitable its output and employment of resources would tend to (expand, contract) ______________
but in the Soviet Union this would not occur; these unplanned profits would, however, indicate that the Soviet plant or industry was (more, less) ______________ efficient than average.

12. The gross national product of the U.S.S.R. is about (what percentage) ______ of the GNP of the U.S. and grew during the 1950–1980 period at a rate of about ______% per year.

13. List five specific reasons for the past economic growth of the Soviet economy.

a. ______________

b. ______________

c. ______________

d. ______________

e. ______________

14. What four factors have retarded economic growth in the Soviet Union since the late 1960s?

a. ______________

b. ______________

c. ______________

d. ______________

15. The recent decline in the rate at which worker productivity in the Soviet Union has increased is the result of the depletion of ______________, the lack of incentives for ______________ and ______________ advances, poor worker ______________, and the possible obsolescence of the ______________ mechanism.

16. What have been the two most significant accomplishments of the U.S.S.R. since central planning began?

a. ______________

b. ______________
The two chief shortcomings of the Soviet economy over the past years have been ______________ and ______________

■ PROBLEMS AND PROJECTS

1. On the left of the table on the top of page 398 are several of the major institutions or characteristics of American capitalism. In the spaces to the right, name the institution or characteristic of the Soviet economy which compares with the American institution or characteristic.

American institution or characteristic	Russian institution or characteristic
Private ownership of economic resources	______
Consumer freedom to spend income as he or she sees fit	______
Consumer sovereignty	______
Worker freedom to select occupation and place of work	______
Profit motive	______
Entrepreneurial freedom to select product, output, price, etc.	______
System of prices and markets	______
Self-interest	______
Privately owned farms	______
Privately owned industrial firms and retail stores	______

2. Below is a market demand schedule for product X.

Price, rubles	Quantity demanded (million)
90	25
80	30
70	35
60	40
50	45
40	50
30	55

a. If Soviet planners decide to produce 50 million units of product X, the price of the product *plus* the turnover tax will be set at ______ rubles.

b. If the accounting cost of producing product X is 25 rubles, the turnover tax *rate* will be set at ______%.

■ SELF-TEST

Circle the T if the statement is true, the F if it is false.

1. The Soviet government sets the economic objectives of the economy, directs the resources of the economy toward the achievement of these objectives, and uses the price system as one of the means of achieving these objectives. **T F**

2. Consumers in the U.S.S.R. are free to spend their incomes on any of the consumer goods provided by the economy's central plan. **T F**

3. The government of the U.S.S.R. determines the composition and the allocation of the labor force by setting the wage rates paid for different types of workers and by controlling the educational system. **T F**

4. A One-year Plan is less general and more detailed and specific than a Five-year Plan. **T F**

5. *Gosplan* is the agency in the Soviet Union primarily responsible for preparing the economic plan. **T F**

6. The basic planning problem in the Soviet Union is the determination of the overall goals of the economy. **T F**

7. The equation of the planned requirements with the available supplies of different inputs and commodities in the One- and Five-year Plans of the Soviet Union is called "material balance." **T F**

8. In the U.S.S.R. individual plants and industries play no part in the formulation of the final economic plan. **T F**

9. Application of the priority principle means that when production bottlenecks develop in the economy, inventories are used to prevent a chain reaction. **T F**

10. The communist nations of Eastern Europe to whom

the U.S.S.R. exports and from whom it imports goods and services are the "second economy." **T F**

11. "Control by the ruble" is a device utilized by *Gosbank* to supervise the activities of the plants that produce goods in the Soviet economy. **T F**

12. Most workers in the Soviet Union are paid on a piece-rate basis. **T F**

13. The labor-force participation rates of both men and women are greater in the Soviet Union than in other industrialized nations. **T F**

14. The turnover tax does not affect the price of consumer goods, but it does affect the consumer income available for the purchase of consumer goods. **T F**

15. The GNP of the U.S.S.R. is about 60% as large as the GNP in the United States, and the rate of growth of the GNP in the Soviet Union has been greater than the rate of growth of GNP in the United States. **T F**

16. The productivity of labor is 40% greater in the Soviet economy than in the American economy. **T F**

Circle the letter that corresponds to the best answer.

1. Which of the following is *not* an element in the ideology of the Soviet Union? (*a*) A dictatorship of the working class; (*b*) the creation of surplus value by government; (*c*) the labor theory of value; (*d*) the public ownership of property.

2. Marxian (or communist) ideology is highly critical of capitalist societies because in them (*a*) property is privately owned by the capitalists; (*b*) capitalists pay workers a wage that is less than the value of their production; (*c*) capitalists obtain surplus value; (*d*) all of the above are true.

3. In the U.S.S.R.: (*a*) all property is owned by the state or by collective farms and cooperatives; (*b*) all property except urban housing and farms is owned either by the state or by cooperatives; (*c*) all property except retail and wholesale enterprises is owned either by the state or by collective farms and cooperatives; (*d*) all property except small tools, clothing, household furnishings, and some housing is owned by the state or by collective farms and cooperatives.

4. Which of the following helps to make central economic planning work in the Soviet Union? (*a*) The existence of the "second economy"; (*b*) application of the priority principle; (*c*) planning by negotiation; (*d*) all of the above.

5. Which of the following is the most important agency in enforcing and carrying out the central economic plan in the Soviet Union? (*a*) *Gosplan;* (*b*) *Gosbank;* (*c*) the Communist Party; (*d*) the secret police.

6. Labor unions in the Soviet Union do *not* (*a*) exist; (*b*) engage in strikes or slowdowns; (*c*) bargain collectively with their employers to determine wage rates; (*d*) encourage workers to be more productive.

7. Prices in the Soviet Union: (*a*) are used as a device for rationing consumer goods; (*b*) are determined by the demands for and the supplies of products and resources; (*c*) are used to allocate resources among different firms and industries; (*d*) perform a guiding function, but not a rationing function.

8. Profits and losses in the U.S.S.R. are used to determine whether: (*a*) the production of various consumer goods should be expanded or contracted; (*b*) various goods are being produced efficiently or inefficiently; (*c*) more or fewer resources should be devoted to the production of various goods; (*d*) a product should be exported or imported.

9. Suppose the Soviet government determined that the annual output of a certain quality of wristwatch would be 100,000 and that the accounting cost of producing a watch is 300 rubles. If the demand schedule for these watches were as given in the table below, what turnover rate would be placed on watches? (*a*) 33⅓%; (*b*) 66⅔%; (*c*) 100%; (*d*) 133⅓%.

Price, rubles	Quantity demanded
700	85,000
600	90,000
500	100,000
400	120,000
300	150,000
200	190,000
100	240,000

10. The annual rates of growth in real output in the Soviet Union and in the United States during the 1950–1980 period were, respectively (*a*) 4.7 and 3.4%; (*b*) 5.2 and 3.9%; (*c*) 5.7 and 4.4%; (*d*) 6.2 and 4.9%.

11. In comparing the composition of GNP in the U.S.S.R. and the United States it can be said that (*a*) over 25% of the GNP in the United States is devoted to capital goods while less than 20% is so devoted in the U.S.S.R.; (*b*) government in the U.S.S.R. absorbs over 20% and in the United States absorbs less than 10% of the GNP; (*c*) over 75% of the GNP in both nations is represented by consumer goods; (*d*) gross investment in the U.S.S.R. is about twice again as large a percentage of the GNP as it is in the United States.

12. Which of the following is *not* true? (*a*) The standard of living in the U.S.S.R. is below the standard of living of the U.S.; (*b*) the output of the Russian economy exceeds the output of the American economy; (*c*) the output of the Russian economy is growing at a more rapid rate than the output of the American economy; (*d*) the Soviet economy devotes a larger percentage of its output to capital accumulation than does the American economy.

13. Which of the following is *not* a significant factor in explaining the past economic growth in the Soviet Union? (*a*) Extensive investment by foreigners in the Soviet economy; (*b*) high levels of domestic investment in basic industries; (*c*) adoption of the advanced technological methods employed in Western nations; (*d*) the reallocation of labor from the agricultural to the industrial sector of the economy.

14. All but one of the following contributed to the slower rate of growth of the Soviet after the late 1960s. Which one? (*a*) The onerous burden of military expenditures; (*b*) agricultural drag; (*c*) an overall shortage of labor; (*d*) a decline in the productivity of labor.

15. The two major accomplishments of the Soviet economic system have been (*a*) improvements in education and the standard of living; (*b*) improvements in education and the social-insurance system; (*c*) improvements in the standard of living and the social-insurance system; (*d*) improvements in the standard of living and the extent of personal freedom.

16. Which of the following has been one of the two principal shortcomings of the Soviet economic system? (*a*) A slow rate of economic growth; (*b*) a slow rate of growth in the output of consumer goods; (*c*) a rising rate of unemployment; (*d*) a rising rate of illiteracy.

■ DISCUSSION QUESTIONS

1. What are the essential features of the Marxian ideology on which the command economy of the U.S.S.R. is based?

2. What are the two principal economic institutions of the U.S.S.R.? How do these institutions compare with the economic institutions of the United States?

3. In what ways are the freedoms of consumers and workers circumscribed in the Soviet Union?

4. What is the basic planning problem in the U.S.S.R.? What techniques are used to overcome this problem and make central planning workable?

5. How is an economic plan drawn up in the Soviet Union? How is such a plan made "realistic and workable"? Why is the process of obtaining the final plan referred to as a "down-and-up evolution"?

6. What is meant by the priority principle of resource allocation? What sectors of the Soviet economy have received high priorities in the past?

7. What means and agencies are used in the Soviet Union to facilitate the achievement of the objectives of the economic plan? What types of incentives and inducements are offered to encourage the achievement of these objectives?

8. Explain the role *Gosbank* plays in the enforcement of the central economic plan in the U.S.S.R.

9. What functions do prices perform in the U.S.S.R.? How does the Russian government use the turnover tax to set the prices of consumer goods?

10. Plants and firms in the U.S.S.R. can earn profits or suffer losses just as plants and firms can in the United States. What role do profits and losses play in the U.S.S.R. and what role do they play in the United States?

11. How is the turnover tax used in the Soviet Union to match the quantities demanded of various consumer goods with the quantities of these goods which *Gosplan* has decided to produce?

12. Compare the GNPs of the Soviet Union and the United States with respect to size, composition, and rate of growth.

13. Why was it possible for the U.S.S.R. to achieve economic growth in the past?

14. Why has the growth of the Soviet economy slowed since the late 1960s? Why in particular has the rate at which labor productivity rises slowed?

15. What have been the major accomplishments of central planning in the U.S.S.R.? What are its chief shortcomings?

16. Why does Marshall Goldman believe the Soviet Union is headed for a crisis? What kind of crisis does he predict and why do his critics contend that this crisis will not materialize?

Answers

CHAPTER 1 THE NATURE AND METHOD OF ECONOMICS

Fill-in questions

1. *a.* production, distribution, consumption; *b.* limited (scarce), maximum

2. citizens, vocational

3. descriptive

4. generalizations, abstraction

5. "other things equal" (*ceteris paribus*)

6. *a.* failure to distinguish between relevant and irrelevant facts; *b.* failure to recognize economic models for what they are—useful first approximations; *c.* tendency to impute ethical or moral qualities to economic models

7. control, prepare

8. *a.* economic growth; *b.* full employment; *c.* price stability; *d.* economic freedom; *e.* equitable distribution of income; *f.* economic security; *g.* balance of trade

9. *a.* a clear statement of the objectives and goals of the policy; *b.* a statement and analysis of all possible alternative solutions to the problem; *c.* an evaluation of the results of the policy selected after it has been put into operation

10. total, general, individual industry, particular product

Problems and projects

1. An increase in the demand for an economic good will cause the price of that good to rise.

2. *a.* The validity of the statement depends upon the phase of the business cycle; *b.* the fallacy of composition; *c.* loaded terminology; *d.* the *post hoc, ergo propter hoc* fallacy.

3. *a.* direct, up-; *b.* inverse, down-; *c.* (1) are, is not, (2) coincidental, incomes (standard of living, or some other such answer).

Self-test

1. T; **2.** F; **3.** F; **4.** T; **5.** T; **6.** F; **7.** T; **8.** F; **9.** T; **10.** F; **11.** F; **12.** F

1. *b*; **2.** *b*; **3.** *c*; **4.** *a*; **5.** *d*; **6.** *a*; **7.** *b*; **8.** *a*; **9.** *d*; **10.** *d*; **11.** *b*; **12.** *a*

CHAPTER 2 AN INTRODUCTION TO THE ECONOMIZING PROBLEM

Fill-in questions

1. *a.* society's material wants are unlimited; *b.* economic resources, which are the ultimate means of satisfying these wants, are scarce in relation to these wants

2. *a.* property resources; (1) land or raw materials, (2) capital; *b.* human resources; (1) labor, (2) entrepreneurial ability

3. directly, indirectly

4. rental income, interest income, wages, profits

5. the social science concerned with the problem of using or administering scarce resources to attain maximum fulfillment of unlimited wants

6. employment, production

7. *a.* the economy is operating at full employment and full production; *b.* the available supplies of the factors of production are fixed; *c.* technology does not change during the course of the analysis; *d.* the economy produces only two products

8. *a.* fewer, more; *b.* unemployed, underemployed; *c.* more, more; *d.* increase resource supplies, improve its technology

9. values, nonscientific

10. opportunity cost

11. economic resources are not completely adaptable among alternate uses

12. less

13. *a.* at what level to utilize resources in the productive process; *b.* what collection of goods and services best satisfies its wants; *c.* how to produce this total output; *d.* how to divide this output among the various economic units of the economy; *e.* how to make the responses required to remain efficient over time

14. *a.* consumer tastes; *b.* the supplies of resources; *c.* technology

15. *a.* privately, market; *b.* publicly, planning

Problems and projects

1. *a.* land; *b.* C; *c.* land; *d.* C; *e.* EA; *f.* land; *g.* C; *h.* C; *i.* labor; *j.* EA

2. *b.* 1, 2, 3, 4, 5, 6, 7 wheat

4. *a.* DEP; *b.* CAP; *c.* CAP; *d.* CAP; *e.* CAP; *f.* CAP; *g.* DEP; *h.* DEP; *i.* DEP; *j.* DEP; *k.* CAP; *l.* DEP

Self-test

1. T; **2.** F; **3.** F; **4.** T; **5.** T; **6.** T; **7.** T; **8.** F; **9.** T; **10.** T; **11.** F; **12.** F

1. *d*; **2.** *d*; **3.** *b*; **4.** *c*; **5.** *d*; **6.** *a*; **7.** *b*; **8.** *b*; **9.** *b*; **10.** *d*; **11.** *a*; **12.** *c*

CHAPTER 3 PURE CAPITALISM AND THE CIRCULAR FLOW

Fill-in questions

1. private property

2. enterprise, choice

3. do what is best for itself, competition

4. *a.* large numbers of independently acting buyers and sellers operating in the markets; *b.* freedom of buyers and sellers to enter or leave these markets

5. control (rig, affect)

6. markets, prices

7. a limited

8. the extensive use of capital, specialization, the use of money

9. efficient

10. interdependent, exchange (trade)

11. inefficient

12. medium of exchange

13. coincidence of wants

14. generally acceptable by sellers in exchange

15. *a.* product, resource; *b.* real, money (either order); *c.* cost, income

Problems and projects

1. *a.* goods and services; *b.* expenditures for goods and services; *c.* money income payments (wages, rent, interest, and profit); *d.* services of resources (land, labor, capital, and entrepreneurial ability)

Self-test

1. F; **2.** T; **3.** T; **4.** T; **5.** T; **6.** F; **7.** T; **8.** T; **9.** T; **10.** F; **11.** T; **12.** F

1. *b*; **2.** *a*; **3.** *c*; **4.** *b*; **5.** *a*; **6.** *d*; **7.** *c*; **8.** *d*; **9.** *d*; **10.** *a*

CHAPTER 4 THE MECHANICS OF INDIVIDUAL PRICES: DEMAND AND SUPPLY

Fill-in questions

1. buyers (demanders), sellers (suppliers) (either order); *a.* business firms, households; *b.* demand decisions of households, supply decisions of business firms

2. indirect, direct

3. diminishing marginal utility

4. *a.* income; *b.* substitution

5. vertical, horizontal

6. *a.* the tastes or preferences of consumers; *b.* the number of consumers in the market; *c.* the money income of consumers; *d.* the prices of related goods; *e.* consumer expectations with respect to future prices and incomes

7. smaller, less

8. demand for, a change in the quantity demanded of the product

9. *a.* the technique of production; *b.* resource prices; *c.* taxes and subsidies; *d.* prices of other goods; *e.* price expectations; *f.* the number of sellers in the market

10. quantity demanded and quantity supplied are equal

11. below, shortage, rise

12. *a.* +, +; *b.* −, +; *c.* −, −; *d.* +, −; *e.* ?, +; *f.* +, ?; *g.* ?, −; *h.* −, ?

13. rationing

14. other things being equal

15. surplus, shortage

Problems and projects

1. *b.* 6.60; *c.* 25; *e.* surplus, 20

2. Total: 5, 9, 17, 27, 39

3. Each quantity in column 3 is greater than in column 2, and each quantity in column 4 is less than in column 2.

4. *a.* 30, 4; *b.* (1) 20, 7; (2) inferior; (3) normal (superior)

5. *a.* complementary; *b.* substitute

6. *a.* 45,000; 33,000; 22,500; 13,500; 6,000; 0 *b.* shortage, 28,500

7. *a.* decrease demand, decrease price; *b.* decrease supply, increase price; *c.* decrease supply, increase price; *d.* increase demand, increase price; *e.* decrease supply, increase price; *f.* increase demand, increase price; *g.* increase supply, decrease price; *h.* decrease demand, decrease price; *i.* increase demand, increase price; *j.* decrease supply, increase price

Self-test

1. T; **2.** F; **3.** F; **4.** F; **5.** F; **6.** T; **7.** F; **8.** F; **9.** F; **10.** F; **11.** T

1. *d*; **2.** *a*; **3.** *b*; **4.** *b*; **5.** *a*; **6.** *c*; **7.** *d*; **8.** *a*; **9.** *c*; **10.** *d*; **11.** *b*

CHAPTER 5 THE PRICE SYSTEM AND THE FIVE FUNDAMENTAL QUESTIONS

Fill-in questions

1. communicating, synchronizing (coordinating)

2. is, must, entrepreneurs, is not, need not

3. receipts (revenues), costs

4. *a.* normal; *b.* pure (economic)

5. enter, fall, more, larger, decrease, zero

6. *a.* dollars; *b.* sovereign; *c.* restrict

7. cost

8. *a.* income; *b.* prices

9. *a.* preferences (tastes), technology, resources; *b.* guiding

10. *a.* profit; *b.* losses (bankruptcy)

11. profits, borrowed funds

12. private, public (social), invisible hand

13. it efficiently allocates resources, it emphasizes personal freedom

14. *a.* competition; *b.* (1) unequal, (2) costs, benefits, social, (3) full employment, prices

15. big, government

Problems and projects

1. $6, −$5, $10; *a.* C; *b.* produce A and have an economic profit of $14; *c.* it would increase

2. *a.* method 2; *b.* 15; *c.* (1) 13, 8; 3, 4; 2, 4; (2) 15, 4

Self-test

1. F; **2.** T; **3.** T; **4.** T; **5.** T; **6.** T; **7.** T; **8.** T; **9.** T; **10.** T; **11.** T; **12.** T

1. *c;* **2.** *b;* **3.** *c;* **4.** *d;* **5.** *d;* **6.** *c;* **7.** *a;* **8.** *a;* **9.** *c;* **10.** *b;* **11.** *a;* **12.** *d*

CHAPTER 6 MIXED CAPITALISM AND THE ECONOMIC FUNCTIONS OF GOVERNMENT

Fill-in questions

1. market, centrally planned (either order)

2. *a.* provide legal foundation and social environment; *b.* maintain competition; *c.* redistribute income and wealth; *d.* reallocate resources; *e.* stabilize the economy

3. *a.* regulate, natural, ownership; *b.* antitrust (antimonopoly)

4. unequal; *a.* public assistance (welfare); *b.* market; *c.* income

5. market; *a.* produces the "wrong" amounts of certain goods and services; *b.* fails to allocate any resources to the production of certain goods and services whose production is economically justified

6. spillover

7. people other than the buyers and sellers (third parties)

8. *a.* over; *b.* under

9. *a.* (1) enact legislation, (2) pass special taxes; *b.* (1) subsidize production, (2) finance or take over the production of the product

10. exclusion, indivisible, benefits

11. taxing, spends the revenue to buy

12. *a.* increases, increasing, decreasing; *b.* decreases, decreasing, increasing

13. stabilizing the economy

14. benefits, costs

15. estimate (measure)

16. public, failure

17. *a.* special; *b.* clear, hidden; *c.* select; *d.* incentives, test (measure)

18. choice

19. *a.* private sector; *b.* imperfect; *c.* assigned

20. limited decisions

Problems and projects

1. *a.* reallocates resources; *b.* redistributes income; *c.* provides a legal foundation and social environment *and* stabilizes the economy; *d.* reallocates resources; *e.* maintains competition; *f.* provides a legal foundation and social environment *and* maintains competition; *g.* redistributes income; *h.* reallocates resources; *i.* provides a legal foundation and social environment; *j.* redistributes income

2. *a.* (1) businesses, resources, households, (2) households, products, businesses, (3) government, products, businesses, (4) businesses, (5) government, resources, households, (6) households; *b.* (1) 3, 5 (either order), 4, 6 (either order), (2) 3, 4, 6 (either order), (3) increase, decrease, 6

3. *a.* under; *b.* over; *c.* Q_2, optimum

4. *a.* (1) supply of, taxing, (2) decreases, increases; *b.* (2) subsidize, lower, (4) greater than, below

5. *a.* marginal cost: $500, $180, $80, $100; marginal benefit: $650, $100, $50, $25; *b.* yes; *c.* (1) 2, (2) $500, (3) $650, (4) $150

Self-test

1. F; **2.** F; **3.** F; **4.** F; **5.** T; **6.** T; **7.** F; **8.** T; **9.** T; **10.** T; **11.** T; **12.** F; **13.** F; **14.** F; **15.** F; **16.** T; **17.** F; **18.** F; **19.** T; **20.** F

1. *a;* **2.** *a;* **3.** *b;* **4.** *d;* **5.** *c;* **6.** *b;* **7.** *a;* **8.** *b;* **9.** *b;* **10.** *d;* **11.** *c;* **12.** *c;* **13.** *b;* **14.** *a;* **15.** *d*

CHAPTER 7 THE FACTS OF AMERICAN CAPITALISM: THE PRIVATE SECTOR

Fill-in questions

1. sixty-three, furnish resources, buy the bulk of the total output of the economy

2. wages and salaries, 74

3. 5, 43

4. composition of national output, levels

5. contribution of resources

6. personal consumption, personal saving, personal taxes

7. sixteen, income, Federal

8. security, speculation

9. services, nondurable goods, durable goods

10. sixteen and one-half, sole proprietorship, corporation

11. unlimited, limited

12. *a.* CORP; *b.* PRO and PART; *c.* PRO; *d.* CORP; *e.* CORP; *f.* CORP; *g.* PART; *h.* PART; *i.* CORP

13. *a.* agriculture, forestry, and fishing; services; *b.* manufacturing, wholesale and retail

14. eight

15. few, large

Problems and projects

1. 73.3, 2.9

2. A. 60; B. 12; C. 17; D. 9; E. 51; F. 81

4. *a.* Firms *a, c, d,* and *f* are in wholesale and retail trade; firms *b, g, h, i,* and *j* are in manufacturing; firms *h* and *i* are in mining; firm *e* is in transportation, communications, and public utilities; *b.* the Aluminum Company of America is engaged in the production of primary aluminum; the General Electric Company produces locomotives (and parts), electric lamps (bulbs), and household laundry equipment; William Wrigley produces chewing gum and Revere produces primary copper

Self-test

1. F; **2.** T; **3.** T; **4.** T; **5.** T; **6.** T; **7.** T; **8.** F; **9.** T; **10.** F; **11.** F; **12.** T; **13.** F; **14.** T; **15.** F

1. *d;* **2.** *a;* **3.** *b;* **4.** *d;* **5.** *b;* **6.** *a;* **7.** *a;* **8.** *c;* **9.** *b;* **10.** *d;* **11.** *a;* **12.** *a;* **13.** *b;* **14.** *d;* **15.** *b*

CHAPTER 8 THE FACTS OF AMERICAN CAPITALISM: THE PUBLIC SECTOR

Fill-in questions

1. expenditures, taxes

2. voluntary, compulsory

3. *a.* increase, 20; *b.* increased; *c.* 33

4. expenditures for which government currently receives no good or service in return, nonexhaustive

5. private, social, composition

6. personal income, payroll, income security, national defense, public debt

7. revenue, redistribute, stabilize

8. complex, equity, incentives

9. tax-exempt, capital gains

10. underground, 100

11. sales and excise, personal income, education, public welfare

12. property, education

13. Federal, sharing

14. benefits-received, ability-to-pay

15. is constant, increases, decreases

16. *a.* P; *b.* R; *c.* R; *d.* U; *e.* P

17. *a.* the persons upon whom it is levied; *b.* those who buy the taxed product; *c.* either the firm or its customers; *d.* owners when they occupy their own residences, tenants who rent residences from the owners, consumers who buy the products produced on business property

18. progressive; *a.* small; *b.* incidence; *c.* less; *d.* transfer

19. *a.* (1) Proposition 13, (2) Economic Recovery Tax; *b.* productivity, (1) decreased, increased, (2) corporate, value-added; *c.* personal, flat, (1) deductions, exemptions, loopholes, (2) same

20. decrease, three

Problems and projects

1. *a.* tax: $770, 1,060, 1,400, 1,800; average tax rate: 22%, 23.6%, 25.5%, 27.7%; *b.* (1) increases, (2) decreases

2. Tax A: 3, 3, 3, 3, proportional; Tax B: 3, 3, 2.5, 2, combination; Tax C: 8, 7, 6, 5, regressive

3. *a.* $264, 296, 328, 360; *b.* 3.8, 3.7, 3.64, 3.6; *c.* regressive

Self-test

1. T; **2.** F; **3.** F; **4.** T; **5.** F; **6.** T; **7.** T; **8.** F; **9.** F; **10.** F; **11.** F; **12.** T; **13.** F; **14.** T; **15.** F; **16.** T; **17.** T; **18.** T; **19.** F; **20.** T

1. *d;* **2.** *b;* **3.** *a;* **4.** *a;* **5.** *d;* **6.** *d;* **7.** *d;* **8.** *d;* **9.** *b;* **10.** *d;* **11.** *b;* **12.** *c;* **13.** *d;* **14.** *a;* **15.** *a;* **16.** *b;* **17.** *b;* **18.** *b;* **19.** *b;* **20.** *a*

CHAPTER 9 NATIONAL INCOME ACCOUNTING

Fill-in questions

1. production, policies

2. market prices

3. double counting

4. value added

5. market, final, gross national

6. durable, nondurable (either order), services

7. all final purchases of machinery, tools, and equipment by business firms; all construction; changes in inventories; the capital consumption allowance

8. negative, declining

9. exports, imports

10. C, I_g, G, X_n

11. nonincome

12. supplements, insurance, private

13. corporate income taxes, dividends, undistributed corporate profits

14. capital goods, capital consumption allowance

15. indirect business taxes

16. *a.* transfer payments, social security contributions, corporate income taxes, undistributed corporate profits; *b.* personal consumption expenditures, personal taxes, personal saving

17. *a.* personal taxes; *b.* personal consumption expenditures plus personal saving

18. the price level changes

19. *a.* nonmarket, leisure; *b.* quality, output, environment, underground; *c.* per capita

20. falls

Problems and projects

1. *a.* (1) 1722, (2) 29, (3) 130; *b.* see table below; *c.* (1) 2546, (2) 2291, (3) 2320, (4) 1948

Receipts: expenditures approach		Allocations: income approach	
Personal consumption expenditures	$1810	Capital consumption allowance	$ 307
Gross private domestic investment	437	Indirect business taxes	255
Government purchases of goods and services	577	Compensation of employees	1722
Net exports	29	Rents	33
		Interest	201
		Proprietors' income	132
		Corporate income taxes	88
		Dividends	60
		Undistributed corporate profit	55
Gross national product	2853	Gross national product	2853

2. *a.* (1) 200,000, (2) 200,000; *b.* (1) 250,000, (2) 50,000; *c.* (1) 10,000, (2) 10,000; *d.* (1) 315,000, (2) 55,000; *e.* (1) 409,500, (2) 94,500; *f.* 409,500, 409,500

3. *a.* personal income and disposable income, a public transfer payment; *b.* none; a second-hand sale; *c.* all, represents investment (additions to inventories); *d.* all, illegal production and incomes are included when known; *e.* none, a purely financial transaction; *f.* all; *g.* none, a nonmarket transaction; *h.* all; *i.* none, a private transfer payment; *j.* all; *k.* none, a nonmarket transaction; *l.* all; *m.* all, represents additions to the inventory of the retailer; *n.* personal income and disposable income, a public transfer payment; *o.* all; estimate of rental value of owner-occupied homes is included in rents as if it were income and in personal consumption expenditures as if it were payment for a service

4. *a.* 1939; *b.* (1) deflation, (2) inflation; *c.* 86, 62, 91; *d.* (1) deflated, (2) inflated, (3) neither

Self-test

1. F; **2.** T; **3.** T; **4.** T; **5.** F; **6.** T; **7.** F; **8.** T; **9.** F; **10.** T; **11.** T; **12.** F; **13.** T; **14.** T; **15.** F; **16.** T; **17.** F; **18.** F

1. *b;* **2.** *d;* **3.** *a;* **4.** *b;* **5.** *a;* **6.** *c;* **7.** *c;* **8.** *b;* **9.** *d;* **10.** *a;* **11.** *d;* **12.** *a;* **13.** *a;* **14.** *d;* **15.** *d;* **16.** *a;* **17.** *b;* **18.** *d*

CHAPTER 10 MACROECONOMIC INSTABILITY: UNEMPLOYMENT AND INFLATION

Fill-in questions

1. unsteady, inflation, output, employment

2. ups (increases), downs (decreases), recession, trough, recovery

3. spending, demand

4. seasonal, secular

5. durable, capital, nondurable, low-

6. *a.* frictional unemployment; *b.* structural unemployment; *c.* cyclical unemployment (any order)

7. *a.* natural; *b.* frictional, structural (either order); *c.* cyclical, actual, potential (either order); *d.* 6

8. equal to, constant

9. the number of unemployed persons, labor force

10. the potential, the actual, increase, 2.5

11. black, teenage, blue-collar, less

12. rise (increase), prices, 1987, 1986, 1986

13. *a.* an increase; *b.* market, labor unions, business firms (corporations)

14. *a.* fixed; *b.* unexpected; *c.* creditors, debtors; *d.* households, the public sector

15. *a.* increase; *b.* decrease; *c.* breakdown (collapse)

Problems and projects

1. 1970: 4,093, 4.8; 1975: 7,929, 8.3; *a.* the labor force increased more than employment increased; *b.* because unemployment and employment in relative terms are percentages of the labor force and *always* add to 100%, and if one increases the other must decrease; *c.* no economist would argue that the full-employment unemployment rate is as high as 8.3% and 1975 was not a year of full employment; *d.* the number of people looking for work expands

2. *a.* B, B, C, A; *b.* B, B, C, B; *c.* A, D, A, D

3. *a.* D; *b.* I; *c.* B; *d.* D; *e.* D; *f.* I; *g.* B

4. *a.* 0; *b.* 95, 412.5; *c.* 97.5, (1) 2.5, (2) 7; *d.* 90, (1) 10, (2) 10

5. *a.* 12, 10, 5; *b.* 5.83, 7, 14

6. *a.* equal, the national output demanded and supplied at the equilibrium price level; *b.* (1) increase, (2) demand-pull; *c.* (1) rise, fall, (2) cost-push inflation

Self-test

1. T; **2.** F; **3.** F; **4.** T; **5.** F; **6.** T; **7.** F; **8.** T; **9.** T; **10.** F; **11.** T; **12.** F; **13.** T; **14.** T; **15.** T; **16.** F; **17.** F; **18.** F; **19.** T; **20.** F; **21.** T; **22.** F; **23.** T; **24.** T; **25.** F

1. *a;* **2.** *d;* **3.** *b;* **4.** *c;* **5.** *a;* **6.** *b;* **7.** *a;* **8.** *c;* **9.** *c;* **10.** *d;* **11.** *d;* **12.** *c;* **13.** *d;* **14.** *b;* **15.** *a;* **16.** *c;* **17.** *b;* **18.** *d;* **19.** *d;* **20.** *d;* **21.** *d;* **22.** *a;* **23.** *b;* **24.** *d;* **25.** *d*

CHAPTER 11 MACROECONOMICS: AN OVERVIEW

Fill-in questions

1. output, level

2. purchased (demanded), levels; *a.* downward; *b.* real-balances, interest-rate, foreign-purchases (any order)

3. produced (supplied), levels; *a.* horizontal; *b.* upsloping; *c.* vertical

4. intersection; *a.* purchased (demanded), produced (supplied) (either order); *b.* accept, pay

5. *a.* increasing, reduce; *b.* decreasing, expand

6. *a.* increase, have no effect on; *b.* increase, increase; *c.* have no effect on, increase

7. smaller, ratchet

8. *a.* (1) expansionary, increasing, decreasing, (2) easy, increasing; *b.* (1) contractionary, decreasing, increasing, (2) tight, decreasing

9. increase, a decrease in the costs of producing goods and services; *a.* raise, prevent, increase; *b.* lower, raise

10. *a.* increase; *b.* decrease

11. increase, real output, inflation

12. increase, rise, decrease, fall in real output

Problems and projects

1. *a.* (1) 0, 1000, (2) 2000, 6.00, (3) 1000, 2000; *c.* (1) 1700, 4.00, (2) 2000, 6.00, (3) 900, 2.00

2. *a.* increases, (1) real national output, price level, (2) raise, expand, (3) increase the price level but will not affect national output; *b.* decreases, (1) Decrease the price level in the classical and intermediate ranges and decrease national output in the intermediate and Keynesian ranges, (2) Decrease only output in the intermediate and Keynesian ranges

3. *a.* increase, (1) lower, expand, (2) increase, will not; *b.* decrease, increase, decrease

Self-test

1. T; **2.** T; **3.** F; **4.** F; **5.** F; **6.** T; **7.** T; **8.** F; **9.** T; **10.** T; **11.** T; **12.** T; **13.** F; **14.** F; **15.** F; **16.** T

1. *d;* **2.** *a;* **3.** *b;* **4.** *d;* **5.** *a;* **6.** *b;* **7.** *a;* **8.** *b;* **9.** *b;* **10.** *a;* **11.** *b;* **12.** *b;* **13.** *a;* **14.** *b;* **15.** *c;* **16.** *b*

CHAPTER 12 CLASSICAL AND KEYNESIAN THEORIES OF EMPLOYMENT

Fill-in questions

1. fully, less than fully, laissez faire, activist

2. closed, personal, taxes, transfer, spend; *a.* national income, personal income, disposable income; *b.* consumption, investment

3. Say's, flexibility

4. demand for these goods and services

5. the rate of interest

6. fall, rise, saving, investment

7. fall, unemployment, downward, increase, all who are willing to work at the going wage rate are employed and total output equals total spending

8. *a.* groups, reasons (motives); *b.* accumulated money balances, commercial banks; *c.* balances, loans (debts)

9. do not, smaller, fall, decrease, employment (output)

10. fallacy of composition

11. vertical, horizontal, Keynesian, classical

12. rise, expand

13. *a.* directly, expenditures; *b.* disposable income; *c.* directly

14. rise, fall

15. *a.* real, financial (either order); *b.* the price level; *c.* expectations; *d.* consumer indebtedness; *e.* taxation of consumer income

16. the amount consumers plan to consume (save) will be different at every level of income, the level of income has changed and that consumers will change their planned consumption (saving) as a result

17. capital goods; *a.* expected, profits; *b.* interest

18. greater

19. inverse; *a.* decrease; *b.* increase

20. *a.* the cost of acquiring, maintaining, and operating the capital goods; *b.* business taxes; *c.* technological change; *d.* the stock of capital goods on hand; *e.* expectations

21. stable, unstable

22. durability, irregularity, variability

Problems and projects

1. *a.* *S:* −40, −20, 0, 20, 40, 60, 80, 100; APC: 1.000, 0.970, 0.955; APS: 0.000, 0.030, 0.045; *b.* 1700; *c.* 80, 100, 80; *d.* 20, 100, 20

2. *a.* −; *b.* −; *c.* +; *d.* +; *e.* +; *f.* none; *g.* −; *h.* −

3. *a.* 0, 10; *b.* 20, 30; *c.* 30, 60; *d.* 100, 150, 210, 280; *f.* inverse, (1) decrease, (2) increase; *g.* (1) lower, (2) raise; *h.* investment-demand

4. *a.* +; *b.* −; *c.* +; *d.* +; *e.* −; *f.* −; *g.* −; *h.* +; *i.* −

5. *a.* investment; *b.* constant (given); *c.* (1) unrelated, (2) directly related; *d.* decrease, downward

Self-test

1. T; **2.** T; **3.** F; **4.** T; **5.** F; **6.** F; **7.** T; **8.** F; **9.** T; **10.** F; **11.** F; **12.** F; **13.** T; **14.** T; **15.** T; **16.** F; **17.** T; **18.** F; **19.** F; **20.** T

1. *a;* **2.** *c;* **3.** *b;* **4.** *c;* **5.** *a;* **6.** *b;* **7.** *d;* **8.** *d;* **9.** *a;* **10.** *c;* **11.** *b;* **12.** *c;* **13.** *a;* **14.** *d;* **15.** *b;* **16.** *c;* **17.** *c;* **18.** *d;* **19.** *c;* **20.** *d;* **21.** *b*

CHAPTER 13 EQUILIBRIUM NATIONAL OUTPUT IN THE KEYNESIAN MODEL

Fill-in questions

1. *a.* Keynesian, constant; *b.* real, NNP

2. (aggregate) expenditures-(national) output, leakages-injections

3. *a.* expenditures, output; *b.* consumption, planned net investment; *c.* 45-degree

4. *a.* saving, net investment; *b.* (1) taxes, imports; (2) government expenditures, exports

5. *a.* less, disinvestment, rise; *b.* greater, investment, fall; *c.* equal to, zero, neither rise nor fall

6. actual; *a.* (1) disinvestment, (2) rise; *b.* (1) investment, (2) fall

7. *a.* the equilibrium real NNP; *b.* marginal propensity to save, the marginal propensity to consume

8. *a.* income; *b.* consumption, marginal propensity to consume

9. increases, decreases; *a.* greater; *b.* directly

10. decrease, decrease; paradox of thrift

11. less, increase, multiplier

12. inflationary, the aggregate-expenditures schedule, the amount by which equilibrium money NNP exceeds the full-employment noninflationary real NNP

13. variable, constant; *a.* real-balances, raise, rise; *b.* lower, fall; *c.* inverse, demand

14. *a.* right, multiplier; *b.* left, downward shift in aggregate expenditures times the multiplier

15. *a.* greater, smaller; *b.* smaller, greater

Problems and projects

1. *a.* *I*: 22, 22, 22, 22, 22, 22, 22; *C* + *I*: 1328, 1336, 1344, 1352, 1360, 1368, 1376; *UI*: −8, −6, −4, −2, 0, +2, +4; *b.* 1360; *c.* 0.8, 0.2; *d.* 5; *e.* increase, 3, increase, 15; *f.* decrease, 4, decrease, 20

2. change in income: 8.00, 6.40, 5.12, 4.10, 50,000; change in consumption: 8.00, 6.40, 5.12, 4.10, 3.28, 40.000; change in saving: 2.00, 1.60, 1.28, 1.02, 0.82, 10.00

3. *a.* 350, 15; *b.* 0.20, 5; *c.* 10, 20; *d.* 10; *e.* (1) decrease, 340, 15; (2) decrease, 330, 13; (3) decrease, decrease, leave unchanged the amount of, paradox of thrift; (4) the multiplier

4. *a.* 2½; *b.* 620, 30, inflationary, 12; *c.* 570, 20, recessionary, 8

5. *a.* 2200; *b.* 2400; *c.* 2600; *d.* 2200, 2400, 2600, (1) aggregate-demand, (2) inversely

6. *a.* (1) 2390, 2.00, (2) 1840, 1.00; *b.* 1640, 1.00, 100, remain constant; *c.* 2300, 1.80, 2350, 1.90; *d.* 2390, 2.20, 2.40, remain constant

Self-test

1. T; **2.** F; **3.** F; **4.** T; **5.** T; **6.** T; **7.** T; **8.** F; **9.** T; **10.** F; **11.** F; **12.** F; **13.** F; **14.** T; **15.** F; **16.** F; **17.** F; **18.** T

1. *a;* **2.** *d;* **3.** *c;* **4.** *d;* **5.** *a;* **6.** *b;* **7.** *a;* **8.** *c;* **9.** *d;* **10.** *a;* **11.** *b;* **12.** *b;* **13.** *b;* **14.** *a;* **15.** *c;* **16.** *b;* **17.** *c;* **18.** *b*

APPENDIX TO CHAPTER 13 INTERNATIONAL TRADE AND EQUILIBRIUM OUTPUT

Fill-in questions

1. *a.* exports, imports; *b.* directly, total income (NNP); *c.* directly, its own total income (NNP)

2. *a.* net exports; *b.* aggregate expenditures; save, import (either order)

3. *a.* −; *b.* +; *c.* +; *d.* −

4. tariffs, quotas, increase; *a.* reduce international specialization and the efficiency with which resources are allocated; *b.* are likely to result in retaliation by other nations

5. national income (NNP), imports

6. *a.* fall, fall; *b.* fall

Problem

1. *a.* $16, 12, 8, 4, 0, −4, −8; *b.* $792, 828, 864, 900, 936, 972, 1,008; *c.* $900; *d.* 0.08; *e.* 3.57; *f.* (1) increase, $35.7, (2) decrease, $35.7

Self-test

1. T; **2.** F; **3.** T; **4.** F; **5.** F; **6.** T

1. *b;* **2.** *b;* **3.** *a;* **4.** *c;* **5.** *d;* **6.** *a*

CHAPTER 14 FISCAL POLICY

Fill-in questions

1. Employment; *a.* Economic Advisers, Joint Economic; *b.* Humphrey-Hawkins (Full Employment and Balanced Growth), goals, plan (program)

2. marginal propensity to consume, marginal propensity to save

3. *a.* expenditures, output; *b.* consumption, planned net investment, government purchases of goods and services; *c.* planned net investment, government purchases of goods and services, saving, net taxes

4. decrease; the decreases in taxes and government purchases

5. decreased, increased, increased, decreased

6. deficit, surplus

7. borrowing from the public, creating new money, latter

8. increase, taxes, decrease, taxes

9. a. taxes, transfer payments; *b.* increase, decrease

10. built-in; *a.* increase, increase, decrease; *b.* decrease, increase, decrease

11. employment, full employment

12. *a.* budget surplus or deficit, full employment; *b.* expansionary, contractionary

13. recognition, administrative, operational

14. other, deficits, political

15. deficit, borrows; *a.* raise, contract; *b.* crowding-out, weaken

16. raise; *a.* weaken; *b.* increase, increase, increase, decrease, strengthen

Problems and projects

1. *a.* (1) 0.9, 90, C_a: 1160, 1250, 1340, 1430, 1520, 1610, 1700, (2) 0.1, 10, S_a: 240, 250, 260, 270, 280, 290, 300; *b.* 340, 350, 360, 370, 380, 390, 400; *c.* $I + G$: 350, 350, 350, 350, 350, 350, 350, $C_a + I + G$: 1510, 1600, 1690, 1780, 1870, 1960, 2050; *d.* 1600; *f.* rise, 100; *g.* fall, 90; *h.* raise, 10

2. *a.* (1) increase, $10, (2) decrease, $20, (3) direct; *b.* (1) $100, (2) increase, (3) less, (4) lessened; *c.* (1) $5, (2) decrease, (3) less, (4) lessened, more; *d.* (1) government expenditures are $200 at all NNPs, government surplus: −30, −20, −10, 0, 10, 20, 30, (2) $30, (3) deficit, $20, (4) expansionary, recession, (5) deficit, $40, (6) deficit, $50

3. *a.* 2300, 1.80; *b.* (1) 2400, (2) 1.90, 2350; *c.* (1) 2400, (2) remain constant

Self-test

1. T; **2.** T; **3.** T; **4.** F; **5.** T; **6.** F; **7.** F; **8.** T; **9.** F; **10.** F; **11.** F; **12.** F; **13.** F; **14.** T; **15.** F; **16.** F

1. *b;* **2.** *c;* **3.** *b;* **4.** *b;* **5.** *a;* **6.** *b;* **7.** *b;* **8.** *a;* **9.** *d;* **10.** *c;* **11.** *c;* **12.** *d;* **13.** *b;* **14.** *b;* **15.** *b;* **16.** *d*

CHAPTER 15 BUDGET DEFICITS AND THE PUBLIC DEBT

Fill-in questions

1. expenditures, revenues, deficits, surpluses

2. pro-, raise, lower

3. recession, inflation

4. full employment without inflation, deficits, public debt

5. wars, recessions, rates

6. *a.* 2112, 46, 140, 3.2; *b.* internal

7. *a.* agencies, central; *b.* 11

8. debts, assets; *a.* greater; *b.* decreases, deficit, surplus

9. reduce, refinancing, money

10. asset, consumption, the present

11. externally, increase, incentives, crowding-out

12. increases, decreases, capital; *a.* consumer, present; *b.* capital, less than full

13. size, costs, peace, full employment

14. increase; *a.* contracts, more; *b.* increases, raises; *c.* contracts, expands, contracts; *d.* contractionary

15. Constitutional, Gramm-Rudman, taxes, privitization

16. saving, growing, full employment

Problems and projects

1. *a.* increase, 100; *b.* (1) increased, 20, (2) (a) decreased, 25, (b) decreased, 125, (c) decrease, 25; *c.* increase, 25

Self-test

1. F; **2.** T; **3.** T; **4.** T; **5.** F; **6.** F; **7.** F; **8.** F; **9.** T; **10.** T; **11.** T; **12.** F; **13.** F; **14.** F; **15.** F; **16.** F; **17.** T; **18.** T

1. *c;* **2.** *a;* **3.** *d;* **4.** *a;* **5.** *a;* **6.** *b;* **7;** *a;* **8.** *d;* **9.** *a;* **10.** *c;* **11.** *b;* **12.** *d;* **13.** *d;* **14.** *b;* **15.** *a;* **16.** *c;* **17.** *d;* **18.** *b*

CHAPTER 16 INFLATION, UNEMPLOYMENT, AND AGGREGATE SUPPLY

Fill-in questions

1. full employment, excess, either

2. *a.* increase, demand-pull; *b.* decrease, cost-push

3. *a.* greater, greater, smaller; *b.* inverse

4. *a.* full employment is reached; *b.* business firms, labor unions, labor

5. *a.* price level, unemployment; *b.* negative

6. *a.* inflation, unemployment; *b.* increase, increase

7. select a point on the Phillips Curve

8. *a.* the dramatic rise in the oil prices of OPEC; *b.* agricultural shortfalls throughout the world (higher agricultural prices); *c.* the devaluation of the dollar; *d.* the abandonment of wage-price controls; *e.* the fall in the rate of growth of labor productivity; *f.* inflationary expectations

9. *a.* increase; *b.* increase

10. higher, rise, decrease, higher, higher

11. *a.* decreased; *b.* price, unemployment; *c.* stagflation

12. *a.* right; *b.* exist

13. *a.* (1) vertical, less, (2) increases; *(b)* (1) inflation, real, increase, money, (2) a rise, no change

14. *a.* market, wage, price, supply-side; *b.* left

15. *a.* manpower; *b.* competition

16. *a.* incomes; *b.* (1) guideposts, (2) controls

17. productivity, unit labor

18. *a.* (1) cost, wedge, (2) incentives, (3) regulation; *b.* decrease

19. *a.* substantial reduction in Federal expenditures except for those for defense; *b.* reduction in government regulation of private business; *c.* limitation of the rate of growth in the money supply; *d.* sharp reduction in personal and corporate income tax rates

20. *a.* the U.S. is increasingly linked to the world economy and this growing international interdependence is an added source of macroeconomic instability; *b.* expectations of inflation play a causal role in inflation and make it difficult for government policy to control it; *c.* both aggregate demand and aggregate supply affect the state of the economy and the kinds of policy that may be used to control it

Problems and projects

1. *a.* 20; *b.* 9; *c.* (it's your choice)

2. 2300; *a.* (1) 6, 2000, (2) 75, 5, 6.25; *b.* (1) 7, 2200, (2) 3, 2.5, (3) 16.67; *c.* (1) 5, 1700, (2) 3, 10, (3) negative

3. P_1, Q_4; *a.* (1) (*a*) rise, P_2, (*b*) rise, Q_5, (*c*) fall, (2) (*a*) rise, P_3, (*b*) fall, Q_4, (*c*) rise; *b.* (1) (*a*) P_1, (*b*) fall, Q_4, (*c*) rise, (2) (*b*) fall, Q_2, (*c*) rise, (3) (*a*) smaller, (*b*) larger

4. *a.* 4; *b.* (1) increase, 1, rise, 1; (2) decrease, 2, fall, 2; (3) increase, 6, rise, 6

Self-test

1. T; **2.** T; **3.** F; **4.** F; **5.** T; **6.** F; **7.** T; **8.** T; **9.** T; **10.** T; **11.** T; **12.** T; **13.** T; **14.** T; **15.** F; **16.** F; **17.** T; **18.** T; **19.** F; **20.** T; **21.** T; **22.** F; **23.** F; **24.** F; **25.** F; **26.** T

1. *c;* **2.** *d;* **3.** *a;* **4.** *a;* **5.** *b;* **6.** *c;* **7.** *a;* **8** *d;* **9.** *b;* **10.** *a;* **11.** *b;* **12.** *d;* **13.** *d;* **14.** *a;* **15.** *d;* **16.** *b;* **17.** *d;* **18.** *c;* **19.** *a;* **20.** *a;* **21.** *d;* **22.** *d;* **23.** *a;* **24.** *c;* **25.** *b;* **26.** *d*

CHAPTER 17 MONEY AND BANKING

Fill-in questions

1. *a.* medium of exchange; *b.* standard of value; *c.* store of value

2. *a.* currency, coins, money; *b.* checkable, depository institutions; *c.* Federal Reserve, Federal

3. *a.* savings and loan, mutual savings, credit; *b.* NOW, ATS (either order), share

4. *a.* (1) noncheckable, (2) small; *b.* large; *c.* certificates, 100,000

5. *a.* Treasury, bonds; *b.* currency, checkable, loss

6. *a.* their existence influences consuming-saving habits; *b.* conversion from near-money to money or from money to near-money may affect the stability of the economy; *c.* important when monetary policy is to be employed

7. depository, Federal Reserve

8. *a.* are not; *b.* exchange, legal, scarce

9. desirable goods and services, inversely, price

10. *a.* directly, money GNP; *b.* inversely, rate of interest

11. supply, interest, money

12. Open Market Committee, Federal Advisory Council

13. *a.* they are central banks; *b.* they are quasi-public banks; *c.* they are bankers' banks

14. deposits, loans, depository institutions

15. deposits, loans, increase

16. *a.* holding the deposits (reserves) of banks and thrifts; *b.* providing for the collection of checks; *c.* acting as fiscal agents for the Federal government; *d.* supervising member banks; *e.* regulating the money supply; regulating the money supply

Problems and projects

1. *a.* 170, 448 (either order), 618; *b.* 300, 1,630 (either order), 2,548; *c.* 645, 3,193

2. *a.* rise, 25; *b.* fall, 9.

3. *a.* (1) ¼ (25%), (2) 500; *b.* (1) 520, 540, 560, 580, 600, 620, 640; *c.* (2) 10; *d.* (1) fall, 8, (2) rise, 14; *e.* (1) increase, 20, rise, 2, (2) decrease, 30, fall, 3

Self-test

1. F; **2.** T; **3.** F; **4.** T; **5.** F; **6.** T; **7.** T; **8.** F; **9.** F; **10.** F; **11.** F; **12.** T; **13.** T; **14.** F; **15.** T; **16.** T; **17.** T; **18.** F; **19.** T; **20.** T

1. *a;* **2.** *d;* **3.** *d;* **4.** *d;* **5.** *c;* **6.** *a;* **7.** *b;* **8.** *d;* **9.** *c;* **10.** *b;* **11.** *b;* **12.** *d;* **13.** *b;* **14.** *c;* **15.** *b;* **16.** *a;* **17.** *b;* **18.** *d;* **19.** *d;* **20.** *d*

CHAPTER 18 HOW BANKS CREATE MONEY

Fill-in questions

1. assets, liabilities, net worth (capital)

2. vault, till

3. not changed

4. Federal Reserve Bank in its district, deposit liabilities, reserve ratio

5. actual reserves, required reserves

6. fractional

7. decreased, increased, decreased, increased

8. excess reserves

9. increases, 10,000

10. decreases, 2000

11. profits, liquidity (safety)

12. monetary multiplier (reciprocal of the reserve ratio), reserves

13. smaller

14. decrease, 36 million

15. currency (cash), excess

16. *a.* recession, prosperity; *b.* more

Problems and projects

1.

	(a)	(b)	(c)	(d)
Assets:				
Cash	$100	$100	$100	$100
Reserves	150	150	260	300
Loans	500	500	500	500
Securities	200	200	200	100
Liabilities and net worth:				
Demand deposits	850	850	960	900
Capital stock	100	100	100	100

2.
a.

	(1a)	(2a)	(3a)	(4a)	(5a)
A. Required reserve	$35	$40	$30	$36	$44
B. Excess reserve	5	0	−5	4	1
C. New loans	5	0	*	4	1

b.

	(1b)	(2b)	(3b)	(4b)	(5b)
Assets:					
Cash	$ 10	$ 20	$20	$ 20	$ 15
Reserves	40	40	25	40	45
Loans	105	100	*	104	151
Securities	50	60	30	70	60
Liabilities and net worth:					
Demand deposits	180	200	*	184	221
Capital stock	25	20	25	50	50

* If an individual bank is $5 short of reserves it must either obtain additional reserves of $5 by selling loans, securities, or its own IOUs to the reserve bank or contract its loans by $25.

3. column 2: 8, 6, 5, 4, 3⅓, 3; column 3: 1,1, 1, 1, 1, 1; column 4: 8, 6, 5, 4, 3⅓, 3

4.

	(1)	(2)	(3)	(4)	(5)	(6)
Assets:						
Cash	$ 50	$ 50	$ 50	$ 50	$ 50	$ 50
Reserves	105	105	108	108	110	110
Loans	200	220	200	240	200	250
Securities	200	200	192	192	200	200
Liabilities and net worth:						
Demand deposits	505	525	500	540	500	550
Capital stock	50	50	50	50	50	50
Loans from Federal Reserve	0	0	0	0	10	10
Excess reserves	4	0	8	0	10	0
Maximum possible expansion of the money supply	20	0	40	0	50	0

Self-test

1. F; **2.** F; **3.** F; **4.** T; **5.** F; **6.** T; **7.** T; **8.** F; **9.** F; **10.** F; **11.** T; **12.** T; **13.** T; **14.** T; **15.** T; **16.** F

1. *d;* **2.** *d;* **3.** *a;* **4.** *d;* **5.** *b;* **6.** *b;* **7.** *b;* **8.** *b;* **9.** *a;* **10.** *d;* **11.** *d;* **12.** *c;* **13.** *c;* **14.** *a;* **15.** *c;* **16.** *c*

CHAPTER 19 THE FEDERAL RESERVE BANKS AND MONETARY POLICY

Fill-in questions

1. full-employment noninflationary, Board of Governors, Banks

2. decrease, decrease, increase, decrease

3. securities, loans to commercial banks (either order), reserves of commercial banks, Treasury deposits, Federal Reserve Notes (any order)

4. open-market operations, reserve ratio, the discount rate (any order)

5. money, interest

6. 10 million, 10 million, 7.5 million, 0, 10 million, 10 million

7. excess reserves, multiplier

8. more, increase

9. lower, buy, decrease

10. open-market operations

11. margin requirements, the terms of credit available for consumer durable goods, moral suasion

12. *a.* money; *b.* investment-demand; *c.* saving; *d.* decrease, increase, increase

13. steeper, flatter

14. demand, right; *a.* large, small; *b.* small, large; *c.* flatter, steeper

15. *a.* flexible, acceptable, effective; *b.* inflation, recession, velocity, opposite, cost-push, investment

16. unable; *a.* increase; *b.* increase

17. expenditures, consumption, investment, government

18. fiscal, monetary (either order)

Problems and projects

1. *a.* (1) decrease, 20, (2) buy, 25; *b.* (1) increase, $28\frac{4}{7}$, (2) sell, $12\frac{1}{2}$

2.

	(2)	(3)	(4)	(5)	(6)
			Federal Reserve Banks		
Assets:					
Gold certificates	$ 25	$ 25	$ 25	$ 25	$ 25
Securities	27	34	30	30	30
Loans to commercial banks	10	10	10	10	4
Liabilities:					
Reserves of commercial banks	47	54	50	55	44
Treasury deposits	5	5	5	0	5
Federal Reserve Notes	10	10	10	10	10
			Commercial Banks		
Assets:					
Reserves	$ 47	$ 54	$ 50	$ 55	$ 44
Securities	$ 70	66	70	70	70
Loans	90	90	90	90	90
Liabilities:					
Demand deposits	197	200	200	205	200
Loans from Federal Reserve	10	10	10	10	4
A. Required reserves	49.25	50	40	51.25	50
B. Excess reserves	−2.25	4	10	3.75	−6
C. How much has the money supply changed?	−3	0	0	+5	0
D. How much more can the money supply change?	−9	+16	+50	+15	−24
E. What is the total of D and E?	−12	+16	+50	+20.25	−24

3. *a.* (2) 8; *b.* 20; *c.* (2) 850; *d.* (1) 6, (2) 30, (3) 900; *e.* (1) 25, (2) 25, (3) 7, (4) 350; *f.* (1) 0.20, 5, (2) increase, 5, increase, 25, (3) 50

4. *a.* 1700; *b.* 2120; *c.* 1600, .30; *d.* rise to $1700 billion, remain constant; *e.* rise from $1870 billion to $2000 billion, rise from .50 to .70; *f.* remain constant at $2120 billion, rise from 1.10 to 1.20

5. *a.* 5; *b.* increase, 500; *c.* rise, 6; *d.* increase, decrease, rise, fall

Self-test

1. F; **2.** T; **3.** F; **4.** T; **5.** F; **6.** T; **7.** T; **8.** T; **9.** T; **10.** T; **11.** F; **12.** F; **13.** F; **14.** F; **15.** T; **16.** F

1. *b;* **2.** *b;* **3.** *b;* **4.** *a;* **5.** *c;* **6.** *d;* **7.** *c;* **8.** *b;* **9.** *a;* **10.** *c;* **11.** *c;* **12.** *a;* **13.** *a;* **14.** *d;* **15.** *b;* **16.** a

CHAPTER 20 ALTERNATIVE VIEWS: MONETARISM AND RATIONAL EXPECTATIONS

Fill-in questions

1. unstable, noncompetitive, government intervention, fiscal, monetary

2. stable, competitive, laissez faire, nondiscretionary, monetary

3. $MV = PQ$; *a.* equation of exchange; *b.* (1) the money supply, (2) the (income or circuit) velocity of money, (3) the average price of each unit of physical output, (4) the physical volume of goods and services produced

4. *a.* total spending (aggregate demand), *MV*; *b.* *PQ*

5. *a.* increase; *b.* increase; (*c*) increase, *P*

6. *a.* medium of exchange, transactions, money NNP, stable; *b.* store of value, asset, interest rate, unstable

7. *a.* (1) more, (2) increase, (3) increase, (4) *P, Q*; *b.* (1) decrease, (2) increase, (3) decrease, (4) uncertain

8. *a.* *M, PQ*; *b.* directly, decreases, inversely

9. *a.* fiscal; *b.* raise, crowding-out

10. real GNP, 3, 5

11. destabilize

12. *a.* flat, small, large; *b.* steep, large, small

13. *a.* self-interests; *b.* purely competitive, flexible; *c.* inflation, no change, an increase

14. vertical, the price level, the real output

15. *a.* pro-; *b.* policy rules

16. less, less, sticky, stabilize, real

Problems and projects

1. *a.* 100, 220, 360, 520, 700, 900, 1120; *b.* 360, 360, 360, 360, 360, 360, 360, (1) 360, (2) 3.00, (3) 130; *c.* 700, (1) 700, (2) 5.00, (3) 140

2. *a.* (1) 50, (2) 75, (3) 125, (4) equal to, (5) 4; *b.* (1) 60, 100, (2) 160, equal to, (3) 3.75; *c.* (1) 80, 80, 160, (2) 5; *d.* decrease, increase

3. *a.* rational-expectations, classical, Keynesian; *b.* Q_1, P_1; *c.* (1) increase, Q_2, increase, P_3, (2) increase, Q_3, increase, P_2, (3) remain constant, Q_1, increase, P_4

Self-test

1. T; **2.** T; **3.** F; **4.** T; **5.** F; **6.** F; **7.** T; **8.** T; **9.** T; **10.** F; **11.** T; **12.** F; **13.** F; **14.** F; **15.** F; **16.** F

1. *d;* **2.** *b;* **3.** *b;* **4.** *d;* **5.** *a;* **6.** *b;* **7.** *d;* **8.** *c;* **9.** *c;* **10.** *d;* **11.** *d;* **12.** *c;* **13.** *b;* **14.** *d;* **15.** *b;* **16.** *d*

CHAPTER 21 THE ECONOMICS OF GROWTH

Fill-in questions

1. fixed, increases

2. total real output (NNP or GNP), real output (NNP or GNP) per capita

3. increases, decreases

4. 180, 108, 72

5. quantity and quality of natural resources, quantity and quality of human resources, the supply or stock of capital goods, technology, demand, allocative

6. output, average

7. optimum population

8. population, decrease

9. productivity, capital, technology, labor

10. aggregate expenditures (or investment)

11. aggregate expenditures, productive capacity, capital-output ratio

12. reallocate

13. *a.* demand, low, investment, contract; *b.* saving, investment, work effect, risk-taking, capacity output; *c.* structure, composition, industrial

Problems and projects

1. *a.* 9; *b.* 8

2. *a.* 80, 100, 110, 100, 90, 80, 70, 60; *b.* third, fourth; *c.* 3, average

3. *a.* 100; *b.* 100, 110, 120, 125, 120, 110, 100, 90; *c.* 25; *d.* increased, 4; *e.* (1) increased, 120, (2) remained constant, (3) decreased to 90

4. *a.* (1) 1100, 1210; (2) consumption: 880, 968; saving: 220, 242; (3) investment: 220, 242; aggregate expenditures: 1100, 1210; *b.* (1) 10; (2) 10; *c.* (1) 0.8, (2) 0.2; *d.* 1050; (1) 5; (2) less than; (3) recession; *e.* 1150; (1) greater than, cannot; (2) inflation; *f.* increases

5. *a.* 270, 270; *b.* 90; *c.* 990, 297, 297, 99; *d.* 1089, 326.7, 326.7, 108.9; *e.* (1) investment; (2) average propensity to save, capital-output ratio; *f.* 2.5

Self-test

1. T; **2.** F; **3.** T; **4.** F; **5.** T; **6.** T; **7.** F; **8.** T; **9.** F; **10.** F; **11.** T; **12.** F

1. *a;* **2.** *b;* **3.** *d;* **4.** *b;* **5.** *a;* **6.** *c;* **7.** *b;* **8.** *c;* **9.** *b;* **10.** *b;* **11.** *b;* **12.** *d*

CHAPTER 22 ECONOMIC GROWTH: FACTS AND ISSUES

Fill-in questions

1. five, three

2. 3.1, 1.8

3. quantity, productivity; *a.* hours of labor; *b.* worker, hour (either order)

4. labor, length, population, participation

5. 2.9, 1, labor, 2, productivity, labor

6. increases, increases; *a.* progress (advance); *b.* capital, worker; *c.* education, training; *d.* scale; *e.* allocation

7. investment, more

8. output (production), investment

9. regulations, investment, productivity

10. natural, environment

11. recessionary, slower

12. fallen; *a.* fall, living, real, rise, inflation, foreign; *b.* fall, investment, fall, capital, deterioration, technological, managers, employees; *c.* increased

13. pollutes, domestic problems, anxiety, insecurity, good life

14. living, unlimited wants-scarce resource, pollution, equitable, income, a better life

15. *a.* population, natural resources, pollution, food output per capita, industrial output per capita; *b.* 100, population, industrial output (or capacity)

16. unrealistic, technological, feedback

Problems and projects

1. *a.* 400, 500, 550, 600, 550, 500; *b.* 150 million; *c.* $15 billion; *d.* 46⅔%

2. *a.* 100,000, 105,000, 115,500; *b.* (1) 5, (2), 5; *c.* (1) 10, (2) 10; *d.* (1) 15.5, (2) quantity, productivity

Self-test

1. T; **2.** F; **3.** F; **4.** T; **5.** F; **6.** T; **7.** F; **8.** F; **9.** T; **10.** T; **11.** F; **12.** F; **13.** F; **14.** T; **15.** T

1. *d;* **2.** *c;* **3.** *b;* **4.** *b;* **5.** *b;* **6.** *b;* **7.** *d;* **8.** *d;* **9.** *a;* **10.** *c;* **11.** *a;* **12.** *c;* **13.** *b;* **14.** *b;* **15.** *d*

CHAPTER 23 GROWTH AND THE UNDERDEVELOPED NATIONS

Fill-in questions

1. poverty (i.e., a low standard of living)

2. Asia, Latin America, Africa, $2/3$

3. Third World, 50, 15, 3

4. natural resources, human resources, capital goods, technology

5. natural resources

6. *a.* overpopulation; *b.* widespread unemployment; *c.* the poor quality of the labor force

7. consumer goods (food) production, population, aspirations, standard of living

8. output, invest

9. saving potential, investors, incentives

10. agriculture, social

11. *a.* skilled, scarce, abundant, capital; *b.* unskilled, abundant, scarce, labor

12. saving

13. institutions, social

14. income, investment, productivity, output (income)

15. *a.* the existence of widespread banditry and intertribal warfare in many underdeveloped nations; *b.* the absence of a sizable and vigorous entrepreneurial class; *c.* the great need for social goods and services; *d.* government action may be the only means of promoting saving and investment; *e.* government can more effectively deal with the social-institutional obstacles to growth

16. by expanding trade with the underdeveloped nations (lowering the barriers to trade), private flows of capital, foreign aid (public loans and grants)

17. *a.* rules; *b.* trade, tariff treatments; *c.* exploitation, dependence; *d.* terms, trade, stabilization, indexing; *e.* debts, cancelled, rescheduled; *f.* insufficient, 0.7, strings, automatic

18. *a.* population, standard of living; *b.* cartels, raw materials; *c.* redistribution

Problems and projects

1. *a.* 7500; *b.* (1) 8400, (2) 525, (3) widen, 7875

2. *a.* low; *b.* short; *c.* widespread; *d.* low; *e.* primitive; *f.* large; *g.* large; *h.* high; *i.* poor; *j.* small; *k.* low; *l.* absent; *m.* small; *n.* small; *o.* small and poor; *p.* small; *q.* low; *r.* common

3. *a.* food supply: 400, 600, 800, 1000, 1200, 1400; population: 40, 80, 160, 320, 640, 1280; *b.* the food supply is just able to support the population; *c.* the inability of the food supply to support a population growing at this rate; *d.* (1) 200, (2) 240, (3) 280; *e.* the population increased as rapidly as the food supply

Self-test

1. F; **2.** F; **3.** F; **4.** F; **5.** T; **6.** F; **7.** F; **8.** T; **9.** F; **10.** F; **11.** F; **12.** T; **13.** T; **14.** F; **15.** T; **16.** F; **17.** T; **18.** T; **19.** T; **20.** F

1. *d;* **2.** *d;* **3.** *d;* **4.** *b;* **5.** *d;* **6.** *a;* **7.** *b;* **8.** *b;* **9.** *c;* **10.** *d;* **11.** *d;* **12.** *b;* **13.** *d;* **14.** *b;* **15.** *a;* **16.** *c;* **17.** *d;* **18.** *b;* **19.** *d;* **20.** *d*

CHAPTER 24 DEMAND, SUPPLY, AND ELASTICITY: SOME APPLICATIONS

Fill-in questions

1. fully, allocated; *a.* latter, micro-; *b.* price, prices

2. inelastic, elastic

3. inelastic, vertical, perfectly elastic, horizontal

4. *a.* greater than; *b.* less than; *c.* equal to

5. inversely, directly

6. elastic: greater than 1, decrease, increase; inelastic: less than 1, increase, decrease; of unitary elasticity: equal to 1, remain constant, remain constant

7. *a.* the number of good substitute products available; *b.* the relative importance of the product in the total budget of the buyer; *c.* whether the good is a necessity or a luxury; *d.* the period of time in which demand is being considered

8. the amount of time which a seller has to respond to a price change

9. *a.* 7.00, 15,000; *b.* shortage, 4000; *c.* surplus, 2000.

10. war, shortages, rationing

11. minimum wages, agricultural price supports

12. surplus, attempt to reduce supply or increase demand, purchase the surplus and store or dispose of it

13. rationing

14. the amount the price of the commodity rises as a result of the tax; *a.* less, more; *b.* more, less

Problems and projects

1. total revenue: $300, 360, 400, 420, 420, 400, 360; elasticity coefficient: $2\frac{5}{7}$ (2.71), $1\frac{8}{9}$ (1.89), $1\frac{4}{11}$ (1.36), 1, $\frac{11}{15}$ (0.73), $\frac{9}{17}$ (0.53); character of demand: elastic, elastic, elastic, unitary elasticity, inelastic, inelastic

2. Elasticity coefficient: $1\frac{4}{15}$ (1.27), $1\frac{4}{13}$ (1.31), $1\frac{4}{11}$ (1.36), $1\frac{4}{9}$

(1.44), 1 4/7 (1.57), 1 4/5 (1.8); character of supply: elastic, elastic, elastic, elastic, elastic, elastic

3. *a.* (1)S_3; (2) S_2; (3) S_1; *b.* p_1, q_1; *c.* (1) p_4, remain at q_1; (2) p_3, q_2; (3) p_2, q_3; *d.* more; *e.* less, greater

4. *a.* $3.60; *b.* (reading down) 600, 500, 400, 300, 200, 100; *c.* $4.00; *d.* (1) $.40, 66⅔; (2) $.20, 33⅓

5. *a.* (2) not changed; (3) none, all; (4) smaller, larger; (5) larger, smaller; *b.* (2) increased by the amount of the tax; (3) all, none; (4) larger, smaller; (5) smaller, larger

Self-test

1. F; **2.** T; **3.** F; **4.** T; **5.** T; **6.** F; **7.** F; **8.** F; **9.** T; **10.** T

1. *c;* **2.** *b;* **3.** *a;* **4.** *a;* **5.** *c;* **6.** *b;* **7.** *b;* **8.** *c;* **9.** *a;* **10.** *b*

CHAPTER 25 FURTHER TOPICS IN THE THEORY OF CONSUMER DEMAND

Fill-in questions

1. increase, decrease, income

2. more, lower, less, more, substitution

3. decrease

4. rational, preferences

5. limited, prices, budget restraint

6. ratio of the marginal utility of the last unit purchased of a product to its price

7. increase, decrease

8. *a.* MU of product X; *b.* price of X; *c.* MU of product Y; *d.* price of Y

9. *a.* the income of the consumer; *b.* the prices of other products

10. time; *a.* scarce; *b.* the income that can be earned by using the time for work; *c.* market price, value of the consumption time

Problems and projects

1. *a.* (1) increase, 1½; (2) inelastic; *b.* (1) decrease, 1; (2) elastic

2. marginal utility of good A: 21, 20, 18, 15, 11, 6, 0; marginal utility of good B: 7, 6, 5, 4, 3, 2, 1. 2; marginal utility of good C: 23, 17, 12, 8, 5, 3, 2

3. *a.* marginal utility per dollar of good A: 4⅕, 4, 3⅗, 3, 2⅕, 1⅕, 0; marginal utility per dollar of good B: 7, 6, 5, 4, 3, 2, 1⅕; marginal utility per dollar of good C: 5¾, 4¼, 3, 2, 1¼, ¾, ½; *b.* the marginal utility per dollar spent on good B (7) is greater than the marginal utility per dollar spent on good A (3), and the latter is greater than the marginal utility per dollar spent on good C (2); *c.* he would be spending more than his $37 income; *d.* (1) 4; (2) 5; (3) 3; 151, 3; *e.* A, he would obtain the greatest marginal utility for his dollar (2⅕)

4. *a.* 2, 3, 4, 6, 8; *b.* the demand schedule (for good D)

5. *a.* yes; *b.* (1) 10, (2) 3; *c.* no, the marginal utility to price ratios are not the same for the two goods; *d.* of *M*, because its MU/*P* ratio is greater; *e.* less

Self-test

1. F; **2.** T; **3.** T; **4.** F; **5.** F; **6.** T; **7.** F

1. *c;* **2.** *b;* **3.** *a;* **4.** *b;* **5.** *c;* **6.** *c;* **7.** *b*

APPENDIX TO CHAPTER 25 INDIFFERENCE CURVE ANALYSIS

Fill-in questions

1. money income, the price of X, price of Y

2. *a.* right; *b.* inward, F

3. total satisfaction (utility); *a.* downward, rate, substitution; *b.* convex

4. smaller, decreases

5. greater

6. tangent to an indifference curve, the ratio of the price of the product the quantity of which is measured on the horizontal axis to the price of the product the quantity of which is measured on the vertical axis

7. up

8. is, does not

9. *a.* outward, right; *b.* higher; *c.* more

10. demand

Problems and projects

1. *b.* (1) 30, 25, 20, 15, 10, 5, 0; (3) 5; *c.* (1) 3, 15; (2) 36, 36

2. *a.* (1) 5, 10; (2) 50, 50; *b.* (1) 12, 4; (2) 80, 20; *c.* (1) 19, 1; (2) 95, 5; *e.* elastic, substitutes

Self-test

1. F; **2.** T; **3.** T; **4.** T; **5.** F; **6.** F; **7.** F; **8.** T; **9.** T; **10.** T

1. *d;* **2.** *b;* **3.** *b;* **4.** *b;* **5.** *c;* **6.** *b;* **7.** *a;* **8.** *d;* **9.** *b;* **10.** *b*

CHAPTER 26 THE COSTS OF PRODUCTION

Fill-in questions

1. other, opportunity

2. attract, explicit, implicit

3. entrepreneur(s); *a.* revenues, costs; *b.* explicit

4. variable, fixed, short, long

5. variable, fixed, marginal

6. *a.* rising; *b.* falling; *c.* maximum

8. fixed, variable, variable

10. average variable, average total, marginal

11. total variable, total cost

12. falling, rising

13. *a.* falling; *b.* rising; *c.* maximum; *d.* minimum; *e.* (1) marginal, equal, (2) marginal, equal

14. plant

16. *a.* increased specialization in the use of labor; *b.* better utilization of and increased specialization in management; *c.* more efficient productive equipment; *d.* better utilization of by-products

17. managerial complexities (problems)

18. size, number

Problems and projects

1. *a.* 80, 120, 130, 70, 50, 30, 10, −10; *b.* third, fourth; *c.* positive, negative; *d.* 80, 100, 110, 100, 90, 80, 70, 60

2. *a.* $0, 10, 20, 30, 40, 50, 60, 70, 80, 90, 100; *b.* $2.00, 1.67, 1.43, 1.67, 2.00, 2.50, 3.33, 5.00, 10.00; *c.* (1) decreases, (2) increases; *d.* 2.00, 1.82, 1.67, 1.67, 1.72, 1.82, 1.94, 2.11, 2.31, 2.56; *e.* (1) decreases, (2) increases

3. *a.*

Total cost	Average fixed cost	Average total cost	Marginal cost
$ 200	—	—	—
250	$200.00	$250.00	$ 50
290	100.00	145.00	40
320	66.67	106.67	30
360	50.00	90.00	40
420	40.00	84.00	60
500	33.33	83.33	80
600	28.57	85.71	100
720	25.00	90.00	120
870	22.22	96.67	150
1,100	20.00	110.00	230

4. *a.* $7.00, 6.00, 5.00, 4.00, 4.00, 3.00, 4.00, 5.00, 6.00, 5.00, 7.00, 10.00; *b.* (1) 10, 40; (2) 50, 80; (3) 90, 120

Self-test

1. T; **2.** F; **3.** T; **4.** F; **5.** F; **6.** F; **7.** T; **8.** F; **9.** T; **10.** T; **11.** T; **12.** F; **13.** F; **14.** F; **15.** T

1. *b;* **2.** *b;* **3.** *d;* **4.** *a;* **5.** *b;* **6.** *a;* **7.** *d;* **8.** *a;* **9.** *c;* **10.** *d;* **11.** *c;* **12.** *b;* **13.** *b;* **14.** *a;* **15.** *d*

CHAPTER 27 PRICE AND OUTPUT DETERMINATION: PURE COMPETITION

Fill-in questions

1. *a.* pure competition, pure monopoly, monopolistic competition, oligopoly (any order); *b.* number, standardized, differentiated (either order), enter

2. *a.* a large number of independent sellers; *b.* a standardized product; *c.* no single firm supplies enough to influence market price; *d.* no obstacles to the entry of new firms or the exodus of old firms

3. taker, elastic, equal to

4. total revenue minus total cost

5. total-receipts–total-cost, marginal-revenue–marginal-cost

6. profit, fixed costs; *a.* maximum, minimum; *b.* cost, revenue (either order)

7. variable

8. that portion of the firm's marginal-cost curve which lies above the average-variable-cost curve, the sum of the short-run supply curves of all firms in the industry

9. total quantity demanded, total quantity supplied (either order), the quantity demanded and supplied at the equilibrium price

10. fixed, variable

11. average, marginal (either order), minimum

12. the firms in the industry are realizing profits in the short run, the firms in the industry are realizing losses in the short run

13. increasing-, upsloping

14. productive, allocative (either order)

15. average, minimum

16. marginal

17. *a.* the competitive price system does not necessarily result in an ideal distribution of money income in the economy; *b.* the competitive price system does not accurately measure costs and benefits when spillover costs and benefits are significant or provide social goods; *c.* the competitive price system does not entail the use of the most efficient productive techniques; *d.* the competitive price system may not provide for a sufficient range of consumer choice or for the development of new products

Problems and projects

1. number of firms: d, a, c, b; type of product: e, n, f, e or f; control over price: m, h, g, g; entry: i, j, k, l; nonprice competition: m, g, h, g or h

2. *a.* average revenue: all are $10.00; total revenue: $0, 10.00, 20,000, 30,000, 40,000, 50,000, 60,000; marginal revenue: all are $10,000; *b.* yes, because price (average revenue) is constant and equal to marginal revenue; *d.* infinity; *e.* they are equal

3. *a.* (see table below); *b.* (1) 0, −$300; (2) 5, −$100; (3) 7, $380;

Market price = $55		Market price = $120		Market price = $200	
Revenue	Profit	Revenue	Profit	Revenue	Profit
$ 0	$ −300	$ 0	$ −300	$ 0	$ −300
55	−345	120	−280	200	−200
110	−340	240	−210	400	−50
165	−345	360	−150	600	90
220	−370	480	−110	800	210
275	−425	600	−100	1,000	300
330	−510	720	−120	1,200	360
385	−635	840	−180	1,400	380
440	−810	960	−290	1,600	350
495	−1,045	1,080	−460	1,800	260
550	−1,350	1,200	−700	2,000	100

c.

Price	Quantity supplied	Profit
$360	10	$1,700
290	9	1,070
230	8	590
180	7	240
140	6	0
110	5	−150
80	4	−270
60	0	−300

d. (1) quantity supplied: 1000, 900, 800, 700, 600, 500, 400; (2) (*a*) 180; (*b*) 7; (*c*) 240; (*d*) enter, profits in the industry will attract them into the industry

4. *a.* 140; *b.* 6; *c.* 133 = 800 (the total quantity demanded at $140) ÷ 6 (the output of each firm); *d.* 150 = 900 ÷ 6; *e.* (1) the curve is a horizontal line, (2) the curve slopes upward

Self-test

1. F; **2.** T; **3.** T; **4.** T; **5.** F; **6.** T; **7.** T; **8.** T; **9.** T; **10.** F; **11.** T; **12.** T; **13.** F; **14.** T; **15.** T; **16.** T

1. *d;* **2.** *d;* **3.** *b;* **4.** *b;* **5.** *a;* **6.** *a;* **7.** *a;* **8.** *c;* **9.** *c;* **10.** *a;* **11.** *b;* **12.** *b;* **13.** *b;* **14.** *c;* **15.** *c;* **16.** *b;* **17.** *a;* **18.** *b;* **19.** *d*

CHAPTER 28 PRICE AND OUTPUT DETERMINATION: PURE MONOPOLY

Fill-in questions

1. close substitutes, blocked

2. *a.* the economies of scale; *b.* natural monopolies; *c.* ownership of essential raw materials; *d.* patents and research; *e.* unfair competition; *f.* the economies of being established

3. greater, money capital

4. natural, regulated

5. less than, less, decrease

6. marginal revenue, marginal cost, greater

7. *a.* highest possible; *b.* a maximum; *c.* profit

8. a minimum, price (or average revenue), marginal cost

9. costs (or cost schedules); *a.* scale; *b.* X-inefficiency

10. techniques (technology), costs (or cost schedules), products

11. upper

12. prices, cost

13. *a.* the seller has some monopoly power; *b.* the seller is able to separate buyers into groups which have different elasticities of demand for the product; *c.* the original buyers cannot resell the product

14. increase, increase

15. marginal cost, average (total) cost

16. average (total) cost, misallocation

Problems and projects

1. *a.* total revenue: $0, 650, 1200, 1650, 2000, 2250, 2400, 2450, 2400, 2250, 2000; marginal revenue: $650, 550, 450, 350, 250, 150, 50, −50, −150, −250; *b.* inelastic; *c.* (1) 6; (2) 400; (3) 1560; *d.* (1) total revenue: $0, 650, 1250, 1800, 2300, 2750, 3150, 3500, 3800, 4050, 4250; marginal revenue: $650, 600, 550, 500, 450, 400, 350, 300, 250, 200; (2) price; (3) 8, 300, 2550; (4) larger, larger

2. *a.* 4, 11.50, 4.00; *b.* 6, 8.50, −7.50, bankrupt, subsidize; *c.* 73.50, 58.50, 15.00; *d.* 5, 10.00, zero; *e.* b, a, d

Self-test

1. F; **2.** T; **3.** F; **4.** T; **5.** F; **6.** T; **7.** T; **8.** F; **9.** F; **10.** T; **11.** T; **12.** F; **13.** F; **14.** T; **15.** F; **16.** T

1. *b;* **2.** *c;* **3.** *d;* **4.** *a;* **5.** *c;* **6.** *d;* **7.** *c;* **8.** *a;* **9.** *d;* **10.** *b;* **11.** *d;* **12.** *b;* **13.** *a;* **14.** *b;* **15.** *b;* **16.** *a*

CHAPTER 29 PRICE AND OUTPUT DETERMINATION: MONOPOLISTIC COMPETITION

Fill-in questions

1. relatively large number of, differentiated, do not, price, nonprice, fairly easy

2. limited, rivalry

3. *a.* more, less; *b.* number of rivals the firm has, the degree of product differentiation; *c.* marginal cost, marginal revenue

4. reduce, increase

5. average cost, zero, greater

6. average cost is greater than minimum average cost, price is greater than marginal cost

7. product differentiation, product promotion

8. variety, quality

9. both

10. product, promotion

Problems and projects

2. *a.* marginal cost: $30, 10, 20, 30, 40, 50, 60, 70, 80, 90; marginal revenue: $110, 90, 70, 50, 30, 10, −10, −30, −50, −70; *b.* (1) 4; (2) $80; (3) $180; *c.* (1) decrease; (2) average cost; (3) equal to zero

Self-test

1. F; **2.** T; **3.** F; **4.** T; **5.** F; **6.** T; **7.** F; **8.** T; **9.** F; **10.** F

1. *c;* **2.** *b;* **3.** *c;* **4.** *d;* **5.** *d;* **6.** *b;* **7.** *d;* **8.** *b;* **9.** *b;* **10.** *a*

CHAPTER 30 PRICE AND OUTPUT DETERMINATION: OLIGOPOLY

Fill-in questions

1. few, standardized, differentiated, difficult

2. the economies of scale, other barriers to entry, the advantages of merger

3. mutually interdependent, the reactions of rivals, no, so many

4. many, uncertain

5. inflexible, simultaneously

6. elastic, elastic, inelastic

7. not raise their prices, lower their prices

8. gap, price the oligopolist will charge

9. by a pure monopolist

10. price, output, share

11. an informal, prices, the ingenuity of each seller (i.e., nonprice competition)

12. *a.* demand and cost differences; *b.* a large number of firms; *c.* cheating (secret price cutting); *d.* a recession; *e.* legal obstacles (antitrust laws)

13. tacit, price leadership

14. markup, average

15. price, nonprice, share of the market, *a.* price cuts can be quickly matched by rival firms; *b.* oligopolists tend to have the greater financial resources required to engage in nonprice competition

16. higher, smaller, slower

17. *a.* means, incentives; *b.* product improvement, costs, prices, output, employment

18. have not

Problems and projects

1. *a.* total revenue: 290, 560, 810, 1040, 1250, 1260, 1265, 1265, 1260; *b.* marginal revenue: 2.70, 2.50, 2.30, 2.10, 0.40, 0.20, 0, −0.20; *c.* 2.50, 500; *e.* (1) 2.50, 500; (2) 2.50, 500, they have decreased; (3) 2.50, 500, they have increased

2. *a.* marginal cost: $30, 20, 30, 40, 50, 60, 70, 80; marginal revenue: $130, 110, 90, 70, 50, 30, 10, −10; *b.* $90; *c.* (1) 5; (2) $280; *d.* (1) 15; (2) $840; *e.* no; *f.* $90

3. *a.* 400; *b.* 800; *c.* (1) 533.33, (2) 7033.33, (3) 8.2

Self-test

1. T; **2.** F; **3.** T; **4.** F; **5.** T; **6.** F; **7.** F; **8.** F; **9.** T; **10.** T; **11.** F; **12.** T

1. *b;* **2.** *d;* **3.** *d;* **4.** *d;* **5.** *c;* **6.** *c;* **7.** *d;* **8.** *c;* **9.** *c;* **10.** *b;* **11.** *d;* **12.** *d;* **13.** *a;* **14.** *d*

CHAPTER 31 PRODUCTION AND THE DEMAND FOR ECONOMIC RESOURCES

Fill-in questions

1. resources, incomes, costs

2. derived, productivity, value (price)

3. marginal, revenue, product, marginal resource cost, price, marginal resource cost (either order)

4. marginal revenue product, prices

5. lower, less

6. adding the demand curves for the resource of all the firms hiring the resource

7. product, productivity, prices

8. *a.* +; *b.* −; *c.* +; *d.* −; *e.* +

9. more, less, substitution, more, output

10. marginal physical product, substituted, price-elasticity, portion of total production costs accounted for by the resource

11. marginal physical product, price

12. marginal revenue product, price

13. one

14. *a.* marginal physical product, marginal resource cost; *b.* marginal revenue product, marginal resource cost, marginal revenue product, marginal resource cost, one

15. marginal revenue product (marginal contribution to the firm's revenue)

Problems and projects

1. *a.* marginal physical product of A: 12, 10, 8, 6, 4, 2, 1; *b.* total revenue: 0, 18.00, 33.00, 45.00, 54.00, 60.00, 63.00, 64.50; marginal revenue product of A: 18.00, 15.00, 12.00, 9.00, 6.00, 3.00, 1.50; *c.* 0, 1, 2, 3, 4, 5, 6, 7

2. *a.* total product: 22, 43, 62, 78, 90, 97, 98; *b.* (1) total revenue: 22.00, 38.70, 49.60, 54.60, 54.00, 48.50, 39.20; (2) marginal revenue product of B: 22.00, 16.70, 10.90, 5.00, −0.60, −5.50, −9.30; *c.* 0, 1, 2, 3, 4, 4

3. *a.* (1) 1, 3; (2) 3, 5; *b.* 5, 6; *c.* the marginal physical product of C divided by its price, the marginal physical product of D divided by its price; *d.* purely, $.50; *e.* (1) 114; (2) $57; (3) $28; (4) $29

Self-test

1. T; **2.** T; **3.** F; **4.** T; **5.** T; **6.** T; **7.** F; **8.** F; **9.** T; **10.** F; **11.** T; **12.** F; **13.** F; **14.** F; **15.** T

1. *d;* **2.** *c;* **3.** *a;* **4.** *d;* **5.** *c;* **6.** *a;* **7.** *c;* **8.** *c;* **9.** *a;* **10.** *b;* **11.** *c;* **12.** *d;* **13.** *a;* **14.** *b;* **15.** *b*

CHAPTER 32 THE PRICING AND EMPLOYMENT OF RESOURCES: WAGE DETERMINATION

Fill-in questions

1. time, wage rate, the amount of time worked, the goods and services money wages will purchase

2. *a.* strong; *b.* capital equipment, natural resources, technology, quality

3. *a.* wages, alternative employment; *b.* marginal-revenue-product (demand) schedules; *c.* total quantity of labor demanded, total quantity of labor supplied (either order)

4. perfectly, wage rate

5. marginal revenue product, wage rate, marginal labor cost

6. marginal revenue product, marginal labor cost, greater, marginal revenue product, labor cost

7. lower, less

8. increase wages, demand, supply, above-equilibrium

9. restricting the supply of labor, imposing above-equilibrium wage rates; *a.* decreased; *b.* decrease; *c.* growing, inelastic

10. products they produce, productivity, prices

11. marginal revenue product of labor, competitive and monopsonistic equilibrium wage, the relative bargaining strength of the union and the monopsonist

12. *a.* increase, decrease; *b.* increase, increase; *c.* increase, decrease

13. homogeneous, attractiveness, imperfect

14. noncompeting, equalizing differences

15. immobilities, geographical, sociological, institutional

16. *a.* education, health, mobility; *b.* productivity, wage rates (income); *c.* real wages; *d.* noncompeting, differences

Problems and projects

1. *a.* quantity of labor demanded: 100, 200, 300, 400, 500, 600, 700, 800; *b.* (1) 10.00; (2) 600; *c.* (1) 10.00; (2) 6; (3) 10.00; *f.* 400

2. *a.* total labor cost: 0, 4.00, 12.00, 24.00, 40.00, 60.00, 84.00, 112.00, 144.00; marginal labor cost: 4.00, 8.00, 12.00, 16.00, 20.00, 24.00, 28.00, 32.00; *b.* (1) 5; (2) 12.00; (3) 20.00; *d.* 6, 14.00

3. *a.* wage rate: 16.00, 16.00, 16.00, 16.00, 16.00, 16.00, 16.00, 18.00; *b.* total labor cost: 16.00, 32.00, 48.00, 64.00, 80.00, 96.00, 112.00, 144.00; marginal labor cost: 16.00, 16.00, 16.00, 16.00, 16.00, 16.00, 16.00, 32.00; *c.* (1) 6; (2) 16.00; (3) 96.00; *d.* increased, increased, increased

Self-test

1. F; **2.** T; **3.** T; **4.** T; **5.** T; **6.** T; **7.** F; **8.** F; **9.** T; **10.** F; **11.** T; **12.** T; **13.** T; **14.** T; **15.** T

1. *a;* **2.** *a;* **3.** *a;* **4.** *c;* **5.** *d;* **6.** *d;* **7.** *d;* **8.** *c;* **9.** *a;* **10.** *d;* **11.** *c;* **12.** *b;* **13.** *a;* **14.** *b;* **15.** *d*

CHAPTER 33 THE PRICING AND EMPLOYMENT OF RESOURCES: RENT, INTEREST, AND PROFITS

Fill-in questions

1. land, natural resources, fixed (perfectly inelastic)

2. demand, supply, incentive, surplus

3. unearned, nationalized, single tax

4. land differs in productivity (quality), individual, alternative uses

5. money, risk, the length of loan, the amount of the loan, market imperfections

6. *a.* transactions, money GNP; *b.* asset, rate of interest

7. *a.* the monetary authority (the Federal Reserve Banks); *b.* quantity of money demanded, the money supply (stock) (either order)

8. decrease, increase, increase

9. *a.* elastic; *b.* marginal revenue product of capital, the rate of interest

10. real, nominal, inflation, real

11. administered, investment, rations

12. entrepreneurial ability, resources, nonroutine, innovates, risks

13. uncertain, insurable, uninsurable, economy as a whole, innovation

14. *a.* investment, employment, output; *b.* allocation, monopoly

15. *a.* 80; *b.* rent, interest, corporate profit, 20; *c.* (1) remained constant, (2) remained constant

16. *a.* profits; *b.* productivity, the prices of the products they produce; *c.* labor's share of the national income

Problems and projects

1. *a.* 250; *b.* 300,000; *d.* 0, 300,000

2. *b.* (1) 180; *c.* 240, 260, 280, 300, 320, 340, 360; *d.* (2) 280, 280, 280, 280, 280, 280, 280, (3) 6; *e.* 300,000; *f.* (1) (*a*) fall, 5 (*b*) increase, 400,000, (2) (*a*) rise to 8%, (*b*) decrease the quantity of capital demanded to $100,000

3. *a.* 6; *b.* 10

4. *a.* 73.8; *b.* 81.3, 18.7

Self-test

1. F; **2.** T; **3.** F; **4.** F; **5.** F; **6.** T; **7.** T; **8.** T; **9.** F; **10.** T; **11.** F; **12.** T; **13.** T; **14.** F; **15.** F

1. *a;* **2.** *d;* **3.** *b;* **4.** *d;* **5.** *b;* **6.** *b;* **7.** *d;* **8.** *a;* **9.** *b;* **10.** *b;* **11.** *b;* **12.** *d;* **13.** *c;* **14.** *d;* **15.** *d*

CHAPTER 34 GENERAL EQUILIBRIUM: THE PRICE SYSTEM AND ITS OPERATION

Fill-in questions

1. particular, interrelationships

2. equilibrium, product, resource

3. *a.* the resources used to produce Z; *b.* other products which use these same resources; *c.* products which are substitutes for or complements to product Z; *d.* resources which are substitutes for the resources used to produce Z and other products

4. tastes, availability of resources, technology

5. downward, upward; *a.* (1) diminishing marginal utility, (2) diminishing marginal productivity; *b.* (1) increasing marginal cost, (2) work-leisure preferences

6. *a.* increase, decrease; *b.* P, Q; *c.* increase, decrease; *d.* C, D

7. *a.* P, Q; *b.* increase, decrease; *c.* increase, decrease; *d.* C, D; *e.* increase, decrease

8. *a.* substitutes, complements; *b.* increase, decrease; *c.* Q, P

9. satisfaction of the wants (welfare); *a.* marginal cost; *b.* minimum, least-cost; *c.* the same

10. imperfectly, ideal, incomplete, slow

11. technological progress, product variety

12. *a.* spillover costs, spillover benefits, social; *b.* distribution

13. producing, consuming (using), input, outputs

14. 7.5

15. performance, problems, policies

Problems and projects

2. *a.* From left to right: 75, 0, 75, 10, 400; *b.* 25; *c.* (1) 37½; (2) 15; (3) 8¾; (4) 35; *d.* (1) 8.8; (2) 13.6; (3) 2.9; (4) 8.97; *e.* each sector will have to increase its inputs in order to increase its output, and this will require still further increases in the outputs of the various sectors

Self-test

1. F; **2.** T; **3.** T; **4.** F; **5.** T; **6.** T; **7.** T; **8.** F; **9.** F; **10.** T; **11.** F; **12.** T

1. *b;* **2.** *a;* **3.** *d;* **4.** *c;* **5.** *b;* **6.** *d;* **7.** *c;* **8.** *a;* **9.** *c;* **10.** *c;* **11.** *d;* **12.** *a*

CHAPTER 35 ANTITRUST AND REGULATION

Fill-in questions

1. *a.* a few firms, both absolutely and relatively

2. misallocation, slows, unequal, dangers

3. interindustry, foreign (either order), scale, technological progress

4. competition, monopoly

5. monopol-, trade

6. discrimination, stock, tying, interlocking

7. unfair, hearings, cease-and-desist

8. Wheeler-Lea

9. Celler-Kefauver, Clayton

10. structure, narrowly, broadly (either order); *a.* reason, Alcoa; *b.* packaging materials

11. antitrust; *a.* (labor) unions, agricultural; *b.* patent, tariffs

12. natural, agencies, commissions (either order)

13. Interstate Commerce Commission, railroads

14. *a.* cost, capital, labor; *b.* the industry (firms) it is supposed to regulate; *c.* natural, competitive

15. monopoly, cartel

16. quality; *a.* conditions, society, character; *b.* industrial, economic (either order)

17. *a.* greater; *b.* inflation, slower, less

18. less

Problems and projects

1. *a.* C; *b.* F; *c.* A; *d.* E; *e.* D; *f.* B

2. *a.* S; *b.* S; *c.* L; *d.* L; *e.* S; *f.* L

Self-test

1. F; **2.** F; **3.** T; **4.** F; **5.** F; **6.** F; **7.** T; **8.** T; **9.** F; **10.** F; **11.** F; **12.** F; **13.** F; **14.** F; **15.** T; **16.** T; **17.** T; **18.** T

1. *d;* **2.** *b;* **3.** *d;* **4.** *a;* **5.** *b;* **6.** *d;* **7.** *a;* **8.** *a;* **9.** *d;* **10.** *c;* **11.** *c;* **12.** *d;* **13.** *c;* **14.** *d;* **15.** *d;* **16.** *a;* **17.** *b;* **18.** *b*

CHAPTER 36 RURAL ECONOMICS: THE FARM PROBLEM

Fill-in questions

1. *a.* prosperity; *b.* prosperity; *c.* depression; *d.* prosperity; *e.* depression; *f.* prosperity; *g.* depression

2. less, diverse; *a.* 12, 68; *b.* 71, 12; *c.* 16, 19

3. lag behind, instability

4. inelastic, greater, immobility

5. substitutes

6. technological

7. increased rapidly enough, less

8. immobile

9. inelastic, small, large, small, large

10. resources, the agricultural, nonagricultural

11. *a.* progress (economic growth); *b.* competitive, unable

12. enhance, stabilize (either order)

13. fixed

14. surpluses, purchase; *a.* incomes; *b.* prices, taxes to finance the government purchases

15. increase, decrease

16. allotment, reserve, in-kind, uses, consumption, export

17. target, surplus

18. *a* the target and the market price; *b.* the amount spent by consumers for the product; *c.* (1) the same, (2) less, inelastic, (3) greater than, (4) less, (5) like, over-

19. do not; *a.* reallocate, high, contradictions, decreasingly, more; *b.* macroeconomic, interest, (1) debts, (2) dollar, export

20. *a.* buy, sell; *b.* contract, allocation, taxpayers, export

Problems and projects

1. *a.* 4.20, 7.00; *b.* 90, 75

2. *a.* inelastic; *b.* decrease, 1,200.00, 700.00, 16⅔, decrease, 41⅔; *c.* fall, 1.00, 0.80, fall, 700.00, 560.00; *d.* (1) 100, (2) 180, (3) 1296, (4) 0.80, 576, (5) 720, (6) 1.00, 100

3. *a.* increase, 153,750.00, 200,000.00; *b.* increase, 153,750.00, 205,000.00

4. *a.* (1) 850, 1150, 300, (2) 1105, 390, 1495; *b.* (1) 1150, 0.70, (2) 805, 0.60, 690, 1495; *c.* 1495, (1) more, 300, (2) 300, 0.60, 300

5. *a.* .50, buy, 40; *b.* 1.00, sell, 60

Self-test

1. T; **2.** F; **3.** T; **4.** F; **5.** T; **6.** F; **7.** T; **8.** F; **9.** T; **10.** F; **11.** T; **12.** T; **13.** T; **14.** F; **15.** F; **16.** F; **17.** T; **18.** T; **19.** F; **20.** F; **21.** T; **22.** F

1. *c;* **2.** *d;* **3.** *a;* **4.** *d;* **5.** *a;* **6.** *c;* **7.** *d;* **8.** *c;* **9.** *d;* **10.** *d;* **11.** *b;* **12.** *c;* **13.** *a;* **14.** *b;* **15.** *b;* **16.** *c;* **17.** *a;* **18.** *b;* **19.** *b;* **20.** *d;* **21.** *b;* **22.** *c;* **23.** *a*

CHAPTER 37 URBAN ECONOMICS: THE PROBLEMS OF THE CITIES

Fill-in questions

1. 180, 76

2. how, transport, resources, buyers

3. surplus, labor

4. near (close to); *a.* internal economies of scale; *b.* locational (transport) economics; *c.* external economies of scale; *d.* infrastructure

5. higher, external, society, spillover

6. advantages, disadvantages, fragmentation, imbalance

7. *a.* property, rates; *b.* large, densely, high

8. *a.* trained and educated, suburbs, buildings; *b.* educated, low; *c.* central city, suburbs, mass transit, discrimination

9. jobs, education, training, maintenance

10. spiral, discrimination, controls

11. *a.* jobs; *b.* transportation; *c.* highways, congestion, pollution; *d.* highways, suburbs, automobiles, highways; *e.* public mass transit

12. *a.* user charge, peak-pricing; *b.* public mass-transit systems

13. wastes, nature (the ecological system), absorb (reabsorb or recycle), population, per capita income, technology, incentives

14. consolidation, revenues

15. decision, needs, means

16. sharing, the Federal government, land, buildings

Problems and projects

1. *a.* grossly inadequate; *b.* high; *c.* low; *d.* inadequate; *e.* old, deteriorated, crowded; *f.* high; *g.* deplorable; *h.* high

2. 300, 15, 30, 10, 510, 30, 5; *a.* 1800, 900; *b.* $.50; *c.* $.50; *d.* (1) 810, (2) total revenue: 225, 67.50, 90, 45, 270, 90, 22.50; 810, (3) 7am–9am, 4pm–6pm; *e.* (1) 55, (2) 64

3. *a.* 4,000, 2,500; *b.* 5,000; *c.* 7,500,000; *d.* 1,000, 1,500,000

Self-test

1. T; **2.** F; **3.** T; **4.** T; **5.** F; **6.** F; **7.** F; **8.** T; **9.** F; **10.** T; **11.** F; **12.** F; **13.** T; **14.** T; **15.** T; **16.** F; **17.** T; **18.** F; **19.** T; **20.** T

1. *c;* **2.** *c;* **3.** *a;* **4.** *a;* **5.** *b;* **6.** *a;* **7.** *c;* **8.** *b;* **9.** *d;* **10.** *a;* **11.** *b;* **12.** *d;* **13.** *a;* **14.** *c;* **15.** *b;* **16.** *b;* **17.** *d;* **18.** *c*

CHAPTER 38 INCOME DISTRIBUTION: INEQUALITY, POVERTY, AND DISCRIMINATION

Fill-in questions

1. considerable; *a.* decreased, increased, significant; *b.* has not

2. Lorenz; *a.* families, income; *b.* lower, upper; *c.* Lorenz curve, line of complete equality (either order)

3. narrow, short, less, smaller

4. reduce

5. ability, education, training, tastes, property, power

6. *a.* utility; *b.* income

7. equality, efficiency (either order); *a.* smaller; *b.* more

8. *a.* 10,609, 5,278; *b.* x, 34

9. *a.* young; *b.* blacks and Hispanics; *c.* women

10. invisible (hidden)

11. *a.* wage discrimination; *b.* employment discrimination; *c.* human-capital discrimination; *d.* occupational discrimination; 4, 160

12. crowding; *a.* low; *b.* more, expansion

13. insurance, assistance; *a.* (1) OASDI, care, (2) unemployment; *b.* (1) SSI, AFDC (either order), (2) food-stamp, (3) caid; *c.* efficient, equitable, centives

14. guaranteed, benefit-loss

15. *a.* poverty, incentives, costs; *b.* conflicting

Problems and projects

1. *a.* (1) column 4: 18, 30, 44, 61, 80, 91, 100; (2) column 5: 4, 10, 22, 36, 51, 71, 100; *b.* (1) 30, 10; (2) 20, 49

2. *a.* (1) 3, (2) 9; *b.* (1) (*a*) 7, (*b*) 18, (2) (*a*) 7, (*b*) 15, 30 (*c*) 12

3. *a.* NIT subsidy: 4,000, 3,000, 2,000, 1,000, 0; Total income: 9,000, 13,000, 17,000, 21,000, 25,000; (1) 4,000, (2) 25,000; *b.* NIT subsidy: 3,750, 2,500, 1,250, 0; Total income: 6,250, 7,500, 8,750, 10,000; (1) 10,000, (2) 2,500; *c.* NIT subsidy: 6,000, 4,500, 3,000, 1,500, 0; Total income: 9,000, 10,500, 12,000, 13,500, 15,000; (1) 15,000, (2) 18,750; *d.* (1) greater, greater, (2) greater, (3) increase, decrease

Self-test

1. T; **2.** T; **3.** F; **4.** T; **5.** F; **6.** T; **7.** F; **8.** F; **9.** T; **10.** T; **11.** T; **12.** F; **13.** T; **14.** T; **15.** F

1. *d;* **2.** *d;* **3.** *c;* **4.** *d;* **5.** *d;* **6.** *b;* **7.** *b;* **8.** *a;* **9.** *c;* **10.** *a;* **11.** *b;* **12.** *d;* **13.** *c;* **14.** *b;* **15.** *d*

CHAPTER 39: LABOR UNIONS AND THEIR ECONOMIC IMPACT

Fill-in questions

1. 17, 15

2. courts, recognize, bargain

3. criminal conspiracy, injunctions

4. discriminatory discharge, blacklisting, lockout, strikebreakers, yellow-dog contracts, paternalism, company unions

5. business unionism, political neutrality, craft unionism

6. Norris-LaGuardia, Wagner, CIO, industrial, both skilled and unskilled

7. organize, bargain collectively, National Labor Relations, management

8. Taft-Hartley, Landrum-Griffin, merger

9. decreased, decreased

10. structural-change, substitution, managerial-opposition (any order)

11. *a.* the degree of recognition and status accorded the union and the prerogatives of management; *b.* wages and hours; *c.* seniority and job opportunities; *d.* a procedure for settling grievances (any order)

12. not only, continuous, dynamic

13. increase, decrease, have no effect on

14. *a.* (1) featherbedding, work, (2) strikes, (3) above-, misallocation; *b.* (1) shock, capital, labor, decrease, (2) decrease, (3) seniority, informal, younger, older

15. *a.* high, unionized, low, nonunionized; *b.* the same, the same

16. *a.* result, cause; *b.* demand, supply; *c.* perpetuates, more, long-

Problems and projects

1. 1. K; 2. D; 3. Q; 4. E; 5. I; 6. G; 7. A; 8. C; 9. F; 10. J

2. *a.* T; *b.* W; *c.* W; *d.* N; *e.* L; *f.* T; *g.* T; *h.* W

3. *a.* 70, 40; *b.* (1) fall, 20, (2) contract, 150; *c.* (1) fall, 50, (2) expand, 110; *d.* contracted, 40

Self-test

1. F; **2.** F; **3.** T; **4.** F; **5.** F; **6.** F; **7.** F; **8.** F; **9.** F; **10.** T; **11.** T; **12.** F; **13.** T; **14.** T; **15.** F; **16.** F; **17.** T; **18.** F; **19.** F; **20.** T

1. *a;* **2.** *b;* **3.** *d;* **4.** *a;* **5.** *a;* **6.** *d;* **7.** *b;* **8.** *c;* **9.** *b;* **10.** *b;* **11.** *a;* **12.** *b;* **13.** *a;* **14.** *c;* **15.** *a;* **16.** *d;* **17.** *a;* **18.** *c;* **19.** *d;* **20.** *d*

CHAPTER 40 THE RADICAL CRITIQUE: THE ECONOMICS OF DISSENT

Fill-in questions

1. nature; *a.* other; *b.* bourgeois, proletariat

2. property, employment (a livelihood), surplus value, wage, value

3. competition, profits (surplus value), national, labor, profit

4. exploitation

5. *a.* the monopolization of; *b.* imperialism

6. revolution, proletariat, capital, capitalistic, socialistic (classless)

7. *a.* harmony, conflict; *b.* narrow, political

8. *a.* large (monopolistic), state (government), markets, workers, consumers; *b.* inequality, imperialism; *c.* socialism

9. *a.* It fails to control monopolies; *b.* It uses revenues from regressive taxes to subsidize them; *c.* It provides markets for them

10. marginal revenue product, national income; *a.* competitive; *b.* labor; *c.* unearned

11. *a.* private, power; *b.* dual, primary, secondary

12. *a.* lives, decision; *b.* large corporations

13. *a.* profit; *b.* environment, military, imperialistic

14. socialism, democratic, profits

15. reality, objective, ideology, option

Problems and projects

1. *a.* 8, 7, 6, 5, 4, 3, 2; *b.* 5; *c.* 20; *d.* 30, 10; *e.* 6; *f.* 2

2. *a.* 400, 394, 388.6; *b.* 70, 69, 68; *c.* 120, 118, 116.6; *d.* (1) 380, 386, 392.4, (2) .316, .306, .297; *e.* (1) decreases, increases, (2) decreases

Self-test

1. F; **2.** T; **3.** T; **4.** F; **5.** T; **6.** F; **7.** T; **8.** F; **9.** T; **10.** T; **11.** F; **12.** T; **13.** F; **14.** F; **15.** T; **16.** F; **17.** F; **18.** T; **19.** F; **20.** T

1. *b;* **2.** *d;* **3.** *a;* **4.** *c;* **5.** *d;* **6.** *a;* **7.** *c;* **8.** *d;* **9.** *b;* **10.** *d;* **11.** *d;* **12.** *b;* **13.** *c;* **14.** *d;* **15.** *b;* **16.** *b;* **17.** *a;* **18.** *d*

CHAPTER 41 INTERNATIONAL TRADE: COMPARATIVE ADVANTAGE AND PROTECTIONISM

Fill-in questions

1. 10

2. less, money (currency), greater

3. uneven, different

4. comparative advantage, comparative advantage

5. *a.* inexpensive, expensive; *b.* expensive, inexpensive; *c.* hats, bananas; *d.* 3, 4, world demand and supply for hats and bananas; *e.* (1) ⅓, 2/7, (2) 4, 3½; *f.* increases

6. allocation, standard

7. tariffs, import, tariff, voluntary export

8. special interest, decrease, less

9. *a.* increase; *b.* decrease; *c.* (1) increase, (2) decrease; *d.* decrease, decrease

10. *a.* military self-sufficiency; *b.* infant industry; *c.* increase domestic employment; *d.* diversification for stability; *e.* cheap foreign labor; military-self-sufficiency, infant-industry

11. upward, Reciprocal Trade Agreements, downward, tariff, 50, most-favored-nation

12. *a.* equal, nondiscriminatory treatment of all trading nations; *b.* reduction of tariffs by negotiation; *c.* elimination of import quotas

13. tariffs and import quotas, nonmember, capital, labor

14. *a.* the freer trade that resulted from past reductions in trade barriers; *b.* the increased competition from abroad that resulted from a more open economy; *c.* the increased competitiveness of foreign products that resulted from lower labor costs and prices abroad; *d.* the increased international value of the dollar; *e.* worldwide recession

15. prices; *a.* greater; *b.* lowest

Problems and projects

1. *a.* constant; *b.* (1) 8, 2, (2) 4, 2; *c.* (1) it has a comparative advantage in producing wheat (its cost of producing wheat is less than Chile's), (2) it has a comparative advantage in producing copper (its cost of producing copper is less than the United

States'), *d.* one of the two nations would be unwilling to trade if the terms of trade are outside this range; *f.* (1) 1, 0, (2) 1, 0

2. *a.* 750, 700, 650, 600, 550, 500, 450, 300, 0; *b.* $2.00, 600; *c.* 375, 350, 325, 300, 0, 0, 0, 0, 0; *d.* 650, 600, 550, 500, 175, 150, 125, 0, 0; *e.* $2.20, 550; *f.* (1) increased, 25, (2) decreased, 75; *g.* (1) increased, $95, (2) decreased, $345; *h.* increased, $10; *i.* increased, $260; *j.* decreased, $345, decrease, $345

Self-test

1. F; **2.** T; **3.** T; **4.** F; **5.** F; **6.** T; **7.** T; **8.** T; **9.** F; **10.** F; **11.** T; **12.** T; **13.** F; **14.** T; **15.** F; **16.** T; **17.** T; **18.** T; **19.** T; **20.** T

1. *d;* **2.** *a;* **3.** *b;* **4.** *a;* **5.** *c;* **6.** *c;* **7.** *d;* **8.** *a;* **9.** *a;* **10.** *c;* **11.** *b;* **12.** *d;* **13.** *a;* **14.** *a;* **15.** *c;* **16.** *d;* **17.** *d;* **18.** *c;* **19.** *d;* **20.** *d;* **21.** *d*

CHAPTER 42 EXCHANGE RATES AND THE BALANCE OF PAYMENTS

Fill-in questions

1. francs, dollar

2. 3⅓

3. *a.* supply of, demand for, increase, decrease; *b.* demand for, supply of, decrease, increase

4. transportation, insurance (either order), interest, dividends (either order)

5. the other nations of the world; *a.* credit, +; *b.* debit, −

6. *a.* less, merchandise; *b.* greater; *c.* investment, remittances, negative

7. *a.* in that nation, other nations, in other nations, that nation, real, financial (either order); *b.* greater

8. *a.* selling, borrowing; *b.* buy, lend

9. foreign monies, central; *a.* decrease; *b.* increase; *c.* zero

10. negative, decrease, positive, increase

11. *a.* depreciate, appreciate; *b.* decrease, increase, decrease

12. *a.* depreciate; *b.* appreciate; *c.* depreciate; *d.* depreciate; *e.* depreciate

13. diminish, worsened, recession, inflation (either order)

14. *a.* sell; *b.* buy

15. *a.* taxing, subsidizing; *b.* import, export, government

16. contractionary, recession

17. gold, money, stock, exported, imported

18. *a.* stable; *b.* (1) out of, (2) decreased, rose, (3) fell, recession

19. fixed, adjustable-peg; *a.* gold, dollars (either order); *b.* buying, exchange-stabilization, selling, borrowing from; *c.* devalue; *d.* gold, dollars (either order); *e.* stable, flexible

20. *a.* deficits; *b.* gold; *c.* decreased; *d.* eliminated, continued

21. gold, market forces (demand and supply), fixed, floating

22. managed floating; *a.* stable; *b.* imbalances

Problems and projects

1. *a.* (1) 3, (2) (*a*) 3, dollars, (*b*) 150, pesos; *b.* (1) 3, (2) (*a*) 3, (*b*) 3; *c.* (1) demand for, supply of, (2) increased, decreased

2. *a.* −50, −35, −30, +25, −5, +5; *b.* deficit, 5

3. *a.* (1) 4.00, (2) ¼, (3) 300, (4) 1200; *b.* buy, 300, 1500; *c.* sell, 380, 950

Self-test

1. T; **2.** F; **3.** T; **4.** F; **5.** T; **6.** F; **7.** T; **8.** F; **9.** T; **10.** T; **11.** T; **12.** F; **13.** T; **14.** T; **15.** T; **16.** F; **17.** T; **18.** F; **19.** F; **20.** T; **21.** T; **22.** T; **23.** T; **24.** T; **25.** T; **26.** F; **27.** F; **28.** F

1. *c;* **2.** *d;* **3.** *a;* **4.** *c;* **5.** *c;* **6.** *d;* **7.** *d;* **8.** *b;* **9.** *b;* **10.** *c;* **11.** *b;* **12.** *b;* **13.** *d;* **14.** *c;* **15.** *a;* **16.** *d;* **17.** *a;* **18.** *b;* **19.** *c;* **20.** *d;* **21.** *d;* **22.** *d;* **23.** *d;* **24.** *c;* **25.** *a;* **26.** *a;* **27.** *a;* **28.** *a*

CHAPTER 43 INTERNATIONAL ECONOMIC ISSUES

Fill-in questions

1. increases, deficits, imports, exports

2. *a.* strong; *b.* rapid; *c.* reduced

3. *a.* more, less, decreased, increased; *b.* high, deficits, tight, low

4. *a.* rose; *b.* restrictive, devalue, exports, imports

5. contract, slow, lower, increase, creditor, debtor

6. fall, contraction

7. *a.* full employment without inflation; *b.* a zero current-account balance; *c.* domestic

8. *a.* conflicts; *b.* conflicts

9. *a.* tariffs, currency; *b.* fluctuate; *c.* monetary

10. 500,000, 500,000 to 1 million

11. *a.* increase, decrease, increase; *b.* decrease, increase, decrease; *c.* increase

12. *a.* including the costs of migration; *b.* remittances and backflows; *c.* the amounts of unemployment in the two nations; *d.* the fiscal aspects in the country receiving the immigrants

Problems and projects

1. *a.* (1) contractionary, tight, (2) (*a*) increase, (*b*) decrease, (*c*) decrease, (3) reduce, (4) widened; *b.* (1) expansionary, easy, (2) (*a*) decrease, (*b*) increase, (*c*) increase, (3) widen, (4) narrowed

2. *a.* (1) 14, (2) 8; *b.* (1) 1540, 600, (2) 320, 270; *c.* (1) fall, 12, (2)

rise, 10; *d.* (1) increase, 60, (2) decrease, 40, (3) 20; *e.* increased, 220, decreased, 70

Self-test

1. F; **2.** T; **3.** T; **4.** F; **5.** T; **6.** T; **7.** F; **8.** F; **9.** F; **10.** T; **11.** F; **12.** T; **13.** T; **14.** T; **15.** F; **16.** T; **17.** T; **18.** T; **19.** T; **20.** F

1. *c;* **2.** *d;* **3.** *b;* **4.** *a;* **5.** *d;* **6.** *a;* **7.** *c;* **8.** *c;* **9.** *d;* **10.** *c;* **11.** *d;* **12.** *c;* **13.** *c;* **14.** *c;* **15.** *b;* **16.** *b;* **17.** *b;* **18.** *c*

CHAPTER 44 THE ECONOMY OF THE SOVIET UNION

Fill-in questions

1. *a.* labor; *b.* privately, subsistence, surplus; *c.* publicly, class, proletariat

2. state, central economic

3. *a.* government; *b.* educational, wage

4. government (state), Communist

5. Five, One (either order)

6. coordination, bottleneck, chain

7. balances, materials (inputs), negotiation, priority, reserve stocks (inventories), second economy

8. *Gosplan, Gosbank*

9. monetary, nonmonetary (either order), work

10. efficiency, rationing

11. expand, more

12. 60, 3.4

13. *a.* the large natural resource base; *b.* the totalitarian government has allocated resources to promote growth; *c.* the surplus of farm labor; *d.* the employment of the superior technologies developed in Western nations; *e.* the absence of cyclical unemployment

14. *a.* the diversion of resources to military uses; *b.* a manpower (labor) shortage; *c.* the backwardness of Soviet agriculture; *d.* a lower rate of increase in labor productivity

15. natural resources, innovation, technological, discipline, planning

16. *a.* the increased quantity and quality of education; *b.* the development of a complete system of social insurance; the failure of the consumer's standard of living to increase by as much as is possible; the limited freedom of Soviet citizens

Problems and projects

1. state ownership of property resources; relative consumer freedom to spend income as he or she sees fit; central economic planning; workers are generally free to choose occupation and place of work; central economic planning and various forms of incentives; central economic planning; central economic planning with prices playing an implemental role; central economic planning and various forms of incentives which appeal to self-interest; state and collective farms; state-owned and cooperative firms and retail stores

2. *a.* 40; *b.* 60

Self-test

1. T; **2.** T; **3.** T; **4.** T; **5.** T; **6.** F; **7.** T; **8.** F; **9.** F; **10.** F; **11.** T; **12.** T; **13.** T; **14.** F; **15.** T; **16.** F

1. *b;* **2.** *d;* **3.** *d;* **4.** *d;* **5.** *b;* **6.** *c;* **7.** *a;* **8.** *b;* **9.** *b;* **10.***a;* **11.** *d;* **12.** *b;* **13.** *a;* **14.** *d;* **15.** *b;* **16.** *b*

Glossary

Ability-to-pay principle The belief that those who have the greater income (or wealth) should be taxed absolutely and relatively more than those who have less.

Abstraction Elimination of irrelevant and noneconomic facts to obtain an economic principle.

Accelerationist hypothesis The contention that the negatively sloped Phillips curve (*see*) does not exist in the long run and that attempts to reduce the Unemployment rate bring about an accelerating rate of Inflation.

Acreage-allotment program The program which determined the total number of acres that was to be used to produce various agricultural products and allocated these acres among individual farmers who were required to limit their plantings to the number of acres allotted to them if they wished to obtain the Support price for their crops.

Acreage-reserve program A program in which the Federal government made payments to farmers who took land away from the production of crops.

Actual budget The amount spent by the Federal government (to purchase goods and services and for transfer payments) less the amount of tax revenue collected by it in any (fiscal) year; and which is *not* to be used to determine whether it is pursuing an expansionary or contractionary fiscal policy. Compare with (*see*) the Full-employment budget.

Actual investment The amount which business Firms do invest; equal to Planned investment plus unplanned investment.

Actual reserve The amount which a Member bank has on deposit at the Federal Reserve bank of its district (plus its Vault cash).

Adjustable pegs The device utilized in the Bretton Woods system (*see*) to change Exchange rates in an orderly way to eliminate persistent Payments deficits and surpluses: each nation defined its monetary unit in terms of (pegged it to) gold or the dollar, kept the Rate of exchange for its money stable in the short run, and changed (adjusted) it in the long run when faced with international disequilibrium.

AFDC (*See* Aid to families with dependent children.)

Aggregate demand A schedule or curve which shows the total quantity of goods and services that will be demanded (purchased) at different levels.

Aggregate demand-aggregate supply model The macroeconomic model which uses Aggregate demand and Aggregate supply (*see both*) to determine and explain the Price level and the real National output.

Aggregate expenditures The total amount spent for final goods and services in the economy.

Aggregate expenditures-national output approach Determination of the Equilibrium net national product (*see*) by finding the real NNP at which Aggregate expenditures are equal to the National output.

Aggregate-expenditures schedule A schedule or curve which shows the total amount spent for final goods and services at different levels of real NNP.

Aggregate supply A schedule or curve which shows the total quantity of goods and services that will be supplied (produced) at different price levels.

Agricultural Adjustment Act The Federal act of 1933 which established the Parity concept (*see*) as the cornerstone of American agricultural policy and provided Price supports for farm products, restriction of agricultural production, and the disposal of surplus output.

Aid to families with dependent children A state-administered and partly Federally funded program in the United States which provides aid to families in which dependent children do not have the support of a parent because of his or her death, disability, or desertion.

Alcoa case The case decided by the Federal courts in 1945 in which the courts ruled that the possession of monopoly power, no matter how reasonably that power had been used, was a violation of the antitrust laws; and which overturned the Rule of reason (*see*) applied in the U.S. Steel case (*see*).

Alienation The inability of individuals to take part in the process by which the decisions that affect them are made and to control their own lives and activities.

Allocative efficiency The apportionment of resources among firms and industries to obtain the production of the products most wanted by society (consumers): the output of each product at which its Marginal cost and Price are equal.

Allocative factor The ability of an economy to reallocate resources to achieve the Economic growth which the Supply factors (*see*) make possible.

American Federation of Labor The organization of affiliated Craft unions formed in 1886.

Annually balanced budget The equality of government expenditures and tax collections during a year.

Anticipated inflation Inflation (*see*) at a rate which was equal to the rate expected in that period of time.

Applied economics (*See* Policy economics.)

Arbitration The designation of a neutral third party to render a decision in a dispute by which both parties (the employer and the labor union) agree in advance to abide.

Asset Anything with a monetary value owned by a firm or individual.

Asset demand for money The amount of money people want to hold as a Store of value (the amount of their financial assets they wish to have in the form of Money); and which varies inversely with the Rate of interest.

ATS account Automatic transfer service account (*see*).

Authoritarian capitalism An economic system (method of organization) in which property resources are privately owned and government extensively directs and controls the economy.

Authoritarian socialism (*See* Command economy.)

Automatic transfer service account The combination of a Checking account and an interest-bearing Savings account at a Commercial bank that automatically transfers funds from the latter to the former account when checks are written against it.

Average fixed costs The total Fixed cost (*see*) of a Firm divided by its output (the quantity of product produced).

Average product Average physical product; the total output produced per unit of a resource employed (total product divided by the quantity of a resource employed).

Average propensity to consume Fraction of Disposable income which households spend for consumer goods and services; consumption divided by Disposable income.

Average propensity to save Fraction of Disposable income which households save; Saving divided by Disposable income.

Average revenue Total revenue from the sale of a product divided by the quantity of the product sold (demanded); equal to the price at which the product is sold so long as all units of the product are sold at the same price.

Average tax rate Total tax paid divided by total (taxable) income; the tax rate on total (taxable) income.

Average (total) cost The Total cost of a Firm divided by its output (the quantity of product produced); equal to Average fixed cost (*see*) plus Average variable cost (*see*).

Average variable cost The total Variable cost (*see*) of a Firm divided by its output (the quantity of product produced).

Backflows The return of workers to the countries from which they originally migrated.

Balanced-budget multiplier The effect of equal increases (decreases) in government spending for goods and services and in taxes is to increase (decrease) the Equilibrium net national product by the amount of the equal increases (decreases).

Balance of payments deficit The sum of the Balance on current account (*see*) and the Balance on the capital account (*see*) is negative.

Balance of payments surplus The sum of the Balance on current account (*see*) and the Balance on the capital account (*see*) is positive.

Balance on current account The exports of goods (merchandise) and services of a nation less its imports of goods (merchandise) and services plus its Net investment income and Net transfers.

Balance on goods and services The exports of goods (merchandise) and services of a nation less its imports of goods (merchandise) and services.

Balance on the capital account The Capital inflows (*see*) of a nation less its Capital outflows (*see*).

Balance sheet A statement of the Assets (*see*), Liabilities (*see*), and Net worth (*see*) of a Firm or individual at some given time.

Bankers' bank A bank which accepts the deposits of and makes loans to Depository institutions; a Federal Reserve Bank.

Barrier to entry Anything that artificially prevents the entry of Firms into an industry.

Barter The exchange of one good or service for another good or service.

Base year The year with which prices in other years are compared when a Price index (*see*) is constructed.

Basic social capital Public utilities, roads, communication systems, railways, housing, and educational and public health facilities; the Capital goods which must exist before there can be profitable (productive) investments in manufacturing, agriculture, and commerce.

Benefit-cost analysis Deciding whether to employ resources and the quantity of resources to employ for a project or program (for the production of a good or service) by comparing the benefit with the cost.

Benefit-loss rate The percentage of any increase in earned income by which subsidy benefits in a Negative income tax plan (*see*) are reduced.

Benefits-received principle The belief that those who receive the benefits of goods and services provided by government should pay the taxes required to finance them.

Big business A business Firm which either produces a large percentage of the total output of an industry, is large (in terms of number of employees or stockholders, sales, assets, or profits) compared with other Firms in the economy, or both.

Big tradeoff (*See* Equality vs. efficiency tradeoff.)

Bilateral monopoly A market in which there is a single seller (Monopoly) and a single buyer (Monopsony).

Black capitalism The creation of new business Firms owned and operated by Negroes.

Blacklisting The passing from one employer to another of the names of workers who favor the formation of labor unions and who ought not to be hired.

"Block" grant An Unrestricted grant (*see*).

Board of Governors The seven-member group that supervises and controls the money and banking system of the United States; formally, the Board of Governors of the Federal Reserve System; the Federal Reserve Board.

Bourgeois The capitalists; the capitalistic class; the owners of the machinery and equipment needed for production in an industrial society.

Break-even income The level of Disposable income at which Households plan to consume (spend) all of their income (for consumer goods and services) and to save none of it.

Break-even point Any output which a (competitive) Firm might produce at which its Total cost and Total revenue would be equal; an output at which it has neither profit nor a loss.

Bretton Woods system The international monetary system developed after World War II in which Adjustable pegs (*see*) were employed, the International Monetary Fund (*see*) helped to stabilize Foreign exchange rates, and gold and the Key currencies (*see*) were used as International monetary reserves (*see*).

Budget deficit The amount by which the expenditures of the Federal government exceed its revenues in any year.

Budget line A curve which shows the different combinations of two products a consumer can purchase with a given money income.

Budget restraint The limit imposed upon the ability of an individual consumer to obtain goods and services by the size of the consumer's income (and by the prices that must be paid for the goods and services).

Built-in stability The effect of Nondiscretionary fiscal policy (*see*) upon the economy; when Net taxes vary directly with the Net national product the fall (rise) in Net taxes during a recession (inflation) helps to eliminate unemployment (inflationary pressures).

Business cycle Recurrent ups and downs over a period of years in the level of economic activity.

Business unionism The belief that the labor union should concern itself with such practical and short-run objectives as higher wages, shorter hours, and improved working conditions and should not concern itself with long-run idealistic changes in the capitalistic system.

Capacity-creating aspect of investment The effect of investment spending on the productive capacity (the ability to produce goods and services) of an economy.

Capital Man-made resources used to produce goods and services; goods which do not directly satisfy human wants; Capital goods.

Capital account The section in a nation's International balance of payments (*see*) in which are recorded the Capital inflows (*see*) and the Capital outflows (*see*) of that nation.

Capital account deficit A negative Balance on the capital account (*see*).

Capital account surplus A positive Balance on the capital account (*see*).

Capital consumption allowances Estimate of the amount of Capital worn out or used up (consumed) in producing the Gross national product.

Capital gain The gain realized when securities or properties are sold for a price greater than the price paid for them.

Capital goods (*See* Capital.)

Capital inflow The expenditures made by the residents of foreign nations to purchase real and financial capital from the residents of a nation.

Capital-intensive commodity A product in the production of which a relatively large amount of Capital is employed.

Capital outflow The expenditures made by the residents of a nation to purchase real and financial capital from the residents of foreign nations.

Capital-output ratio The ratio of the stock of Capital to the productive (output) capacity of the economy; and the ratio of a change in the stock of Capital (net investment) to the resulting change in productive capacity.

Capital-saving technological advance An improvement in technology that permits a greater quantity of a product to be produced with a given amount of Capital (or the same amount of the product to be produced with a smaller amount of Capital).

Capital-using technological advance An improvement in technology that requires the use of a greater amount of Capital to produce a given quantity of a product.

Cartel A formal written or oral agreement among Firms to set the price of the product and the outputs of the individual firms or to divide the market for the product geographically.

"Categorical" grant A Restricted grant (*see*).

Causation A cause-and-effect relationship; one or several events bring about or result in another event.

CEA (*See* Council of Economic Advisers.)

Cease-and-desist order An order from a court or government agency (commission or board) to corporation or individual to stop engaging in a specified practice.

Ceiling price (*See* Price ceiling.)

Celler-Kefauver Act The Federal act of 1950 which amended the Clayton Act (*see*) by prohibiting the acquisition of the assets of one firm by another firm when the effect would be to lessen competition.

Central bank A bank whose chief function is the control of the nation's money supply.

Central economic planning Determination of the objectives of the economy and the direction of its resources to the attainment of these objectives by the national government.

CETA Comprehensive Employment and Training Act of 1973 (*see*).

***Ceteris paribus* assumption** (*See* "Other things equal" assumption.)

Change in amount consumed Increase or decrease in consumption spending that results from an increase or decrease in Disposable income, the Consumption schedule (curve) remaining unchanged; movement from one line (point) to another on the same Consumption schedule (curve).

Change in amount saved Increase or decrease in Saving that results from an increase or decrease in Disposable income, the Saving schedule (curve) remaining unchanged; movement from one line (point) to another on the same Saving schedule (curve).

Change in the consumption schedule An increase or decrease in consumption at each level of Disposable income caused by changes in the Nonincome determinants of consumption and saving (*see*); an upward or downward movement of the Consumption schedule.

Change in the saving schedule An increase or decrease in Saving at each level of Disposable income caused by changes in the Nonincome determinants of consumption and saving (*see*); an upward or downward movement of the Saving schedule.

Checkable deposit Any deposit in a commercial bank or Thrift institution against which a check may be written; includes Demand deposits and NOW, ATS, and Share draft accounts.

Checking account A Demand deposit (*see*) in a Commercial bank.

Circuit velocity of money (*See* Income velocity of money.)

Circular flow of income The flow of resources from Households to Firms and of products from Firms to Households accompanied in an economy using money by flows of money from Households to Firms and from Firms to Households.

Classical range The vertical segment of the Aggregate-supply curve along which the economy is at Full employment.

Classical theory The Classical theory of employment (*see*).

Classical theory of employment The Macroeconomic generalizations which were accepted by most economists prior to the 1930s and which led to the conclusion that a capitalistic economy would tend to employ its resources fully.

Class struggle The struggle for the output of the economy between the Proletariat (*see*) and the Bourgeois (*see*) in a capitalistic society.

Clayton Act The Federal antitrust act of 1914 which strengthened the Sherman Act (*see*) by making it illegal for business firms to engage in certain specified practices.

Closed economy An economy which neither exports nor imports goods and services.

(The) close-down case The circumstances which would result in a loss greater than its Total fixed cost if a (competitive) Firm were to produce any output greater than zero and which would induce it to cease (close down) production (the plant); when the price at which the Firm can sell its product is less than Average variable cost.

Closed shop A place of employment at which only workers who are already members of a labor union may be hired.

Club of Rome An international group of scientists, businessmen, and academicians which contends that future economic growth in the world is impossible; which bases its predictions on a Doomsday model (*see*); and which advocates ZEG (*see*) and ZPG (*see*).

Coincidence of wants The item (good or service) which one trader wishes to obtain is the same item which another trader desires to give up and the item which the second trader wishes to acquire is the same item the first trader desires to surrender.

COLA (*See* Cost-of-living adjustment.)

Collection of checks The process by which funds are transferred from the checking accounts of the writers of checks to the checking accounts of the recipients of the checks; also called the "clearing" of checks.

Collective voice The function a union performs for its members as a group when it communicates their problems and grievances to management and presses management for a satisfactory resolution to them.

Collusive oligopoly An Oligopoly in which the Firms act together and in agreement (collude) to set the price of the product and the output each firm will produce or to determine the geographic area in which each firm will sell.

Command economy An economic system (method of organization) in which property resources are publicly owned and Central economic planning (*see*) is used to direct and coordinate economic activities.

Commercial bank Firm which has a charter from either a state government or the Federal government to engage in the business of banking.

Commercial banking system All Commercial banks as a group.

Communism (*See* Command economy.)

Company union An organization of employees which is dominated by the employer (the company) and does not engage in genuine collective bargaining with the employer.

Comparable worth doctrine The belief that women should receive the same salaries (wages) as men when the levels of skill, effort, and responsibility in their different jobs are comparable (the same).

Comparative advantage A lower Comparative cost (*see*) than another producer.

Comparative cost The amount the production of one product must be reduced to increase the production of another product; Opportunity cost (*see*).

Compensation to employees Wages and salaries paid by employers to workers plus Wage and salary supplements (*see*).

Competing goods (*See* Substitute goods.)

Competition The presence in a market of several independent buyers and sellers and the freedom of buyers and sellers to enter and to leave the market.

(The) competitive industry's short-run supply curve The horizontal summation of the short-run supply curves of the Firms in a purely competitive industry (*see* Pure competition); a curve which shows the total quantities that will be offered for sale at various prices by the Firms in an industry in the Short run (*see*).

(The) competitive industry's short-run supply schedule The summation of the short-run supply schedules of the Firms in a purely competitive industry (*see* Pure competition); a schedule which shows the total quantities that will be offered for sale at various prices by the Firms in an industry in the Short run (*see*).

Competitive labor market A market in which a large number of (noncolluding) firms demand a particular type of labor from a large number of nonunionized workers.

Complementary goods Goods or services such that there is an inverse relationship between the price of one and the demand for the other; when the price of one falls (rises) the demand for the other increases (decreases).

Complex multiplier The Multiplier (*see*) when changes in the Net national product not only change Saving but also change Net taxes and Imports.

Comprehensive Employment and Training Act of 1973 Federal legislation which provides for grants to state and local governments to develop manpower training programs appropriate to their areas of jurisdiction.

Concentration ratio The percentage of the total sales of an industry made by the four (or some other number) largest sellers (Firms) in the industry.

Conglomerate combination A group of Plants (*see*) owned by a single Firm and engaged at one or more stages in the production of different products (of products which do not compete with each other).

Conglomerate merger The merger of a Firm in one Industry with a Firm in another Industry (with a Firm that is neither supplier, customer, nor competitor).

Congress of Industrial Organizations The organization of affiliated Industrial unions formed in 1936.

Constant-cost industry An Industry in which the expansion of the Industry by the entry of new Firms has no effect upon the prices the Firms in the industry pay for resources and no effect, therefore, upon their cost schedules (curves).

Consumer goods Goods and services which satisfy human wants directly.

Consumer sovereignty Determination by consumers of the types and quantities of goods and services that are produced from the scarce resources of the economy.

Consumption schedule Schedule which shows the amounts Households plan to spend for Consumer goods at different levels of Disposable income.

Contractionary fiscal policy A decrease in Aggregate demand brought about by a decrease in Government expenditures for goods and services, an increase in Net taxes, or some combination of the two.

"Control by the ruble" The requirement in the U.S.S.R. that each plant's receipts and expenditures be completed through the use of checks drawn on *Gosbank* (*see*) which enables *Gosbank* to record the performance and progress of each plant toward the fulfillment of the production targets assigned it by *Gosplan*.

Corporate income tax A tax levied on the net income (profit) of Corporations.

Corporation A legal entity ("person") chartered by a state or the Federal government, and distinct and separate from the individuals who own it.

Correlation Systematic and dependable association between two sets of data (two kinds of events).

Cost-of-living adjustment An increase in the incomes (wages) of workers which is automatically received by them when there is inflation in the economy and guaranteed by a clause in their labor contracts with their employer.

Cost-plus pricing A procedure used by (oligopolistic) Firms to determine the price they will charge for a product and in which a percentage markup is added to the estimated average cost of producing the product.

Cost-push inflation Inflation that results from a decrease in Aggregate supply (from higher wage rates and raw material prices) and which is accompanied by decreases in real output and employment (by increases in the Unemployment rate).

Cost ratio The ratio of the decrease in the production of one product to the increase in the production of another product when resources are shifted from the production of the first to the production of the second product; the amount the production of one product decreases when the production of second product increases by one unit.

Council of Economic Advisers A group of three persons which advises and assists the President of the United States on economic matters (including the preparation of the economic report of the President to Congress).

Craft union A labor union which limits its membership to workers with a particular skill (craft).

Credit An accounting notation that the value of an asset (such as the foreign money owned by the residents of a nation) has increased.

Credit union An association of persons who have a common tie (such as being employees of the same Firm or members of the same Labor union) which sells shares to (accepts deposits from) its members and makes loans to them.

Criminal-conspiracy doctrine The (now outdated) legal doctrine that combinations of workers (Labor unions) to raise wages were criminal conspiracies and, therefore, illegal.

Crowding model of occupational discrimination A model of labor markets that assumes Occupational discrimination (*see*) against women and blacks has kept them out of many occupations and forced them into a limited number of other occupations in which the large Supply of labor (relative to the Demand) results in lower wages and incomes.

Crowding-out effect The rise in interest rates and the resulting decrease in planned net investment spending in the economy caused by increased borrowing in the money market by the Federal government.

Currency Coins and Paper money.

Currency appreciation (*See* Exchange rate appreciation.)

Currency depreciation (*See* Exchange rate depreciation.)

Current account The section in a nation's International balance of payments (*see*) in which are recorded its exports and imports of goods (merchandise) and services, its net investment income, and its net transfers.

Current account deficit A negative Balance on current account (*see*).

Current account surplus A positive Balance on current account (*see*).

Customary economy (*See* Traditional economy.)

Cyclically balanced budget The equality of Government expenditures for goods and services and Net taxes collections over the course of a Business cycle; deficits incurred during periods of recession are offset by surpluses obtained during periods of prosperity (inflation).

Cyclical unemployment Unemployment caused by insufficient Aggregate expenditures.

Debit An accounting notation that the value of an asset (such as the foreign money owned by the residents of a nation) has decreased.

Declining economy An economy in which Net private domestic investment (*see*) is less than zero (Gross private domestic investment is less than Depreciation).

Declining industry An industry in which Economic profits are negative (losses are incurred) and which will, therefore, decrease its output as Firms leave the industry.

Decrease in demand A decrease in the Quantity demanded of a good or service at every price; a shift of the Demand curve to the left.

Decrease in supply A decrease in the Quantity supplied of a good or service at every price; a shift of the Supply curve to the left.

Deduction Reasoning from assumptions to conclusions; a method of reasoning that tests a hypothesis (an assumption) by comparing the conclusions to which it leads with economic facts.

Deflating Finding the Real gross national product (*see*) by decreasing the dollar value of the Gross national product produced in a year in which prices were higher than in the Base year (*see*).

Deflation A fall in the general (average) level of prices in the economy.

Deglomerative forces Increases in the cost of producing and marketing that result from the growth of cities and the concentration of firms and industries within a geographic area.

Demand A demand schedule or a Demand curve (*see both*).

Demand curve A curve which shows the amounts of a good or service buyers wish to purchase at various prices during some period of time.

Demand deposit A deposit in a Commercial bank against which checks may be written; a Checking account or checking-account money.

Demand-deposit multiplier (*See* Monetary multiplier.)

Demand factor The increase in the level of Aggregate demand which brings about the Economic growth made possible by an increase in the productive potential of the economy.

Demand management The use of Fiscal policy (*see*) and Monetary policy (*see*) to increase or decrease Aggregate demand.

Demand-pull inflation Inflation which is the result of an increase in Aggregate demand.

Demand schedule A schedule which shows the amounts of a good or service buyers wish to purchase at various prices during some period of time.

Depository institution A Firm that accepts the deposits of Money of the public (businesses and persons); Commercial banks, Savings and loan associations, Mutual savings banks, and Credit unions.

Depository Institutions Deregulation and Monetary Control Act Federal legislation of 1980 which, among other things, allowed Thrift institutions to accept Checkable deposits and to use the check-clearing facilities of the Federal Reserve and to borrow from the Federal Reserve Banks; subjected the Thrifts to the reserve requirements of the Fed; and provided for the gradual elimination of the maximum interest rates that could be paid by Depository institutions on Savings and Time deposits.

Depreciation (*See* Capital consumption allowances.)

Derived demand The demand for a good or service which is dependent upon or related to the demand for some other good or service; the demand for a resource which depends upon the demand for the products it can be used to produce.

Descriptive economics The gathering or collection of relevant economic facts (data).

Devaluation A decrease in the defined value of a currency.

DI (*See* Disposable income.)

Dictatorship of the proletariat The rule by the working class which is to follow the revolution overthrowing capitalism and the introduction of socialism in the Marxian vision of the future.

DIDMCA (*See* Depository Institutions Deregulation and Monetary Control Act.)

Differentiated oligopoly An Oligopoly in which the firms produce a Differentiated product (*see*).

Differentiated product A product which differs physically or in some other way from the similar products produced by other Firms; a product which is similar to but not identical with and, therefore, not a perfect substitute for other products; a product such that buyers are not indifferent to the seller from whom they purchase it so long as the price charged by all sellers is the same.

Dilemma of regulation When a Regulatory agency (*see*) must establish the maximum legal price a monopolist may charge it finds that if it sets the price at the Socially optimum price (*see*) this price is below the Average cost (and either bankrupts the Firm or requires that it be subsidized) and if it sets the price at the Fair-return price (*see*) it has failed to eliminate the underallocation of resources that is the consequence of unregulated monopoly.

Directing function of prices (*See* Guiding function of prices.)

Directly related Two sets of economic data that change in the same direction; when one variable increases (decreases) the other increases (decreases).

Discount rate The interest rate which the Federal Reserve Banks charge on the loans they make to Depository institutions.

Discouraged workers Workers who have left the Labor force (*see*) because they have not been able to find employment.

Discretionary fiscal policy Deliberate changes in taxes (tax rates) and government spending (spending for goods and services and transfer payment programs) by Congress for the purpose of achieving a full-employment noninflationary Net national product and economic growth.

Discriminatory discharge The firing of workers who favor the formation of labor unions.

Diseconomies of scale The forces which increase the Average cost of producing a product as the Firm expands the size of its Plant (its output) in the Long run (*see*).

Disposable income Personal income (*see*) less Personal taxes (*see*); income available for Personal consumption expenditures (*see*) and Personal saving (*see*).

Dissaving Spending for consumer goods and services in excess of Disposable income; the amount by which Personal consumption expenditures (*see*) exceed Disposable income.

Division of labor Dividing the work required to produce a product into a number of different tasks which are performed by different workers; Specialization (*see*) of workers.

Dollar votes The "votes" which consumers and entrepreneurs in effect cast for the production of the different kinds of consumer and capital goods, respectively, when they purchase them in the markets of the economy.

Domestic capital formation Adding to a nation's stock of Capital by saving a part of its own national output.

Domestic economic goal Assumed to be full employment with little or no inflation.

Doomsday model An economic model which predicts that within the next one hundred years there will be a sudden collapse in the world's food and industrial output and its population.

Double counting Including the value of Intermediate goods (*see*) in the Gross national product; counting the same good or service more than once.

Double taxation Taxation of both corporate net income (profits) and the dividends paid from this net income when they become the Personal income of households.

Dual labor market A labor market divided into two distinct types or submarkets; a primary labor market in which workers fare well and a secondary labor market in which they fare poorly.

DuPont cellophane case The antitrust case brought against DuPont in which the U.S. Supreme Court ruled (in 1956) that while DuPont (and one licensee) had a monopoly in the narrowly defined market for cellophane it did not monopolize the more broadly defined market for flexible packaging materials, and was not guilty, therefore, of violating the antitrust laws.

Durable good A consumer good with an expected life (use) of one year or more.

Dynamic progress The development over time of more efficient (less costly) techniques of producing existing products and of improved products; technological progress.

Earnings The money income received by a worker; equal to the Wage (rate) multiplied by the quantity of labor supplied (the amount of time worked) by the worker.

Easy money policy Expanding the Money supply.

Economic analysis Deriving Economic principles (*see*) from relevant economic facts.

Economic cost A payment that must be made to obtain and retain the services of a resource; the income a Firm must provide to a resource supplier to attract the resource away from an alternative use; equal to the quantity of other products that cannot be produced when resources are employed to produce a particular product.

Economic efficiency The relationship between the input of scarce resources and the resulting output of a good or service; production of an output with a given dollar-and-cents value with the smallest total expenditure for resources; obtaining the largest total production of a good or service with resources of a given dollar-and-cents value.

Economic growth (1) An increase in the Production possibilities schedule or curve that results from an increase in resource supplies or an improvement in Technology; (2) an increase either in real output (Gross national product) or in real output per capita.

Economic integration Cooperation among and the complete or partial unification of the economies of different nations; the elimination of the barriers to trade among these nations; the bringing together of the markets in each of the separate economies to form one large (a common) market.

Economic law (*See* Economic principle.)

Economic model A simplified picture of reality; an abstract generalization.

Economic policy Course of action that will correct or avoid a problem.

Economic principle Generalization of the economic behavior of individuals and institutions.

Economic profit The total receipts (revenue) of a firm less all its Economic costs; also called "pure profit" and "above normal profit."

Economic Recovery Tax Act The Federal act of 1981 which reduced Personal income tax rates, lowered Capital gains tax rates, allowed a more rapid writeoff against taxes of business expenditures for new plants and equipment, lowered the rates at which corporate incomes are taxed, and provided for the elimination of Bracket creep (*see*) beginning in 1985.

Economic regulation (*See* Industrial regulation.)

Economic rent The price paid for the use of land and other natural resources, the supply of which is fixed (perfectly inelastic).

Economics Social science concerned with using scarce resources to obtain the maximum satisfaction of the unlimited human wants of society.

Economic theory Deriving Economic principles (*see*) from relevant economic facts; an Economic principle (*see*).

Economies of agglomeration The reduction in the cost of producing or marketing that results from the location of Firms relatively close to each other.

(The) economies of being established Advantages which Firms already producing a product have over potential producers of the product.

Economies of scale The forces which reduce the Average cost of producing a product as the Firm expands the size of its Plant (its output) in the Long run (*see*); the economies of mass production.

EEC European Economic Community; (*see* European Common Market).

Efficient allocation of resources The allocation of the resources of an economy among the production of different products that leads to the maximum satisfaction of the wants of consumers.

Elastic demand The Elasticity coefficient (*see*) is greater than one; the percentage change in Quantity demanded is greater than the percentage change in price.

Elasticity coefficient The number obtained when the percentage change in quantity demanded (or supplied) is divided by the percentage change in the price of the commodity.

Elasticity formula The price elasticity of demand (supply) is equal to

$$\frac{\text{percentage change in quantity demanded (supplied)}}{\text{percentage change in price}}$$

which is equal to

$$\frac{\text{change in quantity demanded (supplied)}}{\text{original quantity demanded (supplied)}}$$

$$\text{divided by } \frac{\text{change in price}}{\text{original price}}$$

Elastic supply The Elasticity coefficient (*see*) is greater than one; the percentage change in Quantity supplied is greater than the percentage change in price.

Emission fees Special fees that might be levied against those who discharge pollutants into the environment.

Employment Act of 1946 Federal legislation which committed the federal government to the maintenance of economic stability (Full employment, stable prices, and Economic growth); established the Council of Economic Advisers (*see*); and the Joint Economic Committee (*see*); and provided for the annual economic report of the President to Congress.

Employment discrimination The employment of whites before blacks (and other minority groups) are employed and the discharge of blacks (and other minority groups) before whites are discharged.

Employment rate The percentage of the Labor force (*see*) employed at any time.

Entrepreneurial ability The human resource which combines the other resources to produce a product, makes nonroutine decisions, innovates, and bears risks.

Equality vs. efficiency tradeoff The decrease in Economic efficiency (*see*) that appears to accompany a decrease in income inequality (*see*); the presumption that an increase in Income inequality is required to increase Economic efficiency.

Equation of exchange $MV = PQ$; in which M is the Money supply (*see*), V is the income velocity of money (*see*), P is the Price level, and Q is the physical volume of final goods and services produced.

Equilibrium national output The real National output at which the Aggregate-demand curve intersects the Aggregate-supply curve.

Equilibrium NNP The Net national product at which the total quantity of final goods and services produced (the National output) is equal to the total quantity of final goods and services purchased (Aggregate expenditures).

Equilibrium position The point at which the Budget line (*see*) is tangent to an Indifference curve (*see*) in the indifference curve approach to the theory of consumer behavior.

Equilibrium price The price in a competitive market at which the Quantity demanded (*see*) and the Quantity supplied (*see*) are equal; at which there is neither a shortage nor a surplus; and at which there is no tendency for price to rise or fall.

Equilibrium price level The Price level at which the Aggregate-demand curve intersects the Aggregate-supply curve.

Equilibrium quantity The Quantity demanded (*see*) and Quantity supplied (*see*) at the Equilibrium price (*see*) in a competitive market.

Equalizing differences The differences in the Wages received by workers in different jobs which compensate for nonmonetary differences in the jobs.

ERP (*See* European Recovery Program.)

ERTA (*See* Economic Recovery Tax Act.)

European Common Market The association of thirteen European nations initiated in 1958 to abolish gradually the Tariffs and Import quotas among them, to establish common Tariffs for goods imported from outside the member nations, to allow the eventual free movement of labor and capital among them, and to create other common economic policies.

European Economic Community (*See* European Common Market.)

Excess reserve The amount by which a Member bank's Actual reserve (*see*) exceeds its Required reserve (*see*); Actual reserve minus Required reserve.

Exchange control (*See* Foreign exchange control.)

Exchange rate The Rate of exchange (*see*).

Exchange rate appreciation An increase in the value of a nation's money in foreign exchange markets; a decrease in the Rates of exchange for foreign monies.

Exchange rate depreciation A decrease in the value of a nation's money in foreign exchange markets; a decrease in the Rates of exchange for foreign monies.

Exchange rate determinant Any factor other than the Rate of exchange (*see*) that determines the demand for and the supply of a currency in the Foreign exchange market (*see*).

Excise tax A tax levied on the expenditure for a specific product or on the quantity of the product purchased.

Exclusion principle The exclusion of those who do not pay for a product from the benefits of the product.

Exclusive unionism The policies employed by a Labor union to restrict the supply of labor by excluding potential members in order to increase the Wages received by its members; the policies typically employed by a Craft union (*see*).

Exhaustive expenditure An expenditure by government that results directly in the employment of economic resources and in the absorption by government of the goods and services these resources produce; Government purchase (*see*).

Exit mechanism Leaving a job and searching for another one in order to improve the conditions under which a worker is employed.

Expanding economy An economy in which Net private domestic investment (*see*) is greater than zero (Gross private domestic investment is greater than Depreciation).

Expanding industry An industry in which Economic profits are obtained by the firms in the industry and which will, therefore, increase its output as new firms enter the industry.

Expansionary fiscal policy An increase in Aggregate demand brought about by an increase in Government expenditures for goods and services, a decrease in Net taxes, or some combination of the two.

Expectations What consumers, business Firms, and others believe will happen or what conditions will be in the future.

Expected rate of net profits Annual profits which a firm anticipates it will obtain by purchasing Capital (by investing) expressed as a percentage of the price (cost) of the Capital.

Expenditures approach The method which adds all the expenditures made for Final goods and services to measure the Gross national product.

Expenditures-output approach (*See* Aggregate expenditures-national output approach.)

Explicit cost The monetary payment a Firm must make to an outsider to obtain a resource.

Exploitation Paying a worker a Wage which is less than the value of the output produced by the worker; obtaining Surplus value (*see*) or unearned income.

Exports Spending for the goods and services produced in an economy by foreign individuals, firms, and governments.

Export transaction A sale of a good or service which increases the amount of foreign money held by the citizens, firms, and governments of a nation.

External benefit (*See* Spillover benefit.)

External cost (*See* Spillover cost.)

External debt Public debt (*see*) owed to foreign citizens, firms, and institutions.

External economic goal (*See* International economic goal.)

External economies of scale The reduction in a Firm's cost of producing and marketing that results from the expansion of (the output or the number of Firms in) the Industry of which the Firm is a member.

Externality (*See* Spillover.)

Face value The dollar or cents value stamped on a coin.

Factors of production Economic resources: Land, Capital, Labor, and Entrepreneurial ability.

Fair-return price The price of a product which enables its producer to obtain a Normal profit (*see*) and which is equal to the Average cost of producing it.

Fallacy of composition Incorrectly reasoning that what is true for the individual (or part) is therefore necessarily true for the group (or whole).

Farm problem The relatively low income of farmers (compared with incomes in the non-agricultural sectors of the economy) and the tendency for their incomes to fluctuate sharply from year to year.

FDIC (*See* Federal Deposit Insurance Corporation.)

Featherbedding Payment by an employer to a worker for work not actually performed.

Federal Advisory Committee The group of twelve commercial bankers which advises the Board of Governors (*see*) on banking policy.

Federal Deposit Insurance Corporation The federally chartered corporation which insures the deposit liabilities of Commercial banks (Member and qualified nonmember banks).

Federal Open Market Committee (*See* Open Market Committee.)

Federal Reserve Bank Any one of the twelve banks chartered by the United States government to control the Money supply and perform other functions; (*see* Central bank, Quasi-public bank, *and* Bankers' bank).

Federal Reserve Note Paper money issued by and debts of the Federal Reserve Banks.

Federal Savings and Loan Insurance Corporation The federally chartered corporation which insures the deposit liabilities of Savings and loan associations.

Federal Trade Commission The commission of five members established by the Federal Trade Commission Act of 1914 to investigate unfair competitive practices of business Firms, to hold hearings on the complaints of such practices, and to issue Cease-and-desist orders (*see*) when Firms were found to engage in such practices.

Federal Trade Commission Act The Federal act of 1914 which established the Federal Trade Commission (*see*).

Feedback effects The effects which a change in the money supply will have (because it affects the interest rate, planned investment, and the equilibrium NNP) on the demand for money which is itself directly related to the NNP.

Feedback mechanism A change in human behavior which is the result of an actual or predicted undesirable event and which has the effect of preventing the recurrence or occurrence of the event.

Female participation rate The percentage of the female population of working age in the Labor force (*see*).

Fewness A relatively small number of sellers (or buyers) of a good or service.

Fiat money Anything that is Money because government has decreed it to be Money.

Final goods Goods which have been purchased for final use and not for resale or further processing or manufacturing (during the year).

Financial capital (*See* Money capital.)

Financing exports and imports The use of Foreign exchange markets by exporters and importers to receive and make payments for goods and services they sell and buy in foreign nations.

Firm An organization that employs resources to produce a good or service for profit and owns and operates one or more Plants (*see*).

(The) firm's short-run supply curve A curve which shows the quantities of a product a Firm in a purely competitive industry (*see* Pure competition) will offer to sell at various prices in the Short run (*see*); the portion of the Firm's short-run Marginal cost (*see*) curve which lies above its Average variable cost curve.

(The) firm's short-run supply schedule A schedule which shows the quantities of product a Firm in a purely competitive industry (*see* Pure competition) will offer to sell at various prices in the Short run (*see*); the portion of the firm's short-run Marginal-cost (*see*) schedule in which Marginal cost is equal to or greater than Average variable cost.

Fiscal drag The difficulty encountered in reaching and maintaining Full employment when the revenues from Net taxes vary directly with the Net national product.

Fiscal federalism The system of transfers (grants) by which the Federal government shares its revenues with state and local governments; Revenue sharing (*see*).

Fiscal policy Changes in government spending and tax collections for the purpose of achieving a full-employment and noninflationary Net national product.

Five Fundamental Economic Questions The five questions which every economy must answer; what to produce, how to produce, how to divide the total output, how to maintain Full employment, and how to ensure Economic flexibility (*see*).

Five-year Plan A statement of the basic strategy for economic development and resource allocation which is prepared by *Gosplan* (*see*) and which includes target rates of growth for the Soviet economy and its major sectors and the general composition of the national output for a five-year period.

Fixed cost Any cost which in total does not change when the Firm changes its output; the cost of Fixed resources (*see*).

Fixed exchange rate A Rate of exchange that is prevented from rising or falling.

Fixed resource Any resource employed by a Firm the quantity of which the firm cannot change.

Flat-rate income tax A tax which taxes all incomes at the same rate.

Flexible exchange rate A Rate of exchange that is determined by the demand for and supply of the foreign money and is free to rise or fall.

Floating exchange rate (*See* Flexible exchange rate.)

Food for peace program The program established under the provisions of Public Law 480 which permits less developed nations to buy surplus American agricultural products and pay for them with their own monies (instead of dollars).

Food stamp program A program in the United States which permits low-income persons to purchase for less than their retail value, or to obtain without cost, coupons that can be exchanged for food items at retail stores.

Foreign exchange control The control a government may exercise over the quantity of foreign money demanded by its citizens and business firms and over the Rates of exchange in order to limit its outpayments to its inpayments (to eliminate a Payments deficit, *see*).

Foreign exchange market A market in which the money (currency) used by one nation is used to purchase (is exchanged for) the money used by another nation.

Foreign exchange rate (*See* Rate of exchange.)

Foreign purchases effect The inverse relationship between the Net exports (*see*) of an economy and its Price level (*see*) relative to foreign Price levels.

Foreign-trade crisis The large and expanding trade (merchandise and current-account) deficits of the United States during the 1980s.

45-degree line A curve along which the value of the NNP (measured horizontally) is equal to the value of Aggregate expenditures (measured vertically).

Fractional reserve A Reserve ratio (*see*) that is less than 100 percent of the deposit liabilities of a Commercial bank.

Freedom of choice Freedom of owners of property resources and money to employ or dispose of these resources as they see fit, of workers to enter any line of work for which they are qualified, and of consumers to spend their incomes in a manner which they deem to be appropriate (best for them).

Freedom of enterprise Freedom of business Firms to employ economic resources, to use these resources to produce products of the firm's own choosing, and to sell these products in markets of their choice.

Freely floating exchange rates Rates of exchange (*see*) which are not controlled and which may, therefore, rise and fall; and which are determined by the demand for and the supply of foreign monies.

Free-rider problem The inability of those who might provide the economy with an economically desirable and indivisible good or service to obtain payment from those who benefit from the good or service because the Exclusion principle (*see*) cannot be applied to it.

Free trade The absence of artificial (government imposed) barriers to trade among individuals and firms in different nations.

Frictional unemployment Unemployment caused by workers voluntarily changing jobs and by temporary layoffs; unemployed workers between jobs.

Fringe benefits The rewards other than Wages that employees receive from their employers and which include pensions, medical and dental insurance, paid vacations, and sick leaves.

FSLIC (*See* Federal Savings and Loan Insurance Corporation.)

Full employment (1) Using all available resources to produce goods and services; (2) when the Unemployment rate is equal to the Full-employment unemployment rate and there is Frictional and Structural but no Cyclical unemployment (and the Real output of the economy is equal to its Potential real output).

Full Employment and Balanced Growth Act of 1978 The Federal act which supplements the Employment Act of 1946 (*see*), and requires the Federal government to establish five-year goals for the economy and to make plans to achieve these goals (in particular, a 4% unemployment rate and a 3% rate of inflation by 1983).

Full-employment budget What the government expenditures and revenues and its surplus or deficit would be if the economy were to operate at Full employment throughout the year.

Full-employment rate of growth The rate at which an economy is able to grow when it maintains Full employment; equal to the Average propensity to save (*see*) divided by the Capital-output ratio (*see*).

Full-employment unemployment rate The Unemployment rate (*see*) at which there is no Cyclical unemployment (*see*) of the Labor force (*see*); and because some Frictional and Structural unemployment is unavoidable, equal to about 6%.

Full production The maximum amount of goods and services that can be produced from the employed resources of an economy; the absence of Underemployment (*see*).

Functional distribution of income The manner in which the economy's (the national) income is divided among those who perform different functions (provide the economy with different kinds of resources); the division of National income (*see*) into wages and salaries, proprietors' income, corporate profits, interest, and rent.

Functional finance Use of Fiscal policy to achieve a full-employment noninflationary Net national product without regard to the effect on the Public debt (*see*).

GATT (*See* General Agreement on Tariffs and Trade.)

General Agreement on Tariffs and Trade The international agreement reached in 1947 by twenty-three nations (including the United States) in which each nation agreed to give equal and nondiscriminatory treatment to the other nations, to reduce tariff rates by multinational negotiations, and to eliminate Import quotas.

General equilibrium analysis A study of the Price system as a whole; of the interrelations among equilibrium prices, outputs, and employments in all the different markets of the economy.

Generalization Statistical or probability statement; statement of the nature of the relation between two or more sets of facts.

Gentleman's agreement An informal understanding on the price to be charged among the firms in an Oligopoly.

Given year Any year other than the Base year (*see*) for which a Price index (*see*) is constructed.

GNP (*See* Gross national product.)

GNP deflator The Price index (*see*) for all final goods and services used to adjust the money (or nominal) GNP to measure the real GNP.

GNP gap Potential Real gross national product less actual Real gross national product.

Gold export point The rate of exchange for a foreign money above which—when nations participate in the International gold standard (*see*)—the foreign money will not be purchased and gold will be sent (exported) to the foreign country to make payments there.

Gold flow The movement of gold into or out of a nation.

Gold import point The Rate of exchange for a foreign money below which—when nations participate in the International gold standard (*see*)—a nation's own money will not be purchased and gold will be sent (imported) into that country by foreigners to make payments there.

Gold standard (*See* International gold standard.)

Gosbank The state owned and operated (and the only) bank in the U.S.S.R.

Gosplan The State Planning Commission in the U.S.S.R.

Government purchase Disbursement of money by government for which government receives a currently produced good or service in return.

Government purchases of goods and services The expenditures of all governments in the economy for Final goods (*see*) and services.

Government transfer payment Disbursement of money (or goods and services) by government for which government receives no currently produced good or service in return.

Grain reserve program A program in which grain is put into a reserve to reduce market supply when prices are low and sold from the reserve when prices are unusually high in order to increase the market supply.

Gramm-Rudman Act Legislation enacted in 1985 by the Federal government requiring annual reductions in Federal budget deficits and a balanced budget by 1991;

and mandating an automatic decrease in expenditures when Congress and the President cannot agree on how to meet the targeted reductions in the budget deficit.

Green revolution The major technological advance which created new strains of rice and wheat and increased the output per acre and per worker-hour of these crops.

Grievance procedure The methods used by a Labor union and the Firm to settle disputes that arise during the life of the collective bargaining agreement between them.

Gross national product The total market value of all Final goods (*see*) and services produced in the economy during a year.

Gross private domestic investment Expenditures for newly produced Capital goods (*see*)—machinery, equipment, tools, and buildings—and for additions to inventories.

Guaranteed income The minimum income a family (or individual) would receive if a Negative income tax (*see*) were to be adopted.

Guiding function of prices The ability of price changes to bring about changes in the quantities of products and resources demanded and supplied; (*see* Incentive function of price).

Homogeneous oligopoly An Oligopoly in which the firms produce a Standardized product (*see*).

Horizontal combination A group of Plants (*see*) in the same stage of production and owned by a single Firm (*see*).

Horizontal merger The merger of one or more Firms producing the same product into a single Firm.

Household An economic unit (of one or more persons) which provides the economy with resources and uses the money paid to it for these resources to purchase goods and services that satisfy human wants.

Human-capital discrimination The denial of the same quality and quantity of education and training received by whites to blacks (and other minority groups).

Human-capital investment Any action taken to increase the productivity (by improving the skills and abilities) of workers; expenditures made to improve the education, health, or mobility of workers.

Humphrey-Hawkins Act (*See* Full Employment and Balanced Growth Act of 1978.)

Hyperinflation A very rapid rise in the price level.

Illegal immigrant A person who unlawfully enters a country.

IMF (*See* International Monetary Fund.)

Immobility The inability or unwillingness of a worker or another resource to move from one geographic area or occupation to another or from a lower-paying to a higher-paying job.

Imperfect competition All markets except Pure competition (*see*); Monopoly, Monopsony, Monopolistic competition, Oligopoly, and Oligopsony (*see all*).

Imperialism The Exploitation (*see*) of the less economically developed parts of the world by Capitalists (*see*) in the industrially advanced nations; and characterized by colonialism, the employment of the labor and raw materials of the less developed nations by the capitalistic nations, the sale of manufactured goods to them by the advanced nations, and investment by the developed nations in the underdeveloped ones.

Implicit cost The monetary income a Firm sacrifices when it employs a resource it owns to produce a product rather than supplying the resource in the market; equal to what the resource could have earned in the best-paying alternative employment.

Import quota A limit imposed by a nation on the maximum quantity of a good that may be imported from abroad during some period of time.

Imports Spending by individuals, Firms, and governments of an economy for goods and services produced in foreign nations.

Import transaction The purchase of a good or service which decreases the amount of foreign money held by the citizens, firms, and governments of a nation.

Incentive function The inducement which an increase (a decrease) in the price of a commodity offers to sellers of the commodity to make more (less) of it available; and the inducement which an increase (decrease) in price offers to buyers to purchase smaller (larger) quantities; the Guiding function of prices (*see*).

Inclusive unionism The policies employed by a Labor union that does not limit the number of workers in the union in order to increase the Wage (rate); the policies of an Industrial union (*see*).

Income approach The method which adds all the incomes generated by the production of Final goods and services to measure the Gross national product.

Income-creating aspect of investment The effect of net investment spending upon Aggregate expenditures and the resulting effect upon the income (output) of an economy.

Income effect The effect which a change in the price of a product has upon the Real income (purchasing power) of a consumer and the resulting effect upon the quantity of that product the consumer would purchase after the consequences of the Substitution effect (*see*) have been taken into account (eliminated).

Income inequality The unequal distribution of an economy's total income among persons or families in the economy.

Income-maintenance system The programs designed to eliminate poverty and to reduce the unequal distribution of income.

Incomes policy Government policy that affects the Money incomes individuals (the wages workers) receive and the prices they pay for goods and services and thereby affects their Real incomes; (*see* Wage-price policy).

Income velocity of money (*See* Velocity of money.)

Increase in demand An increase in the Quantity demanded of a good or service at every price; a shift in the Demand curve to the right.

Increase in supply An increase in the Quantity supplied of a good or service at every price; a shift in the Supply curve to the right.

Increasing-cost industry An Industry in which the expansion of the Industry through the entry of new firms increases the prices the Firms in the Industry must pay for resources and, therefore, increases their cost schedules (moves their cost curves upward).

Increasing returns An increase in the Marginal product (*see*) of a resource as successive units of the resource are employed.

Independent goods Goods or services such that there is no relationship between the price of one and the demand for the other; when the price of one rises or falls the demand for the other remains constant.

Indifference curve A curve which shows the different combinations of two products which give a consumer the same satisfaction or Utility (*see*).

Indifference map A series of Indifference curves (*see*) each of which represents a different level of Utility; and which together are the preferences of the consumer.

Indirect business taxes Such taxes as Sales, Excise, and business Property taxes (*see all*), license fees, and Tariffs (*see*) which Firms treat as costs of producing a product and pass on (in whole or in part) to buyers of the product by charging them higher prices.

Individual demand The Demand schedule (*see*) or Demand curve (*see*) of a single buyer of a good or service.

Individual supply The Supply schedule (*see*) or Supply curve (*see*) of a single seller of a good or service.

Induction A method of reasoning that proceeds from facts to Generalization (*see*).

Industrial policy Any policy in which government takes a direct and active role in shaping the structure and composition of industry to promote economic growth.

Industrial regulation The older and more traditional type of regulation in which government is concerned with the prices charged and the services provided the public in specific industries; in contrast to Social regulation (*see*).

Industrial reserve army A Marxian term; those workers who are unemployed as a result of the substitution of Capital for Labor, the growing capacity of the economy to produce goods and services, and the inadequate purchasing power of the working class.

Industrial union A Labor union which accepts as members all workers employed in a particular industry (or by a particular firm) and which contains largely unskilled or semiskilled workers.

Industry The group of (one or more) Firms that produce identical or similar products.

Inelastic demand The Elasticity coefficient (*see*) is less than one; the percentage change in price is greater than the percentage change in Quantity demanded.

Inelastic supply The Elasticity coefficient (*see*) is less than one; the percentage change in price is greater than the percentage change in Quantity supplied.

Inferior good A good or service of which consumers purchase less (more) at every price when their incomes increase (decrease).

Inflating Finding the Real gross national product (*see*) by increasing the dollar value of the Gross national product produced in a year in which prices are lower than they were in the Base year (*see*).

Inflation A rise in the general (average) level of prices in the economy.

Inflationary expectations The belief of workers, business Firms, and consumers that there will be substantial inflation in the future.

Inflationary gap The amount by which the Aggregate-expenditures schedule (curve) must decrease (shift downward) to decrease the money NNP to the full-employment noninflationary level.

Inflationary recession (*See* Stagflation.)

Infrastructure For the economy, the capital goods usually provided by the Public sector for the use of its citizens and Firms (e.g., highways, bridges, transit systems, waste-water treatment facilities, municipal water systems, and airports). For the Firm, the services and facilities which it must have to produce its products, which would be too costly for it to provide for itself, and which are provided by governments or other Firms (e.g., water, electricity, waste treatment, transportation, research, engineering, finance, and banking).

Injection An addition of spending to the income-expenditure stream; Investment, Government purchases of goods and services, and Exports.

Injunction An order from a court of law that directs a person or organization not to perform a certain act because the act would do irreparable damage to some other person or persons; a restraining order.

In-kind investment Nonfinancial investment (*see*).

In-kind transfer The distribution by government of goods and services to individuals and for which the government receives no currently produced good or service in return; a Government transfer payment (*see*) made in goods or services rather than in money.

Innovation The introduction of a new product, the use of a new method of production, or the employment of a new form of business organization.

Inpayments The receipts of (its own or foreign) money which the individuals, Firms, and governments of one nation obtain from the sale of goods and services. Investment income, Remittances, and Capital inflows from abroad.

Input-output analysis Using an Input-output table (*see*) to examine interdependencies among different parts (sectors and industries) of the economy and to make economic forecasts and plans.

Input-output table A table which lists (along the left side) the producing sectors and (along the top) the consuming or using sectors of the economy and which shows quantitatively in each of its rows how the output of a producing sector was distributed among consuming sectors and quantitatively in each of its columns the producing sectors from which a consuming sector obtained its inputs during some period of time (a year).

Insurable risk An event, the average occurrence of which can be estimated with considerable accuracy, which would result in a loss that can be avoided by purchasing insurance.

Interest The payment made for the use of money (of borrowed funds).

Interest income Income of those who supply the economy with Capital (*see*).

Interest rate The rate of interest (*see*).

Interest-rate effect The tendency for increases (decreases) in the Price level to increase (decrease) the demand for money; raise (lower) interest rates; and, as a result, to reduce (expand) total spending in the economy.

Intergovernmental grant A transfer payment (gift) from the Federal government to a state or local government or from a state to a local government.

Interindustry competition Competition or rivalry between the products produced by Firms in one industry (*see*) and the products produced by Firms in another industry (or in other industries).

Interlocking directorate A situation in which one or more of the members of the board of directors of one Corporation are also on the board of directors of another Corporation; and which is illegal when it tends to reduce competition among the Corporations.

Intermediate goods Goods which are purchased for resale or further processing or manufacturing during the year.

Intermediate range The upsloping segment of the Aggregate-supply curve that lies between the Keynesian range and the Classical range (*see both*).

Internal economic goal (*See* Domestic economic goal.)

Internal economies The reduction in the cost of producing or marketing a product that results from an increase in output of the Firm; (*see* Economies of (large) scale).

Internal growth Increase in the size of a Firm accomplished by using the firm's earnings and by selling securities to obtain the funds to construct new Plants.

Internally held public debt Public debt (*see*) owed to (United States government securities owned by) American citizens, Firms, and institutions.

International balance of payments Summary statement of the transactions which took place between the individuals, Firms, and governments of one nation and those in all other nations during a year.

International balance of payments deficit (*See* Payments deficit.)

International balance of payments surplus (*See* Payments surplus.)

International Bank for Reconstruction and Development (*See* World Bank.)

International economic goal Assumed to be a current-account balance of zero.

International gold standard An international monetary system employed in the nineteenth and early twentieth centuries in which each nation defined its money in terms of a quantity of gold, maintained a fixed relationship between its gold stock and money supply, and allowed the free importation and exportation of gold.

International Monetary Fund The international association of nations which was formed after World War II to make loans of foreign monies to nations with temporary Payments deficits (*see*) and to administer the Adjustable pegs (*see*).

International monetary reserves The foreign monies and such other assets as gold a nation may use to settle a Payments deficit (*see*).

International value of the dollar The price that must be paid in foreign currency (money) to obtain one American dollar.

Interstate Commerce Commission The commission established in 1887 to regulate the rates and monitor the services of the railroads in the United States.

Interstate Commerce Commission Act The Federal legislation of 1887 which established the Interstate Commerce Commission (*see*).

Intrinsic value The value in the market of the metal in a coin.

Inversely related Two sets of economic data that change in opposite directions; when one increases (decreases) the other decreases (increases).

Investment Spending for (the production and accumulation of) Capital goods (*see*) and additions to inventories.

Investment curve A curve which shows the amounts firms plan to invest (along the vertical axis) at different income (Net national product) levels (along the horizontal axis).

Investment-demand curve A curve which shows Rates of interest (along the vertical axis) and the amount of Investment (along the horizontal axis) at each Rate of interest.

Investment-demand schedule Schedule which shows Rates of interest and the amount of Investment at each Rate of interest.

Investment in human capital (*See* Human-capital investment.)

Investment schedule A schedule which shows the amounts Firms plan to invest at different income (Net national product) levels.

Invisible hand The tendency of Firms and resource suppliers seeking to further their self-interests in competitive markets to further the best interest of society as a whole (the maximum satisfaction of wants).

JEC (*See* Joint Economic Committee.)

Joint Economic Committee Committee of Senators and Congressmen which investigates economic problems of national interest.

Jurisdictional strike Withholding from an employer the labor services of its members by a Labor union that is engaged in a dispute with another Labor union over which is to perform a specific kind of work for the employer.

Keynesian economics The macroeconomic generalizations which are today accepted by most (but not all) economists and which lead to the conclusion that a capitalistic economy does not tend to employ its resources fully and that Fiscal policy (*see*) and Monetary policy (*see*) can be used to promote Full employment (*see*).

Keynesianism The philosophical, ideological, and analytical views of the prevailing majority of American economists; and their employment theory and stabilization policies.

Keynesian range The horizontal segment of the Aggregate-supply curve along which the economy is in a depression or severe recession.

Keynesian theory Keynesian economics.

Kinked demand curve The demand curve which a noncollusive oligopolist sees for its output and which is based on the assumption that rivals will follow a price decrease and will not follow a price increase.

Labor The physical and mental talents (efforts) of people which can be used to produce goods and services.

Labor force Persons sixteen years of age and older who are not in institutions and who are employed or are unemployed and seeking work.

Labor-intensive commodity A product in the production of which a relatively large amount of Labor is employed.

Labor-Management Relations Act (*See* Taft-Hartley Act.)

Labor-Management Reporting and Disclosure Act (*See* Landrum-Griffin Act.)

Labor productivity Total output divided by the quantity of labor employed to produce the output; the Average product (*see*) of labor or output per worker per hour.

Labor theory of value The Marxian notion that the economic value of any commodity is determined solely by the amount of labor required to produce it.

Labor union A group of workers organized to advance the interests of the group (to increase wages, shorten the hours worked, improve working conditions, etc.).

Laffer curve A curve which shows the relationship between tax rates and the tax revenues of government and on which there is a tax rate (between zero and 100%) at which tax revenues are a maximum.

Laissez faire capitalism (*See* Pure capitalism.)

Land Natural resources ("free gifts of nature") which can be used to produce goods and services.

Land-intensive commodity A product in the production of which a relatively large amount of Land is employed.

Landrum-Griffin Act The Federal act of 1959 which regulates the elections and finances of Labor unions and guarantees certain rights to their members.

Law of capitalist accumulation The tendency seen by Marx for capitalists to react to competition from other capitalists by investing profits (Surplus value) expropriated from workers in additional and technologically superior machinery and equipment (Capital goods).

Law of demand The inverse relationship between the price and the Quantity demanded (*see*) of a good or service during some period of time.

Law of diminishing marginal utility As a consumer increases the consumption of a good or service the Marginal utility (*see*) obtained from each additional unit of the good or service decreases.

Law of diminishing returns When successive equal increments of a Variable resource (*see*) are added to the Fixed resources (*see*), beyond some level of employment, the Marginal product (*see*) of the Variable resource will decrease.

Law of increasing cost As the amount of a product produced is increased the Opportunity (*see*)—Marginal cost (*see*)—of producing an additional unit of the product increases.

Law of supply The direct relationship between the price and the Quantity supplied (*see*) of a good or service during some period of time

Leakage (1) A withdrawal of potential spending from the income-expenditures stream: Saving (*see*), tax payment, and Imports (*see*); (2) a withdrawal which reduces the lending potential of the Commercial banking system.

Leakages-injections approach Determination of the Equilibrium net national product (*see*) by finding the Net national product at which Leakages (*see*) are equal to Injections (*see*).

Least-cost combination rule (of resources) The quantity of each resource a Firm must employ if it is to produce any output at the lowest total cost; the combination in which the ratio of the Marginal product (*see*) of a resource to its Marginal resource cost (*see*) (to its price if the resource is employed in a competitive market) is the same for all resources employed.

Legal cartel theory of regulation The hypothesis that industries want to be regulated so that they may form legal Cartels (*see*) and that government officials (the government) provide the regulation in return for their political and financial support.

Legal immigrant A person who lawfully enters a country.

Legal reserve (deposit) The minimum amount which a Depository institution (*see*) must keep on deposit with the Federal Reserve Bank in its district, or in Vault cash (*see*).

Legal tender Anything that government has decreed must be accepted in payment of a debt.

(The) lending potential of an individual commercial bank The amount by which a single Commercial bank can safely increase the Money supply by making new loans to (or buying securities from) the public; equal to the Commercial bank's Excess reserve (*see*).

(The) lending potential of the banking system The amount by which the Commercial banking system (*see*) can increase the Money supply by making new loans to (or buying securities from) the public; equal to the Excess reserve (*see*) of the Commercial banking system multiplied by the Monetary multiplier (*see*).

Liability A debt with a monetary value; an amount owed by a Firm or an individual.

Limited liability Restriction of the maximum that may be lost to a predetermined amount; the maximum amount that may be lost by the owners (stockholders) of a Corporation is the amount they paid for their shares of stock.

Liquidity Money or things which can be quickly and easily converted into Money with little or no loss of purchasing power.

Liquidity preference theory of interest The theory in which the demand for Liquidity (the quantity of Money firms and households wish to possess) and the supply of Liquidity (the quantity of Money available) determine the equilibrium Rate of interest in the economy.

Loaded terminology Terms which arouse emotions and elicit approval or disapproval.

Lockout The temporary closing of a place of employment and the halting of production by an employer in order to discourage the formation of a Labor union or to compel a Labor union to modify its demands.

Long run A period of time long enough to enable producers of a product to change the quantities of all the resources they employ; in which all resources and costs are variable and no resources or costs are fixed.

Long-run competitive equilibrium The price at which the Firms in Pure competition (*see*) neither obtain Economic profit nor suffer losses in the Long run and the total quantity demanded and supplied at that price; a price equal to the minimum long-run average cost of producing the product.

Long-run farm problem The tendency for the incomes of farmers to decline relative to incomes in the rest of the economy.

Long-run supply A schedule or curve which shows the prices at which a Purely competitive industry will make various quantities of the product available in the Long run.

Lorenz curve A curve which can be used to show the distribution of income in an economy; and when used for this purpose the cumulated percentage of families (income receivers) is measured along the horizontal axis and the cumulated percentage of income is measured along the vertical axis.

(The) loss-minimizing case The circumstances which result in a loss which is less than its Total fixed cost when a competitive Firm produces the output at which total profit is a maximum (or total loss is a minimum): when the price at which the firm can sell its product is less than Average total but greater than Average variable cost.

Lump-sum tax A tax which is a constant amount (the tax revenue of government is the same) at all levels of NNP.

***M*1** The narrowly defined Money supply; the Currency and Checkable deposits (*see*) not owned by the Federal government, Federal Reserve Banks, or Depository institutions.

***M*2** A more broadly defined Money supply; equal to *M*1 (*see*) plus Noncheckable savings deposits and small Time deposits (deposits of less than $100,000).

***M*3** A still more broadly defined Money supply; equal to *M*2 (*see*) plus large Time deposits (deposits of $100,000 or more).

Macroeconomics The part of economics concerned with the economy as a whole; with such major aggregates as the household, business, and governmental sectors and with totals for the economy.

Managed floating exchange rate An Exchange rate that is allowed to change (float) to eliminate persistent Payments deficits and surpluses and is controlled (managed) to eliminate day-to-day fluctuations.

Managerial-opposition hypothesis The explanation that attributes the relative decline of unionism in the United States to the increased and more aggressive opposition of management to unions.

Managerial prerogatives The decisions, often enumerated in the contract between a Labor union and a business Firm, that the management of the Firm has the sole right to make.

Marginal cost The extra (additional) cost of producing one more unit of output; equal to the change in Total cost divided by the change in output (and in the short run to the change in total Variable cost divided by the change in output).

Marginal labor cost The amount by which the total cost of employing Labor increases when a Firm employs one additional unit of Labor (the quantity of other resources employed remaining constant); equal to the change in the total cost of Labor divided by the change in the quantity of Labor employed.

Marginal product The additional output produced when one additional unit of a resource is employed (the quantity of all other resources employed remaining constant); equal to the change in total product divided by the change in the quantity of a resource employed; Marginal physical product.

Marginal productivity theory of income distribution The contention that the distribution of income is equitable when each unit of each resource receives a money payment equal to its marginal contribution to the firm's revenue (its Marginal revenue product).

Marginal propensity to consume Fraction of any change in Disposable income which is spent for Consumer goods; equal to the change in consumption divided by the change in Disposable income.

Marginal propensity to import The fraction of any change in income (Net national product) spent for imported goods and services; equal to the change in Imports (*see*) divided by the change in income.

Marginal propensity to save Fraction of any change in Disposable income which households save; equal to change in Saving (*see*) divided by the change in Disposable income.

Marginal rate of substitution The rate (at the margin) at which a consumer is prepared to substitute one good or service for another and remain equally satisfied (have the same total Utility); and equal to the slope of an Indifference curve (*see*).

Marginal resource cost The amount by which the total cost of employing a resource increases when a Firm employs one additional unit of the resource (the quantity of all other resources employed remaining constant); equal to the change in the total cost of the resource divided by the change in the quantity of the resource employed.

Marginal revenue The change to the Total revenue of the Firm that results from the sale of one additional unit of its product; equal to the change in Total revenue divided by the change in the quantity of the product sold (demanded).

Marginal-revenue–marginal-cost approach The method which finds the total output at which Economic profit (*see*) is a maximum (or losses a minimum) by comparing the Marginal revenue (*see*) and the Marginal cost (*see*) of additional units of output.

Marginal revenue product The change in the Total revenue of the Firm when it employs one additional unit of a resource (the quantity of all other resources employed remaining constant); equal to the change in Total revenue divided by the change in the quantity of the resource employed.

Marginal tax rate The fraction of additional (taxable) income that must be paid in taxes.

Marginal utility The extra Utility (*see*) a consumer obtains from the consumption of one additional unit of a good or service; equal to the change in total Utility divided by the change in the quantity consumed.

Margin requirement The minimum percentage down payment which purchasers of shares of stock must make.

Market Any institution or mechanism that brings together the buyers (demanders) and sellers (suppliers) of a particular good or service.

Market demand (*See* Total demand.)

Market economy An economy in which only the private decisions of consumers, resource suppliers, and business Firms determine how resources are allocated; the Price system (*see*).

Market failure The failure of a market to bring about the allocation of resources that best satisfies the wants of society (that maximizes the satisfaction of wants). In particular, the over- or underallocation of resources to the production of a particular good or service (because of Spillovers) and no allocation of resources to the production of Social goods (*see*).

Market for pollution rights A market in which the Perfectly inelastic supply (*see*) of the right to pollute the environment and the demand for the right to pollute would determine the price which a polluter would have to pay for the right.

Market-oriented income stabilization The proposal to shift the goal of farm policy from the enhancement to the stabilization of farm prices and incomes; allow farm prices and incomes to move toward their free-market levels in the long run; and have government stabilize farm prices and incomes from year to year by purchasing farm products when their prices fell below and by selling surplus farm products when their prices rose above their long-run trend of prices.

Market period A period of time in which producers of a product are unable to change the quantity produced in response to a change in its price; in which there is Perfect inelasticity of supply (*see*); and in which all resources are Fixed resources (*see*).

Market policies Government policies designed to reduce the market power of labor unions and large business firms and to reduce or eliminate imbalances and bottlenecks in labor markets.

Market socialism An economic system (method of organization) in which property resources are publicly owned and markets and prices are used to direct and coordinate economic activities.

Marxian economics The Economic theories and perceptions of Karl Marx (and his followers); an explanation of the forces and contradictions that would cause the breakdown of a capitalistic economy.

"Material balance" Preparation of the Five- and One-year Plans (*see each*) by *Gosplan* (*see*) so that the planned requirements and the available supplies of each input and commodity are equal.

Materials balance approach A method of dealing with pollution problems which compares the production of waste materials with the capacity of the environment to absorb these materials.

Medicaid A Federal program in the United States which helps to finance the medical expenses of individuals covered by the Supplemental security income (*see*) and the Aid to families with dependent children (*see*) programs.

Medicare A Federal program in the United States which provides for compulsory hospital insurance for the aged and is financed by Payroll taxes (*see*) and for low-cost voluntary insurance to help the aged pay physicians' fees.

Medium of exchange Money (*see*); a convenient means of exchanging goods and services without engaging in Barter (*see*); what sellers generally accept and buyers generally use to pay for a good or service.

Member bank A Commercial bank (*see*) which is a member of the Federal Reserve system; all National banks (*see*) and the State banks (*see*) which have chosen to join the system.

Member bank deposits The deposits which Member banks (*see*) have at the Federal Reserve Banks (*see*).

Member bank reserves Member bank deposits (*see*) plus their Vault cash (*see*).

Microeconomics The part of economics concerned with such individual units within the economy as Industries, firms, and Households; and with individual markets, particular prices, and specific goods and services.

Minimum wage The lowest Wage (*rate*) employers may legally pay for an hour of Labor.

Mixed capitalism An economy in which both government and private decisions determine how resources are allocated.

Monetarism An alternative to Keynesianism (*see*); the philosophical, ideological, and analytical views of a minority of American economists; and their employment theory and stabilization policy which stress the role of money.

Monetary multiplier The multiple of its Excess reserve (*see*) by which the Commercial banking system (*see*) can expand the Money supply and Demand deposits by making new loans (or buying securities); and equal to one divided by the Required reserve ratio (*see*).

Monetary policy Changing the Money supply (*see*) in order to assist the economy to achieve a full-employment, noninflationary level of total output.

Monetary rule The rule suggested by the Monetarists (*see*); the Money supply should be expanded each year at the same annual rate as the potential rate of growth of the Real gross national product; the supply of money should be increased steadily at from 3 to 5% per year.

Money Any item which is generally acceptable to sellers in exchange for goods and services.

Money capital Money available to purchase Capital goods (*see*).

Money income (*See* Nominal income.)

Money interest rate The Nominal interest rate (*see*).

Money market The market in which the demand for and the supply of money determine the Interest rate (or the level of interest rates) in the economy.

Money supply Narrowly defined (*see*) *M*1, more broadly defined (*see*) *M*2 and *M*3.

Money wage The amount of money received by a worker per unit of time (hour, day, etc.).

Money-wage rate (*See* Money wage.)

Monopolistic competition A market in which many Firms sell a Differentiated product (*see*), into which entry is relatively easy, in which the Firm has some control over the price at which the product it produces is sold, and in which there is considerable Nonprice competition (*see*).

Monopoly (1) A market in which the number of sellers is so few that each seller is able to influence the total supply and the price of the good or service; (2) a major industry in which a small number of Firms control all or a large portion of its output.

Monopoly capitalism A Marxian term; the ownership and control of the economy's Capital (machinery and equipment) by a small number of capitalists.

Monopsony A market in which there is only one buyer of the good or service.

Moral suasion The statements, pronouncements, and appeals made by the Federal Reserve Banks which are intended to influence the lending policies of Commercial banks.

Most favored nation clause A clause in a trade agreement between the United States and another nation which provides that the other nation's Imports into the United States will be subjected to the lowest tariff rates levied then or later on any other nation's Imports into the United States.

MR = MC rule A Firm will maximize its Economic profit (or minimize its losses) by producing the output at which Marginal revenue (*see*) and Marginal cost (*see*) are equal—provided the price at which it can sell its product is equal to or greater than Average variable cost (*see*).

MRP = MRC rule To maximize Economic profit (or minimize losses) a Firm should employ the quantity of a resource at which its Marginal revenue product (*see*) is equal to its Marginal resource cost (*see*).

Multiplier The ratio of the change in the Equilibrium NNP to the change in Investment (*see*), or to the change in any other component in the Aggregate-expenditures schedule or to the change in Net taxes; the number by which a change in any component in the Aggregate-expenditures schedule or in Net taxes must be multiplied to find the resulting change in the Equilibrium NNP.

Multiplier effect The effect upon the Equilibrium net national product of a change in the Aggregate-expenditures schedule (caused by a change in the Consumption schedule, Investment, Net taxes, Government expenditures for goods and services, or Exports).

Mutual interdependence Situation in which a change in price (or in some other policy) by one Firm will affect the sales and profits of another Firm (or other Firms) and any Firm which makes such a change can expect the other Firm(s) to react in an unpredictable (uncertain) way.

Mutually exclusive goals Goals which conflict and cannot be achieved simultaneously.

Mutual savings bank A Firm without stockholders which accepts deposits primarily from small individual savers and which lends primarily to individuals to finance the purchases of residences.

National bank A Commercial bank (*see*) chartered by the United States government.

National income Total income earned by resource suppliers for their contributions to the production of the Gross national product (*see*); equal to the Gross national product minus the Nonincome charges (*see*).

National income accounting The techniques employed to measure (estimate) the overall production of the economy and other related totals for the nation as a whole.

National Labor Relations Act (*See* Wagner Act.)

National Labor Relations Board The board established by the Wagner (National Labor Relations) Act (*see*) of 1935 to investigate unfair labor practices, issue Cease-and-desist orders (*see*), and to conduct elections among employees to determine if they wish to be represented by a Labor union and which union they wish to represent them.

National output The Net (or gross) national product; the total output of final goods and services produced in the economy.

Natural monopoly An industry in which the Economies of scale (*see*) are so great that the product can be produced by one Firm at an average cost which is lower than it would be if it were produced by more than one Firm.

Natural rate of unemployment (*See* Full-employment unemployment rate.)

Near-money Financial assets, the most important of which are Noncheckable savings accounts, Time deposits, and U.S. government short-term securities and savings bonds, that are not a medium of exchange but can be readily converted into Money.

Negative income tax The proposal to subsidize families and individuals with money payments when their incomes fall below a Guaranteed income (*see*); the negative tax would decrease as earned income increases (*see* Benefits-loss rate).

Negotiable order of withdrawal account An account (deposit) in a Savings and loan association (*see*) or Mutual savings bank (*see*) against which a check may be written and which pays interest to the depositor.

Neocolonialism Domination and exploitation (*see*) of the economies in the Third World by private business Firms and governments in the United States and the industrially developed nations of Europe.

Net capital movement The difference between the real and financial investments and loans made by individuals and Firms of one nation in the other nations of the world and the investments and loans made by individuals and Firms from other nations in a nation; Capital inflows less Capital outflows.

Net exports Exports (*see*) minus Imports (*see*).

Net investment income The interest and dividend income received by the residents of a nation from residents of other nations less the interest and dividend payments made by the residents of that nation to the residents of other nations.

Net national product Gross national product (*see*) less that part of the output needed to replace the Capital goods worn out in producing the output (Capital consumption allowances, *see*).

Net private domestic investment Gross private domestic investment (*see*) less Capital consumption allowances (*see*); the addition to the nation's stock of Capital during a year.

Net taxes The taxes collected by government less Government transfer payments (*see*).

Net transfers The personal and government transfer payments made to residents of foreign nations less the personal and government transfer payments received from residents of foreign nations.

Net worth The total Assets (*see*) less the total Liabilities (*see*) of a Firm or an individual; the claims of the owners of a firm against its total Assets.

New International Economic Order A series of proposals made by the Third World (*see*) for basic changes in its relationships with the advanced industrialized nations that would accelerate the growth of and redistribute world income to the Third World.

New Left The radical economists; those who hold the views called Radical economics (*see*); the present-day followers of Marx and proponents of Marxian economics (*see*).

NIEO New International Economic Order (*see*).

NIT (*See* Negative income tax.)

NLRB (*See* National Labor Relations Board.)

NNP (*See* Net national product.)

Nominal income The number of dollars received by an individual or group during some period of time.

Nominal interest rate The rate of interest expressed in dollars of current value (not adjusted for inflation).

Nominal national output (NNP) The NNP (*see*) measured in terms of the price level at the time of measurement (unadjusted for changes in the price level).

Nominal wage rate The Money wage (*see*).

Noncheckable savings account A Savings account (*see*) against which a check may not be written; a Savings account which is not a NOW, ATS, or share draft account.

Noncollusive oligopoly An Oligopoly (*see*) in which the Firms do not act together and in agreement to determine the price of the product and the output each Firm will produce or to determine the geographic area in which each Firm will sell.

Noncompeting groups Groups of workers in the economy that do not compete with each other for employment because the skill and training of the workers in one group are substantially different from those of the workers in other groups.

Nondiscretionary fiscal policy The increases (decreases) in Net taxes (*see*) which occur without Congressional action when the Net national product rises (falls) and which tend to stabilize the economy.

Nondurable good A Consumer good (*see*) with an expected life (use) of less than one year.

Nonexhaustive expenditure An expenditure by government that does not result directly in the employment of economic resources or the production of goods and services; *see* Government transfer payment.

Nonfinancial investment An investment which does not require households to save a part of their money incomes; but which uses surplus (unproductive) labor to build Capital goods.

Nonincome charges Capital consumption allowances (*see*) and Indirect business taxes (*see*).

Nonincome determinants of consumption and saving All influences on consumption spending and saving other than the level of Disposable income.

Noninterest determinants of investment All influences on the level of investment spending other than the rate of interest.

Noninvestment transaction An expenditure for stocks, bonds, or second-hand Capital goods.

Nonmarket transactions The production of goods and services not included in the measurement of the Gross national product because the goods and services are not bought and sold.

Nonprice competition The means other than decreasing the prices of their products which Firms employ to attempt to increase the sale of their products; and which includes Quality competition (*see*), advertising, and sales promotion activities.

Nonprice determinant of demand Factors other than its price which determine the quantities demanded of a good or service.

Nonprice determinant of supply Factors other than its price which determine the quantities supplied of a good or service.

Nonproductive transaction The purchase and sale of any item that is not a currently produced good or service.

Nontariff barriers All barriers other than Tariffs (*see*) which nations erect to impede trade among nations: Import quotas (*see*), licensing requirements, unreasonable product-quality standards, unnecessary red tape in customs procedures, etc.

Nonunion shop A place of employment at which none of the employees are members of a Labor union (and at which the employer attempts to hire only workers who are not apt to join a union).

Normal good A good or service of which consumers will purchase more (less) at every price when their incomes increase (decrease).

Normal profit Payment that must be made by a Firm to obtain and retain Entrepreneurial ability (*see*); the minimum payment (income) Entrepreneurial ability must (expect to) receive to induce it to perform the entrepreneurial functions for a Firm; an Implicit cost (*see*).

Norris-LaGuardia Act The Federal act of 1932 which made it more difficult for employers to obtain Injunctions (*see*) against Labor unions in Federal courts and which declared that Yellow-dog contracts (*see*) were unenforceable.

NOW account Negotiable order of withdrawal account (*see*).

NTBs (*See* Nontariff barriers.)

OASDHI (*See* Old age, survivors, and disability health insurance.)

Occupational discrimination The arbitrary restrictions which prevent blacks (and other minority groups) from entering the more desirable and higher-paying occupations.

Occupational licensure The laws of state governments which require a worker to obtain a license from a state licensing board (by satisfying certain specified requirements) before engaging in a particular occupation.

Official reserves The foreign monies (currencies) owned by the central bank of a nation.

Okun's law The generalization that any one percentage point rise in the Unemployment rate above the Full-employment unemployment rate will increase the GNP gap by 2.5% of the Potential output (GNP) of the economy.

Old age, survivors, and disability health insurance The social security program in the United States which is financed by Federal Payroll taxes (*see*) on employers and employees and which is designed to replace the Earnings lost when workers retire, die, or become unable to work.

Old Left Karl Marx and his followers during the latter part of the nineteenth and the early part of the twentieth century.

Oligopoly A market in which a few Firms sell either a Standardized or Differentiated product, into which entry is difficult, in which the Firm's control over the price at which it sells its product is limited by Mutual interdependence (*see*) (except when there is collusion among firms), and in which there is typically a great deal of Nonprice competition (*see*).

Oligopsony A market in which there are a few buyers.

One-year Plan A detailed operational plan which is prepared by *Gosplan* (*see*) and which specifies the inputs and outputs of each enterprise in the U.S.S.R. for a one-year period.

OPEC An acronym for the Organization of Petroleum Exporting Countries (*see*).

Open economy An economy which both exports and imports goods and services.

Open-economy multiplier The Multiplier (*see*) in an economy in which some part of any increase in the income (Net national product) of the economy is used to purchase additional goods and services from abroad; and which is equal to the reciprocal of the sum of the Marginal propensity to save (*see*) and the Marginal propensity to import (*see*).

Open-Market Committee The twelve-member group that determines the purchase-and-sale policies of the Federal Reserve Banks in the market for United States government securities.

Open-market operations The buying and selling of United States government securities by the Federal Reserve Banks.

Open shop A place of employment at which the employer may hire either Labor union members or workers who are not (and need not become) members of the union.

Opportunity cost The amount of other products that must be forgone or sacrificed to produce a unit of a product.

Optimal distribution of income The distribution of income that would result in the greatest possible (maximum) satisfaction of consumer wants (Utility) in the economy.

Optimum population The population size at which the real output per person (real output per worker or Average product, *see*) is a maximum.

Organization of Petroleum Exporting Countries The cartel formed in 1970 by thirteen oil-producing countries to control the price at which they sell crude oil to foreign importers and the quantity of oil exported by its members and which exports approximately 90% of the world's export of oil.

"Other things (being equal)" assumption Assuming that factors other than those being considered are constant.

Outpayments The expenditures of (its own or foreign) money which the individuals, Firms, and governments of one nation make to purchase goods and services, for Remittances, as investment income, and Capital outflows abroad.

Output effect The impact which a change in the price of a resource has upon the output a Firm finds it most profitable to produce and the resulting effect upon the quantity of the resource (and the quantities of other resources) employed by the Firm after the consequences of the Substitution effect (*see*) have been taken into account (eliminated).

Paper money Pieces of paper used as a Medium of exchange (*see*); in the United States, Federal Reserve Notes (*see*) and Treasury currency.

Paradox of thrift The attempt of society to save more results in the same amount or less Saving.

Parity concept The notion that year after year a given output of a farm product should enable a farmer to acquire a constant amount of nonagricultural goods and services.

Parity price The price at which a given amount of an agricultural product would have to be sold to enable a farmer to obtain year after year the money income needed to purchase a constant total quantity of nonagricultural goods and services.

Parity ratio The ratio (index) of the price received by farmers from the sale of an agricultural commodity to the (index of the) price paid by them; and also equal to ratio of the price received to the Parity price (*see*).

Partial equilibrium analysis The study of equilibrium prices and equilibrium outputs or employments in a particular market which assumes prices, outputs, and employments in the other markets of the economy remain unchanged.

Participatory socialism A form of socialism in which individuals would take part in the process by which the decisions that affect them are made and would be able to control their own lives and activities.

Partnership An unincorporated business Firm owned and operated by two or more persons.

Patent laws The Federal laws which grant to inventors and innovators the exclusive right to produce and sell a new product or machine for a period of seventeen years.

Payment-in-kind A payment to farmers who take additional farmland out of production by transferring to them some of the surpluses of agricultural commodities held by the Federal government.

Payments deficit (*See* Balance of payments deficit.)

Payments surplus (*See* Balance of payments surplus.)

Payroll tax A tax levied on employers of Labor equal to a percentage of all or part of the wages and salaries paid by them; and on employees equal to a percentage of all or part of the wages and salaries received by them.

Peak pricing Setting the price charged for the use of a facility (the User charge, *see*) or for a good or service at a higher level when the demand for the uses of the facility or for the good or service is greater and at a lower level when the demand for it is less.

Perfect elasticity of demand A change in the Quantity demanded requires no change in the price of the commodity; buyers will purchase as much of a commodity as is available at a constant price.

Perfect elasticity of supply A change in the Quantity supplied requires no change in the price of the commodity; sellers will make available as much of the commodity as buyers will purchase at a constant price.

Perfect inelasticity of demand A change in price results in no change in the Quantity demanded of a commodity; the Quantity demanded is the same at all prices.

Perfect inelasticity of supply A change in price results in no change in the Quantity supplied of a commodity; the Quantity supplied is the same at all prices.

Personal consumption expenditures The expenditures of Households for Durable and Nondurable consumer goods and services.

Personal distribution of income The manner in which the economy's Personal or Disposable income is divided among different income classes or different households.

Personal income The income, part of which is earned and the remainder of which is unearned, available to resource suppliers and others before the payment of Personal taxes (*see*).

Personal income tax A tax levied on the taxable income of individuals (households and unincorporated firms).

Personal saving The Personal income of households less Personal taxes (*see*) and Personal consumption expenditures (*see*); Disposable income less Personal consumption expenditures; that part of Disposable income not spent for Consumer goods (*see*).

Phillips curve A curve which shows the relationship between the Unemployment rate (*see*) (on the horizontal axis) and the annual rate of increase in the Price level (on the vertical axis).

PIK (*See* Payment-in-kind.)

Planned economy An economy in which only government determines how resources are allocated.

Planned investment The amount which business firms plan or intend to invest.

Plant A physical establishment (Land and Capital) which performs one or more of the functions in the production (fabrication and distribution) of goods and services.

***P* = MC rule** A firm in Pure competition (*see*) will maximize its Economic profit (*see*) or minimize its losses by producing the output at which the price of the product is equal to Marginal cost (*see*), provided that price is equal to or greater than Average variable cost (*see*) in the short run and equal to or greater than Average (total) cost (*see*) in the long run.

Policy economics The formulation of courses of action to bring about desired results or to prevent undesired occurrences (to control economic events).

Political business cycle The tendency of Congress to destabilize the economy by reducing taxes and increasing government expenditures before elections and to raise taxes and lower expenditures after the elections.

Political fragmentation The existence within the larger urban (metropolitan) areas of a great number of separate political entities (states, counties, cities, etc.) which have their own governments.

***Post hoc, ergo propter hoc* fallacy** Incorrectly reasoning that when one event precedes another the first event is the cause of the second.

Potential output The real output (GNP) an economy is able to produce when it fully employs its available resources.

Poverty An existence in which the basic needs of an individual or family exceed the means available to satisfy them.

Precautionary demand for money The amount of money Households and Firms wish to have to protect themselves against unforeseen losses of income and unforeseen expenses; a demand for money that is directly related to the Net national product.

Preferential hiring A practice (often required by the provisions of a contract between a Labor union and an employer) which requires the employer to hire union members so long as they are available and to hire nonunion workers only when union members are not available.

Preferential tariff treatment Setting Tariffs lower for one nation (or group of nations) than for others.

Premature inflation Inflation (*see*) which occurs before the economy has reached Full employment (*see*).

Price The quantity of money (or of other goods and services) paid and received for a unit of a good or service.

Price ceiling A legally established maximum price for a good or service.

Price-decreasing effect The effect in a competitive market of a decrease in Demand or an increase in Supply upon the Equilibrium price (*see*).

Price discrimination The selling of a product (at a given time) to different buyers at different prices when the price differences are not justified by differences in the cost of producing the product for the different buyers; and a practice made illegal by the Clayton Act (*see*).

Price elasticity of demand The ratio of the percentage change in Quantity demanded of a commodity to the percentage change in its price; the responsiveness or sensitivity of the quantity of a commodity buyers demand to a change in the price of a commodity.

Price elasticity of supply The ratio of the percentage change in the Quantity supplied of a commodity to the percentage change in its price; the responsiveness or sensitivity of the quantity sellers of a commodity supply to a change in the price of the commodity.

Price guidepost The price charged by an industry for its product should increase by no more than the increase in the Unit labor cost (*see*) of producing the product.

Price-increasing effect The effect in a competitive market of an increase in Demand or a decrease in Supply upon the Equilibrium price (*see*).

Price index A ratio (expressed as a percentage) of prices in a Given year (*see*) to prices in the Base year (*see*).

Price leadership An informal method which the Firms in an Oligopoly (*see*) may employ to set the price of the product they produce: one firm (the leader) is the first to announce a change in price and the other firms (the followers) quickly announce identical (or similar) changes in price.

Price level The weighted average of the Prices paid for the final goods and services produced in the economy.

Price maker A seller (or buyer) of a commodity that is able to affect the price at which the commodity sells by changing the amount it sells (buys).

Price support The minimum price which government allows sellers to receive for a good or service; a price which is a legally established or maintained minimum price.

Price system All the product and resource markets of the economy and the relationships among them; a method which allows the prices determined in these markets to allocate the economy's scarce resources and to communicate and coordinate the decisions made by consumers, business firms, and resource suppliers.

Price taker A seller (or buyer) of a commodity that is unable to affect the price at which a commodity sells by changing the amount it sells (or buys).

Price-wage flexibility Changes in the prices of products and in the Wages paid to workers; the ability of prices and Wages to rise or to fall.

Price war Successive and continued decreases in the prices charged by the firms in an oligopolistic industry by which each firm hopes to increase its sales and revenues and from which firms seldom benefit.

Priority principle The assignment of priorities to the planned outputs of the various sectors and industries in the economy of the U.S.S.R. and the shifting of resources, when bottlenecks develop, from low- to high-priority sectors and industries to ensure the fulfillment of the production targets of the latter sectors and industries.

Private good A good or service to which the Exclusion principle (*see*) is applicable and which is provided by privately owned firms to those who are willing to pay for it.

Private property The right of private persons and Firms to obtain, own, control, employ, dispose of, and bequeath Land, Capital, and other Assets.

Private sector The Households and business firms of the economy.

Product differentiation Physical or other differences between the products produced by different Firms which result in individual buyers preferring (so long as the price charged by all sellers is the same) the product of one Firm to the Products of the other Firms.

Production possibilities curve A curve which shows the different combinations of two goods or services that can be produced in a Full-employment (*see*), Full-production (*see*) economy in which the available supplies of resources and technology are constant.

Production possibilities table A table which shows the different combinations of two goods or services that can be produced in a Full-employment (*see*), Full-production (*see*) economy in which the available supplies of resources and technology are constant.

Productive efficiency The production of a good in the least-costly way: employing the minimum quantity of resources needed to produce a given output and producing the output at which Average total cost is a minimum.

Productivity slowdown The recent decline in the rate at which Labor productivity (*see*) in the United States has increased.

Product market A market in which Households buy and Firms sell the products they have produced.

Profit (*See* Economic profit and Normal profit); without an adjective preceding it, the income of those who supply the economy with Entrepreneurial ability (*see*) or Normal profit.

(The) profit-maximizing case The circumstances which result in an Economic profit (*see*) for a (competitive) Firm when it produces the output at which Economic profit is a maximum or losses a minimum: when the price at which the Firm can sell its product is greater than the Average (total) cost of producing it.

Profit-maximizing rule (combination of resources) The quantity of each resource a Firm must employ if its Economic profit (*see*) is to be a maximum or its losses a minimum; the combination in which the Marginal revenue product (*see*) of each resource is equal to its Marginal resource cost (*see*) (to its price if the resource is employed in a competitive market).

Progressive tax A tax such that the tax rate increases as the taxpayer's income increases and decreases as income decreases.

Proletariat The workers; the working class; those without the machinery and equipment needed to produce goods and services in an industrial society.

Property tax A tax on the value of property (Capital, Land, stocks and bonds, and other Assets) owned by Firms and Households.

Proportional tax A tax such that the tax rate remains constant as the taxpayer's income increases and decreases.

Proposition 13 A proposal approved by the voters of California to limit the level and growth of property taxes within the state.

Proprietors' income The net income of the owners of unincorporated Firms (proprietorships and partnerships).

Prosperous industry (*See* Expanding industry.)

Protective tariff A Tariff (*see*) designed to protect domestic producers of a good from the competition of foreign producers.

Public assistance programs Programs which pay benefits to those who are unable to earn income (because of permanent handicaps or because they are dependent children) which are financed by general tax revenues, and which are viewed as public charity (rather than earned rights).

Public choice theory Generalizations that describe how government (the Public sector) makes decisions for the use of economic resources.

Public debt The total amount owed by the Federal government (to the owners of government securities) and equal to the sum of its past Budget deficits (less its budget surpluses).

Public interest theory of regulation The presumption that the purpose of the regulation of an Industry is to protect the public (consumers) from the abuse of the power possessed by Natural monopolies (*see*).

Public Law 480 The Federal law which permits less developed nations to purchase surplus American agricultural products and to pay for them with their own monies (rather than with dollars).

Public sector The part of the economy that contains all its governments; government.

Public-sector failure The failure of the Public sector (government) to resolve socio-economic problems because it performs its functions in an economically inefficient fashion.

Public utility A Firm which produces an essential good or service, has obtained from a government the right to be the sole supplier of the good or service in the area, and is regulated by that government to prevent the abuse of its monopoly power.

Pure capitalism An economic system (method of organization) in which property resources are privately owned and markets and prices are used to direct and coordinate economic activities.

Pure competition (1) A market in which a very large number of Firms sell a Standardized product (*see*), into which entry is very easy, in which the individual seller has no control over the price at which the product sells, and in which there is no Nonprice competition (*see*); (2) a market in which there is a very large number of buyers.

Pure monopoly A market in which one Firm sells a unique product (one for which there are no close substitutes), into which entry is blocked, in which the Firm has considerable control over the price at which the product sells, and in which Nonprice competition (*see*) may or may not be found.

Pure profit (*See* Economic profit.)

(The) *pure* rate of interest (*See The* rate of interest.)

Pursuit and escape theory An explanation of the

stability of labor's relative share of the National income (*see*) in which Labor tries to obtain (pursues) higher money wages by decreasing the Economic profits of capitalists and capitalists avoid (escape) a reduction in their profits by increasing the productivity of labor or the prices they charge for products.

Quantity-decreasing effect The effect in a competitive market of a decrease in Demand or a decrease in Supply upon the Equilibrium quantity (*see*).

Quantity demanded The amount of a good or service buyers wish (or a buyer wishes) to purchase at a particular price during some period of time.

Quantity-increasing effect The effect in a competitive market of an increase in Demand or an increase in Supply upon the Equilibrium quantity (*see*).

Quantity supplied The amount of a good or service sellers offer (or a seller offers) to sell at a particular price during some period of time.

Quasi-public bank A bank which is privately owned but governmentally (publicly) controlled; each of the Federal Reserve Banks.

Quasi-public good A good or service to which the Exclusion principle (*see*) could be applied, but which has such a large Spillover benefit (*see*) that government sponsors its production to prevent an underallocation of resources.

Radical economics The modern version of Marxian economics (*see*) which criticizes the methods of orthodox economists, contends that large monopolistic Corporations dominate American capitalism and government, argues that the expansion of capitalism produces society's major problems, and advocates some form of socialism.

R&D Research and development; activities undertaken to bring about Technological progress.

Ratchet effect The tendency for the Price level to decline by less when Aggregate demand decreases than an equal increase in Aggregate demand increased the Price level.

Rate of exchange The price paid in one's own money to acquire one unit of a foreign money; the rate at which the money of one nation is exchanged for the money of another nation.

Rate of interest Price paid for the use of Money or for the use of Capital; interest rate.

Rational An adjective that decribes the behavior of any individual who consistently does those things that will enable him to achieve the declared objective of the individual; and that describes the behavior of a consumer who uses money income to buy the collection of goods and services that yields the maximum amount of Utility (*see*).

Rational expectations theory The hypothesis that business firms and households expect monetary and fiscal policies to have certain effects on the economy and take, in pursuit of their own self-interests, actions which make these policies ineffective.

Rationing function of price The ability of price in a competitive market to equalize Quantity demanded and Quantity supplied and to eliminate shortages and surpluses by rising or falling.

Reaganomics The policies of the Reagan administration based on Supply-side economics (*see*) and intended to reduce inflation and the Unemployment rate (Stagflation).

Real-balances effect The tendency for increases (decreases) in the price level to lower (raise) the real value (or purchasing power) of financial assets with fixed money values; and, as a result, to reduce (expand) total spending in the economy.

Real capital (*See* Capital.)

Real gross national product Gross national product (*see*) adjusted for changes in the price level; Gross national product in a year divided by the GNP deflator (*see*) for that year.

Real income The amount of goods and services an individual or group can purchase with his, her, or its Nominal income during some period of time; Nominal income adjusted for changes in the Price level.

Real interest rate The rate of interest expressed in dollars of constant value (adjusted for inflation); and equal to the Nominal interest rate (*see*) less the rate of inflation.

Real national output (NNP) The NNP (*see*) measured in terms of a constant price level (adjusted for changes in the price level).

Real rate of interest The Real interest rate (*see*).

Real wage The amount of goods and services a worker can purchase with his or her Money wage (*see*); the purchasing power of the Money wage; the Money wage adjusted for changes in changes in the Price level.

Real wage rate (*See* Real wage.)

Recessionary gap The amount by which the Aggregate-expenditures schedule (curve) must increase (shift upward) to increase the real NNP to the full-employment noninflationary level.

Reciprocal Trade Agreements Act of 1934 The Federal act which gave the President the authority to negotiate agreements with foreign nations and lower American tariff rates by up to 50% if the foreign nations would reduce tariff rates on American goods and which incorporated Most-favored-nation clauses (*see*) in the agreements reached with these nations.

Refinancing the public debt Paying owners of maturing United States government securities with money obtained by selling new securities or with new securities.

Regressive tax A tax such that the tax rate decreases (increases) as the taxpayer's income increases (decreases).

Regulatory agency An agency (commission or board) established by the Federal or a state government to control for the benefit of the public the prices charged and the services offered (output produced) by a Natural monopoly (*see*).

Remittance A gift or grant; a payment for which no good or service is received in return; the funds sent by workers who have legally or illegally entered a foreign nation to their families in the nations from which they have migrated.

Rental income Income received by those who supply the economy with Land (*see*).

Reopening clause A clause in an agreement between an employer and a Labor union that requires each to give the other sixty days notice of its intent to modify or terminate the agreement.

Required reserve ratio (*See* Reserve ratio.)

Reserve ratio The specified minimum percentage of its deposit liabilities which a Member bank (*see*) must keep on deposit at the Federal Reserve Bank in its district, or in Vault cash (*see*).

Resource market A market in which Households sell and Firms buy the services of resources.

Restricted grant A transfer of funds from the Federal government to state and local governments to finance a specific program; a "categorical" grant.

Retiring the public debt Reducing the size of the Public debt by paying money to owners of maturing United States government securities.

Revaluation An increase in the defined value of a currency.

Revenue sharing The distribution by the Federal government of some of its tax revenues to state and local governments.

Revenue tariff A Tariff (*see*) designed to produce income for the (Federal) government.

Reversibility problem The failure of the Price level to decrease when Aggregate demand decreases (because prices are inflexible downward) and a decline in the Unemployment rate which is smaller than the fall in the Unemployment rate that would have resulted from an equal increase in Aggregate demand.

Right-to-work law A law which has been enacted in twenty states that makes it illegal in those states to require a worker to join a Labor union in order to retain his or her job with an employer.

Roundabout production The construction and use of Capital (*see*) to aid in the production of Consumer goods (*see*).

Rule of reason The rule stated and applied in the U.S. Steel case (*see*) that only combinations and contracts that unreasonably restrain trade are subject to actions under the antitrust laws and that size and the possession of monopoly were not themselves illegal.

Rule of 70 A method by which the number of years it will take for the Price level to double can be calculated; divide 70 by the annual rate of inflation.

Sales tax A tax levied on expenditures for a broad group of products.

Saving Disposable income not spent for Consumer goods (*see*); not spending for consumption; equal to Disposable income minus Personal consumption expenditures (*see*).

Savings account A deposit in a Depository institution (*see*) which is interest-earning and which can normally be withdrawn by the depositor at any time (though the institution may legally require fourteen days notice for withdrawal).

Savings and loan association A Firm which is owned by stockholders, accepts deposits primarily from small individual savers, and lends primarily to individuals to finance the purchases of residences.

Saving schedule Schedule which shows the amounts Households plan to save (plan not to spend for Consumer goods, *see*) at different levels of Disposable income.

Savings institution A Thrift institution (*see*).

Say's Law The (discredited) macroeconomic generalization that the production of goods and services (supply) creates an equal Aggregate demand for these goods and services.

Scarce resources The fixed (limited) quantities of Land, Capital, Labor, and Entrepreneurial ability (*see all*) which are never sufficient to satisfy the wants of humans because their wants are unlimited.

Schumpeter-Galbraith view (of oligopoly) The belief shared by these two economists that large oligopolistic firms are necessary if there is to be a rapid rate of technological progress (because only this kind of firm has both the means and the incentive to introduce technological changes).

Seasonal variation An increase or decrease during a single year in the level of economic activity caused by a change in the season.

Secondary boycott The refusal of a Labor union to buy or to work with the products produced by another union or a group of nonunion workers.

"Second economy" The semilegal and illegal markets and activities which exist side by side with the legal and official markets and activities in the U.S.S.R.

Secular trend The expansion or contraction in the level of economic activity over a long period of years.

Selective controls The techniques the Federal Reserve Banks employ to change the availability of certain specific types of credit.

Self-interest What each Firm, property owner, worker, and consumer believes is best for itself and seeks to obtain.

Self-limiting adjustment A change which eliminates the reason or motive for the change as the change occurs.

Seniority The length of time a worker has been employed by an employer relative to the lengths of time the employer's other workers have been employed; the principle which is used to determine which workers will be laid off when there is unsufficient work for them all and which will be rehired when more work becomes available.

Separation of ownership and control Difference between the group that owns the Corporation (the stockholders) and the group that manages it (the directors and officers) and between the interests (goals) of the two groups.

Service That which is intangible (invisible) and for which a consumer, firm, or government is willing to exchange something of value.

Share draft account A deposit in a Credit union (*see*) against which a check may be written and which earns interest for the depositor (member).

Sherman Act The Federal antitrust act of 1890 which made monopoly, restraint of trade, and attempts, combinations, and conspiracies to monopolize or to restrain trade criminal offenses; and allowed the Federal government or injured parties to take legal action against those committing these offenses.

Short run A period of time in which producers of a product are able to change the quantity of some but not all of the resources they employ; in which some resources—the Plant (*see*)—are Fixed resources (*see*) and some are Variable resources (*see*); in which some costs are Fixed costs (*see*) and some are Variable costs (*see*); a period of time too brief to allow a Firm to vary its plant capacity but long enough to permit it to change the level at which the plant capacity is utilized; a period of time not long enough to enable Firms to enter or to leave an Industry (*see*).

Short-run competition equilibrium The price at which the total quantity of a product supplied in the Short run (*see*) by a purely competitive industry and the total quantity of the product demanded are equal and which is equal to or greater than the Average variable cost (*see*) of producing the product; and the quantity of the product demanded and supplied at this price.

Short-run farm problem The sharp year-to-year changes in the prices of agricultural products and in the incomes of farmers.

Simple multiplier The Multiplier (*see*) in an economy in which government collects no Net taxes (*see*), there are no Imports (*see*), and Investment (*see*) is independent of the level of the level of income (Net national product); equal to one divided by the Marginal propensity to save (*see*).

Simpson-Mazzoli bill The bill introduced in Congress during 1984 (but not passed) which would have reformed the immigration laws of the United States.

Single-tax movement The attempt of a group which followed the teachings of Henry George to eliminate all taxes except one which would tax all Rental income (*see*) at a rate of 100 percent.

Social accounting (*See* National income accounting.)

Social good A good or service to which the Exclusion principle (*see*) is not applicable; and which is provided by government if it yields substantial benefits to society.

Socially optimum price The price of a product which results in the most efficient allocation of an economy's resources and which is equal to the Marginal cost (*see*) of the last unit of the product produced.

Social regulation The newer and different type of regulation in which government is concerned with the conditions under which goods and services are produced, their physical characteristics, and the impact of their production upon society; in contrast to industrial regulation (*see*).

Social security programs The programs which replace the earnings lost when people retire or are temporarily unemployed, which are financed by Payroll taxes (*see*), and which are viewed as earned rights (rather than charity).

Soil bank program A program in which the Federal government made payments to farmers who took land away from the production of crops which were sold for cash and used the land either to grow cover crops or for timber.

Sole proprietorship An unincorporated business firm owned and operated by a single person.

Special-interest effect Effect on public decision making and the allocation of resources in the economy when government promotes the interests (goals) of small groups to the detriment of society as a whole.

Specialization The use of the resources of an individual, a Firm, a region, or a nation to produce one or a few goods and services.

Spillover A benefit or cost associated with the consumption or production of a good or service which is obtained by or inflicted without compensation upon a party other than the buyer or seller of the good or service; (*see* Spillover benefit and Spillover cost).

Spillover benefit The benefit obtained neither by producers nor by consumers of a product but without compensation by a third party (society as a whole).

Spillover cost The cost of producing a product borne neither by producers nor by consumers of the product but without compensation by a third party (society as a whole).

SSI (*See* Supplemental security income.)

Stabilization fund A stock of money and of a commodity that is used to prevent the price of the commodity from changing by buying (selling) the commodity when its price decreases (increases).

Stabilization policy dilemma The use of monetary and fiscal policy to decrease the Unemployment rate increases the rate of inflation and the use of monetary and fiscal policy to decrease the rate of inflation increases the Unemployment rate.

Stagflation Inflation accompanied by stagnation in the rate of growth of output and a high unemployment rate in the economy; simultaneous increases in both the Price level and the Unemployment rate.

Standardized product A product such that buyers are indifferent to the seller from whom they purchase it so long as the price charged by all sellers is the same; a product such that all units of the product are perfect substitutes for each other (are identical).

Standard of value A means of measuring the relative worth (of stating the prices) of goods and services.

State bank A Commercial bank chartered to engage in the business of banking by a state government.

State ownership The ownership of property (Land and Capital) by government (the state); in the U.S.S.R. by the central government (the nation).

Static economy (1) An economy in which Net private domestic investment (*see*) is equal to zero—Gross private domestic investment (*see*) is equal to the Capital consumption allowances (*see*); (2) an economy in which the supplies of resources, technology, and the tastes of consumers do not change and in which, therefore, the economic future is perfectly predictable and there is no uncertainty.

Store of value Any asset (*see*) or wealth set aside for future use.

Strike The withholding of their labor services by an organized group of workers (a Labor union).

Strikebreaker A person employed by a Firm when its employees are engaged in a strike against the firm.

Structural-change hypothesis The explanation that attributes the relative decline of unionism in the United States to changes in the structure of the economy and of the labor force.

Structural unemployment Unemployment caused by changes in the structure of demand for Consumer goods and in technology; workers who are unemployed either because their skills are not demanded by employers or because they lack sufficient skills to obtain employment.

Subsidy A payment of funds (or goods and services) by a government, business firm, or household for which it receives no good or service in return. When made by a government, it is the reverse of a tax or Government transfer payment (*see*).

Substitute goods Goods or services such that there is a direct relationship between the price of one and the Demand for the other; when the price of one falls (rises) the Demand for the other decreases (increases).

Substitution effect (1) The effect which a change in the price of a Consumer good would have upon the relative expensiveness of that good and the resulting effect upon the quantity of the good a consumer would purchase if the consumer's Real income (*see*) remained constant; (2) the effect which a change in the price of a resource would have upon the quantity of the resource employed by a firm if the firm did not change its output.

Substitution hypothesis The explanation that attributes the relative decline of unionism in the United States to the replacement of the benefits once provided workers by unions by benefits provided by government.

Superior good (*See* Normal good.)

Supermultiplier The Multiplier (*see*) when Investment is directly related to the level of income (Net national product); when the Investment curve (*see*) is positively sloped.

Supplemental security income A program Federally financed and administered which provides a uniform nationwide minimum income for the aged, blind, and disabled who do not qualify for benefits under the Old age, survivors, and disability insurance (*see*) or Unemployment insurance (*see*) programs in the United States.

Supply A Supply schedule or a Supply curve (*see both*).

Supply curve A curve which shows the amounts of a good or service sellers (a seller) will offer to sell at various prices during some period of time.

Supply factor An increase in the available quantity of a resource, an improvement in its quality, or an expansion of technological knowledge which makes it possible for an economy to produce a greater output of goods and services.

Supply schedule A schedule which shows the amounts of a good or service sellers (a seller) will offer to sell at various prices during some period of time.

Supply-side economics The part of modern macroeconomics that emphasizes the role of costs and Aggregate supply in its explanation of Inflation and unemployed labor.

Supply-side shock One of several events of the 1970s and early 1980s which increased production costs, decreased Aggregate supply, and generated Stagflation in the United States.

Supply-side view The view of fiscal policy held by the advocates of Supply-side economics which emphasizes increasing Aggregate supply (*see*) as a means of reducing the Unemployment rate and Inflation and encouraging Economic growth.

Support price (*See* Price support.)

Surplus value A Marxian term; the amount by which the value of a worker's daily output exceeds his daily Wage; the output of workers appropriated by Capitalists as profit.

Sympathy strike Withholding from an employer the labor services of its members by a Labor union that does not have a disagreement with the employer but wishes to assist another Labor union that does have a disagreement with the employer.

Tacit collusion Any method utilized in a Collusive oligopoly (*see*) to set prices and outputs or the market area of each firm that does not involve outright (or overt) collusion (formal agreements or secret meetings); and of which Price leadership (*see*) is a frequent example.

Taft-Hartley Act The Federal act of 1947 which marked the shift from government sponsorship to government regulation of Labor unions and which contained provisions that fall into four major categories.

Target price A minimum price for a basic agricultural product guaranteed to farmers by having the Federal government pay them a subsidy equal to the amount by which the Target price exceeds the market price.

Tariff A tax imposed (only by the Federal government in the United States) on an imported good.

Tax A nonvoluntary payment of money (or goods and services) to a government by a Household or Firm for which the Household or Firm receives no good or service directly in return and which is not a fine imposed by a court for an illegal act.

Tax-based incomes policies An Incomes policy (*see*) which would include special tax penalties for those who do not comply and tax rebates for those who do comply with the Wage-price guideposts (*see*).

Tax incidence The income or purchasing power which different persons and groups lose as a result of the imposition of a tax after Tax shifting (*see*) has occurred.

Taxpayers' revolt A movement in the United States during the late 1970s to impose ceilings on government expenditures and taxes.

Tax shifting The transfer to others of all or part of a tax by charging them a higher price or by paying them a lower price for a good or service.

Tax-transfer disincentives Decreases in the incentives to work, save, invest, innovate, and take risks that allegedly result from high Marginal tax rates and Transfer-payment programs.

Tax "wedge" Such taxes as Indirect business taxes (*see*) and Payroll taxes (*see*) which are treated as a cost by business firms and reflected in the prices of the products produced by them; equal to the price of the product less the cost of the resources required to produce it.

Technology The body of knowledge that can be used to produce goods and services from Economic resources.

Terms of trade The rate at which units of one product can be exchanged for units of another product; the Price (*see*) of a good or service; the amount of one good or service that must be given up to obtain one unit of another good or service.

The economizing problem Society's human wants are unlimited but the resources available to produce the goods and services that satisfy wants are limited (scarce); the inability of any economy to produce unlimited quantities of goods and services.

Theory of human capital Generalization that Wage differentials (*see*) are the result of differences in the amount of Human-capital investment (*see*); and that the incomes of lower-paid workers are increased by increasing the amount of such investment.

***The* rate of interest** The Rate of interest (*see*) which is paid solely for the use of Money over an extended period of time and which excludes the charges made for the riskiness of the loan and its administrative costs; and which is approximately equal to the rate of interest paid on the long-term and virtually riskless bonds of the United States government.

Third World The semideveloped and underdeveloped nations; nations other than the industrially advanced market economies and the centrally planned economies.

Thrift institution A Savings and loan association, Mutual savings bank, or Credit union (*see all*).

Tight money policy Contracting the nation's Money supply (*see*).

Till money (*See* Vault cash.)

Time deposit An interest-earning deposit in a Depository institution (*see*) which may be withdrawn by the depositor without a loss of interest on or after a specific date or at the end of a specific period of time.

TIP (*See* Tax-based incomes policies.)

Token money Coins which have a Face value (*see*) greater than their Intrinsic value (*see*).

Total cost The sum of Fixed cost (*see*) and Variable cost (*see*).

Total demand The Demand schedule (*see*) or the Demand curve (*see*) of all buyers of a good or service.

Total demand for money Sum of the Transactions demand for money (*see*) and Asset demand for money (*see*); the relationship between the total amount of money demanded and money GNP and the Rate of Interest.

Total product The total output of a particular good or service produced by a firm (a group of firms or the entire economy).

Total-receipts–total-costs approach The method which finds the output at which Economic profit (*see*) is a maximum or losses a minimum by comparing the total receipts (revenue) and the total costs of a Firm at different outputs.

Total revenue The total number of dollars received by a Firm (or Firms) from the sale of a product; equal to the total expenditures for the product produced by the Firm (or Firms); equal to the quantity sold (demanded) multiplied by the price at which it is sold—by the Average revenue (*see*) from its sale.

Total-revenue test A test to determine whether Demand is Elastic (*see*), Inelastic (*see*), or of Unitary elasticity (*see*) between any two prices: demand is elastic (inelastic, unit elastic) if the Total revenue (*see*) of sellers of the commodity increases (decreases, remains constant) when the price of the commodity falls; or Total revenue decreases (increases, remains constant) when its price rises.

Total spending The total amount buyers of goods and services spend or plan to spend.

Total supply The Supply schedule (*see*) or the Supply curve (*see*) of all sellers of a good or service.

Trade balance The exports of merchandise (goods) of a nation less its imports of merchandise (goods).

Trade controls Tariffs (*see*), exports subsidies, Import quotas (*see*), and other means a nation may employ to reduce Imports (*see*) and expand Exports (*see*) in order to eliminate a Balance of payments deficit (*see*).

Trade deficit The amount by which a nation's imports of merchandise (goods) exceed its exports of merchandise (goods).

Trade surplus The amount by which a nation's exports of merchandise (goods) exceed its imports of merchandise (goods).

Trading possibilities line A line which shows the different combinations of two products an economy is able to obtain (consume) when it specializes in the production of one product and trades (exports) this product to obtain the other product.

Traditional economy An economic system (method of organization) in which traditions and customs determine how the economy will use its scarce resources.

Traditional view (of oligopoly) The belief that oligopoly (because it is similar to Monopoly) will result in smaller outputs, higher prices and profits, and slower technological progress.

Transactions demand for money The amount of money people want to hold to use as a Medium of exchange (to make payments); and which varies directly with the money GNP.

Transfer payment A payment of money (or goods and services) by a government or a Firm to a Household or Firm for which the payer receives no good or service directly in return.

Truth in Lending Act Federal law enacted in 1968 that is designed to protect consumers who borrow; and that requires the lender to state in concise and uniform language the costs and terms of the credit (the finance charges and the annual percentage rate of interest).

Turnover tax The tax added to the accounting price of a good in the U.S.S.R. to determine the price at which the quantity of the good demanded will equal the quantity of the good it has been decided to produce, the rate of taxation being higher on relatively scarce and lower on relatively abundant goods.

Tying agreement A promise made by a buyer when allowed to purchase a patented product from a seller that it will make all of its purchases of certain other (unpatented) products from the same seller; and a practice forbidden by the Clayton Act (*see*).

Unanticipated inflation Inflation (*see*) at a rate which was greater than the rate expected in that period of time.

Underdeveloped nation A nation in which per capita Real income (output) is low.

Underemployment Failure to produce the maximum amount of goods and services that can be produced from the resources employed; failure to achieve Full production (*see*).

Undistributed corporate profits The after-tax profits of corporations not distributed as dividends to stockholders; corporate or business saving.

Unemployment Failure to use all available Economic resources to produce goods and services; failure of the economy to employ fully its Labor force (*see*).

Unemployment compensation (*See* Unemployment insurance.)

Unemployment insurance The insurance program which in the United States is financed by state Payroll taxes (*see*) on employers and makes income available to workers who are unable to find jobs.

Unemployment rate The percentage of the Labor force (*see*) that is unemployed at any time.

Unfair competition Any practice which is employed by a Firm either to eliminate a rival or to block the entry of a new Firm into an Industry and which society (or a rival) believes to be an unacceptable method of achieving these ends.

Uninsurable risk An event, the occurrence of which is uncontrollable and unpredictable, which would result in a loss that cannot be avoided by purchasing insurance and must be assumed by an entrepreneur (*see* Entrepreneurial ability); sometimes called "uncertainty."

Union shop A place of employment at which the employer may hire either labor union members or workers who are not members of the union but who must become members within a specified period of time or lose their jobs.

Unitary elasticity The Elasticity coefficient (*see*) is equal to one; the percentage change in the quantity (demanded or supplied) is equal to the percentage change in price.

Unit labor cost Labor costs per unit of output; equal to the Money-wage rate (*see*) divided by the Average product (*see*) of labor.

Unlimited liability Absence of any limit on the maximum amount that may be lost by an individual and that the individual may become legally required to pay; the maximum amount that may be lost and that a sole proprietor or partner may be required to pay.

Unlimited wants The insatiable desire of consumers (people) for goods and services that will give them pleasure or satisfaction.

Unplanned investment Actual investment less Planned investment; increases or decreases in the inventories of business firms that result from production greater than or less than sales.

Unprosperous industry (*See* Declining industry.)

Unrestricted grant A transfer of funds from the Federal government to state and local governments to be used by the latter governments as they wish; a "block" grant.

Urban sprawl The movement of people and firms from the central city and into the suburbs of a metropolitan area and the resulting expansion of the geographic area of the metropolitan area.

User charge A price paid by those who use a facility which covers the full cost of using the facility.

U.S. Steel case The antitrust action brought by the Federal government against the U.S. Steel Corporation in which the courts ruled (in 1920) that only unreasonable restraints of trade were illegal and size and the possession of monopoly power were not violations of the antitrust laws.

Utility The want-satisfying power of a good or service; the satisfaction or pleasure a consumer obtains from the consumption of a good or service (or from the consumption of a collection of goods and services).

Utility-maximizing rule To obtain the greatest Utility (*see*) the consumer should allocate his Money income so that the last dollar spent on each good or service yields the same Marginal utility (*see*); so that the Marginal utility of each good or service divided by its price is the same for all goods and services.

Value added The value of the product sold by a Firm less the value of the goods (materials) purchased and used by the Firm to produce the product; and equal to the revenue which can be used for Wages, rent, interest, and profits.

Value-added tax A tax imposed upon the difference between the value of the goods sold by a firm and the value of the goods purchased by the firm from other firms.

Value judgment Opinion of what is desirable or undesirable; belief regarding what ought or ought not to be (regarding what is right or just and wrong or unjust).

Value of money The quantity of goods and services for which a unit of money (a dollar) can be exchanged; the purchasing power of a unit of money; the reciprocal of the Price level.

Variable cost A cost which in total increases (decreases) when the firm increases (decreases) its output; the cost of Variable resources (*see*).

Variable resource Any resource employed by a firm the quantity of which can be increased or decreased (varied).

VAT Value-added tax (*see*).

Vault cash The Currency (*see*) a bank has in its safe (vault) and cash drawers.

Velocity of money The number of times per year the average dollar in the Money supply (*see*) is spent for Final goods (*see*).

VERs (*See* Voluntary export restrictions.)

Vertical combination A group of Plants (*see*) engaged in different stages of the production of a final product and owned by a single Firm (*see*).

Vertical merger The merger of one or more Firms engaged in different stages of the production of a final product into a single Firm.

Voice mechanism Communication by a worker or workers with an employer to improve working conditions and resolve grievances.

Voluntary export restrictions The limitation by firms of their exports to particular foreign nations in order to avoid the erection of other trade barriers by the foreign nations.

Wage The price paid for Labor (for the use or services of Labor, *see*) per unit of time (per hour, per day, etc.).

Wage and salary supplements Payments made by employers of Labor into social insurance and private pension, health, and welfare funds for workers; and a part of the employer's cost of obtaining Labor.

Wage differential The difference between the Wage (*see*) received by one worker or group of workers and that received by another worker or group of workers.

Wage discrimination The payment to blacks (or other minority groups) of a wage lower than that paid to whites for doing the same work.

Wage guidepost Wages (*see*) in all industries in the economy should increase at an annual rate equal to the rate of increase in the Average product (*see*) of Labor in the economy.

Wage-price controls A Wage-price policy (*see*) that legally fixes the maximum amounts by which Wages (*see*) and prices may be increased in any period of time.

Wage-price guideposts A Wage-price policy (*see*) that depends upon the voluntary cooperation of Labor unions and business firms.

Wage-price inflationary spiral Increases in wage rates which bring about increases in prices which in turn result in further increases in wage rates and in prices.

Wage-price policy Government policy that attempts to alter the behavior of Labor unions and business firms in order to make their Wage and price decisions more nearly compatible with the goals of Full employment and stable prices.

Wage rate (*See* Wage.)

Wages The income of those who supply the economy with Labor (*see*).

Wagner Act The Federal act of 1938 which established the National Labor Relations Board (*see*), guaranteed the rights of Labor unions to organize and to bargain collectively with employers, and listed and prohibited a number of unfair labor practices by employers.

Wastes of monopolistic competition The waste of economic resources that is the result of producing an output at which price is less than marginal cost and average cost is less than the minimum average cost.

Welfare programs (*See* Public assistance programs.)

Wheeler-Lea Act The Federal act of 1938 which amended the Federal Trade Commission Act (*see*) by prohibiting and giving the commission power to investigate unfair and deceptive acts or practices in commerce (false and misleading advertising and the misrepresentation of products).

(The) "will to develop" Wanting economic growth strongly enough to change from old to new ways of doing things.

World Bank A bank supported by 135 nations which lends (and guarantees loans) to underdeveloped nations to assist them to grow; formally, the International Bank for Reconstruction and Development.

X-inefficiency Failure to produce any given output at the lowest average (and total) cost possible.

Yellow-dog contract The (now illegal) contract in which an employee agrees when he or she accepts employment with a Firm that he or she will not become a member of a Labor union while employed by the Firm.